❧ ALFONSO X,
THE JUSTINIAN OF HIS AGE

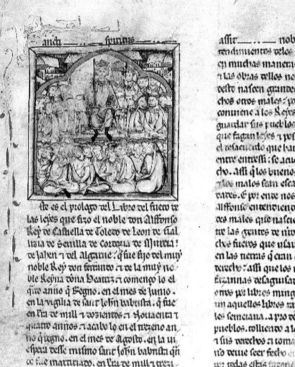

Alfonso X, el Sabio, the Lawgiver, from *The Law Code of King Alfonso X ('el Sabio'), Primera Partida*. Courtesy of the British Library, Additional MS 20787.

ALFONSO X, THE JUSTINIAN OF HIS AGE

LAW AND JUSTICE IN THIRTEENTH-CENTURY CASTILE

JOSEPH F. O'CALLAGHAN

CORNELL UNIVERSITY PRESS
Ithaca and London

First published 2019 by Cornell University Press

Library of Congress Cataloging-in-Publication Data

Names: O'Callaghan, Joseph F., author.
Title: Alfonso X, the Justinian of his age : law and justice in
    thirteenth-century Castile / Joseph F. O'Callaghan.
Description: 1st edition. | Ithaca [New York] : Cornell
    University Press, 2019. | Includes bibliographical
    references and index.
Identifiers: LCCN 2018040210 (print) | LCCN 2018041263
    (ebook) | ISBN 9781501735905 (pdf) | ISBN 9781501735912
    (epub/mobi) | ISBN 9781501735899 (cloth)
Subjects: LCSH: Law—Spain—Castile—History—To 1500. |
    Alfonso X, King of Castile and Leon, 1221–1284—
    Influence. | Law, Medieval.
Classification: LCC KKT125 (ebook) | LCC KKT125 .O23
    2019 (print) | DDC 349.46/309022—dc23
LC record available at https://lccn.loc.gov/2018040210

Onde conuiene al rey que a de tener e guardar ssus pueblos en paz e en iustiçia e en derecho, que ffaga leys e posturas por que los departimientos e las voluntades de los omnes sse acuerden todas en vno por derecho, por que los buenos biuan en paz e en iustiçia e los malos ssean castigados de sus maldades con pena de derecho.
—Espéculo, prólogo

Now it is appropriate for the king, who has to maintain and safeguard his people in peace, justice, and righteousness, to make laws and decisions so that men's divergent wills may all come together in unity in the law, so that good men may live in peace and justice and the wicked may be punished for their evil deeds with the penalty of the law.

❧ CONTENTS

❧ ACKNOWLEDGMENTS

As a student of institutional history, I became aware many years ago of Alfonso X's influence on the development of law and government in thirteenth-century Castile. My interest in this subject was first stirred when I encountered the writings of several eminent Spanish scholars who helped to develop the history of Spanish law as an academic discipline. The initial impetus came from the priest Francisco Martínez Marina (1754–1833), whose liberal views, formed in the post-Napoleonic era, infused his two major contributions to the history of Spanish law. His *Ensayo histórico-crítico sobre la antigua legislación y principales cuerpos legales de los Reynos de León y Castilla, especialmente sobre el Código de las Siete Partidas de Don Alfonso el Sabio*, first published in two volumes in 1808 and reissued in a second edition in 1834, was intended as an introduction to the edition of the *Siete Partidas* by the Real Academia de la Historia in 1808.[1] Five years later, after the Cortes of Cádiz promulgated the Constitution of 1812 establishing a constitutional monarchy, he published his *Teoría de las Cortes o Grandes Juntas Nacionales*, the first significant attempt to study Spanish parliamentary history.[2] Both works exhibit a thorough knowledge of the narrative and documentary sources. Many years elapsed, however, before the history of Spanish law received serious scholarly attention again. Meanwhile, German scholars began to publish and subject to rigorous examination the principal sources of Roman and Germanic law, including the *Liber Iudiciorum* or Visigothic Code.

Influenced by their ideas and methods, Eduardo de Hinojosa (1852–1919) published his study of *El elemento germánico en el derecho español* and developed a new generation of scholars who continued the scientific study of Spanish legal history.[3] Members of the so-called Escuela de Hinojosa, or School of Hinojosa, included Galo Sánchez (1892–1969) and Claudio Sánchez Albornoz (1893–1984), who, with others, gave further impetus to the subject by founding the *Anuario de Historia del Derecho Español* (*AHDE*) in 1924. Their publications will be cited throughout this work. I owe a special debt to two of Sánchez Albornoz's students, Luis García de Valdeavellano (1904–85) and

Alfonso García Gallo (1911–92), whose works I encountered when I first studied in Spain. The former's *Historia de España* and his *Curso de historia de las instituciones españolas* shaped my understanding of medieval Spain and its institutional development,[4] while the latter's *Manual de la Historia del Derecho Español* opened up to me the legal history of Spain.[5] Together with the many other Spanish scholars whose works are cited throughout my book, they helped my understanding of the king and his impact on the law.

Here I want to record my debt of gratitude to two colleagues and friends of many years, both now deceased. Robert A. MacDonald of the University of Richmond, whose editions of several Alfonsine legal texts are without parallel, shared with me his unrivaled knowledge of el Rey Sabio. An invitation from Robert I. Burns, SJ, of UCLA, to contribute an introductory chapter to his edition of Samuel Parsons Scott's English translation of the *Siete Partidas* enabled me to explore Alfonso X's legal achievement in detail and led me to plan the present volume.[6] Father Burns's introductions to each of the *Partidas* exhibit his characteristic wisdom and clarity of thought and have been most helpful to me.

I am also grateful to Jerry R. Craddock of UC Berkeley and Jesús Rodríguez Velasco of Columbia University who read my manuscript and offered many valuable insights.

I must also thank the British Library for permission to use the illustration of Additional MS 20787.

I also express my gratitude to Yvonne Marchese for her photographic artistry.

During my studies of constitutional history I discovered that English historians had dubbed Edward I as the English Justinian because of the extensive statutes that he enacted. That prompted me to identify Alfonso X as the Justinian of his age because, alone among his royal contemporaries, he created a true code of law, comprehensive and systematic, on the model of Justinian's Code.

In 1975 Cornell University Press published my first book, *A History of Medieval Spain*, and I am now immensely pleased that the press offers this book to the public. I very much appreciate the work of Mahinder Kingra, editor in chief, and all the editors who made it possible.

❧ ABBREVIATIONS

AD	*Anales de Derecho*
AEM	*Anuario de Estudios Medievales*
AHDE	*Anuario de Historia del Derecho Español*
BAE	*Biblioteca de Autores Españoles*
BRAH	*Boletín de la Real Academia de la Historia*
C	*Justinian's Code*
CAX(GJ)	*Crónica de Alfonso X*, ed. González Jiménez
CEM	*Cuadernos de Estudios Medievales*
CHD	*Cuadernos de Historia del Derecho*
CHE	*Cuadernos de Historia de España*
CLC	*Cortes de los antiguos reinos de Castilla y León*
CLCHM	*Cahiers de Linguistique et de Civilisation Hispaniques Médiévales*
CLHM	*Cahiers de Linguistique Hispanique Médiévale*
CSM	*Cantigas de Santa Maria*
D	*Digest of Justinian*
DAAX	*Diplomatario Andaluz de Alfonso X*
DO	Jacobo de las leyes, *Dotrinal*
E	*Espéculo*
EHR	*English Historical Review*
ELEM	*En la España Medieval*
ES	*España Sagrada*
ETF	*Espacio, Tiempo y Forma*, 3rd series, Historia Medieval
FD	Jacobo de las leyes, *Flores del derecho*
FJ	*Fuero Juzgo*
FR	*Fuero real*
FV	*Fuero viejo*
Glossae	*Glossae: Revista de Historia del Derecho Europeo*
HID	*Historia, Instituciones, Documentos*
Inst.	*Justinian's Institutes*
Jerez 1268	Assembly of Jerez, in *CLC*, 1:64–86
LEst	*Leyes del estilo*

LFC	*Libro de los fueros de Castilla*
MHE	*Memorial Histórico Español*
MMM	*Miscelánea Medieval Murciana*
OA 1348	Ordinance of Alcalá 1348
OZ 1274	Ordinance of Zamora 1274
PCG	*Primera Crónica General*
POL	*Pseudo Ordenamiento de León*
PON	*Pseudo Ordenamiento II de Nájera*
PPBM	*Primera Partida*, British Museum
PPHS	*Primera Partida*, Hispanic Society
RABM	*Revista de Archivos, Bibliotecas y Museos*
REHJ	*Revista de Estudios Histórico-Jurídicos*
RFDUC	*Revista de la Facultad de Derecho de la Universidad Complutense*
RFE	*Revista de Filología Española*
Seville 1252	Cortes of Seville 1252 (Gross)
Seville 1253	Cortes of Seville 1253 (López Ferreiro, *Fueros municipales*)
Seville 1261	Cortes of Seville 1261 (González Jiménez)
Seville 1264	Cortes of Seville 1264 (Iglesia Ferreirós, "El Privilegio general concedido a las Extremaduras")
SNTP	Jacobo de las leyes, *Summa de los nueve tiempos de los pleitos*, ed. Roudil
SP	*Siete Partidas*
SPGL	*Siete Partidas*, ed. Gregorio López
SPRAH	*Siete Partidas*, ed. Real Academia de la Historia
Valladolid 1258	Cortes of Valladolid, in *CLC*, 1:54–63

❦ Note on Citations and Coinage

In citing the Alfonsine Codes the initial number refers to the book, the second to the title, and the third to the law or laws. For example, *E* 4, 2, 7–9 means *Espéculo*, bk. 4, tit. 2, laws 7–9. For other legal compilations not divided into books and titles the numbers refer to specific laws. In citing the Cortes I refer to the place, year, and article, for example, Seville 1252, art. 1. Among the various editions, I cite Georg Gross for Seville 1252, Antonio López Ferreiro for Seville 1253, Manuel González Jiménez for Seville 1261, and *Cortes de los antiguos reinos de Castilla y León* for Valladolid 1258 and Jerez 1268.

All translations of biblical passages are from *The Saint Joseph Edition of the New American Bible with Revised New Testament and Psalms* (New York: Catholic Book Publishing Co., 1992).

In chapter 12 I discuss Alfonso X's various permutations of the coinage, but it will help the reader to know that ordinarily prices were calculated in terms of the *maravedí* (lat. *morabetinus*), the *sueldo* (lat. *solidus*), and the *dinero* (lat. *denarius*). Both a gold coin and a money of account, the *maravedí* theoretically consisted of 15 *sueldos* or 180 *dineros*.

ALFONSO X, THE JUSTINIAN OF HIS AGE

Chapter 1

El Rey Sabio

Prefulget etiam Omnimoda Libertate Yspania, cum in Agendis Causis Ciuilibus Propriis Utitur Legibus

Alfonso X, el Sabio, king of Castile and León (1252–84), and Holy Roman Emperor-elect, excelled among his contemporaries as a distinguished scholar and patron of scholars, and as a great lawgiver in the tradition of the Roman emperor Justinian (525–65).[1] Intent on creating a body of law applicable to all his people, he assembled a company of jurists who composed the *Libro de las leyes*, also known as the *Espéculo* and, in its revised form, as the *Siete Partidas*, a comprehensive and systematic code of law. They also wrote the *Fuero real*, a code of municipal law. The *Partidas*, one of the greatest legal monuments of medieval Europe, significantly transformed the substance and practice of law in his realms, and though he encountered strong opposition, his work has had an enduring impact on the development of law and institutions, not only in the Iberian Peninsula but also throughout the Spanish-speaking world and in the states of the American west once ruled by Spain.[2]

The Study of Roman and Canon Law

Alfonso X's achievement ultimately sprang from the study of Roman and canon law in the eleventh and twelfth centuries that prompted the development of a European *ius commune* or common law.[3] Although Justinian's Code did not gain general acceptance during his reign in the western provinces of the empire lost to Germanic barbarians, centuries later scholars discovered in the libraries of Italy the Code and the ancillary books (the *Digest, Institutes*, and *Novels*), later known collectively as the *Corpus Iuris Civilis*.[4] Through their efforts Justinian's Code was accepted as the law of the Holy Roman Empire, which claimed universal dominion in Western Europe as the legitimate continuation of the ancient institution.[5] Other scholars, impelled by the Gregorian Reform, assembled the diverse sources of ecclesiastical law, a process that reached a significant stage around 1140 when the monk Gratian published his *Concordance of Discordant Canons*, or the *Decretum*. A century later Pope Gregory IX (1227–41) entrusted Ramon de Penyafort (d. 1275), the great Catalan Dominican, with the task of compiling the *Decretales* or laws enacted since Gratian's day.[6]

The revival of Roman law and the concomitant development of canon law had significant consequences for Western European legal history. The study of law was transmuted into a science, and a learned jurisprudence—the theory and philosophy of law—was brought into being. Two distinct groups of jurists, armed with a professional knowledge of civil law, a universal secular law, or of canon law, an equally universal ecclesiastical law, graduated from the nascent universities, especially at Bologna or Montpellier. The civilians or legists, experts in Roman law, were mostly laymen, and the canonists, mainly ecclesiastics. Often enough, individuals studied both laws.

Some new masters of law became professors and explicated difficult legal passages by writing interlinear and marginal notes or glosses. Their work reached its culmination around the middle of the thirteenth century. Thereafter professors of jurisprudence composed lengthy commentaries on the law. Other law graduates found employment serving emperors, kings, popes, and bishops, while others practiced law in the courts. All of them helped to change the substance of law, the courts, and legal procedures and to formulate the new idea of the state and the responsibilities of kingship. The canonists, by viewing spiritual and religious issues through the lens of the law, helped to give a juridical cast to the life of the church.

Civilians and Canonists in Spain

Spanish students, after attending the University of Bologna, brought home their newfound knowledge of Roman and canon law.[7] Masters of law, summoned by Alfonso VIII of Castile (1157–1214) and Alfonso IX of León (1188–1230) to teach in the recently established Universities of Palencia in Castile and Salamanca in León, influenced the Spanish legal system.[8] The Catalan

Pere of Cardona, *doctor legum magnificus* and chancellor of Castile (1178–82), introduced the concepts of Roman and canon law into Castilian usage.[9] Several *magistri* of Italian origin served in the Castilian royal court, and *iurisperiti* or experts in the law also appeared in León.[10] After teaching at Bologna, the canonist Laurentius Hispanus returned home to occupy the see of Orense (1218–48).[11] Bequests of books of Roman and canon law also testify to the study of law in the late twelfth century.[12]

Vincentius Hispanus, another canonist who taught at Bologna, became bishop of Guarda in Portugal around 1217. Declaring that "Blessed Lady Spain" had her own laws, he denied that Spain was subject to the Holy Roman Empire.[13] Echoing Vincentius, Lucas, bishop of Túy (d. 1249), proclaimed: "Prefulget etiam omnimoda libertate Yspania, cum in agendis causis ciuilibus propriis utitur legibus et Yspanorum rex nulli subditur imperio temporali" (Spain shines forth in full liberty because she uses her own laws in adjudicating civil suits and the king of the Spaniards is not subject to any temporal empire).[14] The "king of the Spaniards" was the king of Castile-León. A generation later, Fray Juan Gil de Zamora, tutor to the king's son and heir, Infante Sancho, repeated that sentence.[15]

Although the University of Palencia gradually ceased to function, the University of Salamanca survives until this day. In 1254, Alfonso X provided for a master of civil law, paid an annual salary of five hundred *maravedís*; an assistant, a bachelor canon; a master of decretals or canon law, paid three hundred *maravedís*; and a stationer receiving one hundred *maravedís* who saw to the transcription of necessary texts. In 1255 Pope Alexander IV granted the *licentia ubique docendi* or license to teach everywhere to Salamanca's graduates and authorized the teaching of civil law there.[16]

A Thirteenth-Century Justinian

In the thirteenth century the study of law stimulated the production of books describing or codifying the law of various European kingdoms. Often-cited examples include Emperor Frederick II's *Liber Augustalis* or *Constitutions of Melfi*, a brief code for his kingdom of Sicily;[17] Philippe de Beaumanoir's *Coutumes de Beauvaisis*, a record of French provincial law;[18] Henri de Bracton's *De legibus et consuetudinibus Angliae*, describing English court practice;[19] and the statutes of Edward I, which brought him acclaim as the English Justinian.[20] Yet, aside from the *Constitutions of Melfi*, none of those works can properly be called a code of law.

On the contrary, Alfonso X's *Libro de las leyes* was organized systematically in books, titles, and laws in the manner of Justinian's Code. Although he did not mention Justinian, Alfonso X and his jurists were well acquainted with the emperor's legal achievement and used it as a model for their work.[21]

That Alfonso X consciously perceived himself as emulating the great Roman legislator is visibly manifested in a miniature in the *Libro de las leyes* composed in the royal scriptorium and now conserved in the British Library (Add. MS 20787).[22] Seated on a throne surrounded by his courtiers, the king holds a sword in his right hand and in his left a book, presumably a book of laws. The portrait is a deliberate evocation of Justinian's declaration when confirming his Code (*C, De Iustiniano Codice Confirmando*):

> Summa rei publicae tuitio de stirpe duarum rerum, armorum atque legum . . . istorum etenim alterum alterius auxilio semper viguit, et tam militaris res legibus in tuto collocata, quam ipsae leges armorum praesidio servatae sunt.

> [The highest protection of the republic derives from two things, arms and laws . . . because each always requires the help of the other, and military matters are placed in safety by the laws, and the laws are preserved by the force of arms.]

Inspired by the emperor's example and, like him, bearing arms and the law, Alfonso X created a *Libro de las leyes*, a code of law that has endured over the centuries to the present day. On that account, he is worthy to be called the Justinian of his age.

The Purpose of this Study

My initial intention is to describe Alfonso X's struggle to create a new, coherent, inclusive, and all-embracing body of law binding on everyone. However, human beings by their nature are resistant to change, especially in matters of law that affect their daily lives. Given the historical development of his realms and the consequent diversity of their laws and customs, his innovations met with resistance. Secondly, I plan to consider his understanding of his role as king and lawgiver, entrusted to him by God, and his concurrent responsibility for the well-being of his people, the defense of the faith, and the security of the realm. Thirdly, I will evaluate the impact of his legal works on the administration of justice through an elaborate system of courts, judges, and attorneys. Next, I will review royal legislation regulating such fundamental issues as marriage, family, and inheritance; the status of persons, freemen and slaves, lords and vassals; the ownership and possession of property; trade and commerce; crime and punishment; and the juridical status of the non-Christian peoples. Whereas the law books present an ideal, that ideal must be compared to the reality depicted in the everyday transactions recorded in other contemporary sources, including royal charters, the enactments of the Cortes, and private documents. Thus, after expounding the substance of the Alfonsine Codes on a given topic, wherever possible I will point out other documents or literary remains that illustrate the practical application of the law. I trust that the reader will be able to distinguish my exposition and commentary on the law from the examples of its usage in everyday life. The challenges facing the king who wished to carry out a radical alteration of the legal system will provide an illustration, however imperfect, of the essential political, social, economic, and religious characteristics of thirteenth-century society. A brief overview of Alfonso X's reign will provide the context necessary for understanding and assessing his accomplishment.

The Learned King

At Alfonso X's accession, the Castilian reconquest of Islamic Spain had reached its culmination under the leadership of his father, Fernando III (1217–48), who conquered Córdoba, Jaén, and Seville.[23] Only the emirate of Granada remained in Muslim hands, but the emir, Ibn al-Aḥmar, had to acknowledge his vassalage to Castile and pay an annual tribute. While busy colonizing Seville and the recently reconquered regions of Andalucía,[24] Alfonso X pursued the crown of the Holy Roman Empire and planned an African crusade. After his imperial election in 1257, he expended considerable treasure over nearly twenty years in a vain effort to secure recognition.[25] His African adventure was intended to deprive the Moroccans of easy access to the Iberian Peninsula but had to be abandoned when Ibn al-Aḥmar, realizing the threat to his own realm, in 1264 stirred up rebellion among the Mudéjars, Muslims living under Christian rule in Andalucía and Murcia.

Several years later Alfonso X encountered strong opposition from the nobility who accused him of denying their right to be judged by their peers according to their customs. The townsmen also complained about his new municipal law code and the burden of extraordinary taxation. Although he confirmed the customs of both nobles and townsmen during the Cortes of Burgos in 1272, the nobles, still dissatisfied, withdrew to Granada and did not return to his service until two years later.

After surviving that crisis, in 1275 the king journeyed to southern France, in a futile attempt to persuade Pope Gregory X to acknowledge his imperial status. When the Marinids, a new Moroccan dynasty, took advantage of his absence and invaded Castile, his son and heir Fernando de la Cerda determined to halt their advance but died suddenly en route to the frontier.

Although the Marinids thereafter twice routed Castilian forces, the king's second son, Sancho, organized the defense and arranged a truce. When the Marinids invaded again in 1277, the king, hoping to prevent future invasions, unsuccessfully laid siege to the seaport of Algeciras.

Meanwhile, following the death of his firstborn son, Alfonso X had to resolve the problem of succession. Although he could recognize as his heir Fernando de la Cerda's oldest son, still a child, he opted to follow older custom giving preference to a king's surviving sons and acknowledged Sancho in the Cortes of Burgos in 1276. Fernando de la Cerda's widow, concerned about the security of her two sons, sought the protection of Pedro III of Aragón and appealed for help to her brother Philip III of France. Under French pressure, Alfonso X decided to partition his kingdom for the benefit of Alfonso de la Cerda, the elder of his two grandsons. Infuriated, Sancho, after exchanging harsh words with his father during the Cortes of Seville in 1281, summoned the estates of the realm to Valladolid in 1282. The king's recent erratic behavior, probably caused by the excruciating pain of cancer, led many to believe that he was no longer capable of governing. Thus, the assembled estates transferred royal authority to Sancho, leaving his father with the empty title of king. Abandoned by his family, Alfonso X turned to the Marinids, his erstwhile enemies, who invaded Spain once more, but now as his allies. In his last will he disinherited Sancho and died at the age of sixty-two on 4 April 1284 at Seville. His son succeeded as Sancho IV.[26]

Amid these political and social upheavals, el Rey Sabio directed a scholarly enterprise without parallel in thirteenth-century Europe that produced works of law, poetry (the *Cantigas de Santa Maria*), history (the *Estoria de Espanna* and the *General Estoria*), astronomy, and astrology (including translations from Arabic).[27] His contemporaries lauded his good qualities. Jofré de Loaysa affirmed that "he was very generous, a lover and doer of justice, handsome in figure and quite graceful in appearance."[28] Juan Gil de Zamora commented that he was a man of "sharp intellect, attentive in study, with an excellent memory . . . discreet in speech, distinguished by his elegance, moderate in laughter, honest in his gaze, easy in his gait, and temperate in eating." His generosity, however, "clothed a sort of prodigality."[29] Astronomers remarked that he "surpassed in wisdom, intelligence, understanding, law, kindness, piety, and nobility all other wise kings."[30] His nephew Juan Manuel (d. 1348) remarked that he caused the translation into Castilian of "all the sciences, both theology and logic, and all the seven liberal arts and all the art known as mechanics." Besides translating the teachings of Muslims and Jews, he "turned into romance all the ecclesiastical and secular laws." Juan Manuel added: "What more can I say? . . . No man did so much good especially in increasing and illuminating knowledge as this noble king."[31] In our time Robert I. Burns described him as "the greatest poet-king of Western Europe, and by his various legal texts its greatest philosopher-king." He "richly . . . deserves his titles 'El Sabio' and 'emperor of Culture'" and, "much more than his contemporary" Frederick II, "he is the true *Stupor mundi*—a royal wonder of the world."[32]

El Rey que es Fermosura de Espanna et Thesoro de la Filosofia

Through his law codes Alfonso X gave governmental institutions a form and character that they would retain for many years after his death.[33] In all his scholarly endeavors, he strove to educate his people, so much so that Francisco Márquez Villanueva rightly described him as "El Rex Magister" (the Teacher King).[34] The poetic eulogy preceding his *Estoria de Espanna* expressed that desire. While its purpose was to encourage his people to learn about their history, his words could also refer to his creation of a new body of law:

> O Espanna, si tomas los dones que te da la sabiduría del rey, resplandeçeras, otrosi en fama et fermosura creçeras.
>
> El rey que es fermosura de Espanna et thesoro de la filosofia, ensennanças da a los yspanos; tomen las buenas los buenos et den las vanas a los vanos.

> [O Spain, if you take the gifts that the wisdom of the king gives you, you will shine forth and you will grow in fame and beauty. The king, who is the glory of Spain and the treasure of philosophy, gives instruction to the Spanish people. Let good men take what is good, and leave what is vain to those who are vain.][35]

CHAPTER 2

The Law and the Lawgiver

Onde por Todas Estas Rrazones Auemos Poder Conplidamente de Ffazer Leys

In order to fashion a common law to supplant the prevailing disparate forms of law, Alfonso X employed a company of jurists trained in Roman and canon law to compose the *Espéculo*, the original form of the *Siete Partidas*, and the *Fuero real*. Once that task was finished, he promulgated his new codes and declared them binding on his people.

That achievement had its roots in the Roman and Visigothic tradition. After subjugating the Iberian Peninsula,[1] the Visigothic kings published several legal compilations culminating in the *Liber Iudiciorum* or *Book of Judges*, a comprehensive territorial law promulgated around 654.[2] Imitating Roman practice, it was divided into twelve books, and these in turn into titles and laws.[3] After the Muslims destroyed the Visigothic kingdom in the eighth century, the *Liber Iudiciorum* survived as a principal element of its legacy.[4]

The Mozarabic Christians subject to Islamic rule continued to be governed by the *Liber Iudiciorum*, and those who fled to the northern realm of León introduced it there. Unwritten customary law predominated in neighboring Castile,[5] but in time collections of *fazañas* or judicial sentences based on custom were assembled.[6] Castilian territorial customary law was also recorded in the *Libro de los fueros de Castiella*,[7] the *Fuero viejo de Castilla*,[8] and similar works. *Fuero* comes from *forum*, a low Latin word for law. The text of an ordinance purportedly enacted by Alfonso VIII in the Curia of Nájera in 1185[9] is not extant but may be comprised in the *Pseudo-Ordenamiento II de Nájera*.[10] Alfonso XI adapted it in the Ordinance of Alcalá in 1348 (cap. 73).[11] In the eleventh and twelfth centuries, written charters or *fueros* regulated life in the municipalities extending southward from the Duero River to the Tagus.[12] Much fuller than most, Alfonso VIII's *Fuero* of Cuenca, published in 1177, was later given to towns in Extremadura and Andalucía.[13] The *Fuero viejo* supposedly originated when Alfonso VIII, after his triumph at Las Navas de Tolosa in 1212, confirmed the municipal *fueros* and asked the nobles to summarize their customs, but it is doubtful that they did so.[14] Recognizing the desirability of having a common body of law, Fernando III commissioned the *Fuero Juzgo*, a Castilian translation of the *Liber Iudiciorum* or *Forum Judicum*, and gave it to many towns in Andalucía and Murcia.[15]

The Alfonsine Codes

Given the need to clarify the inevitable confusion arising from this legal miscellany, Fernando III initiated work on a new law code but died before he could complete it. In the second prologue (*Dios es comienço*) to the *Partidas*, and in the *Setenario*,[16] a final attempt to revise the *Partidas*, Alfonso X stated that his father commanded him to finish it. The mid-fourteenth century *Chronicle of Alfonso X* affirmed that he did so.[17] The tendency to identify the royal law codes by the same or similar names, *Libro de las leyes*, *Libro del fuero de las leyes*, *Libro del fuero*, or *Fuero del libro*, inevitably prompted misunderstanding.[18] The prologue to each text asserts that Alfonso X was the author and I will refer to him as such, but one should understand that these codes were the result of a collaborative effort by anonymous jurists. The king's role, as Evelyn Procter commented, was that of a general editor, as he himself explained:

> The king makes a book, not because he writes it with his hands, but because he sets forth the reasons for it, and amends and corrects and improves them and shows how they ought to be done; and although the one whom he commands may write them, we say, nevertheless, for this reason that the king makes the book.[19]

Among his likely collaborators was Master Jacobo de las leyes (d. 1294), a member of the Giunta family of Italy, who settled in Castile at an uncertain date.[20] Three works are attributed to him.[21] The *Summa de los nove tienpos delos pleitos* (*Summary of the Nine Seasons of Pleas*), treating summonses, court appearances, postponements, proofs, and sentences, is a translation of the *Ordo iudiciarius ad summariam notitiam* of Petrus Hispanus.[22] For the instruction of his son Bonajunta, he composed the *Dotrinal que fabla delos juyzios* (*Textbook that Speaks of Judgments*), or *Dotrinal de pleitos* (*Textbook on Pleas*), a tract on legal procedure. As this work closely resembles the *Third Partida*, Antonio Pérez Martín regards Jacobo as the principal author of the *Partidas*. Stressing the value of a legal career, Jacobo remarked that one who learned "the science of law" would be honored by kings and other great lords. The three books of his *Flores de derecho* also known as *Flores de las leyes* (*Flowers of Law*) discussed judges and litigants (1); court procedure (2); and sentences and appeals (3). Pérez Martín demonstrated that it was written around 1274–75 for the king's illegitimate son Alfonso Fernández, known as Alfonso el Niño, then entrusted with the government of Seville.[23] Another possible contributor was Master Fernando Martínez (d. 1275), archdeacon of Zamora, who, after studying at Bologna, served as royal notary for León and bishop of Oviedo (1269–75). His writings include the *Summa aurea de ordine iudiciario* or *Suma del orden judicial* (*Summary of Judicial Order*), and probably the *Margarita de los pleitos* (*Miscellany of Pleas*), written about 1263.[24] Robert A. MacDonald suggested other names.[25]

The *Espéculo* survives in one codex, MS 10,123 of the Biblioteca Nacional in Madrid, copied about 1390.[26] The king made the laws "in this book, which is a mirror of law," to guide his judges in judging correctly and assuring everyone's rights. Intended as the fundamental law of the royal court, it was the standard by which all other laws would be judged. The text, however, is incomplete, as only five books, each divided into titles and these into laws, are extant. Book 1 treats law in general and the articles of the Catholic faith; book 2, the king's role, the royal family and household, and custody of royal castles; book 3, royal vassals, military organization, and warfare; book 4, the administration of justice; and book 5, judicial procedure and appeals. The nonexistent books 6 and 7 reportedly concerned ecclesiastical jurisdiction, the family, manumission, and inheritance. Gonzalo Martínez Díez suggested that a missing book 8 dealt with property and commercial activity, and that book 9 may have discussed criminal law.[27]

Both Martínez Díez and Aquilino Iglesia Ferreirós concluded that the *Espéculo* was never terminated and was abandoned in 1256 after Alfonso X was acknowledged as Holy Roman Emperor and work was begun on the *Partidas*.[28] On the contrary, Jerry Craddock argued that it was complete and in force until completion of the *Partidas* in 1265.[29] I agree. The king's inclusion of excerpts from the *Espéculo* in ordinances given to Valladolid in 1258 (*E* 4, 2, 7–9, 11, 13–14, 16, 18),[30] and Santiago de Compostela in 1261 (*E* 4, 10, 3; 4,

11, 1, 5–10, 12, 14) prove that point.[31] As he reserved the right to amend the *Espéculo* (pr.) with the counsel of his court, I believe that, given his imperial election, he transformed the text into the *Siete Partidas*.

Although most historians believe that the *Espéculo* was never promulgated, the king commanded his successors to observe it and threatened violators with an enormous fine of ten thousand *maravedís*. Robert MacDonald argued that he promulgated the *Espéculo* in 1254 when he asked the Cortes of Toledo to acknowledge his daughter Berenguela as his successor. The king, at Palencia on 5 May 1255, notified Louis of France, her husband-to-be, that that had been done and expressed their marriage contract in language similar to the law in the *Espéculo* (2, 16, 1) recognizing the right of succession of the king's oldest daughter, in default of his oldest son.[32] Alfonso X surely perceived the symbolic value of promulgating the *Espéculo* in Toledo, his birthplace and the ancient seat of the Visigoths and the emperors of Spain.[33]

Some scholars, citing the so-called Ordinance of Zamora in 1274 (art. 40), have identified the *Espéculo* with a book establishing chancery fees "made *por corte* in Palencia" in the year that Prince Edward of England married the king's sister Leonor in November 1254. That seems to imply that the *Espéculo* was completed in May 1255 at Palencia. However, the ordinance did not mention a book of laws, a *Libro de las leyes*. The book referred to was likely a list of chancery fees taken from the *Espéculo* (4, 13, 4) for easy reference.

In the prologue to the *Espéculo*, Alfonso X, after describing the confusing legal situation, argued the need for a new body of law common to everyone:

> E por esto damos ende libro en cada villa sseellado con nuestro sseello de plomo e touiemos este scripto en nuestra corte, de que sson ssacados todos los otros que diemos por las villas, porque sse acaesçiere dubda ssobre los entendemientos de las leys e sse alçassen a nos que sse libre la dubda en nuestra corte por este libro que ffeziemos con consseio e con acuerdo de los arçobispos e de los obispos de Dios e de los ricos omnes e de los más onrrados ssabidores de derecho que podiemos auer e ffallar e otrossí de otros que auie en nuestra corte e en nuestro rregno.

> [For this reason, therefore, we give a book, sealed with our leaden seal, to each town and we kept this written text in our court, from which all the others that we gave to the towns are taken. Wherefore if a doubt should arise concerning the understanding of the laws and appeal should be made to us, the doubt might be resolved in our court by this book that we made with the counsel and consent of the archbishops and bishops of God and the magnates and the most honored scholars

of law that we could have and find and also of others in our court and
our kingdom.]

The book given to the towns was the *Fuero real*, probably promulgated
simultaneously with the *Espéculo*. In the prologue to the *Fuero real*, the king
explained that many municipalities petitioned him for a *fuero*, probably in the
Cortes of Seville in 1252. Thus, "taking counsel with our court and with men
knowledgeable in the law, we gave them this *fuero*" and commanded everyone to observe it. Book 1 deals with the Catholic faith, the status of the king,
laws in general, and the administration of justice. Book 2 considers legal
procedure. Marriage, inheritance, and commerce are discussed in book 3,
and criminal law in book 4.[34] Although men might study other laws, the king
required all pleas to be adjudicated according to this book (*FR* 1, 6, 5).

Assuming that the passage quoted above referred only to one law book,
Alfonso García Gallo, contrary to common opinion, argued that the book,
"sealed with my leaden seal," was the *Espéculo*.[35] If that were true, one would
expect that there would be many extant copies rather than one incomplete
text. If the *Espéculo* was intended as a municipal code, the *Fuero real* would
be unnecessary. In my judgment, two different books were mentioned. One,
"sealed with our leaden seal" and given to the towns, was taken from another
written text (*este escripto*) preserved in the royal court. Royal charters of 1256
confirming the concession to the towns of the book "sealed with my leaden
seal" prove the identity of that book as the *Fuero real*, whose structure and
content derived from the *Espéculo*.[36] As an unfinished work would not likely
serve as a model for laws given to the municipalities or be used to clarify
doubts or settle appeals, the passage quoted demonstrates that the *Espéculo*
was completed.

Unlike the *Espéculo*, there are numerous copies of the *Fuero real*, which
the king granted to the towns of Castile and Extremadura, especially those
lacking a *fuero*. As the *Fuero Juzgo* served the kingdom of León, a separate
code was not required there. The physical labor of transcribing by hand
perhaps fifty to one hundred copies probably occupied many months. The
first references to the *Fuero real* are dated in 1255, leading many scholars to
believe that that was the date of composition.[37] None of those dates was the
date of promulgation, but rather the date on which a copy was issued to a
particular municipality. That accorded with the chancery practice of giving
each town a record of the acts of the Cortes dated on the day when it was
written. Recalling that he had previously granted the towns "that *fuero* that
I made with the counsel of my court, written in a book and sealed with my
leaden seal," Alfonso X, in 1256 and later, granted tax exemptions to urban

knights.[38] In 1264 he confirmed the privileges of the towns of Extremadura, including the *"Libro del fuero* that we gave them."[39] Various references to the *Fuero castellano, Fuero de las leyes, Libro del fuero,* or *Fuero del libro* eventually gave way to *Fuero real.*[40]

Having reserved the right to amend the *Espéculo* (pr.), Alfonso X, after being recognized by Pisa as Holy Roman Emperor in March 1256 and elected by the German princes in 1257, commenced a revision emphasizing his new imperial status.[41] Descended from Alfonso VII, *emperador de España,* and Frederick Barbarossa, *emperador de Roma,* he hoped to revive the claims of his predecessors to rule over all of Spain and to secure papal recognition as Holy Roman Emperor.[42] The *General Estoria* likened him to Jupiter, "king of this world," the ancestor of the kings of Troy and Greece, the Caesars and emperors of Rome.[43] Although the primary audience of his revised code, written in the vernacular and later known as the *Siete Partidas,* was the people of Castile-León, he may have intended to have it translated into Latin to give it wider circulation especially within the empire.[44]

The extant codices of the *Partidas* (with one partial exception) date from the fourteenth or fifteenth centuries, and at least 115 manuscripts of the entire text or one or more of its parts in Castilian, Galician, Portuguese, and Catalan survive.[45] Two texts amplifying book 1 of the *Espéculo* represent the initial version of this new code: the British Library manuscript Additional 20787,[46] and HC 397/573 in the library of the Hispanic Society of America.[47] The prologue (beginning *A Dios deue*) identified the text as the *Libro del fuero de las leyes.* Composition commenced on the vigil of the Nativity of St. John the Baptist, in the era 1294 [23 June 1256] and was completed on the eve of the Passion of St. John the Baptist in the era 1303 [28 August 1265]. The text (identified as Biblioteca Real 3), printed at the foot of the Real Academia de la Historia's edition of the *Partidas,* is essentially the same as Additional 20787 and has the same dates of composition.[48] Craddock argued that the *Libro del fuero de las leyes* was an intermediary stage between the *Espéculo* and the *Partidas* and that it is incorrect to refer to it as the *Primera Partida.*[49]

None of the three editions of the *Partidas* exemplifies the criteria of modern scholarship.[50] Alfonso Díaz de Montalvo published the first in 1491;[51] Gregorio López, the second with an extensive gloss in 1555;[52] and the Real Academia de la Historia, the third in 1807.[53] López's edition gained general use in the courts, and I will usually cite it.[54] Given its impact on several southwestern states, the American Bar Association commissioned Samuel Parsons Scott to translate López's text.[55]

Although the second prologue (*Dios es comienço*) to the *Partidas* dated the work between 23 June 1256 and 1263, Craddock asserted that the earlier dates (23 June 1256 to 28 August 1265) are correct and that the later dating reflected the king's increasing fascination with the number seven.[56] In Alfonso X's honor, the first letter of each *Partida* was one of the seven letters in his name. The section entitled *Septenario*, following the second prologue, highlighted the significance of the number seven and explained that the book was divided into seven parts. Accordingly, the *Libro de las leyes* has been known as the *Siete Partidas* since the end of the thirteenth century (*SP* 1, 1, 1). Citing Alfonso X's last will, dated 10 January 1284, in which he bequeathed to his successor "the book that we made with the name *Setenario*,"[57] Craddock maintained that *Septenario* or *Setenario* was the title preferred by the king and that the incomplete work known as *Setenario* is a final revision of a portion of the *First Partida* carried out after 1272.[58]

The *Setenario* relates that it was begun by Fernando III who, on his deathbed, commanded Alfonso X to complete it (leyes 2, 4, 10).[59] The royal predilection for the number seven is evident in the discussion of the divine attributes, but also in the reduction of Fernando's name to Ferando. Moreover, the seven letters of Alfonso are said to exemplify the seven names of God (ley 1). Alfonso X inscribed a poignant eulogy of his father and praise of Seville, "the most noble [city] of Spain" and "anciently the household and dwelling place of the emperors who were crowned there."[60] An extensive commentary on worshippers of the elements of earth, water, wind, and fire, the planets and astrological signs, and the odd mixture of astrology and Christian theology (leyes 12–34, 43–68) reflects the preoccupation of his last years, but seems at variance with the intent of a law book. The remainder (leyes 35–42, 69–108), summarizing church teaching and the seven sacraments, corresponds to the *First Partida*.[61]

The *Siete Partidas* consists of seven parts, each divided into titles and then into laws. The prologue to each title explains its purpose and the content of the laws. After a general disquisition on law, the *First Partida* (24 titles, 518 laws) discusses the Christian faith and the organization of the church. The *Second* (31 titles, 359 laws) concerns the king, his court, his people, and his military organization; the *Third* (32 titles, 543 laws), the administration of justice; the *Fourth* (27 titles, 256 laws), marriage and the family; the *Fifth* (15 titles, 374 laws), trade and commerce; the *Sixth* (19 titles, 272 laws), wills and inheritances; and the *Seventh* (34 titles, 363 laws), on crime and punishment, concludes this extraordinary enterprise.

A thorough study of the sources remains to be undertaken. In addition to Justinian's *Corpus Iuris Civilis*,[62] the king's men, citing *sabios antiguos* (including Aristotle, Cicero, and Seneca), drew on Roman and canon law, philosophy and theology,[63] the Bible, the *Fuero antiguo de España*, the *Fuero Juzgo*, and other texts. The skillful incorporation of ideas and principles from these sources and the didactic tone has given the *Partidas* a distinctly doctrinal character. At times the Latin form of a word is given and defined and several reasons might be adduced to explain it. As his people's educator, Alfonso X realized that if they understood the rationale for a law they would be inclined to obey it.[64] García Gallo compared the *Partidas* to the *Summa Theologica* of the king's contemporary Thomas Aquinas.[65] MacDonald characterized this "juridical *summa*" in these words:

> The *Siete Partidas* represents an encyclopedic and systematic integra-
> tion of definition, prescription, explanation, and amplification of
> materials from many sources—classical and contemporary, canoni-
> cal and secular, Roman and Castilian, legal and literary. . . . In intent
> and character the law becomes instructive and preventive, rather than
> penal, as definitions and moral maxims are used skillfully to clarify,
> exhort, or admonish.[66]

In the Ordinance of Alcalá (cap. 64) in 1348, Alfonso XI, believing that there was no evidence that the *Partidas* had been promulgated, proclaimed that henceforth the code would have the force of law.[67] Although his state-ment has generally been accepted, I believe that he was incorrect. His chan-cellor Fernán Sánchez de Valladolid, the probable author of the *Chronicle of Alfonso X*, remarked that the king completed the *Partidas* begun by his father and commanded everyone to accept them as the law and required judges to judge according to them.[68] As I argued above, Alfonso X likely promulgated the *Espéculo* in the Cortes of Toledo in 1254 and, having reserved the right to amend it, transformed it into the *Siete Partidas*. As a revision of the original code, the *Partidas* did not require a separate act of promulgation.[69] Never-theless, Alfonso XI's declaration in 1348 dispelled any ambiguity about the validity of the *Partidas*.

Several other legal compilations should be noted. The so-called Ordinance of Zamora survives in a sixteenth-century copy. An introductory statement (*Siguense*) asserted that Alfonso X enacted it during the Cortes of Zamora in 1274 with the consent of the people. The text relates that in June 1274, the king (whose name is not mentioned) consulted bishops, religious, magnates, and judges concerning the settlement of pleas. After he presented a written statement of his views, they took counsel among themselves and submitted written responses. The scribes and lawyers, though not asked to do so, also offered written opinions. In response, the king directed attention to advo-cates, judges, scribes, and the king. Eleven *casos de corte*, cases reserved to royal jurisdiction, were identified.[70]

This document lacks the typical intitulation and salutation of legislative acts promulgated by the king, to whom it refers in the third person. Nor does it follow the usual form of dating royal documents. The final clause states that it was made on the king's command nineteen years after he gave the *fuero castellano* to Burgos at Valladolid on 25 August 1255. I do not believe that the introductory statement (*Siguense*) or the dating clause were part of the original text. Omitting them, we have a fragment of a memorandum recording the agreement reached by the king and his court concerning the processing of pleas. I do not believe that the king convened the Cortes in Zamora in 1274 or that he promulgated this ordinance in the Cortes. He issued numerous charters at Zamora between 5 June and 27 July 1274, but none records actions taken in the Cortes or states that he convened the Cortes. The ordinance does not mention municipal representatives who were ordinarily summoned to the Cortes.[71]

Master Roldán, whose name suggests that he may have been an Italian legist, commissioned by the king, composed the *Libro de las Tafurerías*, a code of forty-six laws regulating gambling houses, a topic omitted in the other codes. MacDonald suggested that the king promulgated it during the Cortes of Burgos in 1276.[72]

The five *Leyes para los adelantados mayores* described the duties of territorial administrators in Andalucía and Murcia.[73] Lacking any indication of authorship or date of publication, this probably was a private collection.[74] The *Leyes nuevas* is also a private compilation of royal responses to questions posed by the judges of Burgos concerning the application of the *Fuero real*.[75] The 252 laws of the *Leyes del estilo*, completed around 1310, concern the practice of the royal court from the time of Alfonso X to that of Fernando IV (1295–1312).[76]

King Alfonso as Lawgiver

The diversity of laws and the usage of incomplete and altered texts impeded Alfonso X's task of enacting just laws and rendering certain judgment. His laws facilitated knowledge and understanding of the law and guaranteed everyone's rights (*E* pr.). The *Fuero real* (1, pr.) and the first (*A Dios deue*) and second (*Dios es comienço*) prologues to the *Partidas* (PPBM; PPHS; SPGL) expressed similar ideas.[77] Although the *Partidas* seems like an academic treatise or legal encyclopedia, Alfonso X surely intended it to have the force of law. As its laws were written to serve God and the common good, everyone had to obey them and be judged by them (*SP* 1, 1, pr.). The language of command manifested that purpose: "mandamos" (we command) (*SP* 3, 3, 8; 7, 1, 20);

"tenemos por bien" (we hold it as right) (*SP* 6, 3, 18; 7, 2, 5); "tenemos por bien e mandamos" (we hold it as right and we command) (*SP* 3, 2, 43); "porende diximos" (therefore we state) (*SP* 5, 2, 2); "otrossi dezimos" (we also state) (*SP* 5, 2, 3); "ca derecho es" (because it is the law) (*SP* 6, 1, 23); "assi como mandan las leyes deste libro" (as the laws of this book command) (*SP* 3, 3, 1; 3, 3, 9). Judges had "to adjudicate [pleas] . . . by the laws of this book and not by any other" (*SP* 3, 4, 6), and the people had to know its laws (*SP* 5, 14, 31).

Ruling by God's grace, and having no temporal superior ("por la merçed de Dios non auemos mayor ssobre nos en el tenporal"), Alfonso X argued that only emperors and kings could make laws (*E* 1, 1, 3, 13; *PPBM* 1, 1, 4, 13; *SPRAH* 1, 1, 12). King Alfonso and his predecessors exercised the legislative function in a limited way by granting charters of rights and privileges to individuals, communities, and municipalities. His laws enacted in the Cortes with the counsel and consent of the three estates were recorded in *cuadernos* or notebooks given to municipal representatives at the conclusion of each session. The extant records of the Cortes of Seville in 1252,[78] and 1253,[79] Valladolid in 1258,[80] and Seville in 1261,[81] and the Assembly of Jerez in 1268,[82] reveal that sometimes he took the initiative, but in other instances, the townsmen presented petitions that he enacted into law. Some of those laws made their way into or otherwise influenced the Alfonsine Codes.[83]

As a law applicable to everyone, the Alfonsine Codes aspired to advance the common good and encourage obedience to God and the king. The king ought to make law with the counsel of knowledgeable men, and with "the consent of those upon whom it is imposed" (*SP* 1, 2, 8). That accorded with the Roman legal principle "quod omnes tangit, ab omnibus approbari debet" (what touches all should be approved by all).[84] Inspired by the love of justice and truth, the legislator ought to assure everyone his due ("que aya cada uno lo ssuyo").[85] Listening attentively to everyone, he should explain the law with well-reasoned argument and measured language. While standing firmly against the cruel and the proud, he ought to show mercy to the guilty and unfortunate (*E* 1, 1, 4; *PPBM* 1, 1, 5; *SPRAH* 1, 1, 6).

Laws should be carefully drafted so that they were free of error and contradictions. As a law contrary to divinity, royal sovereignty, and the common good required correction, the king, after consulting legal scholars and good men from many regions, should publish the amended laws. Included in the *Partidas*, a new law would have the same validity as other laws (*SP* 1, 1, 17–19). Without exception all residents of the kingdom, including foreigners, had to obey the laws (*SP* 1, 1, 15). No one could plead ignorance of the law (*FR* 1, 6, 4), except minors, peasants, shepherds, madmen, women, and knights (*E* 1, 1, 11–12; *PPBM* 1, 1, 11–12; *SPRAH* 1, 1, 14; *SPGL* 1, 1, 20–21).

The king, too, ought to observe the law, even though "all laws and all rights are subject to him and no other human being has his power except God whose place he has in all temporal affairs" (*FR* 4, 25, 5). Nevertheless, he should obey the laws because they honor and protect him, and assist him in doing justice, and, as the maker of laws, he should be the first to keep them. The people should do so because he commands them and the laws are good and overcome injury and are beneficial to them (*E* 1, 1, 9; *PPBM* 1, 1, 9; *SPRAH* 1, 1, 11). The lawmaker's failure "to live according to the laws" would encourage others to disregard them (*SP* 1, 1, 15–16). Those remarks reflect two Roman legal principles, namely, "Princeps legibus solutus est" (the prince is released from the laws) (*D* 1, 3, 31); and "Digna vox maiestate regnantis legibus alligatum se principem profiteri: adeo de auctoritate iuris nostra pendet auctoritas" (It is a statement worthy of the majesty of a reigning prince for him to profess to be subject to the laws; for our authority is dependent upon the authority of the law) (*C* 1, 14, 4).[86] Recognizing the hypocrisy of exempting the prince from obeying the laws, while requiring everyone else to do so, the royal jurists acknowledged that the laws would be more effective if the prince, as well as the people, submitted to them.

As law was the essential foundation for an orderly society, Alfonso X's task was to declare what law was. Following Roman tradition, he acknowledged *jus naturale* or natural law, inhering in all creatures, and *jus gentium*, the law of nations, restricted to human beings. The latter, derived from human reason, constrained violence and required everyone to obey governing authorities.[87] The teachings of saints and wise men also gave rise to spiritual and temporal laws, which, taken together, reflected the union of body and soul (*SP* 1, 1, 2–3).

Terms used for law included *ley, derecho, fuero, postura, establecimiento*, and *ordenamiento*.[88] The generic term *ley* (lat. *lex*) was a written direction to do right and avoid evil, but it could also refer to a religion, for example, Christianity, Islam, or Judaism (*E* 1, 1, 7; *SP* 1, 1). *Derecho* (lat. *directum*), meaning what was right, also signified law in general.[89] *Fuero* (lat. *forum*) was a law observed for a long time, whether written or not (*E* 1, 1, 7). *Postura* (lat. *positura*) denoted an agreement, contract, judicial decision, or the enactments of the Cortes.[90] *Paramiento* (lat. *parare*), an agreement made for the common good (*E* 1, 1, 7), was used by Fernando III to describe the acts of the Cortes of Seville in 1250.[91] *Establecimiento* (lat. *stabilimentum*) referred to a statute. The word *establecemos* was used throughout the Alfonsine Codes to declare the law.[92] The king did not usually refer to *ordenamientos* or ordinances, but he did so in 1278 and 1281 and the word came into use thereafter.[93] Except for *paramiento* and *ordenamiento*, the *Espéculo* (1, 1, 1) brought all these terms together by affirming that "these laws (*leyes*) are decisions (*posturas*), statutes (*establecimientos*), and laws (*fueros*)" enacted so that men might observe the Christian faith and live together in "right (*derecho*) and justice" (*PPBM* 1, 1, 2; *SPRAH* 1, 1, 2). The *Partidas* (1, 1, 1) declared that "these laws (*leyes*) are statutes (*establecimientos*) enabling men to live well and in an orderly manner." Law (*ley*), whose commands are loyal and right (*derecho*), not only teaches one to do good, but also to avoid evil (*SP* 1, 1, 4).

The law, embodying all that was right and true, and in accord with reason and nature, should be complete and free from error. Avoiding verbosity that encourages tortured interpretations, it should be written clearly and accurately in easily understood language. Abbreviations should be avoided and every word fully written out. Laws ought not to contradict one another. The legislator could clarify obscure or uncertain passages and, if necessary, enact new laws. Law punishes evil, rewards good; assists people to know, love, and fear God; teaches them to be obedient and loyal to their natural lord, to love one another, to assure each one's rights; and dissuades them from doing what they should not do (*E* 1, 1, 2, 5–6, 8; *FR* 1, 6, 2; *PPBM* 1, 1, 3, 6, 8; *SPRAH* 1, 1, 4, 7–8, 10; *SP* 1, 1, 10, 13–14).

Neither the *Espéculo* nor the British Library and Hispanic Society texts refer to unwritten law, but the López and Academia editions considered usage (*uso*), custom (*costumbre*; lat. *consuetudo*), and *fuero*. Usage, or human activity over a long time, leads to local or general custom, a practice followed for ten or twenty years and confirmed by two court judgments. Conforming to reason, custom should not contravene divine law, royal sovereignty, natural law, or the common good. Custom was often incorporated in written *fueros*. A recently enacted *fuero* could override an older custom. That sentence emphasized that the *Fuero real* superseded earlier customs. A *fuero*, reasonable, equitable, right, just, and serving the common good, should be made with the counsel of intelligent men and the agreement of the king and the people subject to it. If it no longer served that purpose, it should be abolished (*SP* 1, 2, 1–10).

The Academia edition added a final law demonstrating the superiority of written laws (*SPRAH* 1, 2, 11). Written laws were certain and not subject to interpretation by men of little intelligence or to the arbitrary judgment of *fazañas*. Not swayed by love or hate, promises or threats, the law guarded the rights not only of the lowliest person, but also of the king. The law equally served one who was mad, or sane; one who was intelligent, or not; one who was well spoken, or not. Written law was endowed with great honor because emperors and kings commanded learned men to make it, using well-chosen words, and by virtue of being written it would not fall into oblivion. Whereas custom might be changed at will, written law could only be corrected by enacting an amendment. Given the works of literature, history, and science published in the king's name, the statement that the law "speaks of noble and honored deeds more so than all other written texts" (*SP* 1, 2, 11) suggests a predilection for the law. Though sanctioned by long usage, customs and *fueros* were defective and would be corrected, or supplanted by the more honorable laws of the *Libro de las leyes*.

As one might expect, people found it difficult to adjust to the new juridical regime and asked for guidance in interpreting difficult or obscure points of law. Both Cuenca in 1256[94] and Escalona in 1261 sought further explanation of the privilege given to urban knights. Three years later, the king admonished the people of Escalona to abide by the *Libro del fuero*, and in 1269 he recalled that he had given them the *Fuero real* and the tax exemptions of 1256.[95] In order to resolve disputes concerning the administration of justice, he sent excerpts from the *Espéculo* to Valladolid in 1258 and to Compostela in 1261.[96] When Miranda de Ebro in 1262 and again in 1272 expressed its aggravation with "the *Libro del ffuero nuevo*," he confirmed the town's previous *fuero*.[97] He responded to queries from Burgos in 1263 and 1268 concerning difficult passages in the *Fuero real*.[98] When Vitoria complained in 1271 of certain matters in the *Fuero real*, he ordered his *alcalde*, Diago Pérez, to meet with the city council and to propose reforms. He also commanded that lawsuits be adjudicated according to the *Libro del fuero*.[99]

The negative reaction to his legal innovations prompted the magnates to voice three juridical grievances during the Cortes of Burgos in 1272. First, they objected to being judged by the *Fuero real* used in towns adjacent to their lordships. Secondly, protesting the absence of *alcaldes de Castilla* in his court, they demanded the appointment of two noble judges (*alcaldes fijos-dalgo*) to adjudicate their disputes. Thirdly, disparaging the *merinos mayores*, they insisted that he replace them with *adelantados*. In asserting their right to be judged by their peers according to their ancient customs, they implicitly rejected the legists trained in Roman law serving in the royal court. The king, eager to pursue his imperial ambitions, confirmed the magnates' customary *fueros*; assured them that they would not be judged, without their consent, according to municipal *fueros*; and pledged to appoint *alcaldes de Castilla* to resolve their lawsuits. He also agreed that if any noble had a quarrel against him it would be adjudicated by his fellow nobles in accordance with the "ancient *fuero*." Although he promised to correct the excesses of the *merinos mayores*, he refused to replace them until the country was settled. After the magnates went into exile to Granada, he appointed a commission headed by Queen Violante to negotiate their return. Insisting that he ratify their customs and privileges, and objecting to the presence of legists and canonists in his court, they reiterated their demand to be judged by laymen. According to the *Fuero viejo* (pr.), he restored their traditional *fueros* at Martinmas (11 November 1272) and instructed Burgos to use its old *fuero*. Charters issued to Madrid, Soria, Béjar, Cuenca, and Sepúlveda in October 1272 suggest that he restored the traditional *fueros* of the Castilian and Extremaduran towns.[100] In 1273 he restored to Baeza the *Fuero* of Cuenca used there "until we gave them this other *fuero*."[101] The towns, in return for permission to appoint their own judges, granted an annual tribute to complete his imperial quest. At the end of 1273 the magnates renewed their allegiance and in the Cortes of Burgos in 1274 agreed to support his proposed journey to the empire.[102]

Although the king ostensibly modified his original plan to create a common royal law, the Alfonsine Codes continued to shape the course of the law. The citation of two laws from the *Seventh Partida* (7, 12, 3; 7, 14, 7) in the *Leyes del estilo* (4, 144) indicates that the royal legists persisted in applying the great law code.[103] The *Fuero real* also remained in use. For example, in 1279 he provided Alba de Tormes with a new copy to replace the one that was lost.[104]

La Ley Ama e Ensenna las Cosas que Son de Dios

Alfonso X and his jurists, after long years of labor, produced two major codes of law, the *Libro de las leyes* and the *Fuero real*, that altered the juridical landscape of Castile-León forever. The *Libro de las leyes*, conceived as a body of law by which all others would be judged, was revised successively in order to clarify the meaning of the laws. The comparatively brief *Espéculo*, probably promulgated in the Cortes of Toledo in 1254, gave way to the more elaborate *Siete Partidas*. As he reserved the right to amend his code, the *Partidas* did not require a separate promulgation. Rejecting the older customs and *fazañas* as arbitrary and irrational, he stressed that the principal goal of the *Libro de las leyes* was to foster the common good, by assisting his judges to adjudicate cases and assure everyone's rights. The people, too, were instructed not only in receiving the law, but also in their duty to obey the king who enacted it and enforced it for the good of everyone. As the law reflected God's will, and as the king ruled by God's grace, refusal to abide by the laws was an offense against God.

By means of the *Libro de las leyes*, the *Fuero real*, and the *Fuero Juzgo*, Alfonso X hoped to forge a common body of law for his realms. He expressed his understanding of law's purpose in this way:

> La ley ama e ensenna las cosas que son de Dios, e es fuente de ensenna-miento, e maestra de derecho, e de justicia, e ordenamiento de buenas costumbres, e guiamiento del pueblo e de su vida, e es tan bien para las mugeres como para los varones, tambien para los mancebos como para los viejos, tan bien para los sabios como para los non sabios, asi para los de la cibdat como para los de fuera, e es guarda del rey e de los pueblos.

> [The law loves and teaches the things that are of God. It is a fountain of learning, a teacher of righteousness and justice and the regulation of good customs, a guide for the people and their life. It is both for women and for men, both for the young and the old, for the wise and the not-so-wise, for those living in the city and those without. It is pro-tection for the king and the people.] (*FR* 1, 6, 1)

Despite that ideal, opposition compelled the king to confirm the tradi-tional customs of the nobility and the townsmen, but he never fully aban-doned his plan to create a new law for everyone that "all could understand, that deceived no one . . . that was honest, equal, and beneficial" (*FR* 1, 6, 2). As the purpose of the *Libro de las leyes* was to enable his people to live in peace and justice, we must now consider its practical application in everyday life.

❦ Chapter 3

Creating a Dynasty

Rey Tanto Quiere Dezir Commo Rregidor

Alfonso X defined his office in simple terms: "Rey tanto quiere dezir commo rregidor, ca sin falla, a el pertenesce el gouernamiento del reyno" (King means ruler, for certainly, the government of the kingdom is entrusted to him) (*SP* 2, 1, 6). The Alfonsine Codes described the qualities of a good king who attained that rank by hereditary succession and ruled by God's grace. An overview of the accession ritual and the symbols of kingship may further elucidate his understanding of his position. As kingship was the family business, he had to carefully choose a queen to be his faithful companion and share the task of nurturing their children. In contrast to the ideal portrayed by the royal jurists, his brothers challenged his authority, and the plan of succession was subverted by the untimely death of his son and heir. The king's task as lawgiver must be seen in those circumstances.

The Making of a King

Upon the king's death, prelates, magnates, masters of the military orders, and good men of the towns should attend his funeral, give alms, and pray for his entrance into paradise. His debts and bequests should be paid and his wrongs redressed. Acknowledging his rightful heir as king, and declaring their vassalage, they should promise obedience, loyalty, and protection. In recognition of his sovereignty, they should kiss his foot and hand and surrender all offices, estates, and revenues that they held of his predecessor, so he could entrust them to persons having his confidence (*E* 2, 16, 2–3, 6; *SP* 2, 13, 19–20).

Those rituals seem to have been observed when Fernando III died at Seville on 31 May 1252 and Alfonso X, after a long apprenticeship, came to power at the age of thirty-one.[1] Jofré de Loaysa, who was present, related that after the interment on 1 June, those assembled "raised up Don Alfonso as king and he became a knight."[2] That ought to be understood figuratively, as it is unlikely that Alfonso X, given his sense of the majesty of kingship, was literally raised on a shield in accord with ancient Germanic custom.[3] The fifteenth-century continuator of Lucas of Túy narrated that Alfonso X, after a triumphal procession through the streets, promised to give the people good *fueros*, to confirm their privileges, and not to impose any undue burden upon them. Although not a contemporary account, that is probably a reasonably accurate description of what transpired.[4] Perhaps royal chamberlains scattered gold and silver coins or jewels among the crowds, as directed in the *Partidas* (3, 28, 48). During the Cortes of Seville in October 1252 the estates likely pledged allegiance, and he may have assured them of good *fueros* and confirmed their rights and privileges.[5]

At his accession, according to Jofré and the king himself, he received knighthood.[6] Although Antonio Ballesteros proposed that, like Alfonso XI, he was knighted by a mechanical statue of Santiago, that seems improbable.[7] As the recipient of knighthood was subordinated to the person conferring that honor, it is unlikely that anyone knighted him. Considering his neglect of the shrine of Santiago de Compostela, there is scant reason to believe that he would establish a special bond with that see (and, by implication, subservience to the archbishop) by receiving knighthood from a statue of St. James.[8] As he remarked, the king or his heir, though not knights, could confer knighthood, "because they are the head of the knighthood" (*SP* 2, 21, 11). Imitating his father, he probably girded himself with his arms after one of the bishops blessed them.[9]

The accession lacked the religious characteristics associated with other monarchies. The French and English kings, anointed and crowned by an archbishop, were believed to receive a sacramental or priestly character and were endowed with the power to heal scrofula. In contrast, the Castilian ceremony consisted of acclamation and a pledge of allegiance by the assembled estates. Thus, Teofilo Ruiz spoke of a secular monarchy.[10] Anointing, introduced in seventh-century Spain, was intended to protect the Visigothic kings against assassination. Several kings of Asturias-León were anointed in the ninth, tenth, and early eleventh centuries. In 1135 Alfonso VII crowned himself as emperor of León, but there is no record of his being anointed, nor were any of his immediate successors anointed or crowned.[11] The troubadour Raimon Vidal de Bezaudon commented that Alfonso VIII "was neither anointed nor consecrated."[12]

The royal jurists, citing Isaiah's prophecy (Is 9:5–6) that the king of heaven and earth would bear his empire on his shoulders, and affirming that Jesus carried his cross on his right shoulder, declared that Christian kings holding Christ's place on earth were anointed on the shoulder or back of the right arm. That "should be done as stated in the second book" (PPBM 1, 4, 13). The text from Biblioteca Real, 2 and 3, printed at the foot of the Academia edition, repeated that phrase (SPRAH 1, 4, 13), but SPGL did not. Neither the Espéculo nor the Second Partida mention anointing.[13] After distinguishing the spiritual anointing of priests from the temporal anointing of kings, the Setenario (ley 89) stated that Jesus was anointed as priest and king and that anciently kings, occupying his place, were anointed. However, the Setenario did not say that the Castilian kings were anointed or should be.[14] Thus, the ritual of anointing and coronation by an archbishop never become customary in Castile-León. European contemporaries commented on that anomaly.[15]

As Alfonso X seemed determined not to allow any ecclesiastic to claim superiority over him, he probably crowned himself at his accession, but I believe that he also did so during the Cortes of Toledo in the spring of 1254. In attendance were prelates, nobles, and townsmen, and his vassals, the Muslim emirs of Granada, Niebla, and Murcia. In 1274, when transferring the remains of the Visigothic king Wamba to the city, he declared that Toledo was the head of Spain, "where anciently the emperors were crowned."[16] None of the Visigothic kings employed the imperial title, but some tenth- and eleventh-century rulers of Asturias-León-Castile, claiming to be their heirs, did so. After conquering Toledo in 1085, Alfonso VI styled himself "imperator toletanus" (emperor of Toledo), but there is no record of his coronation there.[17]

Toledo, with its memories of peninsular hegemony, would have been an appropriate site for Alfonso X's coronation. The placement of Toledo immediately after Castile in the royal intitulation acknowledged its importance. The poet Gil Pérez Conde's reference to an undated instance "in Toledo, when you took the crown there," suggests that the king crowned himself during the Cortes in 1254.[18] That he did so is also implied by the fact that Sancho IV, after being acclaimed at Ávila, hastened to Toledo where he received the crown from four bishops and declared that his successors should be crowned there.[19] Although his son Fernando IV was acclaimed at Toledo, it is not evident that he was crowned or anointed.[20] By opting to crown himself in Toledo, Alfonso X may have wished to emphasize that he, like his Visigothic predecessors, exercised supreme authority over the entire peninsula, but his Christian neighbors did not consider themselves his subordinates.

Not only did Alfonso X reject the quasi-priestly character conferred on a king by episcopal anointing and coronation, but he also repudiated the notion of the royal touch, the claim that the French and English kings could cure scrofula by touching the afflicted person.[21] In *CSM* 321 he dismissed as "nonsense" the idea that a king could heal a Córdoban girl suffering from *lanparones*, a tumor of some sort, or scrofula.[22] That probably reflected his natural skepticism but may also have been provoked by the intrusion of Philip III of France into Castilian affairs after 1275.

When speaking of the secular character of the Castilian monarchy, one does not mean that it was irreligious or lacking a spiritual element. The preambles to royal charters, the numerous royal donations to churches, and the text of the *First* and *Second Partidas* make clear that the Castilian kings, ruling by God's grace, believed that the promotion of true religion was a paramount obligation. They expressed their religious fervor by founding monasteries, going on pilgrimage, or dedicating themselves to the war against Islam. Presenting himself as defender of the orthodox faith, Alfonso X also upheld the spiritual authority of the pope. Thus, Alfonso X, whose *Cantigas de Santa Maria* reveal his devotion to the Virgin Mary, was no less devout than any of his contemporaries.[23]

The chancery formula "rex Dei gratia" or "rey por la gracia de Dios" (king by the grace of God) signified the religious character of monarchy. The claim to rule by God's grace stressed that the king was appointed by God to whom he was directly accountable. As God's temporal representative on earth, he was expected to govern his people justly, but as he did not derive his authority from them, he was not answerable to them. To challenge him was tantamount to challenging God. Only God could remove him from office.[24]

Following that formula, Alfonso X identified himself as king of Castile, Toledo, León, Galicia, Seville, Córdoba, Murcia, Jaén, and the Algarve.[25] That list summarized several centuries of historical development and Fernando III's and Alfonso X's more recent extension of the frontier into Andalucía and Murcia.[26] Alfonso X described this accumulation of kingdoms as "nuestros rregnos" and "nuestro sennorio" ("our kingdoms" and "our lordship") (*E* pr.). The list seemed to suggest that his power and prestige were greater because of the many states subject to his rule. Although he proclaimed that king and people formed one body, he did not govern a unified state. Not only were the legal and institutional differences between Castile and León significant, but so too were the differences between them and the southern realms that had once been petty Muslim kingdoms. The task of unifying those diverse elements was challenging, but Alfonso X, while accepting the disparities, attempted to make them function in a coherent harmony.

Contemporary portrayals of the king and the symbols of kingship provided a visual illustration of his power.[27] So that his royal status would be readily manifest, the *Partidas* instructed that he should wear silken garments with gold and jewels, as well as spurs and saddles of gold and silver and precious stones. When holding the Cortes, he should wear richly adorned golden crowns (*SP* 2, 5, 5).

The *PPBM* depicted a seated king, bearded and crowned, bearing a sword in his right hand and a book in his left. Around him were gathered bishops, magnates, courtiers, and others seated at his feet who were probably townsmen assembled in the Cortes. This royal pose is reminiscent of Justinian's statement that "imperial majesty ought to be adorned not only by arms but also by laws."[28] Sancho IV painted an extraordinary picture of a king (perhaps his father) whom he said he had seen. His golden crown was set with rubies, emeralds, and sapphires, symbolizing the virtues of fear of God, true belief, good habits, benignity, chastity, knowledge, and memory. Robed in cloth of gold and silk set with jewels, the king wore golden armlets and sat on a seat covered with gold, silver, and precious stones. In his right hand he held a sword "to display the justice in which [he] ought to maintain his people." In his left hand was a golden apple surmounted by a cross representing the kingdom. To enable the king "to render to each one his law," a servant presented him with a book of laws while another held a scepter used to punish the wicked.[29]

In the *Cantigas de Santa Maria* the king often appears on his knees with his hands clasped in supplication before Mary's statue. His clothing, though simple in form, was richly made and intended to differentiate him from his people.[30] In some miniatures, the clean-shaven king, with brown shoulder-length hair, wears a golden crown and a blue tunic trimmed with gold and a red mantle (*CSM* pr. A and B). Other texts portray a crowned king, seated or mounted on a horse, and wearing a tunic quartered in castles and lions, the symbols of Castile and León.[31] His great seal of 1255 shows him, mounted and crowned, with a sword in one hand and in the other a shield marked with castles and lions.[32] The royal throne was usually depicted as a simple chair or bench.[33] A statue of the king in the cathedral of Toledo holds a scepter topped by an imperial eagle in his right hand and the sword of justice in his left.[34] A stained-glass portrait in the cathedral of León also shows the scepter with an eagle.[35]

In 1282, after being abandoned by his family and fellow monarchs, Alfonso X, in return for a loan of one hundred thousand gold dinars, pledged his crown to the Marinids. Although Ibn Khaldūn (d. 1406) saw it in the royal palace in Marrakech, it has since disappeared.[36] In his last will the king bequeathed to his heir crowns with stones, cameos, and jewels.[37] His effigy in the cathedral of Seville, according to an account of 1345, wore a golden crown set with precious stones; in his right hand was a silver scepter with an imperial eagle on top and in his left hand a golden apple surmounted by a cross. In 1579, a "sword, scepter, crown, a staff of emperor," and an "imperial crown with stones" were found in his tomb, but those objects subsequently disappeared.[38] These depictions stressed the duties of his office: the enactment of laws, the administration of justice, the defense of the realm, his learning, and the task of educating his people.

A Primer of Queenly Conduct

In order to transfer his power to his heirs, the king had to choose a suitable spouse. The union of Alfonso and Violante, the daughter of Jaime I, was intended to draw Castile and Aragón together. Their spousal mass was celebrated at Valladolid in 1246, and their marriage was solemnized there three years later, when he was twenty-eight and she was thirteen.[39] Eventually they had eleven children: Berenguela (1253–1313?); Beatriz (1254?–1280); Fernando de la Cerda (1255–75); Leonor (1256?–75); Sancho (1258–95); Constanza (1259?–?); Pedro (1261–83); Juan (1264–1319); Isabel (1265?–?); Violante (1266?–?); and Jaime (1267–84).

Prior to his marriage Alfonso X had several illegitimate children, including Berenguela (b. 1240–41), born to María Alfonso, an illegitimate daughter of Alfonso IX; and Alfonso Fernández, or Alfonso el Niño (ca. 1242–81), the son of Elvira Fernández de Villada. Mayor Guillén de Guzmán, probably the love of his life, gave birth to Beatriz (1244–1303) who married Afonso III of Portugal and became the mother of Dinis (1279–1325).[40] Urraca Alfonso and Martín Alfonso were mentioned in his will.[41]

Violante represented her husband in several critical situations. In 1264 she appealed to her father to suppress the Mudéjar uprising in Murcia. In the Cortes of Burgos in 1272 she headed a commission to consider the demands of the prelates and magnates, and she negotiated the return of the exiled magnates from Granada. Mistreated by the king who was afflicted with a debilitating illness, in 1278 she fled to her brother Pedro III of Aragón. Although she was reconciled to her husband and returned to Castile, she broke with him again in 1282 and supported Sancho's rebellion. Alfonso X did not mention her by name in his poetry, but it would be unwise to assume that he was indifferent to her. After making a pilgrimage to Rome in 1300, she died at Roncesvalles on the return journey.[42]

Prior to considering the queen's role, the royal jurists cautioned the king against relationships with dissolute women. If he had children by them, he would commit a grave sin, set a poor example, and dishonor himself and his realm. Whereas the children of a man "blessed by God stand around his table like the branches of new olive trees" (Ps 128:3–4), illegitimate children shamed them and him. Moreover, should he "overindulge in wine and women" (Sir 19:2–3), God would withhold his blessing in this life and punish him in the next (SP 2, 5, 3). Sancho IV repeated those admonitions when counseling his son.[43] However, the Espéculo (2, 3, 1), admitting the king's liaisons with several women, stressed that if he had a mistress, though that was contrary to church law, she ought to be protected against all harm.

The harmonious union between king and queen was perceived as a source of stability and good government.[44] If his bride was endowed with good lineage, beauty, virtuous habits, and riches, he would love her more deeply; their children would be comely and genteel and the family held in great esteem; and her wealth would redound to his benefit and that of the kingdom. Beauty and riches were transitory and might be dispensed with, but good lineage and honest character were essential. The queen who was loved, honored, and protected by her husband would love, honor, and care for him, and thus offer a good example to everyone. Placed in the company of virtuous men and women, she would learn to conduct herself appropriately and to avoid anything unseemly (SP 2, 6, 1–2). Anyone who induced her to betray her husband by engaging in promiscuous behavior committed treason. Should she have an affair, she would offend the king's honor, dishonor herself, and bring into question the legitimacy of her children (E 2, 3, 1–3; SP 2, 14, 1). A double standard prevailed, however, because Alfonso X suffered no punishment for his disloyalty to her.

As described in the Alfonsine Code, the queen's court was much like that of her husband. Chaplains said daily mass and the liturgical hours; a chancellor handled her correspondence, and a mayordomo managed her finances. Minor functionaries performed other tasks. Female relatives and noble wives and daughters attending upon her or being raised under her direction also resided with her. Sheltered from wicked men and women, their honor and security was guaranteed. Peeping toms or illicit lovers were charged with treason. The misconduct of a woman nursing the royal children was particularly reprehensible because of the possibility, according to ancient wise men, that her milk might cause illness or death—a notion foreign to modern medicine (*E* 2, 15, 1–13; *SP* 2, 14, 3–4). Immoral behavior by the queen, her children, or the ladies of her household affected the king because of the indissoluble bond of marriage and, in the most extreme cases, was punishable as treason.

Although the royal jurists did not describe the dress appropriate to a queen, Alfonso X, determined to curb extravagance, in the Cortes of Seville in 1252 (arts. 5–10) curtailed luxurious feminine apparel. Perhaps these restrictions did not apply to the queen. No woman was permitted to wear a dress or belt of gold, pearls, a chemise embroidered with gold or silver, serge or embroidered clothing, or a toque or headdress bordered with gold or silver, or of any color but white. She might wear ermine or otter fur and, if she wished, the sleeves of her gown might be wide open. The fine for violating this law was twenty *maravedís* per day. The price for a silk headdress, with or without golden decoration, was three *maravedís*. The fine for charging or paying more was ten *maravedís* and the buyer lost the toque. The price for six pairs of gilded women's shoes was one *maravedí* (arts. 6–7, 10). *CSM* 64 illustrates women's clothing.[45]

Educating Royal Children

Responsibility for rearing their children and arranging suitable marriages for them rested with the king and the queen, but perhaps more so with the queen in the early years. The progeny of a lawful marriage were called *fijos* (lat. *filii*). As *fijos* included sons and daughters, much of what was said about raising children applied to both sexes, though training appropriate for boys was distinguished from that for girls. Even when adults, princes were called infantes, and princesses, infantas. Loving them as "members of his own body," the king expected them to continue his good deeds. If they proved better than he, he should not think less of himself, but rather take pride in their accomplishments (*SP* 2, 7, 1). That comment recalls the deathbed counsel of his father, Fernando III:

> My son, you are richer in lands and good vassals than any other king in Christendom. Strive to do well and to be good, for you have the wherewithal. My Lord, I leave you the whole realm from the sea hither that the Moors won from Rodrigo, king of Spain. All of it is in your dominion, part of it conquered, the other part tributary. If you know how to preserve in this state what I leave you, you will be as good a king as I; and if you win more for yourself, you will be better than I; but if you diminish it, you will not be as good as I.[46]

Impressed by that lesson, Alfonso X quoted Proverbs 23:24: "The father of a just man will exult with glee; he who begets a wise son will have joy in him."

As his children guaranteed the future of the dynasty, they had to be cared for by honest and refined persons. Just as animals strive to give their young what is needed for survival, so human beings, who surpass animals in wisdom and intelligence, should do likewise. Children who were carefully reared would be healthy and strong, and learn to attend to important matters, leaving aside those of lesser concern. If the king neglected this and they fell into error, he had no one to blame but himself (*SP* 2, 7, 2; *E* 2, 4, 1–7; 2, 15, 1–8).

Once the child (*niño*) left its mother's womb, a healthy woman of good habits and family should be selected as a nurse (*ama*),[47] to suckle it until it was weaned.[48] If the nurse was handsome, graceful, and even-tempered, the child would love her and be more easily guided. Frightened by harsh words and blows, a child could become depressed and succumb to sickness and perhaps die. When boys reached puberty (*mancebía*), and became *moços*,[49] they were commended to a tutor (*ayo*), a person of good family, well mannered, discreet, intelligent, and loyal, and possessing a calm temperament and sound judgment. As the monarch was a peripatetic ruler, children, for reasons of tranquility and security, were cared for in a quiet place often far away from the court. However, as visits probably were restricted to great festivals, the process of bonding between parent and child was limited. Only in his teens did the child reside at court and travel with the king.[50] The most notable tutor was Juan Gil de Zamora (d. 1318), a Franciscan friar and a graduate of the University of Paris, assigned the task of educating the future Sancho IV. His *Liber de preconiis Hispanie*, dedicated to his pupil, is a mirror of princes extolling the glories of Spain.[51] As small boys were like wax on which an engraved seal could leave its mark, the tutor had to teach them to act with propriety (*SP* 2, 7, 3–4).

Given their social position and the obligation to give good example, royal princes had to learn proper table manners. A law summarizing the admonitions of parents in every age cautioned children to avoid gluttony and to chew their food thoroughly, not stuffing it into their mouths, or speaking or singing with their mouths full. Before and after eating, they should wash their hands and dry them on towels and not on their clothing.[52] Learning how to drink wine in moderation, mixing it with water, was important. Wine was a demon that produced harmful effects that are all so familiar: irritation, insubordination, indolence, headaches, lightheadedness, blurred vision, slurred speech, bodily weakness, trembling of the limbs, poor judgment, drowsiness, irrational behavior, and lasciviousness. Modern medicine, I suspect, would reject the conclusion that too much drink causes brain tumors or that intercourse in a state of intoxication leads to small and weak children (*SP* 2, 7, 5–6).[53]

Young men had to be taught to speak properly and politely. As speech and reason distinguish men from animals, human beings, but especially those in high position, should strive to be rational, because people remember what they say more than others. One ought not to speak loudly, too low, too rapidly or slowly, or flail one's arms, a sign of boorishness. As the situation required, one should use words necessary to convey one's meaning, but not so few as to impede understanding. As a confident air was a sign of nobility and grace, the tutor also had to teach them good manners. Thus, when spoken to, they should not gape with their mouths open. They ought to walk with assurance, not stooping, dragging their feet, or slumping in a chair. Their clothing, bridles, saddles, and horses ought to be elegant and suitable to the seasons. The tutor ought to speak to them in a kindly tone, because persons of good breeding learn more easily by words rather than by blows (*SP* 2, 7, 7–8).

Besides God and their teachers, the infantes should learn to know, love, and fear their parents and their oldest brother, their natural lords. The reference to their brother indicates that this law was written after the birth in 1255 of Fernando de la Cerda, the heir to the throne. As Sirach (23:7–15) warned against habitual cursing and swearing, they should always speak truthfully and swear only when undertaking obligations that they could meet. Cursing ill became any man and suggested little respect for God or oneself. Should the king and queen fail to teach their sons, they would sin gravely against God, themselves, their sons, and the people (*SP* 2, 7, 9).

Just as one had to lengthen a boy's clothes as he grew, so the king's sons, on entering young manhood and becoming *donceles*,[54] had to learn many new things. Literacy was essential because it facilitated learning and better enabled them to keep their secrets. Lest they focus entirely on the unattainable, they ought not to covet what they could not or should not have. They ought to desire what was good; to be merry, but not immoderately so; and to be protected from sadness. Learning about the lineage, station, and character of other men and how to talk to them was also important. As befitted a king's sons, they should be instructed in the arts of chivalry, learning how to ride and hunt, to play games, and to wield all sorts of weapons. They ought not be overly given to eating and drinking, nor should they make use of women, as such behavior was unbecoming and harmful. If they were educated in this manner, they would be men of good habits who would not treat others improperly. In that case their tutors would have fulfilled their responsibilities (*SP* 2, 7, 10).

As well as educating his sons, the king should settle them in good marriages and give them estates so they could live honorably. If he failed to endow them suitably so that they were not as wealthy as his other vassals, they might seek compensation elsewhere or perhaps go into exile. That notion perhaps reflected the minimal endowment that Fernando III conferred on his youngest son Infante Manuel. Lastly, the king should use their services in peace and war and punish them when they erred (SP 2, 7, 13).

Although he had much more to say about the education of his sons, King Alfonso also discussed the upbringing of his daughters. Whereas his sons might learn much by traveling about the realm, the infantas were more closely guarded. Great care had to be taken in choosing nurses and governesses to be their daily companions. As women of intelligence, loyalty, and honesty, they not only had to protect the young ladies, but also instruct them in good manners, so that they would respect themselves and their husbands and give good example. They should be taught to read, especially the canonical hours and the psalms, to eat, drink, and speak in a refined manner, and to dress suitably. They should especially learn to curb their anger, a sign of a wicked disposition that "more than anything else, leads women to do wrong." On the contrary, by learning the tasks proper to noble ladies, they would be happy and free of wicked thoughts (SP 2, 7, 11).

Perhaps the most significant responsibility of the king and queen toward their daughters was the selection of suitable husbands. By virtue of marriage, a girl passed from her father's protection to that of her husband. Thus it was all the more important that as soon as she reached the appropriate age, an honorable marriage should be arranged. Just as good lineage, beauty, upright habits, and wealth were qualities desirable in a prospective queen, so too were they valued in the young man chosen to marry an infanta. At minimum he ought to be a man of virtue from a good family. As a final admonition, the king was cautioned to guard his daughters against any occasion of sin, and they were warned not to engage in dishonest alliances that might result in the birth of illegitimate children (SP 2, 7, 12). Anyone who had illicit intercourse with an infanta would be condemned as a traitor. She would be disinherited and imprisoned at the king's mercy. By losing her good reputation, she could not marry appropriately to her rank (E 2, 4, 2; SP 2, 14, 2).

Political considerations were of primary importance when marriages were negotiated. If the couple developed a mutual love, that was a bonus. In 1254, for example, the king arranged the marriage of his sister Leonor to Prince Edward of England, but his expectation of English aid for his African crusade was unfulfilled.[55]

Considering an alliance with France as paramount, in 1256 Alfonso X betrothed his oldest child, Berenguela, then two, to Louis IX's son Louis, a boy of twelve, but the latter's death in 1259 ended the proposed union.[56] A later account stated that about a year later the Mamlūk sultan of Egypt asked for Berenguela's hand in marriage, but she reportedly refused on account of the religious difference.[57] As she was only about seven or eight, her parents likely rejected such a fantastic idea. Even in the desperation of his last years, it is hard to imagine that Alfonso X would consent to marry his daughter to a Muslim prince. Endowed with the lordship of Guadalajara, Berenguela appears never to have married.[58] The king made another attempt at a French alliance by marrying his oldest son, Fernando de la Cerda, to Blanche, Louis IX's daughter, at Burgos in 1269. The marriage was cut short, however, by Fernando's sudden death in 1275. In the subsequent dispute over the succession, Philip III of France became Alfonso X's archenemy rather than his ally.[59]

To advance his claims to Gascony, the king betrothed Sancho, his second son, to Guillerma de Moncada, daughter of Gastón VII, viscount of Béarn, but Sancho refused to marry her. In 1282 he wed his cousin María de Molina, daughter of Alfonso de Molina, a younger brother of Fernando III.[60] Hoping to solidify support for his imperial ambitions, in 1271 Alfonso X married his daughter Beatriz, then seventeen, to William, marquess of Montferrat, a widower in his forties. The king's fourth son, Juan, wedded William's daughter Margarita in 1275. The purpose of the union of his third son, Pedro, and Marguerite, sister of Aimery, viscount of Narbonne, was to secure assistance in opposing Philip III.[61]

The most significant royal marriages were intended to establish a firm relationship with France, but in the end, because of the quarrel over the succession, the opposite occurred. Political calculation prompted the other marriages, but none of them (other than the marriage of his illegitimate daughter Beatriz to Afonso III of Portugal) linked Castile with another royal house. Spouses from Béarn, Montferrat, and Narbonne were persons of distinction, wealth, and good family, but not among the most distinguished in Europe.

Brotherly Love

The bond of consanguinity obliged the king to love, honor, and protect his relatives and utilize their services. In return for the benefits he bestowed on them, they ought to love, obey, and protect him. However, just as one might amputate a rotting part of one's own body lest it corrupt the rest, so ought the king to dissociate himself from a disobedient and disloyal relative (*SP* 2, 8, 1–2).

The reality prompting that law was as follows. Fernando III granted Enrique, his third son, lordship of Morón and Cote and promised to exchange it for Jerez, Arcos, Lebrija, and Medina Sidonia once they were captured. However, in 1249 Enrique refused to do homage for that lordship to his older brother Alfonso. Thus, Alfonso X, considering Enrique's lordship a threat to his authority and a likely obstacle to his projected African crusade, canceled his father's charters in 1253. Dispossessed, Enrique was forced into exile in 1255 and entered the service of the emir of Tunis. While opposing Charles of Anjou's ambitions in southern Italy, he was captured in 1268 and released only in 1294. Returning home, he participated in the regency of Fernando IV, until his death in 1304.[62]

Around 1240 Fernando III sent his second son, Fadrique, to the court of his cousin Frederick II in southern Italy to obtain the duchy of Swabia, his mother's inheritance, but without success. Joining Enrique in Tunis in 1260, Fadrique also opposed Charles of Anjou in Sicily and helped to defend Tunis in 1270 against Louis IX's crusade. Returning to Castile in 1272, he was executed five years later for reasons never fully explained. The king's other brothers Felipe and Sancho were intended for ecclesiastical careers. Felipe, educated at Paris and archbishop-elect of Seville, had no inclination to the priestly life and, with the king's consent, married Kristin, daughter of the king of Norway, in 1258. That projected Norwegian alliance came to naught when she died in 1262. Felipe later led the rebellious magnates against the king, but died about 1274. Sancho, archbishop-elect of Toledo, died in 1261. Manuel, the youngest brother and Alfonso X's favorite, also joined Sancho's revolt and died in 1283.[63]

Thus, Alfonso X's relationships with his brothers steadily worsened and led to Enrique's exile, Fadrique's execution, Felipe's rebellion and alliance with the king of Granada, and, at the end, Manuel's repudiation of his allegiance. The royal herald expressed the king's sense of the disgrace brought on the family when he upbraided Felipe: "You, as the son of King Fernando and Queen Beatriz and brother of King Alfonso, ought to better guard the lineage whence you come and the duty that you have toward it."[64] The king might have similarly reproached his other brothers who betrayed him in equal measure. Although he accepted his familial and legal obligation to love them, he was adamant in declaring that if they turned against him he would sever all ties with them. That he did.

The Heir to the Throne

Aside from the queen, the king's most important relationship was with his eldest son and heir (E 2, 4, 1–7). Justifying the principle of primogeniture, the royal jurists emphasized that every firstborn male was holy and belonged to

God (Ex 13:1–2) and cited Isaac's words directing Jacob, whom he thought, in his blindness, to be his oldest son, to be master of his brothers (Gen 27:29). Alfonso X's hand is evident in those laws that were written when his relations with his brothers Enrique and Fadrique were fractured. One can imagine him apprising them of his superiority and their obligation to obey him. The royal jurists also argued that the custom of every realm where kingship was reserved to the eldest son precluded division of the kingdom among his siblings. As Jesus said, "every kingdom divided against itself will be laid waste" (Mt 12:25; Lk 11:17; Mk 3:24–25). Therefore, the kingdom, undivided, should pass to the eldest son or, in default of sons, to the oldest daughter. If the oldest son died before ascending the throne, the principle of representation stipulated that his legitimate son or daughter should inherit his rights, but if all his children died, his nearest male relative should do so (E 2, 16, 1–3; SP 2, 15, 2).

This law touched on two crucial issues, namely, the territorial integrity of the realm and the right of female succession. The dangers of partitioning the kingdom were revealed when Alfonso VII divided León and Castile between two sons in 1157. Unity was not restored until Fernando III, king of Castile since 1217, also became king of León in 1230.[65] Alfonso X, however, fearing that his kingdom might be dismembered, nullified his brother Enrique's lordship. Ironically, in later years, despite his insistence on maintaining unity, he proposed to divide his dominions.

The right of succession was not exclusive to males. In the twelfth century Urraca ruled as queen of León-Castile in her own right.[66] Alfonso VIII's heir presumptive was his daughter Berenguela, but her place was taken by her brother Enrique I (1214–17). After his sudden death, she was acknowledged as queen but opted to cede authority to Fernando III, her son by Alfonso IX of León. However, her regal status was recorded in his charters until her death in 1246.[67]

Thus, Berenguela, Alfonso X's first child, born in 1253, was accepted as heir to the throne by a General Curia or Cortes at Toledo in March 1254, in accordance with "royal sanctions and the custom of Spain." If the king should die without leaving a legitimate son, the assembled archbishops, bishops, barons, and chief men of his court and the procurators of the cities and towns pledged to accept her as his heir and successor. The king explained on 5 May 1255 that according to the general and approved custom of Spain, inheritance of the undivided kingdom belonged to the firstborn child if all the children were male or if all were female. However, if there were both males and females, the oldest son would always take precedence. Lamenting the desolation that would occur if his dominions were divided, he referenced the Gospel admonition concerning a house divided against itself and cited Lucan's phrase "every power is known to be impatient of having a partner."[68] Here the king repeated the principles set down in the Alfonsine Codes (*E* 2, 16, 1; *SP* 2, 15, 2).[69] Jerry Craddock suggested that the law in the *Espéculo* recognizing the right of the king's oldest daughter was written when Berenguela was his only heir.[70]

The royal jurists also stated that lest the tranquility of the realm be imperiled during a royal minority, everyone had to obey the guardians to whom the deceased king, either orally or in writing, entrusted his heir and the kingdom. If he had not done so, then the prelates, magnates, and good men of the towns should assemble and choose one, three, or five guardians. Natives of the realm and royal vassals, they should be intelligent and reputable men, who would not treat the king's property as their own. Whatever the majority decided should be valid. They should swear to protect the child-king, to act for his best interest and that of the realm, to uproot evil, to preserve the unity of the realm, and to maintain it in peace and justice until the king reached the age of twenty. If a daughter inherited the crown, they would serve until her marriage. If the child's mother were alive, she should be the most important of his guardians, provided that she did not remarry (*SP* 2, 15, 3).

These laws were prompted by recent dynastic history. In 1158 Alfonso VIII, then just two years old, became king after the sudden death of his father Sancho III. During the ensuing eleven years the Lara and Castro families contended for custody of the child, and for a time his uncle Fernando II of León was recognized as his tutor but never had control of his person. After Alfonso VIII's death, his eleven-year-old son Enrique I became king, under the guardianship of his older sister Berenguela. She entrusted him to Count Álvaro Núñez de Lara, provided that he not wage war against any adjacent kingdom, confiscate anyone's estates, or impose any tribute without her consent. However, as the self-styled *procurator regis et regni* he followed his own aims until the boy-king's accidental death.[71]

The succession attained critical importance in July 1275, while the king was absent from the realm seeking papal recognition as emperor. Fernando de la Cerda, not yet twenty, died suddenly while preparing to halt the Marinid invasion. Marinid victories over the Castilians at Écija on 7 September and at Martos on 10 October compounded that disaster. Infante Sancho, then seventeen, reorganized the defense, and hostilities were temporarily suspended.[72]

Thus, Alfonso X had to prepare for a new invasion and decide whether to acknowledge Sancho as his heir, instead of Fernando de la Cerda's son Alfonso, a five-year-old. The *Partidas* (2, 15, 2) favored the latter, stating that if the king's oldest son predeceased him, his son (the king's grandson), representing the direct line of succession, should inherit the kingdom. (The corresponding law in *E* 4, 16, 3 does not mention the right of representation.) However, an interpolation inserted after 1276, perhaps with the king's consent, affirmed the rights of the king's second son. The original version (*SP* 2, 15, 3) stated that a royal minority should end when the king reached the age of twenty, but the interpolation, as Jerry Craddock pointed out, fixed it at sixteen. As Sancho was already seventeen and would be twenty in May 1278, there would be no need for a regency upon his father's death.[73] Manuel González Jiménez remarked that this law demonstrates that the *Partidas* were regarded as the law of the land and that the supposition that they were not operative during Alfonso X's reign is incorrect.[74] Moreover, the alteration of the text reflects the king's assertion that he could amend the law when necessary.

Alfonso de la Cerda's pretensions seemed strong on legal grounds. During the Cortes of Burgos in 1274, Alfonso X, planning his papal visit, designated Fernando de la Cerda as regent. The Cortes pledged to accept him as king if his father should die. It is also likely that the Cortes, in accordance with an agreement between Alfonso X and Philip III, the boy's maternal grandfather, acknowledged Alfonso de la Cerda as the presumptive heir in case of his father's death.[75] Commenting on that agreement, Infante Manuel made the case for Sancho, in what González Jiménez called "una bella sentencia":

> Lord, the tree of kings is not ended by an agreement; nor is the one who descends according to nature disinherited thereby. If the oldest one descending from the tree dies, the branch under him ought to rise to the top. Three things there are that are not subject to an agreement: law, king, and kingdom. Anything done contrary to any one of these is not valid and ought not to be held or observed.[76]

Rejecting the law of the *Partidas* (2, 15, 2), Manuel upheld an earlier tradition favoring the succession of brother to brother. He also knew that Sancho, given his age, would be better able than the child Alfonso de la Cerda to face the Marinid challenge, especially considering the king's recurring illness. Also comprehending that reality, Alfonso X, in the Cortes of Burgos in 1276, set aside the law of the *Partidas* and appointed Sancho as his heir.[77] In 1283 he explained that he followed "the ancient law and the law of reason according to the law of Spain."[78]

As his health deteriorated, in the Cortes of Segovia in 1278 he conferred greater authority on Sancho, who, according to Juan Gil de Zamora, began to reign jointly with his father. In 1283 Alfonso X stated that he gave Sancho "greater power than any king's son had in his father's lifetime." He probably made that decision because Sancho, now twenty years old, would be able, according to the *Partidas* (2, 15, 3), to reign without a regency should his father die.[79] Nevertheless, the king, anxious to secure French assistance against the Marinids, proposed to cede the kingdom of Jaén to Alfonso de la Cerda to hold in vassalage of Castile. He had previously rejected partition as destructive of the unity of the realm, stating that "anciently they made a *fuero* and statute in Spain that the sovereignty of the kingdom should not be divided nor alienated" (*SP* 2, 15, 2, 5).

When he announced that intention during the Cortes of Seville in 1281, Sancho strenuously objected. In the spring of 1282, backed by the estates assembled at Valladolid, he deprived his father of royal authority, though leaving him the title of king. Responding bitterly, Alfonso X denounced and disinherited him.[80] In his final will in January 1284, he made matters worse by failing to name anyone as his heir, referring only to "the one who will inherit our kingdoms." He further dismembered his dominions by granting the kingdoms of Seville and Badajoz to his son Juan, and the kingdom of Murcia to his son Jaime, both to be held in vassalage of Castile.[81] When Alfonso died in April 1284, Sancho succeeded as Sancho IV, but the partisans of the Infantes de la Cerda kept their claims alive into the early fourteenth century. By favoring Alfonso de la Cerda and allotting Infantes Juan and Jaime a share in his inheritance, Alfonso X assured that Castile and León that he had done so much to develop would be thrown into disorder for many years.

Cabeça del Reyno llamaron los Sabios al Rey

The preceding pages describe an ideal order in which the king, as *cabeça del reyno* or head of the kingdom, as wise men called him (*SP* 2, 9, 16), presided over a carefully structured society seeking the common good. To facilitate that, the law prescribed the ritual of king-making, the virtues of a good queen and the ladies of her household, the proper upbringing of royal children, the qualities desirable in their tutors and future spouses, the bond of love between the king and his brothers, the right to the throne of the oldest son or, lacking male heirs, of the oldest daughter, and the regulation of a royal minority. The law codified the behavior appropriate to the king and his family and sought to guarantee the transmission of power from one generation to the next with the least upset. If that ideal had become reality, Castile-León would likely have enjoyed an era of peace and tranquility. Yet the everyday world impacted the life of the king and his family in ways that made the achievement of that ideal elusive. The orderly house erected in the *Partidas* collapsed with the invasion of the Marinids, the king's ongoing illness, and the succession crisis precipitated by Fernando de la Cerda's death. In order to save his kingdom from devastation by the Marinids, he set aside the law in the *Partidas* and declared Sancho as his heir. However, the law had not taken into account the possibility that an ailing king might not be able to fulfill his duties. To resolve that dilemma, Sancho, abetted by Violante and Infante Manuel and with the assent of the estates, divested the king of his authority. Thus, the well-ordered and prosperous kingdom that he envisioned in the *Partidas* dissolved into chaos.

✄ CHAPTER 4

The King and His People

Vicarios de Dios Son los Reyes

Acknowledging that kingship is divinely ordained, Alfonso X believed that as God's temporal representative on earth, he was responsible for governing the people confided to his care so they might live in peace and justice. Those ideas, set forth in the *Espéculo*, were greatly expanded in the *Second Partida*, which has been called the most original of the *Partidas*.[1] In persuasive and didactic language, the text, citing an array of "ancient sages and saints," explains the essential relationship of king and people. Frequent reminders that certain actions or inactions are treasonable emphasize the book's serious legal intent. While the king's men wrote the text, its very personal nature suggests that he took a close interest in it and that it reflects his thinking.

Royal Authority

An extensive *speculum regum* or mirror for kings expounds the nature, functions, responsibilities, and obligations of kingship.[2] The authors utilized Aristotle's *Politics* and the Pseudo-Aristotelian *Secreto de los secretos* and the *Poridat de las poridades*, texts translated from Arabic and purporting to be the philosopher's instructions to his pupil Alexander the Great.[3] The *Bocados de oro*, another translation from Arabic, was also cited.[4] Georges Martin suggested that the royal jurists initiated a new political genre, the neo-Aristotelian *De regimine principum*, and may have influenced Thomas Aquinas who penned his treatise on kingship around 1265.[5]

In the *Fuero real* (1, 5, 4), and in charters of 1255, Alfonso X affirmed "that the temporal and spiritual powers that both come from God ought to be in accord with one another."[6] In the twelfth century the two powers were identified with the two swords presented to Jesus at Gethsemane (Lk 22:38; Mt 26:51–52; Jn 18:11).[7] The spiritual sword "uproots hidden evils and the temporal those that are manifest." Discord between them was contrary to God's commandment and undermined both faith and justice, so that the land could not long remain in "good estate or in peace" (*SP* 2, pr.).[8]

As Holy Roman Emperor-elect,[9] Alfonso X, like other kings and emperors, was endowed by God with *imperium*, "a great dignity, nobler and more honored" than any other temporal office (*SP* 2, 1, 1).[10] That statement acknowledged a fundamental principle of Christian political theory, namely, that all power comes from God (Rom 13:1). However, the *lex regia* cited by the Roman jurist Ulpian (*D* 1, 4, 1) declared that the Roman people transmitted that power to the emperor:

> Quod placuit principi legis habet vigorem, utpote cum lege regia, quae de imperio ejus lata est, populus ei et in eum omne suum imperium et potestatem conferat.

> [What pleases the prince has the force of law because, by the *lex regia* that was enacted concerning his authority, the people conferred on him and in him all their authority and power.][11]

The royal jurists emphasized that the emperor, as God's vicar in the empire, "is not obliged to obey anyone, except the pope in spiritual matters."[12] Commenting on the divided imperial election of 1257, they paraphrased Lucan's remark that power ought not to be shared,[13] and argued that there should only be one emperor. Only the emperor could exercise de jure certain powers. He could make new laws, alter and amend old ones for the common good, abolish harmful customs, and sit in judgment and impose punishment. He could levy tolls, authorize fairs, coin money, delimit provinces and towns, make war and peace, resolve disputes, appoint provincial governors and judges, and collect provisions, tributes, and taxes. He could not arbitrarily dispossess anyone, but if he seized property for the common good, he had to compensate the owner. In order to govern effectively, he should gain the affection of his generals and territorial governors, seek the counsel of wise, intelligent, and loyal men, prepare for war by gathering sufficient treasure and consulting military experts, and administer justice and show mercy. He enjoyed the greatest power when he loved his people and was loved by them, but he was warned that he would lose their love and his ability to govern if he acted unjustly or treated them harshly (*SP* 2, 1, 1–4). Surely when those words were written, Alfonso X had no thought that they would come back later to haunt him. Ironically, by abusing his power and failing to guarantee due process of law, he lost the love of his people who rejected him.

Everything said of the emperor applied also to the king:

> Vicarios de Dios son los Reyes, cada uno en su reyno, puestos sobre las gentes para mantener las en justicia e en verdad, quanto en lo temporal, bien assi como el Emperador en su imperio. . . . El Rey es puesto en la tierra en lugar de Dios para conplir la justicia e dar a cada uno su derecho.

> [Kings are vicars of God, each in his own kingdom, placed over the people to maintain them in justice and truth in temporal affairs, just as the emperor is in his empire. . . . The king is placed on earth in the place of God to do justice and to render to each one his due.] (*SP* 2, 1, 5)[14]

The idea of the king as God's vicar can be traced to Paul's assertion that all power comes from God and that the ruler is God's minister to punish the wicked (Rom 13:1–10).[15] The royal jurists wrote that by standing in God's place on earth, the king, the "heart and soul of the people," was charged with doing justice so the people might live in peace and love. Just as the soul animates the body, so justice giving life to the people resides in the king. Similarly, as the heart unifies the members of the body, the people receive God's gift of being made one through the king, "the head of his kingdom." He is the bond uniting them; a wall protecting them; the sustainer of lesser folk, lest they perish; the suppressor of the mighty, lest they become proud; the animator of the downtrodden, lest they lose heart; and a curb on evildoers. As the feelings that stir the body originate in the head, so too the people should be guided by his commands. Because "he is the soul and head" of the kingdom "and they are the members," they should be in accord with him (*E* 2, 1, 1; *SP* 2, 1, 5).

In pagan times, according to Aristotle's *Politics* (bk. 3, chap. 14),[16] the king was not only a military commander and judge, but also lord over spiritual affairs. In the Christian dispensation, he took his title from God, the "king of kings," who maintained him on earth to do justice.[17] He might also be compared to a rule or ruler because he straightens crooked ways and corrects errors. As human beings inevitably disagree, one person was needed by whose wisdom they might live in justice and harmony. Just as the soul gives life to the body, and the head guides it, so the king gives the people health, wisdom, knowledge, and, through his laws, the facility to discern right and wrong, and the desire to do good and shun evil (E 2, 1, 2–5; SP 2, 1, 6–7).

These passages accentuate several ideas common to medieval political thought. First, the king, as God's temporal representative on earth, is responsible for administering justice and according to each person his due. Secondly, the body politic with its diverse members is compared to the human body whose various parts perform functions essential to the well-being of the whole. As the soul gives life to the human body and the head directs its activities, so the king unifies and commands the body politic.[18]

Throughout this discussion, the royal jurists stressed that kings possessed the same authority in their realms as the emperor had in his empire (SP 2, 1, 5). That reflected the principle "rex in regno suo imperator est" (the king is emperor in his own kingdom)—cited by medieval lawyers to affirm royal sovereignty and to attribute to the king the powers assigned to the emperor in Justinian's Code.[19] Quoting Innocent III's statement "cum rex non recognoscit superiorem in temporalibus" (as the king does not recognize a superior in temporal matters), the legists also asserted the king's independence of the Holy Roman Emperor.[20]

Repudiating any suggestion that Spain was ever subject to the empire, the canonist Vincentius Hispanus (d. 1248) remarked that Charlemagne never dominated the Iberian Peninsula. He added that the Spaniards were creating their own empire and had their own laws and had no need of imperial laws.[21] Lucas of Túy also emphasized that Spain had her own laws and that her kings "are not subject to any temporal empire." Infante Sancho's tutor, Juan Gil de Zamora, repeated that language.[22] As a hereditary monarch, Alfonso X claimed to have greater powers than an elected emperor, including the right to take from the kingdom whatever was necessary for the common good (SP 2, 1, 8).[23]

He also rejected any temporal subordination to the papacy or the empire by saying: "por la merçed de Dios non auemos mayor ssobre nos en el tenporal" (by the grace of God we do not have anyone greater than us in temporal affairs) (E 1, 1, 14).[24] His jurists affirmed that principle when they disallowed an appeal from a judgment rendered by a king or emperor because "ellos non han mayorales sobre si quanto es en las cosas temporales" (they have no superiors over themselves with respect to temporal matters) (SP 3, 23, 17). His predecessors, imitating the practice of the Roman emperors, often described their authority as maiestas, but that term appears only infrequently in Alfonsine texts. Nevertheless, the words mayor or mayoral, derived from the abstract noun mayoría, conveyed the same idea of sovereign authority.[25]

Royal sovereignty was usually described as señorío, a word originally meaning lordship or dominion.[26] Sometimes señorío del regno was used.[27] In

1283 and 1284 Alfonso X referred to his "sennorío mayor de Castella e de León" and his "sennorío de España."[28] *Señorío* was "the supreme power that emperors and kings have to punish evildoers and to render to each one his due" (*SP* 3, 28, 1). At the king's accession, the people should swear to preserve the unity of his *señorío* (*E* 2, 16, 2–3; *SP* 2, 13, 20). *Señorío* was one, because "according to nature, [it] does not want a companion" (*SP* 2, 1, 1). Here Lucan's *potestas* was translated as *señorío*.[29] Certain rights pertaining to the *señorío del rey* should never be alienated: the right to coin money (including *moneda forera*, a tribute paid in return for his pledge not to alter the coinage); the administration of justice; the right to make war and peace; *fonsadera*, a tribute paid in lieu of military service; and hospitality (*yantar*).[30] An affair might touch "the person of the king or his *señorío*" or be "against the king or against his *señorío*" (*E* 2, 7, 3; 5, 12, 4; *FR* 2, 1, 3; 2, 8, 8; 2, 12, 2; 2, 13, 4; 3, 9, 2).

The jurist Jacobo de las leyes linked several key terms when he advised Alfonso Fernández, the king's illegitimate son, "to guard your dignity and your *señorío* which is called in Latin office or jurisdiction" (*FD* pr.). *Señorío* was an *officium*, a *dignitas*, or public duty conferring on the incumbent jurisdiction, namely, the right to declare the law. The *imperium* or authority given to kings and emperors by God was a great dignity (*SP* 2, 1, 1). According to Ernst Kantorowicz, dignity "referred chiefly to the singularity of the royal office, to the sovereignty vested in the king by the people and resting individually in the king alone."[31] By virtue of his office, the king, no matter his personal qualities, should be treated with honor and respect. As he held God's place on earth and, like Jesus, bore the royal title, his duty was to do good to his people and guard them from evil. They, in turn, should honor him, his family, and his officials (*E* 2, 1, 5).

True kings gained sovereignty through inheritance by the deceased monarch's eldest son or nearest relative, by the consent of the people when there was no clear heir, by marriage to a royal heiress, or by papal or imperial concession. However they came to power, kings were obliged to foster the common good. They ought to love and honor people of every station, enjoy the company of learned and intelligent persons, promote love and concord, do justice by giving to each one his due, and confide in their own people rather than in foreigners (*SP* 2, 1, 9).

The Character of a King

A good king, according to the royal jurists, ought to be a man of high character and excellent personal qualities. In order to govern intelligently, he ought to know, love, and fear God, whose place he occupies on earth. Protecting the people commended to him by God, he should rule with compassion and assure "each one of justice and right." He must uphold the faith, suppress its enemies, and protect churches and ecclesiastics. If the king governs in this manner, God will prompt his people to know, love, and fear him. A good king will be rewarded in paradise, but a wicked one will be punished severely. As the desire for riches is "the root of all evils" (1 Tm 6:10), he ought to use his fortune for good (*SP* 2, 2, 1–4; 2, 3, 1–5).

In reasonable and temperate tones, he should articulate his words clearly so as not to be misunderstood. Always adhering to the truth, he should never deliberately tell a lie, for if he is given to lying, his people will not believe him when he speaks the truth. As his words will betray his intellectual shortcomings, he ought to avoid foolish talk, never boast, never praise others beyond their merits, never blaspheme, or defame an innocent person (*SP* 2, 4, 1–5).

Moderation should guide his personal habits. Eating and drinking for his good health, he should guard against excess. Indeed, the Cortes of Valladolid in 1258 urged him to eat "as he thinks best for his body," but as a money-saving measure, the daily expenditure for food for the king and queen (not counting foreign guests) should be no more than 150 *maravedís*. The cost of meals for the royal household should be more modest than it was (arts. 1, 3). Overindulgence in wine might cause him to offend God, reveal secrets, and make faulty judgments; it could also lead to disease and death. The admonition not to engage in promiscuous sexual conduct and beget illegitimate children, thereby dishonoring himself and his sovereignty, is quite ironic as Alfonso X had at least four bastards by several women. So that men might recognize him, he should carry himself well and dress stylishly in silk clothing. During great feasts and during the Cortes, he should wear a golden crown set with precious stones (*SP* 2, 5, 1–5). The Cortes of Valladolid in 1258 affirmed that he should dress as he thought proper and have as many outfits as he wished (art. 2).

By developing good habits and exhibiting the manners of a well-bred man, the king would exemplify an honorable life. The virtues of faith, hope, and charity would enable him to win the love of God and man, while prudence, temperance, fortitude, and justice would help him to live well and justly. In his daily life he should strive to be patient and equable and never yield to anger or hatred. He must maintain a calm demeanor until anger passes, for only then will he be able to perceive the truth and act fairly. Provoked by anger, he might inflict unjust punishment, and so incur the wrath of God and of the people. Although he should extend good will to men of good will, he should hate enemies of the faith and those guilty of treason, forgery, and other great crimes. As it was his duty to proceed justly, he ought not to act hastily, attempt to do something inappropriate, or desire something that could not occur, such as the practice of alchemy. As Solomon said, "a just king and a lover of justice governs his land uprightly, but the one who is overly covetous destroys it."[32] Therefore the king should not be greedy or make unjust and unreasonable demands (SP 2, 5, 6–15).

Reflecting on the proverb "the one who is sparing toward himself and generous to his people is just,"[33] Juan Gil de Zamora extolled the virtue of largesse, but warned that the ruler who filled his own pockets while emptying those of his people destroyed his kingdom. Ancient princes ruled, not for money, but rather glory and the utility and protection of the republic. Avarice causes kings to lie and break off friendships and alliances and ultimately to lose their kingdoms. God expected kings to counsel, assist, and defend their people, not to oppress the poor, widows, orphans, and children with unaccustomed exactions. Aristotle reportedly counseled Alexander: "whoever advises you to extort money from your people is advising them to hate you, and is advising your destruction." Juan Gil concluded with a blessing for the king who lived temperately. "For the strong kings of Spain temperance served as a brake on greed."[34] Those words of caution were likely inspired by Juan Gil's awareness of Alfonso X's extravagance and the burden of taxes imposed on his people.

A wise king should be literate and familiar with the *saberes* or fields of knowledge useful for the business of kingship. That would allow him to form his own judgments and not be overly dependent on any of his counselors. By studying scripture he would deepen his understanding of the faith, while knowledge of other subjects would help him govern his people. Aside from the wisdom to be gained from books, he should familiarize himself with other men, studying their lineage, habits, and deeds in order to identify those on whom he could rely and those of whom he should be wary. Developing skill in the use of arms, he ought also to find diversion in hunting, a pleasant form of recreation illustrated in *CSM* 142. He should also spend time listening to music and song, playing chess and other games, but never gambling, and reading histories and romances and other books that give pleasure (SP 2, 5, 16–21).

The King's Court and Household

In order to execute his duties, the king required the assistance of the officials constituting his court and household. In the twelfth century the term *curia regis*, referring to his ordinary entourage, came into general use,[35] but gave way in the thirteenth century to *corte del rey*. According to the royal jurists, the sword of justice was kept there to cut away evil. Although *casa del rey* was often used interchangeably with *corte del rey*, in time the former referred to the domestic services of the royal household, while the latter emphasized the public functions of administration and justice. Wherever the king might be was also his palace, so-called because one could speak openly and truthfully there. By whatever name it was called, the royal court was the chief instrument whereby Alfonso X exercised his authority.[36]

Surrounded by his counselors, the king gave audience to men who came to honor him, plead for justice, seek favors, discuss their concerns, and offer advice or their services. At the royal court, men and women and the children of magnates learned the habits of *cortesía* (courtesy), namely, kindness, good manners, and proper language. Shunning secrecy, deceit, mockery, vilification, and loud argument, they were rightly described as *corteses* (courteous) (*SP* 2, 9, 27, 29–30).

As there was no capital city, in order to be effective, the king, accompanied by his court, traveled throughout his realm, spending weeks, months, or even years in places requiring attention. Thus, in 1252–53 he resided at Seville, organizing his government and repopulating the city and its district. He was there again in 1261–63 tending to the Mudéjar revolt and the African crusade. In 1270–71 he lived at Murcia settling that recently rebellious region. The closing years of his reign were spent mainly at Seville because of the Marinid threat.[37] As an expression of honor and respect, everyone was expected to kiss his hand upon his arrival or departure (*SP* 4, 25, 5). The *besamanos* became a commonplace of royal ceremonies throughout the centuries.

As Aristotle counseled Alexander,[38] officials should serve the king as their lord and defend the kingdom as they would his body. They should not be overly poor, lest they be susceptible to bribery, nor powerful nobles, scornful of daily service and likely to do harm and demean the king. Rather, they should be men of middle rank, of decent origin, with some property, and endowed with intelligence, good sense, and unswerving loyalty. Measured in conduct, unmoved by feelings of love, hate, or envy, impervious to bribes, they should always strive to be of one will with him. As a superior man, according to Seneca, would always seek counsel before acting, the king ought to appoint as counselors men whom he loved and trusted.[39] Intelligent, prudent, and discreet men of good judgment, who would never reveal his secrets, they should know how to manage important affairs. Nothing worse could befall the king than to have an enemy as his counselor (Sir 37:7–10). Despite the advice attributed to Aristotle, magnates appointed to the highest offices were the king's most prominent counselors (*SP* 2, 9, 1–2, 5–6).

All royal officials had to take an oath to the king. Kneeling before him with their hands in his, they swore to protect his life, to serve his honor and advantage, to give him loyal counsel, to guard his secrets, to protect whatever property they held of him or that pertained to his dominion, to obey his commands, to fulfill the duties of their office well and loyally, and never to do anything contrary to this oath. The king then invested each man with the symbol of his office, but the text does not describe those symbols (SP 2, 9, 26).

Visitors were assured of secure access to the royal court, and also during their journey to and from the court. Whoever killed or wounded another in the king's presence, or in the town where he resided, or within three miles thereof, would be executed as a traitor (E 2, 14, 1–9; SP 2, 16, 1–4). Just prior to the Cortes of Burgos in 1272, the nobles alleged their fear of entering the city unless the king granted them a truce and allowed them to bear arms. Although he asserted that everyone was safe in his court and had no need of arms there, he agreed to meet them outside the walls.[40]

The king's court included both clerics and laymen, the former charged with his spiritual welfare and the latter with temporal affairs. The chief chaplain, for example, was the king's spiritual advisor, who celebrated mass and the liturgical hours, heard his confession, and expounded the scriptures to him (E 2, 12, 1, 5; SP 2, 9, 3). Juan Martínez, capellán mayor, witnessed the king's will in 1283.[41]

The principal place of honor, according to ancient custom, belonged to the alférez (ar. al-faris), a noble of high rank who carried the royal standard in the king's presence, led troops into battle in his absence, and bore the sword of justice in his court. As the king's advocate, he demanded reparation from those who diminished royal sovereignty, brought great men to justice, defended those accused falsely, and appointed advocates for noble widows and orphans. For many years the king's brother Manuel held this post, but after his defection in 1282, the king appointed his youngest son Juan as alférez. Second in rank was the mayordomo mayor who supervised the entire household, especially the financial accounts (E 2, 13, 1–2; SP 2, 9, 16–17). The king named Fernando de la Cerda to this position after his birth, but a subordinate carried out its functions. After Fernando's death in 1275, Infante Manuel briefly held the office. The names of the alférez and mayordomo mayor customarily were included in the circumference of the wheel depicted at the bottom of royal privileges.[42]

Other officials of state, whose activities will be discussed in later chapters, included alcaldes or judges, the adelantado mayor del rey supervising the administration of justice, and the alguacil or justicia mayor who maintained security and enforced their judgments. Territorial administration was the responsibility of the *adelantados mayores* and *merinos mayores*. The *almirante* or admiral commanded the fleet (*E* 2, 13, 3–7; *SP* 2, 9, 18–24). The *almojarife* (ar. *al-mushrif*) directed an army of tax collectors who had to render accounts annually (*SP* 2, 9, 25). The post was often filled by Jews, such as Solomon ibn Zadok (Don Çulema) and Meir ibn Shoshan. The former's son Isaac ibn Zadok (Zag de la Maleha) and the latter's sons Isaac and Joseph served as tax farmers.

As everyone benefited when the king was in good health, the physicians who cared for his physical well-being and tended to him when ill had a significant responsibility (*E* 2, 12, 4; *SP* 2, 9, 10). After suffering a kick in the head by a horse at Burgos in 1269, Alfonso's health began to deteriorate as reports of his illnesses at Ávila (1273), Requena (1273), Beaucaire (1275), Vitoria (1276), and Seville (1281) suggest. Modern examination of his remains revealed that he developed a cancerous growth below his eyes, perhaps the cause of his increasingly irascible behavior that ultimately led to his deposition in 1282. In his last days he was attended by his personal physician, Master Nicolás.[43]

The *repostero mayor* or butler oversaw service at the royal table,[44] while the *despensero mayor* or dispenser purchased victuals and other necessities The *camarero mayor* or chamberlain guarded the king's bedchamber, clothing, and other belongings. The *portero mayor* or chief herald supervised a group of *porteros*, heralds or ushers who admitted people to the king's presence, and otherwise carried out his orders.[45] The *posadero mayor* or lodging master arranged lodgings for the king and his company when they traveled (*SP* 2, 9, 11–15). During the Cortes he requisitioned rooms from local people who often found these visitors to be unwelcome guests. Nevertheless, the king assured the townspeople that they would not have to lodge anyone without their consent. Lodgers were expected to pay rent and were forbidden to steal anything from householders.[46] *Mandaderos*, perhaps best described as ambassadors, were men capable of articulating the king's wishes and keeping his secrets. Pseudo-Aristotle called them the king's eyes and ears (*SP* 2, 9, 21).[47] The *mesnada del rey* or household cavalry guarded the king's person by day and night (*E* 2, 13, 5–6; *SP* 2, 9, 9).

The household also included chamberlains and chambermaids, cupbearers, cooks, and other kitchen personnel. An indeterminate number known collectively as the *criazón del rey* were young people reared in the court and assigned to such tasks as archers, falconers, cellarers, or guardians of royal granaries. At any given time, the court probably included more than a hundred people. Penalties for attacking the king's officials varied depending upon the person assailed and the status of the attacker. A fine of five hundred *maravedís* was common, but it could be one thousand to two thousand payable to the king and an equal amount to the injured person. The perpetrator might also be deprived of his estates, banished, or executed (*E* 2, 13, 8–9, 12–13).

Although Alfonso X was a prodigal king, he attempted to restrain extravagance at court and curb the growing consumer mentality and taste for luxury. As it was important that he maintain a dignified appearance and dress appropriately for his rank, the Cortes of Valladolid in 1258 (art. 14) reserved to the king (and to a bridegroom) the right to wear garments of scarlet, *cendal* (a finely woven cloth), or silk. Eliminating excessive display, the Cortes also limited the types of clothing worn by courtiers and nobles. Royal scribes, crossbowmen, falconers, and porters (with the exception of the chief official of each group) were forbidden to wear white garments, scarlet breeches, gilded shoes or spurs, hats with brass markings, saddles adorned with gold or silver, and silken garments. Household clerics had to wear the full tonsure and avoid the use of bright colors, as well as open sleeves and cord shoes. They should wear dark breeches and use plain saddles and bridles, though some exceptions were made for clerical procurators and cathedral canons (arts. 4–5).

Bernard Reilly remarked that the chancery was "the one undoubted institution of government . . . the oldest institution of royal, central government, after the office of king itself."[48] The chancery served as an essential means of communicating royal directives to the entire realm. By the thirteenth century a professional staff, mostly clerics, developed procedures for composing, issuing, and recording royal documents.[49] As the majority of his people did not understand Latin, the language employed for centuries for serious discourse, Alfonso X opted to use Castilian for chancery documents and law codes, and also for many of the literary works carried out under his aegis. Nevertheless, his imperial chancery, headed by a *protonotarius sacri imperii*, issued Latin documents under its own seal.[50]

Under Fernando III the archbishop of Toledo held the title of *chanciller mayor de Castilla* and the archbishop of Compostela that of *chanciller mayor de León*, but those were honorific positions. The Alfonsine Codes do not associate the office of chancellor with the archbishops, though royal charters do refer to the archbishop of Toledo by that title. Only once was the archbishop of Compostela identified as chancellor. Although the *Espéculo* spoke about chancellors in the plural form, the *Partidas* mentioned only a single chancellor who approved the issuance of all charters and privileges. A member of the *consejo del rey* or royal council, he ought to enjoy the king's confidence, keep his secrets, and protect him against shame or injury. Able to read and write Latin and Romance, he ought to be a person of good lineage, common sense, good memory, and good habits (*E* 2, 12, 2; *SP* 2, 9, 4).

The Alfonsine Codes sketched an ideal chancellor, but in reality the daily business of the chancery was directed by three *notarios mayores* or chief notaries, one each for Castile, León, and Andalucía (this last an innovation of Alfonso X). Both clerics and laymen, they were expected to be prudent, intelligent, and reasonably prosperous, so they would not be tempted by bribes. Those having the title of *magister* were university graduates (*E* 2, 12, 3; *SP* 2, 9, 7). Faithful service in this capacity was often rewarded by ecclesiastical preferment. For example, Master Fernando, *notario mayor de Castilla*, was named bishop of Palencia in 1256, and Suero Pérez, bishop of Zamora, served as *notario mayor de León*. Master Juan Alfonso, archdeacon of Santiago and notary for León, was later named bishop of Palencia. Master Gonzalo García de Gudiel, notary for Castile, later became bishop of Cuenca, then of Burgos, and finally archbishop of Toledo.

After taking notes for a document, the notary directed the process of drafting, sealing, and registering royal charters. Scribes (*escribanos*) who composed the texts were expected to be intelligent men of good reputation who could write neatly and legibly (*E* 2, 2, 6).[51] They had to swear to draw up charters loyally and without delay and to preserve the king's secrets and not be swayed by fear or favor to do otherwise. A scribe who violated that oath could be executed for treason. As evidence of his work, he recorded his name at the foot of the document; if another did so at his request, that had to be noted (*E* 4, 12, 2; *SP* 2, 9, 8). If a document was incorrectly drafted, the notary would destroy it and demand a new one. Registrars (*registradores*) recorded the document in registers so that if the original was lost, defaced, or misunderstood, or if a false charter were offered, the register copy could be presented (*E* 4, 12, 7).[52] Custodians of the royal seals (*seelladores*) used to authenticate chancery documents had to swear that they would seal only those charters authorized by the king, the chancellor, the notary, or the judge, and that they would not reveal any secrets. Nor would they seal an unregistered charter; if a charter did not conform to chancery practice, they would alert the notaries (*E* 4, 13, 1–4). These regulations remained in effect for many years and were confirmed by later monarchs in the Cortes.

The most solemn document was the *privilegio rodado* written on parchment and so called because of the *rueda* or wheel at the foot of the text bearing the names of the king, the *alférez*, and the *mayordomo*. Divided into quarters by a cross, and often brightly colored, the wheel sometimes displayed castles and lions symbolic of Castile and León.[53] Following the subscription of the king and the members of his family, and the names of royal vassals, the bishops, magnates, and principal officials were listed in parallel columns to the right and left of the wheel. As these lists were stereotyped, one cannot say that each confirmant was physically present when the document was drafted. The date might also record a notable event, such as the marriage of Prince Edward to the king's sister Leonor in 1254.[54] Privileges were used for the appointment of royal officials; the concession of tax exemptions, *fueros*, pardons, leases, and contracts; the definition of boundaries; the rendering of accounts; the secure passage of animals; and permission to circulate papal and episcopal petitions.

Most royal business was recorded in charters (*cartas*). Whereas privileges should be written on parchment, paper was used for charters (*SP* 3, 18, 5).[55] Less elaborate than the *privilegios rodados*, charters dispensed with the wheel and the list of confirmants and were used for many purposes: the grant of estates; the legitimation of children; the recording of agreements; the authorization of the export of horses and other *cosas vedadas*; orders for arrests, the collection of taxes, or building castles; recommendations; the conduct of inquests; and the grant of safe conduct to royal envoys (*E* 4, 6, 1–25; *SP* 3, 18, pr., 1–25). The leaden seal appended to privileges and charters with a silken cord was visible evidence of their authenticity. A wax seal was used on most charters. The seal might display a castle and a lion on the obverse and reverse or a mounted king on the obverse and castles and lions quartered on the reverse.[56] In addition to their regular salary, the scribe and the custodian of the seal received one *maravedí* each for every privilege and half a *maravedí* for every charter. There are numerous examples of how different types of documents should be drafted (*E* 4, 12, 12–45; *SP* 3, 18, 4–121).

As noted in chapter 2, it is likely that chancery officials, at Palencia in May–June 1255, compiled a book recording fees to be charged for documents. According to the Ordinance of Zamora in 1274 (art. 40), the royal scribes proposed that chancery fees should be no more than those established in that book. Quite possibly, material from the *Espéculo* and the putative book of fees and chancery practice was incorporated into those sections of the *Partidas* (3, 18–20) dealing with documents, notaries, registration, and sealing.

As the royal court was an itinerant body and there was no permanent depository for its records, the perils of travel and nature inevitably took their toll, and the royal registers and other archival materials were lost. Consequently, the original privileges and charters must be sought in cathedral, monastic, noble, and municipal archives.

God, King, People, and Country

Charged by God to love and defend his people and to uphold justice and law, the king, as their head and loving father, should share their sorrows, chastise them with kindness, and be merciful to them. Elaborating on the

Pseudo-Aristotle's comparison of the kingdom to a garden, the royal jurists described the people as trees, the king as the owner, his officials as workmen, magnates and knights as watchmen, laws and customs as an encircling palisade, and judges as protective walls and hedges. Just as water facilitates growth, so the king should reward everyone according to his merits, but he should also wield the sword of justice to purge wrongdoers.[57] A good king would love, honor, and protect the estates of the realm: the clergy who preached the faith; magnates and knights who ennobled his court and defended the realm; masters of the sciences whose counsel pointed to the straight path; townspeople, the root and treasure of the kingdom; merchants who imported needed products; and craftsmen without whose labor no one could live. If he did so, prosperity would abound and he would be loved, praised, and feared. If not, he would have much to suffer both in this world and the next (SP 2, 10, 1–3). Before the end of his reign, Alfonso X would learn the truth of that statement.

The king was also bound to love and protect his country. The measures that Alfonso proposed to populate and cultivate it so that it would produce the essentials of life and contribute to the prosperity of his people will be discussed in chapter 12.

Paralleling the king's commitments were the people's obligations to love God, king, and country.[58] Endowed by God with understanding beyond all other creatures, the people who have faith and hope in God and love and fear God will be happy in this life and rewarded with the joys of paradise (SP 2, 12, 1–9). They must also love, honor, obey, and fear the king who receives his name from God and stands in God's place. Alluding to the divine command "do not touch my anointed" (Ps 105:15), the royal jurists condemned as a traitor anyone who assaulted or killed the king. Regicides and their families should be forever despised, their property confiscated, their houses torn down, and their fields uprooted. The kingdom whose king was murdered would lose its good name. No one should lie to him, defame him, intentionally mislead him, importune him for something he did not merit, or cause him to expend time and money in vain pursuits (E 2, 1, 6–10; SP 2, 13, 1–11).

Expressing their love for him by offering wise counsel, the people should also fear him, in accordance with the admonition: "fear God, honor the king" (1 Pt 2:17). As God conferred temporal authority upon him, anyone who disobeyed him contravened God's ordinance and would suffer perdition (Rom 13:1–7). The people should willingly obey him, answer his summons, and render military service, financial accounts, and justice. Always speaking truthfully and courteously to him, they ought to correct him quietly and discreetly if he were in error. While standing, sitting, or riding, they should always show him proper deference. No one should lie on his bed or jump over it when he was in it (*E* 2, 2, 1–6; *SP* 2, 13, 12–18). The people also honored him by honoring the queen, his family, and officials (*E* 2, 3–5, 12–16; *SP* 2, 14–16). The people's duty to protect royal estates, maintain his castles, and shield him against his enemies will be discussed in a later chapter (*E* 2, 6–11; *SP* 2, 17–19).

The people ought also to improve their native land by using its resources wisely. Following the biblical injunction to increase and multiply (Gen 1:28), they were encouraged to marry early, beget offspring, and teach them to love their country. Cultivating the land so that it abounds with all necessities, they should maintain their property in good order. Idlers who refused to work should be banished and, if healthy, denied alms. Craftsmen were exhorted to be honest, to avoid the use of false materials, and to complete their work promptly. Recommending a program of public works, the royal jurists urged people to break up rocks, cut tunnels through mountains, level highlands, and fill in lowlands. In order to defend their country, they should build castles, organize military forces, and provide funds for the expenses of war (*SP* 2, 20, 1–8).

Treason and Tyranny

The bond between king and people might by broken when they engaged in treason or when he ruled tyrannically. Treason (*crimen laesae maiestatis*; *crimen perduellionis*)[59] was a crime against the king's person, but also against God, the people, and the realm. The list of treasonable crimes was long: attempting to kill the king, or deprive him of his honor and dignity; conspiring to make someone else king; aiding his enemies; fomenting rebellion; deterring another ruler (the emir of Granada) from becoming his vassal and paying tribute; abandoning him in battle; revealing his plans to his enemies; killing his officials or hostages; violating royal sureties; assisting a traitor to escape; refusing to yield an office to someone else appointed by the king; and mutilating his charters and images or counterfeiting his coinage or seals. These acts were punishable by confiscation, exile, and death (*E* 2, 1, 6–8; 3, 5, 9, 12; *FR* 1, 2, 1–2; 1, 4, 1; 3, 12, 5; 4, 25, 26–27; *SP* 2, 13, 6, 9–25; 2, 18, 3, 5; 2, 19, 6–7; 2, 28, 2; 7, 2, 1).[60]

A traitor's children, forever branded as infamous, could not receive knighthood, hold office, or receive a bequest. His daughters, however, could inherit a quarter of their mother's estate, because women were not as likely to commit treason. The king might pardon a man who planned to commit treason but repented, and even reward him if he identified other traitors. The king would not punish a man who defamed him while intoxicated or out of his mind, but if he was lucid and had a legitimate grievance, he might attend to it (*SP* 7, 2, 2–6; *FR* 4, 4, 21).

The vehemence pervading the discussion of threats to the king reveals an intensity of feeling emanating from Alfonso X himself. Soon after his accession, he had to contend with the hostility of his *alférez* Diego López de Haro, and of his brother Enrique, but there is no evidence that they attempted to assassinate him. His brother Fadrique, given the king's poor health and Sancho's young age, probably committed treason by making a bid for power. In March 1277 the king, "on account of certain things that he knew about them," abruptly ordered the arrest and execution of Fadrique and his son-in-law Simón Ruiz de los Cameros. Without mentioning either man, *CSM* 235 related that some magnates, including the king's "closest relatives," conspired to overthrow him and partition the kingdom. Although Fadrique may have thought to make himself king, that would be contrary to custom and the law of the *Partidas*. It seems more probable, as Manuel González Jiménez suggested, that he intended to declare himself regent for the king whose recurrent illnesses indicated that he was no longer capable of carrying out his duties. Perhaps he would yield the regency when Sancho became eighteen and could govern on his own, but he probably would not have withdrawn graciously.[61] By executing Fadrique and Simón, Alfonso X opened himself to the charge, repeated in his own time and later, that he denied them due process of law. His blatant violation of that fundamental royal duty was a sign of his increasing irascibility that would lead Sancho to deprive him of royal authority five years later.

After describing treasonous activities by the nobility in past centuries, Juan Gil de Zamora related that at Segovia at some unspecified date "treacherous men fired three arrows at King Alfonso," but he escaped unharmed.[62] The king was in Segovia on several occasions, but I suspect that nobles, outraged by the execution of Fadrique and Simón and disgruntled by the king's failure to declare Alfonso de la Cerda as his heir in the Cortes of Segovia in 1278, attempted the assassination in that year. Juan Gil lamented that "miserable Spain is tormented by unaccustomed oppressions," and "today, on account of our sins, princes do not ask vassals for what is due, but for what is undue, not for what is just and customary, but for what is unjust and not customary." By contrast, he recalled the Roman legal maxim *Digna vox* admonishing the king to observe the law. His remarks clearly point to contemporary protests against Alfonso X's legal innovations and his imposition of extraordinary taxation. In the expectation that his student would amend abuses, Juan Gil declared that the name Sancho derived from the Latin *sancio* or sanction.

Adding that "lex est sancio iustiniana" (law is Justinian's sanction), he stressed
Sancho's obligation to do justice by giving everyone his due.[63]

A few years later, Sancho, in his father's mind, committed the gravest
of treasons. During the Cortes of Seville in 1281, the king announced his
intention to allot the kingdom of Jaén to his grandson Alfonso de la Cerda
to hold in vassalage of Castile. When Sancho denounced that idea, his father
threatened to disinherit him. In April 1282, Sancho, supported by Queen
Violante, his younger brothers, and his uncle Manuel, assembled the estates
at Valladolid and stripped his father of royal authority, leaving him only with
the royal title.[64]

In November 1282, the king, in the form of a judicial sentence, bitterly
condemned Sancho.[65] Seated in the tribunal in the palace of Seville, he
accused Sancho of "treasonably and falsely" conspiring against him, causing
him "grave and multiple injuries," concluding a friendship pact with the emir
of Granada, and seizing the tribute owed by the emir. Moreover, Sancho
charged his father with violating the *fueros*, liberties, and good customs of
his people and of impoverishing them with his financial demands. Surely
worst of all, Sancho said many "unworthy" things about him, namely, that
he was "demented and a leper, false, and a perjurer . . . who killed men
without cause, as he killed don Fadrique and Simón." In his fury, the king
accused Sancho of seizing castles and cities, ousting royal judges and other
officials, arresting his familiars and confiscating their property, intercepting
his correspondence and his envoys, and appropriating his treasure. Despite
that, the king, moved by "paternal love," and hoping to dissuade Sancho
from his erroneous path, invited him to meet him at Toledo or Villarreal,
"to order the good estate of the realm." With Sancho's counsel, and that of
the prelates, barons, and good men of the cities, he promised to amend all
outstanding grievances and to "arrange everything for the good of the state,
peace, and tranquility."

Nevertheless, Sancho, "unable to hide his malevolence toward us, and
blinded by the fire of ambition," summoned prelates, barons, knights, and
citizens to Valladolid to a *curia general*—"if one can call it a curia." By bribery
and threats Sancho induced them to "rebel against us and our authority."
"Without citing us, advising us, hearing us, or convicting us, he caused us to
be condemned, not by a judge, but by enemy conspirators." He was deprived
of the administration of justice, the custody of fortresses, and the revenues
of the realm, and was not to be received in any city, town, or castle. Furthermore, Sancho and his accomplices, by striving to have Sancho named king,
violently usurped the honor and dominion that he did not deserve, and disinherited the king. As the "culmination of all those evils," Sancho threatened

the king's life and encouraged the people of Andalucía to seize his person. In the hope of capturing the king, he launched an attack on Seville, and thus revealed himself as a parricide. However, God thwarted his "cruel intent" by encouraging the resistance of the people, and, "what is most admirable, the opportune help of the enemies of our faith," the Moors of Granada, or Marinids of Morocco. As a final insult, Sancho and his men shot arrows against the royal standard.

Without fear of God and entirely forgetting the reverence owed to his father, Sancho "impiously" inflicted grave injuries on him. Therefore, Alfonso X cursed his son, "as worthy of a father's malediction, as God's reprobate, and as worthy of being vituperated by all men. May he live henceforth as a victim of this divine and human curse." The king disinherited him as disobedient, contumacious, and ungrateful, "more so than the most ungrateful and degenerate son." Divested of whatever right he may have had as the king's heir, neither Sancho nor any of his descendants would ever succeed to the kingdom. This irrevocable sentence was sealed with the royal seal in the presence of witnesses, including bishops, nobles, and officials, and many clergy, soldiers, citizens, and an immense multitude of people.[66] That harsh tirade seemed to preclude any peaceful resolution of this dispute. A year later, when the king drew up his last will, he repeated his denunciation of Sancho as a traitor who cruelly dishonored him and even plotted his death. Calling down the malediction of God, the Virgin Mary, and the whole celestial court, he defamed Sancho as a traitor and again disinherited him.[67]

Nevertheless, just as Alfonso X could castigate his son as a traitor, Sancho could assail him as a tyrant. When a king abused his power, his people had to consider what recourse they had. In the early Middle Ages kings were often assassinated, and the assassin sometimes gained the throne. The nobles claimed a right of resistance, which usually took the form of rebellion as they attempted to compel the king to right perceived wrongs. One might also seek redress in the courts or petition the king in the Cortes. From the twelfth century onward scholars discussed whether it was licit to depose or even kill a king. Interpreting the *lex regia*, the legists argued that as the Roman people conferred their authority on the emperor, they might also reclaim it by deposing a tyrannical ruler and choosing another. Deposition, however, was an extreme measure that threatened the established order. Killing another person was morally reprehensible, but to kill a king, God's anointed, God's vicar ruling by God's grace, was construed as an offense against God. Initially, John of Salisbury (d. 1180) argued that a tyrant was a public enemy who might be killed, but ultimately he decided that it was best to leave him to divine punishment.[68] In general, the latter became the preferred doctrine.

In contrast to a true king, a tyrant gained power by force, deceit, or treason and, rather than serve the common good, used that power for his own benefit often to the detriment of the realm. Tyrants maintained themselves by sowing discord among the people, keeping them ignorant and in fear and in poverty. Lacking courage, unity, and the means, the people could not oppose tyrants who plundered the powerful, killed the wise, and prohibited confraternities and assemblies. That reference recalls Fernando III's prohibition in the Cortes of Seville in 1250 of evil confraternities, an injunction repeated by Alfonso X in the Cortes of Seville in 1252 and again in 1258, 1261, and 1268.[69] Tyrants also employed domestic spies and relied on the counsel of foreigners. Citing Aristotle's *Politics* (bk. 4, chaps. 10–11), Alfonso X commented that a king who legitimately gained power might abuse it, so that his lawful sovereignty would become unlawful. In that case the people could declare him to be a tyrant (*SP* 2, 1, 10). However, he left unanswered the question whether the people could overthrow a tyrant or execute him. This discussion of tyranny seems abstract and was probably included in the text for the sake of completeness. In 1282, however, when Sancho broke with his father, the issue of tyranny became very real.

In his condemnation of Sancho in November 1282 the king mentioned several charges that might be construed as signs of tyranny. In addition to trampling on his people's *fueros* and customs, he was accused of ruining them by frequent taxation, and of executing Fadrique and Simón without cause. Those accusations, originally attributed to Sancho and his supporters, were repeated in the Assembly of Valladolid in May. The *hermandad* of Leonese bishops and monasteries implied that the king had threatened them.[70] The town of Chinchilla urged Sancho to ask his father to maintain their good *fueros* and customs and to cancel the copper money in circulation.[71] In July, the Leonese *hermandad*, to which the Castilians adhered, denounced the king for "many acts contrary to law, many injuries, acts of coercion, killings, imprisonments, and excessive taxes, without being heard, and dishonorable acts, and many other things contrary to God, contrary to justice, and contrary to law and to the great harm of all the realms." Complaining that "we were deprived of law and maltreated . . . such that we could not endure it," they turned to Sancho to uphold their *fueros*, customs, and liberties.[72]

Treason and tyranny, then, proved to be opposite sides of the same coin. Although some attempt at reconciliation was made, father and son never met again. Though the king pardoned Sancho and asked Pope Martin IV to do so, Sancho may never have learned that.[73] His father's curse weighed heavily upon him. Many years later he remarked that he was dying not so much because of illness, but because of "the curse that my father gave me for the many reasons that I deserved it."[74]

The Idea of the State

Throughout the Alfonsine Codes, but especially in the *Partidas*, there are frequent references to the kingdom, not merely as a geographical area, but also as an entity distinct from both king and people.[75] There one can detect the emerging concept of the state, established, not on feudal ties, but on the corporate unity of king and people. Many early Christians believed that the state, with its coercive power, arose because of the sinful behavior of men. Rather than appeal to sacred scripture, however, royal theorists found much more congenial Aristotle's argument that the idea of the state was inherent in human nature, and thus essentially good.[76] Given that independent origin, the state was freed from any temporal subordination to the spiritual power.[77] Civil society arose naturally from birth or long residence in the kingdom, and helped to forge family connections and a loving relationship among the people (*SP* 2, 18, 32; 4, 24, 1–5). The king was the *señor natural* or natural lord of the people, who were *naturales* or natives of the kingdom and his natural vassals. That natural bond (*naturaleza*) superseded the feudal link between lord and vassal (*E* 2, 1, 9; 2, 6, 1; 2, 8, 1; *PPBM* pr., 1, 1, 6).[78]

The Roman term for the state was *res publica*, the public business. An abstract idea, it was also a corporate entity, a juridical person, with its own reason for being and its own public law. Although Juan Gil de Zamora used that word,[79] the royal jurists preferred *regno, tierra*, and *señorío*, often in the same passage with essentially the same meaning. Those terms not only identified the territory ruled by the king, but also expressed that abstraction, the state.[80] A kingdom (*regno*) is a country (*tierra*) that has a king as lord (*señor*) (*SP* 2, 19, 3). In his denunciation of Sancho in 1282, Alfonso X's reference to revenues that "belong to the kingdom" indicated his awareness of the separate identity of the state.[81] The classification of certain actions as treasonable offenses against both the king and the kingdom made the same point. On the other hand, the *Libro de los cien capítulos*, probably written toward the end of his reign, commented that the king and the kingdom were two persons, but one thing.[82] In contemporary usage *tierra* meant a benefice or fief, but also the kingdom. *Señorío*, meaning lordship, had feudal connotations, but it also referred to royal sovereignty. The term *corona*, in the sense of an invisible crown linking king and kingdom, but distinct from both, does not seem to be used in Alfonsine texts, but it was known to his collaborators. Sancho IV, for example, in 1285 cited a village belonging to the *corona real*. Nuño González de Lara, according to the early fourteenth-century *Chronicle of Alfonso X*, declared that he would never advise the king to release Portugal from the tribute owed to "the crown of your kingdoms."[83] Juan Gil de Zamora spoke of "the diadem of the three kingdoms" of Castile, León, and Galicia.[84]

The preferred description of the state and its component elements, king, kingdom, and people, was the body politic, which John of Salisbury described in the twelfth century.[85] Although Alfonso X did not use the word *cuerpo político* or body politic, he compared himself and his people to the human body (*E* 2, 6, 2; *SP* 2, 1, 5; 2, 10, 2).[86] The very concept of the body implies unity, an idea accentuated by the statement that the king is the one "through whom all the men of the realm receive the gift of God in being one thing" (*E* 2, 6, 1; *SP* 2, 1, 5; 2, 15, 5). Just as St. Paul stressed the interdependence of the diverse members of Christ's body, the church (1 Cor 1:12), so too Alfonso X affirmed the unity of the body politic, whose members depended on one another to perform functions essential to the well-being of the whole. As the soul gives life to the human body and the head directs its activities, so the king commands the body politic, unifying it under his leadership. By implication, disobedience would cause disorders throughout the body. An attack on the king, for example, was "against the kingdom because it removes from them that head that God gave them and the life whereby they live as one" (*E* 2, 1, 6).

As unity was a fundamental characteristic of the body politic, the king should not diminish it, especially by partition or alienation. In 1255 when Alfonso X required his people to acknowledge his daughter Berenguela as his heir, he stated that a private estate might be divided among heirs, but that succession to a kingdom was indivisible and entire. Quoting Lucan's comment that power ought not to be shared, he stressed that division would bring about the desolation foretold in the Gospel (Mk 3:25).[87] He also commented that "anciently they made a *fuero* and a statute in Spain that the *señorío del regno* should not be divided or alienated" (*E* 5, 11, 33; *SP* 2, 15, 5). The *Estoria de Espanna* remarked: "In ancient times the Goths agreed among themselves that the empire of Spain should never be divided, but that all of it should always be under one lord."[88] Ironically, in his last years, Alfonso X violated that principle when he attempted to partition his dominions among his contending heirs. In opposition, Sancho IV asserted that a king should not "diminish or partition his kingdom among his sons after his death, nor is it appropriate for him to alienate or to diminish the goods of his kingdom. The kingdom that is partitioned and diminished will be desolated to the root, as Jesus Christ said in the Gospel." Without mentioning his father, he reminded his own son to "observe how much evil occurred and how much bad fortune befell those kings who divided their realms among their sons, and, after the death [of those kings], the discord, wars, killings, and evils that came upon them on account of that partition."[89]

Conservation of the good estate of a unified kingdom was the king's essential responsibility. That idea was expressed by the words *utilitas* or *neces-sitas regni*—the utility or necessity of the kingdom. Juan Gil commented, for example, that the Roman consuls ruled "for the utility of the republic."[90] In 1282 Alfonso X spoke of his desire to achieve peace with Granada that would "redound to the service of God, the utility of the kingdom, and our honor."[91] In that year, the bishops and abbots, assembled for "the common utility and good estate" of the church and the kingdoms of León and Castile, prayed that Sancho would rule "for the utility of his realm."[92]

In order to satisfy the needs of the realm, the king had to assess its state. During the Cortes of Seville in 1250, Fernando III declared his desire to regulate the "buen paramiento de la tierra" (good condition of the realm).[93] In 1260 Alfonso X spoke of putting "in good estate the business of our kingdoms" and expressed the hope that the "realm would return to laws and good estate."[94] Appealing to the pope in 1277 to release the king from his oath not to alter the coinage, the bishops asserted that it was for "the good estate of the realm." The *hermandad* of 1282 was anxious that "the realm would be pacified and would return to the good estate in which it was accustomed."[95] In 1282 the king asked Sancho to meet him so they might "order the good estate of the realm."[96]

In trying to maintain the kingdom in good estate, Alfonso X sought to achieve the common good.[97] In 1282 he said that he hoped that the alliance between France and Castile would serve "the common good . . . not only of our dominion, but of the whole of Christendom."[98] He made the laws "for the service of God and the common good" (*PPBM* pr.; 1, 1, 1; 1, 1, 7; 1, 2, 9; 1, 6, 85; *E* 1, 1, 7; 3, 7, 8).[99] In 1277 the bishops emphasized that the alteration of the coinage would "be to the service of God and to the benefit of the king and of his kingdom."[100] Conversely, certain actions might be injurious to the kingdom (*E* 1, 1, 6; 2, 8, 1; 2, 16, 5). The *Espéculo* (5, 11, 33) stipulated that "if the king should swear anything that might injure or diminish the realm, he is not bound to observe that oath." Just as he might have enemies, so also might the kingdom, though usually they were the same people (*E* 2, 6, 2). Thus, in November 1282 Alfonso X condemned "a conspiracy against us and against our dominion" that was "a grave prejudice to our realms."[101] What was injurious to the realm might also be treasonable to the king and the kingdom (*E* 2, 1, 6; 5, 5, 7; *FR* 3, 12, 5; *PPBM* 1, 9, 57).

In asserting his obligation to preserve the good estate of the realm and the people's duty to love their country, the king and his scholars were attempting to inculcate a spirit of patriotism. Love of country, arising from the natural bond created between the land and the people, demanded that everyone attempt to cultivate it, exploit its pasturage, mines, and other natural resources, and develop it in good order so that "men will have a greater desire to live and to dwell in it" (*SP* 2, 11, 1–3; 2, 12, pr.; 2, 20, 1–8).[102]

El Buen Estado de la Tierra

As a we have seen, both the *Espéculo* and the *Second Partida*, in a more elaborate form, emphasized that the king, holding God's place on earth, was obliged to do justice to his people and to show them mercy. His authority was described as *señorío*, a word literally meaning lordship or dominion, but better interpreted as sovereignty, an inalienable right or power. In enunciating the two swords theory, the royal jurists distinguished between the spiritual and temporal powers, but as both powers came from God, they insisted that they should be in concord. Nevertheless, they were emphatic in asserting the king's temporal independence of all other rulers, including the pope and the emperor. Given Alfonso X's status as Holy Roman Emperor-elect, they were at pains to delineate the terms of imperial authority, but they also declared that the king in his kingdom had the same power as the emperor.

Although the notion of the king as God's vicar, ruling by God's grace, seemed to exalt him above all others and free him from any accountability to his people, there were practical limitations on his power. Like his people, he was expected to observe the laws. The Roman maxim *Digna vox*, which declared that the prince ought to abide by his laws because his authority depended on them, was well known to Alfonso X and his jurists. Furthermore, on multiple occasions he acknowledged his obligation to do justice and guaranteed the principle of due process, namely, that no action could be taken against any man until he had first been judged in a court of law. In addition, the long-standing principle that the king was expected to take counsel before undertaking any action was reaffirmed. The prelates, magnates, knights, and men learned in the law who constituted the royal court not only offered counsel but also implemented his decrees. If circumstances required a broader consultation, the king could summon the Cortes that included representatives of the cities and towns.

In explicating the nature of kingship, the royal jurists developed the concept of the state, an entity constituted by the unity between the king and his people and commonly described as the body politic. Ideally, king and people, motivated by their mutual love for their homeland, worked together to foster "el buen estado de la tierra" (the good estate of the realm). In expressing their patriotism in that way, they made the kingdom a desirable place to live. If the people resisted the king's authority and engaged in treasonable activity, he was justified in punishing them by execution, confiscation, or exile. On the other hand, if he wielded authority in an arbitrary or tyrannical manner, it was lawful for them to resist. Led by Infante Sancho, the estates of the realm reclaimed the authority entrusted by God to the king, effectively deposed him, and chose another, as Alfonso X learned to his sorrow.

❦ CHAPTER 5

Defender of the Faith

El Rey es Defendedor e Amparador de la Fe

As a thirteenth-century Christian ruling over a largely Christian population, Alfonso X assumed that Christianity was true and that all good-thinking people would adhere to it.[1] At that time the notion of separation of church and state was unknown. Believing that one of his fundamental duties was to defend the Christian faith, he reminded his Christian people of their obligation to follow church teachings and to acknowledge the pope's spiritual supremacy. As Jews and Muslims did not accept Christianity, he permitted them to worship freely and to be governed by their own laws. Although the Castilian bishops might be pleased by his defense of Christianity, they chafed under his domination and protested to Pope Nicholas III who called him to account.[2]

The articles of the Christian faith summarized in the *Espéculo* (1, 2–3) were compressed into a lengthy paragraph in the *Fuero real* (1, 1). Utilizing Gratian's *Decretum*, the decrees of the Fourth Lateran Council, and Pope Gregory IX's *Decretales*, the *First Partida* discussed the entire range of theological, structural, and canonical issues (*SP* 1, 3–24).[3] The text, generally written in the third person, emphasizes the authority of the church rather than that of the king.[4] The inclusion of this religious content in the *Partidas* suggests Alfonso X's conception of the unity of the law and of society and his obligation to guarantee observance of the church's mandates.

The *Setenario*, an incomplete revision of the *Partidas* compiled during his last years, attempted to show that Christianity was superior to other religions.[5] Proposing that all wisdom, science, and knowledge is one in God, the book argued that God is revealed in the seven liberal arts, the planets and stars, the signs of the zodiac, the articles of the creed, and the seven sacraments.[6] The *Setenario* (104) also includes a vernacular rendition of the canon of the mass.[7]

The substance of the *First Partida* applied to the universal church. Therefore, attention will be directed only to laws referring specifically to Spain and embodying royal enactments, namely, the obligation to observe the Christian faith, reverence for the Eucharist, and the protection of pilgrims. Issues in contention between the king and the bishops will also be considered.

The Christian Faith, the Eucharist, and Pilgrims

Acknowledging that law has its origin in God, Alfonso X briefly explained the doctrine of the Trinity (*E* 1, 2; *FR* 1, 1). In stating that the three persons are but one God, he rejected the Muslim charge that Christians were polytheists. Salvation was restricted to those who accepted the articles of the faith (*SP* 1, 3, pr., 1; *Setenario*, 42). The ancient doctrine "extra ecclesiam nulla salus" (there is no salvation outside the church), voiced by the Fourth Lateran Council,[8] found expression in the *Espéculo* (1, 2, pr.; 1, 3, 1; *PPBM* 1, 2, 1) and in the prologue to the *First Partida* (*SPGL* 1, 3, 1). The official interpretation of that principle emphasizes that those not visibly members of the church are not denied salvation; nor, indeed, is every Christian guaranteed salvation merely by virtue of membership in the church.[9] The king, however, condemned as a heretic who could not be saved anyone who did not accept the articles of the faith (*E* 1, 2, 1; *FR* 1, 1; *PPBM* 1, 2, 2; *SPGL* 1, 3, pr.).

Heretics were dismissed as madmen who perverted Christ's teachings. There were two principal heresies: any doctrine differing from the true faith taught by the Church of Rome; and the denial of an afterlife of rewards and punishments. The adherents of those heresies were worse than wild beasts and brought great harm to the kingdom, but if an accused heretic, persuaded by kind words and good arguments, repented, he should be pardoned. Otherwise, he should be handed over to a secular judge for imposition of the civil penalty for heresy. Depending on the extent of his participation, he could be burned at the stake, banished, imprisoned, fined, or whipped (*SP* 7, 26, 1–2).

The principal heresy of the time was Catharism, then widespread in southern France.[10] The Cathars may have disseminated their opinions along the pilgrimage route to Santiago de Compostela, but evidence of their existence in Castile is scanty. Bishop Lucas of Túy denounced them, but the accuracy of his account has been questioned.[11] Bishop Tello of Palencia imprisoned several heretics and appealed to Fernando III, who banned them and confiscated their property. Arguing that their property belonged to him as lord of the city, the bishop complained to Gregory IX, who upheld his position in 1236. He also ordered the bishop to absolve repentant heretics who could not afford the journey to Rome to obtain absolution. Furthermore, he confirmed the royal edict banishing heretics. When a citizen of Burgos, visiting Rome, expressed concern about his salvation because he had maintained contact with heretics, though he was not one of them, the pope directed Bishop Mauricio to absolve him.[12]

A heretic could not hold any public office, and his will, sales, or donations were void; but his Catholic children could inherit his property. The church acquired the estate of a cleric guilty of heresy. A man who knowingly allowed heretics to use his house would lose it. Anyone sheltering heretics would be excommunicated. A nobleman would suffer confiscation and exile. Persons of lower rank would be penalized as the king saw fit. There is little evidence, however, that heresy was a serious issue or that Alfonso X ever punished a heretic.[13] Nevertheless, his law condemning certain heretics to death by fire was the first law of its kind enacted in Castile and provided a legal foundation for the punishment of heretics in later centuries (*SP* 7, 26, 2–6).

In his later years, Alfonso X pleaded with non-Christians to acknowledge the truth of Christianity, the only true religion (*Setenario*, 37). In his will of November 1283, in language reminiscent of the *First Partida*, he expressed his personal faith. "Knowing that a man cannot be saved in any other way than by our Catholic faith," he declared his belief in the Trinity, Mary, the mother of Jesus, "who assumed human flesh to save us," and all the other church teachings. Fearful of divine judgment on account of his sins, he called on Mary, his advocate, St. Clement, on whose feast day (23 November) he was born, St. Ildefonse, whose name he bore, and Santiago, his lord and defender, to intercede for him, so that the angels would carry his soul to his Lord Jesus.[14]

While believing the articles of the faith, "a complete Christian" should also receive the sacraments (*SP* 1, 4, pr.). The *Espéculo* (1, 3, 3–5) allocated only a short paragraph to the sacraments and declared that anyone who did not accept them and all the teachings of the church should be punished as a heretic. The *Fuero real* omitted the sacraments entirely. The *First Partida* discussed only six of the seven; to avoid repetition the sacrament of marriage was placed in the *Fourth Partida* (1–12). The *First Partida*'s account of the sacraments is almost encyclopedic, but there is no need to discuss it in detail. There are, however, several laws that reflect the peculiar situation of Christian Spain. References to the baptism of Jews or Muslims (*SP* 1, 4, 5–6), royal anointing (*SP* 1, 4, 13), and possible treason by a royal confessor (*SP* 1, 4, 35) can best be discussed in other chapters. The sudden appearance of the words *mando*, or *nos don Alfonso rey*, or *mandamos* signals the incorporation into the *Partidas* of laws enacted apart from it.

One example concerns the proper behavior of Christians, Jews, and Muslims when a priest carried the Eucharist through the streets to the sick. After noting that canon law required Christians to kneel as the priest passed by, the king commanded everyone to accompany him to the end of the street. Anyone on horseback should dismount. Jews and Muslims, though nonbelievers, should kneel. If not, they would be arrested and imprisoned for three days. This law was enacted to safeguard Jews and Muslims from wrongful arrest and unjust punishment. The law did not apply to foreigners who were unaware of it (*PPBM* 1, 4, 59–61; *SP* 1, 4, 61–63).

This law coincides with an enactment in the *cuaderno* of the Cortes of Seville given to Talavera on 12 October 1252.[15] Sr. D. Rafael Gómez Díaz, the distinguished municipal archivist, informed me, however, that the *cuaderno* could not be found in the local archive.[16] Nor does the text in question appear in the other known *cuadernos* of the Cortes of 1252.[17] I have illustrated the concurrence of the texts elsewhere.[18]

The twelfth and thirteenth centuries witnessed a parade of pilgrims to Santiago de Compostela, purportedly the last resting place of the Apostle James. Their influx promoted the prosperity of Compostela and other towns on the *camino de Santiago*, but it also raised several legal issues.[19]

The *Espéculo* refers only incidentally to pilgrims, stating that they could not be summoned to court or deprived of their property during their absence (4, 6, 17; 5, 5, 15). However, one of the missing books probably contained the substance of the title on pilgrims in the *Fuero real* (4, 23, 1–4). In language reminiscent of a law enacted in 1228 by his grandfather, Alfonso IX of León,[20] the king guaranteed the security of pilgrims. Allowed to lodge safely wherever they wished and to purchase necessities, they were protected against anyone attempting to cheat them by using false weights and measures.[21] A pilgrim could draw up his will, and after his death his goods would be delivered to his heirs. Should he die intestate, local judges should use a portion of his property for his burial; the king would dispose of the remainder.[22] Judges who failed to punish innkeepers or others who injured pilgrims would pay twice the damages to the pilgrim and other legal costs. The *fazañas* record several instances of the abuse of pilgrims (*LFC* 265, 273–74). Unscrupulous toll gatherers reportedly extorted money from them at the frontier.[23] In a constitution granted to the archbishopric of Compostela in 1254, Alfonso X reiterated the rights accorded to pilgrims in the *Fuero real*.[24]

Pilgrimage was treated more amply in the *Partidas* (1, 24, 1–4), though not in *PPBM*. The *Partidas* distinguished between the *romero* who traveled to Rome and the *pelerín* who visited the Holy Sepulcher or Compostela. Among other shrines was Sainte Marie de Rocamadour in Languedoc often mentioned in the *Cantigas de Santa Maria* (SP 1, 8, 7). As pilgrims set out to serve God and honor the saints, or to fulfill a vow, or perform a penance, they were urged to make their pilgrimage with great devotion, not engaging in commerce, and traveling in company for protection. The substance of the *Fuero real* guaranteeing their safety and their rights was repeated (SP 5, 8, 27; 6, 1, 30–32), with two notable additions. First, should anyone seize a pilgrim's property during his absence, his relatives, friends, and neighbors could demand restitution, even though they did not have a letter of procuration authorizing them to act on his behalf. Secondly, no action could be taken against his property and no toll or other duty could be levied on his animals or goods (SP 1, 24, 3; E 4, 6, 17).

Pilgrims, then and now, seeking souvenirs, found them in abundance in the cathedral plaza. The cathedral profited from the sale of metal shells, the symbol of St. James, but other entrepreneurs sought to gain from this trade. Although several popes forbade pilgrims to buy or carry shells not made in Compostela, and prohibited their manufacture outside the city, that did not deter anyone.[25] In 1260 Alfonso X ordered the towns on the *camino de Santiago* to be alert to anyone daring to "make representations of Santiago out of tin or lead and sell them to pilgrims."[26] Whether that proved to be an effective deterrent seems unlikely.

The Challenge of the Bishops

The bishops had little reason to quarrel with the king's explanation of the faith, but they protested his actions concerning other issues. They did so during the Cortes of Burgos in 1272, so angering him that he threatened to expel them from the realm, but as he was eager to seek Gregory X's recognition of his imperial status, he designated Fernando de la Cerda to attend to their complaints.[27] Meeting him at Peñafiel in April 1275, they listed their grievances, which were likely identical to those presented in the Cortes. They will be discussed below.[28]

Evidently still dissatisfied, the bishops appealed to Pope Nicholas III, who, on 23 March 1279, chastised the king for his illicit exactions from the clergy, his seizure of church property, and intrusion into ecclesiastical jurisdiction.

In order to convey the gravity of the situation, he dispatched his legate, Bishop Pietro of Rieti, to urge the king to amend his ways.[29] A *Memoriale secretum* given to the legate specified seven principal concerns: (1) the *tercias*; (2) custody of vacant churches and monasteries; (3) harassment of Archbishop Gonzalo Gómez of Compostela and (4) Bishop Martín Fernández of León, both of whom had been driven into exile; (5) grievances detailed in several subheadings; (6) ecclesiastical liberties in Portugal; and (7) oppression of the king's subjects.[30] Subsumed under article 5 were assorted accusations: ignoring or violating royal privileges given to the church; abusing papal privileges granted to the king; establishing on his own authority a new religious order (the Order of Santa María de España, founded in 1273 and merged with the Order of Santiago in 1280);[31] preventing the publication of papal or episcopal indulgences; forbidding the bishops to meet in council or appeal to the pope; forbidding the clergy to take money out of the kingdom for necessary expenses, thereby effectively preventing them from traveling abroad for study or other purposes; and appointing Jews to positions of authority over Christians, a reference to Jewish tax collectors (*Memoriale*, art. 5, E, G, H, I, K, N). An article (M) that did not appear in the original *Memoriale* alleged that ignorant and vulgar persons were intruded into ecclesiastical offices, illicit marriages were contracted, and astronomers and augurs were consulted, a charge implying that the king was not entirely orthodox.[32]

Informed of the legate's mission in May, Alfonso X on 29 July asked Infante Sancho to consult prelates and other good men. A document restating and expanding somewhat the articles in the *Memoriale* (except 6–7), and accompanied by a partial Castilian translation and responses, probably represents the thinking of Sancho and his counselors concerning articles 1, 2, and parts of 5A. The main issues were royal seizure of ecclesiastical revenues, custody of vacant churches, episcopal elections, ecclesiastical jurisdiction, and the church's right to acquire property.[33] The *Memoriale* and the text sent to Sancho, together with his replies, do not provide supporting evidence for most of the charges. Even so, other sources reveal that there were substantial grounds for accusing the king of maltreating churchmen, interfering with ecclesiastical jurisdiction, restricting the church's property rights, and utilizing its resources as though they were his own. Perhaps in order to stir up popular support, Alfonso X authorized Sancho, who had little useful advice to give, to summon the Castilian towns to Valladolid in October 1279. The meeting was postponed to Salamanca in November, and thence to Badajoz, where the king evidently met the municipal representatives in February 1280.[34] The outcome is unknown, but it is likely that the townsmen, who had only disdain for ecclesiastical privileges, supported royal policy. Possibly at this time, in accordance with Nicholas III's wishes, Alfonso X encouraged his grandson Dinis, the new king of Portugal, to treat the church there more kindly than his father had done. In the long run, the legate's mission was unsuccessful and ended with Nicholas III's death in August 1280. His successor Martin IV was disinclined to pressure the king.[35]

The Election of Bishops

The king's attempt to control episcopal elections was a continuing irritant.[36] With a notable modification, he accepted the Fourth Lateran Council's regulation of the electoral procedure (canons 23–24). When a see fell vacant, the cathedral canons had to request his authorization to conduct a free election. Although he might propose his own candidate, he promised not to coerce the electors, unless he believed that they would elect someone harmful to him or his kingdom. He enjoyed these rights "porque es defendedor et amparador de la fe, et de las eglesias, et de los que las sirven, et de sus bienes e otrossí porque es sennor natural de la tierra ó son fundadas las eglesias" (because he is the defender and protector of the faith and of the churches and of those who serve them and of their goods and also because he is the natural lord of the land where the churches are founded).[37] Once the election was completed, the pope should be notified (*PPBM* 1, 5, 18, 26).[38] Although that law does not appear in the Montalvo, López, or Academia editions, they provide an alternate text stating that according to the ancient custom of Spain, the cathedral chapter had to notify the king in writing of an episcopal vacancy and ask his permission to hold a free election. Meanwhile, he would assume responsibility for the diocesan temporalities and surrender them to the newly elected bishop. The kings of Spain possessed those rights because they conquered the land from the Moors, transforming mosques into churches, substituting Jesus's name for Muḥammad's, founding new churches where there had previously been none, and endowing others. For whatever temporal goods he held of the king, the new bishop had to do homage, and he was admonished not to burden his diocese with debt, lest he be unable to meet commitments to the papacy or the king (*PPBM* 1, 5, 16–17, 28; *SP* 1, 5, 17–25, 29).

The right to conduct a free election was limited in practice by the intrusion of the king and the pope. As a means of providing for his younger sons, and of rewarding clerics for faithful service, the king often nominated his candidate. The canons usually accepted him and the pope confirmed him, but he could reserve a disputed election. Ambitious clerics soon realized that royal service was a sure path to ecclesiastical advancement, and the king expected that once promoted to an episcopal see, they would be docile servants.

The king endeavored to place suitable candidates in the three archiepiscopal sees. Fernando III named his sons Felipe (1249–58) and Sancho (1252–61) to the archbishoprics of Seville and Toledo respectively, but Felipe was never consecrated.[39] After Felipe's resignation, Alfonso X secured the election of Remondo (1259–86), bishop of Segovia.[40] Following the death of Sancho I of Toledo, the king persuaded Pope Clement IV to designate Jaime I's son, Sancho II, in 1266.[41] When Sancho was killed by the Marinids in 1275, the king nominated Fernando de Covarrubias, but Nicholas III reserved the election. In 1280 he appointed Gonzalo García de Gudiel, the royal notary for Castile, who, on the king's initiative, had previously been elected as bishop of Cuenca, and then as bishop of Burgos.[42] Fernando de Covarrubias was given the bishopric of Burgos.[43] On the death of Juan Arias, archbishop of Compostela (1237–66), the canons refused to elect the royal notary for León, Juan Alfonso, and the see remained vacant until Gregory X appointed Gonzalo Gómez in 1272.[44] After Gonzalo's death in 1281, Martin IV reserved the appointment, but the see remained vacant for five more years.[45] Nomination to a bishopric was often a reward for service in the royal court. Both Suero Pérez, bishop of Zamora (1255–86), and Martín Fernández, bishop of León (1254–89), served as notaries for León.[46] In 1279 Bishop Martín was exiled for protesting the king's treatment of the church (*Memoriale*, art. 4, B").[47] Fernando, notary for Castile, was elected bishop of Palencia in 1256 and was succeeded in 1266 by another notary, Juan Alfonso, illegitimate son of the king's uncle Alfonso de Molina.[48] Pedro Lorenzo and Agustín, elected respectively bishops of Cuenca and Osma, had also served the king.[49] Pedro Fernández, the royal chaplain, was bishop of Astorga, and Fernando, the royal physician, was bishop of Coria, and Fray Pedro Gallego, the king's confessor, was bishop of Cartagena. Although García Martínez, another royal servant, was elected to succeed him, Nicholas III nullified the election in 1278, naming Diego Martínez instead.[50] Lope Pérez, elected bishop of Córdoba in 1252, was a royal servant, and his successor, Fernando de Mesa, elected in 1257, was the king's chaplain.[51] Fernando Velázquez, formerly the royal procurator, was bishop of Segovia (1265–78).[52] A disputed election in Sigüenza prompted Alfonso X to banish several canons, probably because they opposed his candidate Andrés, elected in 1261. Martín Gómez, named by Gregory X in 1275, probably owed his election to the king's intercession.[53] With papal permission the king filled benefices with subordinate clerks of the royal court.[54] Thus, while conserving his own resources, he was able to provide his faithful servants with an income from the church.

Despite royal–papal collaboration, Nicholas III objected in 1279 that the king nominated his own candidates for bishoprics and other ecclesiastical offices and used threats to impose them. Sancho's suggestion that this ought not to be done in the future changed nothing (*Memoriale*, art. 5, C).[55] As a consequence of the king's intrusion of his own candidates, from 1272 to the end of the reign, the number of vacant sees ranged from a minimum of four to a maximum of ten. Salamanca appears to have been vacant throughout that time and Ávila for at least eight years. Although tension among the pope, the king, and the cathedral canons was a principal factor, Alfonso X may have deliberately tried to gain financial advantage by allowing sees to remain vacant.

Church Property

The church's acquisition of property was a persistent source of tension. Bishops and abbots were forbidden to alienate ecclesiastical property without the consent of their chapters. As security against future losses, when a new bishop was installed an inventory of charters, property, credits, and debits should be prepared. The king occupied diocesan temporalities during an episcopal vacancy to safeguard them from unscrupulous persons (*FR* 1, 5, 1–5).[56] During the seven-year vacancy following the death of Archbishop Juan Arias of Compostela in 1266, Alfonso "took the church under his protection" and occupied its temporal possessions.[57] The Council of Brihuega, convened by Archbishop Sancho II of Toledo in 1267, vainly protested the king's use of the revenues of vacant sees.[58] As his precursors had done,[59] Alfonso X, in October 1255, renounced the *jus spolii* or right to reserve the personal property of a deceased bishop,[60] and in 1274 he directed Burgos to return property taken during an episcopal vacancy.[61] As an alternative to royal custody of vacant churches, a practice opposed by the bishops (*Memoriale*, art. 2), Sancho proposed that the king have lifetime use of the *mesa episcopal*, revenues intended for the bishop's support. The deceased bishop's goods should be used to pay his debts or left to his successor (art. B).[62]

Like his predecessors, Alfonso X feared the loss of revenue if the church acquired royal domain lands. During the Curia of Nájera in 1184, Alfonso VIII forbade the alienation of royal lands to the church and nobility, as both were exempt from taxation.[63] Alfonso IX, in the Curias of León in 1188 and Benavente in 1228, issued similar prohibitions.[64] Likewise, in 1254 Alfonso X commanded Badajoz not to permit churches to obtain tributary property. In the same year, however, he allowed his uncle Alfonso de Molina to sell land to the Order of Calatrava, despite the royal ban on transferring property to religious orders.[65] The king ordered an inquest in Ledesma in 1258 to recover royal lands.[66] Fernando de la Cerda in 1275 condemned the seizure of church lands by nobles and others, on the pretext that they belonged to the crown.[67] Three years later, the king ordered an inquest concerning royal estates acquired by the church and church lands incorporated into the royal domain.[68] The *Leyes del estilo* (ley 231), after mentioning the Curias of Nájera and Benavente, recorded that Alfonso X prohibited ecclesiastical institutions from obtaining royal lands and directed David Mascarán to execute the inquest in the kingdom of León.[69] Responding to the bishops' complaint in 1279, Sancho, after citing the Curia of Nájera, proposed that no tribute would be demanded if the church acquired previously exempt property. Tributary land already held by the church would remain unchanged. Future purchases, however, could only be made with the king's permission and would be subject to tribute (*Memoriale*, art. 5, F). Perceiving the church's accumulation of property as a threat to royal power, Alfonso X endeavored to curb future acquisitions by insisting on his right to give consent and to levy tribute on lands newly acquired by the church.

Jurisdictional Disputes

Conflicts between ecclesiastical and secular jurisdiction were also common. The church claimed jurisdiction over clerics, church property, tithes, marriage, legitimacy, excommunication, perjury, and usury. Temporal pleas concerned movable and immovable property; men, money, and animals; agreements, contracts, and exchanges. The bishop ordinarily resolved temporal cases between clerics, but a secular judge would adjudicate suits between clerics and laypersons. A bishop could not be compelled to appear before a secular judge, unless so ordered by the king (*PPBM* 1, 5, 31; 1, 6, 59, 75–85; *SP* 1, 5, 65; 1, 6, 48, 56–62).

Clerics were forbidden to act as judges in secular pleas, to serve as royal justices, to sue in secular court, or to participate in inquests concerning laypeople (*SP* 3, 4, 4; 3, 17, 4). However, they could argue their own cases or those of the church (*FR* 1, 9, 2). In 1278 Alfonso X explained that clerics could not act in secular pleas as advocates, counselors, or judges because the *Fuero real* did not include canon law, and by introducing it clerics prolonged litigation.[70] However, in a secular court clerics could defend church property, the rights of orphans, the mentally disabled, and spendthrifts. A bishop having temporal jurisdiction could exercise it, and if he believed that a secular judge was negligent, he could call that to the king's attention (*PPBM* 1, 6, 59; *SP* 1, 6, 48). Attempting to delineate the boundaries between competing jurisdictions, Alfonso X declared that temporal appeals should be brought to him rather than a bishop, but the latter could hear spiritual appeals, "as we said in the sixth book" of the *Espéculo* (5, 14, 11). The sixth book is not extant, but its substance was likely incorporated into the *Partidas*. In 1255 the king confirmed the right of the bishop of Sigüenza to hear appeals from municipal judges; but rather than allow a further appeal to the archbishop, he asserted his own authority as a final judge of appeals.[71] Upholding the temporal jurisdiction of the bishop of Zamora in 1271, the king directed his judges not to oust judges appointed by the bishop. In the next year he commanded the municipal council not to protect murderers and other criminals condemned by ecclesiastical authorities, nor to try them again.[72]

The prelates complained at Peñafiel in 1275 that although clerics should be tried in church courts, they were hailed before secular judges, and that secular officials often ignored ecclesiastical censures and, in order to have them lifted, seized church property. Fernando de la Cerda ratified the clergy's right to be tried only in ecclesiastical tribunals, and he directed public officials to observe judgments rendered by ecclesiastical authorities.[73] He also confirmed his father's charter of 1258 forbidding secular officials to arrest clerics without the consent of the bishop of Zamora, and his charter of 1264 upholding the jurisdiction of ecclesiastical courts.[74]

The quarrel over ecclesiastical jurisdiction was perhaps no more intense than in Santiago de Compostela, where the townspeople, seeking greater autonomy, challenged the archbishop's lordship. Although Fernando III resolved many disputed issues in 1250,[75] litigation was brought before Alfonso X in 1253, 1261, 1263, and 1264. He prohibited the archbishop from summoning to his court suits already initiated in the municipal court and forbade clerical judges to hear criminal cases. As judgment had to be rendered according to municipal usages and the *Libro de León* (the *Fuero Juzgo*), clerical advocates were barred from citing Roman and canon law. He also affirmed the right of appeal to his court.[76]

When the king demanded in 1273 that Gonzalo Gómez, the newly appointed archbishop, pledge homage and fealty, the latter refused, arguing that none of his predecessors had done so, and he accused the king of usurping ecclesiastical jurisdiction. In 1278 Nicholas III chastised the king for persecuting the archbishop and sending an army to subject to royal authority tenants of various districts in the Tierra de Santiago.[77] As Alfonso X ignored these admonitions, in 1279 the pope accused him of impeding the archbishop in the exercise of his lordship and of attempting to reserve to himself appointment of the *pertiguero mayor*, an archiepiscopal official (*Memoriale*, art. 3, B').[78] Despite those complaints, the king forced the archbishop into exile in 1279.

Among the injustices cited by Nicholas III in 1279, clerics were summoned before secular tribunals, arrested, imprisoned, and even sentenced to death. Without being summoned, they were subject to secret inquests and punished without being convicted or having confessed (*Memoriale*, art. 5, E).[79] The bishop of Burgos objected in 1278 that royal officials failed to summon the clergy and their vassals to testify in closed inquests concerning the export of prohibited goods. Although the king admonished his officials, the practice of closed inquests seems to have continued.[80] Sancho saw no possibility of resolving this to the king's advantage, other than to say that a cleric caught in a criminal act and degraded by his bishop could be punished by a secular judge. He acknowledged ecclesiastical jurisdiction over property intended for the church's use (*Memoriale*, art. 5, E). The king was also charged with usurping jurisdiction over wills and the crime of usury. By requiring prelates to affix their seals to blank charters, he compelled them to testify to matters that they had not seen nor heard (*Memoriale*, art. 5, L).[81]

Given Alfonso X's efforts to codify the laws and minimize legal differences, it is not surprising that he should attempt to limit ecclesiastical jurisdiction. As a king claiming to have no temporal superior, he could hardly tolerate the existence of a separate legal system over which he had no control. From his point of view, it was imperative to impose restraints on that system, without necessarily repudiating it.

The church used excommunication and interdict to compel obedience and expected the civil power to enforce that judgment (*SP* 1, 6, 59). The king ordered royal officials to aid the bishops in punishing those who violated churches or cemeteries (*FR* 1, 5, 7) and assured the bishops in 1255 that any sentence of excommunication imposed on those who failed to pay tithes would be upheld.[82] The *Partidas* included an extensive summary of the canon law concerning excommunication (*PPBM* 1, 9, 1–57; *SP* 1, 9, 1–38).

At times, however, Alfonso X perceived excommunication as a special irritant. Early in his reign he enacted a law prohibiting the excommunication of his officials if they neglected to defend ecclesiastical privileges. Although that law is not extant, Fernando IV, in the Cortes of Zamora in 1301 (art. 11), reported that his grandfather, having assembled his Cortes (probably at Valladolid in 1258), determined that in cases of temporal jurisdiction, the prelates should not excommunicate royal officials who failed to safeguard ecclesiastical privileges. If the clergy felt aggrieved, they should complain to the king. If, on the contrary, a prelate refused to lift an ecclesiastical censure at the king's request, royal officials were authorized to enforce compliance by taking pledges of church property. Although the prelates protested to the pope, Alexander IV in 1259 declared that only he could excommunicate the king or members of his family.[83] On the other hand, the king, in 1275, ordered municipal judges in Seville to enforce the rulings of the archiepiscopal court and in 1277 directed the city council to arrest anyone excommunicated for more than thirty days and surrender him to the archbishop for punishment and absolution.[84]

In 1279 Nicholas III accused the king of forbidding bishops to render judgments or to use the power of excommunication, except in case of violation of churches, assault on the clergy, and nonpayment of tithes. The king also demanded that prelates revoke censures, that interdicts not be observed, and that the exception of excommunication (barring excommunicates from testifying) be disallowed in his court (*Memoriale*, art. 5, L).[85] Secular judges, however, continued to disregard excommunication, and the fourteenth-century Cortes complained that bishops abused its use.[86]

Taxation, Tithes, and *Tercias*

The church was exempt from taxation except in certain circumstances. For example, if a cleric died intestate, and without heirs, the church would inherit his property but would have to continue paying taxes on any part of his estate subject to tribute. Justifying his right to taxation, the king cited Jesus's admonition when presented with the coin of the tribute: "Then repay to Caesar what belongs to Caesar and to God what belongs to God" (Mt 22:20–22; Mk 12:17). Moreover, "according to the usage and custom of Spain," he had a right to tax church property, although he had not previously done so (*PPBM* 1, 6, 65; *SP* 1, 6, 53). Clerics also had to contribute to the construction of new bridges and the upkeep of old ones (*SP* 1, 6, 54). Royal taxation annoyed the bishops, but priests were also subjected to irritating episcopal taxation. When he was making war against the "enemies of the faith" or for some other just reason, the king commanded the bishops not to tax the churches or their priests, lest he be blamed for oppressing them (*SP* 1, 2, 14).

Churchmen had reason to be pleased in 1253 when the king extended Alfonso IX's exemption of cathedral clergy from *moneda forera*, a tax payable every seven years in return for his promise not to alter the coinage.[87] Two years later, however, he asked the prelates to grant a special tax or *servicio*, to pay his father's debt to the papacy. In the future he pledged not to demand it as a matter of right but to accept it only as their freewill offering.[88] Although they consented, he failed to pay the debt, which was still owed in September 1263.[89]

When the bishops protested the continuous taxation of clerical estates in 1275, Fernando de la Cerda temporarily placated them by confirming royal tax exemptions granted to them.[90] Yet when Gregory X authorized collection of the *decima*, or tenth of ecclesiastical revenue, for six years to oppose the Marinids, their hostility resurfaced.[91] If that were not enough, the king asked them in the Cortes of Burgos in 1276 for a *servicio* to repel the intruders, promising not to levy it again as a matter of right but only with their consent. To allay their resentment, in the Cortes of Burgos 1277 he exempted cathedral chapters from payment of a new tax.[92] Nevertheless, the archbishop of Compostela in 1279 objected that frequent tax levies greatly damaged the church (*Memoriale*, art. 3). Although Sancho admitted that the king was wrong to tax them (*Memoriale*, art. 5, D, P),[93] the bishops learned that he never yielded his claims to their resources and that whenever he granted them a concession, he insisted on something significant in return. Together with the rest of Europe, they discovered that extraordinary taxation was a novelty from which there was no escape.

The tithe, theoretically a tenth of every Christian's income, was a principal source of ecclesiastical revenue, payable by everyone. The payment of tithes on transhumant sheep migrating twice yearly, from northern to southern pastures and back again, was complicated. If the sheep passed the year on their lord's estate, the tithe was due to his parish church, but if they spent the year in another bishopric, it was payable to that bishop. It would be divided equally if the sheep divided the year between two dioceses. Shepherds tried to defraud the bishops by pasturing sheep during the day in one bishopric and crossing into another at night. As tithe collectors sometimes demanded more than they were entitled to, men appointed by the bishops had to list the animals taken and give a schedule to the collector and the chief shepherd (*PPBM* 1, 21, 1–14; *SP* 1, 20, 1–11). During the Cortes of Seville in 1261 townsmen complained that the tithe was collected twice as flocks passed from the archbishopric of Toledo into the archbishopric of Seville and that fully grown sheep and cows were taken rather than lambs and calves. Ordering observance of the law in the *Partidas*, the king declared that shepherds who presented a list of animals already taken would not have to pay the tithe again.[94] That statement contradicts the idea that the *Partidas* did not have the force of law until 1348.

When the Extremaduran towns complained in 1264 about the tithe, Alfonso commanded royal and ecclesiastical officials to take their respective shares at the same time and to avoid any unnecessary inconvenience.[95] An agreement between the bishop-elect of Cartagena and the municipal council of Lorca in 1275 illustrates the practical application of the law. For every ten animals, one was owed as a tithe; if there were more, a monetary tithe of varying amount was imposed. A scribe recorded the tithes collected at the gates of each town, as was done in Toledo, Seville, and Córdoba.[96] As the tithe was an important source of royal income, the king upheld the church's right to it, issuing charters to the archbishop of Seville, and the bishops of Córdoba,[97] Salamanca,[98] Burgos, Valladolid, Ávila, and Cartagena.[99]

The tithe was divided into three parts: one for the bishop, one for the clergy, and the third for the *fabrica* or upkeep of churches.[100] Known as the *tercias*, the last was usually two-ninths of the total. In 1246 Innocent IV was the first pope to approve use of the *tercias* for the reconquest.[101] After the fall of Seville in 1248, the bishops probably hoped that Alfonso X would yield the *tercias*, but in the Cortes of Seville in 1252 (art. 44) he postponed a decision. Soon after he enacted a law concerning the tithe in the *Fuero real* (1, 5, 4). Recalling that Jesus upheld Caesar's claim to the tribute, he affirmed the church's right to the tithe but noted that it could also be used for the service of kings and their kingdom. In order to curb deception, once the harvest was gathered, *terceros* or royal tithe collectors and ecclesiastical representatives were authorized to take their respective shares.[102] Failure to pay the tithe was punishable by excommunication and a fine to be shared equally by the king and the bishop. Thus, while consistent payment of the tithe would benefit the clergy, it would also fill the royal coffers. In the Cortes of Toledo in 1254, the king required Jews and Muslims to pay tithes on property acquired from Christians so the church would not lose income.[103] His citation of "my *posturas*" clearly refers to the law enacted in the *Fuero real*, which he reiterated in charters issued to several municipalities in 1255.[104]

When the king appealed for help to suppress the Mudéjar revolt, Clement IV, in 1265, granted him the *decima*, provided that he forsake "that most vile robbery," the *tercias*. Despite the possibility of being relieved of the hated *tercias*, the bishops were distressed by the imposition of this new financial burden.[105] Of course the king did not abandon the *tercias*. Between 1271 and 1274 the bishop of Cuenca paid ten thousand *maravedís* to the king,[106] and in 1277 Isaac and Mayr Abenxuxén contracted to collect the *tercias* and pay the king seventy thousand *maravedís*.[107] When Gregory X authorized the *decima* for six years in 1275, he demanded that the king give up the *tercias*, but Nicholas III protested four years later that he had not done so.[108] Replying to the accusation that papal authorization to take the *tercias* had lapsed (*Memoriale*, art. 1), Sancho proposed a compromise that would allow the king to retain the *tercias* for life (art. A).[109] Nothing came of that. Though the prelates groaned that they were impoverished by the *tercias*, the *decima*, and the *servicios* that they approved in the Cortes, the king continued to exploit their resources.

Que el Poder Temporal e Espiritual, que Viene Todo de Dios, Se Acuerde en Uno

Alfonso X, presenting himself as a loyal son of the church, declared "que el poder temporal e espiritual, que viene todo de Dios, se acuerde en uno" (that the temporal and spiritual powers, that both come from God, should accord with one another) (FR 1, 5, 4). For that reason he incorporated the substance of canon law in the *First Partida*. Although he recognized his obligation to defend the church, and accepted the spiritual supremacy of the pope, he intended to dominate the church and expected its leaders to be submissive to his will. He acknowledged that episcopal elections should be free but, with papal acquiescence, filled the principal sees with loyal servitors. Asserting his orthodoxy, he affirmed church teachings and, insisting that there was no salvation outside the church, admonished Muslims, Jews, and heretics to accept Christianity. Although heresy was not widespread, he declared that heretics should be burned to death, thereby providing the Spanish Inquisition of a later date with a legal justification for executing them. As a faithful Christian, he also extended his protection to pilgrims, a source of revenue for his kingdom and everyone on the pilgrimage routes. Though he consistently confirmed the property holdings of bishops and monasteries, he attempted to prevent them from acquiring lands of the royal domain, lest his revenues be diminished. His claim to the spoils of a deceased bishop, his exclusion of clerics from any role in secular courts, his efforts to limit ecclesiastical jurisdiction, and his objection to the bishops' use of excommunication, especially of royal officials, proved to be ongoing vexations. Arguing that he and his predecessors had founded or restored bishoprics and monasteries, he believed that, when necessary, he could dispose of the church's temporal resources. The bishops protested not only his appropriation of the *tercias*, but also his imposition of extraordinary levies. As their grievances accumulated, they appealed to Nicholas III. Although the king was attentive to papal admonitions, he seems not to have changed his policies.

Eventually, many bishops supported Sancho's rebellion in 1282. Meeting in Valladolid, the abbots of monasteries formed an *hermandad* or brotherhood in defense of their privileges. The bishops of Astorga, Zamora, Mondoñedo, Túy, Badajoz, and Coria also entered an *hermandad* with twenty-five Leonese monasteries to support Sancho.[110] Bishops Fernando of Burgos and Juan of Palencia, however, protested the actions taken against the king.[111] During the ensuing civil war, the archbishop of Seville and the bishops of Burgos, Ávila, Cádiz, and Oviedo remained loyal to him,[112] but others backed Sancho or remained neutral. In 1283 the bishops of Astorga and Zamora renewed their pact with the monasteries, but urged Sancho to seek peace.[113] The civil war continued, however, until the king's death in 1284. Despite the challenge of the bishops, royal ascendancy over the church was unchanged, as King Alfonso's immediate successors continued to follow his policies.

✺ CHAPTER 6

The Defense of the Realm

A la Tierra Han Grand Debdo de Amarla e de Acrescentarla e Morir por Ella

In order to maintain his people in peace, the king had to protect them against external enemies (*E* 2, 1, 5; *SP* 2, 1, 5; 2, 10, 1–3).[1] The *Espéculo* (3, 1–8) and, more fully, the *Partidas* (2, 18–29) offered a thorough exposition of military doctrine, based partly on the fourth-century Roman author Vegetius, whose book Juan Gil de Zamora summarized.[2] Also infusing the discussion of warfare were practices developed during the reconquest and recorded in municipal *fueros*.[3] The king explained that warfare has two natures, evil and good, in that it caused great destruction, but when properly conducted led to peace, happiness, and friendship. Echoing St. Augustine's notion that "the purpose even of war is peace" (*De Civitate Dei*, 15.4), he remarked that it "seems a great marvel . . . that peace should be gained by war" (*E* 3, 5, pr.). A war fought to repossess a man's land or rights or to protect himself and his property was just, but a war lacking a righteous cause was always unjust (*SP* 2, 23, pr., 1).[4] Surely the king believed that the reconquest, fought to recover Christian lands usurped by the Muslims, was justified and that he would be assured of the help of God and of his friends (*SP* 2, 23, 2).[5]

Responding to Alfonso X's request for help in suppressing the Mudéjar revolt in 1264, Jaime I, after citing familial obligations, acknowledged the power politics of the situation and the wisdom of diverting war from his own realm:

> First, because I do not wish to betray my daughter [Queen Violante of Castile], nor my grandchildren, nor do I wish to disinherit them. Secondly, although I need not aid him out of valor or duty, yet I should help him because he is one of the most powerful men in the world, and if I do not aid him now and he emerges safely from this conflict in which he now finds himself, he will always hold me as his mortal enemy . . . and if he can pressure me he will do so as often as he can and he will have good reason. Thirdly . . . if the king of Castile loses his kingdom we will be badly off in our own kingdom. Therefore it is better to hasten to defend his kingdom now, than to have to defend ours later.[6]

Defending One's Country and Dying for It

The royal jurists noted that there were three reasons that justified going to war: to defend the faith; to serve one's lord; and to protect oneself and one's country. A people who acted otherwise dishonored their king, committed treason, and forever gave the kingdom and its inhabitants an evil reputation (*SP* 2, 19, pr., 1–2). The natural bond between the land and its people, the king's natural vassals, required everyone to participate in the defense of the realm that "touches the king himself and the kingdom" (*E* 3, 4, pr.; 3, 5, 2). No one was excused because "the injury and damage touches all" (*SP* 2, 19, 3) and "it is the defense of the king who is lord of the kingdom that is common to all" (*E* 3, 5, 10). The Asturian *hermandad* of 1277 pledged "to defend and to protect the land of our lord the king," and the bishops declared that the king intended "to guard his kingdoms from the dangers" on the frontier.[7]

Defense of the realm, moreover, might require that a man lay down his life for his country. Indeed, "a la tierra han grand debdo de amarla e de acrescentarla e morir por ella, si menester fuere" (men have a great debt to the land to love it, and increase it, and to die for it, if that should be necessary) (*SP* 4, 24, 4). "Those who die for the faith, or defending their country, or for the honor of their king" ought to receive greater compensation than those who only suffered bodily wounds. They also merited an eternal reward in paradise and a guarantee of undying fame (*E* 3, 7, 11; *SP* 2, 25, 3).[8] The contemporary *Poema de Fernán González* also expressed that sentiment.[9]

In numerous charters requiring his vassals "to make war and peace," King Alfonso reserved the right to demand military service, an inalienable attribute of sovereignty (*FV* 1, 1, 1).[10] Everyone had to act quickly to quell rebellion, which, like poison, went directly to the heart of the kingdom and killed it. Failure to do so emboldened rebels, diminished royal authority, and besmirched the reputation of the kingdom and its people. That insistent tone was undoubtedly due to Enrique's rebellion at the outset of the reign. Equally urgent was the obligation to oppose an invading army. No one was exempt from service, except those under fourteen or over seventy, the infirm, or those impeded by harsh weather. The call to arms might be made orally, or with bells or other noisemakers. Nevertheless, without awaiting a formal summons, everyone capable of bearing arms had to resist the enemy who threatened them all. The usual term of service was three months from departure from home, though in case of a siege, that term began upon arrival. If, for good reason, the king could not dismiss the troops at the end of three months, they had to remain. Troops stationed on the frontier had no fixed term and could not leave without permission (*E* 3, 1, 3; 3, 5, 1–6, 11; *SP* 2, 19, 3–9; 2, 26, 24).

The king sharply condemned as traitors those who fled at sight of the enemy or before an order to retreat was given, or neglected to defend the royal standard, or abandoned the host without permission, or dismissed the troops before his command (*E* 3, 3, 3; 3, 5, 5, 9–19; 3, 6, 1–6; *FR* 4, 19, 1–5). Deprived of their rank, faint-hearted knights suffered the ignominy of having their spurs, swords, and belts stripped (*SP* 2, 21, 25).[11] The *Poema de Fernán González* expressed the wish that whoever fled in battle "should lie in hell with Judas."[12] In his songs of derision, the king mocked poorly equipped soldiers, wearing old and worn-out battle jackets, and vassals who neglected to answer the summons or to bring the required number of knights. He vented his wrath at cowards too terrified to go into battle and deserters who fled the horrors of war.[13]

Military Components

In order to conduct war effectively, men, horses, and arms had to be organized, supplies and engines of war requisitioned, and the enemy's intentions and movements ascertained (*SP* 2, 23, 2–3). Military forces included the king, the adult male members of his family, the *mesnada del rey*, bishops, members of the military orders, magnates, knights, and urban militias.[14] The *mesnada* was an elite corps of knights assigned to protect the king (*E* 2, 13, 5–6; *SP* 2, 9, 9).[15] Prelates holding land from the king owed the service of a certain number of knights, but not if he was at war with Christians. Clerics traditionally were exempt from service, but they had to aid the defense of a town attacked by the Moors (*PPBM* 1, 6, 64, 74; *SP* 1, 6, 52). Although the prelates' primary function was to offer spiritual sustenance, in October 1275, Archbishop Sancho II of Toledo lost his life battling the Marinids near Martos. Though his head was severed from his body and his hand cut off, the Moors returned his remains for burial in Toledo. The day of the warrior-bishop was not yet over.[16]

The military orders of Santiago, Calatrava, and Alcántara (and, to a lesser extent, the Templars and Hospitallers), founded in the second half of the twelfth century, garrisoned frontier castles and provided contingents for the royal army. The title of master given to the superior of each order emphasized his military leadership. Although Alfonso X attempted to persuade Santiago and Calatrava to transfer their principal seats to Andalucía, they were reluctant to do so. Determined to protect the coastline, in 1270 he created the Order of Santa María de España and named his son Sancho as *alférez* and admiral, but in 1274 Pedro Núñez held the military title of master. After the Moors massacred the knights of Santiago at Moclín in 1280, the king merged the Orders of Santiago and Santa María and appointed Pedro Núñez as master.[17]

Magnates and noble knights, whose primary duty was to defend the realm, were expected to possess the virtues of energy, honor, and strength (*SP* 2, 21, pr.).[18] As a privileged military caste, exempt from direct taxation, magnates had to counsel the king and serve him in war. To maintain them, he gave them lands in full ownership or monetary stipends (*soldadas*). Alfonso X reportedly increased their stipends "in order to bind them more surely to his service." The Cortes of Valladolid in 1258 (art. 17) mentioned a stipend of ten thousand *maravedís*. When a magnate came to court, he could bring no more than ten knights and had to pay his own expenses.[19] The relationship between lords and vassals, treated in the *Fourth Partida* (4, 25, 1–13), will be discussed in chapter 10.

In combat, some knights were heavily armored and rode *a la brida*, that is, with their legs stretched straight out in the stirrups so they could use maximum force when attacking. Striving for speed and mobility, others, lightly armed with a lance and a sword, a thin coat-of-mail, and an iron cap, rode *a la jineta* in the Moorish style, with their legs bent in short stirrups. Knights with elongated shields, lances, cylindrical or bowled helmets, chain mail and armor, and horses with protective leather or mail are depicted in *CSM* 63.[20]

Although the *Espéculo* speaks only incidentally of knighthood, the *Partidas* (2, 21, 1–25) offers a long disquisition, the first in Castilian, on the *Orden de caualleria*.[21] Georges Martin argued that by associating the nobility with the ideals of knighthood, Alfonso X hoped to direct their tendency to indiscriminate violence to the defense of faith, king, and country.[22] As men of substance, knights were called *fijosdalgo*, literally sons of wealth. Endowed with the virtues of gentility, prudence, loyalty, understanding, courage, moderation, and justice, they prepared to endure the hardships of war for the common good (*SP* 2, 21, 1–10; 2, 23, 27; 2, 26, 18).

Ordinarily, only a knight could create another knight. In the Cortes of Valladolid in 1258 (art. 23), and again at Seville in 1261 (art. 9), the king required a magnate to receive knighthood before he could marry or create knights. The king and his son and heir, though not knights, could confer knighthood because they were "heads of the knighthood." For example, in 1219, during mass at Burgos, Fernando III "took from the altar the military sword as a sign of knighthood," which the bishop had previously blessed.[23] Like his father, Alfonso X, who stated that "I became king and received knighthood" at Seville, probably girded himself with his arms after they were blessed by a bishop.[24] In celebrations intended to express the honor and esteem accorded to knights, he knighted Prince Edward in 1254, and in 1269 his grandson Dinis, the future king of Portugal.[25] An empress or queen could not confer knighthood, nor could priests and monks. Knighthood could not be purchased. Barred from receiving knighthood were women, priests, monks, the insane, boys under fourteen, the poor, the physically incapacitated, merchants, traitors, anyone condemned to death, or those receiving knighthood as a joke (*SP* 2, 21, 11–12).

The ceremony was endowed with religious significance as knighthood was compared to the priesthood and the investiture of arms was likened to priestly ordination. The royal jurists advised future knights to cleanse their minds and bodies and focus on beautiful things, "especially as their craft is harsh and cruel, as they have to wound and kill." On the eve of investiture, the candidate's fellow squires should bathe him, dress him in handsome clothes, and accompany him to church. There he spent the night in the vigil of arms asking God to protect him as one "entering on a career of death." At daybreak, after mass, with spurs fastened and holding his sword in his right hand, he swore a threefold oath to give up his life for his faith, his lord, and his country. As a reminder of that oath, his sponsor gave him a ceremonial slap on the neck and kissed him as a sign of the brotherhood observed among knights. Then, an eminent knight removed the novice's sword, thereby becoming his *padrino* or godfather. Georges Martin suggested that that act of disarmament reflected his amicable relationship with his fellow knights.[26] A special bond, comparable to that between a newly baptized person and his godparent, was created between the new knight and his *padrino*, whom he was bound to obey and protect, and also between him and the one who knighted him (*SP* 2, 21, 13–16).[27] During the Cortes of Burgos in 1269 Alfonso X, after knighting Fernando de la Cerda, asked him to knight his brothers; but Jaime I, seeing the possibility of future contention, dissuaded Infante Sancho from receiving knighthood from Fernando, lest he seem to be subordinated to him.[28]

The new knight had to observe an appropriate code of conduct. Mounted on horseback, wielding his sword, the mark of knighthood, he should dress elegantly in bright clothing signifying joy. His mantle, symbolizing humility, was his distinctive raiment. Temperate in his habits, the knight, while taking his meals, should seek inspiration by reading about great feats of arms and listening to minstrels singing songs of war. He ought never to use vulgar or arrogant language, except in battle to encourage or reprimand his followers. As motivation, he might call out the names of their sweethearts. As a sign of respect, he was entitled to sit at the front of the church, just below the clergy, and should only dine with another knight (Valladolid 1258, art. 24). His house was safeguarded against violent entry, and ordinarily, his horses and arms could not be seized as a pledge. Anyone seeking restitution from a knight absent on royal business or fulfilling his knightly duties had to await his return home. A knight accused of crime could not be tortured, except in case of treason. Should he be found guilty, he was spared the indignity of being dragged, mutilated, or hanged, but he might be beheaded or starved to death. It is difficult, however, to think of those alternatives as privileges. Aside from execution, his worst humiliation was forfeiture of his knighthood. If he sold or abused his horse or arms, or gambled them away, or gave them to wicked women, or pledged them, or engaged in commerce or a vile trade, he could be deprived of his knighthood. He would incur the death penalty if he fled in battle, abandoned a castle he was bound to defend, deserted his lord, or failed to rescue him or to give him his horse when his lord's horse was killed. Before being executed, he was expelled from the order of knighthood. In a ceremony reminiscent of his initial investiture, a squire put his spurs on his feet and girded him with his sword, and then cut them off. Stripped of the honor and privileges of knighthood, he no longer had the right to be called a *caballero*. If the king spared his life, he could never again hold any public office (*SP* 2, 21, 17–25).

Municipal militia forces consisted of nonnoble knights (*caballeros villanos*) and foot soldiers (*peones*).[29] As the towns of Castile and Extremadura were now far removed from the frontier, many were reluctant to serve in Andalucía. Needing them for his wars against the Moors, Alfonso X, in the Cortes of Seville in 1252 (art. 45), required every man with a horse and arms to be prepared for war. Determined to make military service more attractive, in

1255 he granted tax exemptions to residents of Burgos who had a horse, arms, and body armor. In the following year he extended those exemptions to urban knights with arms and horses worth at least thirty *maravedís* and their dependents whose estimated wealth was less than one hundred *maravedís*. A knight's widow was exempt unless she married a taxpayer, and so too was a knight's son who, at age sixteen, chose to follow his father's profession. A biannual muster usually held on 1 March and 29 September determined whether knights had the required horses and arms.[30] The expense could be considerable. The Assembly of Jerez in 1268, for example, set the price of a *perpunte* or quilted battle jacket at one to one and a half *maravedís*; a shield with cords, straps, and a painted cap was twenty-five; and a painted saddle for a warhorse, with a bit and harness and gilded spurs, was twelve (arts. 10, 12). Tax exemptions were later given to other Castilian and Extremaduran towns.[31]

In April 1264 the Extremaduran towns, assembled in Seville, petitioned Queen Violante to intercede with the king concerning onerous taxation. In reporting his response, the *Chronicle of Alfonso X* incorrectly summarized the privileges of 1255–56.[32] In fact, the king, in the Ordinance of Extremadura, clarified some aspects of those privileges and some laws in the *Fuero real*. He conceded tax exemptions to the brothers, sons, and nephews of knights until they came of age, and pledged a large sum of money and other privileges to those whom he personally knighted (arts. 4–5, 7–9, 12–15).[33] In subsequent years he confirmed the privileges of 1255–56 and the Ordinance of Extremadura.[34] Intent on fostering settlement in Arcos de la Frontera, in 1268 he exempted residents from military service except in the zone from the Guadalquivir to the Mediterranean, and conferred on knights the franchises enjoyed by knights in Seville. In 1273 he exempted the latter from several tributes.[35] Facing the Marinid invasion in 1275, he confirmed the exemptions given to municipal knights and their dependents.[36] Two years later he exempted them from the *servicio* then being collected in the kingdom of León.[37] While enjoying these benefits, some knights claimed exemptions for unqualified dependents or failed to attend the muster properly equipped.[38] Outraged by this dereliction, in 1276 the king authorized Zag de la Maleha to collect appropriate fines.[39]

Aside from knights, infantrymen were important, not only in garrisoning castles, but also because they could move more easily in difficult terrain. Capable of enduring excessive heat and other hardships, they were armed with lances, javelins, knives, and daggers. Crossbowmen were especially effective, because their weapon could inflict great damage on a mounted knight. During sieges, foot soldiers expert in the use of artillery built and manned siege engines, including trebuchets and catapults, as well as wooden siege towers (*SP* 2, 22, 7; 2, 23, 24).

Military success often depended on the wisdom and judgment of the commander, who, by creating a cohesive force, "could best overcome the enemy" (*E* 3, 6, 1). The king was the supreme commander, or in his absence, the *alférez*, but in 1278–79 Infante Pedro directed the siege of Algeciras, and Sancho led the invasion of Granada in 1280.[40] As "warfare is full of dangers and mishaps," the king ought to seek the counsel of a master of the art of war, who could instill confidence in his troops and instruct them in the use of weapons and the care of horses and in the importance of avoiding quarrels and obeying promptly. Before engaging the enemy, he ought to pursue every advantage, including numerical superiority, the placement of troops, and the impact of atmospheric changes. Wise leadership opened possibilities, prevented troops from becoming a disorderly mob, and pointed toward victory (*SP* 2, 23, 4–11).[41]

Serving under the general officers were the *adalid* and the *almocadén*. The *adalid* (ar. *al-dalil*) had to guide his troops through familiar terrain, select encampments, appoint sentries, secure provisions, arrange foraging parties, set ambushes, and command infantry and *almogávares* (ar. *al-mughāwir*), usually lightly mounted warriors skilled in quick strikes.[42] The king, on the recommendation of twelve *adalides*, would promote a man to this office and give him a banner, clothing, a horse, and weapons. Raised on a shield by twelve *adalides* and making the sign of the cross with his sword in all four directions, he should defy the enemies of faith, king, and country. The *almocadén* (ar. *al-muqāddam*) was an infantry commander appointed by the *adalid* on the recommendation of twelve *almocadenes*. As a sign of his office, the king gave him new clothing and entrusted him with a lance and a small pennant bearing his insignia. His twelve sponsors lifted him up four times on the shafts of their lances, and raising his lance and pennant, he made the same declaration as the *adalid*. Emphasizing the importance of promotion through the ranks, the royal jurists commented that just as a good foot soldier makes a good *almocadén*, a good *almocadén* makes a good *almogávar*, and the latter makes a good *adalid* (*SP* 2, 22, 1–6). Numerous *adalides* and *almocadenes* shared in the partition of Seville.[43]

Standards or banners identified various military elements. The royal standard was square, and a magnate's had scalloped edges. A commander of fifty to one hundred men used a triangular banner, and a long, narrow banner marked one with ten to fifty men. Each military order displayed its distinctive cross on its standards.[44] In the Cortes of Seville in 1250 Fernando III declared that a knight, rather than an artisan, should carry the municipal banner.[45] Serving as a rallying point, the banner had to be defended at all costs. Flight with a standard was an act of treason, because it could incite everyone to flee. Banners were prized trophies of war and brought rewards to those who captured them (*E* 3, 5, 13–15, 18–19; *SP* 2, 23, 12–15).

Each company commander was responsible for punishing lapses of discipline and major crimes, namely, informing the enemy about troop movements, desertion, disobedience, fomenting dissension, fleeing in battle, attacking one another, stealing, losing or wasting supplies, interfering with justice, and violating contracts. Lest an informer infiltrate the host, each captain had to keep a written record of the men in his company. Anyone not listed would be killed immediately. Minor transgressions might draw an oral reprimand, a laceration, or a blow with a baton. Penalties for more serious crimes included confiscation, execution, starvation, imprisonment, denial of burial in sacred ground, disinterment, dismemberment, branding, and loss of a share in booty (*SP* 2, 28, 1–11; *E* 3, 6, 1–10; 3, 8, 1–9; *FR* 4, 19, 5).[46]

Military and Naval Actions

Custody of the hundreds of castles dotting the landscape was of major importance.[47] By law all cities, towns, and fortresses belonged to the king and the kingdom and everyone had to defend them. Upon the king's death, every *alcaide* (ar. *al-qāʾid*) or castellan had to surrender his fortress to the new king who could assign it to whomever he wished. The *alcaide* pledged to maintain the fortress in a state of readiness and defend it, to serve the king and welcome him, and to accept his coinage. Asserting the principle that every fortress was ultimately held from the king, the law required everyone holding a castle from another lord to do homage to the king (*SP* 2, 13, 21–23).

Ordinarily, a royal herald gave custody of a castle to an *alcaide* who would be charged with treason if he lost it. When the king visited, his banner was raised on the highest tower as a sign that he had taken possession. Forbidden ever to surrender the castle, the *alcaide* had to maintain a garrison, post sentries, and provide food, water, clothing, weapons, and stones to be used as missiles. No one was to undertake a sally except by his order, and while relying on his own expertise, he should heed the counsel of skilled warriors. During a siege, he ought to conceal his losses and immediately repair any breach in the walls.[48] If he believed that he could not hold the castle and asked the king to relieve him, but was persistently refused, he could depart after dismissing his company, locking the gates, and returning the key to the king, or throwing it over the walls into the castle. Once he informed the local town council that he had yielded custody, he would not be liable if the castle was lost. Occasionally, as security for fulfillment of treaty obligations, kings pledged castles to one another. Whenever anyone conquered a city or castle, he had to cede it to the king on penalty of treason. The royal jurists, perhaps with Infante Enrique in mind, declared that the reason for this was to prevent any of the king's relatives from seizing his lands (E 2, 7, 1–5; 2, 8, 1; 2, 9, pr., 1; SP 2, 18, 2–32).

Two stories perhaps having a historical basis suggest the hazards facing an *alcaide*. CSM 191 tells of a poor *alcaide* "who went to get his pay" and left his castle untended, except by his wife. Unfortunately, she fell off a cliff but was saved by the Virgin. CSM 185 relates that the Muslim *alcaide* of Belmez seized the *alcaide* of Chincoya and handed him over to the emir of Granada. Learning that only fifteen men guarded Chincoya, the emir demanded their surrender; rather than do so, they placed a statue of the Virgin on the walls and compelled the Moors to withdraw. The historicity of another example is unquestioned, as the king himself reported it. According to CSM 345, when the Mudéjars of Jerez revolted in 1264, Nuño González de Lara, the *alcaide*, appealed for help. When a small relieving band arrived, he abandoned the citadel, leaving behind a few ill-equipped men. Though the king reproached Nuño, his good friend, he failed to punish him as a traitor, as the *Partidas* required.[49]

Troops preparing for action were organized in different formations. A rounded block, for example, provided an effective defense against an enveloping enemy, while a wedge divided the enemy; a square protected the baggage train, and a corral of infantry guarded the king. As troops advanced, commanders maintained strict discipline lest the enemy pick off stragglers and stray animals. A vanguard and a rearguard protected against surprise attack (SP 2, 23, 16–17).

Typical military operations were raids, skirmishes, sieges, and pitched battles. Raids (*algara*, ar. *al-gārah*), carried out quickly and often at night, destroyed harvests, disrupted water supplies, foraged for food, and seized booty (SP 2, 23, 25–30).[50] In the spring of 1273, the king, hoping to subdue the Moors, ordered Fernando de la Cerda to destroy orchards and vineyards, the economic heart of Granada.[51] CSM 344 and 374 described raiding parties, but, however destructive they might be, they could not bring the enemy to his knees.

A siege was more protracted, often requiring weeks or months.[52] Sieges are illustrated in CSM 15, 28, and 99. Protected by a ditch, and sometimes by a palisade, the besiegers laid out their tents in streets marked by the officers' banners. The royal tent was always in the center. Though skirmishes occurred, they were never decisive. Siege engines included the counterweight trebuchet, a wooden beam on a rotating axle, with a sling attached to the end of the beam, and capable of launching a projectile over the walls. The traction trebuchet was powered by a crew pulling ropes, and the hybrid trebuchet employed both the counterweight and the pulling crew.[53] While battering rams attempted to demolish walls, miners worked to undermine them, and soldiers used ladders to scale them. Wooden castles moved up on wheels or logs enabled the besiegers to climb onto the walls. If not overcome by assault, the defenders, when deprived of food and water, would be compelled to surrender (*SP* 2, 23, 18–23, 26; *E* 3, 6, 8–9).

In 1261, after besieging Jerez for a month, Alfonso X, realizing that the siege would drag on, negotiated an accord allowing the Moors to remain, while a Castilian garrison was admitted into the citadel. Next, in February 1262, after a siege of nine and a half months, he received the surrender of Niebla. During the Mudéjar revolt, he besieged Jerez again but probably did not recover it until 1266.[54] Resolved to oust the Marinids from Algeciras, in August 1278 he sent Pedro Martínez de Fe, with eighty galleys and twenty-four ships, to establish a blockade. In the following February, he dispatched troops commanded by his son Pedro to complete the siege. As siege engines and cannons battered the walls, the Castilians attempted to sever the food supply, but after three months many men, believing their obligatory term of service was over, returned home. Those remaining suffered, unpaid, through a cold and wet winter. After a Muslim fleet of seventy-two ships destroyed four hundred Castilian ships on 24 July 1279, the remnants of the army abandoned the siege and retreated to Seville.[55]

Pitched battles were rare, especially as the outcome could be disastrous (*SP* 2, 23, 27).[56] At Écija on 7 September 1275, the Marinids crushed the Castilians commanded by Nuño González de Lara and sent his severed head as a trophy to the emir of Granada. Then, on 20 October, at Martos, Archbishop Sancho II of Toledo was routed and killed.[57] A third battle at Moclín on 23 June 1280 also ended in disaster. Despite their victories, the Muslims made no significant territorial gains.[58] Infante Sancho achieved a measure of recompense when he overwhelmed the Moors near Granada on 25 June 1281.[59] The *Cantigas de Santa Maria* depict numerous scenes of warfare.[60]

The Castilian kings had little need of a fleet until Fernando III engaged Ramón Bonifaz of Burgos to bring thirteen galleys and some smaller vessels to blockade Seville in 1247. Although he has been described as the first admiral of Castile he was never officially designated as such.[61] In 1251, Fernando III authorized the "men of the sea," settled in the *barrio de la mar* in Seville, to have their own *alcalde de la mar*, who, assisted by six experts in maritime law, would "judge every affair of the sea." One could then appeal to the king. The mariners owed three months' service at sea; beyond that he would pay their expenses. Twenty carpenters, three blacksmiths, and three *alfajemes* (ar. *al-ḥajjām*), barbers or surgeons, assisted them. Granted the honor of knights, they were exempt from sales taxes and were permitted to have a slaughterhouse.[62]

Expressing the hope that "he might have a fleet at sea so that he might be more feared" (*CSM 376*), Alfonso X summoned the ports on the Bay of Biscay to provide ships for a Moroccan invasion and later for the siege of Algeciras. Besides rebuilding the shipyards in Seville,[63] he contracted with twenty-one mariners from Cantabria, Catalonia, France, and Italy to serve as *cómitres* or ship captains. In return for lands, houses, and money, each one promised to maintain an armed galley for service.[64] In 1256 he contracted with Pisa and Marseilles to provide ten galleys for three months' service,[65] and two years later he urged the Galician and Asturian towns to send their sailing ships and galleys to Cádiz on 1 May for the "affair of the crusade."[66] He also appointed Roy López de Mendoza as the first *almirante de la mar* or admiral.[67] After Roy's death, he named Juan García de Villamayor as *adelantado de la mar* with "all the rights that an admiral ought to have."[68] In the expedition against Salé in Morocco in 1260, Pedro Martínez de Fe, incorrectly identified as admiral by the *Chronicle of Alfonso X*, held the fleet offshore while Juan García led the assault. Later, while commanding the fleet besieging Algeciras, Pedro Martínez was captured.[69]

In the *Partidas*, Alfonso X, "the true creator of the Castilian naval force,"[70] described naval warfare. Mariners had to have a thorough knowledge of the sea and the winds. Their vessels had to be well constructed, adequately provisioned, and manned by loyal crews. As the fleet was comparable to an army, the admiral had the same power as if the king were present. An honorable person of good lineage, knowledgeable in maritime and landed affairs, he should be a courageous leader. As disobedience could lead to disaster, his crew, on penalty of death, should immediately execute his orders. By generously sharing booty with them, he would win their respect and loyalty. Prior to assuming office, he ought to keep a vigil in church. On the next day, dressed in rich silks, he would receive from the king a ring, a sword, and a royal standard, signifying the power of command. He should promise to defend the faith, the king, and the common good, even to the point of death (*SP 2, 9, 24; 2, 24, 3*). The *Espéculo* did not discuss the admiral's functions, although it did have a formula of appointment for various officials, including an admiral; the fee for issuing the charter was two hundred *maravedís* (*E 4, 12, 17, 55*). Ship captains had similar authority. After twelve experienced seamen assessed the qualifications of a man aspiring to command, he would be clothed in red, be given a royal standard, and take possession of his galley. A navigator, familiar with currents, winds, weather, islands, and harbors, received a tiller and a rudder as a sign of his office. Also essential were marines armed with crossbows and other weapons, and mariners who handled the everyday business of propelling the ship with oars or sails (SP 2, 24, 4–6).[71]

Ships should be constructed with duly seasoned wood and properly equipped with banks of oars, a rudder, sails, masts, anchors, ropes, and cables for towing. Also necessary were weapons, iron hooks to latch onto enemy ships, jars of lime to blind the enemy, jars of soap to make him slip, and liquid pitch or Greek fire (alquitrán, ar. al-qiṭrān) to burn his ships. Conserving food supplies, the crew should eat and drink in moderation and guard against too much wine. Given the hazards of naval warfare, it was essential that the crew be paid promptly and receive their share of booty (SP 2, 24, 7–10). Sailing ships of various types are illustrated in the Cantigas.[72]

Lacking enough ships of his own, Alfonso X turned elsewhere. In 1264, for example, he persuaded Bonagiunta de Portovenere, a Genoese merchant, to build three galleys for the "admiral of Castile." Two weeks later, Raimundo Danza di Vintimiglia promised Hugo Vento, "admiral of the king of Castile," a loan for armament of the ships. As we hear no more of Admiral Hugo, Florentino Pérez Embid seems to be correct in noting that this was an isolated instance when the king attempted to secure Genoese collaboration.[73]

Fleets guarding the strait intercepted enemy invaders and supplies sent to relieve ports under siege. When battle was imminent, oarsmen maneuvered their galley and attempted to ram the enemy galley, perhaps disabling it, running it aground, or seizing it with grappling hooks. Marines then leaped into it and assaulted the enemy. The winds of the Atlantic and the strait, however, could be particularly treacherous, and heavy rain in the fall and winter made life miserable for seamen.

The Aftermath of War

Booty made warfare a profitable business.[74] The rewards of victory included jewelry, gold, silver, rich garments, weapons, livestock, horses, and people, who might be ransomed or sold into slavery. The Poem of the Cid (canto 74), after recording the fall of Valencia, remarked that with an abundance of horses, foot soldiers became knights; that there was so much gold and silver that everyone became rich; and that the Cid's fifth amounted to thirty thousand marks. Those lines likely stirred the imagination of listeners hoping to become wealthy.

The process of distributing the spoils elaborated in the municipal *fueros* was the foundation of the Alfonsine discussion.[75] A soldier who abandoned pursuit of the enemy in order to plunder might be deprived of his estates, denied a share in the booty, and disgraced by having to ride on an ass, holding its tail in his hand. Once hostilities ended, the spoils were gathered in a public space for inspection and carefully guarded. *Quadrilleros*, one from each of four divisions of the army, arranged a public auction. Imitating the caliphs of Córdoba, the king received a fifth as an inalienable attribute of sovereignty. Cities, towns, castles, lands, ships, prominent captives, and a prisoner sold for one thousand *maravedís* were reserved for him. If the defenders of a city, town, or castle surrendered, he could allow them to depart with their movable goods; but if they had to leave their goods behind, he would retain half and give the other half to his troops. If he organized a fleet and provided supplies, arms, and the crew, he was entitled to all the booty; but if someone else paid the crew, the royal share would be three-fourths, or a half if he only provided the ships. The admiral's share was one seventh (*E* 3, 7, 8–9, 12; *SP* 2, 26, pr., 1–8, 12, 19, 29–31).

After the royal *mayordomo* received the king's share, and compensation for injuries was arranged and royal officers were paid, the remainder was apportioned among the victors. Goods recovered from enemy raiders had to be restored to their owners if they could be identified. Then, depending upon the extent of his service and the number of men, arms, and animals that he brought to the campaign, each soldier would receive his allotment. In order to prevent fraud, everyone had to pass under a lance held by two men, so that each soldier and his equipment could be counted, and absentees, deserters, and strangers identified. A single share or *cavallería* was allotted to soldiers with a horse, lance, and sword, or varying types of armor. Foot soldiers, horses, and pack animals received a half, but an ass got only a quarter. A commander was entitled to two *cavallerías*. If there were many *adalides*, each would receive only one share (*E* 3, 7, 1–6, 10, 14–17; *SP* 2, 26, 9–18, 20–28).

An auctioneer offered articles for sale to the highest bidder. A scribe recorded the final bid, noting the buyer's name, the article purchased, the price, the date, and the place. Given a receipt with the royal seal, the buyer could remove the article provided he paid for it immediately or gave surety that he would do so within three to nine days. Otherwise, the *quadrilleros* could repossess the item. An auctioneer who took more than he was entitled to would be fined double the amount and banned for a year; for a second offense, he would be executed (*SP* 2, 26, 32–34).

The king might reward deeds of exceptional valor by ennobling a warrior, granting him estates or tax exemptions, knighting him, or arranging a good marriage for him. There were also ample financial rewards. The soldier who first gained entrance to a city, town, or castle by force would receive 1,000 *maravedís* and one of the best houses, except the *alcázar* or other houses reserved by the king. The second man would be given 500 *maravedís* and the next best house; the third man, 250 *maravedís* and another good house. Each would also receive two prisoners who could be held for ransom. Men who gained entrance into a fortress by stealth were also remunerated, as were mariners who seized an enemy ship (E 3, 5, 2, 7–8; SP 2, 27, 1–10).

The military orders and large towns usually maintained hospitals to attend to the wounded.[76] A portion of the booty was allocated to compensation (*erecha*, lat. *erecta*) for injuries and loss of life. In determining the amount, assessors considered the disfigurement caused by facial or head wounds (10–12 *maravedís*), the loss of front teeth (40 *maravedís* per tooth), and the incapacity resulting from the loss of body parts (an eye, nose, hand, or foot, 100 *maravedís*; an arm or a leg, 120 *maravedís*). As loss of life was most grievous, money was set aside (150 *maravedís* for a knight, 75 for a foot soldier) so that God would pardon the sins of the dead warrior and console his heirs. Prior to setting out on an expedition weapons, animals, and other equipment should be appraised so that appropriate compensation might be made in case of loss. If an initial appraisal was not carried out, compensation was meted out according to the value attested by the owner and confirmed by two knights. For example, as much as twenty *maravedís* could be given for a lost mule or horse, or five for an ass (E 3, 7, 11–12; SP 2, 25, 1–4).

The loss of "liberty, which is the most precious thing that people can have in this world" (SP 2, 29, pr.), not only separated the captive from his family and friends, but also subjected him to a "double martyrdom" (CSM 83.18). Wearing chains about their legs and necks, captives were beaten regularly, given little to eat and drink, and had to endure attempts to convert them.[77] Their only hope was to regain their freedom by an exchange of prisoners or the payment of ransom. Those sold into slavery in Morocco likely never returned home. Pedro Marín, around 1284–87, collected stories of the miraculous deliverance of captives by Santo Domingo de Silos.[78]

The royal jurists distinguished prisoners, that is, Christians taken in wars between Christians, from captives or Muslims. The former might be confined but should not be killed, tortured, or sold into slavery, but Muslims, because of the contempt in which their religion was held, could be maltreated. Although the bond of marriage was regarded as indissoluble, captors could inflict even greater cruelty by separating husbands from wives, as well as children from parents (SP 2, 29, 1–2).[79]

Christians were expected to contribute to the liberation of their fellow Christians, but some persons, seeking their own advantage, chose to leave relatives and friends in captivity. A son, for example, could refuse to secure his father's release, but the latter, on being set free, could disinherit him. A vassal who failed to liberate his lord could be executed and his property confiscated. A vassal abandoned by his lord could offer allegiance to another. If a person died in captivity because no one ransomed him, a notary would inventory his property to be sold at auction and the proceeds used to ransom other captives. A captive's relatives were required to maintain the value of his property until he was liberated. On the assumption that a captive acted under compulsion, his will was usually declared invalid. A child born in captivity and later set free was entitled to inherit the property of its parents. If the child of a Christian captive and a Muslim woman was reared as a Christian, and acknowledged by its father, it could inherit his estate. The relatives of a person who died in captivity could dispose of his estate, provided they had not deliberately neglected to ransom him. Laws protecting the property of Christian captives did not apply to those who chose to live among the Moors, but were imprisoned by them. Christians who, without royal authorization, entered the service of the Moors and were captured could be sold into slavery, but only to Christians. That law was prompted by the fact that Spanish Christians had often served in the army of the Moroccan rulers.[80] A man who ransomed another was allowed to retain him, not as a slave, but in service for five years or until he was reimbursed (*SP* 2, 29, 3–12).

The business of ransoming was not for amateurs. Merchants were often employed by families to ransom their relatives, but by the twelfth century the task was in the hands of professionals. Families could purchase Muslim slaves to exchange for Christians. Twelve good men appointed by the king or a municipality would choose a person familiar with the Arabic language as a ransomer or *alfaqueque* (ar. *al-fakkāk*, redeemer) and entrust him with a royal pennant. After negotiating the ransom or exchange of captives, he would be compensated by the king or the municipality and would also be paid by the captive or his family. His commission was usually 10 percent of the ransom or a gold *maravedí* for each prisoner exchanged. *Alfaqueques* who carried out their duty responsibly "should be greatly honored and protected because they accomplish works of piety for the common good of all" (*SP* 2, 30, 1–3).[81]

Deffender lo Ssuyo e Ganar de lo de los Henemigos

In thirteenth-century Castile, war or preparation for war was the natural order of events. Not only did Alfonso X hope to subjugate the emirate of Granada, but he also planned to seize the ports on both sides of the Strait of Gibraltar so as to prevent invasion from Morocco. As he explained, the people needed to do two things: "deffender lo ssuyo et ganar de lo de los hen-emigos" (to defend their own and to seize the enemy's) (*E* 3, 6, pr.). Although wars fought to defend the faith and recover lands believed to be rightly his were thought to be just, they necessarily caused grief and destruction. For that reason, it was essential that war be undertaken only after careful preparation.

The duty of military service, arising from the natural bond between every person and his native land, was shared equally by all, because it affected all. In fulfilling that duty, a man might have to lay down his life, thereby gain-ing everlasting glory and entrance into paradise. While prelates provided spiritual counseling and contingents of knights, nobles, as royal vassals and members of the order of knighthood, had a special responsibility for defense of the realm, as did the military orders. The municipal militias provided valu-able cavalry and infantry elements. Under the direction of experienced com-manders, castles were maintained as the first line of defense, and offensive operations such as raids, sieges, or pitched battles were carried out. From time to time, fleets were deployed to secure the strait. The penalties for fail-ing to respond to the summons to war or to come properly equipped were harsh, but deserters were charged with treason and punished by loss of life and property, and everlasting infamy. When a campaign ended successfully, booty was apportioned in a prescribed manner and monetary compensation was given to the wounded or the families of those who died. Professional ransomers were employed to rescue captives.

While acknowledging the harm accompanying warfare, the king also argued that, by conquering the enemy, peace could be achieved. However, until the Moors were entirely vanquished and Morocco, as part of the Visigothic inheritance, was recovered, there could be no permanent peace. Given those suppositions, the Alfonsine Codes emphasized war rather than peace.

❧ CHAPTER 7

Litigants, Judges, and Lawyers

Dar a Cada Vno su Derecho

By the twelfth century the administration of justice was recognized as a public function of the king as head of the body politic. As Alfonso X pointed out, "there can be no king without a kingdom nor a kingdom without a king, because the king is the head and the kingdom is the body" (*E* 2, 6, 2). Just as the human body was a union of heart and members, so also the bond between king and people forged the unity of the kingdom:

> Saints declared that the king is put on earth in the place of God to carry out justice and to give each one his rights (*dar a cada vno su derecho*). And so they called him [the king], the heart and soul of the people. Thus, as the soul resides in man's heart and the body lives and is sustained by it, so justice, which is the life and sustenance of the people, resides in the king. (*SP* 2, 1, 5)

In other words, justice was essential to the people's well-being, and the king, as the earthly vicar of God, from whom justice ultimately derived, was its immediate source. He dispensed justice personally, but also through his judges. As the law became more complex, however, public officials, who were often legal amateurs, yielded the task of interpretation and judgment to professional jurists.[1]

The acts of the Cortes, the Alfonsine Codes, and the Ordinance of Zamora in 1274 gave ample attention to the administration of justice. The *Third Partida*, utilizing material from books 4 and 5 of the *Espéculo*, bears a close relationship to the *Dotrinal de pleitos* of Jacobo de las leyes, so much so that Alfonso García Gallo regarded him as its principal author. The clear and logical exposition makes the *Third Partida* one of the most admirable parts of the Alfonsine corpus.[2]

By showing earthly judges how to dispense justice, the royal jurists observed that God linked the human desire for justice with his own. Loving justice with all their hearts (Ws 1:1), judges were admonished to show mercy or severity as the case required. They should resist outside interference and administer justice with good sense and wisdom. Allocating rights equally to everyone, justice, "a fountain from which all rights flow," is always oriented toward Jesus Christ, the sun of justice (Mal 3:20). Justice rewards good men for the good they do and induces wicked men to be good. Justice requires that one live honestly, not harming another, and rendering to each one his rights ("que de su derecho a cada vno") (*SP* 3, 1, 1–3). That statement sums up the classic definition of justice by the Roman jurist Ulpian: "Iustitia est constans et perpetua voluntas ius suum cuique tribuendi" (Justice is the constant and perpetual desire to render his right to each one) (*D* 1, 1, 10). Both Alfonso VIII, in 1181, and Alfonso IX, in 1188 in the Curia of León, confirmed that principle.[3] After repeating that phrase, the *Espéculo* (4, 1, pr.) emphasized that the king, more than all others, should love justice.[4] Ironically, the *hermandad* of 1282 upbraided him for denying due process to Fadrique and Simón Ruiz de los Cameros whom he executed without trial in 1277. Although the king objected that he was deprived of authority without a hearing, his failure to adhere to the legal standards articulated in his own law codes brought him to that pass.[5]

Plaintiffs and Defendants

The business of doing justice involved litigants, judges, scribes, advocates, and procurators (*E* 4, 4, pr.). The right of a plaintiff (*demandador*) to initiate a lawsuit might be limited by family, seigneurial, or professional relationships and social status. Under certain conditions, however, a son could sue his father or a brother his brother. Spouses could proceed against one another in case of adultery or treason or to recover property. Slaves could only accuse their masters of treason. Just as a knight could sue his lord for his stipend, university masters, judges, and other public officials, who "are like warriors and opponents of those interfering with justice, which is another form of great war," could sue to gain their salaries (*SP* 3, 2, 1–13; *LEst* 2, 6).

In demanding the return of property, the plaintiff had to describe it in detail: the location and boundaries of real estate; the extent of injuries suffered; the name, sex, and color of slaves and animals; the color, size, weight, and measure of objects. The defendant (*demandado*) was forbidden to destroy items in contention but could not be penalized if they were lost through no fault of his own. If he refused to produce them, the judge could order their seizure (*E* 4, 4, 1–8; *SP* 3, 2, 15–31; *FR* 1, 11, 1–8; 1, 12, 1–4).

The plaintiff should submit his written claim or *libellus* to a judge with jurisdiction by reason of residence, social condition, or location of the contested property. A claim worth less than ten *maravedís* could be stated verbally. The plaintiff should name the judge, himself, the defendant, the property at issue, the sum demanded or redress to be granted, and the rationale for it (*E* 4, 4, 9–12; *SP* 3, 2, 32–47; *DO* 1, 2).[6] In responding, the defendant had to be wary of falsely denying possession or ownership. He ought to determine whether the plaintiff was acting for himself, or represented another, or was the guardian of a minor. Ordinarily the defendant was subject to the jurisdiction of the judge where he resided, but he could not object when summoned before the king (*E* 4, 5, 1–5; *SP* 3, 3, 1–11; *DO* 1, 3; *LEst* 1–5). The rule that he was answerable to the judge of his district court (*SP* 3, 3, 4) was one of several elements of Spanish law acknowledged later in the state of Texas.[7]

Courts and Judges

Although the king was the immediate source of justice, a diversity of jurisdictions existed. Aside from his court and the territorial and municipal tribunals that he authorized, secular and ecclesiastical lords, recipients of immunities granted by his predecessors, adjudicated disputes among their tenants. Bishops similarly claimed jurisdiction over their clergy and church property.

The royal tribunal (*corte del rey*), with jurisdiction over "great affairs," was the most important (*E* 4, 2, pr.).[8] Comparing the court to the sea, the royal jurists emphasized that it ought to be spacious enough to handle all the business brought before it. Like seafarers in good weather, litigants could travel safely to and from the court, knowing that no one could appeal from its just judgment. Conversely, those who made unreasonable demands, like seagoing travelers caught in a storm, would find themselves rejected, and some, on account of their crimes, might have to "swallow the bitterness of justice" and lose their lives. Like the magnetic needle guiding sailors, justice should always direct the king to reward the good and punish the wicked. His counselors ought to be prudent, unswayed by oratory, prejudice, or envy, and encourage him to act according to justice and law (*SP* 2, 9, 28; *E* 2, 14, 1–2).

Casos de corte or pleas reserved to the royal court included, according to the *Espéculo* (4, 2, 12) and an ordinance given to Valladolid in 1258, the defiance of one noble by another (*riepto*), treason among nobles (*aleve*), violation of a royal truce or surety, and counterfeiting the royal seal, charter, or coinage.[9] In addition, the *Partidas* (3, 3, 5) cited destruction of highways,[10] rape, theft, outlawry, debasement of gold, silver and other metals, treason against the king or the kingdom, and a lawsuit against a powerful individual by a minor or a poor or wretched person. As these cases touched the king's sovereignty, they could not go unpunished. The Ordinance of Zamora in 1274 (art. 46) added arson.[11] In 1279 the king reminded the *alcaldes* of Burgos that they did not have jurisdiction over these issues.[12]

Traditionally, the king presided over his court, but as judicial business increased, the burden grew. He informed the Cortes of Valladolid in 1258 (art. 8) that he would sit in judgment each week on Mondays, Tuesdays, and Fridays, but in 1274 he promised to do so until midday on Mondays, Wednesdays, and Fridays. No one was to disturb him with other business during that time. The *alcaldes* assisting him were expected to articulate the issues without engaging in stubborn disputations (OZ 1274, arts. 42–45). As he had no temporal superior, no one could appeal from his judgment, though one could always seek his mercy (SP 3, 23, 17).

Ordinarily, *alcaldes de la corte del rey* conducted most of its business. As they ought to possess a wholesome fear of God and of the king, and a knowledge of the law, the royal jurists urged them to administer justice promptly and evenhandedly, making it accessible to everyone (E 2, 13, 7; 4, 2, 7; SP 3, 4, 1–35).[13] In the Cortes of Valladolid in 1258 (arts. 16, 18), and again at Seville in 1261 (arts. 3, 18), the king prohibited his brothers, and other great men, without first notifying him, from taking the side of someone whose case was before the royal court. Once their cases were heard, litigants were obliged to depart, doubtless because he did not wish them to take advantage of his largesse.

The royal court, according to the Ordinance of Zamora in 1274, would consist of twenty-three judges, all laymen, from three principal geographical areas: nine from Castile, six from Extremadura, and eight from León. The Castilian judges would take turns, three at a time, serving for three months each year. One of the Leonese judges had to be a knight familiar with the Visigothic Code still used in that kingdom. The day began with mass at matins (about 6 a.m.) and, in the summer, concluded with mass at tierce (about 9 a.m.), but in the winter at midday (arts. 17, 35).

Drawn from the class of knights and good men of the towns, the king's judges were expected to be Christian laymen of good reputation, over the age of thirty. If married, their union should be in accordance with church law. Clerics, foreigners, ignorant persons, the blind and the deaf, madmen and slaves, excommunicates, criminals or their abettors, counterfeiters, traitors, and perjurers were disqualified. Clerics could not serve as advocates, counselors, or judges of appeals because they might allege laws (presumably canon law) other than those in the book (apparently the *Espéculo* and the *Fuero real*).[14] Also barred were women, though a queen or lady who inherited a public office could act as a judge with the counsel of learned men, who, if necessary, could correct her (*E* 4, 2, 1–3; *SP* 2, 9, 18; 3, 4, 1–6; *DO* 2, 1; 3, 3–4).

Before taking office a judge had to swear a six-part oath: (1) to obey oral or written royal directives; (2) to protect the king's sovereignty; (3) to keep his secrets; (4) to guard him against injury; (5) to adjudicate cases quickly and only in accordance with the laws in the *Partidas*, and not to be diverted from truth and justice by hostility, fear, gifts, or promises; and (6) never to accept a bribe. He also had to give sureties that after his term ended, he would be available for fifty days to respond to grievances (*E* 4, 2, 3; *SP* 3, 4, 6; 3, 16, 1).[15]

According to the Ordinance of Zamora in 1274, the judge should oblige the advocates to swear that they would not maliciously prolong the proceedings. Judgment should be rendered no later than the third day, so that cases could be settled quickly. A judge should never permit an advocate to reside with him, nor allow one advocate to plead his case privately without hearing the other. He ought to conclude a case before taking up another. If he failed, without a legitimate excuse, to appear in court, or attempted to hear more pleas in a day than he could, he had to pay the costs to the parties. If he had to transfer a case to another judge, he should provide him with the pertinent documentation. Admonished to hear cases gently, judges and the scribes should not participate in offensive exchanges with litigants. Judges should settle cases by themselves and not trouble the king unless they had a question for him. Six bailiffs and two porters were charged with maintaining order and removing those with no business before the court (OZ 1274, arts. 21–30). Jacobo de las leyes advised Alfonso Fernández, the king's illegitimate son, that in order to uphold "the honor of your dignity," he should hold court in an appropriate location, surrounded by judges, wise men, and scribes (*FD* 1, 1, 1). Anyone addressing the judge should be well spoken and avoid excessive familiarity that "breeds depreciation of the dignity" (*DO* 3, 3). On Fridays and Saturdays the judges would hear charges against prisoners, but in deference to Jesus's death on Good Friday, they were forbidden to use torture on Fridays. Petitions unrelated to the administration of justice should be remitted to the Order of Santa María de España, and the order should receive fines levied in the *casos de corte* for "the affair of the sea."[16] Judges, scribes, and attorneys who accepted bribes would be at the king's mercy (OZ 1274, arts. 31–34, 47).

Robert MacDonald identified many of the *alcaldes del rey*, including Jacobo de las leyes and Fernando Mateos.[17] Fifteen judges shared in the partition of Seville.[18]

In order to foster a common system for recording court proceedings, the king reserved the right to appoint scribes. Intelligent, principled men, they should write legibly, understand what they were writing, and guard the king's secrets. Municipal scribes should be residents who knew their neighbors and their concerns. As scribes often had to compose documents involving the death penalty or corporal punishment, clerics were excluded because canon law forbade them to shed blood. Royal scribes had to swear that they would faithfully, impartially, and without prolixity draft the king's charters, and guard his privacy, sovereignty, family, and property. Urban scribes should take a similar oath. Both royal and municipal scribes registered documents, so that if the original were lost, the register copy could be produced (*E* 2, 12, 2–3, 6; 4, 12, 1–12; *DO* 3, 3).[19]

The Ordinance of Zamora added further detail concerning scribal work. Every Sunday the scribe would obtain sufficient parchment from the chancery for the following week's work. Before a suit began, he would present all relevant documents to the judge. After the midday meal, he exhibited his notes to the judge who affixed his seal and signature. In the evening the scribe presented the record to the notary for review. The official record was issued the next day so that the litigants would not suffer any delay (arts. 36–41). Fees for sealing documents were listed in the *Espéculo* (4, 12, 54–59). A scribe who accepted a bribe would lose his office and pay a heavy fine (*E* 4, 12, 18).

The *alguacil* (ar. *al-wazīr*) or *justicia de la casa del rey* or *justicia mayor* maintained order in the court, carried out arrests on the king's command, and had custody of prisoners. When required, he administered torture in the presence of a judge and a scribe who recorded the prisoner's words so they might be used in the judicial proceeding (*E* 2, 13, 5; 4, 3, pr., 1, 8, 14–15; *SP* 2, 9, 20; *LEst* 113, 120).

Whereas in earlier times, a court judgment was final, the right of appeal, derived from Roman law, permitted one to turn to the king's court.[20] In the Assembly of Seville in 1264 the king assured the Extremaduran towns of that right (art. 11).[21] Whether one or more judges were assigned to hear appeals is problematic. In an undated case in the reign of Fernando III, don Diego, *adelantado del rey*, and the other *adelantados* heard an appeal (*LFC* 3). The *Espéculo* (2, 13, 3) stated that the *adelantados mayores de la corte del rrey* heard appeals and adjudicated major pleas (*E* 4, 2, pr., 11). These passages suggest that there were multiple *adelantados mayores* in the king's court, but the section treating appeals refers to a single *adelantado mayor de la corte* (*E* 5, 14, 12, 14). The *Partidas* (2, 9, 19) referred to only one *adelantado mayor de la corte* or *sobrejuez*, a superior judge who attended to major pleas and functioned as a judge of appeals. His decisions could not be appealed (*E* 5, 14, 12; *SP* 3, 23, 17, 19). Jacobo de las leyes confirmed that his rulings were final (*DO* 6, 1, 1; 6, 1, 16). However, there is no documentary evidence of anyone holding that position, and the Ordinance of Zamora's omission of any reference to it suggests that it may have been eliminated. Possibly, one of the royal *alcaldes* fulfilled that function on an ad hoc basis.

The people had access to royal justice through officials entrusted with territorial administration.[22] From Fernando III's time, the king was represented in Old Castile, León, and Galicia by a *merino mayor*, assisted by subordinate *merinos*. In addition to collecting royal revenues, he executed judgments of the royal court, secured the king's highways, and prevented riots and the erection of fortresses without royal permission (*E* 2, 13, 4–5; 4, 3, 1–7, 11–13, 18; *SP* 2, 9, 23). In the Cortes of Seville in 1253 (arts. 14–15, 18–20) the king forbade *merinos* in León to seize property without a judge's authorization, to delegate their responsibility to negligent persons, and to enter immune lordships, except in four cases specified by Alfonso IX: homicide, rape, pursuit of known criminals, and highway robbery.[23]

There were no *merinos* in Extremadura, the kingdom of Toledo, and the lordships of the military orders between the Tagus and Guadalquivir Rivers, but Fernando III assigned a *merino mayor* to the kingdom of Murcia. In 1253, Alfonso X appointed the *adelantado mayor de la frontera* with appellate jurisdiction in Andalucía. Five years later, he replaced the *merinos mayores* of Old Castile, León, and Galicia with *adelantados mayores*. In 1263 Murcia received an *adelantado mayor*, whose judgments could be appealed to the king. Whereas the *merino mayor* enforced judicial decisions, the *adelantado mayor* was a judge with territorial jurisdiction.[24] More than likely the king's intent was to guarantee uniform administration of justice.[25] A royal letter of appointment charged the *adelantado mayor* to dispense justice, punish criminals, and hear appeals (*E* 4, 3, 2; 4, 12, 17; *SP* 2, 9, 22; 3, 18, 6).[26] Eventually, as his financial needs escalated, the king restored the *merinos mayores*, perhaps thinking they could best collect his revenues. In the Cortes of Burgos in 1272, the magnates objected, but their expressed preference for *adelantados* had more to do with their unwillingness to be taxed than the administration of justice. While the king promised to correct the excesses of the *merinos mayores*, he refused to replace them, and the nobles did not press their demand.[27]

Probably during this time a private person composed the *Leyes para los adelantados mayores*.[28]

Bishops, monasteries, nobles, and military orders enjoying the privilege of immunity in their lordships were authorized to grant *fueros*, appoint judges, and administer justice. The king reserved the right to intervene in cases of treason, robbery, destruction of highways, and homicide, though his officials occasionally overstepped their authority.[29] For example, in 1257 he forbade any *merino* to demand hospitality or levy fines in villages belonging to the Order of the Hospital, and in 1265, he barred any *merino* or *adelantado* from entering the order's lands to arrest evildoers, unless the order failed to do justice.[30] Although the king in 1271 ordered municipal judges to respect the bishop of Zamora's privileges, Infante Fernando had to admonish them in 1275 not to prevent the bishop from appointing judges. He also directed the municipality of León to allow a judge appointed by the bishop to hear cases, except those involving the shedding of blood.[31]

The archbishop and the municipality of Santiago de Compostela engaged in a long-standing conflict concerning jurisdiction, the administration of justice, and economic matters. The jurisdictional battle pitted old usages against Roman and canon law. The parties quarreled over the proper relationship between secular and ecclesiastical judges, the role of clerical and lay advocates, the archbishop's right to hear suits already initiated in the municipal court, his jurisdiction over royal pleas, appeals to the king, the pursuit and punishment of criminals, and the imposition of fines. Also in contention was the town's right to receive peasants as new citizens, the cultivation of municipal lands, and the obligations of tenants to their urban landlords and to the archbishop. These topics will be reviewed in the course of this study.[32]

A bitter quarrel erupted in Alfonso X's last decade as the nobility protested that he ignored their traditional customs. Despite his assurance, in the Cortes of Seville in 1253 (art. 3) that he would punish anyone who dishonored them, they became increasingly wary of royal justice.[33] As they observed the influence of Roman law and the presence of legists in his court, they realized that the old customs were giving way to the new juridical order. In 1272 prior to the Cortes of Burgos, they complained that they and their vassals were judged according to the *fueros* of the towns in which they lived. Insisting on the principle of trial by peers, they remarked on the absence of *alcaldes de Castilla* or noble judges in the royal court. Upholding their traditional *fueros*, the king promised to appoint *alcaldes de Castilla* and declared that nobles would not be judged according to municipal *fueros* unless they wished. If any noble had a charge against him, it would be resolved according to "the ancient *fuero*." When the Cortes assembled, the magnates demanded that they be tried only by two *alcaldes de fijosdalgo* or noble judges. The king promised to appoint them, although he commented that his predecessors had not done so. Despite his assurances, they repudiated their vassalage and went into exile to Granada. In negotiating with Queen Violante, they insisted that he confirm traditional customs, objected to the presence of legists and canonists in his court, and reiterated their demand that their suits be adjudicated by lay judges of Castile and León. The prologue to the *Fuero viejo* stated that at Martinmas (11 November 1272), he confirmed that they would be judged according to their traditional *fueros*. He also reportedly set aside the *Fuero del libro* that he had given to the Castilian towns and directed Burgos to use its old *fuero*. At the end of 1273 they renewed their allegiance and in the Cortes of Burgos in 1274 agreed to support his proposed journey to the empire.[34] Notwithstanding the outward appearance of calm, they remained suspicious of the king and joined Infante Sancho in his rebellion in 1282.

Justice was ordinarily dispensed in municipal courts. Many municipalities depended directly upon the king who set down their rights, privileges, and obligations in charters or *fueros*.[35] In the Cortes of Seville in 1252 (art. 35), Alfonso X expressed his irritation with local *alcaldes* who failed to do justice and required them to pay the plaintiff double the amount of his plea as well as the cost of traveling to and from the court. Through the *Fuero real* he determined to exert greater control over the administration of justice and to overcome the difficulties caused by the miscellany of municipal *fueros*. Thus, in 1255 he gave Aguilar de Campóo "el fuero del mio libro aquel que estava en Cervatos" (the *fuero* of my book that was in Cervatos), a nearby village, and appointed two *alcaldes* to judge according to it. He also ordered several villages in the municipality of Burgos to follow the *Fuero real*.[36] Reserving the right to nominate judges, he demanded that they swear before the town council to uphold the rights of the king, the people, and the litigants, and to judge according to the *Fuero real* and no other book. If a judge was ill or absent for a legitimate reason, he could name a substitute (*FR* 1, 7, 1–2). In 1263 the king stated that the decision of a substitute judge could be appealed, first to the *alcaldes mayorales* of Burgos, and then to him.[37] References to *mio alcalde* in municipal charters usually meant the judge whom he appointed.[38] The chancery formula for appointing a judge mentioned Fernando Mateos, *alcalde* of Seville (*SP* 3, 18, 7).

Court should be held in a certain place every morning until midday from 2 October to 31 March, and until the celebration of mass at tierce, or 9 a.m., from 1 April to 1 October. The court was closed on feast days, fair days, royal birthdays, days commemorating the beginning of a reign, the birth of an heir, or a victory over enemies, and during the wheat and grape harvests (E 4, 2, 15; 5, 6, 1–8; FR 1, 7, 2; 2, 5, 1; LEst 209–10).

Only judges named by the king could impose the death penalty. Once a suit began, the parties could not settle privately without official approval. A judge who overstepped his jurisdiction or failed to summon the accused or favored one of the parties was subject to a fine and damages. If he proved to be biased, another judge would replace him. Should a plea arise that was not dealt with in the *Fuero real*, the towns could ask the king to provide a law to be inserted in their copy of the text (FR 1, 7, 4–10).

Several charters illustrate the practical application of the Code. In 1264 the king appointed two judges and a *justicia* or police officer in Escalona. Swearing to execute his commands, the judges had to hold court in a fixed place and at the times established and to render judgment promptly according to "our *libro del fuero*." As he paid their salaries, they had to be impartial, not sharing fines or accepting gifts or services.[39] Four years later, he commanded the judges of Burgos, during construction of the tower, to hold court in the plaza where wood was sold, but with the consent of the litigants, they could also do so in their homes. As some judges came late and left early, they were ordered to rise at the sound of the bell for mass at prime (about 6 a.m.) and to sit in judgment until the hour mandated by the *Fuero real* (9 a.m. in the spring and summer and midday in the fall and winter). If a case had to be dealt with quickly, they should sit again after the midday meal. Judges should punish anyone who maliciously summoned another and chastise advocates who wandered off topic. Clerics, except in those instances permitted by the *Fuero real*, were forbidden to counsel judges, thereby prolonging lawsuits. On Saturdays the fate of prisoners was decided. Fines established in the *Fuero real* for abusive language and assault had to be levied. Making justice accessible to everyone continued to be difficult, as both the king in 1279 and his son Sancho in 1279 and 1282 had to remind judges to hear cases in the tower of Burgos or in another public place, as the *Fuero real* required, and not in their own homes (as he had allowed in 1268).[40] In 1271 Vitoria raised identical issues.[41]

Municipal judges often called on the king to defend their jurisdiction against competing claims. In 1277 he forbade the *merino mayor* of Castile, for example, to exercise jurisdiction in villages pertaining to Burgos. Emphasizing that original jurisdiction belonged to the municipal judges, in 1279 he banned members of his household from settling their disputes with citizens of Burgos in the royal court. He also prohibited judges from adjudicating matters reserved to his court.[42] Rejecting ecclesiastical jurisdiction over wills, he commanded the *alcaldes* of Badajoz in 1270 to hear testamentary cases and to ignore threats of excommunication. He also barred the bishop and chapter from interfering with municipal judges exercising jurisdiction.[43] Several times he sustained the jurisdiction of judges of the city of León in villages in the municipal district.[44]

The variety of laws created jurisdictional problems in the kingdom of Toledo. Whereas the Mozarabs used the *Fuero Juzgo*, the Castilians followed the *Fuero de los castellanos*. In order to avert juridical chaos, in 1254 Alfonso X upheld usage of the *Fuero Juzgo* in Talavera, and three years later gave the Castilians the *Fuero real*. However, it is not clear which law book was followed when litigants adhering to one or the other came into conflict. In 1282 Infante Sancho confirmed his father's privilege to Talavera and ordered the *alcalde* and the *alguacil* to render judgment in the same manner as in Toledo. Whether that clarified the issue is uncertain.[45]

The municipal council of Compostela complained of the partiality of clerical judges appointed by the archbishop, who held the city in lordship, and his attempt to restrict appeals. In 1263, the archbishop's representative asserted the archbishop's temporal jurisdiction and his right to appoint both clerical and lay justices. However, both sides agreed that the archbishop would name a neutral judge to resolve pleas between the townspeople and the archdiocese (ley 5). While confirming that litigation among townspeople should first be adjudicated by municipal judges before an appeal could be directed to the archbishop, the king ordered the archbishop to present any royal charters authorizing him to do so (ley 6).[46]

The municipal council of Oviedo and the bishop, who held partial lordship of the city, quarreled over the appointment of judges. In 1261 the council asserted its right to freely appoint two *jueces* (administrators) and two *alcaldes*, while the bishop named one *juez* and one *alcalde*. Although Fernando III's charter of 1234 ordered the council to ask the bishop's advice concerning judicial appointments, Alfonso X declared that it had been obtained contrary to law and tore it up. Henceforth, he determined that the council did not have to consult the bishop.[47]

The king appointed as many scribes as necessary to record judicial proceedings in the municipal courts. They had to prepare accurate notes for drafting charters and register documents. Their fees depended on the value of the matter involved. When a scribe died, his register would be given to his replacement (FR 1, 8, 1–7). In 1264 Madrid complained about custody of the municipal seal and the role of the scribes in preserving registers.[48]

The law recognized two types of extraordinary judges, namely, *jueces delegados* or judges delegate, and *jueces de avenencia* or arbiters. The idea of judges delegate, with temporary jurisdiction to hear special cases, was borrowed from papal practice. A royal judge could delegate to a subordinate responsibility for resolving a case. The charter appointing him ought to identify the issues, the judges, and the persons involved (*E* 4, 2, 4). Ordinary judges were not authorized to designate judges delegate. If two parties (or only one) asked the king to name a delegate, he should appoint someone acceptable to both sides. A judge delegate could not adjudicate any other quarrel between the litigants, but if the defendant, after first responding to the original charge against him, wished to sue the plaintiff, the delegate could hear that. The delegate might lose his authority if his superior revoked it or died before the issue was joined (*SP* 3, 4, 19–22).[49]

Jueces de avenencia were arbiters freely chosen by the litigants. They were of two types: *auenidores* who functioned in the same manner as ordinary judges; and *arbitratores* or *aluedriadores* who decided contested matters as they thought best. Persons submitting to arbitration should identify the issue, authorize the arbiters to resolve it, and promise to accept their decision. If one refused to do so, he had to pay a penalty. Prior to agreeing to arbitrate, the arbiters should determine whether the case was such that it could legally be settled in that way, and a written statement of their responsibility and authority should be prepared. Not subject to arbitration were cases involving the death penalty, loss of limbs, exile, slavery and freedom, marriage, or the common good of a particular region or of the entire realm. No one could allow his opponent to arbitrate their quarrel unless he wished to make reparation for his actions. A minor under twenty-five could not ask for arbitration without his guardian's consent, but a minor over fourteen, lacking a guardian, could do so (*SP* 3, 4, 23–26).

The authority of the arbiters expired on the day specified, unless an extension was permitted. When no time limit was stated, the matter should be resolved within three years. Should the arbiters needlessly prolong the suit, the ordinary judge could shut them up in a house until they decided it. If they were equally divided, another person could be chosen to help them. The case should be heard in the place assigned or in the town where it arose, and the ordinary court calendar should be observed. Arbitration ended if one of the arbiters died or entered a religious order, unless the parties agreed that the surviving arbiters could decide the case. Arbitration also ended if the property in dispute was lost or died, or if one party willingly relinquished it to the other. Arbiters were not required to hear the case if the parties also submitted it to the judgment of the ordinary judge. Arbiters could be excused if they went on pilgrimage or had to attend to the king's business, or were otherwise impeded, or were harshly treated by one of the parties. An arbiter who was hostile to one party or accepted a bribe would be disqualified. All the arbiters had to state their individual opinions before the decision of the entire group was rendered. They could demand that one or both of the parties take some action by a specified date, or within four months, if no date was cited. An order contrary to royal law, natural law, or good customs, or based on fraud or false testimony, or dealing with a matter not subject to arbitration need not be obeyed. If a penalty was agreed upon initially, no one could appeal the decision. If there were no penalty, one had to object to the decision immediately or within nine days (*SP* 3, 4, 27–35).[50] A dispute between the monastery of San Salvador de Oña and the town of Frías illustrating the work of arbiters will be discussed in the following chapter.

Personeros and Advocates

Men learned in the law played a prominent part in the administration of justice. During the early Middle Ages, a man had to plead his own cause or appoint a spokesman to do so (*FJ* 2, 3, 3). The emergence of Roman and canon law, however, spurred the development of the legal profession.[51] Drawing on Justinian's Code, jurists compared the *militia legum*, the knighthood of laws, to the *militia armata*, the knighthood of arms, and demanded recognition as knights.[52] Today's attorney using the title of esquire perpetuates the notion that lawyering is a form of knighthood. As their function was professionalized, jurists concluded that given the king's lack of formal knowledge, he should yield the responsibility of pronouncing judgment to judges trained in the law.[53] Asserting that "the science of the laws is another form of knighthood," Alfonso X declared that masters of law were entitled to the honors of knights (*SP* 2, 10, 3). Wielding the weapons of the law, jurists "are like warriors and adversaries of those who thwart justice" (*SP* 3, 2, 2). Jacobo de las leyes described himself as "juez et cauallero del rrey de Castilla."[54]

Summoned to court, a litigant might be represented by a *personero*, the equivalent of a procurator.[55] Whereas the *personero* physically stood in place of his principal (*dominus, dueño de la voz*), an advocate argued his case in court. In Roman law a procurator or proctor was ordinarily endowed with *plena potestas*, that is, full power to act for and bind his principal, so that the principal could not later claim that his procurator exceeded his authority.[56] By the early thirteenth century, kings, bishops, cathedral chapters, monasteries, and municipalities were adopting the system of proctorial representation. Although ecclesiastics usually preferred the term *procurator*, municipalities commonly used *personarius* or *personero*, a word with the same meaning. Indeed, the terms were often used interchangeably.[57] In 1250 the *personeros* of the municipality of Santiago de Compostela carried *cartas de personería*, letters of procuration, granting them *lleno poder*, full power, and binding the city by their actions. To my knowledge this is the first document referring to the *plena potestas* of municipal representatives.[58]

Any freeman over the age of twenty-five, and a minor on his guardian's advice, could designate a *personero*. Excluded were madmen, deaf mutes, accused criminals, slaves, and women, though women could represent aged and infirm family members. Monks could act for their communities and ecclesiastics for the church. Knights serving the king and royal officials were forbidden to act as *personeros*. However, the king, his sons, and other powerful men, so as not to intimidate an inferior adversary, should be represented by *personeros*. A *personero* could be appointed for every civil suit, but in a criminal case involving the death penalty, mutilation, or exile, the principal had to stand alone (*SP* 3, 5, 1–12; *E* 4, 8, 1–6, 13; *FR* 1, 10, 2–5, 7, 16; *LEst* 11–17).

A valid letter of procuration, naming the principal, the *personero*, the suit for which he was appointed, and the judge, had to be drawn up by a public scribe, witnessed, dated, and sealed. The principal should give his *personero* power to demand, respond, acknowledge, and deny, and to bind him by whatever he did. For example, Ferrand García granted his *personero* "free and full power (*libre e llenero poder*)" to manage his property, and promised to hold as firm whatever was done in his name. Similarly, Rodrigo Esteban and Alfonso Díaz, *alcaldes* of Seville, with the consent of the city council, appointed a *personero* for their suit with the archbishop. Granting their "true *personero*" the power to ask questions, to respond, to defend, to appeal, and to do whatever else a "true *personero*" might do, the council pledged to "hold as firm and stable" whatever he might do and never to challenge it (*SP* 3, 18, 97–98).[59]

One could also appoint a *personero* verbally in the judge's presence. If someone had several *personeros*, each one's role could be limited by the terms of the *carta de personería* or by the judge (*SP* 3, 5, 13–21; *E* 4, 8, 7–14; *FR* 1, 10, 1–2, 5). In the Cortes of Valladolid in 1258 (art. 8), and again at Seville in 1261 (art. 17), the king limited to two the number of municipal *personeros* and ordered them and their principals to leave his court once their case was settled.

Unless his principal gave him full power, the *personero* could not take certain actions without his consent, but the principal could give retroactive approval. If a *personero*'s power seemed questionable, the judge could permit him to proceed if he gave sureties that his principal would confirm his decisions. A *personero* was expected to answer questions fully and truthfully and not delay the proceedings. The letter of procuration was terminated if the principal died before the suit began; if he died during it, the *personero* had to complete it. The principal, after notifying the judge and his opponent, could replace his *personero*, who could also ask to be relieved. If he lost the case, he should enter an appeal, but he could not pursue it without the principal's consent. He had to deliver to his principal anything awarded by the court, but he also owed reparations for any loss incurred through his fault or negligence. The principal had to pay his just and reasonable expenses (*E* 4, 8, 15–19; *FR* 1, 10, 8, 10–11; *SP* 3, 5, 20–27).

In the second half of the thirteenth century, proctorial representation was commonplace. In 1256, for example, the archbishop and chapter of Compostela dispatched two canons with a *carta de personería* to acknowledge the king's daughter as heir to the throne.[60] The procurators of the municipal council of Orense also pledged fidelity, but the bishop and chapter, claiming lordship over the city, appointed three procurators to protest and promised to ratify their actions.[61] In subsequent years the municipalities of La Coruña, Cuéllar, Tardajos, Burgos, Frías and the abbey of Oña, and the Order of the Hospital appointed procurators and pledged to abide by their actions.[62] In 1281 the king summoned all the cities and towns to send their "procurators with *personerías complidas*" to the Cortes of Seville "to grant all that should be decided" there.[63] From his point of view, it was imperative that *personeros* should have *plena potestas* or *lleno poder* legally binding their principals to accept judgments rendered in court.[64]

While a procurator might represent a litigant in court, the task of arguing his case was entrusted to an advocate (*aduocatus*).[65] Known in the vernacular as *abogado* or *vocero*, and sometimes as an *omne bono* or good man, an advocate was a person of upstanding character authorized to speak on behalf of his client.[66] Familiar with customary law and the municipal *fueros*, he was expected to provide effective and honest representation.[67] Lest justice be delayed, the king, in the Cortes of Seville in 1252 (art. 37), forbade any advocate to refuse to settle a case when his principal wished to do so and imposed a heavy fine. Anyone meddling in the proceedings was also penalized and excluded from court. In order to avoid confusion, no one was permitted to have more than one advocate. If the advocate and his principal wished to consult others, they were to do so privately.[68]

The *mester de los voceros*—the craft or trade of the advocates, who were professional jurists—offered certain benefits.[69] Pleas could be adjudicated more surely, because an advocate could effectively present the case of a litigant who, out of fear, intimidation, or lack of skill, could not. Furthermore, the advocate's familiarity with the law and court procedure and ability to engage in verbal argument served his client's interest and assisted judges in the quest for truth. The *vocero*, so-called "because he uses his voice and words in carrying out his office" (*SP* 3, 6, 1), should know the laws, *fueros*, and customs and could only argue pleas according to the *fuero* of the region where he lived. He ought not to take a case unless he was able to present it before a judge. Minors under the age of seventeen, deaf mutes, blind men, madmen, absentminded people, and criminals could not act as advocates. Monks and cathedral canons could only act on behalf of their communities. Foreigners were also excluded (*E* 4, 9, pr., 1–3; *FR* 1, 9, 2, 4; *SP* 3, 6, pr., 1–3; *OZ* 1274, arts. 1–2, 9, 16; *DO* 2, 2, 1).

Reference to the *mester de los voceros* indicates the existence of a formal guild of lawyers, but how it was organized is not clear. Obviously, the court could call upon designated advocates familiar with pleas ("sabidores del fuero e usando en los pleitos") (*E* 4, 9, 1). If a litigant did not have an advocate, he could ask the judge "to give him one from among those who are accustomed to take pleas" (*FR* 1, 9, 1). In his laws for Toledo in 1254, the king repeated that point. If the *vocero* refused to accept the assignment, he would be barred from acting as an advocate for a year, except in his own case.[70] No one whose ignorance of the law might disturb the proceedings should function as an advocate. Rather, an advocate should be selected by the "judges and the experts in law in our court" or from the region where he wished to function. If he were found to be knowledgeable and suitable for the task, he had to swear to loyally assist his client, and not to participate knowingly in a false suit, or protract litigation maliciously. Once approved, his name would be written "in the book where the names of other advocates are written." Anyone not so designated could not act as an advocate (*SP* 3, 6, 13). Thus, a prospective advocate had to pass an examination, in much the same way as a modern lawyer is examined before being admitted to the bar. After taking an oath to do right by his client, his name was recorded in a book listing those permitted to practice law in the courts. In preparation for a career as an advocate a young man may have been accepted as an apprentice and set to learn the law under the guidance of experienced advocates. After completing his studies and successfully passing the examination described above, he was likely admitted to full standing in the guild of advocates. By the middle of the thirteenth century, therefore, a professional class of advocates existed in Castile (*LEst* 19).

In 1253 the king prohibited clerics from acting as advocates against laypersons in Compostela. By their subtleties and by citing Roman law contrary to the *Libro de León* (the *Fuero Juzgo*) and municipal usages and customs, they were accused of delaying justice for three or four years, effectively denying it (leyes 2–3).[71]

A woman was also barred, because it was inappropriate for her to assume the "office of a man" and to mix publicly with men. In ancient times, a learned woman named Calpurnia (Ulpian, *D* 3, 1, 5) spoke so shamelessly in court that the judges could not abide her. Distressed by her lack of decorum and finding it difficult to listen to her and to contend with her, they forbade a woman to act as an advocate. That passage acknowledges the possibility that a woman, like a man, might be knowledgeable in the law, but ancient wise men, perhaps embarrassed by her superior legal knowledge and skill in argument, decided to ban all women from court. On the supposition that he might be susceptible to bribery, a man paid to fight wild animals was also forbidden to act as an advocate. A Jew or a Moor could not represent a Christian. The judge had to appoint advocates for widows, orphans, and poor people. If his client could not afford his fee, the advocate might have to serve "for the love of God" (*E* 4, 9, 3; *SP* 3, 6, 3–6).

When making their arguments, advocates, unless prevented by infirmity, had to stand before the seated judge. The plaintiff's advocate spoke first and then the defendant's. If several advocates appeared for one party, only one was to speak. Avoiding provocative or offensive language, not shouting or insulting his opponents, the advocate should address the judge calmly and courteously. If he did not conduct himself properly, the judge could prohibit him from representing anyone. Should he make an error in his argument, he could correct it before the final sentence. If he revealed his client's secrets to the other party or committed any fraudulent act, he could be barred from ever acting as an advocate. Irritated by an obstreperous or overly garrulous advocate, the judge could set a time when he could speak (*SP* 3, 6, 7–12; *E* 4, 9, 4–7; *FR* 1, 9, 5; *OZ* 1274, art. 4). Following the prescriptions in the *Partidas* (3, 6, 7), Texas law also required advocates to speak plainly in understandable language.[72] The Ordinance of Zamora required the advocate, prior to beginning his case, to swear that he would not act maliciously and would not lie. If he swore falsely, he would be permanently excluded from the office of advocate and could not serve as a witness or a judge. He would also be fined twice the amount at issue and subjected to confiscation of property, exile, and condemnation as a perjurer. Other fines were imposed if he extended the proceedings unnecessarily, and if he were absent without a legitimate excuse he had to pay the expenses of both parties (arts. 3–7, 12).

As compensation, the *vocero* in Toledo in 1254 was entitled to a tenth of the value of the plea, to be paid in thirds during the course of the suit.[73] Although the *Espéculo* (4, 9, 8–9) and the *Fuero real* (1, 9, 1, 5) allotted a fee of one-twentieth, the *Partidas* (3, 6, 14; *LEst* 18, 20), acknowledging that an advocate should be paid in accordance with the nature of the case and his own learning, fixed the fee at one hundred *maravedís*. The Ordinance of Zamora cited the figure of one-twentieth, but also set a maximum of one hundred *maravedís*. If the value of the case were uncertain, the judge, in consultation with others, would determine fair recompense (art. 14). In 1280 the king ordered Burgos to pay its *vocero* his salary for four years at the annual rate of one hundred *maravedís*.[74]

Under penalty of being forever declared infamous, the advocate was prohibited from making an agreement with his client to receive a share in the property at issue, lest that induce him to use inappropriate methods to win the case. If he deliberately aided his client's adversary, or introduced forged documents or false witnesses, he would be executed and his property turned over to his client (*SP* 3, 6, 14–15; *FR* 1, 9, 5). In the expectation of reducing unnecessary litigation, the king required an advocate who believed that a judge's decision was correct to swear that he would not advise his client to appeal it (OZ 1274, art. 13).

Bien et Leal mente Deue Fazer su Ofiçio el Judgador

In order to do justice to everyone, Alfonso X endeavored to create an effective judicial system and insisted that judgment be in accord with his law codes. Judges were chiefly laymen trained in the *ius commune*, the civil and canon law taught in the universities, and knowledgeable in the substance of the Alfonsine Codes. As assurance that his law would be applied throughout the realm, King Alfonso appointed the judges of the royal court and the provincial *adelantados mayores*, as well as municipal judges and scribes. By requiring judges to hold court at certain hours and seasons, he tried to establish a judicial calendar that would make justice available on a regular basis. The burden on the ordinary courts was relieved somewhat by permitting arbiters to settle many cases, but ultimately they acted on royal authority and their decisions could be appealed to the king. Litigants could appoint *personeros* to appear on their behalf and to make binding decisions, and they could also be represented by a professional class of advocates familiar with the royal law codes.

The king, as God's temporal representative, had the primary responsibility to dispense justice and promised to hear lawsuits three days every week, but it seems likely that he could not always do so. The cases presented to him probably concerned great men and *grandes ffechos*, or the so-called *casos de corte*. He also reserved the right to attend to appeals from every jurisdiction. Hoping to assure fair judgment, he ordered his judges to act promptly and not to tolerate unnecessary delay. As a guarantee of justice for all, legal counsel had to be provided to the poor and downtrodden. The smooth working of the judicial system depended on the sense of honesty and responsibility shared by judges, procurators, advocates, scribes, and litigants.

As a judge of the royal court, Jacobo de las leyes admonished his fellow judges: "Bien et leal mente deue fazer su ofiçio el judgador et deue trabajar de saber la verdad del pleito que es antel quanto mas pudiere, et no se deue partir dela carrera del derecho" (Every judge should fulfill his office well and loyally and should strive to know the truth of the case before him, insofar as he can, and he should not depart from the pathway of the law) (DO 1, 3, 3). If the other participants in the legal process behaved similarly, justice would be done.

Although the king believed that by entrusting the administration of justice to skilled professionals the right of every man would be defended, it is clear that many of the failings in the modern judicial system were present in the thirteenth century. Human nature being what it is, one should not be surprised to learn of fraud, cheating, collusion between judges and advocates, laziness, absenteeism, grandstanding by advocates, and other abuses.

✿ CHAPTER 8

The Judicial Process

Ffazer Derecho

When litigants, duly summoned, appeared before a judge through their procurators and advocates, they wanted him to *ffazer derecho* (to make right) (*SP* 3, 7, 1). If a defendant admitted the charge, the judge's task was made easier, but in most instances that did not occur. After hearing arguments, the judge called for proof in the form of witnesses, sworn testimony, and documents. He could then *ffazer derecho*. Three passages from the *Third Partida* underscored the importance of making things right. Expressing a negative view of human behavior, the royal jurists stated that "the wickedness of human beings . . . is so great . . . that if justice and law did not prevent them, good men could not live in peace or secure their rights." Moreover: "One of the things of this world about which kings and other lords, who hold the place of God on earth, should most exert themselves, in order to maintain it in justice, is to oppose the malice of human beings so that law may not be thwarted by them." As a shield against malevolence, the king's court was "a place where things ought to be done with greater accord and greater counsel so that they might not be lightly undone" (*SP* 3, 7, 9–10, 15). Thus, the Alfonsine Codes outlined procedures to restrain evil and uphold right and justice.[1]

Under the influence of Roman and canon law the distinctive Germanic character of the judicial process was modified.[2] Henceforth the *ordo iudiciarius*, as the Romano-canonical process was called, was written rather than oral. Judges were encouraged to intervene actively by interrogating litigants and witnesses and to evaluate the truth of evidence. Ordeals and purgation as forms of proof were cast aside when the Fourth Lateran Council (canon 8) prohibited the clergy from blessing them. Instead, the inquest was commonly employed to gather evidence in both civil and criminal cases. Despite the judge's efforts to render a just decision, his judgment could be appealed ultimately to the king.[3]

The Summons to Court

A lawsuit began when a defendant was summoned verbally or in writing by the king, a public official, or the plaintiff (*E* 5, 1, 1–3; *SP* 3, 7, 1; *FR* 2, 3, 1). In January 1264, for example, Alfonso X commanded the archbishop of Compostela and the city council to send their *personeros* with supporting materials to appear before him on the feast of St. Andrew (30 November).[4]

Although everyone was obliged to respond, certain persons, depending on their rank and circumstances, could not be required to appear immediately on a specified date. Among them were a priest saying mass, soldiers on military service, agents on a public mission, policemen restoring order, the sick and wounded, prisoners, those attending weddings or funerals, and the town crier. A judge summoned by an inferior could ignore the order. A summons to a member of a religious community should be directed to his or her superior. Minors, the insane, spendthrifts, freedmen, honorable women living at home, and even a woman who refused to marry a judge who summoned her out of spite could respond through a guardian or procurator. The summons should not be issued during festival days (*SP* 3, 7, 2–6).[5]

With the judge's approval, the parties might agree to postpone the hearing, but if the plea "touches the king or the kingdom," it could not be deferred without the king's consent. If a defendant attempted to evade a summons, his name could be proclaimed at his home and in three public markets, and the judge could authorize the seizure of his possessions. The Cortes of Seville in 1252 declared that plowing animals could only be taken as a last resort. Only after a successful plaintiff's claims were satisfied would goods taken as pledges be returned to the defendant.[6] Should anyone adamantly refuse to appear, he would be fined heavily and obliged to pay his opponent's expenses (*LEst* 21, 24, 26). A judge who deliberately refused to issue a summons had to reimburse the plaintiff for expenses and resulting damages. Persons summoned to the king's court were given a grace period of three days (or nine days, if from another kingdom) beyond the date specified and were guaranteed security from the time they left home until they returned (*E* 5, 1, 2–5; *SP* 3, 7, 7–12; *FR* 2, 3, 2–8).

In a chancery formula, Fernando Mateos, the royal *alcalde mayor* in Seville, reported that Esteban Pérez, though summoned three times, by letter and by messenger, once in person, and twice at his residence, failed to appear to answer an allegation by Gonzalo Yuañez. Therefore, after Gonzalo swore that he had not brought suit maliciously, the judge awarded him compensation of one thousand *maravedís* (*SP* 3, 18, 108).

If the defendant did not appear or send a procurator, the judge, by an interlocutory decree, could authorize the plaintiff to temporarily take possession of property in dispute, but he could not alienate it. The property could also be sequestered until final disposition of the case. If, after being summoned three times over thirty days, the defendant failed to respond, he could be deprived of ownership; if he attempted to thwart justice by disposing of property, he would be fined severely (*E* 5, 1, 6–13; *SP* 3, 7, 13–17; 3, 8, 1–8; 3, 9, 1–2; *FR* 2, 3, 2; 2, 4, 1–2). The king applied that law in 1254 when Toledo complained about delays in the administration of justice.[7] In effect, anyone who defied a summons to court was accounted as contumacious and rebellious.[8]

Court Procedure

Once assigned a day in court, the plaintiff was given the opportunity to present his plea or demand orally or in writing (*libellus*), and the defendant, his response (*FR* 2, 6, 1–2; *DO* 3, 1, 1–3).[9] Civil suits ordinarily concerned property or personal obligations. In 1254 the king determined that if a plaintiff in Toledo submitted a written demand, the defendant should have a day to take counsel and prepare a written response. That stage in the proceedings when the issue was joined was known as the *litis contestatio* (*SP* 3, 10, 3).[10] Without delay, the plaintiff was permitted to make a written counterargument. If either party had reason to believe that the judge would not be impartial, that suspicion should be raised immediately and ruled on by other judges (*E* 5, 2, 1–4).

This *exebçion* or *defensión* was one of several exceptions that the parties could present to delay, to exclude from consideration, or to thwart the process. "This is like an arm by which a man defends himself against his enemies" (*E* 5, 4, pr.). By challenging the judge's jurisdiction (*exceptio declinatoria*), the defendant hoped to avoid having to respond to the plaintiff. He might also object that the judge or the plaintiff was excommunicated, or that he that did not owe a debt claimed by the plaintiff. He could delay the proceedings (*exceptio dilatoria*) by arguing that a debt owed was not yet due, or that he should be excused from appearing on a designated date because he was engaged in the king's business or was ill. Moreover, he might prove that a debt had already been paid (*exceptio peremptoria*), or that a court had previously rejected the plaintiff's demand. The declinatory and dilatory exceptions had to be made before the *litis contestatio*, but peremptory exceptions could be raised throughout the process (*E* 5, 4, 1–11; *SP* 3, 3, 8–11).[11]

Before proceeding, the judge had to determine whether the plaintiff was eligible to bring suit. The plaintiff should specify whether his plea concerned real or movable property or services to be performed. In the first case, he should ask for restoration of the property and its income for however many years it was held by his opponent. A movable object in contention ought to be presented in court or otherwise described accurately. If the defendant could not immediately produce it, he could give surety to do so when he had it again in hand, unless it had been stolen or lost through no fault of his own. He would be punished if he deliberately concealed, damaged, or destroyed it. If he failed to complete work on time, he would be penalized and compelled to reimburse the plaintiff for any damage or loss. The defendant might reject the plaintiff's charges (*E* 5, 7, 1–18; *SP* 3, 10, 1–8).[12]

If an assertion could not be proved otherwise, one or both parties might swear to the truth of their allegations. An oath taken against the king's sovereignty or harmful to the realm or to one's soul was invalid (*FR* 2, 12, 1–5). Oaths were of three kinds: voluntary, compulsory, and judicial. A voluntary oath sworn outside the courtroom by one party and accepted by the other could settle a dispute. Once a suit began, both litigants had to swear an oath of *manquadra*, or *sacramentum calumnie* to affirm their rights, to respond truthfully to the judge, not to offer false proofs, and not to delay the proceedings.[13] If a litigant claimed to have been attacked, robbed, or defrauded by his opponent, the judge, so as to assess damages, could require a compulsory oath. The judicial oath was administered in court by one party who agreed to accept as true what the other said. If either party refused to swear, the judge would declare that he had lost his case. Ordinarily the one administering the oath should be twenty-five years old, a freeman of sound mind, living independently. The one taking an oath had to be at least fifteen (*E* 5, 7, 21; 5, 11, 1, 18; *SP* 3, 11, 1–29).[14]

The texts of oaths to be sworn respectively by Christians, Jews, and Muslims conformed to the tenets of each one's religion. In the Cortes of Seville in 1252 (art. 38) Jews and Christians were directed to swear as in the time of Alfonso VIII, but no text was recorded. The formulas for the three oaths were set forth initially in the *Espéculo* (5, 11, 15–17) and were repeated in later texts.[15] Placing his hand on the Gospels, the cross, or the altar, a Christian swore in the name of God the creator, his son Jesus Christ, born of the Virgin Mary, and the Holy Spirit. A Jew, with his hand on the Torah in the synagogue, in the presence of Jewish and Christian witnesses, recalled God's favors to Abraham, Isaac, and David, and swore by the Ten Commandments given to Moses on Mount Sinai. If he swore falsely, he called down on himself the plagues that God visited on the Egyptians. A Muslim, standing at the door of the mosque with his hands raised and facing toward the south, swore that there was no God but God, who revealed himself to Muḥammad, his prophet and messenger. If he perjured himself he would be forever separated from God and Muḥammad, and excluded from Paradise (SP 3, 11, 19–21). For example, the former Muslim inhabitants of Écija, standing in their mosque and facing Mecca, swore to tell the truth concerning the boundaries of the municipality.[16]

After the litigants presented their respective positions, the judge might interrogate them in order to clarify the issues. They might also interrogate one another. The interrogatories were expected to be brief and to the point so that they could be easily understood and elicit a useful reply. Lest the search for truth be impeded, advocates were not permitted to advise their clients during the interrogatories (E 5, 7, 19; SP 3, 12, 1–2).

Next, the court would determine the proofs to be presented. As the burden of proof rested with the plaintiff, his case would be dismissed if he could not present it. Philosophical arguments were unacceptable because they could not be determined by law or judgment. Evidence should relate directly to the point in contention, and time should not be wasted debating extraneous matters. Proofs included admission by the defendant of the plaintiff's demand, the testimony of at least two witnesses, the presentation of appropriate documents, and the presumption by the judge that the position of one of the parties was true, though presumption may often be incorrect and could not be used to prove an accusation of crime. Visual inspection of property or persons by the judge was another form of proof. Although the judicial duel was mentioned, it was not usually admitted as proof because it often resulted in the triumph of error (E 5, 10, 1–14; SP 3, 14, 1–15; 3, 15, 1–3).[17]

A defendant at least twenty years of age might resolve the dispute by an admission (*conoscencia*) of facts. If he implicated others in a crime, his testimony alone was insufficient for them to be charged, except in case of treason against the king or the kingdom or heresy, when only one witness was necessary. A deathbed confession would also be valid. Whereas a client could correct an admission made by his advocate, he could not do so if he was not in court, except in case of error or fraud, because he had authorized his advocate to act on his behalf and agreed to be bound by his actions. A confession made out of court or under torture or fear of death was invalid, but would be accepted if the person afterward, freely and without fear, confirmed it (*E* 5, 12, 1–12; *SP* 3, 13, 1–7). If the defendant admitted the charge, the judge could then proceed to judgment (*FR* 2, 7, 1–3).[18]

The testimony of witnesses was especially valuable, mainly because they could be interrogated, a process that could prove their undoing.[19] The judge had to decide whether a prospective witness was properly qualified and a person of good character, and once he was heard, he had to ascertain the truth of his testimony. The testimony of slaves and disreputable people was inadmissible except in case of treason against the king or kingdom. As slaves were likely to lie, they should be tortured to elicit the truth. Also excluded were perjurers, liars, forgers, counterfeiters, poisoners, abortionists, those who killed another, except in self-defense, married men who kept concubines, rapists, seducers of nuns, persons in incestuous marriages, traitors, those publicly degraded who were not equal in rank to the other party, the insane, thieves, robbers, pimps, gamblers, women dressing as men, wandering monks or nuns, and the very poor worth less than twenty *maravedís* who kept bad company. A woman of good character could testify in all cases except those concerning wills. That was also true for a hermaphrodite, but if the male nature predominated, he could bear witness in testamentary actions. Jews, Moors, and heretics could testify against one another, but not against Christians, except in case of treason against the king or the kingdom. Spouses and family members in a direct line of descent or in a collateral line to the third degree of kindred ordinarily could not testify against one another, nor could business partners. In criminal cases, fathers and grandfathers could not bear witness against their sons or grandsons, nor could a freedman against his former master; the testimony of prisoners, bullfighters, and prostitutes was also inadmissible. As children under fourteen lacked sufficient intelligence to comprehend the truth, they could not testify. In criminal matters a witness had to be twenty years of age. Quite reasonably, judges, advocates, and procurators could not be witnesses in cases in which they were parties. If a witness testified to matters extraneous to the suit, his entire testimony could be thrown out. Prior to trial, out of concern that an aged or infirm witness might die, his testimony could be recorded and introduced later in the proceedings. Testimony could also be taken before the beginning of a trial to gather evidence through an inquest or in preparation for an appeal or another legal procedure, or when a litigant accused a judge of partiality, or when public officials were denounced for misappropriating royal revenues or abusing the people under their jurisdiction (*E* 4, 1–14; *SP* 3, 16, 1–22; 6, 1, 10; *FR* 2, 8, 1–14).[20]

Depending on their distance from court, witnesses had to appear within a reasonable time; for example, three days for a resident, nine for one living within the municipality, and thirty days beyond that. A witness from another realm could be assigned a date, or his written testimony could be forwarded at the expense of the litigant who requested it. The judge or his representative might travel to obtain the testimony of prominent persons, or the sick and elderly. Swearing on the Gospels to tell the truth, the witness declared that his oath was freely given, not prompted by bribery, love, hatred, or any threat. His testimony, given privately to the judge, was recorded by a scribe. He was questioned as to his relationship to the party on whose behalf he testified, whether his evidence was based on what he knew or heard, and when and where the events transpired. Always looking directly at the witness in a kindly manner, the judge should listen quietly and ask the witness to confirm his testimony. In some rare instances hearsay evidence was accepted. Two witnesses of good character were usually required. Recalcitrant witnesses could be compelled to testify, and those who swore falsely would be punished as perjurers. In case of contradictory testimony, the judge could use his discretion as to which witness to believe (*E* 4, 7, 15–36; *SP* 3, 16, 23–43; *FR* 2, 8, 15–21).

The testimony of a pope, emperor, or king was sufficient by itself and did not require corroboration. As the king knew that he would have to account to God for his actions in wielding the temporal sword, he would act and speak truthfully and command what is right (*E* 4, 7, 29). The insertion of this law seems jarring and may indicate the direct intervention of the king, perhaps in reaction to a doubt posed by a judge concerning a charter containing the king's unsworn testimony.

The sworn inquest or inquisition (*inquisitio, pesquisa*) gathered the testimony of witnesses in a more comprehensive manner. Numerous twelfth- and early thirteenth-century documents reveal that the inquest had become a customary means of discovering the truth. King Alfonso used it as a multifaceted tool for administrative and judicial purposes, namely, to gather information about taxes due, alienations of royal lands, the export of prohibited goods, and the identification of criminals; and to settle civil cases concerning municipal boundaries, property disputes, and other matters.[21] The use of the inquest to identify those who committed murder, the desecration of churches, rape, violation of households, arson, and highway robbery greatly expanded royal jurisdiction in criminal cases (*E* 4, 11, 1; *SP* 3, 17, 1).[22]

The king or a judge appointed men of probity known as *pesquisidores* or examiners to execute an inquest. They had to swear to loyally seek the truth and not to be deterred from asking essential questions; nor would they conceal the results of their inquiry by reason of friendship, allegiance, fear, hostility, or bribery. Clerics were barred from serving as examiners. *Pesquisidores* appointed in administrative districts seem to have been permanent officials but were forbidden to conduct an inquest except by order of the king or the *merino mayor*. Abuse of the procedure may have prompted the king in 1254 to direct the *merino mayor* of León not to carry out a *pesquisa* in the towns in the diocese of Oviedo without his authorization.[23] Several months later, he banned the use of the *pesquisa* unless it was general for everyone.[24] In 1261, after an inquest found that the bishop of Oviedo interfered with construction of the city walls, Alfonso X ordered the work to be finished.[25] Similarly, when officials responsible for regulating exports in the diocese of Burgos carried out a closed *pesquisa*, but failed to interrogate the bishop or his clerics, the king in 1278 ordered a new inquiry in which they would participate.[26]

Ordinarily, two *pesquisidores* and a scribe who transcribed the proceedings were appointed. Except for illness or hostility to one of the parties, no one could excuse himself from accepting this responsibility. Depending on their appointment and the scope of their task, they were entitled to the honor and protection accorded to royal or municipal judges. Either the king, the litigants, or the municipality would pay their expenses. An examiner who encouraged witnesses to lie would be severely punished (*E* 4, 11, 2–6, 10–16; *SP* 3, 17, 2–8, 10–12).

The *pesquisidores* summoned upstanding and knowledgeable members of the community to give pertinent information under oath within three to nine days. Each one had to swear to tell the truth concerning what he knew, what he had heard, and what he believed to be true (*E* 4, 7, 16; *SP* 3, 16, 25). Interrogated separately, each witness was forbidden to reveal his testimony until the investigation was complete. The written record, closed and sealed, was submitted to the judge or the king. If a person was accused, he should be informed so that he could prepare his defense. The king would decide how to proceed against a municipality (*E* 4, 11, 8–9; *FR* 2, 8, 3; *SP* 3, 17, 9; *DO* 4, 3, 1–2).

In 1261 Alfonso X, responding to a complaint by the municipality of Santiago de Compostela, chastised ecclesiastical officials for refusing to show the results of *pesquisas generales* to those accused. Instead, he declared that an inquest ought to discover the truth of church robberies, rape, burning of harvests, vineyards, and trees, disruption of highways, and wounding, seizing, or killing people. In explanation of his decision, he provided texts of the *Espéculo* (4, 11, 5–12) relating to these matters.[27] As the *Partidas* was not yet complete, the *Espéculo* remained in force.

The complete transcript of an inquest executed in 1280 in the quarrel between the monastery of Oña and the town of Frías occupies thirty-five printed pages. Marín Pérez, *alcalde* of Burgos, the royal *alcalde* Juan Iñíguez, and Juan Pérez de Frías carried it out. Oña presented seventy witnesses, and Frías, thirty-eight. After each witness was identified by name, residence, and status in the community, he swore to tell the truth. Many mentioned that their knowledge extended back for ten, twenty, thirty, or even forty-five years.[28]

Alfonso X justified his use of the inquest "so that the truth of things might not be hidden" (*SP* 3, 17, pr., 1), but the searching nature of royal inquests prompted the Cortes of Seville in 1281 to object to "enquisas de mascarade" (inquests of deceit).[29] In 1283 he rewarded Murcia's loyalty by cancelling all pending inquests there.[30] The Cortes of Palencia convened by Sancho IV in 1286 declared that parties named in a closed, general inquest should be informed so they could be heard and judged according to law (art. 7).[31]

The presentation of appropriate documents was also an accepted form of proof. Most valuable was an original text bearing the seal of the king, another person, or an institution as a sign of authenticity. Also acceptable was a charter containing a text written on the top and bottom of the page and separated in the middle by the letters ABC. The charter was cut through the letters, and each party received half. Authenticity was demonstrated when the halves were presented later and the letters fitted neatly together. Confirmations of charters issued by the king or his predecessors were also admissible, as was a true copy made by a public scribe or the chancery and properly sealed (*SP* 6, 15, 18). Royal privileges were valid during the king's lifetime, but Alfonso X, during his early years, ratified many charters of his predecessors. Charters contrary to the Catholic faith, natural law, the law of the land, royal rights, the common rights of the people, or copies lacking the royal seal were invalid. Charters issued by excommunicates or obtained by falsehood, fraud, or deceit, or directed against women, minors, and the aged and infirm were rejected. A charter initiating a lawsuit was valid for ten years, provided that all the parties were living (*E* 4, 6, 1–25; *SP* 3, 18, 25–55; *FR* 2, 9, 1–8).[32]

For the guidance of notaries and scribes the *Espéculo* (4, 12, 13–45) and, more elaborately, the *Partidas* (3, 18, 56–110) presented examples of how charters should be drafted for all kinds of transactions: conveyances; sales; exchanges; donations; transfers; leases; loans; rentals of houses, vineyards, and orchards; hiring workers; forming partnerships; division of land among several persons; payment of debts; making peace or a truce; giving one's daughter in marriage; parental consent to marriage; dowries and the marriage portion; entry into a religious order; securing the services of a retainer; emancipation of slaves; adoption; guardianship of minors; letters of procuration; inventory of the property of a deceased person; wills and codicils; compromises and arbitration; the final judgment by a court and appeals. Whereas the examples in the *Espéculo* were couched in generic terms, those in the *Partidas* were often issued in the name of actual royal judges, while others were impersonal. As I suggested previously, these notarial formulas may have been gathered in the king's "book, which was made *por corte* in Palencia" in 1255.[33]

The authentication of documents was essential to determining the truth or falsity of claims. Scribes, therefore, were responsible for accurately recording privileges and charters and the testimony of witnesses. As the seal affixed to a document was another sign of authenticity, custody of the seal and the responsibility of sealing were assigned to trustworthy persons. Just as the king appointed municipal scribes, so too he named sealers and fixed their compensation at six *dineros* of the *moneda comunal*. Sealers in the royal chancery received a *maravedí* for a privilege and a half *maravedí* for a charter (*E* 4, 13, 1–4; *SP* 3, 19–20).

In 1253 Alfonso X required the archbishop of Compostela to submit charters of Fernando III that he cited in support of his case against the municipality.[34] The presentation of charters on behalf of the bishop of Burgos helped royal officials partition a village near the city in 1278.[35] In the quarrel between Oña and Frías, Oña's *personero* presented three privileges, four charters, and four *cuadernos*. However, as two of the charters lacked a seal or sign, and another had two signs but no seal, their authenticity was questioned. The *personero* of Frías had a privilege sealed with Alfonso VIII's leaden seal and a charter sealed with Fernando III's wax seal. All were accepted as authentic.[36]

Judgment and Appeal

In 1254 the king declared that once arguments were completed, the *alcalde* should render judgment "so that each party should have his rights."[37] Before doing so, he was advised, especially in great pleas and those involving the death penalty, to seek the counsel of intelligent, virtuous men who knew the law. If their advice was helpful, he should act on it (*E* 4, 10, 1–3; *SP* 3, 21, 1–3).[38]

The judge's definitive judgment "should be certain and right as the laws of our book command, and the truth of the matter should be examined, scrutinized, and established" (*SP* 3, 22, 3). The litigants should be present, but he could pronounce sentence in the absence of either one. Given the solemnity of the event, he should act in the daytime, while seated in his usual place. He ought to read his decision aloud, but if he could not read, he could ask another person to do so, and then confirm it orally. Each litigant should receive a copy, and the court should retain another. Written in easily understood language, the decision should state clearly that the defendant was released from or held responsible for, either in whole or in part, the claim made against him. After declaring sentence, the judge could not change it except, on the same day, to clarify it by inserting information previously omitted. If a defendant was too poor to pay a fine, the judge, out of compassion, could excuse him, thereby altering his decision (*E* 5, 13, 1–10, 18; *SP* 3, 22, 1–5; *FR* 2, 13, 1–6; 2, 14, 1–3).[39]

According to a chancery formula, Fernán Matheos, the royal *alcalde* of Seville, after hearing the plaintiff's demand and the defendant's response, affirmed that he listened to witnesses, examined documents, reviewed arguments, sought the counsel of men learned in the law, and then summoned the parties to hear his definitive judgment, namely, that Domingo surrender to Pedro a house or land that was rightfully his (*SP* 3, 18, 109; *FD* 3, 1, 7–8).

Following that formula, in 1261, Alfonso X rendered what he hoped would be a final judgment in the controversy between the archbishop of Compostela and the city council:

> We, having heard the arguments, both oral and written, and the pleas already begun by demand and response; . . . and having reviewed the charters and writings and materials that both sides showed us; and having taken our consent and our counsel with . . . our brothers . . . , our magnates and our judges and other good men of our court . . . : we judge and we command and we hold as right that the agreement made by . . . King don Fernando . . . is entirely valid as was stated in the charters sealed with the leaden seal in Seville . . . in the era 1288 [1250]; and that the later agreement made by the archbishop and chapter with the council of Santiago in charters divided by ABC in the era 1288 is not valid.

Using similar language, he pronounced judgment on thirty-six separate issues. Anyone violating his decision would be fined ten thousand *maravedís*. The archbishop and the city council received copies (fourteen printed pages) of the document sealed with his leaden seal.[40]

More than likely, the task of hearing cases and fashioning the definitive judgment fell to professional jurists. For example, a royal charter of 1254 restricting use of the inquest in Oviedo bears a notation that Fernando Fernández, *alcalde del rey*, acting on the king's command, ordered that to be done.[41] If a case involved less than ten *maravedís*, the judge could issue an oral decision. He could also act summarily to place minors, widows, and others in possession of their property. If he could not reach a decision, he should send a sealed copy of the proceedings to the king for judgment. Judges were admonished, however, not to shirk their responsibilities by turning to the king. If a judge concluded that a plaintiff brought suit out of malice, he could decide against him and order him to pay costs incurred by the defendant (*SP* 3, 22, 6–11).

Just as physicians sometimes erred in prescribing medicines, judges also made mistakes. For example, a decision was invalid for these reasons: it was not in the proper form; or was based on false testimony or forged documents; or failed to address the plaintiff's complaint; or was founded on a *fazaña*; or the judge was standing, rather than sitting, or in an inappropriate place, or acting at the wrong time; or he lacked jurisdiction. When several judges disagreed, the majority decision should be followed. If they were equally divided concerning the amount of money required of the defendant, they should exact the lesser amount because they should always be merciful. For the same reason, they should always favor a person's freedom (*E* 5, 13, 12–13, 15–17; *SP* 3, 22, 12–18).

A definitive judgment justly declared had the force of law, and the litigants were obliged to obey it. However, the subsequent loss of property in dispute or accounting errors might necessitate some alteration of the original judgment. If no appeal was undertaken, the judgment would remain in effect even if new documents were discovered that might have caused the judge, if he had seen them, to render a different decision. However, new evidence affecting a judgment against the king could be presented within three years. A just judgment continued in force even after the death of the king or the judge. The heirs of the one in whose favor it was given had thirty years in which to claim any property awarded (*E* 5, 13, 19–22; *SP* 3, 22, 19; *FR* 2, 14, 1–3).[42]

A judicial decision could be appealed to the king. In the Cortes of Seville in 1253 (art. 1), Alfonso X assured the Leonese towns that if a plaintiff could not obtain satisfaction in court, he could appeal to the local bishop; if still not satisfied, he could ask the bishop to petition the king to do justice. In that same year, the city council of Compostela protested that the archbishop would not allow an appeal to the king, but the archbishop's representative contended that an appeal was permissible only after judgment was rendered (ley 5). Determined to uphold his right to hear appeals, King Alfonso demanded that the archbishop produce Fernando III's charter allegedly justifying his position (ley 9).[43] In 1254, the king informed Toledo that if a litigant was displeased with the judge's decision, the judge could review it with a body of good men, so that each party could have his rights.[44]

The Alfonsine Codes outlined the process whereby every free man could make an appeal.[45] No one could appeal a sentence involving the death penalty (FR 2, 15, 1–9; LEst 163). A parent or guardian of an orphan or of someone mentally incapacitated or the owner of a slave could appeal on his behalf. So too could anyone who might be affected negatively by a judgment; for example, a beneficiary who would lose his legacy if a will were nullified. A litigant who failed to attend the appellate court would lose his appeal and be deemed a rebel. If the court upheld the original judgment, the appellant would have to pay his opponent's costs. A municipal council could appeal to the king concerning the negligence of royal officials. An appeal could be carried from a lower court to a higher one, but one could bypass those intermediate steps and appeal directly to the king. No one could appeal from the judgment of the king (or an emperor) because he had no temporal superior and, as a lover of justice and truth, he was surrounded by men learned in the law so that everyone should know that his judgment was right and complete. Yet one could always appeal to his mercy. As the *adelantado mayor* of the royal court was superior to all other judges and could call upon prudent men learned in the law, no one could appeal his decisions (E 5, 14, 1–12). Many appeals to the royal court might be heard by judges who daily adjudicated cases, but if more than five hundred *maravedís* were involved, the king should be informed. If he could not personally attend to it, the *adelantado mayor* should do so. The king could always ask the *adelantado mayor* to suspend his judgment as a matter of mercy. Although the *Fuero real* (2, 15, 5) stated that a judgment involving less than ten *maravedís* could not be appealed to the king, he was expected to personally hear the appeals of widows, orphans, the poor, the aged, and once wealthy persons now impoverished (SP 3, 23, 1–19).[46]

When the aggrieved party asked for an appeal, the judge, within three days, should describe the case in writing and ask the appeals court to assign a date for a hearing (FR 2, 15, 1–2; E 4, 12, 45). Once a decision was announced, a litigant should say "I appeal," or present a letter to the judge asking him to address a letter of appeal to the king within three days. Taking festival days into account, the appeal ought to be heard within two months. If the appellate judge confirmed the original judgment, it was accepted as just and in accordance with the law. The king might set aside a sentence when he wished to show mercy or favor, even if no appeal were made. Judgments against minors under twenty-five or their guardians could also be nullified even though they had not been appealed. Judgments based on false charters, false proofs, or contrary to law were also declared invalid, while true and authentic sentences had to be carried out (SP 3, 23, 22–29; FR 2, 15, 9).

A chancery formula reported that Don Marín, *alcalde* of Burgos, gave judgment in favor of the abbot of Oña against Gonzalo Ruiz, who appealed to the king. Fernando Yuañes (Ibáñez) el Gallego and Domingo Yuañes (Ibáñez),[47] auditors (*oydores*) and judges of appeals (*judgadores de las alçadas*) in the royal court, reviewed the decision, heard the appellant's arguments, consulted good men knowledgeable in the law, and confirmed the original sentence (*SP* 3, 18, 110).[48] In 1271, a trial judge issued a sealed charter granting the appeal of the villagers of Gradefes in their dispute with the monks of Eslonza and set a date for the *personeros* of both parties to appear before Fernando de la Cerda. After hearing their arguments, he rejected the appeal, confirmed the original judgment, and ordered Gradefes to pay court costs of three hundred *maravedís*. Alfonso Martínez, the royal *alcalde*, who probably heard the case in the infante's name, recorded the decision. Also in 1271 Fernando overturned the decision of the trial judge in the quarrel between the monastery of Vega and the men of Benavente. Martín Amador, *alcalde del rey*, probably heard the appeal in the prince's name.[49]

The Ordinance of Zamora in 1274 (arts. 19–21) provided for three judges to hear appeals from the entire realm, except for Castile, where appeals would be carried from the ordinary royal judges to the *adelantado mayor* of Castile and ultimately to the king. Leonese appeals would be resolved according to the *Fuero Juzgo*. The right of appeal to the royal court within three days was guaranteed, but the appellant had to swear that he was not maliciously trying to prolong a suit (*E* 4, 2, 11; *SP* 2, 9, 19; 3, 23, 17–20).

The Courts in Session

The extant records of actual lawsuits reveal that the procedures described above were generally followed. Those records, including arguments, oaths, interrogatories, *cartas de personería*, and other documents, and the testimony of witnesses, likely filled many pages, but complete documentation relating to most cases has disappeared. Nevertheless, the one hundred printed pages recording the suit between Oña and Frías suggest what a comprehensive record looked like. Existing records are generally summaries of the disposition of cases redacted for the benefit of the court and the litigants. As such, they usually adhered to a certain formula. Ordinarily the text began with the phrase "Let all those who see this charter know that, concerning the dispute (*contienda*). . . ." The king then summarized the case and declared that the litigants, responding to his summons, appeared before him in person or through their *personeros* on the assigned day. Whereas the names of *personeros* are always given, those of advocates are never mentioned, despite their prominent role in the Alfonsine Codes. While it is possible that a *personero* may also have acted as an advocate, it is more likely that arguments attributed to the *personero* were actually made by an advocate. Probably following the *libelli* presented by the litigants, the document then outlined the plaintiff's demand and the defendant's response. After oral arguments were heard and closed (the *encerramiento de las razones*), the king examined documents, the testimony of witnesses, and the sureties given, and then consulted with his brothers, sons, prelates, magnates, and *sabidores de derecho* of his court. Employing the formula "tuve por bien et mandé" or "tengo por bien et mando" or "judgamos et mandamos" ("I held [or hold] it to be right and I commanded [or command]," or "we judge and we command"), he pronounced judgment and threatened with a penalty of ten thousand *maravedís* anyone who infringed it. Following the date, one or more *alcaldes del rey* ordered the document to be recorded in the king's name. In all probability they actually heard the pleading, assessed the evidence, and pronounced judgment on his behalf.

Boundary disputes were commonly brought to court. In 1253, for example, the king confirmed the boundaries between lands of the Orders of Alcántara and the Temple in Extremadura. Gonzalo Vicente and Fernando Mateos, *alcaldes del rey*, announced his decision.[50] He also settled boundary conflicts between the Order of Alcántara and Toledo; Alcántara and Badajoz;[51] the Order of Calatrava and Córdoba;[52] Toledo and Talavera;[53] and Cuéllar and Portillo.[54] Sometimes Moors appointed by the emir of Granada were asked to identify boundaries as they existed under Muslim rule.[55]

The royal court resolved other issues. For example, in 1258 Garcí Guillén, commander of the convent of San Clemente of Toledo, and two men from Talavera, with their respective *cartas de personería*, presented their quarrel concerning a bridge built across the Tagus River by the nuns. Pronouncing judgment for the nuns, the king directed Talavera to reconstruct the bridge, restore it to the convent, and pay the nuns twice the cost of knocking it down and all other damages.[56] The bishop of Osma and the city council contended over episcopal rights;[57] Archbishop Remondo of Seville and the magnate Roy López de Mendoza fought over vineyards;[58] Oviedo demanded payment of taxes by servants of the bishop;[59] and the villagers of Humanes protested the lordship claimed by the Order of the Hospital.[60] The king ruled in 1262 that the bishop of Zamora could not claim as vassals persons living within the municipality of Toro.[61] Infante Fernando similarly upheld the rights of the abbey of Samos to certain vassals. Martín Amador, *alcalde del rey*, probably heard the arguments and issued the judgment in his name. Fernando also decided in favor of the bishop of León's possession of a church and upheld the tributary rights of the collegiate church of San Isidoro de León.[62]

The issue of ecclesiastical jurisdiction arose in 1254 when the Orders of Alcántara and the Temple contended for possession of Ronda on the Tagus River. Alfonso X prohibited three judges delegate named by the pope from inquiring into this affair, because issues relating to the royal domain or donations by his predecessors were not subject to the church's judgment. For the first time in a royal document that I know, he added: "Leida la carta, dadgela" (Having read the letter, obey it). Despite that, the judges delegate persisted in their effort to adjudicate the matter.[63] In response to other charges by the Templars against Alcántara, the king directed two judges to investigate and to submit their report to him for judgment.[64]

Resolution by Arbitration

The alternative to adjudication by a court was arbitration, a procedure that was quite common, perhaps more so than a court trial. The main reason for that, as the king remarked, was the expense of bringing suit in a court of law and pursuing it through judgment and a possible appeal. Arbitration might also preserve positive relations between the litigants that might otherwise be frayed by a court trial. At times, the king was asked to act as arbiter, but usually the parties chose one or more persons; the king might add another impartial arbiter. The parties had to agree beforehand to abide by the decision of the arbiters and to give sureties that they would do so. The sureties not only guaranteed acceptance of the decision, but also payment of a fine for failure to agree to it.[65] Arbiters, sometimes employing the inquest, also decided a variety of quarrels concerning tithes, first fruits, and other offerings, tolls, pasturage, the use of woodland, and water rights.[66]

The most extensive record of a lawsuit settled by arbitration concerned the monastery of San Salvador de Oña and the town of Frías and occupies one hundred printed pages. Their dispute originated in the early thirteenth century when Alfonso VIII exchanged certain lands with the monastery and established the royal town of Frías. After initiating their suit in the royal court, the monks agreed to submit it to arbitration. As arbiters, they designated the *alcalde* Juan Iñíguez, and Frías chose the *alcalde* Juan Pérez; both sides added Marín Pérez, one of three *alcaldes* of Burgos nominated by Alfonso X. The three arbiters were directed to carry out an inquest, but it was delayed when Frías demanded that it should be conducted from the death of Alfonso VIII onward. In July 1271 Fernando de la Cerda (or Diego Pérez, *alcalde del rey*, acting in his name) ordered the arbiters to commence the inquest on

1 September and send him their sealed findings. Although the completed inquest was sent to the king, he failed to act on it and the document was lost. When Abbot Pedro complained, Alfonso X, in April 1278, ordered Marín, the royal *alcalde* of Burgos and one of the original *pesquisidores*, to send him the text. This mandate was drawn up by the royal *alcalde* Juan Iñiguez.[67]

Despite that, the issue was still pending several years later. The king delegated it to Infante Sancho, but as he was hastening to the frontier in 1280, he directed the monks and townspeople to submit their quarrel to arbitration. Each side nominated an arbiter, and Sancho added Marín, *alcalde* of Burgos. All three were instructed to review the earlier inquest. The monks and the townspeople agreed to accept the arbiters' decision, on penalty of two thousand *maravedís*. Each party also named four trustees to guarantee acceptance of the decision.[68]

In mid-July the arbiters began to listen to arguments presented by Pedro Pérez, the monastery's *personero*, and Domingo González, *personero* of Frías. The hearing resumed in early September and continued through October. Designating Domingo as "nuestro procurador e nuestro personero cierto," Frías pledged to accept whatever he said or did. In a similar *carta de personería* the monks gave Pedro Pérez "lenero e complido poder," that is, full and complete power, to act on their behalf.[69] Occasionally, the arbiters asked both men to swear the oath of *manquadra*, declaring that they would speak the truth and not resort to falsehood. In addition to presenting documentary evidence, the *personeros* referred to statements made by the more than one hundred witnesses summoned to the inquest.

Pedro Pérez of Oña, among other arguments, cited the prohibition attributed to the Curia of Nájera that ecclesiastical lands should not pass to the royal domain. Domingo González, however, countered that Alfonso VIII, as lord of the realm, was justified in acquiring lands from Oña, through exchange, in order to found the town of Frías. Pedro also argued that Frías used violence to subject many of Oña's tenants to vassalage, but Domingo asserted that they freely chose to submit to Frías. Rejecting Frías's reliance on the *Fuero del libro* or *Fuero real* (2, 11, 1–10), which recognized ownership after occupation for a year and a day, Pedro stated that according to the canonical rule of prescription, the monastery could not lose rights that it had enjoyed for forty years or more. This citation implies that despite the challenges made at the Cortes of Burgos in 1272, the *Fuero real* continued in use in Old Castile. The *Leyes del estilo* (242) also cited this law.

At last, on 13 February 1281 two of the arbiters, Marín Pérez, *alcalde* of Burgos, and Mathe García of Oña, rendered their decision, which generally favored San Salvador de Oña. Infante Sancho confirmed it on 27 February.[70]

Then, on 2 April 1281, Roy Pérez, a *ballestero* in Sancho's service, acting on his command, put the monks in possession of the lands and rights determined by the arbiters.[71] Two days later Alfonso X directed the *merino* of Castile to deliver the lands in question to the monks. In May of the following year, Infante Sancho reiterated that order. Despite that, Frías was dissatisfied with the outcome, and the matter dragged on into the reign of Sancho IV.[72]

Que Cada Una de las Partes Aya Su Derecho

In the foregoing pages we have reviewed the process of *fazer derecho*—doing right—outlined in the Alfonsine Codes. The task of the court was to guarantee "que cada una de las partes aya su derecho" (that each one of the parties should have his rights).[73] The litigants, responding to a formal summons, made their way to court, where, if there was no objection to the impartiality of the judge, the plaintiff initiated his suit by presenting his demand and the defendant responded. The judge might require them to swear the oath of *manquadra* whereby they affirmed their intention to tell the truth and to shun any falsehood. Christians, Jews, and Muslims, when brought before a judge, had to swear an oath tailored to their specific religious beliefs. Throughout the proceeding the judge could attempt to elicit the truth by interrogating the litigants and witnesses. When the issue to be decided became clear, he had to determine the method of proof and then whether the proofs offered were sufficient, conclusive, and valid. A simple acknowledgment of the facts by the defendant might easily resolve the matter, but the judge had to be certain that the defendant acted freely and truthfully. Some cases probably required something more. A few witnesses might be summoned, or a more searching inquest might be undertaken. In each instance, the judge had to consider the witness's demeanor and determine the veracity of his testimony. Documentary proof might seem irrefutable, but forging documents to bolster one's claims was a notorious practice. The task of establishing the authenticity of documents was very serious. When all the arguments were finished and all the evidence presented, the judge had to render sentence, but before doing so, he was advised not to rely solely upon himself, but to seek the counsel of good men, especially men learned in the law. The observance of proper decorum in pronouncing judgment was intended to emphasize the solemnity of the occasion. Once he announced his decision, he was expected to order steps to be taken to enforce it. However, should either party wish to appeal the judgment, the judge had to notify the appellate judge and forward to him a complete record of the suit.

Whether settled by the sentence of a judge in a court of law or resolved by arbitration, the procedures delineated by Alfonso X and his jurists were intended to *fazer derecho* in an orderly and timely manner that would guarantee a fair and honest hearing to both plaintiff and defendant. Ideally, once final judgment was pronounced, each side, whether pleased or not by the verdict, should come away believing that he had received what was rightfully his and that justice was served.

CHAPTER 9

Marriage, Family, and Inheritance

Ordenado por Dios Mismo en el Parayso

Marriage and the family, then as now, were the heart of society, and the wife and mother was the heart of the family. Marriages were often arranged between families hoping to achieve greater wealth, social status, power, and influence. Should husband and wife learn to love one another, that was a welcome outcome, but not a necessary condition of marriage. Women were valued for their fertility, but, whether married or single, they occupied an inferior position under the tutelage of a male relative.[1] Children, the fruit of marriage, gave hope that the lineage would be continued and that its estates would be transmitted from generation to generation. Preserving that inheritance was one of the principal ends of marriage.

Betrothal and Marriage

Marital law, based on ancient custom and Roman law, was embodied in the Visigothic Code and the municipal *fueros*. Marriage was viewed as a civil contract, but in the twelfth and thirteenth centuries the church, emphasizing its sacramental character, attempted to regulate it. Whereas the *Fuero real* reflected customary law, the *Fourth Partida*, following canon law, especially the writings of Ramon de Penyafort and Gregory IX's *Decretales*,[2] commented on betrothal, marriage, dowries, consanguinity, marital impediments, the dissolution of marriage, and related topics (*SP* 4, 1–12). As historians of canon law have thoroughly explored these subjects, I will not do so, except insofar as they reflect conditions in thirteenth-century Castile.[3] The *Espéculo* treated marriage in the missing seventh book.

According to the royal jurists, God honored man above all other creatures by creating him in his own image and likeness and by giving him a woman as his companion. Although their bodies differed according to nature, their love would make them one, and their descendants would populate the world. The exposition of marriage, the first of the seven sacraments, "ordenado por Dios Mismo en el Parayso" (established by God in Paradise), was placed in the midst of the other six *Partidas*, "just as the heart, where the human spirit, whence comes life to all the other members, is placed in the middle of the body" (*SP* 4, 1, pr.).[4]

The marital union was initiated when two people were betrothed in accordance with the wishes of their families. The imposition of a penalty if the marriage was not solemnized was rejected because one should not enter marriage "out of fear of punishment, but out of the love and consent of both parties" (*SP* 5, 11, 39). Though their opportunities to become acquainted before marriage were limited, children were expected to be betrothed to others of equal rank. The church's ban on marriages between persons related up to the seventh degree of kindred complicated the search for a spouse, but the Fourth Lateran Council in 1215 (canon 51) altered the rule to the fourth degree, thereby expanding the pool of eligible partners (*SP* 4, 6, 1–6).[5]

Children could be betrothed as early as seven years of age, because they were deemed capable of giving consent, though they surely did not understand the commitment that marriage entailed. Boys could marry at fourteen and girls at twelve (*SP* 4, 1, 1–6).[6] In 1266 when Fernando de la Cerda was eleven years old, his procurators contracted marriage with Blanche, Louis IX's daughter, then thirteen, but the marriage was not solemnized until three years later.[7] The bridegroom's gift of a ring to his bride, as tangible evidence of his intention to marry her, is illustrated in *CSM* 42. A young man, preparing to play ball, for safekeeping placed his ring on the finger of a statue of Mary. When he married, Mary reminded him that he was pledged to her; thus, leaving his wife, he became a hermit.[8]

A girl could not marry without her parents' consent.[9] Should she do so, she would be disinherited.[10] If only one forgave her, she would share in that parent's estate, or in the estate of both, if only one parent was living. After reaching her majority at twenty-five, she was free to marry as she wished.

The brothers of an orphaned girl, out of a greedy desire to retain her property, could not withhold their consent, unless she intended to marry their enemy. The man who married her without her family's approval became their enemy. She could also be disinherited if she dishonored her family by marrying an unsuitable person (FR 3, 1, 2, 5–6, 8–10, 14). A girl could not be compelled to marry, but if she rejected a worthy suitor, her father could disinherit her. Should she die before marriage, her father ought to offer another daughter to the groom. Although the bishop could compel a recalcitrant party to marry as promised, there were exceptions, for example: if one wished to enter a monastery, disappeared for three years, contracted leprosy, or became blind, deformed, or seriously injured; if the parties became related within the prohibited degrees; if both agreed to separate; if one was guilty of fornication, or was betrothed to more than one person, or ran off with someone betrothed to another; or if, on reaching legal age, they chose not to marry (SP 4, 1, 7–12).

CSM 135 tells of a boy and girl who vowed to be married, but their parents refused permission. Instead, the girl's father arranged her marriage to a rich man, but when she told him of her childhood vow, he did not attempt to consummate the marriage and pledged to help her find her young man. Once he was found in Montpellier, they were duly married in church with a priest presiding. The final illustration shows the newly married couple in bed, nude from the waist up, and the caption tells us that "the bridegroom did as a man does with his bride when they are at their ease."[11]

Given ongoing frontier warfare, many wives were likely widowed at an early age. Husbands, summoned to military service, were often absent for weeks and months, or even longer if they were captured and sold into slavery. Many died, leaving widows behind. No longer subject to a male relative, a widow enjoyed a degree of personal freedom. Supported by her dowry and arras, and having usufruct of her deceased spouse's property, she could maintain her household. In 1256 and 1264 the king guaranteed widows of urban knights tax exemptions granted to their husbands. However, a widow who married a taxpayer would lose those benefits.[12] Widows, seeking the emotional and economic support and legal protection of a new husband, risked losing custody of their children to a near relative. If a husband presumed dead returned home, he could sell both his remarried wife and her new spouse into slavery or punish them as he wished, except kill them. If his death was confirmed, she could remarry without her family's concurrence, provided that she first observed a year of mourning. Should she violate that rule or behave wantonly, she would be condemned as a wicked woman. The king, however, perhaps thinking of potential political alliances, permitted a widow to remarry within the year after her husband's death. If a woman and her lover killed her husband, they could not marry (*FR* 3, 1, 3–4, 11–13; *SP* 4, 12, 3).[13]

Marriages should be carried out publicly according to the rites of the church (*FR* 3, 1, 7). The king effectively yielded jurisdiction over marital cases to the church when he stated that anyone involved in a suit concerning marriage could not marry until it was resolved by an ecclesiastical court. Inasmuch as secret marriages or marriages contracted without parental consent often resulted in enmity, the church prohibited them. The king's use of the word *defendemos* to prohibit secret marriages, and his establishment of a penalty for doing so, suggests that he enacted a separate law on this matter. Perhaps he alluded to the *Fuero real* (3, 1, 1), which fined the guilty parties one hundred *maravedís*, payable to the king, or placed their goods and persons at his disposal. Without mentioning monetary penalties, the *Partidas* declared that a man who dishonored a girl's parents by secretly marrying their daughter should be handed over to them with all his property to serve them throughout his life. They were forbidden, however, to kill, wound, or harm him, but should be content with his permanent disgrace (*SP* 4, 3, 5).

Marriage between Christians and non-Christians was particularly relevant to Spain. As marriage was a sacrament, Christians were forbidden to marry heretics, Jews, or Muslims, but marriages among Jews or Muslims were valid. A marriage could not be dissolved if one spouse became a heretic, a Jew, or a Muslim, or committed adultery. A Christian could marry a Jew or a Muslim if his bride promised to convert to Christianity before marriage. As the rules of consanguinity applied only to Christians, Jews or Muslims related within the prohibited degrees would not be required to separate if they accepted Christianity. If one spouse converted, but the other refused and consistently denigrated Christianity, the Christian spouse could leave the marriage and remarry (*SP* 4, 2, 7, 15; 4, 4, 4; 4, 6, 6; 4, 10, 3). That accorded with the so-called Pauline Privilege enunciated by St. Paul (1 Cor 7:10–15).

A marriage was contracted in language like that used in Murcia in 1268:

> I, Bernat Cadireta, a moneyer, in the name of the Father, the Son, and the Holy Spirit, give to you, Ramoneta, daughter of Ramon de Belloc, by these present words, my body as a loyal husband, and I receive yours as a loyal wife, as the law of Jesus Christ wishes, and as Mary and the Apostles St. Peter and St. Paul confirm it, and as Holy Church established and ordained it. And I, the said Ramoneta, in the same manner, give to you the said Bernat Cadireta, my body as a loyal wife, and I receive yours as a loyal husband.

The couple, out of their mutual love, pledged to live together and share equally whatever property they possessed or would acquire. At the time of death, each could bequeath half of it. Both affixed their sign in the presence of five witnesses, including a priest of Saint Bartholomeu church, who probably presided at their nuptials. Sadly, the marriage ended four years later with Bernat's death. At that time royal judges upheld Ramoneta's claim to half of their estates.[14]

CSM 135 depicted the public celebration of a wedding, as the church required.[15] Kneeling before the altar, the bride and groom received the priest's blessing. A banquet, such as that portrayed in CSM 42, usually followed the ceremony. The burgeoning problem of inflation, however, prompted Fernando III, in the Cortes of Seville in 1250, to curb extravagance at weddings. If a man seeking to arrange the marriage of a female relative, perhaps one less desirable, offered or received a gift, he would be fined double the value and fifty maravedís. A man was forbidden to give more than sixty maravedís for wedding garments to a prospective bride if she were a virgin, or no more than forty if she were a widow. The number of guests at the wedding banquet was limited to ten, divided equally between the bride and groom. If more were present, a fine of ten maravedís was levied, seven for the king and three for the one who made an accusation in good faith.[16] The municipal council of Madrid had enacted a similar ordinance in 1235.[17]

During the Cortes of Seville in 1252 (art. 13), and again at Valladolid in 1258 (art. 45), Seville in 1261 (art. 31), and Jerez in 1268 (art. 40), Alfonso X repeated, with some modifications, his father's strictures. The fine for arranging a marriage was increased to one hundred maravedís. The groom might still spend fifty maravedís for his bride's trousseau, whether she was a virgin or a widow, and each party could invite five guests to the wedding banquet, not counting their parents, witnesses, godparents, and servants. The person who raised an orphaned bride or groom could stand in place of a parent. The wedding celebration was limited to two days. That austerity seems to have been forgotten in 1278 when Infante Sancho asked the city council of Burgos to permit his chamberlain to import fifty casks of new wine for his wedding.[18]

The bride and groom customarily exchanged gifts to establish a foundation on which they might live.[19] Her family provided her with a dowry (dote) that gave her equal standing with her spouse and provided her with essential financial support in her widowhood.[20] The amount was a sign of her family's wealth and position and obviously made rich young women more attractive partners than others. Fernando de la Cerda named a procurator in 1270 to collect the dowry of ten thousand livres tournois that Louis IX promised to his daughter Blanche.[21] In 1282 Juan de Montpellier, a physician, his wife, and her three sisters sold land for two hundred *maravedís* to Pedro Sarracín II, dean of the cathedral of Burgos, to pay the dowry of a fourth sister.[22] In reality, the husband determined how his wife's contribution to the marriage would be used. The *Fuero real* did not discuss her dowry, but the *Fourth Partida*, following Roman law, stated that she might provide the dowry from her own estate (*adventitia*) or that of her parents or other family members (*profectitia*). Should the marriage be terminated by divorce or her husband's death, the dowry would revert to whomever provided it (*SP* 4, 11, 1–2).[23]

The dower or marriage gift (*dotarium*) given by the husband to his bride, and known in Spain as *arras*, has been likened to the Germanic bride-price whereby a man effectively purchased a woman from her family.[24] As the dower's purpose was to support her after her husband's death, it remained under her control. When Fernando III married his second wife, Jeanne of Ponthieu, in 1237, for example, he endowed her with estates in Andalucía, but Alfonso X, soon after his accession, reclaimed those lands for the royal domain.[25]

Following the invocation of the Trinity, a charter concerning *arras* ought to state that marriage was the first ordinance made by God when he created Eve from Adam's rib. Citing biblical passages emphasizing the union of husband and wife (Gen 2:24; Mk 10:9; Mt 19:6; 1 Cor 7:1–16), the man should specify the amount of her *arras* and declare that she would share equally in whatever God granted them as husband and wife. A record of their respective estates on their wedding day should be prepared so that if either one died, all would know what each brought to it. The charter, sealed and witnessed, should be given to his bride (*E* 4, 12, 39). In another formula, Juan García gave five hundred *maravedís* as *arras* for Teresa, the daughter of Martín Esteban, who promised to secure her consent to the marriage within two months and to endow her with estates. If the marriage did not take place, Juan García would forfeit the *arras*. In still another formula Juan García and Teresa agreed to marry, and as customary, he placed a ring on her finger. Teresa gave him a dowry of five hundred *maravedís* that he pledged to return if their marriage was terminated by death or otherwise (*SP* 3, 18, 84–87).

The *Fuero real* limited the amount of *arras* at a tenth of the man's estate. The estate of Juan García of Burgos must have been substantial because, in 1275, he promised to give his bride one thousand *maravedís* as *arras*.[26] After a wife died, a quarter of her *arras* could be offered for her soul, but the remainder would pass to her children. If there were none, the husband could use the *arras* as he wished. If she was under twenty-five, her parents had to preserve her *arras* until she reached her majority. Should her husband die before they were intimate, but he had kissed her, she could retain half his gifts of clothing or other items but had to return the rest to his family. If he had not kissed her, she had to return everything, including *arras*. Conversely, if she gave him anything, whether he kissed her or not, but they were not otherwise intimate, he had to return it. If she died and they had been intimate, he could keep her gifts. If she was guilty of adultery or abandoned him, he could reclaim her *arras* (FR 3, 2, 1–6; FJ 3, 2, 6).

A *fazaña* concerning Elvira, espoused to a knight who gave her several gifts, exemplified that law. As the marriage was never celebrated, he demanded their return. When she refused, he complained to Diego López de Haro, *adelantado* of Castile, who offered Elvira two options. If she had kissed and embraced the knight, she could keep his gifts, but if not, she had to return them. Declaring that she had not, she gave them up (LFC 241; FV 5, 1, 4).[27] The *arras* of twenty thousand *maravedís* given to Berenguela López, the daughter of Lope Díaz de Haro, by her husband, the magnate Rodrigo Gonzálvez Girón, was especially high. In 1258 she sued her deceased spouse's executors to obtain the *arras*, but they argued that after paying his debts, only ten thousand *maravedís* remained. Alfonso X ordered that amount to be given to her as well as the income from the sale of certain properties of the deceased. In accordance with the *Fuero real* (3, 2, 1), he directed her to donate 2,500 *maravedís*, a quarter of the remainder of the estate, for her husband's soul.[28]

In addition to her dowry, the bride might have personal property or *paraphernalia*,[29] which could serve the common purpose of the marriage. Although she retained ownership, she could not dispose of it without her husband's consent (SP 4, 11, 17).

Although the couple should share equally whatever property they acquired, the law did not absolutely establish the principle of communal property.[30] The king might make a gift to both, but if it was intended for one partner, only that one should have use of it. A husband could also use as his own an inheritance, a gift, or a stipend received from the king for military service. However, if he and his wife paid the expenses of his service, they would share whatever he gained from it, for, as the cost was communal, so also should the profits be. This principle also applied to whatever a wife acquired on her own. Although one or the other might bring greater resources to the marriage, they were expected to exploit them together, but each one retained his or her inheritance, which would pass to their heirs (FR 3, 3, 1–3).[31] The law recognizing the right of husband and wife to own property individually was transmitted to California and Texas.[32]

Whereas canon law acknowledged the validity of a marriage solemnized in the presence of a priest, as well as a clandestine marriage by consenting spouses, civil law accepted *barraganía* or concubinage. Like marriage, *barraganía* was a long-lasting relationship based on friendship, love, and fidelity, but it did not have equivalent legal status.[33] While admitting that the church condemned concubinage, the royal jurists argued that ancient wise men decided that it was less wicked for a man to have one concubine, rather than several, so that the parentage of children might be more certain. In effect, *barraganía* regulated by law was a safeguard against polygamy. An unmarried man could take as a concubine a free woman over twelve who was not related within the prohibited degrees. If she were an honorable woman, he should declare his intention in the presence of witnesses; but he need not do so if she were of inferior rank, or an adulterer, or of ill repute. An unmarried *adelantado mayor* could take a concubine, but he could not marry a woman from the province that he governed, lest he be accused of threatening her father to give consent. Although kings and other great men kept concubines, they were advised not to contaminate their noble blood by taking up with slaves, freedwomen, minstrels, barmaids, hucksters, procuresses, or other degraded women. The bastard child of such a woman was not entitled to a share in the father's estate (*SP* 4, 14, 1–3). The *Espéculo* (4, 7, 7) denied a married man who kept a known concubine the right to testify in court. The *Libro de los fueros de Castiella* (175) and the *Fuero Juzgo* (5, 6, 1) stated that a noble could ennoble his children by a concubine by giving them five hundred *sueldos*, but they would have limited rights of inheritance. *CSM* 104 related a tale of sacrilege as a *barragana*, discovering that her lover intended to marry another, planned to win him back by making a love potion with the Eucharistic bread. The Virgin Mary prevented her, however, and to atone for her sin she entered the convent.

Reading these guidelines, one ought to conclude that Mayor Guillén de Guzmán was Alfonso X's *barragana*. In 1244 she gave him a daughter, Beatriz, who proved to be his favorite and, on her mother's death in 1262, inherited her estates.[34] Although he had children by other liaisons, his relationship with Mayor Guillén seems to have had some permanency even after his marriage to Violante of Aragón in 1249.

Like laymen, many clergy, notorious for their failure to observe the rule of celibacy, lived with *barraganas*.[35] *CSM* 151, for example, told the story of a priest who pursued many women, but one night, while visiting his concubine, he was distracted by the sight of a church dedicated to Mary and thereafter gave up his wicked life. The Council of Valladolid convened in 1228 by the papal legate Cardinal John of Santa Sabina condemned concubinary clergy, excluding them from any ecclesiastical office, excommunicating their concubines, consigning them at death to burial with animals, and disinheriting their children.[36] The council's decrees were quickly forgotten, however. Although the *Partidas* (1, 6, 53) prohibited clerics from keeping *barraganas*, in 1262 Alfonso X assured the diocesan clergy of Salamanca that their children and other direct descendants could inherit their estates.[37] Eight years later, he legitimated the children of the clergy of the deanery of Roa in the diocese of Osma, and guaranteed their right of inheritance, provided that none of their property was given to the church or to a religious order.[38] Little had changed when Juan Ruiz, archpriest of Hita (d. ca. 1351), mocked the plan of the clergy of Talavera to appeal to the king against the archbishop of Toledo's decree forbidding them to live with women.[39]

Children, Legitimate and Illegitimate

Just as animals care for their young, the royal jurists argued, human beings should take even greater care of their children. Children, in turn, ought to love and fear their parents and look after them in time of need. The primary responsibility for children rested with the mother during the first three years, but thereafter with the father. If the parents separated, the one at fault had to provide for the children, while the other cared for them. If the mother remarried, her first husband should take charge of their children. Paternal grandparents or great-grandparents should assume that responsibility if the parents were too poor. Whereas the father had to support his mistress's children, their immediate relatives were not obliged to do so, though they might out of courtesy. A father was not required to support a child who accused him of a major crime or a son who could live independently. A man who cared for a stranger's children could not treat them as servants or, when they reached adulthood, demand payment for rearing them. Parents who abandoned a child could not reclaim it, unless they did so immediately and reimbursed those who provided for it (*SP* 4, 19, 1–7; 4, 20, 1–3).

Legitimate children could inherit family estates and aspire to public offices and were not exposed to the shame directed at illegitimate children. If, after a couple married, an impediment was discovered, their children already born would be legitimate, but not if the couple concealed the impediment by marrying in secret. A concubine's children could become legitimate if her lover married her. An illegitimate child was denied any share in its parents' estates. By declaring that the pope could only legitimate someone seeking priestly ordination, and by reserving to emperors and kings the right to grant legitimacy in the temporal sphere, Alfonso X limited spiritual authority. An example of a royal charter legitimating Remondo, the son of Remón Pérez by Doña Perona, guaranteed his right to inherit his father's property and to be treated with the respect accorded to a legitimate son (*SP* 3, 18, 9).[40] A father could legitimate his son in his will or in a notarized document or by offering him to the service of the king or a municipal council. A declaration of legitimacy erased all legal barriers to inheritance and public service (*SP* 4, 13, 1–2; 4, 15, 1–9; *FR* 3, 6, 1–2, 4, 17).[41]

The legitimacy of a child born after the death of a woman's husband might be called into question. Relying upon the Greek physician Hippocrates (ca. 460–ca. 370 BC), who declared that pregnancy lasted no longer than ten months,[42] the royal jurists asserted that if the woman had been living with her husband and gave birth within ten months of his death, the child would be legitimate. However, that would not be so if she gave birth on the first day of the eleventh month. A deformed child had the right to his parents' inheritance, but a creature having the head or limbs of an animal could not. In that instance the king's men perhaps gave too much credence to fairy tales about monstrous births.[43] More realistically, they warned against a woman who, with an eye on a rich estate, tried to pass off her bastard as her deceased husband's child (*SP* 4, 23, 4–5; 6, 6, 17).

Lacking children of their own, couples often resorted to adoption (*porfijamiento*).[44] Roman law recognized two forms of adoption: *adrogatio*, the adoption of someone no longer under his father's authority, and *adoptio*, adoption of one still subject to his father.[45] Adoptive parents could not marry their adopted children; nor could their true children marry their adopted siblings (*SP* 4, 7, 7–8). However, adopted children could marry one another (*FR* 4, 21, 1–7). Any adult freeman could adopt a child eighteen years younger than he, but a woman could adopt only if she lost a son in military service. Minors, monks, and castrated persons could do so only with royal permission. The king's consent was also required to adopt an orphan under seven, or a child between seven and fourteen. A guardian, lest he be suspected of a wicked purpose, could not adopt the boy in his care, though he could do so, with royal approval, after the boy reached twenty-five. If an adoption was annulled, the adoptee was entitled to whatever property he possessed at the time of adoption. An adopted child could also share in his adoptive father's estate (*SP* 4, 16, 1–10).[46] If, after adopting children, a man had legitimate offspring, the latter would inherit his estate, but he could make other provision for those he adopted. If an adoptee died intestate before his adoptive parent, his estate would pass to his nearest relatives. He was also entitled to a fourth of the estate of his adoptive parent who died intestate (*FR* 4, 21, 1, 2–5; 3, 6, 5). The law concerning adoption was also accepted in the state of Texas.[47]

Although the title concerning adoption in the *Espéculo* (4, 7, 11) is not extant, there is a formula for adoption. If the adoptee was a married freeman and not subject to parental control, the adopting person, with the king's assent, could designate him as his heir. If the adoptee was still under his parents' authority, the local judge should grant the adoption (*E* 4, 12, 40). Two charters demonstrated a legal adoption. In the first, the child was still in his father's power, while in the second he was not. Thus, Ruy Pérez, with the consent of Gonzalo Ruyz, *alcalde* of Toledo,[48] adopted Fernando, the son of Garcí Pérez, who consented and, in a symbolic transfer of authority, gave his son's hand to Ruy Pérez. In the second case, Domingo Ruiz adopted Pero Ferrández, the son of Ferrand Velásquez. All declared their consent. As the laws concerning adoption were observed, the adoption was approved and recorded (*SP* 3, 18, 91–92). In neither case were the reasons for adoption expressed.

In their confrontation with the king in 1272 the nobles protested the adoption at some uncertain date of Fernando de la Cerda by Mencía López de Haro. Following Mencía's death in 1271–72, Fernando's representative took possession of her Leonese estates, prompting Infante Felipe to complain that his wife, Leonor Ruiz de Castro, was done out of her inheritance. The king replied that he could not interfere with anyone's right to freely choose an heir.[49] As Mencía had no children and did not lose any in the reconquest, it is evident that the king made an exception to the law of the *Partidas*. It is also unlikely that he allowed her to exercise authority over his son as the law provided. In one sense his comment that he could not override her right to designate her heir was correct, but in another it was disingenuous. She could have simply bequeathed her estates to Fernando, but adopting him evidently seemed a firmer guarantee that he would actually take possession of them. The adoption was a calculated move by the king to secure her inheritance for his son.

In treating the guardianship of minor children, boys under fourteen and girls under twelve, the *Partidas* (6, 16–19) adhered to Roman law.[50] A father might appoint a guardian, a man over twenty-five, in his will, but if he did not, his nearest relative, preferably the mother or grandmother, could act as such. Otherwise, a judge could designate a guardian. The woman had to promise not to marry during the minority, and if she did so, a judge would entrust her minor children to their closest male relative. A widow could appoint a guardian in her will, but a judge had to confirm it. When a boy became fourteen and a girl twelve, the judge should select a curator to serve until the child was twenty-five.[51] Barred from acting as guardians were deaf mutes, the physically or mentally incapacitated, spendthrifts, immoral or impoverished persons, the terminally ill, the child's debtors, enemies of his father, royal officials, knights in royal service, teachers of the liberal arts, royal judges and counselors, and philosophers. Members of the secular clergy could act as guardians for their relatives, but bishops and monks could not (*SP* 6, 16, 1–14; 6, 17, 1–4; *FR* 3, 7, 1–3).

A guardian had two principal obligations: the prudent management of his ward's property, and his proper care and upbringing. Encouraging the child to develop good behavior, the guardian should teach him to read and write, and assist him in finding an occupation appropriate to his character, income, and capability. The guardian could enter binding contracts in his ward's name and represent him in court. He was forbidden to dispose of his ward's real estate except, with a judge's permission, to pay his father's debts, to marry his sisters or the child himself, or for another legal purpose. Although the *Fuero real* (3, 7, 2) allowed the guardian 10 percent of the income from the estate, the *Partidas* did not specify a figure. At the conclusion of the minority, the guardian had to render an accurate account of his stewardship. If he wasted his ward's estate or taught him immoral behavior, a judge could require him to make restitution, convict him of malfeasance, and declare him infamous. His ward could abrogate any contracts made by his guardian that he deemed detrimental to his interest (*SP* 6, 15, 15–21; 6, 18, 1–4; 6, 19, 1–9).

Several chancery formulas concern the role of guardians. Rodrigo Esteban, *alcalde* of Seville,[52] designated two men of good reputation as guardians of their nephew. Swearing to act in his interest, they pledged to render a faithful account at the end of his minority. In another case, Gonzalo Yuañez, *alcalde* of Toledo, appointed a prudent woman, Doña Urraca, as guardian of her minor son. She promised not to marry while he was under age and renounced "the laws in this our book that state that women cannot obligate themselves for others" (*SP* 3,18, 95). She also appointed a *personero* to defend her son in court. As protection against any accusation of malfeasance or misappropriation of funds, García Álvarez prepared an inventory of his ward's estate. Similarly, Álvar Peréz, then over fourteen, on receiving from his guardian a true account of his estate, acknowledged that he had faithfully fulfilled his legal responsibilities. A guardian who overstated his ward's wealth could not minimize it when subsequently rendering accounts (*SP* 3, 18, 94–96, 99, 102, 120).

Living in a patriarchal society, the royal jurists reaffirmed the Roman principle of *patria potestas*, whereby a father had absolute authority over all the members of his family, except for his illegitimate children, because "such as these are not worthy to be called children because they are conceived in sin" (*SP* 4, 17, 1–4).[53] Assuming that Alfonso X read that, one wonders what he thought of his illegitimate children. Ordinarily, a father had a right to his child's income while he was under his control. That included earnings from use of the father's property (*profectitia*), or from the child's own labor, or from gifts and bequests by the child's mother or other relatives (*adventitia*). However, a child had an absolute right to income (*pegujar*, lat. *peculium*) earned in other ways, as, for example, income from military service known as *castrense peculium*. *Quasi castrense peculium* referred to the salary paid by the royal treasury to a master of sciences, a judge, or a scribe.[54] A father on the verge of starvation could sell or pledge his child.[55] He could ask a judge to compel an obstinate son to obey him. A son could sue his father if he attempted to seize his income. If a son was robbed while traveling, he could seek redress in court, without having to ask his father's permission and perhaps lose his rights because of the ensuing delay (*SP* 4, 17, 5–12).

Wishing to acknowledge his son's independence, a father should inform a judge. As compensation for rearing his son, he could retain usufruct of his adventitious property. A father who treated his child cruelly, encouraged his daughter to lead a life of sin, abused a stepson or wasted his property, or accepted a bequest obliging him to emancipate his children had to give them their freedom. A newly independent son who, instead of showing gratitude, dishonored his father would be subjected to his power again. The son's behavior was "one of the greatest evils that a man could do" (*SP* 4, 18, 15–19). In light of Infante Sancho's rebellion and Alfonso X's scathing denunciation, those words seem especially prophetic. An emancipation formula declared that Diego Aparicio, appearing before Gonzalo Yuañez, *alcalde* of Toledo, took his son by the hand and, with his consent, released him from his power and authorized him to do everything that a man could do in or out of court. Renouncing a father's right to his son's property, he granted him an estate to hold by hereditary right (*SP* 3, 18, 93).

A father's authority ceased when he died or suffered civil death, that is, if the king condemned him to compulsory labor, or exiled him for life and confiscated his property. However, a man banished but allowed to retain his property was not civilly dead and would still have power over his children. A father proclaimed an outlaw, or convicted of incest, child abuse, or sexual molestation of his daughters, also lost *patria potestas*. A son appointed to an office in royal service would be emancipated from his father's power (*SP* 4, 18, 1–14).[56]

Wills and Inheritance

The desire to transmit one's estate to one's heirs without challenge encouraged the making of wills.[57] As Harold Berman remarked, under the influence of the canonists a will was regarded as a "religious instrument," whose primary purpose was to secure the testator's eternal salvation.[58] The *Fuero real* (3, 5, 1–14) summarized the law on wills, but the *Espéculo's* discussion of testaments is in the missing seventh book. Robert I. Burns commented that "Alfonso's treatise on wills" in the *Sixth Partida*, adapting Roman and canon law, is "the most comprehensive and instructive from the Middle Ages."[59]

A will might be made orally or written on any suitable material. Although seven witnesses were necessary, a knight on campaign only required two, and a villager could make do with five literate witnesses (*SP* 6, 1, 1–8, 12; *FR* 3, 5, 1–2). A man in possession of his senses should compose his will in the name of God, appoint executors, list his bequests, threaten to disinherit anyone who challenged it, revoke all earlier wills, and record the names of witnesses (*E* 4, 12, 44). In a chancery formula, Esteban Fernández, stating that he was ill but sound in mind, appointed his heirs and executors; made a bequest; provided for his burial, payment of his debts, and correction of any wrongs he had committed; and canceled previous wills. Although a minor could not make a will, if he were in danger of death, he could donate his property with his father's consent. An ailing Nicolás Fernández, for example, still subject to his father, whom he named as his executor, bequeathed money to a hospital, gave his books to a classmate, and left a vineyard to a friend. If he regained good health, those donations would be annulled (*SP* 3, 18, 103, 105).

A blind man could make a will, but others could not: a son under his father's control; a boy under fourteen; a girl under twelve; a deaf mute; someone condemned to death or banished for life; a knight who sold or gambled away his weapons; a hostage, heretic, or traitor; or a monk, unless he did so before entering religious life. According to a formula, Domingo Vicente, after making his will and disposing of his property, made his profession as a Benedictine monk (*SP* 3, 18, 88). Secular clergy, not bound by the vow of poverty, could bequeath their personal possessions but not church property. Should a Christian designate as his heir a Jew, a Muslim, or a heretic, his estate would pass to the king. Barred from witnessing a will were persons convicted of serious crimes or declared infamous, apostates, women, minors under fourteen, slaves, deaf mutes, the insane, wastrels, a hermaphrodite who was more of a woman than a man, and persons condemned for writing *malas cantigas*. Ironically, Alfonso X himself wrote nasty songs. A man could revoke his will and make a new one if his circumstances changed, as, for example, the birth or adoption of a child or death of an heir (*SP* 6, 1, 9, 13–29; *FR* 3, 5, 5–7, 10; 3, 6, 11, 16).

Given the economic importance of the pilgrimage to Compostela, the *Fuero real* (4, 23, 2–4) repeated Alfonso IX's law of 1228 guaranteeing the right of pilgrims to make wills.[60] Alfonso X's inclusion of these provisions in a constitution granted to the cathedral of Santiago in 1254 demonstrates that the *Fuero real* was composed prior to 1255.[61] Reiterating them in the *Partidas* (6, 1, 30–32), he required an innkeeper to inventory the belongings of a guest who died intestate, so the bishop could deliver them to his heirs. If no one claimed them, they would be devoted to pious purposes (*LFC* 58).

Among potential heirs, who should be identified by name, were an emperor, empress, king, or queen; a corporate body; and anyone not excluded by "the laws of this our book." Those who could not be named were men exiled for life, heretics, those knowingly baptized twice, apostates, confraternities banned by royal command, the children of incest or of nuns, or a widow who remarried within a year of her husband's death. If there were several heirs, the estate should be divided, according to Roman law, into twelve parts to be apportioned among them. All would share equally if the testator neglected to specify each one's allotment. If he bequeathed his estate to the poor, the king would designate the beneficiaries.[62] A master might emancipate his slave and declare him as his heir, but if he had no other property and was in debt, he could not do so. An heir could not be required to abide by a condition impossible to accomplish. In case his heir were to predecease him, a testator could designate a substitute; he could also do so if he believed that his original heir would not comply with a conditional bequest (*SP* 6, 3, 1–25; 6, 4, 1–16; 6, 5, 1–14; *FR* 3, 5, 14).

As acceptance of a will could be problematic, especially if the deceased's estate were burdened with debt, a presumptive heir had a year to assess the wisdom of accepting it. Meanwhile, an inventory had to be compiled, and no portion of the estate could be alienated except to pay burial expenses or to fulfill a pressing obligation (*SP* 6, 6, 1–20). Two formulas illustrated this process. In the first instance, in order to determine whether he could satisfy his father's creditors, Domingo had an inventory of his estate prepared. Similarly, Rodrigo Ygneguez, appearing before Gonzalo Yuañez, *alcalde* of Toledo, refused to accept an inheritance from his father because payment of his debts would be overly burdensome (*SP* 3, 18, 100–101).

A presumptive heir might so offend his father or other benefactor as to be disinherited.[63] The classic example was Alfonso X's condemnation and disinheritance of his son Sancho.[64] A son could be disowned if he assaulted his father, dishonored him, accused him of a major crime, plotted his murder, slept with his wife or mistress, spoke ill of him, refused to pay his debts, or tried to prevent him from making a will. A father could cut off a daughter who refused to marry as he wished, or married against his will, or became a prostitute. A stranger caring for an insane person neglected by his family could inherit his estate to the exclusion of the family. A father who fell into enemy hands could disinherit his family if they refused to ransom him. Although a son who became a Muslim, a Jew, or a heretic might be disinherited, a heretical father could not dispossess his son who accepted Christianity. A father's Christian sons would inherit his estate, to the exclusion of non-Christians. An heir could be deprived of his inheritance if he caused the death of the testator. A testator's direct descendants whom he did not name as his heirs might sue to break his will. However, anyone disinherited for any of the reasons cited above could not do so (*SP* 6, 7, 1–17; 6, 8, 1–7; *FR* 3, 9, 1–5).

When the testator made a bequest, he should identify the beneficiary and state any conditions. The validity of all bequests would be determined by "the laws of this our book." Ecclesiastical or royal property, as well as public spaces, could not be disposed of by will. One could not bequeath a slave to a Jew, a Muslim, or a heretic. A knight who received a castle from the king with the obligation to defend it could not bequeath it to someone incapable of that responsibility. A beneficiary could refuse a bequest that he believed was unnecessarily onerous (*SP* 6, 9, 1–48).

A testator's executors (*cabezales*, lat. *capitales*) were responsible for carrying out his wishes and were forbidden to act according to their own whims.[65] Prohibited from serving as executors were slaves, monks, women, minors, madmen, heretics, Jews, and Moors, deaf mutes, traitors, and those condemned to death or banished (*FR* 3, 5, 7). If the executors failed to fulfill their duty within a year of the testator's death, the diocesan bishop could compel them to act or appoint other executors. Absent an executor, the bishop could also implement a bequest for ransoming captives. The local judge should record the sum allotted and the date on which it was received, and at the end of the year the bishop had to report the number of captives ransomed and the amount paid for each one (*SP* 6, 10, 1–8; *FR* 3, 5, 11–13).[66]

An heir was entitled to *falcidia*, a fourth of the estate, and reimbursement for expenses incurred in handling it.[67] After satisfying the testator's debts, bequests had to be distributed, but if there were insufficient funds the amounts allotted could be reduced. If the debts were high, the heir might be left with little or nothing. Pious bequests, however, ought to be paid in full. A man could add a codicil to his will, but he could only change his heir or disinherit his children by preparing another will (*SP* 6, 11, 1–8; 6, 12, 1–3; *FR* 3, 5, 4).[68] As an example of a codicil, Pero Fernández transferred property from one person to another, bequeathed to his heirs a vineyard originally allotted to a church, donated one thousand *maravedís* to a friend, and named a new guardian for his children (*SP* 3, 18, 104).

When a man died intestate, his children or grandchildren, or if there were none, his brothers or closest relatives, would inherit his estate.[69] Parents could inherit the estate of a son who died intestate. If there were no heirs, the estate would pass to the king (*FR* 3, 5, 3). After an heir presented a valid will, a judge could give him possession of the deceased's property. If there were two or more claimants, a judge should decide who had the better right, or he might allow them to share equally. The heir who failed to claim his inheritance within ten years (or twenty if he were in another country) would lose it. Any dangerous items among the deceased's belongings should be burned (*SP* 6, 13, 1–12; 6, 14, 1–7; 6, 15, 1–10; *FR* 3, 6, 1, 10, 13). A testator could create an entailed estate by declaring that his son and his descendants should possess it forever (*SP* 5, 5, 44).

Several extant wills, including Alfonso X's, reflect the laws described above.[70] Usually, after expressing some pious sentiment and asserting his soundness of mind, the testator detailed various bequests, appointed executors, and disinherited anyone who objected. Four to six witnesses often attested the will. Sometimes property was set aside to commemorate the anniversary of the testator's death.[71] For example, Esteban Domingo, royal *alcalde* in Ávila, being of sound mind, with his family's consent, for the salvation of his soul bequeathed property to the cathedral and established an endowment of forty *maravedís* for two chaplains to say daily mass and the canonical hours for him.[72] Mateo Sanz, commending his soul and body to God and Mary, named his executors, annulled previous wills, arranged for payment of his debts and burial expenses, and left the remainder of his estate to his wife and son.[73] Several ecclesiastics bequeathed books of theology and canon and civil law.[74]

In his will of 1283 Infante Manuel, sound of mind, directed his executors to pay his debts and right his wrongs. His beneficiaries included members of his family, servants, and retainers, but his principal heir was his son Juan Manuel. Recalling his own efforts to secure Sancho's right to the throne, Manuel placed his wife and son under Sancho's protection and reminded Juan Manuel of his obligation to serve him. After providing for his burial and masses to be said for his soul, and forbidding any of his heirs to transgress the terms of his will, he revoked all other wills and ordered his last testament to be sealed and witnessed.[75]

Civil and ecclesiastical authorities disputed jurisdiction over wills. As one's last testament was drawn up in expectation of death and a future life of rewards or punishments, churchmen argued that as this was a spiritual matter, they ought to adjudicate it. In 1270, however, the municipal council of Badajoz complained that the bishop excommunicated lay judges hearing contested wills. Expressing astonishment, Alfonso X confirmed the jurisdiction of secular judges and forbade the bishop or any cleric to contravene his decision.[76]

Parentesco de Linaje es Cosa que Ata los Omes en Grand Amor

The royal jurists, recognizing that the family created by the marital union was the cornerstone of society, emphasized that "parentesco de linaje es cosa que ata los omes en grand amor" (kinship by lineage is something that binds men in great love) (*SP* 4, 6, pr.).[77] In order to give the family the greatest stability, the *Fourth Partida* accepted the rules embodied in canon law. Parents hoping to achieve greater economic and social standing betrothed their children and, with their consent, arranged their marriages. Vows were usually exchanged in a church in the presence of a priest, and a banquet followed. While the couple shared their resources, each one might have his or her property. In addition to her personal possessions and gifts from her spouse, the woman had a dowry and *arras* to provide for her after his death or the dissolution of their marriage. The children born of a union blessed by the church could rightfully inherit their parents' estates.

Paralleling Christian marriage was the civil practice of *barraganía* whereby a man might keep a concubine whose children were allowed a share in his estate. Children of illicit affairs, however, were not. The king emphatically asserted his right to legitimate them but admitted that the church could legitimate anyone wishing to become a cleric or a monk. He also recognized that a childless couple might wish to adopt a child, and the possibility that one or both parents might die leaving minor children who would need the care of guardians. Thus, the paternal household might embrace many people, wives, *barraganas*, children, legitimate or not, under age or adopted, and servants. The father, by virtue of *patria potestas*, wielded absolute authority over them all.

One of the purposes of marriage was to ensure the transmission of the family's property to the father's direct descendants. Building on the foundation of Roman law, the proper form of a will was delineated, as well as the disposition of the estate of one dying intestate. Among the issues clarified were the rights of heirs, the appointment of executors, the drafting of codicils, the acceptance or refusal of the will by an heir, the distribution of bequests, and the disinheritance of hostile children.

Although the king proclaimed that marriage was ordained by God in paradise, the many permutations in the relationship between husband and wife, between parents and children, and the convolutions of inheritance reveal the capacity of human beings to create an extraordinarily complex society quite at odds with the idyllic existence of Adam and Eve before the fall. Familial relations were one aspect—a most important one—of the law of persons.

 CHAPTER 10

The Law of Persons

Status Hominum es el Estado o la Condición o la Manera en que los Omes Biuen o Están

Justinian's *Institutes* (1, 2, 12) explained that "all our law is about persons, things, and actions." The law of persons related to freedom and slavery, marriage, family, guardianship, and citizenship. A person's condition in life entailed certain rights and obligations.[1] The Alfonsine Codes touched on all those topics especially as they related to freemen. The previous chapter reviewed the *Fourth Partida*'s treatment of marriage and the family, and the *Sixth Partida*'s discussion of guardianship, wills, and inheritances. Next to be considered is the *Fourth Partida*'s exposition of the legal personality and juridical capacity of freemen and slaves, and the mutual obligations between a man and woman, a parent and child, a guardian and ward, a testator and beneficiary.[2] Rights and obligations arising from birth, vassalage, and friendship must also be examined.

Juridical Capacity

Alfonso García Gallo discussed the acquisition of juridical capacity and the elements shaping it, namely, one's place of birth, age, gender, family membership, health, religion, and social and cultural condition.[3] The term *persona* meant someone recognized as a legal person who could freely exercise rights and incur obligations under the law. Ordinarily one acted in a juridical capacity as a member of a family and/or a citizen of a town. In Roman law the *paterfamilias* or father of a family, having *patria potestas*, wielded almost absolute authority over his family, household, and property.[4] Over time, however, the individual acquired greater legal significance as men became vassals of lords, or achieved independence by colonizing new lands or pursuing their livelihood as merchants and artisans. The revival of Roman and canon law acknowledged the individual freeman as the subject of rights and obligations, thereby minimizing the juridical status of the family. In addition to natural persons or human beings, the law recognized juristic persons, that is, institutions or corporations that enabled a group of individuals to act as one person.[5] The *personero* who occupied "the place of the person of another," whether an individual or a corporation, reflected that idea (*SP* 3, 5, 1).

Directing attention to the *status hominum*, that is, "el estado o la condición o la manera en que los omes biuen o están" (the state or condition or manner in which men live or exist), the royal jurists recognized three conditions: freedom, servitude, or emancipation. While most people were free, many were slaves or freedmen. Although the word *persona* was used of slaves because they were human beings, they did not have juridical capacity and were treated as objects. Comparable distinctions emphasized the legal superiority of nobles over nonnobles, priests over laity, legitimate children over bastards, Christians over Muslims and Jews, and men over women (*SP* 4, 23, pr., 1–5). In effect, the law did not admit the equality of all human beings.

In Roman law a child of free parents acquired a legal personality at birth.[6] The *Fuero real* (3, 6, 3) admitted the right of a baptized child born after his father's death to inherit his property, but the *Partidas* (4, 23, 3–5), following Roman law, stressed the viability of a newborn and eliminated the reference to baptism. Whatever was done for the benefit of the child in the womb was valid, just as if it were born, but anything done to the contrary was not. A child born to a free woman would be free. Although someone might maliciously postpone emancipating a pregnant slave so that her newly delivered child would inherit her status as a slave, the law determined that the child should be free as intended. A pregnant woman should not be executed for a crime until her child was born lest it be penalized for a crime it did not commit. A child born to a married couple within seven to ten months of conception was legitimate. A deformed child could inherit his parents' estate (*SP* 4, 23, 4–5; 6, 6, 17).

A person achieved the fullness of juridical capacity on reaching his majority. According to Roman law, infancy extended to age seven, while puberty was fourteen for boys and twelve for girls. The age of majority was twenty-five, but a boy might be liberated from his father's control at twenty and a girl at eighteen.[7] Initially, Alfonso X seems to have been uncertain about that, but ultimately accepted twenty-five as the age of majority (*SP* 6, 19, 2; *E* 1, 1, 12). The Roman ages for puberty were also recognized (*SP* 6, 16, 13). Although the *Partidas* (2, 15, 3) declared that a royal minority should end at twenty, an interpolation, intended to eliminate the need for a regency for Sancho, put it at sixteen.

The inferior status of women was stated emphatically: "The condition of a man is better than that of a woman in many things and in many ways" (*SP* 4, 23, 2). The word "woman" meant a virgin over twelve and all others beyond that age, whether virgins or not (*SP* 7, 33, 6). Women ordinarily were subject to their male relatives and seldom could act independently, though a single woman or a widow no longer under that authority might be able to do so. A woman could not marry without the consent of her parents or act as surety for certain contracts (*SP* 5, 12, 3). Her right to own and dispose of property depended on her marital status. Unless she was a queen or a countess, she could not sit as a judge, as it was unseemly for a woman to be in a crowd of men. However learned she might be, she could not serve as an advocate (*SP* 3, 4, 4; 3, 6, 3), though she might argue her own plea (*FR* 1, 10, 4).[8] The *Fuero real* (2, 8, 8) limited her testimony to "womanly matters," but the *Partidas* (3, 16, 17) allowed a woman of good reputation to testify in all cases except wills (*SP* 6, 1, 1). In certain cases she was excused from knowing the law (*SP* 5, 14, 29, 31; *E* 1, 1, 12).[9]

A person's place in society, which was hierarchical in nature, also determined the extent of his juridical capacity. By the beginning of the thirteenth century the theoretical division of society into three estates, the clergy, nobility, and workers, was well known. The clergy and members of religious orders, exempt from taxation and military service since Roman times and bound by the vow of celibacy, enjoyed the *privilegium fori* with their own law (*SP* 1, 6, 50) but were banned from many secular proceedings. They could not serve as advocates in civil cases other than their own or engage in commerce or practice medicine (*SP* 1, 6, 45–49). Although secular clergy could own or inherit property, monks and nuns, bound by a vow of poverty, could not.

Among the nobility, distinctions emerged between magnates, possessing great wealth, power, and influence, and the knights or petty nobility. Claiming the right to be judged by their peers, nobles were tried in the royal court, but could not be tortured or subjected to corporal punishment or confiscation if they were banished. In judicial proceedings greater weight was given to their testimony than that of others. They were also exempt from personal or property taxes. As their principal task was to defend the realm, knights were excused from other legal responsibilities and were not required to know the substance of the law (*E* 1, 1, 12). Magnates were entrusted with the principal public offices. Toward the close of the thirteenth century, the wealthier among them began to entail their estates (*mayorazgo*) for the benefit of their firstborn sons.[10]

Freemen could testify in court, make wills, and serve as advocates and judges. Most people lived in rural areas as farmers, laborers, or shepherds. Many were free proprietors, but others were tenants burdened by a variety of rents and labor services. Although their lords attempted to bind them to the soil, the *Partidas* affirmed their right to move freely, taking their movables with them. As a result of the commercial revolution, merchants and artisans lived as freemen in the towns. Early municipal *fueros* accorded juridical capacity to a resident (*vecino*) possessing a *casa poblada* in the town, a house in which he lived with his family. As such, residents were regarded equally before the law. Over time, however, the *caballeros villanos* formed an urban aristocracy that dominated municipal government. As a consequence, most ordinary freemen had little involvement in political affairs.[11]

The state of a person's health also impacted his legal standing. As the insane and mentally deficient were incapable of understanding complex legal issues and making rational decisions, they did not have juridical capacity (*SP* 7, 34, 4). A blind man, incapable of recognizing anyone by sight, could not act as a witness, but he could marry by signing his consent. A deaf mute could not serve as an advocate. Obviously, given their handicaps, none of these persons, as well as those who were chronically ill, could hold public office, sit as a judge, or act as a witness, advocate, or guardian (*SP* 3, 4, 4; 4, 2, 5; 5, 11, 2; 6, 1, 9, 13; 6, 16, 4, 14). As spendthrifts were deemed unfit to act responsibly, their property was entrusted to a curator, and they could not be witnesses, guardians, or advocates, or make a will (*SP* 3, 6, 2; 5, 11, 4–5; 6, 1, 13; 6, 16, 4).[12]

One's level of education and general culture was also a factor in assessing juridical capacity. Scholars trained in law held significant posts in public administration, served as counselors to the king, and helped to shape the Alfonsine Codes. During the early Middle Ages people were more or less considered equal before the law, and the *Fuero real* (1, 6, 1), acknowledging that principle, stated that the law was intended for everyone, men and women, the young and old, the wise and the not so wise, and urban and country dwellers. The *Partidas* (1, 1, 21), however, following the opinion of Roman jurists, declared that peasants or shepherds living in comparative isolation could not be expected to know the law (*E* 1, 1, 12). Nevertheless, over time, the principle that ignorance of the law is no excuse prevailed.[13]

Criminals, heretics, and non-Christians were denied the right to participate fully in civic life. A criminal who suffered mutilation or was declared infamous was deprived of legal standing (FR 3, 5–8, 11; SP 7, 6, 1–8). That was also true of a heretic (SP 7, 26, 1–6). Although Jews and Muslims were permitted to follow their own law, they did not have equal standing with Christians. They could not exercise authority over them or serve as witnesses against them, except in cases of treason (SP 7, 24–25).[14]

Foreigners enjoyed a full legal personality. Although pleas between foreigners could be adjudicated according to their laws (SP 3, 14, 15), they were otherwise subject to Castilian law (SP 1, 1, 15).[15] Aware that foreign merchants helped to enrich his kingdom, the king prohibited anyone to harm them or their property (SP 5, 7, 4–5; 5, 8, 26).[16] For the same reason, pilgrims journeying to Santiago de Compostela were especially deserving of care and protection (FR 4, 23, 1–4; SP 1, 24, 2–3). As a matter of diplomatic reciprocity, envoys from Muslim rulers had to be treated with respect and protected against injury (SP 7, 25, 9).

Juridical capacity, acquired a birth, normally ended with natural death (SP 7, 33, 12), but it might also be terminated by civil death, the result of a judicial sentence of imprisonment, exile, or infamy. Civil death was a legal fiction that abrogated one's rights under the law. Such a person was dead "insofar as honor, nobility, and the affairs of this world." Not only did he lose his authority over his children, but he could not make a will, and if he had done so it would not be valid (SP 4, 18, 2).[17]

Human Rights

Joaquín Cerdá Ruiz-Funes emphasized that in addition to juridical rights, people also enjoyed, in varying degrees, fundamental human rights, namely, personal freedom, security under the law and in one's household, freedom of association, freedom of thought, religious liberty, and the right to participate in government. None of those rights was absolute, as each was limited by the circumstances of one's life. References to them are scattered throughout the Alfonsine Codes rather than assembled in any declaration of human rights.[18]

The security of all the men of the realm was essential to an orderly society (SP 1, 6, 51). By restraining malefactors, the law enabled everyone, no matter his or her status, to live in justice and peace. All the people, both great and small, had to protect one another against injustice, error, violence, and injury. The king ought to suppress the proud and mighty and strengthen the weak and lowly so that all might dwell securely (SP 2, 10, 1–2).

Personal freedom was also of paramount importance. Endowed by nature with free will, men and women desire to be free to do as they wish, to go and come as they please, to live where they choose. However, in order to further the common good, the law restricted the individual's right to do as he liked. No one could intrude on another's person or property, and criminals were condemned. Social and economic circumstances—whether one was rich or poor, resident in town or country—also constrained personal freedom. By commending themselves to the protection and service of the more powerful, men compromised their freedom. Worst of all were slaves who were compelled to give unquestioning obedience to their masters. Nevertheless, the royal jurists, believing that the desire for freedom was inherent in human nature, declared that "all the laws of the world always fostered liberty" (*SP* 3, 5, 4). Moreover, judges were admonished to favor liberty as a rule of law, "because it is a friend of nature, which not only men, but all the other animals, love" (*SP* 7, 34, 1).

A man and his family should also be able to dwell securely in their own home (*SP* 3, 7, 3). The Visigothic Code and the municipal *fueros* enunciated that principle, and in 1188 Alfonso IX of León forbade anyone to violate another's home.[19] Just as everyone was guaranteed security in the royal household, so too nobles (*SP* 2, 18, 32), clerics (*SP* 1, 6, 51), scholars (*SP* 2, 31, 2), and merchants (*SP* 5, 7, 4), and by extension, ordinary families and their guests, were assured of the same right in their homes. As the home was expected to be a safe place, free of crime, a householder was forbidden to harbor counterfeiters, heretics, or arsonists (*SP* 7, 7, 10; 7, 10, 3; 7, 26, 5–6). A man should keep his house in good repair, making certain that it did not impinge on his neighbor's property or interfere with public structures or communal places (*SP* 3, 28, 4, 8, 18). The law did not speak of a house as a possible eyesore or threat to property values, but that surely was the intent.

The right of men to associate freely with whomever they wished was admitted under certain limitations. A freeman was generally free to marry or not, to enter a monastery or the priesthood, to become a knight, to elect a profession, or to participate in the business or agricultural communities. Over centuries men voluntarily chose to live together in villages and municipalities, both old and new, and many settled in the reconquered cities and towns of Andalucía and Murcia. Ordinarily no one was banned from doing so. However, just as the nobility were forbidden to take part in *asonadas*, which could be described as military riots, merchants and artisans could not form confraternities that attempted to fix wages and prices (*SP* 2, 31, 6; 5, 7, 2). On the other hand, the king encouraged the formation of mercantile companies (*SP* 3, 18, 78; 5, 10, pr., 1–17) and assured university scholars of protection against robbers and other criminals (*SP* 2, 1, 2, 6). In both instances he recognized their contribution to the economic and cultural prosperity of his realm.

A scholarly king also valued a man's right to follow his thoughts wherever they led him and to enunciate them clearly and truthfully. Human nature endowed man with the ability to think, to consider the facts before him, their past circumstances, and future possibilities, and then to make the decision that he deemed wisest (*SP* 2, 3, pr., 1–2). Thoughts were often expressed in words and could prompt action. For that reason, the king was advised to take counsel and weigh his words carefully before reaching a decision (*SP* 2, 4, 1–4). Knowing that words have consequences, he prized precision in thinking and speaking, as the many definitions of words in the *Partidas* make clear. Clarity of thought and expression was important in the business of government, but especially for all those involved in the administration of justice. Honest thinking and speech in everyday affairs also helped to foster peace and harmony (*SP* 2, 13, 9; 2, 23, 6). Although wicked thoughts might enter one's mind, they were punished only when acted upon (*SP* 7, 31, 2). Free speech did not permit one to deprecate others, and using derogatory language when speaking of the king could lead to the charge of treason (*FR* 4, 3, 1–2; *SP* 7, 9, pr., 1–2).

Religious liberty was accorded to Jews and Muslims inasmuch as they were permitted to worship freely, but they could not proselytize among Christians. However, they could convert to Christianity. As a general principle, Christians were denied religious liberty, because they were required by law to adhere to the teachings of the church. If they did not, they were condemned as heretics.

Nature and Natural Relationships

The royal jurists next turned attention to the obligation of men to their lords by reason of *naturaleza*, a word meaning naturalness or a natural relationship. The *Espéculo* (3, 4) noted that royal vassals were subordinated to the king and the kingdom by virtue of *naturaleza* and *sennorío*. *Sennorío* referred to his rulership and *naturaleza* to being a native of the realm. One might acquire *naturaleza* in several ways: by birth in the kingdom, inheritance, adoption, residence for two years or more, or emancipation. In contemporary language these were various means of being naturalized.

Naturaleza was a natural bond uniting men and inspiring them to love and care for one another so that they became one (or so the king hoped!).[20] Nature,[21] the force holding everything in the state ordained by God, differed from *naturaleza*, which sustains everything deriving from nature. The ancients recognized ten types of natural relationships: the ties between (1) men and their natural lord; (2) lords and vassals; (3) parents and children; (4) a knight and the one knighting him; (5) a husband and wife; (6) an heir and his benefactor; (7) a captive and his liberator, or between one saved from death or dishonor and his savior; (8) a freedman and his former master; (9) a convert and the one who brought him to the faith; and (10) a resident born elsewhere and the country in which he lived for ten years (*SP* 4, 24, pr., 1–2).[22]

These relationships entailed obligations. The greatest was the natural duty to love and fear God who created and sustained man and gave him hope of eternal life (*SP* 2, 2, 1–4). A man similarly was obliged to love, honor, and protect his parents who gave him birth and reared him, the nurses who nourished him, and the tutor who counseled and directed him. He ought to alleviate their needs, safeguard them from all harm, and never kill, wound, rob, or dishonor them (*SP* 4, 20, 1–4). Natives (*naturales*) of the realm were also bound by the debt of nature to love, honor, and protect their lord who favored, honored, and protected them. If need be, they should gladly suffer death for him. So too they ought to love and increase their country and die for it (*SP* 2, 25, 3). By observing everything that they rightfully owed to one another, natives and their lord would always maintain the natural bond between them. As that obligation arose from nature, it could only be rightfully terminated for four reasons: (1) treason by a native against his lord or country; (2) the lord's attempt to kill a native without just cause; (3) adultery by the lord with a native's wife; and (4) the lord's wrongful disinheritance of a native (*SP* 4, 24, 3–5). The word *desnaturar* described the rupture between a man and his lord or his country.

Georges Martin remarked that the word *natural*, meaning a native, born and raised in the kingdom, was used at least from the twelfth century onward. Natives owed allegiance to the king as their *señor natural*, a term employed early in the thirteenth century (*SP* 4, 24, 2). Although the laws quoted above refer to *sennores* in the plural, the royal jurists obviously were thinking of the king. His rulership, often cited as *sennorío*, was founded on his people's obligation of *naturaleza*, as the king noted in his privilege to the towns of Extremadura in 1264. Among the royal duties, two were especially important: first, to reward those who served him loyally, and second, to do well by them and to favor them, so that they might be more inclined to serve him in the future, even though they were obliged to do so by reason of *naturaleza* and *sennorío*.[23] In the codicil to his last will, Alfonso X directed his heir to carry out his wishes "because of the *sennorío natural* that we have over him through lineage and *naturaleza*."[24] As Martin noted, the king based his authority on dynastic and territorial considerations. *Naturaleza* was an obligation binding men to one another and subordinating them to the royal lordship by virtue of their being natives or naturalized residents of his realm.

Vassalage

The bond between lord and vassal entailed mutual rights and obligations that were elaborated in several anonymous collections of customary law.[25] Prominent among them were the Ordinance of Nájera, probably enacted by Alfonso VIII in the Curia of Nájera in 1185, and the *Fuero viejo* purportedly drafted by the nobility at the king's request after 1212.[26]

A lord, in return for giving his vassal a benefice, often a monetary stipend known as *soldadas*, could require certain services (*SP* 3, 18, 68). Money drawn on the royal treasury was called *tierra*; if it derived from the revenues of a town or castle, it was an *honor*. The royal jurists, perhaps because of the king's hope of securing a base in Lombardy to further his imperial aspirations, explained fiefs by drawing on the twelfth-century Lombard *Libri feudorum*.[27] However, Julio Valdeón commented that although many of the elements of northern European feudalism were present in Castile, they were never fully developed.[28] Therefore, we need not discuss the account of fief-holding in the *Partidas* (4, 26, 1–11).

There were five types of lordship: (1) the king's authority over his people, called *merum imperium*,[29] meaning the unfettered and absolute right to judge and command them; (2) a lord's ascendancy over his vassals; (3) his control over his estates; (4) a father's power over his children; and (5) a master's rule over his slaves (*SP* 4, pr., 1–2).

In northern Castile, custom recognized several other types of lordship dating from the early Middle Ages, namely, *devisa*, *solariego*, and *behetría*. While some free proprietors owned their own land, most men were tenants commended to the protection of powerful lords. *Devisa* was a lordship shared by *deviseros*, members of the same family entitled to provisions, lodging, and other benefits.[30] *Solariego* (*solar*, a settlement) described a tenancy held by a freeman who owed rent and services to his lord. He could leave whenever he wished, taking his movable goods, but he had no right to any improvements (*FV* 1, 7, 1–4). In these lands the king only claimed *moneda*, the tax collected in exchange for his promise not to alter the coinage. In earlier times, because of the availability of land, many freeholders could choose any lord and sever ties with him at any time while retaining their holdings. Because of their advantageous situation, they were known as *hombres de behetría* (lat. *benefactoria*, benefit). Like other tenants, they owed rents, labor services, and hospitality (*SP* 4, 25, 3). By the thirteenth century, whereas some peasants were still free to choose a lord from sea to sea (*behetría de mar a mar*), many more were bound in a hereditary relationship to their lord (*behetría de linaje*).[31]

By pledging homage to his lord a vassal became his man. He sealed that pledge by kissing his lord's hand and did so again when receiving knighthood or renouncing his vassalage. Magnates kissed the king's hand on ceremonial occasions. The most notable example occurred during the Curia of Carrión in 1188 when Alfonso IX of León received knighthood from Alfonso VIII of Castile and kissed his hand as a sign of vassalage.[32] A vassal had to love, honor, protect and serve his lord. Ordinarily he owed three-months' military service in return for his *soldadas*. The lord similarly had to love, honor, and protect his vassal. During the first year, a vassal could not leave the lord who knighted him, unless he tried to kill him, dishonor his wife, or deny him justice. Thereafter, he could leave for whatever reason, but he had to inform his lord personally or ask another to do so if he feared that his lord would kill or dishonor him. Whatever arms or horses a vassal received from his lord and whatever he gained thereby were his to keep; but if he left his lord, he had to return everything except his stipends. If he refused to do so, the lord could invoke the procedure of *riepto* and sue him. The lord was forbidden to harm or speak disparagingly of a vassal who left in the proper manner. After ending their relationship, neither man should attack the other. A vassal who refused to serve his lord could be compelled to pay double the amount of his stipend; conversely, a lord who failed to pay him would owe the same amount. A vassal who failed to attend the summons to war or to bring the required number of knights would lose whatever he held from the king. Although a vassal holding from a secondary lord was not required to become a vassal of his deceased lord's sons, he had to surrender whatever he had received from his lord. Magnates and other royal vassals, however, always had to renew their vassalage to the son of a dead king (*SP* 4, 25, 4–10; *FR* 3, 13, 1–7; *FV* 1, 3, 1–3).

The king could expel a vassal who incurred his wrath, for example, the Cid, banished by Alfonso VI.[33] If the vassal failed to dissuade him, he had to go into exile, but he could live off the land and wage war against the king for refusing to state why he was banished. Meanwhile, the king guaranteed the safety of the vassal's family and the families of his vassals who accompanied him. If he entered another king's service, his vassals had to return home within a month. However, those who chose to go to Muslim lands and aid "the enemies of the faith" would be charged with treason, and their families would also be exiled. A vassal who sought the king's pardon could return home, but he would have to pay double the value of whatever he stole (*SP* 4, 25, 10–13; *FV* 1, 4, 1–2).

The rupture between the king and his vassals during the Cortes of Burgos in 1272 exemplified those laws. Sending emissaries to inform the king that they repudiated their vassalage, the magnates asked for a month's grace to purchase necessities and arranged to surrender royal castles to his *porteros*. Lest they plunder the countryside, the king appointed men to guide them and provide them with lodgings on their journey to Granada. Nevertheless, they stole cattle, burned places, and violated churches. While trying to dissuade their vassals from accompanying them, the king chastised the magnates for their crimes and threatened to bring them to justice. While the magnates and their retainers, numbering about 1,200, took service with the emir of Granada, they continued to negotiate with Alfonso and returned home in the following year.[34]

Friendship

Friendship, which encourages men to love one another (Prv 18:24), was also a legal obligation (*SP* 4, 27, pr.).[35] In this first treatise on friendship in the Castilian language, the royal jurists followed Aristotle's teaching.[36] Although friendship developed when two persons loved one another, it was not identical with love, benevolence, or concord. Love, for example, might not be reciprocated, and one might regard benevolently a person one did not know, or live in harmony with another without loving him or being friends with him. True friends would have no need of courts or judges, because their friendship would prompt them to do what justice required. Friendship was advantageous to everyone. The rich and powerful needed friends to assist them in using their wealth to do good; others required friends to help them in their poverty and support them in time of danger. A child needed friends to rear him, a young person to guide him, and an old man to assist him in dealing with the frailties of age. A friend in whom one could confide conveyed a sense of serenity and security. Cicero warned, however, that one should be wary of flatterers who did not have one's best interest at heart.[37] There was no pestilence worse than having a false friend (Mi 7:5). Aristotle urged the value of taking time to develop a firm acquaintance before making someone a friend (*SP* 4, 27, 1–3).

Aristotle distinguished three types of friendship: (1) the natural friendship between parents and children, husbands and wives, and natives of the same country; (2) affection among friends of long standing; and (3) friendship based on the expectation of gaining some benefit from another. The latter was not true friendship because it might dissipate once the anticipated advantage was won. The custom of Spain recognized another kind of friendship, whereby the nobles pledged not to dishonor or harm one another, without first renouncing their friendship and issuing a challenge, as expressed in the title on challenges (*SP* 7, 3, 1–9). That topic is treated in chapter 13 (*SP* 4, 27, 4).

Three rules sustained friendship: (1) to be loyal always; (2) never to say anything that might cause a friend to be declared infamous; and (3) to strive as much for a friend's well-being as for one's own. Cicero commented that without the firm foundation of good faith, there could be no love between friends.[38] Aristotle observed that one should not believe anything malicious about a friend who had proved his loyalty over a long time.[39] The peril of disparaging a friend was highlighted purportedly in the book of Ecclesiasticus: "whoever dishonors his friend by word destroys his friendship with him."[40] Trust could be lost if a friend revealed his friend's secrets (Sir 7:16). After remarking that only a man motivated by ill will would insult his friend by throwing up to him past services, Cicero argued that a friend should share his good fortune or honors with his friends.[41] Stressing that there were no levels of friendship, St. Augustine declared that friends should always be equal (*SP* 4, 27, 4–5).

Friends ought to love one another truly and without deceit. Cicero likened to a commercial transaction the notion that a man should love his friend as much as his friend loved him or that he should love his friend as much as he loved himself. That could not be a perfect friendship. Yet, as there were few men willing to do things for a friend that they would not do for themselves, perfect friendships were rare. Although a man ought to protect his friend and even risk his life and property for him, he should not commit a crime for him.[42] Friendship might be terminated if someone disinherited his descendants, or became an enemy of his country, or turned to wicked ways. On the other hand, friendship should not be abandoned because of sickness, poverty, or misfortune. Indeed, adversity strengthened true friendship, while false friendship would collapse on its own account (*SP* 4, 27, 6–7).

At first glance this disquisition seems misplaced, but the royal jurists made the point that friendship was a legal obligation like vassalage and *naturaleza*. Without mentioning Justinian, they drew on the rich literature of antiquity, namely, Aristotle, Cicero, Solomon, the prophet Micah, and St. Augustine, so that this treatise has more of a literary than a legal character. The placement of this topic immediately following the discussion of vassalage was deliberate. The purpose was didactic and the pupils were the nobility, whose feuds destroyed lives and property. By encouraging them to think of each other as friends, the king hoped to restrain their penchant for violence and thus foster a more tranquil society. He also realized that if all his people took to heart the lessons of friendship, peace and harmony would prevail. Clearly, that ideal was difficult to achieve, but as Aristotle noted, true friends would try to live justly with one another so that courts and judges would be unnecessary.

Liberty and Servitude

The royal jurists, following Roman law, devoted the greater part of their discussion of the law of persons to those deprived of liberty. All creatures love liberty, "the power that every man naturally has to do whatever he wishes, provided that the force or right of law or *fuero* does not prevent him" (*SP* 4, 22, pr., 1).[43] By contrast, "servitude is the vilest and most despised thing among men because man, the noblest and freest creature among all the creatures made by God, is placed in the power of another who can do with him as he wishes." Divested of control over his person and property, a slave was subject to his master's command (*SP* 4, 5, pr.).

Although slavery existed in Roman and Visigothic Spain and the Muslim world,[44] the open frontier in the northern kingdoms enabled Christian slaves to gain their freedom. By the twelfth century their number had dwindled, but as the reconquest proceeded, frontier warfare became the major source of slaves. Men, women, and children on both sides, caught up in the throes of war, were seized as booty shared by the victors. Isolated from family and community, and laboring as personal servants or cultivating the fields, slaves were often treated harshly and sold or held for ransom. Ownership of slaves was visual evidence of one's wealth and standing.[45]

Servitude, according to the royal jurists, originated in ancient times when it was decided, contrary to natural reason, that freemen might be enslaved. Slaves were known as *siervos*, a word derived from *servare*, supposedly because the emperors resolved that captives should be preserved and used. Slaves might be enemies of the faith taken in war, children of female slaves, and freemen who sold themselves into slavery. The latter had to be at least twenty years old, know that they were free, willingly consent to the sale, and obtain part of the purchase price.[46] As slavery was determined by one's mother, anyone born to a female slave, although the father was free, would be a slave. If she was emancipated, her newborn child would be free and would remain free if she was enslaved again. The child of a free mother and a slave father would also be free. However, if a priest married a free woman, their child would be a slave of his church, forever bound to it, because church property could not be alienated. Although a slave child could inherit his mother's estate, but not his father's, whatever he received ulti-mately belonged to his master. Wicked Christians who abetted the Moors in war could be enslaved. A slave had to protect, honor, and obey his master and his family, and even give up his life for them, unless he was ill, imprisoned, or far away. A master should not kill or wound a recalcitrant slave, unless he discovered him with his wife or daughter. If a slave complained of his mas-ter's cruelty, a judge could sell the slave and give the money to the master. A slave's earnings and any inheritance that he received belonged to his master. Non-Christians could not own a Christian slave; one so owned could gain his freedom by declaring his desire to become a Christian. However, if he con-verted during three months while his owner was trying to sell him, he had to pay the owner twelve *maravedís* or give service as a freeman until the price was paid (*SP* 4, 21, 1–8). Slave owners, whether Jews, Muslims, or Christians, were surely loath to encourage conversions because they knew they would lose control of their slaves.

A slave could not obtain ownership of property by reason of long posses-sion, but he might accumulate a fund over time by keeping a shop belong-ing to his master or working as an artisan. Ultimately, however, all that he earned belonged to his master (*SP* 3, 29, 3). If a slave, on his master's direc-tion, purchased a certain property, believing in good faith that it belonged to the seller, the master could acquire ownership, unless he knew that the seller was not the owner and did not object at the time of the sale. If a slave sold his master's property without his consent, the sale would not be valid (*SP* 5, 5, 60).

Although their masters objected, slaves could be joined in a valid marriage recognized by the church. Marriage became more complicated when slaves married freemen or women or when they belonged to different masters. If a slave married a freewoman who was aware of his status, their marriage would be lawful, but otherwise not, unless, after discovering the truth, she consented. The union of a female slave and a freedman was valid only if they were Christians. Masters were forbidden to sell their married slaves separately. Should a master demand some service from his slave at the same time that the slave's wife asked him to fulfill his conjugal debt, he had to obey his master, unless the husband believed that she would commit adultery. If the couple could not cohabit because their individual masters lived in different regions, the church could require one of them to buy the other's slave. If he was unwilling, the church could arrange the sale in order to unite them. Should a slave wed a freewoman or a freeman marry a female slave in the presence of either one's master and he did not claim his slave, they gained their freedom. When a freeman or a freewoman unknowingly married a slave, the marriage would not be valid, unless, on learning the truth, he or she consented or had intercourse with the slave (*SP* 4, 2, 11). A slave claiming that he did not know that his wife was free could not part from her, but if she learned that he was a slave only after their wedding, she could leave him. A slave who inadvertently married another slave, assuming that she was free, could not terminate the marriage. If a freeman, believing that he was marrying a freewoman, mistakenly wed a slave, the union would not be valid, unless, after learning the truth, he gave his consent. Should her master claim her, her husband, after realizing that she was a slave, should not be intimate with her, lest, by acknowledging their marriage, he could not leave her. A marriage could not be annulled if a husband, wishing to be rid of his wife, became a slave, surely an act of desperation! Determined not to bring dishonor upon herself or her children, she could claim him and emancipate him (*SP* 4, 5, 1–4).

The day slaves were offered for sale was to be dreaded. The sale might be private or through an auction. Married slaves could not be sold apart from their spouses, but that may not always have been observed. If the seller deliberately failed to inform the buyer of a slave's defects or bad habits, he had to return the purchase price, take back the slave, and pay damages (*SP* 5, 5, 64; *FR* 3, 10, 12). As slaves were known to offend their masters, a seller could stipulate that a buyer remove the slave to another area; but if the buyer did not, the seller could recover possession or demand a penalty (*SP* 5, 5, 47).

For example, in 1266, Infante Manuel's representative purchased three *mamelukes* or slaves, a husband, wife, and daughter, for fifty-three gold *maravedís*, from a servant of the *comendador mayor* of Calatrava in Madrid, in accordance with the law concerning purchases. The seller warranted that the slaves were not stolen or illegally acquired and that he was legally competent to sell them and pledged his property to guarantee the sale.[47]

At times a freeman, burdened with debt or anxious to provide for his family, allowed himself to be sold into slavery. Although no one could sell a freeman, if he agreed to the sale he would be entitled to a share of the price, but if he changed his mind and returned the money he would regain his liberty. If he was sold against his will, the seller had to pay him one hundred *maravedís*, unless he was unaware that the man was free. A father faced with grave necessity could not sell or pledge his children or give them away (*FR* 3, 10, 8; *SP* 4, 21, 1). Anyone who knowingly sold a freeman against his will, or imprisoned him to sell him, or put him in the power of his enemies, would be executed. No one could sell another's slave without the owner's consent; if he did so, he had to return him and pay a fine (*FR* 4, 14, 1–2). A slave purchased with his own money would not become free because whatever he had belonged to his owner (*FR* 3, 10, 9–12).

While some slaves accepted their fate, others tried to escape. If anyone concealed a fugitive slave or facilitated his getaway, he had to return him and, as a penalty, give a slave of equivalent value. A householder who discovered that a slave had taken refuge in his house had to turn him over to the local *alcalde*. If a fugitive asserted that he was a freeman, he had to prove that in court. Anyone who encouraged the disobedience or immoral behavior of another's slave had to pay the owner twice the expense of the harm done (FR 4, 15, 1–7; SP 7, 14, 22–29).

In sum, slaves were entitled to basic maintenance: food and drink, clothing, a place to sleep, and fair treatment. They were permitted to marry and have children, who would inherit their status if their mother was a slave. They might receive an inheritance or acquire property, though ownership was vested in their master. Married slaves could not be sold separately. In addition to labor in the fields or in the household, some might be allowed to work as craftsmen or manage a shop; the more trustworthy were used as messengers. Lacking juridical capacity, a slave could not function as a judge, an advocate, or a *personero*, nor could he give testimony unless it concerned treason against the king or the kingdom. If he was asked to bear witness concerning accusations of adultery or heresy, he would be routinely tortured. Though he normally could not sue in court, he could do so if his master was abusive. Unable to endure the life of a slave, some fled in the hope of gaining their liberty, but the life of a fugitive was always perilous.

Manumission

A master could emancipate his slave in a public place, in his will or a charter, or he could command his descendants to do so.[48] Though a minor ordinarily could not free his slaves, one between seventeen and twenty, with his guardian's consent, could liberate his child by a female slave, his parents and siblings, his teacher, tutor, or nurse, or his other slaves. He could also do so if he had the same foster-mother as his slave, or if the slave saved him from death or defended his good name, or if he intended to appoint his slave, who had to be seventeen years of age, as his agent for nonjudicial affairs, or if he wished to marry a female slave within six months (SP 4, 22, 1).[49] Once emancipated, a slave acquired juridical capacity and the status of a freedman.

A charter of manumission had to have five witnesses. The chancery formula commented that although men were naturally free, some were enslaved on account of their wickedness. After declaring that Jesus Christ died to liberate men, the master expressed his intention to restore his slaves "to that freedom that they ought to have by natural law." He then granted the slave and his descendants the freedom enjoyed by any freeman. The formula referred to the title on emancipation in book 7 of the *Espéculo*, which is not extant (*E* 4, 12, 42). The *Partidas* provided a more detailed formula: Gonzalo Yua-ñez, in the presence of a scribe and witnesses, emancipated Muḥammad, his wife Aisha, and their children, giving them true freedom and releasing them and their property from his power. Henceforth they could appear in court, make contracts, agreements, and wills, and do whatever else freemen could do. As the price of freedom, Muḥammad paid Gonzalo one hundred gold *doblas* (*SP* 3, 18, 90). A slave who, in return for his liberty, refused to pay his master a promised sum of money could be compelled to do so (*SP* 5, 11, 6).

If a slave had two masters and one wished to emancipate him, he could buy his colleague's share for an appropriate price set by a judge. Should the second master obstinately refuse to accept the money, it would be deposited in a church, and the slave would be free. In four instances of exceptional service to the king a slave merited his freedom: notifying the king (1) that someone raped a virgin; (2) that someone engaged in counterfeiting; (3) that a military commander abandoned his post or that a knight deserted; or (4) that someone killed his master or committed treason against the king or his kingdom (*SP* 4, 22, 2–3).

Female slaves were often subjected to abuse by immoral masters who, effectively becoming their pimps, prostituted them. Declaring that the women should be free, the king ordered local judges to protect them so their masters could not enslave them again. A slave who, with his master's consent, married a freewoman became free, as did a female slave who married a freeman. If a slave, with his master's knowledge, received holy orders, he would be free; but a master who objected could repossess his slave up to the order of subdeacon. A priest or deacon remained free but had to pay his master his value at the time of his ordination, or give him another slave of comparable worth, or two in the case of a bishop. A slave who believed he was a freeman and lived publicly as such gained his freedom in ten years, if his master resided in the country, or in twenty years, if he lived elsewhere. A fugitive slave dwelling in Christian lands could be reclaimed within twenty years, but after thirty he would be free. However, if he fled to the land of the Moors and lived there as a freeman and then returned to Castile, his former master, having lost his right of ownership, could not enslave him again (*SP* 4, 22, 4–7; 7, 14, 23).

A slave given or sold to another on condition of emancipation on a certain day would become free even if his new owner neglected to liberate him. If no specific date was set, the slave would gain his freedom when his master died. A slave whose buyer promised to free him when he could would be free within two months. An obdurate slave sold with the stipulation that he never be freed could only obtain his liberty if he alerted his master to a plot against his life; or avenged his master's murderer or accused him in court; or if the purchaser used the slave's own money or that of his relatives to buy him (*SP* 5, 5, 45–46).

Though emancipated, a freedman did not enjoy the fullness of freedom. In all humility he was bound "to obey, love, and honor" his former master and his family for the gift of freedom. If his master became impoverished, he ought to relieve him as best he could. He should not sue, defame, or accuse him, except in a matter concerning the king, or if his master assaulted or offended him.[50] If a freedman accused his master of crime, defamed him, aided his enemies, refused to allay his poverty, or displayed ingratitude, the master could ask a judge to reduce him to his former estate. The master was entitled to his freedman's property if he died intestate, without direct heirs, or to a third of his estate worth two hundred gold *maravedís* if he made a will. The master and his descendants up to the fourth degree could lose that right if he neglected to succor a starving freedman or forbade him to marry or have children; if the slave was freed because of a good deed or was freed by the emperor or king; if the master was exiled forever; if he received something from the freedman in lieu of a share in his estate; if he required the freedman to perform a task after manumission; or if he released the freedman from all claims against him (*SP* 4, 22, 8–11).

La Fuerça del Estado de los Omes Se Departe en Muchas Maneras

One of Alfonso X's principal responsibilities was to assure each person of his fundamental rights. That process began by recognizing the legal standing or juridical capacity of every free man and woman born in the kingdom or resident there for several years. That meant that a person possessed certain rights and corresponding obligations under the law, such as the right to testify, to represent another in court, or to make a will. A person who reached his majority at age twenty-five was fully capable of taking legal action.

Nevertheless, not all were equal before the law. As the royal jurists explained, "la fuerça del estado de los omes se departe en muchas maneras" (the importance of the estate of men varies in many ways) (*SP* 4, 23, 2). Women were clearly inferior to men, children to parents or guardians, slaves to freemen, nonnobles to nobles, laity to clergy, and non-Christians to Christians. Standing at the head of a hierarchical society were the clergy, privileged with their own law, exempt from taxation and military service, but also excluded from secular offices and professions. As defenders of the realm, the nobility had a principal role in the king's council and in territorial administration. Exempt from direct taxation, they were entitled to be judged by their peers and were not subject to some of the cruder aspects of the judicial process; nor, because of their military responsibilities, were they expected to be acquainted with the niceties of the law. The majority of freemen dwelling in towns or rural villages also possessed the fundamental right to appear in court as plaintiffs, defendants, witnesses, advocates, *personeros*, and even judges. Peasants living in isolated areas, however, were not presumed to know the law. Slaves, of course, did not have juridical capacity.

In addition to social standing, other situations circumscribed a person's juridical capacity. The *paterfamilias* acted on behalf of the members of his family and his household, and the guardian of a minor child had to protect his legal rights. A spendthrift, or someone who was mentally disturbed or deficient, or blind, deaf and dumb, or chronically ill, could not personally exercise his rights. Criminals and heretics lacked all legal standing. Although Jews and Muslims could practice their religion and live in accordance with their own law, a kingdom that publicly proclaimed itself as Christian could not admit that they had legal equality with Christians. On the other hand, foreigners, many of whom were merchants or pilgrims, were assured of their security but had to obey the laws of the kingdom. The law also guaranteed a man's personal safety and the security of his household and his freedom to go and come as he pleased, to choose his companions, to entertain whatever thoughts came to his head, provided they did not lead him to commit a crime or indulge in heresy, and to take part in local government and represent it in the Cortes. When a person died, his juridical capacity died as well, but it might also be terminated by his civil death if he were condemned to imprisonment, exile, or infamy.

The most basic source of the rights and obligations described above was *naturaleza*, a comprehensive natural relationship embracing everyone born in the kingdom, the *naturales* or natives, and those resident there for many years. On that account, men were bound to God, the king, their families, and their fellow countrymen. *Naturaleza* required everyone to recognize the king as their natural lord and to submit to his authority. Vassalage was a more restricted relationship that compelled a lord's vassals to counsel him and serve him militarily. For their sustenance, he gave each one a benefice, usually a financial stipend, but that relationship might be terminated if either party neglected to fulfill his obligations. By emphasizing the significance of friendship, the king wished to remind his people, but especially the nobility, that friendly relationships were essential to the peace of the realm. With that in mind, the royal jurists also elucidated the rights and obligations of masters and slaves, the process of manumission, and the continuing relationship between freedmen and their former masters.

Throughout his law codes, Alfonso X stressed the necessity of promoting the common good. In order to achieve that purpose, he recognized that a proper balance between the rights and obligations of every person was essential. Thus, while the law acknowledged a diversity of rights and obligations, none were absolute; rather, all were subordinated to the task of maintaining a well-ordered society that would serve the best interests of everyone.

❧ CHAPTER 11

The Law of Property

Señorío es Poder que Ome ha en su Cosa de Fazer della e enella lo que Quisiere

At Alfonso X's accession, the Castilian economy was largely agricultural and pastoral, but trade and commerce, spurred by the general European revival, became increasingly vital. Consequently, the law of property, whether real or personal, movable or immovable, public or private, assumed great importance. The royal jurists, drawing on Roman law, considered ownership and possession and the acquisition and disposal of property in the *Third Partida*, and in the *Fifth*, contractual obligations.

Ownership and Possession

Ownership (*señorío*) and possession (*tenencia*) had fundamental significance (*E* 5, 8, 1–36; *SP* 3, 28–32). Landed property was classified as *realengo*, *abadengo*, and *solariego*. *Realengo* meant the inalienable royal domain: castles, villages, towns, landed estates, forests, tolls, tributes, salt pits, mines, and fisheries. Property held by ecclesiastical institutions was *abadengo*, and lands controlled by secular lords, *solariego*.

Simplifying the definition in the *Espéculo* (5, 8, 4), the *Third Partida* (3, 28, 1) explained that "señorío es poder que ome ha en su cosa de fazer della e enella lo que quisiere segund Dios e segund fuero" (ownership is the power that a man has over his property to do with it and in it whatever he wishes according to God and the law).[1] There were three forms of *señorío*: (1) the power of emperors and kings to punish evildoers and to render to everyone his right; (2) the power that one has over movable and immovable property transmissible to one's heirs; and (3) usufruct or rental of property for life or a fixed term, or over property held as a fief (*SP* 3, 28, 1). In the first instance, *señorío* refers to governmental authority or sovereignty. The other two concern ownership and possession.

In explaining the acquisition of property, the royal jurists relied heavily on Justinian's *Institutes* (2, 2, 1).[2] Natural elements such as air, rainwater, the sea, and its shores were common to all living creatures. Known as *res nullius*, they had no owner, but everyone could use them. Anything found on the shore below the high tide mark belonged to the finder. Fishermen and boatmen could also access river banks, even if someone owned the adjoining land. No one could impede free passage on a river.[3] Fountains, squares, marketplaces, roads, woodland, and pastures in municipal districts were reserved for common use. Income derived from them was used to repair walls and bridges, but customs duties, tolls, revenue from salt pits, fisheries, and iron mines, and other tributes were earmarked for the sustenance of emperors and kings, defense of the realm, and war against enemies of the faith (*E* 5, 8, 1–2; *SP* 3, 28, 1–11). Lest individual claims to water sources cause conflict, Infante Manuel stipulated in 1268 that water in his town of Elche should be held in common by the town council.[4] In disputes over the water supply in California and Texas, lawyers and courts referred to the *Partidas* for guidance.[5]

Churches and cemeteries were sacred spaces administered but not owned by the clergy and could not be alienated except in accordance with the *First Partida* (1, 14). No one, without royal authorization, could disinter a body, other than that of one who had committed treason. Relics and religious objects could only be sold according to the terms set down in the sixth book of the *Espéculo*, which is not extant. City walls and gates were also holy, and no one should ever try to enter a city by climbing over the walls (*E* 5, 8, 3; *SP* 3, 28, 12–16). Legend had it that Romulus, after killing his brother Remus who jumped over the half-finished walls of Rome, vowed to kill anyone else who did so.[6]

The royal jurists spoke at some length about the ownership of human beings, animals, birds, and fish. Although human beings were naturally free and could not be bought or sold, a captive could be reduced to slavery or held for ransom. However, if he escaped to his own country, his captor lost his right of ownership. A man would lose ownership of wild beasts, bees, peacocks, and other tamed animals that escaped out of sight, but ordinary fowl were always considered his. The owner of cows, ewes, and mares also owned their offspring. He could recover fruit that had fallen from his trees into a neighbor's property, but he could not hunt there without permission. In rural areas, peasants hunted small game for food, but for the king and the nobles hunting was often a sport. The vagaries of rivers and streams at times altered the landscape in one's favor or disfavor. Alluvial deposits fell to the man holding the land on which they were made. Islands in the midst of a river should be divided between the landowners on each side, but a man would not lose his property if a river created an island in it or if it were entirely covered by water. If an island arose in the sea (a rare occurrence) it would belong to the one who colonized it (*E* 5, 8, 3, 5–10; *SP* 3, 28, 17–33).[7]

Ownership of raw materials to make something new depended on whether the materials could be replaced and were used honestly. A man who, in good faith, used another's grapes or olives to make wine or oil would own the finished product but should compensate the original owner. If the material was imperishable, the one using it had no right of ownership. A book written on parchment or a painting on a board, for example, belonged to the owner of the material used, but he owed the writer or painter a fair price. Similarly, stone or wood used in a building belonged to the building's owner and not to the builder. Ownership of treasure or abandoned property was vested in the finder, though the king was entitled to half of any "very large" treasure—a vague term indeed (*E* 5, 8, 11–19; *SP* 3, 28, 34–50).[8]

Prescription was the right of ownership acquired by a man who, for a long time, without interruption, lawfully possessed property belonging to another. If he acted in good faith and the property was not stolen, he might gain ownership of movable property after holding it continuously for three years, or thirty years for immovable property. Nevertheless, property belonging to minors, married women, soldiers on military service, captives, pilgrims, and students was protected from loss in this way. Royal property was never subject to prescription, and church property was also sheltered, though immovable property owned by the church could be lost after forty years.[9] Prescription did not confer on anyone the right to administer justice without royal consent, or ownership of the communal property of cities and towns. Ownership of animals, ships, or revenues pertaining to a city, however, could be acquired after possession over forty years. A freeman held as a slave, no matter how many years, could never lose his status, but a slave living openly as a freeman for thirty years and a fugitive remaining free for fifty years could not be enslaved again. A debt not collected within thirty years was canceled (*E* 5, 8, 21; *SP* 3, 29, 1–30; *FR* 2, 11, 1–10).

Possession was the effective occupancy of physical property.[10] Even if a man only occasionally resided on his property, he retained possession, provided that he did not abandon it. Workmen using another's property did not have a right of possession. One could lose possession of real estate through abandonment, expulsion, seizure by another person, floods, or other natural disasters. Moreover, neighbors might demolish a collapsing house if the occupant refused to repair it. If movable objects, birds, and animals were lost, a man retained possession if he continued to search for them (*E* 5, 8, 22–27; *SP* 3, 30, 1–18).

An easement or servitude allowed one to use another's land or buildings, without owning or possessing them.[11] For example, adjacent buildings might share gutters and supporting pillars and their height might be restricted so as not to impede the view or obstruct the light. A rural easement might be the right of way, or use of water from another's irrigation channel, well, pond, or spring. A right of way had to be at least eight feet wide and where the road curved, seventeen feet, so that carts could pass. An easement remained in effect, even if the owner sold his property. An easement could not be placed on sacred property or municipal communal locations. Usufruct was an easement enabling someone to live in an owner's house or land or use his animals or slaves and to reap the profits. The usufructuary had to maintain the property but would lose it if he did not use it over ten years. He could never acquire ownership or possession, and his right ended when the owner died. Usufruct of buildings or lands given to a city or municipality was limited to a hundred years (*SP* 3, 31, 1–27).[12]

The construction of new buildings oftentimes stirred opposition, as it does now. If a new structure intruded on another's property or easements, the possessor could demand that the work be stopped. Essential repairs could not be halted, but if a building was in danger of collapse, a judge could order it to be demolished. He could also require that weak walls be strengthened and trees in danger of falling be cut down. No one could impede passage through the streets or a communal area by erecting a building. There should be at least fifteen feet between a building and the walls of a castle or a town. Nor should one build a house or shop next to a church, unless it was devoted to the works of mercy.[13] As the king was ultimately responsible for maintaining castles, city walls, walkways, bridges, and gutters, he should appoint capable persons to oversee them (*SP* 3, 32, 1–26).

Contractual Obligations

Next, the royal jurists, first in the *Fuero real*, and then at greater length in the *Fifth Partida*, discussed an array of contracts or legal obligations binding both parties, namely, loans, deposits, donations, purchases, exchanges, leases, sureties, pledges, and partnerships. The influence of Roman law and the thirteenth-century glossators is evident throughout. The *Espéculo* examined some of these topics in the missing eighth book.[14]

There were two kinds of loans, namely, the *empréstito* (lat. *mutuum*) and the *préstamo* (lat. *commodatum*) (*SP* 5, 1, 1).[15] The first was a consumptive loan of something that could be counted, weighed, or measured, and required the borrower to return to the lender something of comparable worth at a specified time and place. Everyone could borrow, and all had to repay loans made by their subordinates. The borrower was also responsible for the loss of property loaned and would suffer the penalty agreed upon if he neglected to repay the loan at the appointed time (*SP* 5, 1, 1–10; *FR* 3, 16, 1).[16] For example, in 1268 Bishop Pedro Lorenzo of Cuenca and several Spanish scholars at the University of Bologna promised to repay Bartolomeo Ammanati for the loan of 1,725 Pisan *libras parvas*. Two years later, Archbishop Sancho II of Toledo directed Arnau de Ebrau to pay a debt owed to Sienese merchants at Montpellier. He also promised to compensate Arnau for various services at the fair of Brihuega at All Saints' next. Peter Linehan indicated other instances when Spanish prelates borrowed money from Italian bankers.[17]

The most notable instance of an *empréstito* was the loan solicited by Fernando III from twenty-two Galician towns in 1248 for the siege of Seville.[18] Six men from every parish were chosen to assess everyone's property. As the rate of payment was 5 percent, anyone with holdings worth one thousand *maravedís* would lend fifty; worth five hundred *maravedís*, twenty-five; and worth three hundred *maravedís*, fifteen. Anything less than that was exempt. The king, asserting his need and not any right, promised to repay the loan when he next collected *moneda forera*. Alfonso X's assurance to Burgos in 1255 and to other towns in 1255–56 that he would never require an *empréstito* against their will suggests that he had already done so.[19] His demand, in 1258, that Oviedo, and perhaps other northern towns, give him an *empréstito* of twelve hundred *maravedís* to maintain his fleet indicates that he continued this practice.[20] In the chancery formula for an *empréstito* Garcí Pérez testified that he borrowed twenty *maravedís* from Gonzalo Vicente and, binding himself, his property, and his heirs, promised repayment within six months on penalty of paying double the amount. He authorized Gonzalo to sue him if he did not repay it on the designated date and place (*SP* 3, 18, 70; *E* 4, 12, 37).

The *préstamo* was the loan of an animal, a slave, or an object for a certain time, without expectation of recompense. If the lender failed to mention any defect, he would be liable for any loss incurred by the borrower. The latter was obliged to take care of the property and return it when asked. Should he lose it through no fault of his own, he would not have to pay for it, unless he placed it at risk. If, after reimbursing the owner, he found it, he could keep it. He had to pay the lender's expense in suing for recovery if it was not returned on time (*SP* 5, 2, 1–9; *FR* 3, 16, 2–6).[21] The chancery formula for a *préstamo* stated that Sancho received from Rodrigo a mule of a certain color valued at seventy *maravedís* to be ridden or driven with a load to a certain place. Within one month Sancho had to return it or its appraised value and to compensate any injury or loss. If he failed to return it on time, he would be penalized double the assessed amount (*SP* 3, 18, 71).

In 1254 the king gave the village of Caspuenes to his brother Sancho I, archbishop of Toledo, as a *préstamo* for life, but if Sancho received a higher ecclesiastical dignity, Caspuenes would revert to the king. When María Gutiérrez complained in 1277 that Alfonso Téllez promised to pay a debt owed to her father from his holdings in Córdoba, now in possession of the cathedral chapter, the king directed the chapter to pay her.[22]

The imposition of penalties for late payment of loans was a common device for evading the church's prohibition of interest or usury. Both parties knew that a penalty clause was interest in disguise.[23] In 1272, for example, three citizens of Burgos promised to pay the cathedral chapter 1,520 *maravedís*, half at Christmas, and the other half at Easter; but if they did not, they would be penalized ten *maravedís* for each day overdue. Three years later three clerics agreed to a daily penalty of four *maravedís* if they failed to repay loans of four thousand *maravedís* on the same feast days. Nicolás de Mazuela also pledged to pay a debt of 350 *maravedís* to the chapter of Burgos, with a daily penalty of two *maravedís*.[24] A borrower was not obliged to pay a penalty demanded by a known usurer, as any agreement involving the fraud of usury was not binding (*SP* 5, 11, 40). The right of Jews to lend money at interest was casually acknowledged and will be discussed in the following chapter (*SP* 5, 12, 22).

A deposit (*condesijo*) was a transaction whereby someone entrusted an object to another person or institution for safekeeping. Other than expenses incurred, the custodian received no compensation. He had to return the object when asked, but if he refused, he had to pay double its value and would be declared infamous. If he lost it, he would have to pay for it, but ordinarily not if the loss was accidental. However, he should not return a weapon to an insane owner who might use it to harm someone. If the object was stolen, he should retain it until true ownership was proved (*SP* 5, 3, 1–10; *FR* 3, 15, 1–11).[25] A chancery formula recorded that Velasco deposited one thousand gold *maravedís* with Domingo who promised to return them when asked (*SP* 3, 18, 72). In 1252, Fernando III's widow, Jeanne of Ponthieu, deposited twenty-six royal privileges for safekeeping with the Order of Cala-trava.[26] Infante Enrique also consigned to Calatrava Fernando III's privileges concerning Morón and Jerez, but in 1253 Alfonso X demanded their surren-der and destroyed them.[27]

A freeman over twenty-five could make a donation, but one made under compulsion was invalid.[28] Those who could not make a donation included an insane person, a spendthrift, a man forbidden by a judge to dispose of his property, anyone plotting to kill or injure the king or his counselors or divide his kingdom, a heretic, or a convicted criminal. A son subject to his father's or grandfather's authority could only make a donation with his con-sent, unless he wished to dispose of property gained by military service in accord with the Roman law relating to *peculium castrense*.[29] A man who would be impoverished by promising to make a donation would not have to do so. If a childless man donated any of his property and then married and had legitimate children, his initial donation would be nullified (*SP* 5, 4, 1–8; *FR* 3, 12, 1–11; *FJ* 5, 2, 1–7). The chancery formula required the donor to state that either for life or for a limited time, he willingly donated a house or other property, with its entrances, exits, and appurtenances, to be held by the recipient *por iuro de heredad*, that is, in full ownership with the right to bequeath it to his heirs (*E* 4, 12, 38; *SP* 3, 18, 67).

A donation by an emperor or king, whether written or not, was always valid, but sovereign rights, such as coinage and criminal justice, were never conceded. Donations could be made to ransom captives, rebuild churches or houses, or as a dowry or marriage gift. A gift worth more than five hundred gold *maravedís* to a church, monastery, or hospital should be reported to the local judge.[30] A donation could be revoked if the recipient verbally dishon-ored the donor, accused him of a crime punishable by death or loss of limb, caused him to be declared infamous, damaged his property, attacked him, or tried to kill him. An infirm donor in fear of death could rescind a donation if he recovered or changed his mind, or if the donee predeceased him (*SP* 5, 4, 9–11; *FR* 3, 12, 7).

In repopulating Andalucía, Alfonso X made numerous donations of heri-table estates. Ordinarily he identified the property by its Arabic name or the name of the previous Muslim owner and often assigned a new one. He men-tioned the entrances, exits, woods, streams, pastures, vineyards, and bound-aries of a village or a town. If the donation included an oil press, he reserved a thirtieth of production for himself. When he granted Seville several water-mills, he stipulated that the flow of water through the pipes into the kitchens and gardens of the royal *alcázar* should be uninterrupted.[31] In 1255, when granting several villages to Burgos, he reserved his rights and revenues. The royal *merino* would administer justice in the villages while municipal *alcaldes* whom he appointed would judge townspeople according to the municipal *fuero*. No familiar or officeholder in a religious order was permitted to hold a public office or be involved in the city's affairs.[32] Ceding several villages to the archdiocese of Seville in 1260, he similarly reserved the right to make war and peace, coin money, collect *moneda forera*, and administer justice. The royal *adelantado* could enter the villages, and the municipal *alcaldes* could hear appeals from the archiepiscopal court. A final appeal could be directed to the king himself.[33] Letters of grace were a form of donation whereby the king rewarded a special service or recognized a recipient's outstanding qualities (*SP* 3, 18, 49–51). For instance, in 1256 he gave his brother Archbishop Sancho I of Toledo six thousand *maravedís* annually.[34]

Buying and selling personal and real property was known in Roman law as *emptio venditio* or *compraventa* in Castilian.[35] A sale was a contract whereby an owner transferred ownership of movable or immovable property for a fixed price to a purchaser. No one, other than a man who abused his slave, could be compelled to sell his property. As guardians were forbidden to purchase property belonging to their charges, so also royal officials could not acquire property in districts under their jurisdiction. A written bill of sale should name the seller, the purchaser, the asset being sold, and the price and should be witnessed. A buyer who made a down payment and then changed his mind or failed to pay the price on time would lose his money; a seller who reneged on the sale would have to return twice the amount (*FR* 3, 10, 2–3, 15). One could also sell futures, for example, the future yield of a crop, the offspring of a pregnant slave or animal, or the profits of an expected inheritance. One could not sell a free man, a sacred thing, a public place, rivers, or fountains. The sale of toxic substances was forbidden, but a poisonous drug such as scammony, which could be neutralized by mixing it with other ingredients, could be sold for medicinal purposes. No one should sell weapons to enemies of the faith, or another's property, or fraudulently substitute one property for another. The sale of a house included all its essential parts, though the seller retained movable goods, livestock, wine and oil presses, and wine cellars, unless they were specifically included in the sale (*SP* 5, 5, 1–31; *FR* 3, 10, 8–9). The buyer only acquired ownership after paying the full purchase price (*E* 5, 8, 20; *SP* 3, 28, 46).[36] When repopulating Seville and Murcia, Alfonso X authorized Christians to purchase lands from the Moors.[37]

The chancery formula for a bill of sale required the seller to identify himself, the purchaser, the property sold, its location, boundaries, entrances, exits, and appurtenances. The scribe recorded that the price was just and that the transaction was properly witnessed. Yielding his rights and transferring possession to the buyer, the seller declared that he had not sold the property to anyone else; nor had he given it in pledge or encumbered it in any way (*SP* 3, 18, 56; *E* 4, 12, 35). Bills of sale of holdings in Seville followed the chancery formula.[38] Among them was the sale of an orchard in Seville by Jacobo de las leyes in 1274.[39] Other forms had to be used by sureties guaranteeing a sale, by a wife consenting to a sale by her husband, for sales by a minor or his guardian, a *personero* representing a client, or the executor of a deceased person, or by a church or monastery (*SP* 3, 18, 56–65).

Once a sale was finalized, the buyer, though not yet in possession of the property, was entitled to any increase in value, but provided that the seller was not responsible, he also had to absorb losses. Should the value of goods sold in bulk and on sight increase or decrease, he would reap the benefit or suffer the loss. The seller guaranteed the integrity of the property being sold, but if it deteriorated while in his possession he had to bear the cost. If he neglected to notify the buyer of an encumbrance, or a slave's defect, or an animal's unpleasant trait, disease, or blemish, he had to return the purchase price and compensate the buyer. If a third party claimed ownership of the property being sold, the seller had to make good the loss if a court nullified the sale. When a seller agreed to sell for a certain price but received a better offer, he had to allow the original buyer to meet the higher price. If property given as security was not redeemed on the assigned date, the surety could purchase it. The seller could recover property sold by refunding the sale price (*SP* 5, 5, 23–27, 32–43; *FR* 3, 10, 7).

A buyer or an agent using his own money could purchase property on behalf of another but had to deliver it to him. A buyer could retain property purchased with another's money, except a knight in royal service, a minor, a church or prelate, or a husband using part of his wife's dowry with her consent. When property was sold to two men on different occasions, the one taking possession could keep it, but the seller had to refund the purchase price to the buyer who lost out. If the king sold or donated someone else's property, the owner should be reimbursed for the appraised value. A fraudulent sale should be nullified and the purchase price returned. For example, a seller might deceive a buyer by selling the expected issue of a female slave or an animal known to be sterile, or the yield of a vineyard that he knew would not bear fruit, or a building that he knew had been torn down, or trees that were uprooted. A sale could also be canceled if the seller falsely alleged that he was compelled to sell his property at less than its true value, or if the buyer failed to fulfill his side of the bargain, or if a taxpayer secretly sold his property so as to evade payment of taxes, or if a slave sold his deceased master's property (*SP* 5, 5, 48–67; *FR* 3, 10, 5–6, 13–14, 16).

Teofilo Ruiz pointed out that most of the documentation relating to real estate transactions in northern Castile comes from ecclesiastical institutions. The property sold was usually a freehold. Sellers were individual laymen, married couples, widows with children, or brothers and sisters. The boundaries of fields, vineyards, and orchards were usually recorded, but the extent of the property was seldom specified. The cost is no guide as to size, as the price might vary depending on quality or location.[40] Purchases and sales made by the monastery of San Salvador de Oña and the bishopric of Burgos follow that pattern. Plots of indeterminate size, wheat fields, vineyards, pastures, woodlands, springs, and mills were sold for varying amounts. Boundaries were specified, and the seller confirmed that he had received the entire purchase price and transferred all rights to the purchaser. Violation of the agreement was fined double the amount of the sale price.[41]

The exchange of an animal or an object for another was known as *permutatio* in Roman law (*FR* 3, 11, 1–5). A contract for an exchange, whether verbal or written, required the consent of both parties and was bound by the same rules as a sale.[42] The chancery formula required each person to declare that he lawfully possessed the property he wished to exchange and to specify its boundaries and appurtenances (*SP* 3, 18, 66; *E* 4, 12, 36). Also similar to an exchange were the four kinds of *contractus innominati* or unnamed contracts, each requiring certain actions (*SP* 5, 6, 1–5).[43] In 1257, for example, the king induced the bishop and chapter of Cuenca, in exchange for three salt pits, to abandon a toll on transhumant sheep. A year later, he gave Córdoba the fortress of Cabra in exchange for Poley, known later as Aguilar de la Frontera.[44] The monks of San Salvador de Oña also participated in several exchanges of meadows, wheat fields, and other lands.[45]

In discussing the hiring of services or rental of property, the royal jurists explained the Roman process of *locatio conductio* (location conduction in modern law), whereby a *locator* hired a *conductor* to perform a service or pay rent.[46] A chancery formula stated that Pedro Martínez pledged to copy a book for the dean of Toledo for thirty *maravedís*, and not to copy another book until he finished this one. In another formula Remón rented Guillén a pair of mules worth one hundred *maravedís* to carry a load to a certain place within a certain time. In addition to paying a monthly charge, Guillén would feed them and return them or their equivalent value at the appointed time and place (*SP* 3, 18, 75–76).

Among other instances of contracted services were these. If a judge, a royal official, or a master of sciences receiving an annual salary died during the year, his heirs were entitled to his full stipend because his work was interrupted involuntarily. However, an advocate who failed to complete his client's suit would not receive his fee; if he died during the proceedings, his heirs would receive only a portion of his fee. Artisans, physicians, surgeons, farriers, and others were accountable for mistakes caused by negligence or lack of knowledge. Teachers or master craftsmen who accidentally killed or maimed their students or apprentices had to compensate the victims' families. Owners had to be reimbursed by dyers who damaged cloth, or by men who rented leaky casks or knowingly rented contaminated pasturage. Careless shepherds were responsible for lost or injured sheep, as builders were for performing shoddy workmanship. However, if the owner falsely alleged that the structure was ill made, a judge could compel him to pay the builder what he owed (SP 5, 8, 9–17).

An inattentive renter who lost goods being transported had to make good the loss. If a slave or animal died, or a ship was destroyed by a storm, or a house burned down, or a mill was swept away by a flood, the renter would not be accountable unless he was at fault. However, he would have to pay damages if he promised to do so in his rental agreement, or if he delayed returning the property and it was damaged, or if he caused an accident. A man who rented a warehouse would not be responsible for loss of a product stored there unless he promised to care for it or if he were negligent. Innkeepers and sailors had to safeguard the property of pilgrims and travelers and could be charged for any loss or theft, unless they previously disclaimed responsibility (SP 5, 8, 8, 25–29).

Anyone who could buy and sell real estate could also rent it, but knights and royal officials ought not to rent lands from others because that would interfere with their service to the king. Rental contracts made in accordance with "the laws of this our book" might be for a limited time or for life and could be continued by the heirs of both parties. Usually rent was payable either at the beginning of the lease or at the end of the year. A tenant who was in arrears or neglected to take proper care of a house or allowed unsavory men or women to use it could be evicted. If the owner needed a place to live, or if the rented house was collapsing, he could evict an honest tenant but had to provide him with another dwelling. If the owner sold the house before the lease expired, the buyer could evict the tenant, unless the owner permitted him to remain until expiration of the lease or granted him a perpetual lease. A tenant in possession for three days after the end of the lease had to pay an additional year's rent. Just as the tenant was liable for damages, so the owner had to reimburse the tenant for improvements (SP 5, 8, 1–7, 18–24; FR 3, 17, 1–9; FV 4, 3, 1–5).

The contract known as *emphyteusis* differed from a sale or ordinary lease.[47] It was a long-term lease either for the life of the lessee and his descendants or for a fixed term. Although the lessee paid an annual rent to the lessor who retained ownership, the lessee could sell, alienate, or give the property as security or transmit it to his heirs. If he wished to sell it, he should offer it first to the owner. That seems to undercut the owner's right of ownership, but if he did not buy it back he could not prevent its sale to a new lessee. The owner would be responsible for damage caused by a natural disaster, and the lessee would not have to pay rent unless an eighth of the property remained. The owner would recover possession if the lessee died without heirs or failed to pay rent for three years or if the lease expired (*SP* 5, 8, 28–29).

In the first of three rental formulas, Abbot *Fulan* (So-and-So)[48] and his monks rented a house with all its appurtenances to *Fulan* (So-and-So) and his descendants to the third generation, subject to an annual quitrent of so many *maravedís*. If the tenant wished to sell the property, he had to inform the abbot, who would give the new occupant the keys in return for a pound of wax or a gold *meaja*, a coin worth about half a *maravedí*. The second formula stated that Gonzalo rented houses to Pedro for one year beginning at Michaelmas for thirty *maravedís*, half payable at the outset and the remainder at the end of the year. In another instance, Álvaro rented a vineyard to Diego for one hundred *maravedís* and a pair of capons at Michaelmas (*SP* 3, 18, 69, 73–74).

As examples of the process, in 1251 the monks of Oña rented a house to Pedro López for life at an annual rent of twenty-nine *maravedís* payable at Martinmas. He had to maintain it and was forbidden to sell, lease, or transfer it. The monastery would own any willow or elm trees that he planted. If he lost half the yield or more due to hail, snow, or drought, and could not pay the rent, the monks would provide help with the harvest, to be divided equally between them. Three years later they leased land for life to Miguel Domínguez, who agreed to pay four *maravedís* at Easter for the first two years and thereafter six *maravedís*. He was required to build good houses and dwell there and to fulfill other obligations as set forth in the previous document. The monks also rented houses, wheat fields, vineyards, and mills, usually for life, for money or bushels of wheat or barley, or even wax, payable in March or on the Assumption or Martinmas.[49]

The diverse forms of contract recognized by Roman law included stipulations, or verbal promises to perform a certain act or to observe certain conditions.[50] The language had to be precise, lest there be any confusion. Those who could not make a binding promise included a deaf mute, a wastrel, an insane or retarded person, a child under seven, a ward between seven and fourteen, and a minor under twenty-five without his guardian's consent; but a minor between fourteen and twenty-five lacking a guardian could do so. Neither a father nor a son could compel the other to satisfy a promise, except with respect to the son's profits from military service.[51] One could not make a promise in the name of someone over whom one had no control, but a *personero* could do so in the name of his principal. Promises were of three kinds: (1) a simple promise to give something to another or to perform a service; (2) a promise to be carried out on a certain day; and (3) a conditional promise. The parties had to be present, the object had to be clearly identified, and the schedule for completion and any conditions spelled out. Should one making a promise die before executing it, his heirs had to fulfill it. If an animal died or was injured, the one promising it would not have to pay for it unless the event occurred after the agreed date of delivery. One could promise the fruit of a vineyard or the child of a female slave, but not something that would never exist or a service that could never be performed. One could not promise sacred property or the enslavement of a freeman. A Jew or a Muslim could promise a Christian slave to another Christian, but a Christian could not promise to enslave another Christian. A promise made under duress or not to prosecute a criminal was invalid. The parties could not promise to inherit each other's estate lest that encourage one to cause the other's death. A promise to kill someone, to commit a crime, or to collect usury could not be enforced. For example, a promise to pay thirty or forty *maravedís* for a loan of twenty (a rate of interest of 50 percent to 100 percent) was usurious and would be invalid. Penalties might be imposed for failure to fulfill a promise, unless a legal impediment such as illness or a flood prevented it (*SP* 5, 11, 1–40).

Fulfillment of Contracts

As assurance that a contract would be fulfilled, one might name a surety or trustee (*fiador*; lat. *fidejussor*).[52] If his principal defaulted, the surety's person and property would be at risk, as chancery formulas stated (*SP* 3, 18, 57, 70). Barred from acting as sureties were knights in royal service, bishops, clergy, monks, slaves, minors, and women "because it is not proper for women to be involved in litigation" and "to go to places where many men gather and to do things contrary to chastity or the good customs that women ought to observe" (*SP* 5 12, 2). Though exempt because of her natural simplicity and weakness, a woman could act as surety for money paid for freeing a slave, for a dowry, when she renounced her right not to serve as surety, when she was assumed to be the principal for whom she acted as surety, when she was paid to be a surety, when, by dressing as a man, she deceived others into believing that she was a surety, when she was surety for her own acts, and as surety for another whose property she would inherit. A minor and his surety who were defrauded would not be accountable for any sum involved (*SP* 5, 12, 1–4; *FR* 3, 18, 6; *FV* 3, 6, 1–7).

There were two kinds of suretyship: an obligation according to law and nature, whereby one, though unwilling, could be compelled to fulfill a contract;[53] and a natural obligation that a human being should carry out, but which could not be enforced in court. A surety's obligation might be conditional or limited in time. If a debtor defaulted, his surety could be sued for the amount owed. The surety could be released from his obligation if his principal failed to pay his debt on time or wasted his property. A surety who, as promised, neglected to produce in court a person accused of an offense incurred a penalty. A surety's heirs inherited his responsibility. Several obligations were similar to suretyship. For example, a man, whether orally or in writing, might order another to perform an act on a specific day or under certain conditions. Somewhat different was an obligation willingly assumed. For example, friends might take care of an absent owner's property; if so, he should cover their expenses. An abandoned child, when grown, was not obliged to reimburse a man who reared him, but he should honor him for the rest of his life. However, a mother, grandmother, or stepfather could recover expenses for caring for their children (*SP* 5, 12, 5–37; *FR* 3, 18, 1–14).

A surety guaranteeing a sale was described variously as "fiador de sanar e de redrar a fuero de la tierra," "fiador de redrar e de otorgar a fuero de tierra," "fiador de riedra," "fiador de anno e dia," or "fiador por siempre." Those phrases might be translated as "surety to make good and confirm [the sale] according to the *fuero* of the land," "surety to confirm and grant [the sale] according to the *fuero* of the land," "surety for a year and a day," "surety forever."[54] Aside from the last two phrases, no time limit was imposed. In 1254, for example, when the monks of Oña purchased a plot, two sureties assumed responsibility, one in general terms and the other for a year and a day. Three years later Roy Díaz sold a mill to the monastery for one hundred *maravedís*, payable in two installments on All Saints' Day and 1 March, and named two sureties, one for a year and day and the other forever.[55]

Whereas a surety personally guaranteed a certain action, a pledge (*peño*, lat. *pignus*) was movable property delivered to another for the same purpose.[56] A chancery example noted that Garcí Pérez, as security for repayment of a loan, pledged a house to Gonzalo Vicente, giving him full power to take possession and dispose of it if Garcí did not pay the debt on time (*SP* 3, 18, 70). In 1256 Alfonso X declared that one could only take a pledge from a citizen of Burgos for his personal debts, and not to guarantee payment of tribute owed to the king.[57] In the previous year, perhaps intent on excluding the application of canon law, he required religious orders giving pledges in Burgos to observe the municipal *fuero*.[58]

A pledge might be voluntary or mandated by a judge. Whether conditional or for a specified time, a pledge should be clearly identified. One could pledge the expected yield of a vineyard or debts owed to the one making the pledge. A freeman could not pledge himself, except to secure the release of a captive, or when, suffering from hunger, he pledged his son. Farm animals and implements could not be pledged; nor could sacred property, a concubine and her children, personal servants and slaves, one's personal effects, and a man's horse and weapons. The pledger retained his rights if the pledgee altered or improved the pledge and was entitled to compensation if he removed, lost, or caused it to depreciate. In order to recover it, the pledger had to satisfy the debt it secured and pay the pledgee's expenses for maintaining it. In case of a silent pledge, it was understood that certain property secured an obligation. For example, a husband's property secured his wife's dowry; a guardian's property secured his administration of his ward's estate; and a father's property secured his use of his son's property. The property of a royal tax collector or of a taxpayer was security that taxes owed to the king would be paid (*SP* 5, 13, 1–50; *FR* 3, 19, 1–10; *FJ* 5, 6, 1–4; *FV* 3, 7, 1–5).

Payment of Debts

Once a final payment was made or a release was obtained, the debtor, his sureties, pledges, and heirs were no longer bound by any obligation. There were as many types of payments and releases as there were debts and obligations. For example, in a chancery formula Aparicio acknowledged receipt of one hundred *maravedís* as payment of a debt, tore up the instrument recording it, and released his debtor and his heirs from any further demand. Similarly, Pero Ruyz affirmed that he received one hundred *maravedís alfonsís* from Juan Pérez in payment of a loan or purchase, and returned to him the cancelled document detailing it (*SP* 3, 18, 81).

A debt should be paid in the form originally agreed upon, or in a manner approved by a judge.[59] Similarly, if a man could not do something as promised, a judge could order him to do something else and reimburse the other party for damages. Lest he have to make a payment a second time, a debtor owing a minor, or an insane person, or one suffering dementia, or a wastrel, with a judge's consent should pay him directly or his guardian. Should the creditor be unwilling to accept payment on the due date, the debtor should entrust the money to a good man or to a church sacristy and thereby be free of the debt. Unless he was negligent or committed fraud, a debtor was not liable if an animal or other property died or was lost before the date for its return. When paying one of several debts, he should designate the one to which it should be credited; otherwise, the money would be apportioned equally among all his debts, provided that none were usurious. When he had multiple creditors, the first to win a judgment against him should be paid. When contracts were renewed or extended, previous obligations were annulled. For example, a debtor who, with the consent of his creditor, transferred his debt to a third person would be released from his obligation to pay. If the conditions in a new contract were not met, the debtor could be sued under the terms of the previous contract. A man who inadvertently believed that he owed a debt to another and then assumed an obligation due to a third party was required to pay it, though he could ask his creditor to release him (*SP* 5, 14, pr., 1–19; *FJ* 5, 6, 5).

The Roman process of *compensatio* enabled men who were creditors and debtors to one another to settle their obligations by counterbalancing their debts.[60] That could easily be decided if the debts could be weighed, measured, or counted and were equivalent. Partners could counterbalance damages and losses incurred through each one's fault or fraudulent acts. Sureties could offset debts that they secured, and a son, on his father's behalf, could offset the debts of his father and his creditor if they were of equal amount. No one, by asserting that the king or town council owed him an offsetting debt, could claim exemption from taxation to maintain property set aside for public purposes (*SP* 5, 14, 20–27).

Men occasionally regretted paying a debt and tried to obtain a refund. Excepted from this were minors, women, simple laborers, and knights. Anyone who proved that he mistakenly paid a debt that he did not owe could recover his money; but someone, other than a minor, who knowingly paid a debt that he did not owe could not recover it because it was presumed to be a gift. A man who paid a debt but was unsure whether he owed it could obtain a refund. An heir or executor could not recover bequests on the grounds that a will was improperly drafted or because he was unaware that the law did not require him to pay the bequests. The fault was his because the king expected everyone, other than knights, women, minors, and simple laborers, to know his laws. Money advanced under a condition that might never be fulfilled could not be recouped. Anyone ordered to pay a debt could not later claim that as the judge was in error, the money should be returned, unless he proved that the judge was deceived by false witnesses and forged documents. A man who discounted a portion of a debt or agreed to less advantageous terms could not overturn that contract unless he could prove that he was defrauded (*SP* 5, 14, 28–34).

Numerous other situations involved recovery or nonrecovery of questionable payments. A marriage gift, once given, could not be reclaimed, nor could the cost of rearing someone in one's home. A person could recoup money spent to pay the debts of a deceased person whose heir he mistakenly believed he was, or to pay debts that he did not owe. If he freed a slave that he received in payment of a debt that he did not owe, he had to pay the slave's estimated value. Should he give two things to another person, though he owed only one, he could ask for return of the one he preferred. He was also entitled to payment for work that he mistakenly thought he had to do. In exchange for releasing a man from a contract, he could demand performance of another service. He had to return property accepted on condition of doing a service if he neglected to do it. A rightful heir could demand return of legacies wrongly distributed under a defective will. No one could keep property accepted for committing a crime or an immoral act. A captive could recover money paid to gain his freedom if no action was taken on his behalf. Someone induced by fraud or threats to promise money could not recoup it because no one was bound to abide by a promise unwillingly made. A woman, knowing that she could not marry, could not reclaim money that she gave to a prospective husband. Whatever a prospective husband and wife, knowing they could not marry, gave to one another was forfeited to the king, as was a bribe given to a judge. Money given to a woman to commit sexual acts could not be recovered if she refused to do what she promised. A criminal could recover money paid to silence someone threatening to expose him, because everyone should protect his reputation (*SP* 5, 14, 35–54).

As one might expect, not every debtor could meet his obligations. Unable to do so, and retaining only the clothes on his back, he had to surrender his property to a judge for distribution among his creditors. First, however, the judge should allot certain portions to various persons for their comfort: the debtor's direct descendant or immediate ancestor; his or her spouse; a freedman; a partner; or to settle a suit concerning a gift. The remainder should be sold at auction and the proceeds allocated to the creditors. A debtor who refused to pay his debts or yield his property to the court should be imprisoned until he did so. If a debtor attempted to thwart a court order to surrender his property by alienating everything, no one should purchase it. Property transferred by a debtor to evade payment had to be returned, and his creditors could sue within a year to revoke a fraudulent transfer (*SP* 5, 15, pr., 1–12).

Honrras Señaladas Dio Nuestro Señor Dios al Ome sobre Todas Las Otras Criaturas

The influence of Roman law on Alfonso X's exposition of the law of property is readily apparent. The *Third Partida* distinguished between public property that could be used by everyone and private property, whether movable or immovable, that the owner could use as he wished, provided that he did not intrude on his neighbor. In contrast to ownership, possession referred to the tenancy of property owned by someone else, though a possessor, by virtue of prescription, might acquire full ownership after a term of years. Easements facilitated movement through another's property, and usufruct, a type of easement, allowed one to use another's property for a fixed term or for life, but without ever gaining ownership. The *Fifth Partida* further developed the law of property by considering various contracts with their attendant legal obligations. They included deposits, whereby one temporarily entrusted something to another without offering remuneration, and donations, sales, and exchanges, which conferred ownership of property. A landowner, without ceding ownership, might profit by renting his property for a limited time or for life. *Emphyteusis* was a long-term lease allowing the lessee and his descendants to utilize the property as though it were their own.

The two types of loans were also notable contracts: the *empréstito* requiring the borrower to return something of equal value; and the *préstamo* allowing the borrower to use something for a limited time without cost. Penalties imposed if the terms of the loan were not observed often screened interest or usury. One could also contract for the services of workers who could be held accountable for errors or damages. Also having the binding force of contracts, whether oral or written, were promises to give something to another or to perform a service at a specified time or subject to a condition. Sureties risked their persons and property to guarantee fulfillment of a contract. Pledges of movable property served the same purpose. Once a person satisfactorily performed a service, or paid a required sum of money or rent, he was released from his contractual obligations. So too were his sureties and pledges.

From the earliest times human beings have claimed ownership of land and the animals that populate the earth. Christians and Jews found justification for that in the book of Genesis (1:28–29) wherein God commanded Adam and Eve to "fill the earth and subdue it." The royal jurists who explained the complexities of the law of property were surely familiar with that biblical passage. As they remarked: "Honrras señaladas dio nuestro Señor Dios al ome sobre todas las otras criaturas" (Our Lord God gave man special honors over all other creatures) (*SP* 4, pr.). However, thirteenth-century Castile was not the idyllic world of the Garden of Eden. The Alfonsine laws clearly reveal that human beings, having lost their primitive innocence, were prepared to practice fraud and deception, to commit violence to enforce their claims, and to renege on contractual obligations freely entered into.

❧ CHAPTER 12

Trade and Commerce

De las Mercadurias que Traen los Mercadores se Aprouecha la Tierra dellas Comunalmente

The revival of trade and commerce spawned a new class of merchants and craftsmen who spurred the rapid growth of cities and towns. While the conquest of Andalucía and Murcia gave Castile access to the Mediterranean, maritime contacts linking the Atlantic coast of Andalucía with the Bay of Biscay facilitated commercial enterprise with northern Europe. Yet there were grave economic concerns. The emigration of thousands of skilled Muslim workers resulted in a shortage of manufactured goods, and equally skilled Christian replacements were lacking. The colonization of Andalucía, moreover, depopulated many northern villages. Inflation, resulting in part from these demographic changes, became a serious problem, never effectively controlled. Recognizing the altered economic situation, Alfonso X deliberately attempted to control the economy, so as to alleviate inflation and amass sufficient treasure to finance his African crusade and his imperial quest.[1] Claudio Sánchez Albornoz aptly described this as a "directed economy."[2] In some respects King Alfonso's actions anticipated the early modern theory of mercantilism that sought to augment the wealth of the kingdom by the active intervention of the government.

Regulating the Economy

Alfonso X was one of the first monarchs to enact legislation to protect the environment and conserve natural resources. Urging his people to take pride in their country and to improve it, he stressed their responsibility to cultivate the land, to develop pastures, mines, and other assets in an orderly way, to safeguard trees and vineyards, to facilitate transportation and communication by eliminating unnecessary obstructions, and to guarantee the safety of pilgrims and other travelers. Cities, towns, and castles should be well fortified with strong walls and towers kept in repair (*SP* 1, 24, 1–4; 2, 11, 1–3; 2, 12, pr.; 2, 20, 1–8; *FR* 4, 6, 1–6; 4, 23, 1–4).[3]

The king also articulated that program for economic development in the Cortes of Seville in 1252 and subsequent parliamentary assemblies. By reiterating and amplifying regulations in the municipal *fueros*, he hoped to protect animals, birds, fish, trees, and plants so they would flourish and contribute to the general prosperity. Quarrelsome neighbors were warned not to destroy fields or vineyards, cut down trees not their own, or set woods on fire. Lest agricultural production be impacted negatively, plowing animals could not be slaughtered or taken as pledges for repayment of debt. Hunting fowl and rabbits was restricted, and in order not to deplete the supply of food and hides, all hunting was prohibited from the beginning of Lent until Michaelmas.[4]

Merchants attending markets and fairs were obliged to be honest, to charge a just price, not to defraud their customers with false or imperfect wares, to use lawful weights and measures, and to travel established routes and pay tolls and customs duties (*SP* 5, 7, 1).[5] However, Fernando III, objecting to their efforts to control commerce by forming associations, in July 1250 ordered the dissolution of confraternities or guilds in Santiago de Compostela. In November, during the Cortes of Seville, while approving religious or charitable associations, he prohibited "wicked confraternities" from having their own *alcaldes*.[6]

In the Cortes of Seville in 1252 (arts. 11, 14–16) and other assemblies, King Alfonso repeated his father's condemnation of guilds formed without royal consent and ordered that their quarrels could only be adjudicated by judges whom he appointed.[7] He reaffirmed that injunction in charters granted to several towns in 1255–56.[8] Accusing guilds of fixing prices and measures, restricting membership to certain families, and boycotting those who refused to join their company, he banned all confraternities established without his authorization (*SP* 5, 7, 2).[9] Nevertheless, he recognized the existence of guilds on several occasions. For example, he ordered a master craftsman who struck and killed his apprentice to be tried for homicide (*FR* 4, 17, 8). In 1253 he heard a dispute concerning the appointment of guild officials in Compostela,[10] and in 1280 he ratified ordinances adopted in 1259 by the shoemakers' guild of Burgos.[11] He also confirmed the muleteers and merchants of Atienza, the textile workers of Seville, the textile workers and shopkeepers of Soria, and the blacksmiths of Burgos.[12]

Royal policy was dictated by a desire to maintain the untrammeled authority of the crown and to prevent the development of an autonomous mercantile jurisdiction. In forbidding merchants to fix prices and wages, the king did not intend that the principle of laissez-faire should govern the market, but rather reserved the power of regulation to himself. In the Cortes of Seville in 1252 (arts. 1–3, 7, 9–10, 17–18, 23–28) he established prices for Frisian cloth, shields, saddles, and harnesses, women's silk headdresses, hides, shoes, horses and other livestock, and hawks and falcons. As complaints of the high cost of living and the shortage of goods persisted, he undertook a more extensive effort to control prices in the Assembly of Jerez in 1268. Prices for metals as well as domestic and imported cloth were usually higher in Andalucía (arts. 2–5). The price of mantles, tunics, gowns, and breeches, as well as shields, saddles, and harness had risen since 1252 (arts. 9–12). Hides of horses were reserved for shields and saddles and could not be used by shoemakers or scabbard makers (art. 13).[13] The list of prices for livestock, fowl, rabbits, and fish was extensive (arts. 16–20, 23). Apparently for the first time wages were fixed for workingmen and women. Rates varied throughout the realm but seem to have been highest in Andalucía. As might be expected, women were paid less than men. If a laborer refused to work or to accept the stipulated wages, he would be forced to do so. Vagabonds were restrained, and beggars and robbers were given summary justice (arts. 32–34, 36). How effective this effort to control prices and wages was is uncertain, but the experience of other times suggests that it irritated many people. The *Chronicle of Alfonso X* commented that "everything increased in cost." María del Carmen Carlé pointed out that between 1263 and 1294 prices of certain goods rose as much as 1,000 percent.[14]

In the *Fuero real* (3, 10, 1) Alfonso X declared that weights and measures, guaranteed by municipal inspectors, should be true and equal for everyone. In 1257 he ordered Sepúlveda to observe these directives "until we give them the *fuero*," that is, the *Fuero real*.[15] The *Partidas* (7, 7, 7) ordered the destruction of false weights and measures. During the Cortes of Seville in 1261 (art. 36), he reminded the towns that he had sent them charters obliging them to maintain uniform weights and measures.[16] As "our dominion is one," he emphasized that weights and measures should also be uniform. Lest there be any confusion, he sent archetypes to each town and ordered the destruction of others. The measure for wheat was the *cahíz* (ar. *qafíz*) of Toledo containing twelve *fanegas* (ar. *faníqa*), each divided into twelve *celemines* (ar. *zumniya*), and each of those into twelve *cuchares* (lat. *cochleare*). The *moyo* (lat. *modius*) of Valladolid, containing sixteen *cántaras* (lat. *cantharus*), was the standard for wine, and for meat, the *arrelde* (ar. *arrīṭl*) of Burgos containing ten *libras* or pounds. The *marco alfonsí*, weighing eight ounces, was the standard for weights; a *libra* was two *marcos*. The *arroba* (ar. *arrūb'*) contained twenty-five *libras*. Four *arrobas* equaled a *quintal* or hundredweight. The measure for cloth was the *vara* (lat. *vara*), a stick or metal bar about two feet long. In the Assembly of Jerez in 1268 (art. 26), he repeated this ordinance.[17] Hard pressed financially in later years, Alfonso X intensified the collection of fines for using false weights and measures, and in 1279 insisted that he would never yield this right.[18]

Commercial Activity

Alfonso X's determination to control the economy was nowhere more evident than in the area of domestic trade. The right to a secure market was a royal benefit accorded to many towns.[19] In the Cortes of Seville in 1252 (arts. 15–16), he curbed potential troublemakers such as itinerant hucksters. As free access to the market was essential, he ordered shopkeepers in Sahagún not to block the streets.[20] In 1260 he gave the municipal council of Burgos control of the meat markets, except four tables belonging to the cathedral.[21] In exchange for shops that were being razed, he granted Christian meat markets to the cathedral of Córdoba but reserved the right to the *alcabala* or sales tax.[22] Lest a food shortage occur, he admonished the towns not to restrict the introduction of provisions from other communities.[23] Nevertheless, in order to nurture the development of a municipal fair, he permitted Alba de Tormes to prohibit the sale of wine or grapes produced outside the municipal district.[24]

Unlike town markets where local products were sold at retail, foreign and domestic merchants gathered at fairs to sell goods wholesale.[25] Realizing that fairs would foster population growth and prosperity, Alfonso X, while insisting that the establishment of new fairs required royal authorization, increased their number from six to twenty-five.[26] Merchants, whether Christians, Jews, or Muslims, and their merchandise would be secure at the fair and throughout the realm. Exempted from local exactions, they could not be sued for debts contracted elsewhere or arrested for previous offenses, nor could their property be seized during the fair. However, they could be compelled to fulfill contracts and pay debts incurred during the fair. Anyone who plundered a merchant had to return the stolen merchandise, but if he could not be found, the municipal council where the crime occurred had to make restitution (*SP* 5, 7, 3–4). Fairs usually occurred around festival days. Benavente, for example, held an annual fair for fifteen days after Easter. Seville had two fairs annually, one during the fifteen days before and the fifteen days after the beginning of Lent, and the other at Michaelmas.[27]

The collection of tolls (*portazgo*) on goods in transit was a long-standing custom and a sign of royal sovereignty. Intent on facilitating the free flow of traffic, Alfonso X, in the Cortes of Seville in 1252 (art. 37), limited collection to stations established by Alfonso VIII and Alfonso IX and in Andalucía by Miramamolín, the Almohad caliph.[28] In order to encourage attendance at fairs, he often granted exemption from *portazgo*. Monasteries and cathedrals were similarly favored.[29] Several towns were exempted from *portazgo* throughout the realm, except in Toledo, Seville, and Murcia, where the royal *almojarifazgo*, a toll dating back to Muslim times, was collected.[30] Seville, Carmona, and other towns in Andalucía and Murcia received an exemption valid anywhere.[31]

In return for their personal security, the king argued that merchants should acknowledge his sovereignty by paying a toll of one-eighth the value of goods imported or exported. Items intended for personal or familial use and goods imported for the king were exempt, as were foreign envoys and scholars. Merchants had to give an accurate account of their imports or exports and pay duties. Anyone who attempted to avoid the toll would lose all his merchandise. Wherever the toll was collected from ancient times, the entire amount was the king's, but where tolls were recently established he received two-thirds, and one-third was used to maintain town or castle walls. The right to collect it was auctioned off for a term of three years. Customs collectors were warned not to abuse a merchant, but to accept his sworn statement of his inventory; if they levied more than the appropriate duty, they had to reimburse the merchant double the amount (*SP* 5, 7, 5–9; *LEst* 201).

Although imports from northern Europe, Morocco, and the East were welcomed, the king seriously limited foreign trade by prohibiting the export of certain products—the so-called *cosas vedadas*.[32] Castile was at an economic disadvantage because she had little to offer her neighbors other than raw materials.[33] Acknowledging the need for "an abundance of livestock," Alfonso X, in the Cortes of Seville in 1252 (arts. 19–21) and again at Valladolid in 1258 (art. 12) and Seville in 1261 (art. 19), forbade the export of horses, hides, seeds, silk, mercury, cattle, pigs, goats, sheep, hawks, falcons, and other items. Anyone exporting *cosas vedadas* without permission committed "a very great madness" (*E* 4, 12, 57) and would lose everything (*SP* 5, 7, 5; *LEst* 204). Nevertheless, royal charters authorizing exports were available for a fee (*E* 4, 2, 57; *SP* 3, 20, 10). The charter had to identify the merchant, the number of horses or other products being exported, and whether permission was valid for a year or longer (*SP* 3, 13, 20). In the Assembly of Jerez in 1268 (arts. 14, 21–25) the king again prohibited the export of *cosas vedadas* and, in order to avoid an unfavorable balance of trade, required merchants to import as much as they exported. Masters of foreign ships had to be informed of these regulations and see that they were observed. Customs stations were established at Santander, Laredo, Castro Urdiales, San Sebastián, and Fuenterrabía on the Bay of Biscay; at Avilés, Ribadeo, Vivero, Betanzos, La Coruña, Santa María, Cedeira, Ferrol, Bayona, La Guardia, Pontevedra, Padrón, and Noya in Asturias and Galicia; at Seville, Jerez, Huelva, Cádiz, and Vejer in Andalucía; and at Cartagena, Alicante, and Elche in Murcia.[34]

Reacting negatively to royal policy, the nobles in the Cortes of Burgos in 1272 demanded that Alfonso X abolish customs duties and that the list of prohibited exports should be no greater than in his father's reign. He rejected both demands, and though he promised at Almagro in 1273 to cease collection of customs duties after six years, he never did so. In 1276 he authorized Zag de la Maleha to collect fines for exporting banned items,[35] and in 1277, he forbade the export of gold and silver and the *dineros prietos*, a strong coinage. Merchants and pilgrims traveling to Compostela, however, could take out fifty *sueldos prietos* twice a year. His gold coin could be exported because it could be used to acquire silver needed to mint billon. Anyone leaving the kingdom was permitted to take out only as much money as he brought in. Prelates and nobles had to ask royal permission to take out silver, but in order to encourage the importation of gold, silver, or other coinages, they were exempted from customs duties. Two years later Pedro III of Aragón complained that the prohibition of the export "of almost all merchandise" was injurious to both realms and diminished Castile's potential revenues.[36]

In his closing years Alfonso X, needing money to oppose the Moroccan invasion, assiduously fined violators of the export regulations. Seeking to appease angry merchants who presented their grievances at Burgos in February 1281, he pledged that they would have to pay customs duties only once at the port of entry or exit. They would be exempt from local tolls and customs duties on their personal belongings and would be liable to seizure for payment only of personal debts, but not for debts or taxes owed by the towns where they resided. Imports had still to be balanced against exports, and the ban on the export of prohibited products was repeated. Two days later, he exempted them from *portazgo* on their persons anywhere in the kingdom. They were particularly irritated because he had ordered an inquest to determine whether they were exporting forbidden goods or violating the principle of balancing exports and imports in the ports on the Bay of Biscay. In return for a *servicio* of one hundred thousand *maravedís* and a chancery fee of one thousand, payable in the first coinage of his reign ("la moneda de la primera guerra de Granada"), he pardoned them for previous violations.[37]

Ever since the twelfth century popes had censured Christians who traded with the enemy. Similarly, Alfonso X forbade anyone to sell weapons, wheat, barley, rye, oil, and other foodstuffs to enemies of the faith, "when they are making war against us." Envoys traveling to the royal court, however, were allowed to purchase food and drink for their sustenance. Anyone violating this law would be deprived of his property, and his person would be at the king's mercy, because aiding the enemies of the faith was "a form of treason" (*SP* 5, 5, 22). Those who did so during wartime and were captured by pirates or otherwise injured were reminded that that was their own fault (*SP* 5, 9, 13). When these laws were written, the king was preparing his African crusade, which was aborted in the spring of 1264 by the Mudéjar revolt. Although the submission of the emir of Granada three years later marked the end of the uprising, the threat of Islam remained throughout the reign. This law therefore was solidly grounded in reality.

Maritime Law

As merchant shipping expanded, Alfonso X composed a brief code of maritime law, whose relation to the Rôles of Oléron and the ancient Rhodian Sea Law has been observed.[38] A typical chancery charter stated that the shipmaster Jordán chartered his ship, the *Buenaventura*, to Alemán, a merchant, and promised to transport him and so many hundredweight of wax and so many bales of hides from Seville to La Rochelle on the west coast of France. Jordán guaranteed that the ship was properly equipped with sails, yards, masts, cables, and anchors; a crew of sixty, namely, two pilots, forty mariners, ten marines armed with crossbows, and four servants; and a small boat carrying sufficient provisions. The itinerary included stops at Lisbon, Ribadeo or La Coruña in Galicia, or Santander on the Bay of Biscay, where Jordán would pick up his partners and any merchandise that Alemán might have there. Within eight days of reaching La Rochelle, Alemán had to pay two hundred marks of silver. The ship would be loaded in March so that it could sail from Seville on 1 April, if the weather permitted. The penalty for each infraction of the contract was one hundred marks (*SP* 3, 18, 77).

This example, probably based on an actual charter, suggests that the shipmaster Giordano was one of the many Genoese settled in Seville and that Alemán may have been German as his name indicates.[39] The *Buonaventura*, to give it its Italian name, was a large sailing vessel with a full crew and an auxiliary boat, and carried a cargo of raw materials. A form of international maritime law would come into play if either party violated the charter. As illustrated in the *Cantigas de Santa Maria*, the *nave* had a high prow and even higher stern, with a castle or superstructure for cabins. There were two masts with triangular lateen sails with a crow's nest atop each mast, and a side paddle for steering.[40]

The responsibility for a voyage rested primarily with pilots, masters, and owners. They had to prepare the ship, ensuring that it was properly caulked and that sails, masts, ropes, yards, anchors, and oars were in order. Experienced crewmen, especially navigators who could safely guide the ship through troublesome seas, had to be recruited. A scribe had to keep a log recording everything brought on board. Arms, biscuits, other foods, and fresh water were essential. Agreements between shipmasters, owners, and merchants had to be scrupulously observed. If anyone committed a crime during the voyage, he should be arrested and, on reaching port, presented to the local judge for trial and punishment. Masters and owners could scourge obstreperous crewmembers but had to be careful not to kill or maim them (*SP* 5, 9, pr., 1–2).

Sometimes it was necessary to save the ship from disaster by throwing merchandise overboard. As that served the common good, each merchant had to contribute proportionally to make up the loss suffered by those whose property was cast into the sea. The apportionment outlined in the Alfonsine Codes was based on the shipowner's estimate of the value of the vessel and the value, rather than the weight, of each one's goods, so a merchant carrying gems, gold, or money had to share with everyone else. If the master ordered a mast cut down and thrown overboard to save the ship, the merchants had to make up the loss, but if the mast was broken by lightning or wind, the owner had to pay for it. If the ship was driven aground, merchants were bound to compensate for the loss only if they instructed the master to let it take its course. If the owners recovered their property that fell overboard during a storm, they had to assist the others in making up their loss, as a matter of the common good. Despite contrary custom, ownership of property or pieces of a ship washed up on shore belonged to the original owners and not to those who found it. If a master, fearing that his heavily laden ship might not be able to enter a port's shallow waters, transferred some material to smaller boats and they were lost, all the merchants had to share proportionally in the loss. A master who, contrary to the wishes of the merchants, chose to brave the hazards of sailing between 11 November and

10 March or to pass by a place held by an enemy would be responsible for any loss incurred (*SP* 5, 9, 3–9; *FR* 4, 24, 1–2).

If a shipowner, in the absence of the master or contrary to his directions, wrecked his ship, he would be responsible for loss of the cargo (*SP* 5, 8, 13). A greedy master who deliberately took his ship into dangerous waters so that he could wreck it and seize the goods of merchants should be tried by a local judge and, upon conviction, sentenced to death. Fishermen and others sometimes set fires on shore at nighttime to lure ships into perilous areas where they would be wrecked and plundered. If that charge was proved, the culprits had to pay four times the value of the merchandise and were subjected to bodily punishment. Corsairs, a grave hazard of the sea, after seizing a ship, often released it, the merchants, and their goods in exchange for money. In that case each man had to bear a proportionate share of the expense; even a man with no belongings had to pay for his freedom. Occasionally, corsairs were plundered by other Christians, but the original owners, if they were sailing to or from a Christian country, retained their right to the goods taken from them. The reason for that was "porque de las mercadurias que traen los mercadores se aprouecha la tierra dellas comunalmente" (because the realm benefits in common from merchandise brought in by merchants) (*SP* 5, 9, 13). However, if they were trading with the enemy, contrary to the king's command, whoever stole their property could keep it. Anyone who liberated a pleasure craft seized by the enemy in time of war was entitled to whatever property was on board. Judges in seafaring communities had to resolve such disputes expeditiously so that merchants and ships would not be delayed unnecessarily. While listening to witnesses, judges should give particular credence to the ship's log (*SP* 5, 9, 10–14).

The line between the honest merchantman and the corsair or pirate was often clouded, as mariners engaged in legitimate trade while also attacking enemy shipping. *CSM* 379 related the story of Catalan corsairs driven to Seville by a storm reportedly caused by the Virgin Mary; there they surrendered their booty to the king and entered his service. *CSM* 379 may be dated around December 1281 when the king offered tributary exemptions to corsairs settling in El Puerto de Santa María, provided that they sold at auction whatever goods they seized from his enemies. Corsairs resident elsewhere would enjoy similar privileges if the goods they offered for sale were not taken from the king's friends, whether Moors or Christians.[41]

Mercantile Companies

Merchants often formed companies or partnerships.[42] A mercantile company was an association of two or more merchants seeking their mutual profit through buying and selling, exchanging, or renting and leasing property for a fixed term or for life. A company could be established in two ways. First, the partners in a company with a general purpose agreed to hold their property in common and to share profits and losses equally. Second, a company might be organized to engage in one kind of traffic, for example, the sale of wine or cloth. Profits and losses should be shared equally, unless some other arrangement was made. For example, if one partner endowed with better business acumen took the lead, he might be entitled to a greater share. A so-called Leonine contract (*societas leonina*) whereby one had all the profits and none of the losses or vice versa was invalid.[43] Also invalid was a company in which one party deceived another or unlawfully claimed a greater share of the profits. A company organized for criminal purposes was illegal, and the partners had to make restitution of any profits. A partner who caused any damage or loss had to bear that burden. A contract stating that the partners would share profits from an inheritance (without identifying the benefactor) would be binding; but if the benefactor was named, without his consent, it would not be valid because someone, anxious to secure the inheritance, might attempt to take his life. No one under fourteen or mentally ill could form a company, and a judge could release anyone under twenty-five from his obligations if he was fraudulently persuaded to enter a company (*SP* 5, 10, pr., 1–9).

A chancery formula recorded that Pedro de la Rochela and don Arberat formed a company for ten years to buy cloth and sell it in the *rua de los francos*—the street of the French in Seville, not far from the cathedral. Each one invested one thousand *maravedís* and pledged to share the profits, injuries, and losses; if either violated the pact, he would be fined one thousand *maravedís* (*SP* 3, 18, 78). Both men were probably French: Pedro or Pierre was from La Rochelle, and Arbérats is a town in the southwest corner of France.

A company could be dissolved for several reasons: a partner's death, unless it was agreed that the survivor should continue it; a partner's banishment for life or civil death; the surrender of his property to his colleague by a partner burdened by debt; the death or loss of the property for which the company was formed; or the sacralization of property, for example, a house transformed into a church or a plaza into a cemetery. A company might also be terminated if one of the members declared his desire to leave; if he did so before the expiration date he had to make good any damage or loss caused by his departure. If he withdrew so that he would not have to share some expected gain, as for example, an inheritance, he would be bound to give his partners their rightful share and compensation for any loss or damage. When the company was dissolved all its assets and liabilities should be apportioned among the members according to the company's original charter. A company might be prematurely ended if an obnoxious member could not be tolerated by the others, if the king or a municipal council sent a member on a mission or appointed him to an office, if a member failed to abide by the terms of the charter, or if circumstances such as shipwreck made it impossible to continue (*SP* 5, 10, 10–14).

If a partner controlling the company's property gave a portion to one or two others, leaving nothing for the rest, everything had to be redistributed. Should a partner be unable to pay a debt owed to another member of the company, a judge could allow him to retain sufficient funds to live on but could require him to give security to pay in full when possible. Any expense incurred by a partner on behalf of the company had to be paid from common funds. Should a partner use any of the company's property without the knowledge of the others, he and his heirs were bound to return it, lest they be accused of stealing (*SP* 5, 10, 15–17).

Money and Moneylending

The need for an acceptable medium of exchange was fundamental but proved to be a most difficult task. In the first half of the thirteenth century, the basic coins in circulation were the *dineros burgaleses* in Castile and the *leoneses* in León. Made of billon, an alloy of silver and copper, they were calculated at a ratio of ninety *burgaleses* or ninety-six *leoneses* to the gold *maravedí*, a money of account. As this was a stable coinage, Fernando III maintained it after the union of the kingdoms in 1230. Jean Gautier-Dalché and James Todesca have demonstrated the errors concerning coinage in the *Chronicle of Alfonso X*.[44]

Despite the misstatements of the *Chronicle*, Alfonso X did not alter the coinage until more than a decade after his accession. When he levied *moneda forera* in the Cortes of Valladolid in 1258, he probably promised to maintain the coinage intact for seven years, but as circumstances changed he had to issue new coinages on three different occasions.[45] Sometime after the Mudéjar revolt in 1264, but before 1268, he minted the *dineros alfonsís*, the first coinage common to Castile and León. That coinage was usually known as the *moneda de la guerra* (or *de la primera guerra*) or *blancas* (still later, *blanquillas*). The *dinero alfonsí* bore the legend ALFONSUS REX CASTELLE ET LEGIONIS on the obverse, and castles and lions quartered on the reverse. Although there were ninety *dineros alfonsís* to the *maravedí*, the new money had less purchasing power than the *burgaleses* or *leoneses*. Nevertheless, by replacing a stronger money with a weaker one, the king secured the resources necessary to suppress the Mudéjars.[46] The rise in prices resulting from this effective devaluation prompted the Assembly of Jerez in 1268 (arts. 1–2) to ask the king to guarantee a stable coinage by confirming the *dineros alfonsis* for life. Equivalences were also fixed for other moneys, such as the gold *dobla* (an imitation of an Almohad coin) worth three *maravedís*, and the gold *maravedí alfonsí* (of Alfonso VIII) worth two *maravedís*.[47]

Nevertheless, a demand for a stronger coinage was soon heard, perhaps in the Cortes of Burgos in 1269. After taking counsel with "men wise in the matter of money," the king coined the *dineros prietos*, so-called because of their dark color, and pledged to maintain this coinage for life. The *prieto* was six times greater than the *dinero alfonsí*, as fifteen *dineros prietos* (in contrast to ninety *dineros alfonsís*) equaled one *maravedí*. The *prieto* showed a castle and lion on opposite sides of the coin; the legend ALF REX CASTELLE appeared on the obverse and ET LEGIONIS on the reverse.[48]

Alfonso X also coined a gold *maravedí*, recorded for the first time on 15 June 1272. Although he set its value at ten *maravedís de la moneda de la guerra*, the "many good men knowledgeable in coinage" whom he consulted warned that it was worth much more. Sellers, on the contrary, believing that the gold *maravedí chico* (as it was called) was of lesser value, refused to accept it. This prompted the nobles in 1272 to accuse the king of falsifying the money.[49]

Meanwhile, dissatisfaction with the *dineros prietos* became apparent because only a few, due to the silver shortage, could be minted. As comparatively strong coins, they tended to be hoarded or taken out of the kingdom, and so Alfonso X asked the emir of Granada to pay most of his tribute in silver.[50] In order to mount an effective counteroffensive against the Marinids, the Cortes of Burgos in 1277 asked him to mint a "more common" money, cheaper and more plentiful. However, as he had sworn not to alter the *dineros prietos*, prelates and nobles, on 9 May 1277, asked Pope John XXI to absolve him from his oath.[51] The papal response is unknown but was probably affirmative, as the king issued a third billon coinage, the *moneda nueva* (also called *blancas* and *dineros alfonsís*). Though it had a legal value equal to the *prieto*, it was greatly debased. The *moneda nueva* had the legend MONETA CASTELLE and a castle on the obverse and ET LEGIONIS and a lion on the reverse. It seems strange that the king did not put his name on it, especially as in the *Setenario* (43–44) he noted that the coinage was identified in this way.[52]

As the silver shortage continued, the supply of *moneda nueva*, a weakened billon coinage, was insufficient to meet the kingdom's needs. The war against the Moors strained the king's resources, leading him to propose to the Cortes of Seville in 1281 the minting of two new moneys, one silver and one copper, instead of imposing a new tax. The Cortes acquiesced, "more out of fear than love," but soon asked Sancho to persuade him "not to circulate this copper money."[53]

Shortly after Sancho assumed control of the government, the Assembly of Valladolid in 1282 asked him to reestablish the coinages used in previous reigns. After consulting knowledgeable men, on 19 May 1282 he ordered the minting of *burgaleses* and *pepiones* (half *burgaleses*) in Burgos, *leoneses* in León, and *salamanqueses* in Salamanca and promised never to change them. However, when Burgos expressed its preference for Alfonso X's coinage, Sancho warned the city not to interfere with the minting of the new money.[54]

Alfonso X hoped to curb prices and inflation by creating a sound, stable, and abundant coinage, but his three billon coinages, the *dineros alfonsís* of 1264, the *prietos* of 1271, and the *moneda nueva* of 1277, failed to achieve that goal, mainly because of the chronic silver shortage. Royal monetary policy consequently remained a major source of controversy until the end of the reign.

Prior to the thirteenth century, the extension of credit was evident in agricultural communities. Landed proprietors often lent their tenants livestock or seed to plant wheat or vineyards, but if they could not pay the expected return, the owner confiscated their holdings. By Alfonso X's time, as a consequence of the growth of towns and the increasing use of money, credit was more frequently associated with mercantile operations.[55]

As the church condemned the taking of interest or usury, moneylending was generally conducted by Jews, and to a lesser extent by Muslims.[56] As one might imagine, this caused great friction among the different religious communities. Responding to a chorus of protest against excessive rates of interest, Alfonso X in the Cortes of Seville in 1252 and in the *Fuero real* (4, 2, 6) fixed the annual rate that a Jew could charge at "tres por cuatro" (three for four). That would be a yearly rate at 33⅓ percent.[57] In 1260 he confirmed the right of Jews and Moors to charge that rate but forbade Christians to lend money at interest.[58] During the Assembly of Jerez in 1268 (arts. 29, 44) he reduced the rate to "quatro por cinco" (four for five) or 25 percent and again forbade Christians to take interest. Today that rate would be considered usurious, but the lender's risks were far greater than they are now. No Jew could act for a Christian in a commercial transaction, and a Christian scribe had to prepare documents when a Christian borrowed money from a Jew. Needing money to oppose the Marinid invasion, the king took advantage of the condemnation of Christian usurers by the Council of Lyons in 1274, ordered inquests to identify them, and fined them. Several towns paid substantial sums "for the affair of the frontier" to be quit of any further trouble on this account.[59]

The Mesta

The pasturage of sheep and the production of raw wool was a significant aspect of the economy. Neighboring towns often quarreled over the use of pastures.[60] However, as the frontiers were pushed steadily southward, the annual migration of sheep from winter to summer pastures extended over ever-lengthening distances caused greater conflicts. Sheep owners, determined to protect their interests, organized a guild or Mesta between 1230 and 1265.[61]

In the Cortes of Seville in 1252 (arts. 31–33, 41) the king allowed municipalities or military orders to levy only one toll (*montazgo*) in their pastures, and the tithe only once where customary. Sheep could use streams and traditional sheepwalks (*cañadas*), and no one could enclose previously open pastures.[62] Animals could be pastured in open fields for a day or two, but not in vineyards; trees could not be cut down or fruit taken.[63] Anyone altering a brand and replacing it with his own would be charged with robbery (FR 4, 6, 4–5; 4, 13, 10).

During the Cortes of Seville in 1261, when the sheepmen protested that their flocks had to pay more than one tithe as they moved from the archdiocese of Toledo into that of Seville, the king, while assuring the church of its just due, effected a compromise that would not subject the sheep to a double tithe.[64] The sheep owners also asked the king to relieve them of the municipal toll, offering in return an annual *servicio*, as follows: one hundred out of every one thousand sheep or goats; three out of every one thousand cows; twenty *sueldos de pepiones* for every one hundred pigs, and two *sueldos de pepiones* for every mare, nag, or other animal. This effectively transferred the right of levying *montazgo* from the municipalities to the king.[65]

As towns continued to demand the toll, the sheep owners objected at Badajoz in 1267, and the king again prohibited anyone other than the military orders to take *montazgo*, except for the royal *servicio* already mentioned. This was probably the beginning of one part of the tax later referred to as *servicio y montazgo*. The other part, the *servicio*, likely came about two years later. During the meeting at Badajoz, Alfonso X agreed to appoint two royal officials, later known as *alcaldes entregadores*, in each of five districts to guard the sheepwalks, to resolve disputes with local farmers, to amend all injuries, and to recover pledges unjustly taken from shepherds. For that purpose, they had to convene three annual *mestas* or assemblies and to render accounts either in Lent or at Martinmas. In exchange, the sheep owners offered the king another *servicio* as follows: a half *maravedí* for every one thousand sheep and goats, three *maravedís* for every one thousand cows, and five *maravedís* for every one hundred pigs.[66] The realization that transhumant livestock could be a substantial source of revenue led Alfonso X to impose the *servicio de los ganados* in the Cortes of Burgos in 1269. Seven years later he authorized collection of arrears of this tax owing since 1269.[67]

The sheep owners presented numerous complaints during the Cortes of Burgos in 1272. As the towns persisted in trying to collect *montazgo*, the king reiterated the ban established in 1261. Again he restricted the military orders to the imposition of this toll only once throughout their jurisdiction, and the church to only one tithe. The crown gained by reserving a third of all fines for damages done by migratory sheep and by seizing all lost and unclaimed animals. In order to facilitate transhumance, the sheepwalks would be widened again as in the twelfth century. In wooded areas shepherds were permitted to cut down branches or even trees to open the way. Local farmers were responsible for protecting their own fields from possible damage by the sheep.[68] Objecting to Alfonso X's attempt to profit from transhumant sheep, the magnates in 1273 demanded that the *montazgo* be levied as in Fernando III's time—that is, that the right of the towns to collect it be reinstated—and that the *servicio de los ganados* should not be collected at all. Although the king consented initially, these demands do not seem to have been included in the final settlement.[69]

In the fall of 1273 Alfonso X granted four charters to "the council of the Mesta of the shepherds." Although Julius Klein hailed this as the foundation of the Mesta, Charles Julian Bishko pointed out that it was already in existence.[70] The king reminded his *entregadores* to attend three annual *mestas*, to punish wrongdoers, and to protect the shepherds and their flocks. He also confirmed the shepherds' right to cut paths through woodland and to use wood for cooking and other necessities. Shepherds were exempted from tolls on their clothing and food, and—so that the number of "horses and mules in my realm might increase"—on mares and their foals, and other animals traveling with the flocks. The king also modified his earlier ban on the municipal *montazgo* by permitting towns that had levied it in his father's reign to continue doing so, at the rate of two head per ten thousand.[71]

As trouble between sheepmen and towns continued, the king confirmed his charters of 1272, warning towns not to prevent shepherds from purchasing needed food supplies. In response to complaints in 1278, he ordered his *entregadores* to open blocked sheepwalks and enclosed pastures, levy appropriate fines, punish murderers and robbers, and hear all suits involving shepherds.[72] Charters guaranteeing secure pasturage to monasteries and cathedrals throughout the realm also reflect the tension between sheep owners and towns.[73]

The organization of the Mesta was prompted by the sheep owners' need to defend their interests, but Alfonso X also recognized it as an opportunity to tap new sources of revenue. He stood to profit not only from heavy fines imposed on those who violated the rights of the sheepmen, but also from the *servicio de los ganados* and the *montazgo* that became a regular item in his budget.

Por que Seades Mas Ricos et Mas Abondados

Through economic policies developed in the Cortes and in several privileges, Alfonso X made a concerted effort to raise his kingdom to a greater level of prosperity. His hope was "por que seades mas ricos et mas abondados" (that you may be richer and more prosperous) and thus able to render him greater service (Seville 1252, pr.). Committed to fostering economic growth, he enacted measures safeguarding natural resources and encouraging the responsible exploitation of mineral resources and of land suitable for farming and pasturage. The development of roads, waterways, and bridges was intended to overcome barriers separating communities, to promote domestic trade and facilitate pilgrimage, and, in the broadest sense, to create a spirit of unity among his people that would serve the common good.

As trade and commerce flourished and merchants and artisans became prominent members of urban communities, the king asserted control over their activities. Thus, he banned guilds and confraternities, other than those with a spiritual purpose, and opposed their efforts to limit their membership or to fix prices, a right that he claimed for himself. Indeed, he established prices for a wide range of products and made the first attempt to fix wages. As a means of creating wealth, he encouraged towns to hold regular markets and increased the number of fairs where foreign and domestic merchants could exchange their wares in a secure environment. Moreover, he regulated the formation, operation, and dissolution of mercantile companies and detailed the responsibilities of shipmasters and merchants in his code of maritime law.

While the king recognized the importance of welcoming imported goods, he also established customs duties as a source of revenue. As a means of conserving essential resources, he elaborated a long list of *cosas vedadas* that could not be exported and required merchants to balance imports and exports equally. In order to ease commercial transactions he standardized weights and measures and attempted, without success, to develop a stable coinage. He determined interest rates chargeable by Jewish moneylenders and profited from fines on Christian usurers. He also asserted jurisdiction over disputes between the Mesta and local communities and garnered income from the *servicio y montazgo* levied on flocks.

Alfonso X's ambitious political and cultural enterprises necessitated the expenditure of abundant sums and the careful husbanding of resources. However, despite his efforts, the high cost of living was never brought under control, and as he depleted his ordinary revenues, he became dependent on extraordinary income. At the Cortes of Burgos in 1272 the nobles challenged his economic policies, but his refusal to change and his continued demand for new taxes, his imposition of fines, and his proposed alteration of the coinage aroused intense discontent and ultimately contributed to his downfall.

✿ CHAPTER 13

Crime and Punishment

Ca Razon es que los Fechos Malos e Desaguisados Non Finquen sin Pena

In the early Middle Ages criminal justice was mainly a private affair. The victim had to accuse the perpetrator, but many individuals remained silent rather than risk suffering worse harm from someone more powerful. The victim and his family might seek retribution through violent means or try to prove the charge by an oath of purgation, an ordeal, or a judicial duel. Monetary compensation was intended to alleviate recourse to blood feuds.

Under the influence of Roman and canon law, Alfonso X recognized crime as an offense against the community. Assuming responsibility for maintaining the peace, he claimed jurisdiction over specific crimes, reserved adjudication to judges whom he appointed, and curbed private vengeance by employing the inquest to bring criminals to justice.[1] The *Fuero real* (4, 1–25) penalized a range of crimes, but the *Espéculo's* analysis was in the lost ninth book. The *Seventh Partida*, drawing on Roman law, the municipal *fueros*, and Castilian territorial law, presented an extended treatment of criminal law and portrayed the ideal judge:

> The person of man is the most noble thing in the world and so we decree that every judge who has to hear a case that could lead to death or loss of a limb, ought to take great care that the evidence . . . is loyal

and true without any suspicion, and that the statements and words spoken . . . [by witnesses] are certain and as clear as the light so that there cannot be any doubt about them. And if they [the witnesses] do not speak and testify clearly . . . and the accused is a man of good reputation, the judge . . . ought to acquit him. And if, perchance, the accused is a man of ill fame and the evidence offers certain presumptions against him, he [the judge] can have him tortured in order to learn the truth. And if, either by his confession or the evidence alleged against him, he should find him not guilty of the offense charged against him, he must acquit him. (SP 7, 1, 25)

Charging a Criminal

An accusation or an inquest might initiate a criminal case. Alfonso X, by permitting anyone to make an accusation, shifted responsibility for bringing malefactors to justice to the entire community. Nevertheless, allegations by certain persons were inadmissible: wives, minors under fourteen, judges and public officials still in office, persons expelled from a community, Jews, Muslims, heretics, slaves, perjurers, excommunicates, retarded persons, and convicted criminals. Close family members could not accuse one another; nor freedmen, their former masters; household servants, their patrons; heirs, their benefactors; and benefactors, their heirs. Anyone worth less than fifty *maravedís* could not accuse a wealthier person. With the exception of minors, anyone could denounce treason, counterfeiting, adultery, rape, robbery, theft, heresy, apostasy, and crimes involving the death penalty, bodily punishment, and confiscation. The accuser had to be able to prove his charge lest he suffer the penalty inflicted on a guilty person (FR 4, 20, 1–6; SP 7, 1, 1–5).

One could only accuse a deceased person in case of treason, malfeasance by a royal official, heresy, stealing church property, or a woman's attempt to kill her husband. Lest the dignity of his office be compromised, a royal official still serving could not be charged, unless he committed a serious crime. According to the principle of double jeopardy, no one could be tried again for the same offense unless evidence was suppressed. If several accusers appeared, the judge should select the one best-intentioned to make the complaint (FR 4, 20, 9–10, 13, 15; SP 7, 1, 7–13; LEst 9).

Given the gravity of the proceeding, the complainant had to appear in person and submit a written accusation identifying the accuser, the accused, the judge, the offense, and the month, year, and place of occurrence. He had to swear that his charge was true and that he was not prompted by malice.

Frivolous accusations were severely punished. Neither the plaintiff nor the defendant could be represented by a *personero*, but each could have an advocate (*FR* 4, 20, 5, 7; *SP* 7, 1, 6, 14, 26).[2]

The defendant could be tried in the district where he committed his crime, or where he lived, or where he had taken refuge. The judge could arrest a defendant who attempted to escape, discipline him for obstreperous behavior, and imprison him if he were convicted of a major crime. If the complainant did not appear, the charge would be dismissed; he would be declared infamous and required to pay the accused's expenses and damages and five pounds of gold to the king. He could withdraw his allegation within thirty days unless the judge concluded that it was false and malicious, or the suspect was in prison or tortured, or the crime was treason, desertion by a knight, falsehood, or thievery. The accusation usually died with the death of either party (*SP* 7, 1, 15–25). A suspect might settle out of court and could escape prosecution if the king, wishing to celebrate a notable event, decided not to pursue the matter (*FR* 4, 20, 14).

Responding to a royal inquest, a sworn body of men might accuse those whom they knew to be criminals. As the *Third Partida* discussed the inquest in detail, the *Seventh Partida* did not. However, the *Fuero real* (4, 20, 11–12) stressed that the king could order an inquest, "ca razon es que los fechos malos e desaguisados non finquen sin pena" (because it is right that evil and illegal acts should not go unpunished). If an inquest was general, only the king or his officials should see the jurors' responses; but if it related to specific persons, they had to be informed so they could prepare their defense. If the accusers were upstanding men with no local enemies, whom they might be tempted to accuse, the king could order an inquest; he could also do so to punish forgery, perjury, notorious criminals, those making malicious accusations, or a guardian abusing his responsibility (*SP* 7, 1, 27–28). The *Leyes del estilo* (50–61, 102, 119, 121, 123) cited the use of the inquest in cases of arson, death in another's house, the death of someone in the king's service, rape, fighting, larceny, and robbery.

Men often mistrusted the inquest because it might result in false or spiteful allegations. For example, Antolín Fernández protested that officials of Burgos wrongly carried out a closed inquest accusing him of murder. In 1279, after Antolín presented sureties that he would abide by the law, Infante Sancho ordered his release. Antolín then demanded that the dead man's relatives be summoned to accuse him and that he be given a copy of any inquest executed against him. Sancho ordered the judges to adjudicate the case and to permit an appeal, but the resolution of the case is unknown. Alfonso Durant, the royal *alcalde*, probably rendered this judgment in Sancho's name.[3]

Crimes, Great and Small

The Alfonsine Codes consider the panoply of crimes created by the human mind. One need not repeat, however, the discussion in chapter 4 of treason (*traición*), an offense against God, the king, and the kingdom and, like leprosy, an incurable disease corrupting the entire body (*SP* 7, 2, pr.).

Although noble feuding has age-old roots, nobles anciently bound themselves in friendship (*FR* 4, 25, 1). As noted in chapter 10, the *Fourth Partida* (4, 27, 1–7) encouraged amity among them as a deterrent to violence. Friendship might be undone, however, when a noble charged another with *aleve* or perfidy, a lesser form of treason (*SP* 7, 2, 1).[4] In a procedure known as *riepto*, the aggrieved noble could seek justice by challenging his adversary in the king's court. Only the king could declare a nobleman a traitor.[5] After the accuser declared his readiness to prove his allegation by witnesses, documents, an inquest, or battle, his opponent had three days to issue a denial and choose the method of proof; he could refuse an inquest or trial by battle. If he died before the matter was settled, his reputation and that of his heirs remained unsullied. If he or his representative failed to appear, the king should proclaim him a perfidious traitor and order his execution. However, if he proved that the charge was false, the challenger had to retract it, and if he refused, the king could banish him (*SP* 7, 3, pr., 1–5, 8–9; 7, 11, 1–3; *FR* 4, 25, 2–7).

Trial by battle (*lid*, lat. *lis*), though no longer common, had to be authorized by the king who set a date and time.[6] Judges fixed the boundaries of the battlefield, placed the adversaries in midfield with an equal share of sunlight, explained the rules, and ascertained that they carried the designated weapons. If a disparity of age, size, or strength disadvantaged the accused, he might appoint a substitute. If the challenger defied more than one person, he would have to fight them all at once or one by one. If he refused to fight, his opponent would be acquitted. If either party abandoned the field without consent or was driven from it, he would be defeated, unless he left because of an accident. The accused would be acquitted if he killed the challenger, or if he was killed but did not admit his perfidy. If he successfully defended himself for three days, he would be exculpated, and the challenger would be penalized for making a false accusation. The horses and arms of a man convicted of perfidy who died in battle belonged to the royal *mayordomo* (*SP* 7, 4, pr., 1–6; *FR* 4, 25, 8–13). The vanquished, declared to be "worth less" (*menos valer*), was no longer the equal of his fellow nobles and henceforth could not make an accusation, testify in court, or receive honors. As the restoration of friendship was the king's preferred objective, a truce had to be arranged and the parties had to pardon one another (*SP* 7, 5, 1–3; 7, 12, 1–4).

The *Poem of the Cid* illustrates that procedure. In the royal court, the Cid, declaring that "you are worth less," denounced the Infantes of Carrión as treasonous dogs for abusing his daughters. After the Infantes denied his charge and three of the Cid's knights challenged them to battle, Alfonso VI set a date and appointed judges to supervise the encounter. When the Cid's men defeated the Infantes, the king claimed their arms.[7] The *fazañas* also record several instances of *riepto* in the early thirteenth century (*LFC* 247, 258, 300).

By carefully regulating this procedure, the king hoped to curb wanton violence among the nobility. An orderly society had to be a lawful society.

Closely linked to treason were attempts to deceive. Examples included forging documents or altering authentic ones, revealing the content of court documents that were to be kept secret, an advocate giving an adversary information about his client or citing forged laws, sentencing contrary to law, giving false witness, bribing witnesses and judges, revealing the king's secrets or telling him lies, assuming another's identity, using false weights and measures, falsifying boundary lines, and preparing false financial statements (*SP* 7, 7, pr., 1–8; *FR* 3, 10, 1) As good government depended on the acceptability of authentic records, a scribe who created a false document might lose his hand, his office, or his life and be forever infamous. A cleric who falsified the royal seal would be expelled from the clergy, branded on his forehead, banished, and his property confiscated. A perjurer would lose his teeth, and his testimony would be invalid (*FR* 4, 12, 1–4, 10; *SP* 7, 7, 4, 6).[8]

The most notorious example of falsification concerned Sancho IV. Refusing to marry Guillerma de Moncada, his betrothed, he opted to wed his second cousin María de Molina, but lacking a dispensation, his marriage, in papal eyes, was invalid and his children would be illegitimate. Given Alfonso de la Cerda's claim to the throne, Sancho arranged to have a dispensation forged in the name of Pope Nicholas IV in 1292. Boniface VIII revealed the imposture in 1297, but in response to María de Molina's petition, he legitimated Fernando IV in 1301.[9]

Counterfeiters who intended to deceive by using false gold or silver, or colored copper coins to make them appear more valuable, or clipped coins were burned at the stake and their property confiscated (*FR* 4, 13, 7–8; *SP* 7, 7, 9–10; *LEst* 78).[10] Fernando III twice confiscated villages from counterfeiters.[11]

Homicide, the killing of another human being, was a grave matter.[12] Despite restrictions on the right of accusation, every family member or member of the community could accuse someone of murder (*SP* 7, 8, 14). *Omecillo*, a murder fine, might be imposed on the community where the crime occurred or on a known killer (*FR* 4, 17, 2, 4–8; *LEst* 69, 104, 124). In

1278, Pedro, a carter, identified as a murderer by an inquest, claimed that according to the *Fuero viejo*, he should not be executed but ordered to pay the homicide fine. The king directed the judges of Burgos to send him the inquest, to allow Pedro to give sureties to abide by the law, and not to harm him until he decided the matter. Pedro's fate is unknown.[13]

Deliberate killing was punishable by death. No penalty was imposed, however, if one killed in self-defense or killed someone raping his daughter, sister, or wife, or robbing his house, or burning or destroying his property. A notorious thief, a highway robber, or a knight attempting to desert could be killed with impunity. A madman or a minor who killed someone would not be punished. An accidental death resulting from negligence was punishable. A master who struck his apprentice, thereby causing his death, would be charged with homicide (*FR* 4, 17, 1–9; *SP* 7, 8, 1–5).

Medical malpractice was a medieval problem as well as a modern one. No one could act as a physician or surgeon until his competence was determined by good physicians of the town where he intended to practice, approved by the judges, and certified in writing by the town council (*FR* 4, 16, 1–2). A physician who caused the death of his patient by prescribing incorrect dosages, or blundering at the operating table, would be banished and barred from practicing medicine. If he acted intentionally, he would be executed. He would also incur that penalty if he castrated someone, unless he intended to cure a disease (probably syphilis).[14] An apothecary who knowingly caused the patient's death by giving him lethal drugs would be slain. So too would a woman who tried to induce the abortion of a living child; if it were dead, she would be exiled. As Jews reportedly coerced their Moorish women (probably slaves) to abort their children, the mother would not be punished (*SP* 7, 8, 6–8, 13).[15]

Fathers, masters, and teachers were admonished to take care in chastising their children, slaves, or students lest, by being overly harsh, they might kill them. Anyone who armed a man who was enraged, drunk, or insane so that he could kill himself or someone else would be put to death. A judge who wrongfully sentenced an innocent person to death, exile, or mutilation would also be executed. Parricide, one of the most abhorrent crimes, was similarly punished.[16] Social standing safeguarded some murderers from the most severe punishment. Whereas a guilty noble would be banished forever and his property confiscated, a commoner would be killed. Anyone, however, who killed another in a treasonous or perfidious manner should suffer the death penalty (*SP* 7, 8, 9–12, 15–16).[17] The *fazañas* record some instances of homicide (*LFC* 225, 228).

Although civil society was founded on the notion that everyone was entitled to respect, that principle was breached when individuals were insulted or dishonored by foul language, name-calling, or gestures.[18] Leper, pederast (*fodudincul*),[19] cuckold, traitor, heretic, or whore were common epithets (*FR* 4, 3, 1–2) subject to fines.[20] Defamatory postings, some directed against the king, as well as offensive songs were reprehensible.[21] Stalking, striking, kicking, stripping, spitting, or posting horns on a cuckold's door also brought dishonor (*SP* 7, 9, pr., 1–7). The desecration of graves dishonored the living and the dead (*FR* 4, 18, 1–5; *SP* 7, 9, 12–13; *LFC* 259).[22]

Anyone defamed could seek redress in court, except a knight who deserted, a plaintiff who ignored a judge's summons, someone tortured in accordance with the law, or a man seeking a public office who was passed over for someone better qualified. A woman of good fame who dressed provocatively or visited a brothel could not allege dishonor, because she wore inappropriate clothing and went where she should not (*SP* 7, 9, 8–19). That exemplifies the age-old argument that the woman who was assaulted had only herself to blame. In determining reparations, judges considered several circumstances: injuries to the eyes or the face; whether the act occurred in the royal court, a municipal council, or a church; the status of the one dishonored, for example, a father by his son, a lord by his vassal, a former master by his freedman, or a judge by someone under his jurisdiction; and songs, rhymes, and libels (*SP* 7, 9, 20–23; *LEst* 81).

At times insults preceded violence. Disturbances of the peace by armed men were banned by Alfonso IX in 1188,[23] by the Ordinance of Nájera as recorded in the Ordinance of Alcalá in 1348 (32, 1–2), and in the *Espéculo* (4, 3, 4). However, a man was permitted to defend himself and his property (*SP* 7, 10, pr., 1–7; *FR* 4, 4, 8, 11). In 1252 Alfonso X forbade anyone to commit violence against masters and students at the University of Salamanca, but his prohibition against providing arms to *escolares peleadores* indicates that they were ready to brawl.[24] In 1271 Infante Fernando admonished knights of Toro and neighboring towns engaged in turbulent acts.[25]

Common penalties were banishment, confiscation, a declaration of infamy, restitution, and compensation for damages (*SP* 7, 10, 8–18). Monetary penalties were assigned for various bodily injuries: for example, two *maravedís* for striking the face or twenty-five *maravedís* for loss of a thumb, and lesser amounts for the other fingers in descending order (*FR* 4, 5, 3). That payment schedule, however crude, was an advance from the barbaric past when the law of an eye for an eye prevailed.

Other major crimes were robbery, the forcible seizure of another's property, and larceny, secretly doing so.[26] A robber had to make restitution, pay a fine, name his accomplices, and endure physical punishment (*SP* 7, 13, 1–4; *FR* 4, 4, 15–18; *LEst* 71–72). In 1279 Infante Sancho ruled that an inquest charging Giralt Bernalt with robbery should not have been carried out. Although he allowed the victim to sue, the outcome is unknown. The royal *alcalde* Alfonso Durant probably adjudicated the case in Sancho's name.[27] In 1188 Alfonso IX enacted a law condemning larcenists,[28] who were usually fined or whipped. Rustlers, highwaymen, pirates, and officials who plundered the royal treasury were executed. Although a commoner who kidnapped children, slaves, or freemen to sell them to the Moors would be condemned to death, a nobleman would be put to hard labor for life. Innkeepers, customs officers, and custodians of royal granaries were responsible for losses resulting from theft (*SP* 7, 14, pr., 1–22, 30; *FR* 4, 4, 6; 4, 5, 6–7; 4, 13, 5–15; *LEst* 73–76).

When a criminal act resulted in damage, the one at fault had to make amends.[29] Reparations might not be ordered if an unintended injury occurred, for example, when building a house, digging potholes, or setting traps. However, the original and the appraised value of damaged property had to be assessed and restitution made within thirty days when the act was deliberate, such as causing a ship to sink, polluting a cargo of wine or oil, facilitating a slave's escape, misdiagnosing a patient, cutting down trees or vines, endangering passersby, or throwing bones or garbage into the street (*SP* 7, 15, pr., 1–28; *FR* 4, 4, 1–7, 10, 12–13, 19–20, 22).

Fraud was a deliberate attempt to deceive by lying, keeping silent, or responding ambiguously with the intention of misleading.[30] Deception might be justified to ensnare evildoers or one's enemies, but a promise made in a truce with an enemy, even of another religion, should be kept. If one could prove that a contract was fraudulent, compensation had to be made. One had to sue for reparations within two years, but the victim and his heirs had up to thirty years to recover the estimated loss or depreciation of property suffered as a result of a trick. In addition to that amount, the defendant had to pay the plaintiff's legal costs (*SP* 7, 16, 1–6).

The endless possibilities of fraud included passing off false metal as gold or silver, offering an item for sale and then switching it for something inferior, concealing mediocre merchandise under stuff of good quality, diluting oil, wine, wax, and honey, or selling plain glass as precious stones (*SP* 7, 7, 4; 7, 16, 7–8). One of the more ingenious tricks was to soak bread in red vinegar and, when it was dry, to put it in water that turned red. In that way, the people were tricked into believing that the cheat was a saint (*SP* 7, 16, 10). Also despicable was the man who used a locked chest supposedly filled with valuables as security for a loan. Upon opening the chest later and discovering that it was full of sand, he accused his creditor of stealing, though he knew that it was there from the outset (*SP* 7, 16, 9). The most notorious double-dealer who perpetrated this rip-off was the Cid, who presented two coffers packed with sand to Raquel and Vidas, two Jews of Burgos, who lent him six hundred marks and pledged not to open the coffers during his absence. The royal jurists may have had this story in mind.[31]

On a more sophisticated level, people attempted to manipulate the legal system. For example, when a man wished to buy or sell property, another might attempt to prevent him by maliciously bringing suit for the property. A man fearing prosecution might persuade an accomplice to accuse him so that a third party could not sue him for the same offense. An advocate might assist his client's opponents or otherwise impede the successful prosecution of his client's case. Given the diversity of these fraudulent acts, the judge was advised to take into account the nature of the crime and the status of the victim and the perpetrator (*SP* 7, 16, 11–12).

Intent on controlling criminal activity by gamblers, the king banned private gambling establishments and licensed casinos for a fee. A nobleman, however, was permitted to bet within his own house. No one could pledge the body of another as security for a loan, and a knight was forbidden to pledge his weapons. A wagering cleric in legal trouble could not claim canonical protection but would be subject to the king's law (*Libro de las tahurerías* 23–26, 32).

Among sexual crimes rape was harshly punished.[32] A man who raped a single woman would be killed, but if he abducted her and did not have intercourse he would be fined or imprisoned. If she suffered a gang rape, all her assailants would be killed. The rapist of a married woman would be left to her husband's mercy. A husband could chastise a madam (*alcahuete*; ar. *al-qawwād*) who prostituted his wife, though he could not kill or mutilate her (*FR* 4, 10, 1–8). *CSM* 291 related that a scholar at the University of Salamanca raped a girl, but repented after being captured and composed a song praising the Virgin Mary, who set him free. However that may be, most rapists probably languished in prison or suffered brutal penalties, such as having one's eyes put out, loss of a hand, and hanging (*LFC* 105, 303; *FV* 2, 2, 2).

Adultery was closely linked to the concept of honor.[33] A woman who committed adultery dishonored her husband, but in an obvious instance of a double standard, if he were the adulterer, she suffered no dishonor, because she derived her honor from him (*SP* 7, 17, 1). A woman's husband and male relatives could accuse her, but no one else could, lest her disgrace become widely known. If she proved that she acted at her husband's behest, she and her partner should be acquitted, but her husband would be punished. If, knowing that she committed adultery, he received her into his bed, it would be understood that he pardoned her. If a man was acquitted of adultery, his paramour could not be charged, unless they had intercourse again. An aggrieved husband could punish his wife and her lover, even killing them, but he was forbidden to kill one and spare the other (FR 4, 7, 1–7; SP 7, 17, 7–12, 15).[34] When a knight, for example, discovered his wife and another knight in a compromising position, he cut off the man's genitals, but Fernando III ordered the husband hanged because he did not also punish his wife (LFC 116).

Sexual relationships outside of marriage also drew serious penalties. A father who discovered anyone with his daughter, or a brother with a sister, could kill them. If an unmarried woman willingly committed fornication, her partner would suffer no penalty; nor would a man who had intercourse with a vile woman. A couple related within the prohibited degrees would be sentenced to a life of penance in separate monasteries. Men who seduced nuns, widows, or virgins of good reputation were fined, banished, or scourged. A nun who married, whether willingly or not, was compelled to return to her monastery, and her husband would be banished. A man who slept with his father's wife, or a father with his son's wife, would be charged as a traitor.[35] A bigamist suffered exile. The penalty for incest was the same as for adultery, but a boy under fourteen or a girl under twelve could not be so charged (SP 7, 17, 16; 7, 18, 1–3; 7, 19, 1–3; FR 4, 8, 1–3; 4, 9, 1; 4, 10, 4).

Procurers and pimps, in the king's mind, brought great evil to his realm. Some men exploited prostitutes in brothels, while others prostituted their own wives, or opened their houses to women of good reputation wishing to commit fornication. A man pimping for his own wife would be executed. Although a wicked woman sinned by sleeping with men, she was entitled to keep whatever money they gave her (SP 5, 14, 53). Moreover, she would not have to pay tithes on her earnings because the church would not condone her conduct by accepting her money (SP 1, 20, 12). Though pimps and their women should be expelled from a town, they probably took that as a risk of doing business and established themselves elsewhere. Women enslaved as prostitutes would be given their freedom, and their pimp had to provide them with a dowry (SP 7, 22, 1–2).[36] In one instance, the village authorities of Belorado arrested Mari García, a madam working for Diago Abad, whom they accused of seducing Giralt's wife. While Mari was beaten through the village, Giralt seized Diago's property and wanted to burn his wife, but the judges put her in stocks (LFC 137).

Homosexuality was condemned as a sin against nature that brought *mala fama* and other evils to the kingdom that tolerated it (SP 7, 21, 1). Aggrieved even to have to speak of it, the king commanded that gays be castrated and hanged by their legs until they died. As a public example, their bodies would never be taken down (*FR* 4, 9, 2). Men or women who had intercourse with animals were executed, and the animal was killed to erase any memory of the deed (*SP* 7, 21, 2).[37] *CSM* 235 seemed to imply that either or both Infante Fadrique and Simón Ruiz de los Cameros, whom the king executed in 1277, were gay.[38]

Although astronomers were acknowledged as scholars, sorcerers, soothsayers, fortune-tellers, and diviners who attempted to discern the future and necromancers who summoned evil spirits were condemned to death (*SP* 7, 23, 1–3).[39]

Heresy, a topic discussed in chapter 4, was perceived as a crime menacing the good order of society. As despair was sinful, no one should commit suicide, but some did so because of illness, insanity, loss of inheritance or honor, or shame. Assassins, desperate men who often passed themselves off as monks or pilgrims, were a special danger for kings and magnates and should be executed (*SP* 7, 27, 1–3). Whereas a noble who blasphemed would lose his land, a lowborn person would receive fifty lashes for the first offense, branding with a hot iron on the lips with the letter B for the second, and for the third, lose his tongue. Blaspheming Jews and Moors would be punished as the judge saw fit (*SP* 7, 28, 1–6). The *Libro de las tahurerías* (1) penalized blaspheming gamblers with fines, lashes, or loss of tongue.

Alfonso X was himself accused of blasphemy. Pedro Afonso, count of Barcelos, reported that the king remarked: "if he had been there with God when he made the world, he [the king] would have amended many things so that they would be better made than as he [God] made them, and for that God was angry with him."[40] That comment, taken as a sign of royal arrogance, was said to have stirred the wrath of God, who decreed that the king should be dispossessed and come to a very bad end.[41] Later authors regarded it as proof of his irreligious attitude, implying that it derived from his scientific curiosity, his interest in astrology and alchemy, and his admiration for the wisdom of Muslims and Jews.[42] Whether he ever made such a remark cannot be proven, but he may have done so in jest. However, the conclusion that he was contemptuous of God is unwarranted. His lifelong devotion to the Virgin Mary, his profession of faith and acceptance of church teaching, and his plea for divine guidance in his wills of 1282 and 1284 attest to his orthodoxy.

Arrest, Incarceration, and Punishment

Once charged, a criminal had to be apprehended and brought to trial. Some tried to elude justice by seeking asylum in a church or cemetery.[43] Early church councils acknowledged that right, and the royal jurists summarized canon law on the matter (*SP* 1, 11, 1–5; *PPBM* 1, 11, 1–5).[44] While respecting asylum, civil authorities were expected to protect the church against profanation. For example, during the reign of Fernando III three men fled to a church, but their enemies dragged them out and killed them. Lope Díaz de Haro, acting in the king's name, fined the murderers three hundred *sueldos* and required them to pay the bishop one hundred *sueldos* and to do penance by going to Rome barefoot. Observers of the sacrilege were compelled to fast (*LFC* 262).

Alfonso X reserved the right to seize criminals seeking sanctuary in a church and enacted a law forbidding churchmen to protect them (*FR* 1, 5, 8). In July 1263, he confirmed that criminals fleeing to a church should not be harmed, but he denounced those who sought asylum in the cathedral of Seville where his father was buried. He directed the sacristans to close the doors after religious services so malefactors could not enter. If one did so, he should be dragged out and imprisoned.[45] In November 1263 when the municipal council of Alicante hesitated to seize criminals taking shelter in churches, he quoted the *Libro de las leyes* (*PPBM* 1, 11, 5; *SP* 1, 11, 4) forbidding the church to protect them and authorized their arrest. This decision emphasized his insistence that the *Partidas* was the law of the land and should be enforced.[46]

While awaiting trial, the accused was imprisoned.[47] A decent man or a scholar was treated respectfully and was not confined with other prisoners, but notorious criminals were detained more closely. This resembles the modern distinction between blue collar and white collar criminals. Whereas the former are treated harshly, the latter enjoy the comforts of country club prisons. The Alfonsine Codes instructed that women not be imprisoned with men, but rather in a convent until summoned to court; surely that disrupted the nuns' monastic routine. At night prisoners were confined in stocks or irons under the watchful eyes of guards. At dawn doors were opened and prisoners, one at a time, were permitted to speak with visitors. The chief jailer had to keep a written record noting the charge against each prisoner and make a monthly report to a judge. Prisoners usually had to pay a fee for their food and drink. A prisoner who posted bail (except for a crime punishable by death or loss of limbs) might remain free until his trial, but if he failed to appear in court, his surety would suffer the penalty. If the chief jailer abused prisoners, he could be executed. Guards who killed a prisoner or assisted his escape or suicide would also be executed. After an escapee was recaptured, the judge, taking his flight as evidence of guilt, could sentence him immediately or imprison him more securely. Whereas private prisons had once been used, Alfonso X prohibited anyone from building a prison without royal consent. An act in contravention of royal sovereignty, it was punished by execution (*SP* 7, 29, pr., 1–15; *FR* 4, 5, 4; 4, 13, 12; *LEst* 111, 113).

Torture, as a means of eliciting evidence of a crime, was sanctioned by Roman law and incorporated into the Visigothic Code, but it was unknown to the municipal *fueros* and the *Fuero real*.[48] With the reception of Roman law, torture was reintroduced in the *Espéculo* and the *Partidas* and continued in use until its abolition early in the nineteenth century.[49] Only a judge could authorize torture to ascertain information that might otherwise be kept secret. A prisoner could be scourged, hung by his arms, or have weights piled on his shoulders and legs. Those who could not be tortured included minors under fourteen, knights, masters of laws or other sciences, because of the nobility of the sciences, royal or municipal councilors, and a pregnant woman, lest her unborn child be harmed. A disreputable person of inferior rank, accused by only one witness but generally believed to be guilty, could be tortured. The procedure should be conducted privately in the presence of the judge and a scribe who recorded the accused's responses. If the prisoner subsequently confirmed what he said, the judge could impose sentence, but if he determined that the accused falsely confessed out of fear, insolence, or insanity, he had to release him. However, if the accused retracted his admission of treason, counterfeiting, theft, or robbery, he could be tortured twice again on two different days. And a confession made under torture and not confirmed later was invalid. A judge who maliciously tortured a prisoner, thereby causing his death or loss of a limb, would suffer the same penalty. When having to torture several persons, the judge should begin with the youngest or the one of the most vicious upbringing, because he was most likely to confess. All should be tortured separately, so no one would know what the others said. Torture should be applied with restraint lest anyone be killed or maimed. Slaves could only be tortured to compel them to testify against their masters in case of adultery by the master or mistress, fraud by a royal tax collector, treason, murder, and counterfeiting. If a master or family member was killed in his own house, his slaves and servants should be tortured to determine the killer. As various family members were not obliged to testify in capital cases or those resulting in loss of limb, they could not be tortured (*SP* 7, 30, pr., 1–9; *E* 4, 3, 5; 4, 7, 1, 3).

Conviction inevitably led to punishment.[50] Punishment, in a spiritual sense, was chastisement for sin, but legally its purpose was to castigate the criminal and deter others from committing similar offenses. The royal jurists instructed that only after a thorough procedure determined that the culprit acted intentionally should the judge inflict punishment. If the offense was not deliberate, a lesser penalty should be imposed; and if it was accidental, no penalty was due. A person who did not carry out a planned crime would not be punished, but he would be if he did so, even in part (*SP* 7, 31, 1–2).

Crimes were classified under four headings: (1) murder, theft, or robbery; (2) insults, defamation, perjury, or false advocacy; (3) forgery, wicked songs, or malicious statements; and (4) conspiracy or rebellion. There were seven forms of punishment: (1) execution or loss of limb; (2) confinement in irons for life and labor in the royal mines; (3) confiscation and exile for life to an island, a penalty borrowed from Roman law;[51] (4) imprisonment of a slave awaiting trial; (5) exile to an island without confiscation; (6) declaration of infamy, ouster from public office, or dismissal from the legal profession; and (7) public whipping, placement in the pillory, or exposure to the sun of the naked body seared with honey to attract flies. On one occasion, Diego López de Haro ordered a Gascon who killed a hawk to be stretched on a pillory in the sun until he died (*LFC* 253). An ordinary judge could sentence a criminal to death or loss of a limb and confiscate his property, according to "the laws of this our book." Only the king, however, could banish anyone to an island or confiscate his property in a case not specified in the law code (*SP* 7, 31, 3–5).[52]

As God created man in the divine image, it was deemed inappropriate to disfigure a criminal by branding him on the face with a hot iron, severing his nose, or putting out his eyes; in practice, however, this was often ignored. Punishment could be inflicted on other parts of the body, so that others, seeing it, would be deterred from crime. Capital punishment was carried out by beheading with a sword or a knife, but not with an axe or a sickle used at harvest time. A criminal might be burned to death, hanged, or thrown to wild beasts, but not stoned, crucified, or thrown from a high place (*SP* 7, 3, 6). The *Fuero* of Cuenca (arts. 1.11, 1.25, 2.32, 11.16), however, ordered serious criminals to be cast down from nearby cliffs. *CSM* 107 relates that a Jewish woman, thrown from the cliffs of Segovia by her fellow Jews, cried out to the Virgin Mary who saved her. In gratitude, she became a Christian. Local legend hailed her as Marisaltos, Leaping Mary.[53]

Lest anyone be wrongfully convicted, Alfonso X admonished his judges not to be swayed by suspicions or presumptions, although they might justify the use of torture. Punishment should be founded on incontrovertible proof, because any abuse of the body could never be undone. The nature, circumstances, and seriousness of the crime had to be taken into account, as well as the status and intention of both the perpetrator and the victim. For example, a nobleman or a learned person who committed a capital crime should not be executed ignominiously by being dragged, hanged, burned, or thrown to wild beasts, but made to bleed to death, drowned, or banished. After giving careful attention to all these possibilities, the judge could intensify or lessen the punishment or forego it altogether, but he could not alter it later. Execution ought to be carried out publicly as a deterrent to others. Relatives of the deceased or members of a religious order might claim the body for burial (*SP* 7, 31, 7–11; *FR* 4, 5, 2).

A criminal's reputation might also be destroyed by the brand of infamy. The preservation of one's good name was an ideal, and its loss had dire consequences.[54] *Fama* referred to an honest man who lived in accord with the law and good customs. *Infamia* or *desfamamiento* resulted either from an action over which one had no control or from commission of a crime. A bastard child, for example, was infamous by reason of birth. A father who denounced his son in his will rendered him infamous (*SP* 7, 6, 1–2). That was certainly Alfonso X's intention when, in 1282, he harshly condemned Sancho and disinherited him.[55]

Persons who became infamous as a result of their own conduct included a woman caught in adultery, a widow engaged in "wickedness with her body" within the year of her husband's death, a madam, minstrels, mimes, wandering singers and comics, except those entertaining the king,[56] boxers and men battling wild beasts for money, a knight stripped of his knighthood, usurers, violators of sworn contracts, and homosexuals. A judicial sentence rendered infamous one who committed treason, forgery, adultery, and other crimes. The law distinguished between ill-repute (*nombradía mala*) and infamy. The former was long-lasting and might never be overcome. Once a man gained a bad reputation, people would likely not forget it. On the other hand, an emperor or king could lift a judicial sentence of infamy by pardoning a man, though his reputation might still be tarnished in the popular mind. Infamy not only deprived a man of whatever dignity or honor he held, but also barred him from holding public office. A man who unjustly caused another to be declared infamous and sentenced to death or exile should suffer the same penalty (*SP* 7, 6, 3–8).

In some instances, the king might grant a pardon.[57] The *Fuero real* did not treat the subject specifically, but it likely was included in a missing section of the *Espéculo* that also refers incidentally to pardons. Condemning any attempt on the king's life as the worst of treasons, the royal jurists declared it an unpardonable offense. Should anyone suggest a pardon, he would be expelled from the kingdom. Nevertheless, the king, moved by pity, might pardon a traitor seeking to dispossess him, but should first put his eyes out (*E* 2, 1, 6; 2, 6, 2). That contradicted the law stating that the king could not pardon a traitor or an excommunicated person (*E* 4, 2, 1). There was a chancery formula for issuing a pardon except in cases of *aleve* or treason (*E* 4, 12, 20).[58] The fee for pardoning a crime requiring corporal punishment was ten *maravedís* for a rich man and five for a poor one (*E* 4, 12, 58).

Emperors and kings ought especially to possess the virtues of mercy and grace to dispose them to pardon criminals. The king might issue a general pardon to celebrate the birth of a son or a victory over his enemies, or to commemorate Good Friday. Or he might pardon an individual because of previous service, or because he possessed certain qualities or knowledge beneficial to the realm. Someone pardoned before sentencing would recover his standing and property, though his reputation might never be fully repaired. Unless the king declared otherwise, someone pardoned after being sentenced would not regain his property, fame, or honor (*SP* 7, 32, 1–3).

Two instances, one of insubordination and the other of outright rebellion, surely necessitated pardon. In 1264, during the Mudéjar revolt, the king's long-time friend Nuño González de Lara abandoned the citadel of Jerez without royal permission. He seems not to have suffered any punishment, though years later the king reproached him for his conduct, commenting that he had fined him.[59] In 1272 the nobles, led by the king's brother Infante Felipe, repudiated their vassalage and exiled themselves to Granada, but they returned in 1274 and renewed their allegiance. Although the sources do not mention pardon in either case, the nobles must have made some formal acknowledgment of error in return for the king's pardon.[60]

Conuiene que Saquedes los Malos Omnes de la Tierra

In order to sustain a peaceful society, the legist Master Jacobo de las leyes, in his *Flores de Derecho* (1, 1, 4), counseled Alfonso Fernández, the king's son, that "conuiene que saquedes los malos omnes de la tierra" (it is necessary that you rid the realm of evildoers). That statement confirmed the king's responsibility to purge the kingdom of criminals so that his people might live in peace. By permitting anyone (with certain exceptions) to accuse another of a crime, and by using the inquest to ferret out criminals, Alfonso X broadened the competence of royal justice, while emphasizing that crime was the public's business, as it harmed the entire community.

The catalog of crimes described in the Alfonsine Codes is, rather perversely, a tribute to human cunning and inventiveness. Treason against king and kingdom endangered the institutions intended to maintain the tranquility of the realm. *Aleve* or perfidy disrupted public order, but by regulating the process of *riepto*, the king hoped to restore peace and friendship among the nobility. Forging official documents and counterfeiting the royal coinage or seals were treasonable acts that cast doubt on the trustworthiness of government. The manipulation of false weights and measures was detrimental to economic well-being. Murder, robbery, theft, fraud, and insulting language stirred cries for vengeance and led to violence. Sexual offenses destabilized the life of the family, the nucleus of society. Heresy, communicating with evil spirits, blasphemy, and suicide contravened church teaching and were unacceptable in a Christian society. As all these crimes were regarded as destructive of the common good, the king, whose duty it was to do justice to everyone, had to punish them in the community's name.

Although an accused criminal might seek asylum in a church, Alfonso X authorized his forcible removal. The accused might also be subjected to torture, but he had to confirm his statements when he was no longer under duress. Before meting out an appropriate punishment, the judge had to be convinced of the certitude of the evidence, but he also had to consider the status of the culprit. By treating nobles and scholars with greater respect and leniency than ordinary people, the law recognized the inherent inequality of thirteenth-century society.

Corporal punishment included execution, deprivation of liberty, mutilation, and humiliation. The death penalty, reserved for the most serious crimes, was carried out publicly as a deterrent to others. A wrongdoer sentenced to exile was uprooted from his home and family. Mutilation served as a permanent visible reminder of the offender's crime. Whatever dignity a criminal may have had was lost when he was publicly humiliated by being whipped, pilloried, or put in stocks. Especially degrading was the brand of infamy, of being declared *menos valer*—to be worth less. The malefactor suffered not only the loss of public esteem, but also whatever honor, status, or office he may have possessed. Financial penalties struck the offender in his pocketbook. Confiscation of property impacted his family and his heirs. Should the king be inclined to be merciful, he could mitigate punishment or pardon a criminal.

In an ideal world, if the law was applied honestly, fairly, and justly, crime and criminals would likely be held in check, but as the royal jurists acknowledged, criminals threatened public order and required judges and other officials to take exceptional measures to suppress them.

𝕊 CHAPTER 14

The Law of the Non-Christian Peoples

Los Grandes Señores de los Christianos Siempre Sufrieron que Biuiessen entre Ellos

Although Alfonso X presided over a predominantly Christian society, a significant number of his people professed Judaism or Islam.[1] Rather than describe their beliefs and rituals, he regulated their interaction with Christians. Just as the Islamic rulers treated the Christian minority as a protected people (*dhimmís*), Alfonso regarded Jews and Muslims as privileged minorities, permitted to live according to their own private law, founded on their distinctive religious beliefs. They could worship freely and govern themselves, provided that they did not challenge him. In the *Fuero real* (4, 1–2), after discussing those who abandoned Christianity, he commented briefly on the Jews but ignored the Muslims. Any discussion of either religious community in the *Espéculo* may have been included in one of its lost books. The treatment of Jews and Muslims in the *Partidas* (7, 24–25) relied on the restrictive legislation of the Christian Roman emperors concerning the Jews that was incorporated into the Visigothic *Fuero Juzgo* (12, 2, 3–18; 12, 3, 1–28), as well as the municipal *fueros*, and Ramon de Penyafort's canonical writings.[2] By placing this in the midst of his exposition of criminal law, the king manifested his abhorrence of both religions.

A Question of Identity

In general, Christians knew more about Judaism than Islam. Whereas the *Fuero real* ignored any ideological explanation of the status of the Jews, the *Partidas* (7, 24, pr.) explained that "Iudios son una manera de gente que como quier que no creen la fe de nuestro señor Iesu Christo, pero los grandes señores de los Christianos siempre sufrieron que biuiessen entre ellos" (The Jews are a sort of people, who, though they do not believe in the faith of our Lord Jesus Christ, the great rulers of the Christians always suffered them to live among them). The word "suffered" implies that they were not particularly welcome. As the royal jurists remarked, just as diviners and soothsayers despised God by striving to discern God's innermost secrets, so too did the Jews who refused to acknowledge that God "sent his son our Lord Jesus Christ into the world to save sinners."[3] Following Ramon de Penyafort, the *Partidas* described a Jew as a circumcised believer in the law of Moses, but added that the Jews were descendants of those who crucified Jesus Christ. Rulers suffered them to live among Christians in a state of perpetual captivity as a remembrance of Jesus's crucifixion (*SP* 7, 24, 1). The *Poem of the Cid* (canto 18, lines 347–48) recorded that the Jews placed Jesus on the cross, and the *Cantigas de Santa Maria* charged them with killing him.[4]

Muslims believed that Muḥammad was God's Prophet, but "his religion (*ley*) was, as it were, an insult to God." By following him, Muslims, according to the king's men, foolishly believed that they would be saved. Like the Jews, they were expected to observe their religion and not to disparage Christianity. The stipulation, however, that they were not to "make their sacrifice publicly before men" suggests an ignorance of Muslim practice (*SP* 7, 25, pr., 1).[5]

Castilians ordinarily called Muslims *moros* or Moors, a word derived from *mauri*, the inhabitants of Mauritania, the old Roman province in North Africa, who had invaded Spain in the eighth century. That was an ethnic description lacking any sense of opprobrium, though that developed in time. The royal jurists explained that the word Moor was the equivalent of *Saracenus* or Saracen, a descendant of Sarah, Abraham's free wife. However, as Sarah was unable to conceive, the Moors were descended from Abraham's slave girl Hagar, by whom he had a son, Ishmael. Thus, Muslims were termed Ishmaelites or Agarenes.[6]

Medieval Christians frequently denounced Muḥammad as a false prophet and deprecated his followers as infidels and "enemies of the cross of Christ."[7] The *Poema de Fernán González* (lines 7, 268) condemned Muḥammad as "the man of wicked belief," whose "power isn't worth three fig trees." The *Libro de Alexandre* dismissed Muslims as "a renegade people, who pray to Muḥammad, a proven traitor."[8] Rodrigo Jiménez de Rada incorporated a life of Muḥammad in his *History of the Arabs*.[9] In order to refute Islam, he directed Mark, a canon of Toledo, to prepare a Latin translation of the Qu'rān; but otherwise neither Rodrigo nor his colleagues seem to have troubled themselves about the conversion of the Mudéjars.[10] Bishop Lucas of Túy also provided a rather lurid account of Muḥammad's life and teaching.[11]

Reflecting the prevailing attitude, Alfonso X reviled Islam as "a wicked sect" created by Muḥammad "for the perdition of souls." Utilizing the writings of Rodrigo, Lucas, and others, he summarized the life of Muḥammad in the *Estoria de Espanna*. Born in Mecca, "the false prophet," descended from Ishmael, borrowed many of his ideas from the Jews and Christians he encountered along the trade routes. Accompanied by the Archangel Gabriel, he explored the heavens, ascending even to the seventh heaven, where God chose him as a prophet. Supposedly afflicted with epilepsy, he received revelations from God and began to preach that there was only one God. Rejected by the Quraysh, the ruling tribe in Mecca, who were polytheists, he made his *hijra* or journey to Medina. After subjugating Mecca, he incorporated the pilgrimage to the shrine of the Ka'aba into his religion. His doctrine was said to be drawn from Nicholas of Antioch, one of the original seven deacons, and purportedly the founder of the Nicolaites, a heretical sect. Muḥammad taught that Jesus was born of the Virgin Mary by the Holy Spirit but that he was not divine. Muslims, summoned to prayer, gathered in their mosques and, using a lunar calendar, fasted during the month of Ramadan. Those who killed their enemies would enter paradise where they would enjoy feasting and the embrace of lovely maidens. His words were recorded in the Qu'rān, a book filled with "so much iniquity and falsehood." Though married to Khadija, a wealthy widow, he committed "adultery and fornication" with eighteen women. When he died, he yielded his soul to the devil and, as Lucas remarked, his body was devoured by dogs.[12]

Juan Manuel related that the king caused to be translated into Castilian "the entire sect of the Moors," so as to reveal the errors of Muḥammad, the "false prophet." Those translations included the *Liber scale Machumeti* or *Muḥammad's Ladder*, which recounted his journey to the seventh heaven.[13] The king surely had the opportunity to consult Muslim leaders about their beliefs and to study the Qu'rān, but he seems to have relied on polemical Christian sources for his knowledge of Islam.

The Jewish and Moorish *Aljamas*

By the middle of the thirteenth century, as a consequence of the conquest of Andalucía and Murcia, the Jewish and Muslim populations in Castile had grown substantially. Jewish colonies were located in urban centers where most lived as artisans and shopkeepers. A few gained wealth and prominence as moneylenders, tax collectors, and physicians to the king. Settled in Spain from the earliest times, the Jews were not perceived as a political threat.[14]

Jews, though mainly city dwellers, were never integrated into municipal political and juridical life. Usually residing in a separate urban district called the *judería*, they formed their own community or *aljama* (ar. *al-jama*, the gathering) headed by a *viejo mayor*, "the chief old man."[15] The Jews of Allariz, for example, in 1289 agreed to live within the *judería*, and Christians were forbidden to live there.[16] Although Roman and canon law prohibited Jews from holding public office or exercising authority over Christians, Castilian kings often violated that principle.[17] The *Partidas* (7, 24, 3) explained that the Jews, as God's People, committed treason by failing to recognize Jesus as the Messiah and crucifying him. Thus, emperors forbade them to hold any office with power to oppress Christians. In 1271, for example, Alfonso X barred any non-Christian from public office in Lorca and declared that no Jew or "New Christian," a convert, except a royal *almojarife* or tax collector, should have authority over Christians.[18] Despite that, he ordinarily employed Jews as tax farmers.[19]

In contrast to the Jews, Muslims were viewed as enemies to be driven from Spain. Fernando III, on receiving the surrender of the principal cities, required the Muslim population to evacuate. As Muslim jurisconsults held that a good Muslim ought not to submit to Christian authority, many affluent Muslims emigrated to Granada or Morocco. In 1254 Alfonso X authorized Christians to purchase the holdings of Moors departing from Seville.[20] While the emirs of Murcia, Granada, and Niebla were compelled to become Castilian vassals, thousands of Muslims in Murcia and Andalucía were subject to Christian rule. They were known as Mudéjars, a word derived from *al-mudajjan*, "those allowed to remain."[21] As freemen, some engaged in agricultural and pastoral pursuits, while others were tradesmen or artisans. Still others were held as slaves.[22] In 1260 Alfonso X observed that "the Moors who are in all our realms are ours and we have to guard and protect them and to have our rights from them."[23] Although they had a protected status, their allegiance was always suspect, and their revolt in 1264 confirmed that view.

Moors were also banned from wielding authority over Christians, and there is no evidence that the king employed them in his government. Organized in their own self-governing *aljama*, in the towns they usually lived in certain neighborhoods known as *morerías*, where they were assured of security in their persons and property (*SP* 7, 25, 1). Their *alcaldes* (ar. *al-qādī*) administered justice and collected tributes owed to the crown. Sometimes the *alcalde* was called *alcaide* or *alcayat*, a word derived from *al-qā'id*, a military commander. The similarity of the words, despite their distinct meanings, confused Christian minds. In 1254 Ibn Sabah, *alcayde de moros*, promised the royal *alcalde* Gonzalo Vicente to transfer the *aljama* of Morón southward to Silibar by 31 August. If anyone failed to move by that date, the king would seize his property. Given safe conduct to their new village, the Moors were permitted to build houses, shops, mills, baths, and warehouses. Ibn Sabah would govern them according to their own law, and no Christian was allowed to live there except the royal *almojarife*. For three years from 1 September they were exempt from taxes, but thereafter they would owe the king a tenth of the harvest and varying sums for marshy land (*almarjal*).[24] This was part of a broader plan to reduce the Muslim population in the vicinity of Seville, about forty miles to the northwest. Manuel González Jiménez counted eight *aljamas* in the old kingdom of Jaén, fifteen in the kingdom of Córdoba, and twenty in the kingdom of Seville before the Mudéjar revolt of 1264.[25] There were others in Alicante, Lorca, Elche, and Murcia. Chancery registers for 1284–85 recorded *aljamas* in Badajoz, Moura, Serpa, Valencia, Hornachos, Magacela, Benquerencia, and Alcántara, as well as others in the lands of the military orders.[26] *CSM* 169 related that 'Abd Allāh, "rey de los moros del Arrixaca," a vassal of Alfonso X, vetoed a proposal to remove the Christian church from the Arrixaca of Murcia, even though the king had authorized it.[27]

Social and Legal Constraints

The separation of Jews and Muslims from Christians was intended to inhibit the possibility of conversion. Jewish and Muslim leaders were equally anxious to preserve their community from unnecessary contact with Christians. All three religious traditions opposed intermarriage with persons of other religions, and the ban was incorporated into both Roman and canon law.[28]

All sexual contact between Christians and Jews was forbidden. Lest a Christian woman be seduced by a Jew or persuaded to give up her faith, in 1252 Alfonso X prohibited her from residing with Jews as a servant or nursing their children.[29] Christian and Jewish women were forbidden to nurse children of a different religion, and if a Christian woman married a Jew or a Moor, both would suffer the death penalty (*FR* 4, 2, 4; 4, 11, 3). Declaring that Christian women were spiritually wedded to Jesus Christ, the royal jurists threatened those who had intercourse with Jews or Moors with confiscation, scourging, or death (*SP* 7, 24, 9). The husband of a guilty woman could cast her out, burn her, or punish her however he wished. Moors engaging in liaisons with Christian women would be stoned to death. By contrast, anyone who raped a Muslim woman had only to pay 10 percent of the fine due to a Christian victim of rape (*SP* 7, 25, 10). *CSM* 186 told of a Christian woman, wrongly accused of adultery, who was saved from the flames by the Virgin Mary, though her putative paramour, a Moorish slave, was totally burned. Christian men were also banned from cohabiting with Jews.[30]

A Jew might have Christian servants, provided they did not live in his house where they might be susceptible to proselytization. Christians and Jews were forbidden to eat or drink together, and Christians were warned not to drink wine made by Jews, just as Jewish law forbade the use of wine made by Christians. Nor were Christians to use medicines prepared by Jews, though presumably a Jewish physician might prescribe medication that a Christian could take if it were prepared by a Christian who was familiar with its ingredients. Lest Christians, Jews, or Muslims bathe together, certain days were assigned in the public baths to each of the three religions (*SP* 7, 24, 8).[31]

In order to thwart the assimilation of Jews, they were not permitted to adopt Christian names (Jerez 1268, art. 7). Just as the Almoravids and the Almohads in the eleventh and twelfth centuries obliged Jews to wear distinctive dress, so too did the Fourth Lateran Council in 1215 (canon 68). Thus enabled to identify Jews, Christians presumably would keep their distance from them. Fernando III, protesting that many Jews, rather than submit to this indignity, preferred to withdraw to Muslim lands and that some even conspired against him, appealed to Pope Honorius III in 1219 to suspend the canon. Later evidence reveals that the canon was not observed.[32] In this respect one ought to recall Peter Linehan's judgment that the Castilian Church, dominated by the monarchy, was woefully negligent in implementing the decrees of the Fourth Lateran Council.[33]

The Cortes did not require Jews to wear a badge, but it did regulate colors and types of clothing. In the Cortes of Seville in 1252 (art. 40) Alfonso X required Moors to live in enclosed districts in the towns, to wear their hair parted without a tuft, and their beards as long as their law required. They could not wear brightly colored clothing, or white or gilded shoes, or gold and silver adornments. The penalty for the first offense was one hundred *maravedís* and two hundred for the second. The *Cantigas de Santa María* usually portrayed bearded Moors wearing turbans and long-flowing gowns. This ban was later extended to the Jews.[34] As these ordinances also specified the types and colors of clothing permissible to various ranks in society, including the king, it was not a matter of singling out Jews or Moors.

Nevertheless, the royal jurists, commenting that wicked things occurred when Christians and Jews dressed alike, endorsed canon 68 of the Fourth

Lateran Council and ordered Jews to wear some distinguishing sign on their heads so that they could be easily recognized (*SP* 7, 24, 11). The *Cantigas de Santa María* depict Jews wearing capes and hoods, but there is no identifying badge or other sign on their clothing.[35] The law in the *Partidas*, however, does not seem to have been enforced. When the Cortes of Palencia in 1313 asked Infante Juan, then regent for Alfonso XI, to require Jews to wear a yellow badge as in France, he demurred, saying that he would do what seemed best in this regard (arts. 26 J, 34 J).[36]

Ordinarily judges of each religious community resolved litigation among their own members, but complications occurred when people of different groups came into conflict. For example, Alfonso X declared that Christian judges, rather than Jewish elders, should adjudicate suits between Christians and Jews. Christians were admonished not to take unauthorized pledges or otherwise injure the Jews, but to bring their quarrels before royal judges. No one should summon a Jew to court on the Sabbath, and a Jew could not be constrained to appear on that day (*FR* 4, 2, 7; *SP* 7, 24, 5; *LEst* 87–90). In 1263, the king, rejecting the practice in Burgos of requiring the testimony of a Christian and a Jew in a suit between Christians and Jews, stated that two Christian witnesses were sufficient.[37] When the *aljama* of Burgos complained that judges favored Christians over Jews, he ordered the municipal *alcaldes* to do justice to the Jews, as was customary, and to permit them to appeal to him.[38] The *aljama*, after agreeing to an annual payment of 330⅓ *maravedís* for the city's judges, vainly protested his appointment of Simón Raínez and Garcí Pérez as special *alcaldes* to hear suits between Christians and Jews.[39] In the Cortes of Palencia in 1286 (art. 15) Sancho IV curtailed the right of Jews to be judged by their own judges by declaring that they would be justiciable by royal judges in each town. Subsequent Cortes repeated that principle.[40]

Muslim *alcaldes*, at least in the kingdom of Murcia, were responsible for administering justice among their own people, but occasionally they seem to have been negligent. Alfonso X directed the municipal *alcaldes* of Cartagena to compel the *alcalde moro* to adjudicate pleas between Moors should he fail to do so. That may have been a step toward subjecting litigation among Moors to royal judges. He also assured the people of Alicante and Lorca that only a Christian judge could settle cases between Christians and Moors. As lord of Elche, Infante Manuel also affirmed the authority of the *alcalde de los moros*. However, in Burgos, and perhaps elsewhere, the municipal *alcaldes*, according to Sancho IV, customarily had jurisdiction over the Moors, who evidently did not have their own judge.[41] Mudéjars were also forbidden to act as advocates except in cases involving their coreligionists (*E* 4, 9, 2; *FR* 1, 9, 4; *SP* 3, 6, 5).

In cases involving different religious groups, the law usually required proof by witnesses representing each religion, but the inferior status of Jews and Muslims was manifest. In all pleas the testimony of two Christians of good repute was admissible against Jews or Moors.[42] Moors, Jews, and heretics were forbidden to bear witness against a Christian, unless they could personally testify when there were no Christian witnesses, or in a case of treason in which they personally participated (*E* 4, 7, 5; *SP* 3, 16, 9). Whenever Christians, Jews, or Moors engaged in litigation with one another they were obliged to swear in a prescribed manner. In the Cortes of Seville in 1252 (art. 38) Alfonso X ordered them to do so as in the past, but as noted in chapter 8 above, he specified the exact wording of the oaths in his law codes (*E* 5, 11, 16–17; *SP* 3, 11, 20–21).[43]

The *Leyes del estilo* (83–84, 103) stipulated that monetary penalties for crimes would be levied in accordance with local *fueros* and not Jewish or Muslim privileges. The law favored Christians, whose lives were valued more highly than those of Muslims or Jews. If the dead body of a Jew or a Moor was found within the municipal district, the town would have to pay a homicide fine of one thousand *maravedís*.

Tributes

The Jewish *aljama* was responsible for collecting the annual tribute owed to the king in accordance with the principle enunciated in the *Fuero* of Cuenca (art. 29): "The Jews belong to the king and they are assigned to the treasury."[44] That principle was illustrated in 1270 when he gave a Jewish community to Las Huelgas de Burgos with the stipulation that they would pay tribute to the nuns.[45] The principal tax was a capitation or poll tax, but the Jews also paid a multiplicity of other taxes.[46]

The king also claimed ownership of the Muslims, declaring that those "who live in all our kingdoms are ours." They paid a capitation tax (*pecho de los moros, alfitra, alfitran*). In 1260 he set that at one *maravedí* for sharecroppers, shopkeepers, and craftsmen in Alicante, but at one half for men making their living from the sea.[47] The Moors of Andalucía also paid a land tax (*almarjal*) and a tenth of the harvest (*diezmo*). Some owed labor services, such as Moorish craftsmen, who had to work on the cathedral of Córdoba two days each year.[48] Occasionally, the king obliged the Moorish and Jewish communities to pay an extraordinary tax such as the *oncenas* or eleventh in 1252. When the Jews of Badajoz refused to pay it, in 1253 he ordered them to do so and to pay an additional sum. In 1279 he also required the Jews of San Felices, who refused to pay tribute on taxable property they acquired, to do so.[49]

During the Cortes of Seville in 1252 (art. 41), the king stated that no one was authorized to exempt Moors from taxation, but he sometimes conceded their tributes to the towns. In 1254, for example, he granted Córdoba five hundred *maravedís* from the tribute owed by the *aljama* at Michaelmas for repair of the city walls. Two years later he gave the Muslim tenth to Alicante; in 1261, for the maintenance of the walls he gave the town the capitation tax. Orihuela received a similar concession in 1274.[50]

Both Jews and Moors had to pay tithes on lands formerly belonging to Christians. However incongruous it may seem, the primary reason was economic rather than religious. The transfer of lands from Christians to non-Christians meant a decrease in episcopal revenues from the tithe and would also deprive the king of the *tercias*. Thus, he affirmed the obligation of the Jews and Muslims to pay tithes on lands once Christian.[51]

The Jewish communities paid a much higher tribute than the Moors. Early in 1281 the king arrested all the Jewish *aljamas* and forced them to pay a ransom of 4,380,000 *maravedís* annually.[52] That seems to be twice the usual amount, as the Cortes of Valladolid in 1312 (art. 102) claimed that the *aljamas* paid Alfonso X and Sancho IV 6,000 *maravedís* daily (or 2,190,000 annually); in Fernando IV's time that sum had declined to one fifth (1,200 *maravedís* daily). More than five thousand of the richest Jews were excused from payment, so the burden fell upon poor Jews.[53] In September 1290 the capitation tax was almost 2,000,000 *maravedís* of which the largest portion was paid by Toledo (216,505), followed by Burgos (87,760), and Carrión (73,480). The total for the frontier, including Seville and Córdoba (191,898) was less than for Toledo and for the kingdom of León (218,300). The kingdom of Murcia paid a paltry 22,424 *maravedís*.[54]

The crown's total income from Mudéjar tributes is unknown, though royal accounts for the half year from December 1293 to June 1294 reveal the following sums: Seville, 8,000 *maravedís*; Córdoba, Constantina, and other towns, 5,000; Madrid, 1,300; Burgos, 1,092; Coria, 569; León, 480; Santa Olalla, 423; and Almoguera, 414. Moors in the diocese of Palencia owed 5,692 *maravedís*, and those in the dioceses of Ávila and Segovia taken together, 6,705. The accounts for the year ending in November 1294 show the Moors of Seville paid 5,500 *maravedís*, those of Córdoba, 2,000, and those of Constantina, 1,150. Amounts were given for the combined Jewish and Moorish communities of the archdiocese of Toledo, the kingdom of León, and the dioceses of Plasencia and Cuenca, but there is no way of determining the relative contribution of each community. Most of the money was likely paid by the Jewish *aljamas* who were wealthier than the Moors. The Jews of Ávila, for example, paid 59,592 *maravedís* in 1290 while the Moors of Seville paid 5,500 in 1294.[55]

Religious Freedom

Jews and Muslims were guaranteed religious liberty, but its practical exercise was circumscribed. Jews were admonished to observe the law of Moses peacefully, without speaking ill of the Christian faith. Alfonso X declared: "we do not prohibit the Jews from observing their Sabbaths and the other feasts that their law commands and their usage of all the other things granted by Holy Church and by kings" (FR 4, 2, 7). Saturday was their day of worship, on which they remained in their houses and did not work or engage in business (SP 7, 24, 2).[56]

The king also confirmed their right "to read and to have all the books of their law, as it was given to them by Moses and by the other prophets" (FR 4, 2, 1). Yet they were warned not to read books that might undermine their faith; such books would be burned. While that seems to reflect a concern to preserve authentic Jewish teaching, the law may also have been prompted by fear that the books might contain anti-Christian ideas. Jews were also forbidden knowingly to possess books that attacked Christianity (FR 4, 2, 1). That law may have been inspired by Gregory IX's order in 1239 to seize and scrutinize the Talmud for passages offensive to Christians. Although copies of the Talmud were burned in France, there was no similar expurgation in Castile-León.[57]

The synagogue, a house where Jews praised God's name, was under royal protection, and no one was to destroy it or plunder it. However, the king claimed the right to arrest criminals seeking refuge there, just as he did in Christian churches. Christians were forbidden to use a synagogue as a stable or for lodgings or to interfere with Jews praying there.[58] In accordance with Roman and canon law, already existing synagogues could be repaired but could not be increased in size or height or painted. If that were done, the synagogue would be turned over to the local church. In 1250 Pope Innocent IV prohibited the Jews of Córdoba from erecting a new synagogue.[59] Nevertheless, Alfonso X reserved the right to authorize construction of new synagogues (SP 7, 24, 4), thereby affirming that he did not intend to allow ecclesiastical authorities to determine his policy.

Although the law assured Mudéjars of security in their property, there was always a discrepancy between the letter of the law and its implementation.[60] The Moors were not permitted to have mosques in Christian towns, though they might retain smaller mosques and cemeteries outside the walls. The Christians, however, had no compunction in appropriating mosques and turning them into churches. When Fernando III captured Córdoba, the chief mosque was cleansed of "the filthiness of Muḥammad" and dedicated as a cathedral.[61] That process also occurred in other cities. Alfonso X gave the archbishopric all the mosques in Seville except three in the Jewish quarter that were transformed into synagogues. In 1266 Jaime I demanded that the Mudéjars of Murcia yield the mosque adjacent to the *alcázar* so that it could be consecrated as a church. When they objected, he insisted that he did not wish to hear the muezzin calling the faithful to prayer while he was asleep.[62] Other mosques and cemeteries in the kingdom of Murcia were transferred to Christian hands.[63] The conversion of churches to mosques and mosques to churches symbolized the alternating ascendancy of one religion over the other.

Despite promises of religious liberty, Jews and Muslims were expressly forbidden to propagate their beliefs. The ban on any public display of their religion and the restraints on sexual and social relations among Christians, Muslims, and Jews were intended to obstruct proselytization. The law, furthermore, made it dangerous for anyone to convert to Islam or Judaism. On penalty of death, confiscation, and eternal infamy, Jews and Muslims were prohibited from seeking converts among Christians. If perchance a Christian, losing "his sense and true understanding," committed "the very great treason" of becoming a Muslim or a Jew, his property would be confiscated and he risked losing his life. Should he return to the Christian faith, he would be forever infamous and be banned from testifying in court, holding public office, making a will, inheriting property, or concluding a contract (*SP* 7, 24, 2, 7; 7, 25, 4–8; *FR* 4, 1, 1; 4, 2, 2).

The Cortes of Seville in 1252 (art. 45) explicitly forbade Muslims to convert to Judaism or Jews to become Muslims. Converts or those counseling conversion were fined one hundred *maravedís* and became the king's "captives." Their children would inherit their property, but if there were none, the king would be the beneficiary. The *Partidas* (7, 24, 10), intent on discouraging Jews from seeking converts among slaves, declared that a slave who accepted Judaism would become free. Moors who were captives of Jews could also gain their freedom by becoming Christians. If Jews purchased or owned Christian slaves, which they were forbidden to do by law, those slaves would also be set at liberty.[64]

Jews and Muslims were enjoined not to insult the Christian religion. A Jew who blasphemed God would be fined ten *maravedís* for each offense and would suffer ten lashes (*FR* 4, 2, 3). Reflecting that law, *CSM* 286 related that when Jews laughed at a barking dog interrupting a Christian's prayers, God, on Mary's intercession, caused a door to fall on them and crush them. Muslims and Jews who spit on the cross or the altar, defaced paintings or images, or threw stones at churches would lose a quarter of their goods for the first offense, a third for the second, half for the third, and beyond that they would be banished. If the delinquent was a propertyless minor, his hand would be cut off. A Jew or a Muslim who spoke wrongly of God, the Virgin Mary, or the saints while playing with dice would suffer the lash. On the third offense, his tongue would be cut out, and his body and his goods would be at the king's disposal.[65] While acknowledging that Jews and Moors should not be pressured to accept Christianity, Alfonso X explained that just as the Moors prohibited Christians to insult Muḥammad or Islam, it was only right that Jews and Moors, "whom we permit to live in our realms, though they do not believe in our faith," should be similarly castigated (*SP* 7, 28, 6).

The rumor of ritual murder of Christian children by Jews in northern Europe was echoed in the *Partidas* (7, 24, 2). It was said that Jews, on Good Friday, in contempt of Christ's passion, crucified children or wax images. Anyone convicted of this crime in the king's presence would be executed. Given the possibility of violence against the Jews on Good Friday, the king ordered them to remain inside their district until Saturday morning. Otherwise they would not be entitled to compensation for injuries inflicted by Christians. While the *Cantigas de Santa María* do not include any story of ritual murder, *CSM* 12 related that when the Virgin Mary complained of "the perfidy of the Jews who killed my son," the people of Toledo rushed to the Jewish quarter where they found the Jews crucifying an image of Jesus on the feast of the Assumption.[66]

Unlike Jews and Muslims, Christians were not denied the right to seek converts. They were admonished, however, to win over Jews by good example and the teachings of sacred scripture and not to compel them, because "our Lord Jesus Christ does not wish and does not love service given by force." If a Jew wished to become a Christian, other Jews were not to impede him. If they wounded or killed him, they would be burned to death (*SP* 7, 24, 6). *CSM* 4, describing how a Jewish father was burned for attempting to burn his son, who had received communion with Christian children, may reflect this law.[67]

Nor was anyone to threaten a Muslim wishing to accept Christianity. Echoing Pope Gregory the Great, the royal jurists counseled Christians "to labor by good words and suitable preaching to convert the Moors and cause them to believe in our faith and to lead them to it, not by force or by pressure . . . for [the Lord] is not pleased by service that men give him through fear, but with what they do willingly and without any pressure" (*SP* 7, 25, 2).[68] A generation later Juan Manuel repeated a commonplace of Christian theology: "involuntary and forced services do not please God. . . . Jesus Christ never commanded that anyone should be killed or compelled to accept his religion, because he does not want forced service, but rather that which is done willingly and with the right disposition."[69] Ana Echevarría suggested that the mendicant friars in Seville may have converted those Muslims whom the municipal council described as "new Christians" in 1274.[70]

Converts often found that their situation was not a happy one. Christians were commanded to treat a convert from Judaism with honor and respect, and not to insult him or his descendants because they had once been Jews. Anyone who assaulted a convert would be punished and had to make compensation. A convert was entitled to retain his property and his share in his family's inheritance. No longer excluded from public office, he could hold every office or dignity open to a Christian (SP 7, 24, 6). The Council of Peñafiel in 1302 acknowledged the difficulties facing potential converts who were fearful of losing their goods if they did so.[71]

Muslim converts were often insulted as turncoats. When there was only a handful of Moors in a Christian community, as was probably the case in the north, conversion or assimilation took place inevitably, as the Moors opted to conform to the lifestyle of their neighbors. In the larger towns where the number of Mudéjars was more substantial and they were organized in aljamas, the possibility of maintaining their separate identity was greater. The Cantigas de Santa Maria (167, 192) attributed some conversions to the intercession of the Virgin Mary.

Nevertheless, Alfonso X made no concerted effort to convert either Jews or Muslims. The impetus for missionary activity among the Muslims came from outside the peninsula. Jaime I admonished him for not displaying greater zeal in this respect. While Alfonso X supported the Dominican Arabic language school at Murcia, and in 1254 established a studium generale for Latin and Arabic studies at Seville,[72] he seems to have been prompted chiefly by his interest in Arabic culture rather than a missionary impulse. Still, as the years passed he developed a more hostile attitude toward Muslims and Jews.

Although his son Sancho IV revealed a superficial knowledge of Muḥammad's life and various aspects of Islamic doctrine, Sancho also never suggested that the conversion of the Muslims was a royal responsibility. He stated bluntly that "the Moor is nothing but a dog." The majority of Christians more than likely would have agreed with him.[73]

The Mudéjar Revolt and Its Aftermath

In the second decade of Alfonso X's reign the situation of the Mudéjars changed for the worse. In 1262 the king seized Niebla, dispossessing his vassal Ibn Maḥfūt and forcing the Moors to evacuate the town. Next, he expelled the Mudéjars from Écija and introduced Christian settlers. Then, intent on controlling the Strait of Gibraltar, he demanded that Ibn al-Aḥmar, emir of Granada, surrender Tarifa and Gibraltar. Rather than comply, the emir incited the Mudéjars of Andalucía and Murcia to revolt in 1264. After the emir submitted in 1267, Alfonso X expelled the Moors from the frontier towns and replaced them with Christians. Meanwhile, Jaime I vanquished the Mudéjars of Murcia. In 1272 Alfonso X, fearing a future insurrection, directed the Moors to move from the city to the suburb of Arrixaca. They were forbidden to damage the houses they left or to remove doors, locks, or armoires. Christians living in the Arrixaca had to leave their houses for the Moors. A wall separating the Arrixaca from the city proper was to be built; gates and bridges connecting the city and the suburb were to be sealed or torn down. The Moors of Orihuela were also restricted to the suburb.[74] During his remaining years, the number of Christian settlers steadily increased, while more prosperous Mudéjars emigrated to Granada or North Africa.[75]

In the *Cantigas de Santa Maria* the king described the emir's attempt to seize the castle of Chincoya (*CSM* 185), the uprising in Jerez in 1264 (*CSM* 345), and the proposed removal of the Christian church from the Arrixaca (*CSM* 169). But he also denounced "the false, vain, very crazy villain, the dog Muḥammad" (*CSM* 192.102–4) and expressed the hope that the name of Muḥammad would be erased (*CSM* 328.5–8). He also prayed to "be able to expel the sect of Muḥammad from Spain" (*CSM* 360.27), to "destroy the unbelieving Moors," and "to drive out those who, to my distress, occupy the land of Ultramar and a great part of Spain" (*CSM* 401.12–31; *CSM* 406.33–41).

The Jews, His Other Enemies

As the king's reign drew to a close, the Jews also incurred his wrath. For years Solomon ibn Zadok of Toledo was his *almojarife mayor*, but when he died in 1273, Alfonso X confiscated his estates and gave them to the cathedral of Seville. Despite that, Solomon's son Isaac ibn Zadok, known to the Christians as Zag de la Maleha, served the king in a similar capacity.[76] In five contracts concluded between October 1276 and January 1277, the king authorized Zag de la Maleha, Roy Fernández of Sahagún, a Christian, Abraham ibn Shoshan, son-in-law of the *almojarife* Meir ibn Shoshan, and Meir's sons Zag and Yusuf to collect arrears of taxes owing since the conquest of Niebla in 1262. All told he expected to receive 1,670,000 *maravedís*. The intensive scrutiny of royal accounts dating back fifteen years was bound to exacerbate relations between the king and his people and to rouse hostility toward the Jews.[77]

A few years later, Zag de la Maleha and the Jewish community suffered cruelly at the king's hands. Requiring substantial funds to blockade Algeciras, the king fined Christian usurers and solicited *servicios* from the Cortes. In February 1279, Burgos contracted with the tax collector Yusuf Pimintiella to pay six *servicios* in five years instead of outstanding taxes and fines.[78] Trouble ensued not long after. As the king's behavior became more erratic, probably as a result of a painful cancer in his face, Queen Violante fled to the court of her brother, Pedro III of Aragón. Infante Sancho, anxious to reconcile his parents, compelled Zag de la Maleha to give him tax moneys collected for the siege of Algeciras so that he could bring his mother home. Thereafter, Castilian forces, weakened by illness and hunger, abandoned the siege, and in June 1280 the knights of Santiago were decimated at Moclín. In September, the king vented his fury by ordering the arrest of the Jewish tax collectors. Then, in order to chastise Sancho as well, he had Zag de la Maleha taken to Sancho's residence at the friary of San Francisco in Seville and dragged through the streets to the Arenal on the eastern bank of the Guadalquivir. The *Chronicle of Alfonso X* says nothing of a trial, but the king likely denounced Zag as a traitor deserving the most degrading execution. Although Sancho thought to intervene, his advisers warned him not to. Then, on 19 January 1281, Alfonso X ordered the arrest of all the Jews gathered in their synagogues on the Sabbath and demanded a daily ransom of 12,000 gold *maravedís*, or 4,380,000 annually.[79] In a moving poem written in prison, the courtier-poet Todros b. Judah ha-Levi accepted his imprisonment and impoverishment and the possibility of execution as "a mark of [God's] love."[80]

These events are the hidden story behind CSM 348 telling of a king (obviously Alfonso X) who had insufficient funds for the war against Granada, because those in charge of his revenues failed to assist him. While he was sleeping, the Virgin Mary told him she would reveal a buried treasure, but a search yielded nothing. A year later, however, she showed him an abundance of silver, gold, jewels, silks, and tapestries belonging to the "judeos, seus enemigos, a que quer peor ca mouros" (the Jews, his enemies who are worse than the Moors). This was not buried treasure, but the ransom exacted from the imprisoned Jews. The vehemence of the poet's animosity toward the Jews reflects the king's perception of betrayal by Zag de la Maleha.

Deuen Biuir . . . entre los Christianos . . . Guardando su Ley e Non Denostando la Nuestra

Alfonso X regulated relations among members of the three religions according to this principle: "Deuen biuir los Moros entre los Christianos en aquella mesma manera . . . que lo deuen los judios, guardando su ley e non denostando la nuestra" (the Moors should live among Christians in the same manner . . . as the Jews ought to do, observing their religion [*ley*] and not insulting ours) (*SP* 7, 25, 1). Different religions were designated as *leyes* or laws, because the law was all embracing, including the substance of religious belief, which in turn determined the habits of daily life. Jews and Muslims were assured of religious freedom and jurisdictional autonomy so long as they did not contest Christian ascendancy.

In order to preserve the separate identities of the three religions, the law prohibited Christians from converting to Judaism or Islam, banned Christian women from nursing children of other religions, forbade Christians to cohabit with Jews or Muslims, and required non-Christians to dress in a certain way and not to assume Christian names. The Jewish synagogue was protected as a house of worship and might be repaired, but new ones could not be erected without royal permission. Conversely, the king, perceiving Islam as a greater political threat, routinely transformed mosques into churches, just as the Muslims had once turned churches into mosques. As a clear mark of their inferiority, non-Christians could not hold public office or exercise authority over Christians.

Alfonso X's legislation concerning non-Christians was not particularly original, as it conformed to the centuries-old tradition of Roman and canon law. What is striking is that he seems to have ignored the considerably more hostile anti-Jewish laws in the Visigothic Code and the Councils of Toledo.[81] The condition of the Jews or Muslims seems not to have worsened because of his legislation, but the laws were conveniently summarized in the *Partidas* for future generations to use.

Enforcement of the laws depended largely upon local authorities, but illustrative court records are lacking. Despite the laws and his unflattering depiction of the Jews in the *Cantigas de Santa María*, Alfonso X seems to have been tolerant of them. Contrary to the canonical prohibition, he employed many of them as physicians and tax collectors. Attracted to Islamic culture, he directed many Jews to translate Arabic texts, particularly those of a scientific nature. He even proposed to establish a *studium generale* in Seville where Latin and Arabic would be taught. In his last years, frustrated by the disappointment of his imperial ambitions, threatened by Moroccan invasion, and suffering from various illnesses, he became more hostile to those surrounding him. Lest the Mudéjars threaten his rule again, after their revolt in 1264, he uprooted them from frontier towns. His arrest and execution of Zag de la Maleha and his plundering of the Jewish *aljamas* severed his close relationship with Jewish leaders.

As a final reflection, it is well to recognize that medieval society was not inherently pluralistic. Christianity, Islam, and Judaism were exclusive religions in which religious beliefs and customs were inextricably linked. Unlike our society, which is professedly neutral in matters of religion and in which everyone, irrespective of religious beliefs, is equal before the law, in medieval Europe the law of the dominant religious group prevailed. As Castilian society was fundamentally Christian, only Christians could participate fully in public life. Jews and Muslims, hedged about by legal and social restraints, remained peoples apart. A degree of assimilation was possible in terms of language and external habits, but unless a Jew or a Muslim abandoned his religion, which encompassed the totality of his existence, he could not be wholly integrated into a society proclaiming itself Christian.

❧ CHAPTER 15

The Juridical Achievement of Alfonso X

Guardar Deue el Rey las Leyes como a su Honra e a su Fechura

Alfonso X of Castile, whom generations have acclaimed as el Sabio, the Wise or the Learned, holds a unique place among his fellow monarchs, not only as an eminent scholar and patron of scholars, but also as a great lawgiver in the tradition of Justinian. As a ruler over a complex cluster of kingdoms, each with its own customs and laws, he set out to create a common law or *Libro de las leyes* that would govern all his people and inspire in them a sense of unity transcending regional and provincial boundaries. Though not formally trained as a jurist, Alfonso X, following his father's initiative, directed a company of jurists who created a comprehensive and systematic legal system. While the *Fuero real* was intended for the usage of the cities and towns of Castile and Extremadura, the *Espéculo* was kept in the royal court to serve as the standard by which every other law would be judged. This *Libro de las leyes*, known in its more extensive form as the *Siete Partidas*, was the king's most significant juridical achievement. Aside from Justinian's Code, the *Partidas* stands out as the greatest medieval monument of civil law.

The *Libro de las leyes* presents us with a panoramic view of thirteenth-century Castilian society in its multifaceted forms: political, religious, cultural, social, and economic. Through its pages the whole of humanity passes in review: kings, queens, and princes; courtiers, lords, and ladies; bishops, priests, monks, and nuns; knights, foot soldiers, and mariners; scholars, pilgrims, merchants, moneychangers, tradesmen, farmers, laborers, and shepherds; freemen, slaves, and freedmen; husbands and wives; parents and grandparents; women and children; sons and daughters; boys and girls; widows and orphans; gays and straights; Christians, Jews, and Muslims; judges, lawyers, plaintiffs, defendants, and witnesses; madmen, the halt, the lame, the blind, and the retarded; wastrels, gamblers, cheats, tricksters, frauds, thieves, robbers, and murderers; adulterers, fornicators, prostitutes, pimps, and madams; grave robbers, necromancers, and criminals of every stripe.

Alfonso X left an extraordinary cultural legacy, not only in the works of history, poetry, and science composed at his direction, but especially in his law codes. Choosing to present them in the vernacular, he shaped the language of law and enabled his people to readily understand it. In so doing, he tried to educate them in the law. As he stated "we make this book for the service of God and the common good (*pro comunal*) of the people" (*SP* 1, 1, pr.). Nevertheless, the *Libro de las leyes* did not please everyone, especially those who protested that it superseded ancient customs. That charge coupled with accusations that he violated the Code's assurance that justice would be administered fairly and without prejudice ultimately led to his deposition. Notwithstanding the tragedy of his final years, by creating a common body of law for all his dominions, he gave governmental institutions a form and character that they would retain for many years after his death. One of the greatest kings of medieval Castile, his influence on the development of Spanish law and institutions was profound and lasting. Robert I. Burns remarked that "unlike other codes, [the *Siete Partidas*] is as much a work of literature as law, a catechism of philosophical-moral rumination and behavioral report, exhortative and genial. As a monument of wisdom literature it seems as admirable a construction of human genius as any Gothic cathedral."[1]

The Influence of the *Siete Partidas* beyond Castile

Alfonso XI's explicit declaration that the *Siete Partidas* should have the force of law guaranteed that the legal structure brought into being by Alfonso X would survive him. The subsequent compilations of Spanish law, namely, the *Leyes de Toro* of 1505 (art. 1),[2] and the *Recopilación de Leyes de estos reinos* or *Nueva Recopilación* of 1567 (2, 1, 1),[3] repeated that declaration, and the *Novísima Recopilación* of 1805[4] incorporated various laws from the *Partidas*. Thus the *Siete Partidas* became the foundation of the legal system of the medieval kingdom of Castile-León, and later of modern Spain and of all the countries of the Spanish-speaking world colonized by Spain from the sixteenth century onward.[5]

The existence of at least 115 manuscripts containing the complete or partial text of the *Partidas* suggests its utility in the Middle Ages. The editions of the *Siete Partidas* by Alonso Díaz de Montalvo in 1491, by Gregorio López in 1555 (with an extensive gloss), and by the Real Academia de la Historia in 1807 also attest to the ongoing interest in the Code by lawyers and the courts. In 1555 Carlos I sanctioned the usage of López's edition as the official version to be used not only in Spain, but also in Latin America and the Philippines. In 1818 Fernando VII gave royal approval to the Academia's version, but in 1860 the Spanish Supreme Court declared that when there was a discrepancy between the López and Academia editions, the former should be preferred. In his introduction to Scott's translation, Charles Sumner Lobingier declared that the *Siete Partidas* had "the widest territorial force ever enjoyed by any law book" and that it was an "outstanding landmark" of both Spanish and world law.[6]

The *Partidas* also had a profound impact on the other peninsular kingdoms in the Middle Ages as a result of partial translations into Portuguese, Catalan, and Galician. José Domingues remarked that the *Siete Partidas* "left a unique and indispensable mark on Portugal that centuries have not been able to erase." He concluded that the *Partidas* were first received in Portugal in the reign of Dinis (1279–1325), who cited its laws on at least four occasions (1295, 1305, 1309, and one undated). His son Afonso IV (1325–57) also cited a law from the *Partidas* in 1325. As Dinis was Alfonso X's grandson, it seems reasonable to believe that he would commission a Portuguese translation of the *Partidas* as a sixteenth-century tradition suggested. Thus far, only the complete texts of the *First* and *Third Partidas* and thirty-four fragments of others (except the *Fourth*) are known.[7] The *Third Partida* was copied from an earlier version in the summer of 1341. In the fifteenth century Afonso V enacted the *Ordenações* that, while supplanting the *Partidas*, also utilized many of its laws, especially those concerning military organization, the functions of procurators, commerce, the role of guardians, treason, counterfeiting, and the like.[8]

Not surprisingly, the *Partidas* were known in the Crown of Aragón in the thirteenth century. Various authors have remarked that the treatment of knighthood in the *Partidas* (2, 21) influenced Ramon Llull's Catalan treatise on chivalry, the *Llibre de l'orde de cavalleria* composed around 1274–76.[9] During the second half of the fourteenth century, Pedro IV of Aragón apparently intended to make the *Partidas* the fundamental law of his dominions and directed his protonotary "traslladar en nostra lenguatge per tal que . . . fessem ordenar semblants leyes les quals propriament poguessen esser dites nostres" (to translate [the *Partidas*] into our language . . . so that we might ordain simi- lar laws that could properly be called ours).[10] Sometime before 1365 the *First* and *Second Partidas* were translated into Catalan, but no more. Nevertheless, Pedro IV's *Tractat de cavalleria*, written in 1383, translated the discussion of knighthood in the *Partidas* (2, 21, 1–25). At the end of the fourteenth century, a partial translation of title 18 of the *Second Partida*, concerning the custody of castles, was made.[11]

The *Siete Partidas* also formed part of the legal corpus of the countries of Latin America belonging to the Spanish Empire, but when they declared their independence early in the nineteenth century they had to decide whether to continue following Spanish law. For instance, when Mexico became inde- pendent of Spain in 1821, a table recording the precedence of various bod- ies of law then in force gave sixth place to the *Fuero real* and *Fuero Juzgo* and eighth place to the *Partidas*. In 1857 the Mexican Congress ruled that when the law was uncertain recourse should be made to the Spanish *fueros* and the *Partidas*.[12] In a similar table of precedence enacted in Colombia in 1825 the *Partidas* occupied fifth place. In Chile the *Partidas* were in use until the codi- fication begun in 1857 and completed in 1907. That was also true of Brazil until the adoption of the Civil Code in 1918. The substance of many laws in the *Partidas* was also incorporated into the new law codes of Peru. In 1848 the Congress of Ecuador allotted fifth place in the table of precedence to the *Partidas*. These and other examples illustrate Bernardino Bravo Lira's comment: "The *Partidas* are the juridical corpus that has had the longest and broadest application in Hispanic America."[13]

In the same way the *Partidas* formed part of the law of those territo- ries of the United States that were once part of Spain's overseas dominions. References to the *Partidas* in court cases in Texas, California, and Louisiana illustrate its influence in the nineteenth century and even in the twentieth. Recognizing the significance of this code for American justice, the American Bar Association authorized Samuel Parsons Scott to translate the entire *Siete Partidas*. Though ready for publication as early as 1913, for various reasons his translation was not printed until 1931.[14]

A century earlier a partial translation of the *Partidas* was completed in Louisiana. Originally colonized by France, Louisiana was ceded to Spain in 1762, returned to France in 1800, and sold to the United States in 1803. Dur- ing that time Spanish law, including the *Partidas*, was applicable in Louisiana and continued to be so under American rule. Given that fact, the desirability of an English translation of the *Partidas* became evident and prompted Louis Moreau-Lislet and Henry Carleton in 1818 to translate certain titles relating to promises, obligations, sales, and exchanges (*SP* 5, 5–6, 11). At the direction of the Louisiana legislature, the two jurists published a more complete translation in 1820.[15] As their concern was the laws currently applicable in Louisiana, they did not include the *Second Partida*, which deals primarily with the king, and that part of the *First Partida* relating to canon law. The legislature ordered distribution of the translation to all the state courts, as well as governors of other states and the president of the United States. After publication of the translation, citation of the *Partidas* in the Louisiana courts increased a hundredfold. The translation was also used in the neighboring state of Texas.[16]

Robert I. Burns summarized the work of several scholars concerning the influence of the *Partidas* in the western states.[17] Oftentimes controversy arose over the differing application of Spanish law and English common law introduced by English-speaking settlers in the former Spanish colonies. In Texas English common law was adopted in 1840, but Spanish law concerning the property rights of private parties continued in force. That became an issue in 1995 when private parties holding land titles from the Spanish crown disputed the state of Texas's claim to ownership of an extensive coastal area. In resolving the issue the Texas General Land Office turned to Spanish legal sources and upheld the validity of titles granted by the Spanish crown. A similar issue arose when California and the City of Los Angeles, alleging an easement, sued to acquire rights to coastal lands held by the Summa Corporation. The matter eventually reached the US Supreme Court. In his ruling in 1984, Chief Justice William Rehnquist rejected the claim of an easement and in the footnotes to his decision cited "the expert testimony" of the *Siete Partidas* offered at trial. The *Partidas* (3, 28, 1–8) emphasized that the sea, the seashore, rivers, and harbors are open to everyone and not the property of any individual. The *Partidas* was also cited in resolving claims to water rights.[18] Whereas the *Partidas* (2, 15, 5; 3, 28, 11) asserted that mines pertained to royal sovereignty and should not be alienated to anyone, large mining corporations sought to override the public interest and to encourage privatization of mineral rights. In the mid-nineteenth century, California rejected the principle laid down by the *Partidas* and allowed private bodies to exploit these resources. Arizona and Texas did the same.[19]

Joseph W. McKnight pointed to the influence of the *Partidas* on family law. For example, Texas accepted the rules for adoption outlined in the *Partidas* (4, 7, 7–8) but unknown to English common law. Both Texas and California also acknowledged the principle of communal property. Unlike English common law, the *Partidas* (4, 11, 17) recognized a wife's right to her own property and her right to share equally with her husband in whatever property they acquired together. McKnight also noted that the *Partidas* (5, 13, 4–5) banned the seizure of a debtor's livestock, farm equipment, and slaves, and a knight's horse and arms, as all these were necessary for one's livelihood. Those laws protected homesteaders in Texas from the seizure of their property for debt.[20] King Alfonso's influence on American law was acknowledged in 1950 when a marble relief of el Rey Sabio was included among twenty-three lawgivers honored in the chamber of the House of Representatives in the US Capitol.

This very brief overview suggests something of the ongoing influence of the *Siete Partidas* in those states once subject to Spanish rule. An extensive search of case law will undoubtedly produce further evidence, but that is a task for others to pursue.

The Lessons of el Rex Magister

The study of law and justice in thirteenth-century Castile has an inherent interest, as I hope that the foregoing pages have made clear. Nevertheless, I have always believed that knowing and understanding the past is essential to knowing and understanding the present. As I mentioned in chapter 1, Francisco Márquez Villanueva hailed Alfonso X as el Rex Magister, the Teacher King.[21] Thus, we may ask: What lessons can el Rex Magister teach us about the practice of government? What can his *Libro de las leyes* teach us about our contemporary society? With full awareness of changes wrought by time and circumstance that distinguish the twenty-first century from the thirteenth, I believe that el Sabio, the Learned King, can offer us several lessons.

Promotion of the Common Good

First is the recognition that government exists to foster the *pro comunal*, the common good of everyone. Alfonso X proclaimed that the *Libro de las leyes* was intended "to serve God and the common good of the people," that the legislator ought "to love justice and the common good," that laws "contrary to the grand common good" ought to be repealed, and that the ruler "should always uphold the common good of his people rather than of himself" (*SP* 1, 1, pr., 11, 16–18; 2, 1, 9). Today we live in a highly polarized society that pits one group against another and places a premium on individual rights. As a consequence, the idea of the common good has been shunted aside. Until we again acknowledge that the pursuit of the common good is the foundation for a peaceful, orderly, prosperous, and just society, we are likely to live in contention with one another as each of us seeks to further our own interest to the detriment of everyone else. The danger of excessive polarization is that it can tear apart the body politic. When the ruler uses his office for his own benefit rather than that of his people, or when he disparages any element among his people, whom he is obliged to love and protect, or when his people, who are bound to honor and obey him (*SP* 2, 10, 2), express their contempt for him, the unity of the body politic that exists to promote the common good will be shredded, perhaps irreparably.

Preservation of the Rule of Law

A truly just society must be founded on the rule of law that aims to enable everyone to live in peace and justice. In accordance with the *Libro de las leyes*, judges were directed to administer justice promptly and evenhandedly, with good sense and wisdom. Their task was to implement this principle: "Iustitia est constans et perpetua voluntas ius suum cuique tribuendi" (Justice is the constant and perpetual will to render to each one his right) (*D* 1, 1, 10 pr.; *Inst.* 1, 1). Alfonso X emphasized the ruler's responsibility to see that justice is done to everyone: "El Rey es puesto en la tierra en lugar de Dios para conplir la justicia e dar a cada uno su derecho" (The king is placed on earth in the place of God to do justice and to render to each one his due) (*SP* 2, 1, 5). While that notion is accepted in theory today, marginalized groups in our society (Native Americans, blacks, gays, women, among others) frequently believe that they do not receive their full measure of justice. The harassment or killing of black men by law enforcement officers is often seen as a violation of this principle and has given rise to the Black Lives Matter movement. If justice is to be the hallmark of our society, discrimination of this kind must be ended. Even more far-reaching is the threat to the rule of law about which many have expressed grave concern. Indeed, in May 2018 the vice president of the United States revealed his distorted sense of the rule of law when he extolled as "a tireless champion of strong borders and of the rule of law" a sheriff who brutalized immigrants and, on that account, was convicted of criminal contempt of court.[22] We have also witnessed, at the highest level of government, the denigration of judges and attacks on the integrity and honesty of national officers constitutionally responsible for the administration of justice. If that should continue, the people's trust in the judicial system and their expectation of securing their just due in court will suffer grievous harm. We must be able to believe, as Alfonso X stated, that judges and other officers engaged in the administration of justice are honest persons of upright character whose sole intent is to discover the truth and render judgment without fear or favor. Should any judge or public official abuse his office, he should of course be held accountable (*SP* 2, 9, 28; 7, 1, 11).

Preparation for War

When a nation embarks on a military enterprise it is essential to have well-thought-out goals and objectives. While accepting the notion that a war, especially a war against the "enemies of the faith," was right and just and could ultimately lead to good, King Alfonso also acknowledged that it could result in grief and destruction. As war is "full of perils and fears," it should not be undertaken lightly. Prior to taking action commanders ought to be attentive to the hazards of war lest their troops "incur harm or fall into disgrace." Careful preparation is necessary, and a clear strategy should be worked out (*SP* 2, 23, 6). In view of the seemingly interminable American involvement in wars in Iraq and Afghanistan and more recently in Syria, those words of admonition are most timely. Critics have suggested that the United States blundered into those wars without developing an overarching strategy for bringing them to a conclusion. Fears were also expressed that the lack of detailed planning for the proposed summit with North Korea in June 2018 might lead to a negative outcome. Thus far expectations that the summit would result in the denuclearization of North Korea have not been fulfilled.

Protection of the Environment

At a time when climate change and global warming are becoming an everyday reality, Alfonso X's counsel for caring for the environment ought to prompt us to act conscientiously in using the riches provided by our world. Committed to fostering economic growth, the king enacted measures safeguarding natural resources such as animals, birds, fish, plants, and trees, and encouraging the conscientious utilization of mineral resources and of land suitable for farming and pasturage. The development of roads, waterways, and bridges and the removal of obstructions to passage overland or by water was intended to overcome barriers separating communities, to promote domestic trade and facilitate pilgrimage, and, in the broadest sense, to create a spirit of unity among his people that would serve the common good (*SP* 2, 11, 1–3; 2, 12, pr.; 2, 20, 1–8). Sharing a common love of country, king and people had to further the good estate of the realm by working together to improve the land and exploit its resources responsibly. By doing so, the kingdom would become a pleasing and attractive place to live. Today our environment (and our health) is threatened by potential disasters caused by our own doing, for example, oil spills, the rupture of oil pipelines, air pollution (smog) caused by burning fossil fuels that release carbon dioxide into the air we breathe, and the consequent depletion of the ozone layer. As of April 2018, 195 nations have subscribed to the Paris Agreement to combat climate change, but the American government in 2017 announced its intention to withdraw from that pact by 2020. Meanwhile, the Environmental Protection Agency is dismantling many regulations intended to shield the environment from further pollution.

Welcoming the Stranger

Alfonso X understood that the elimination of unnecessary obstacles would not only facilitate commercial interchange between different regions of the realm and of the known world, but would also contribute to the general prosperity. For that reason he welcomed pilgrims from northern Europe and guaranteed their safety and security. He knew that they brought economic benefits to residents of the towns along the *camino de Santiago* (*SP* 1, 24, 1–4; 5, 8, 27; 6, 1, 30–32). So too, he realized that merchants, whether Christians, Jews, or Muslims, bringing goods from other countries also contributed to the economic well-being of his realm. However, he was not a proponent of free trade, and he regulated mercantile activity, so much so that Pedro III of Aragón complained that the king's prohibition of the export "of almost all merchandise" was injurious to merchants of both realms and diminished Castile's potential revenues.[23] Recently, the president of the United States has railed against trade agreements with other countries that are supposedly detrimental to American interests and has spoken of the possibility of engaging in a trade war. Like Pedro III in the thirteenth century, many twenty-first-century economists have questioned the wisdom of creating unnecessary impediments to free trade. The president has also repeatedly warned of the need to erect an expensive, partial wall on our southern frontier and to impose a ban on travel from certain Islamic countries in order to curb the influx of criminals and terrorists. The frontiers of thirteenth-century Castile were far more fluid, and it is surely likely that criminals crossed them to do mischief, as did Moorish raiders seeking plunder. Castles and other fortifications protected the frontier, but still King Alfonso welcomed strangers who came in peace to his kingdom, in the expectation that they would contribute to the general prosperity.

Acceptance of the Other

Ethnic and religious differences have often served to drive peoples apart. Those differences were especially marked in medieval Spain, a society that was not officially pluralistic. The king and his government were professedly Christian and did not admit the equality of all religions before the law. Only Christians could fully participate in public life. Fenced about by many legal and social barriers, Jews and Muslims could not be wholly integrated into a self-proclaimed Christian society, unless they were willing to abandon their religion and accept Christianity. Despite those restraints, Jews and Muslims were able to live side by side with their Christian neighbors and engage them in the many ordinary interactions of daily life. Living in their own communities, they were permitted to worship freely and to govern themselves, so long as they did not challenge the king's authority. Many Jews served the king as physicians, tax farmers, and tax collectors, despite the canonical prohibition against allowing them to have authority over Christians. The king's attraction to Islamic culture prompted him to sponsor the translation of Arabic texts, especially those of a scientific nature, and he established a *studium generale* or university in Seville where Latin and Arabic would be taught. As he regarded Muslims as less trustworthy than Jews, he expelled the Muslims from the frontier towns following the Mudéjar revolt in 1264. In his later years, as his imperial ambitions were thwarted and the Marinids invaded the kingdom, and his physical woes intensified, he became increasingly hostile to both Muslims and Jews. Unlike ancient and medieval countries, the United States, and most other countries, does not acknowledge any official religion. However, from time to time someone will proclaim that the United States is a Christian nation, thereby ignoring the millions of non-Christian citizens and forgetting that the First Amendment to the Constitution prohibits Congress from enacting a law establishing a state religion or restricting the free exercise of religion. Others, even at the highest level of government, loudly decry the threat of Islam to our civilization and the possibility that *sharia*, or Islamic law, will supplant our Constitution. Statements of this sort betray an ignorance of American history and also of Islam and Islamic law. Medieval Spain was home for many centuries to the greatest concentration of Jews and Muslims in Western Europe. In spite of the limitations placed on them, sporadic outbursts of violence against them, and their ultimate expulsion, the history of medieval Spain, for the most part, is the history of the peaceful coexistence of people belonging to the three religions. Coexistence and religious tolerance have also been characteristic of American society for centuries, and though the threat of terrorism is real, that should not lead to a blind condemnation of Islam whose faithful adherents stop whatever they are doing five times a day to offer prayers in praise of their Creator.

The Qualities of a Political Leader

King Alfonso's disquisition on the role of the king and the qualities that he ought to possess can be read with profit by any modern political leader.

Above all the ruler ought to be a person of outstanding character and ability who understands that his primary obligation is to serve the common good. Ideally, the ruler and his people should be bound by mutual love and respect. Counseled by learned and intelligent persons, he ought to love and honor all his people, no matter their social condition, to protect them, to foster love and unity among them, and to do justice impartially by giving to each one his due. Should he love and honor his people, he would enjoy their esteem, but if he acted abusively or unjustly, or sought to fill his own pockets at the expense of his people, he would lose their love and his ability to govern (SP 2, 2, 1–4, 9; 2, 3, 1–5).

As he often conveyed his ideas and directives verbally, the ruler, before speaking, should carefully consider what he wished to say and then choose his words deliberately, because once they left his mouth they could not be recalled. Not rushing, but clearly enunciating every word so as not to be misunderstood, he should speak in a reasonable and calm manner. He ought not to speak loudly except when circumstances required that he do so. Guarding his tongue, he should not be long-winded, lest he reveal matters best kept secret. Always abiding by the truth, he should never consciously utter a falsehood, because when people discover that he is a habitual liar, they will not believe him when he speaks the truth. As the use of bad language corrupts good habits, he ought not to indulge in foolish and harmful talk or blaspheme. Nor should he brag, but let his good works speak for themselves. He should never praise anyone excessively, wantonly insult anyone, or defame an innocent person. He should watch his tongue in the presence of his enemies, lest they use his words against him, and he ought not to speak over much, lest he unwittingly reveal his secrets. Poorly chosen words expressed in a disjointed manner will expose a ruler's intellectual shortcomings (SP 2, 4, 1–5).

The cultivation of good habits and the practice of the virtues of prudence, temperance, fortitude, and justice would enable the ruler to live honorably and justly and set an example for his people. Guided by the principle of moderation, he should avoid excess in eating and drinking. Always conscious of his position, he should not have sexual intercourse with indecent women. Should he beget illegitimate children, he would bring shame and dishonor upon himself, his family, and his country. Maintaining a patient and serene demeanor, he should strive not to be swayed by rage, anger, or hatred that would interfere with his ability to discover the truth and justice. By giving in to anger and acting hastily, he might violate the law and cause unnecessary harm. A wise ruler was a literate man conversant with the *saberes*, those areas of knowledge useful for the business of government. The wisdom gained from books would assist him in making his own judgments and free him from overdependence on his counselors. He would also be better able to assess their capabilities (*SP* 2, 5, 1–21).

Those words, written in the thirteenth century, can be easily transposed to the twenty-first century to describe the current president of the United States. Unlike Alfonso X, who professed his love for his people and declared his responsibility to govern justly so they might live in peace and harmony, the president seems to take pleasure in sowing division in the body politic by setting one group against another. He seems unwilling or incapable of repairing that divide and offering a unifying purpose to the people. Not only that, but he evidently has little or no knowledge of how our government works and shows little interest in doing the necessary study to overcome that deficit. He refuses to become familiar with the *saberes* and seems incapable of reading anything other than a few paragraphs. His principal aides have questioned his mental acuity. Treating the government as a family business, as an opportunity for personal enrichment, he has surrounded himself with persons whose qualifications for office are often minimal or nonexistent, and who, like him, are prepared to use their offices to gain further riches. We have become accustomed to a president who demeans and debases anyone who questions him or fails to display sufficient loyalty to him. We know that he routinely denies responsibility for his actions, that he lies without hesitation, that he is given to outbursts of rage, that he speaks in hyperbole, without thinking of the consequences of his remarks, that he is often incoherent, that he boasts that his accomplishments are greater than those of his predecessors, that he requires the adulation of huge crowds, and that his private life has become a public scandal.

An autocrat with little understanding or respect for the law, he might give heed to King Alfonso's admonition that the ruler must obey the law: "Guardar deue el rey las leyes como a su honra e a su fechura porque recibe poder e razón para fazer justicia" (The king should observe the laws just as he would his honor and his handiwork, because he is given power and reason to do justice). Should he neglect to do so, his commands and his laws will be scorned. That statement reflects the principle *Digna vox* asserting that the law is the foundation of the prince's authority, and on that account, he should obey it (*C* 1, 14, 4). In a remarkably prescient passage, the king went on to say that no one is above the law: "E desto nunguno puede ser escusado por razon de creencia ni de linage ni de poder, ni de honra, ni avn por demostrarse por vil en su vida o en sus fechos" (No one can be excused from this [obedience to the law] by reason of belief, lineage, power, or honor, not even if he shows himself to be vile in his life and actions) (*SP* 1, 1, 16). Threatened by an ongoing investigation into his conduct, our president has claimed that, while he has done nothing wrong, he has the right to pardon himself. Should he do so, that would be tantamount to acting as judge in his own case, an idea rejected by laws everywhere. King Alfonso explicitly declared: "Dezimos que ningun judgador no puede nin deue oyr ni librar pleyto sobre cosa suya o que a el pertenezca, porque non deue vn ome tener logar de dos, assi como de juez e demandador" (We state that no judge can or ought to hear or decide a case concerning his own business or a matter in which he has an interest, because no man should take the place of two, namely, as the judge and the plaintiff) (*SP* 3, 4, 10). Once again words written more than seven hundred years ago resonate in modern ears.

Unaware or careless of the honor and majesty associated with the exalted office that he holds, our president has inflicted great injury upon it. The task of restoring respect for the presidency after his departure will be an onerous one. His fate is yet to be determined, but the inexorable march of the law may yet call him to account. He might learn a lesson from King Alfonso whose tyrannical behavior cost him his kingship.

A Lawful King Brought Down by the Law

By contrast with our president, el Rey Sabio will always be known as a king who revered the law. Again and again he proclaimed his responsibility to enact just laws that would guarantee the rights of every person and enable everyone to live in peace and justice. In time, however, people objected that his new laws ran counter to traditional customs. Although he attempted to placate his opponents by confirming the customs of the nobility and the traditional *fueros* of the townspeople, he did not abandon the ideas, principles, and aspirations embodied in the *Siete Partidas* and the *Fuero real*. Sadly, however, in the last decade of his reign recurrent illness (apparently a cancer affecting his face and forcing his eye to protrude and producing excruciating pain) made him increasingly irascible and caused him to act more and more arbitrarily. His execution of his brother Fadrique and Simón Ruiz de los Cameros in 1277 without any semblance of a trial, and the execution in 1280 of Zag de la Maleha, a Jew who had long served him faithfully as a tax collector, led to the accusation that he denied due process of law to his subjects. The complaint about "false inquests" in the Cortes of Seville in 1281 gave credence to the notion that he no longer maintained his people in "justice, peace, and law." Thus, having lost the love of his people, in the spring of 1282 his son Sancho and the estates of the realm gathered at Valladolid deprived Alfonso X of royal authority. That proceeding echoed in the late fourteenth century when a royal councilor remarked that the Assembly of Valladolid "with the consent of and at the request of the kingdom," declared that "the sword of justice should be removed from [the king's] hand because he did not use it well, because he killed Infante Don Fadrique . . . and Don Simón de los Cameros without giving them a hearing (*sin ser oídos*)."[24] In effect, guaranteeing due process of law to everyone was a ruler's essential obligation. Whether any of the participants were aware of it or not, the judgment rendered by the Assembly of Valladolid implicitly affirmed the *lex regia* whereby the Roman people conferred on the prince their authority and power (*D* 1, 4, 1). Although Alfonso X claimed to rule by the grace of God, the action taken by the estates intimated that the people, having received power and authority from God, conceded it to the king upon his acclamation and his pledge to uphold the law. Then, finding that he was in violation of his oath to maintain the law and render justice to everyone, the people reclaimed that power and authority. Despite the fidelity of Seville and Murcia, Alfonso X had only a faint hold on his other dominions in the two years before his death at Seville on 4 April 1284. It is a great irony that a king who spoke so eloquently about justice and the law should be brought down by his failure to preserve it.

NOTES

Acknowledgments

1. Francisco Martínez Marina, *Ensayo histórico-crítico sobre la antigua legislación y principales cuerpos legales de los Reynos de León y Castilla, especialmente sobre el Código de las Siete Partidas de Don Alfonso el Sabio*, 2 vols. (Madrid: Hijos de don Joaquín Ibarra, 1808; 2nd ed., Madrid: D. E. Aguado, 1834; 3rd ed., Madrid: Sociedad Literaria y Tipográfica, 1845); 4th ed.: *Obras escogidas de don Francisco Martínez Marina*, ed. José Martínez Cardós, 3 vols. (Madrid: Atlas, 1966–69), vol. 1 (*BAE*, vol. 194).

2. Francisco Martínez Marina, *Teoría de las Cortes o Grandes Juntas Nacionales* (Madrid: Fermín Villalpando, 1813); repr. as *Obras escogidas*, vols. 2–3 (*BAE*, vols. 219–20); Francisco Tomás y Valiente, *Martínez Marina, Historiador del derecho* (Madrid: Real Academia de la Historia, 1991); María de la Concepción Castrillo Llamas, "Francisco Martínez Marina: El hombre y su obra," *Medievalismo* 2 (1992): 219–25.

3. Eduardo de Hinojosa, *El elemento germánico en el derecho español* (Madrid: Imprenta Clásica Española, 1915).

4. Luis García de Valdeavellano, *Historia de España: De los orígenes a la baja edad media*, 2nd ed., 2 vols. (Madrid: Revista de Occidente, 1955), and Valdeavellano, *Curso de historia de las instituciones españolas de los orígenes al final de la edad media* (Madrid: Revista de Occidente, 1968).

5. Alfonso García Gallo, *Manual de la Historia del Derecho Español*, 3rd ed., 2 vols. (Madrid: Artes Gráficas y Ediciones1967).

6. Robert I. Burns, SJ, ed., *Las Siete Partidas*, trans. Samuel Parsons Scott, 5 vols. (Philadelphia: University of Pennsylvania Press, 2001).

1. El Rey Sabio

1. Joseph F. O'Callaghan, *The Learned King: Alfonso X of Castile* (Philadelphia: University of Pennsylvania Press, 1993), and O'Callaghan, *Alfonso X and the Cantigas de Santa Maria: A Poetic Biography* (Leiden: Brill, 1998); Antonio Ballesteros y Beretta, *Alfonso X, el Sabio* (Barcelona: Espasa-Calpe, 1963; repr., Barcelona: El Albir, 1984); Manuel González Jiménez, *Alfonso X, el Sabio* (Barcelona: Ariel, 2004).

2. Jerry R. Craddock, *The Legislative Works of Alfonso X, el Sabio: A Critical Bibliography* (London: Grant & Cutler, 1986), and Craddock, "The Legislative Works of Alfonso el Sabio," in *Emperor of Culture: Alfonso X the Learned of Castile and His Thirteenth-Century Renaissance*, ed. Robert I. Burns (Philadelphia: University of Pennsylvania Press, 1990), 182–97.

3. Manlio Bellomo, *The Common Legal Past of Europe, 1000–1800*, trans. Lydia G. Cochrane (Washington, DC: Catholic University of America Press, 1995); Antonio

Pérez Martín, "La institución real en el 'ius commune' y en las Partidas," *CLHM* 23 (2000): 305–21; and Pérez Martín, "El ius commune: artificio de juristas," in *Història del pensament jurídic: Curs 1996–1997 dedicat a la memoria del professor Francisco Tomás y Valiente*, ed. Tomàs de Montagut (Barcelona: Universitat Pompeu Fabra, 1999), 69–93.

4. *Corpus Iuris Civilis*, ed. Paul Kreuger, Theodor Mommsen, Rudolf Schoell, and Wilhelm Kroll, 3 vols. (Berlin: Weidmann, 1877–88).

5. Harold J. Berman, *Law and Revolution: The Formation of the Western Legal Tradition* (Cambridge, MA: Harvard University Press, 1983), 128–29.

6. James A. Brundage, *Medieval Canon Law* (London: Longman, 1995); Wilfried Hartmann and Kenneth Pennington, eds., *The History of Medieval Canon Law in the Classical Period, 1140–1234: From Gratian to the Decretals of Pope Gregory IX* (Washington, DC: Catholic University of America Press, 2008).

7. Antonio García y García, "En torno al derecho romano en la España medieval," in *Estudios en homenaje a Don Claudio Sánchez Albornoz en sus 90 años*, 3 vols. (Buenos Aires: Instituto de Historia de España, 1985), 3:59–72; Antonio Pérez Martín, ed., "Los colegios de doctores de Bolonia y su relación con España," *AHDE* 48 (1978): 5–90.

8. Rodrigo Jiménez de Rada, *Historia de rebus Hispanie sive Historia Gothica*, ed. Juan Fernández Valverde, Corpus Christianorum, Continuatio Mediaevalis 72 (Turnhout: Brepols, 1987), 256, bk. 7, chap. 34; Lucas of Túy, *Chronicon Mundi*, ed. Emma Falque, Corpus Christianorum, Continuatio Mediaevalis 74 (Turnhout: Brepols, 2003). C. M. Ajo G. y Saínz de Zúñiga, *Historia de las universidades hispánicas*, 11 vols. (Madrid: Centro de Estudios e Investigaciones "Alonso de Madrigal," 1957–79), 1:195–201, 435–36, nos. 1–3.

9. Antonio García y García, *Derecho común en España: los juristas y sus obras* (Murcia: Universidad de Murcia, 1991), 67–68; Ferran Valls Taberner, "Le juriste catalan Pierre de Cardona," in *Mélanges Paul Fournier* (Paris: Recueil Sirey, 1929): 743–46.

10. Julio González, *El reino de Castilla en la época de Alfonso VIII*, 3 vols. (Madrid: Consejo Superior de Investigaciones Científicas, 1960), 1:626–35, and González, *Alfonso IX*, 2 vols. (Madrid: Consejo Superior de Investigaciones Científicas, 1945), 1:453–60, 497, no. 83.

11. Antonio García y García, *Laurentius Hispanus: Datos biográficos y estudio crítico de sus obras* (Rome: Consejo Superior de Investigaciones Científicas, 1956); Alfons Maria Stickler, "Il Decretista Laurentius Hispanus," *Studia Gratiana* 9 (1966): 461–549; Kenneth Pennington, "Laurentius Hispanus," in *Dictionary of the Middle Ages*, ed. Joseph R. Strayer (New York: Scribner's, 1986), 7:385–86.

12. Isaías da Rosa Pereira, "Livros de direito na Idade Média," *Lusitania Sacra* 7 (1964–66): 7–60.

13. Javier Ochoa Sanz, *Vincentius Hispanus: Canonista boloñes del siglo XIII* (Rome: Cuadernos del Instituto Jurídico Español, 1960); Gaines Post, *Studies in Medieval Legal Thought: Public Law and the State, 1100–1322* (Princeton: Princeton University Press, 1964), 482–93.

14. Lucas of Túy, *Chronicon Mundi*, 9, De excellentia Hispaniae.

15. Juan Gil de Zamora, *Liber de preconiis Hispaniae*, ed. Manuel de Castro y Castro (Madrid: Universidad de Madrid, 1955), 183, tract. 7, chap. 3.

16. Ajo G. y Sáinz de Zúñiga, *Historia*, 1:439–40, 441–42, nos. 9, 11; Vicente Beltrán de Heredia, *Cartulario de la Universidad de Salamanca (1218–1600)*, 6 vols. (Salamanca: Ediciones Universidad, 1970–73), 1:604–6, no. 23; Ildefonso Rodríguez de Lama, *La*

documentación pontificia de Alejandro IV (1254–1261) (Rome: Instituto Español de Historia Eclesiástica, 1976), 119–20.

17. *Liber Augustalis*, in Jean L. A. Huillard-Breholles, *Historia Diplomatica Friderici II*, 6 vols. in 12 (Paris: H. Plon, 1852–61), 4.1:1–178; *Liber Augustalis or Constitutions of Melfi Promulgated by the Emperor Frederick II for the Kingdom of Sicily in 1231*, trans. James M. Powell (Syracuse: Syracuse University Press, 1971).

18. Philippe de Beaumanoir, *Coutumes de Beauvaisis*, ed. A. Salmon, 2 vols. (Paris: Picard, 1899–1900); *The Coutumes de Beauvaisis of Philippe de Beaumanoir*, trans. F. R. P. Akehurst (Philadelphia: University of Pennsylvania Press, 1992).

19. Henry de Bracton, *De legibus et consuetudinibus regni Angliae*, ed. Samuel Thorne, 4 vols. (Cambridge, MA: Harvard University Press, 1968–77).

20. *The Statutes of the Realm*, 12 vols. (London: Public Record Office, 1810–28), vol. 1; Edward Jenks, *Edward Plantagenet (Edward I), the English Justinian: or, The Making of the Common Law* (New York: G. P. Putnam's Sons, 1902).

21. Joseph F. O'Callaghan, "Alfonso X," in *Great Christian Jurists in Spanish History*, ed. Rafael Domingo and Javier Martínez-Torrón (New York: Cambridge University Press, 2018), 69–83.

22. Ana Domínguez, "Retratos de Alfonso X el Sabio en la Primera Partida (British Library, Add. Ms .20.787)," *Alcanate* 6 (2008–9): 239–51.

23. Julio González, *Reinado y diplomas de Fernando III*, 3 vols. (Córdoba: Monte de Piedad y Caja de Ahorros, 1980–86); Manuel González Jiménez, *Fernando III el Santo: El Rey que marcó el destino de España* (Seville: Fundación José Manuel Lara, 2006); Joseph F. O'Callaghan, *Reconquest and Crusade in Medieval Spain* (Philadelphia: University of Pennsylvania Press, 2003).

24. Julio González, *Repartimiento de Sevilla*, 2 vols. (Madrid: Consejo Superior de Investigaciones Científicas, 1951; repr., Seville: Ayuntamiento de Sevilla, 1998).

25. Cayetano J. Socarras, *Alfonso X of Castile: A Study on Imperialistic Frustration* (Barcelona: Hispam, 1976); Carlos de Ayala Martínez, *Directrices fundamentales de la política peninsular de Alfonso X (Relaciones castellano-aragonesas de 1252 a 1263)* (Madrid: Universidad Autónoma de Madrid, 1986).

26. José Manuel Nieto Soria, *Sancho IV, 1284–1295* (Palencia: Diputación Provincial de Palencia, 1994); Mercedes Gaibrois de Ballesteros, *Historia del reinado de Sancho IV*, 3 vols. (Madrid: Revista de Archivos, Bibliotecas y Museos, 1922–28).

27. Evelyn Procter, *Alfonso X of Castile: Patron of Literature and Learning* (Oxford: Clarendon Press, 1951).

28. Jofré de Loaysa, *Crónica de los reyes de Castilla, Fernando III, Alfonso X, Sancho IV y Fernando IV, 1248–1305*, ed. Antonio García Martínez (Murcia: Academia Alfonso X el Sabio, 1982), 64, chap. 219.3.

29. Fidel Fita, "Biografías de San Fernando y de Alfonso el Sabio por Juan Gil de Zamora," *BRAH* 5 (1884): 308–28, esp. 319.

30. José Chabas and Bernard R. Goldstein, *The Alfonsine Tables of Toledo* (Dordrecht: Kluwer, 2003), 21, chap. 1.

31. Juan Manuel, *El Libro de la caza*, ed. G. Baist (Halle: Max Niemeyer, 1880), 1–2, prólogo.

32. Robert I. Burns, SJ, "King Alfonso and the Wild West: Medieval Hispanic Law on the U.S. Frontier," *Medieval Encounters* 6 (2000): 83, and Burns, "*Stupor Mundi*: Alfonso X of Castile, the Learned," in Burns, *Emperor of Culture*, 13.

33. Robert A. MacDonald, "Law and Politics: Alfonso's Program of Political Reform," in *The Worlds of Alfonso the Learned and James the Conqueror: Intellect and Force in the Middle Ages*, ed. Robert I. Burns, SJ (Princeton: Princeton University Press, 1985), 150–202.

34. Francisco Márquez Villanueva, *El concepto cultural alfonsí* (Madrid: Mapfre, 1995), 19–27.

35. *Primera Crónica General*, ed. Ramón Menéndez Pidal, 2 vols. (Madrid: Editorial Gredos, 1955), 1:2.

2. The Law and the Lawgiver

1. Joseph F. O'Callaghan, *A History of Medieval Spain* (Ithaca: Cornell University Press, 1975), 1–88; Roger Collins, *Visigothic Spain, 409–711* (Malden, MA: Blackwell, 2004).

2. P. D. King, *Law and Society in the Visigothic Kingdom* (Cambridge: Cambridge University Press, 1972); García Gallo, *Manual*, 1:52–60, 334–40; Francisco Tomás y Valiente, *Manual de historia del derecho español*, 4th ed. (Madrid: Tecnos, 1983), 97–112.

3. *Liber Iudiciorum*, in *Leges Visigothorum*, ed. Karl Zeumer, Monumenta Germaniae Historica, Leges 1 (Hannover: Hahn, 1902), 33–456; *The Visigothic Code (Forum Iudicum)*, trans. Samuel Parsons Scott (Boston: Boston Book Company, 1910).

4. Javier Alvarado Planas, "A modo de conclusiones: el Liber Iudiciorum y la aplicación del Derecho en los siglos VI a XI," *Mélanges de la Casa de Velázquez* 41, no. 2 (2011): 109–27; María Luz Alonso Martín, "La perduración del Fuero Juzgo y el derecho de los castellanos de Toledo," *AHDE* 48 (1978): 335–77.

5. O'Callaghan, *History of Medieval Spain*, 63–68, 171–74, 271–77; García Gallo, *Manual*, 1:361–79; Tomás y Valiente, *Manual*, 113–66; Aquilino Iglesia Ferreirós, "Derecho municipal, derecho señorial, derecho regio," *HID* 4 (1977): 115–98.

6. Alfonso García Gallo, "Una colección de fazañas castellanas del siglo XII," *AHDE* 11 (1934): 522–31; Amalio Marichalar and Cayetano Manrique, *Historia de la legislación y recitaciones del derecho civil de España*, 9 vols. (Madrid: Imprenta Nacional, 1861–72), 2:260–311.

7. *Libro de los fueros de Castiella*, ed. Galo Sánchez (Barcelona, 1924; repr., Barcelona: El Albir, 1981); Sánchez, "Para la historia de la redacción del antiguo derecho territorial castellano," *AHDE* 6 (1929): 260–328; and Sánchez, "Sobre el Ordenamiento de Alcalá (1348) y sus fuentes," *Revista de Derecho Privado* 9 (1922); 351–68.

8. *El Fuero viejo de Castilla*, ed. Ángel Barrios García, Gregorio del Ser Quijano, and Benjamín González Alonso (Salamanca: Junta de Castilla y León-Europa, 1996); Ignacio Jordán de Asso y del Río and Miguel de Manuel y Rodríguez, *El Fuero Viejo de Castilla* (Madrid: Joachín Ibarra, 1771); Juan García González, "El Fuero Viejo asistemático," *AHDE* 41 (1971): 767–86; José Luis Bermejo Cabrero, "Un nuevo texto afín al Fuero Viejo de Castilla: 'El Fuero de los fijosdalgos y las Fazañas del Fuero de Castilla,'" *AHDE* 69 (1999): 240–74.

9. Claudio Sánchez Albornoz, "Dudas sobre el ordenamiento de Nájera," *CHE* 35–36 (1962): 315–34, and Sánchez Albornoz, "Menos dudas sobre el ordenamiento de Nájera," *AEM* 3 (1966): 465–68; Julio González, "Sobre la fecha de las Cortes de Nájera," *CHE* 61–62 (1977): 357–61; Agustín Altisent, "Otra referencia a las Cortes

de Nájera," *AEM* 5 (1968): 473–78; Hilda Grassotti, "El recuerdo de las Cortes de Nájera," *CHE* 70 (1988): 255–72; José Luis Bermejo Cabrero, "En torno a las Cortes de Nájera," *AHDE* 70 (2000): 245–50.

10. Alfonso García Gallo, "Textos de derecho territorial castellano," *AHDE* 13 (1936–41): 308–96, esp. 332–69.

11. *Ordenamiento de Alcalá*, in *CLC*, 1:552–93, cap. 73; Ignacio Jordán de Asso y del Rio and Miguel de Manuel y Rodríguez, *El Ordenamiento de leyes que d. Alfonso XI hizo en las Cortes de Alcalá de Henares el año de mil trescientos y cuarenta y ocho* (Madrid: Antonio Calleja, 1847).

12. Tomás Muñoz y Romero, *Colección de fueros municipales y cartas pueblas de los reinos de Castilla, León, Corona de Aragón y Navarra* (Madrid: José María Alonso, 1847); Alfonso García Gallo, "Aportación al estudio de los Fueros," *AHDE* 26 (1956): 387–446.

13. *Fuero de Cuenca: Formas primitiva y sistemáticas. Texto latín, texto castellano y adaptación del Fuero de Iznatoraf*, ed. Rafael Ureña y Smenjaud (Madrid: Tipografía de Archivos, 1935); *The Code of Cuenca: Municipal Law on the Twelfth-Century Castilian Frontier*, trans. James F. Powers (Philadelphia: University of Pennsylvania Press, 2000).

14. José Manuel Pérez Prendes, "La frialdad del texto: Comentario al prólogo del *Fuero viejo de Castilla*," *CLHM* 22 (1998–99): 297–322.

15. *Fuero Juzgo en latín y castellano*, ed. Real Academia Española (Madrid: Ibarra, 1815).

16. *Setenario*, ed. Kenneth Vanderford (Buenos Aires, 1945; repr., Barcelona: Crítica, 1984), 9–11, 22–23, leyes 2, 4, 10; José Luis Pérez López, "Los prólogos del *Libro de las Leyes* y el fragmento llamado *Setenario* en la obra jurídica alfonsí," *Revista de Literatura Medieval* 14 (2002): 109–43, esp. 119–23; Antonio Pérez Martín, "Hacia un Derecho Común Europeo: La obra jurídica de Alfonso X," in *Alfonso X: Aportaciones de un rey castellano a la construcción de Europa*, ed. Miguel Rodríguez Llopis (Murcia: Editora Regional de Murcia, 1997), 109–35.

17. *CAX(GJ)*, 26, chap. 9.

18. Alfonso García Gallo, "El Libro de las leyes de Alfonso el Sabio: Del Espéculo a las Partidas," *AHDE* 21–22 (1951–52): 345–528; García Gallo, "Nuevas observaciones sobre la obra legislativa de Alfonso X," *AHDE* 46 (1976): 609–70; and García Gallo, "La obra legislativa de Alfonso X: Hechos y hipótesis," *AHDE* 54 (1984): 97–161; Aquilino Iglesia Ferreirós, "Alfonso X el Sabio y su obra legislativa: Algunas reflexiones," *AHDE* 50 (1980): 531–61; Iglesia Ferreirós, "Alfonso X, su labor legislativa y los historiadores," *HID* 9 (1982): 9–113; Iglesia Ferreirós, "Cuestiones Alfonsinas," *AHDE* 55 (1985): 95–149; and Iglesia Ferreirós, "La labor legislativa de Alfonso X el Sabio," in *España y Europa: Un pasado jurídico común. Actos del I simpósio internacional del Instituto de Derecho común*, ed. Antonio Pérez Martín (Murcia: Instituto de Derecho Común, 1986), 275–599.

19. *General Estoria: Primera Parte*, ed. Antonio García Solalinde (Madrid: Centro de Estudios Históricos, 1930), 477b; Procter, *Alfonso X of Castile*, 3.

20. *MHE*, 1:312, no. 140. Juan Torres Fontes, "La familia de Maestre Jacobo de las Leyes," *Glossae* 5–6 (1993–94): 333–49; Rafael Gibert y Sánchez de la Vega, "Jacobo el de las leyes en el estudio jurídico hispánico," *Glossae* 5–6 (1993–94): 255–77.

21. Rafael Ureña y Smenjaud and Adolfo Bonilla San Martín, *Obras del Maestre Jacobo de las leyes, jurisconsulto del siglo XIII* (Madrid: Reus, 1924).

22. Jacobo de las leyes, *Summa de los nueve tiempos de los pleitos*, ed. Jean Roudil (Paris: Klincksieck, 1986); Antonio Pérez Martín, "El *Ordo iudiciarius 'ad summarium notitiam'* y sus derivados: Contribución a la historia de la literatura procesal castellana," *HID* 8 (1981): 195–266, and 9 (1982): 327–423, esp. 232–35.

23. Rafael Floranes, "Flores de las Leyes: Suma legal del Maestre Jacobo Ruiz, llamado de las Leyes," in *MHE*, 2:138–248; Antonio Pérez Martín, "Jacobo de las leyes: datos biográficos," *Glossae* 5–6 (1993–94): 279–331; Pérez Martín, "Jacobo de las leyes: Ureña tenía razón," *AD* 26 (2008): 251–73; and Pérez Martín, "La obra jurídica de Jacobo de las Leyes: las Flores de Derecho," *CLHM* 22 (1998–99): 247–70.

24. Pérez Martín, "El *Ordo judiciarius*," 232, 254–66, esp. 327–417; Joaquín Cerdá Ruiz-Funes, "La Margarita de los pleitos de Fernando Martínez de Zamora," *AHDE* 20 (1950): 634–738.

25. *Espéculo: Texto jurídico atribuido al Rey de Castilla don Alfonso el Sabio*, ed. Robert A. MacDonald (Madison: Hispanic Seminary of Medieval Studies, 1990), 491–504.

26. See *Espéculo*, ed. MacDonald. *Espéculo*, ed. Gonzalo Martínez Díez and José Manuel Ruiz Asencio (Ávila: Fundación Sánchez Albornoz, 1985); *Espéculo*, vol. 1 of *Opúsculos legales del Rey Don Alfonso el Sabio*, ed. Real Academia de la Historia, 2 vols. (Madrid: Imprenta Real, 1836); repr. as vol. 6 of *Los Códigos españoles concordados y anotados*, 2nd ed., 12 vols. (Madrid: Antonio de San Martín, 1873–74); Jerry R. Craddock, "El Texto del *Espéculo* de Alfonso X el Sabio," *Initium: Revista catalana d'Historia del Dret* 3 (1998): 221–74.

27. *Espéculo*, ed. Martínez Díez and Ruiz Asencio, 20–24.

28. *Espéculo*, ed. Martínez Díez and Ruiz Asencio, pp. 31–39; Aquilino Iglesia Ferreirós, "Fuero real y *Espéculo*," *AHDE* 52 (1982): 111–91, esp. 180–84.

29. Jerry R. Craddock, "La cronología de las obras legislativas de Alfonso X el Sabio," *AHDE* 51 (1981): 365–418, esp. 373–75; García Gallo, "El Libro de las leyes," appendix 4, 513–28.

30. *MHE*, 1:139–44, no. 65.

31. Antonio López Ferreiro, *Fueros municipales de Santiago y de su tierra* (Santiago de Compostela: Seminario Central, 1895; repr., Madrid: Ediciones Castilla, 1975), 1:248–61; José Luis Bermejo Cabrero, "En torno a la aplicación de las Partidas: Fragmentos del 'Espéculo' en una sentencia real de 1261," *Hispania: Revista española de historia* 30 (1970): 169–80.

32. *Espéculo*, ed. MacDonald, xlvii–lv, and Robert A. MacDonald, "El Espéculo atribuido a Alfonso X, su edición y problemas que plantea," in Pérez Martín, *España y Europa*, 636–44; Craddock, "Cronología," 367; Iglesia Ferreirós, "Fuero real y Espéculo."

33. In "Sobre la promulgación del Espéculo y del Fuero real," in *Estudios en homenaje a Don Claudio Sánchez Albornoz*, 3:167–79, and *Learned King*, 31–37, I accepted May 1255 as the date of promulgation, but I now agree with MacDonald.

34. *Fuero real*, ed. Gonzalo Martínez Díez, José Manuel Ruiz Asencio, and C. Hernández Alonso (Ávila: Fundación Claudio Sánchez Albornoz, 1988); *Fuero real del rey d. Alonso el Sabio*, in *Opúsculos legales*, 2:1–169; *Fuero real del Rey Don Alonso el Sabio, copiado del Códice del Escorial señalado ij.z.8*, ed. Real Academia de la Historia (Madrid: Imprenta Real, 1836); *Afonso X: Foro real*, ed. José de Azevedo Ferreira, 2 vols. (Lisbon: Instituto Nacional de Investigação Científica, 1987); Craddock, "Cronología," 376–79, and Craddock, "Legislative Works," 184–87; Robert A. MacDonald, "Progress and Problems in Editing Alfonsine Juridical Texts," *La Corónica*

6 (1978): 74–81; Antonio Pérez Martín, "El Fuero Real y Murcia," *AHDE* 54 (1984): 55–96, and Pérez Martín, "Murcia y la obra legislativa alfonsina: pasado y presente," *AD* 8 (1985): 93–128.

35. See note 18 above.

36. O'Callaghan, "Sobre la promulgación," and Joseph F. O'Callaghan, "On the Promulgation of the *Espéculo* and the *Fuero Real*," in my *Alfonso X, the Cortes and Government* (Brookfield, VT: Ashgate, 1998), no. III:1–12.

37. Múñoz y Romero, *Colección*, 313–20; Juan del Alamo, *Colección diplomática de San Salvador de Oña (822–1284)*, 2 vols. (Madrid: Consejo Superior de Investigaciones Científicas, 1950), 2:656–57, no. 537; *Fuero real*, in *Opúsculos legales*; Craddock, "Cronologia," 376–79.

38. *MHE*, 1:89–100, 124–27, 175–80, 202–3, 224–28, nos. 43–45, 59, 83, 91, 102; Antonio Ballesteros, "El Fuero de Atienza," *BRAH* 68 (1916): 264–70, and Ballesteros, "El itinerario de Alfonso X, rey de Castilla," *BRAH* 107 (1935): 59, n. 1; Francisco Layna Serrano, *Historia de la villa de Atienza* (Madrid: Consejo Superior de Investigaciones Científicas, 1945), 503–4; Juan Loperráez, *Descripción histórica del obispado de Osma*, 3 vols. (Madrid: Imprenta real, 1788), 3:86–185, nos. 60–61; Juan Martín Carramolino, *Historia de Ávila, su provincia y obispado*, 3 vols. (Madrid: Librería Española, 1872), 2:491–93, no. 98; Timoteo Domingo Palacio, Agustin Millares Carlo, and Eulogio Varela Hervias, *Documentos del Archivo general de la villa de Madrid*, 6 vols. (Madrid: Imprenta Municipal, 1888–1943), 1:85–91; Antonio Ubieto Arteta, *Colección diplomática de Cuéllar* (Segovia: Diputación provincial de Segovia, 1961), 60–65, no. 1.

39. Aquilino Iglesia Ferreirós, "El Privilegio general concedido a las Extremaduras en 1264 por Alfonso X: Edición del ejemplar enviado a Peñafiel en 15 de abril de 1264," *AHDE* 53 (1983): 456–521; Evelyn Procter, *Curia and Cortes in León and Castille, 1072–1295* (Cambridge: Cambridge University Press, 1980), 286–91, no. 7; Palacio, Millares Carlo, and Varela Hervias, *Documentos del Archivo general de la villa de Madrid*, 1:95–102; *MHE*, 1:250–52, no. 114.

40. *OZ* 1274; *CAX(GJ)*, 26, chap. 9; *FV* pr.; Juan Sanz García, *El Fuero de Verviesca y el Fuero real* (Burgos: Imprenta el Castellano, 1927), 71, 398–99.

41. O'Callaghan, *Learned King*, 198–213.

42. Pérez López, "Prólogos," 139.

43. *General Estoria*, ed. García Solalinde, 198–201; Francisco Rico, *Alfonso X y la General Estoria: Tres Lecciones* (Barcelona: Ariel, 1972), 97–120.

44. Rafael Gibert, *Historia general del derecho español* (Granada: F. Román, 1968), 41–45.

45. *Espéculo*, ed. MacDonald, xvii; Antonio García y García, "Tradición manuscrita de las Siete Partidas," in *Iglesia, Sociedad y Derecho* (Salamanca: Universidad Pontificia de Salamanca, 1985), 249–83; Pérez Martín, "Hacia un Derecho Común Europeo," 133, n. 52; José Luis López Pérez, "Las Siete Partidas según el códice de los Reyes Católicos de la Biblioteca Nacional de Madrid," *Dicenda: Cuadernos de Filología Hispánica* 14 (1996): 235–58; Daniel Panateri, "El Prólogo de *Siete Partidas*: Entropía, edición y uso político," *Medievalia* 47 (2015): 54–81, and Panateri, *El discurso del rey: El discurso jurídico alfonsí y sus implicancias políticas* (Madrid: Universidad Carlos III de Madrid, 2017), 4–94.

46. *Primera Partida según el Manuscrito Add. 20787 del British Museum*, ed. Juan Antonio Arias Bonet (Valladolid: Universidad de Valladolid, 1975).

47. *Primera Partida (MS HC 397/573) Hispanic Society of America*, ed. Francisco Ramos Bossini (Granada: Universidad de Granada, 1984).

48. *SPRAH*, 1:1–177, esp. 5–6.

49. Jerry R. Craddock, "How Many *Partidas* in the *Siete Partidas*?," in *Hispanic Studies in Honor of Alan D. Deyermond: A North American Tribute*, ed. John S. Miletich (Madison: Hispanic Seminary of Medieval Studies, 1986), 83–92; García Gallo, *Manual*, 1:388, 391–93; Procter, *Alfonso X of Castile*, 52–53, 63; MacDonald, "Law and Politics," 180–81; and *Espéculo*, ed. MacDonald, xvii–xviii.

50. García Gallo, "El Libro de las leyes," 350–59; García y García, "Tradición manuscrita," 252.

51. *Las Siete Partidas de Alfonso X el Sabio*, ed. Alfonso Díaz de Montalvo, 2 vols. (Seville: Ungut and Polono, 1491).

52. *Las Siete Partidas del Sabio rey Don Alonso el nono, nuevamente glosadas por el Licenciado Gregorio López*, 4 vols. (Salamanca: Andrea de Portonaris, 1555; facsimile, Madrid: Boletín Oficial del Estado, 1974).

53. *Las Siete Partidas del Rey Don Alfonso el Sabio*, ed. Real Academia de la Historia, 3 vols. (Madrid: Imprenta Real, 1807; repr., Madrid: Atlas, 1972); *Los Códigos españoles*, vols. 2–4; José Sánchez-Arcilla Bernal's *Las Siete Partidas* (Madrid: Reus, 2003) is a modern adaptation for a general audience.

54. García y García, "Tradición manuscrita"; García Gallo, *Manual*, 1:398. Contrary to García Gallo, Iglesia Ferreirós, "Labor legislativa," 283, 513–17, believes that López's edition reflects Alfonso X's original work.

55. Samuel Parsons Scott, trans., *Las Siete Partidas* (Chicago: Commerce Clearing House, 1931); Louis Moreau-Lislet and Henry Carleton, *The Laws of the Siete Partidas which are still in Force in the State of Louisiana*, 2 vols. (New Orleans: James McKarraher, 1820).

56. Jerry R. Craddock, "La nota cronológica inserta en el prólogo de las *Siete Partidas*: edición crítica y comentario," *Al-Andalus* 39 (1974): 363–90; García Gallo, "El Libro de las leyes," 399–402.

57. *DAAX*, 560, no. 521.

58. Jerry R. Craddock, "Setenario: última e inconclusa refundición alfonsina de la primera Partida," *AHDE* 56 (1986): 441–66, and Craddock, "Legislative Works," 184, 192; Peter Linehan, "Pseudo-historia y pseudo-liturgia en la obra alfonsina," in Pérez Martín, *España y Europa*, 259–74, esp. 264–66; Marta Madero, "Formas de justicia en la obra jurídica de Alfonso X el Sabio," *Hispania: Revista española de historia* 56 (1996): 447–66, esp. 449; Pérez López, "Prólogos," 123–34.

59. Kenneth Vanderford, "El 'Setenario' y su relación con las 'Siete Partidas,'" *Revista de Filología hispánica* 3 (1941): 233–62; Procter, *Alfonso X of Castile*, 65–68; MacDonald, "Law and Politics," 173–75.

60. See *PCG*, 1:9, chap. 6, on Julius Caesar's settlement of Seville.

61. Georges Martin, "Alphonse X ou la science politique (*Septénaire*, 1–11)," *CLHM* 18–19 (1993–94): 79–100, and 20 (1995): 7–33; and Martin, "De nuevo sobre la fecha del Setenario," *e-Spania*, 2 December 2006, https://journals.openedition.org/e-spania/.

62. Antonio Pérez Martín, "Fuentes romanas en las Partidas," *Glossae* 4 (1992): 215–46; José Amador de los Ríos, *Historia crítica de la literatura española*, 7 vols. (Madrid: Impr. de J. Rodriguez, 1861–65), 3:546–47, 621–27; Procter, *Alfonso X of Castile*, 64–65.

63. Antonio García y García, "Fuentes canónicas de las Partidas," *Glossae* 3 (1992): 93–101; Ramon Bidagor, "El derecho de las Decretales y las Partidas de Alfonso X el Sabio de España," in *Acta Congressus Iuridici Internationalis VII saeculo a Decretalibus Gregorii IX et XIV a Codice Iustiniano promulgatis* (Rome: Pontificum Institutum Utriusque Iuris, 1936), 297–313.

64. García y García, "Tradición manuscrita," 259–60; Galo Sánchez, *Curso de historia del derecho: Introducción y fuentes*, 9th ed. (Madrid: Reus 1960), 91.

65. García Gallo, *Manual*, 1:393–94.

66. MacDonald, "Law and Politics," 181.

67. *CLC*, 1:541–42; Procter, *Alfonso X of Castile*, 50–51; Alfonso Otero Varela, "Las Partidas y el Ordenamiento de Alcalá en el cambio del ordenamiento medieval," *AHDE* 63–64 (1993–94): 451–548.

68. *CAX(GJ)*, 26, chap. 9.

69. O'Callaghan, *Learned King*, 34–37; MacDonald, "El Espéculo atribuído a Alfonso X," 636–44; Georges Martin, "Alphonse X de Castille, Roi et Empereur: Commentaire du premier titre de la Deuxième Partie," *CLHM* 23 (2000): 323–48, esp. 338, n. 59.

70. *CLC*, 1:87–94, no. 16; Aquilino Iglesia Ferreirós, "Las Cortes de Zamora de 1274 y los casos de corte," *AHDE* 41 (1971): 945–71.

71. Joseph F. O'Callaghan, "On the *Ordenamiento de Zamora*, 1274," *HID* 44 (2017): 297–312.

72. *Libro de las Tahurerías: A Special Code of Law, Concerning Gambling, Drawn Up by Maestro Roldán at the Command of Alfonso X of Castile*, ed. Robert A. MacDonald (Madison: Hispanic Seminary, 1995), 1–17, 285–97; *Ordenamiento de las Tafurerías que fue fecho en la era de mil e trescientos e quatorse años por el rey don Alfonso X*, in *Opúsculos legales*, 2:213–31.

73. *Libro de los Adelantados Mayores: Regulations Attributed to Alfonso X of Castile, Concerning the King's Vicar in the Judiciary and in Territorial Administration*, ed. Robert A. MacDonald (New York: Hispanic Seminary, 2000); *Leyes para los Adelantados mayores dadas por el rey d. Alonso el Sabio*, in *Opúsculos legales*, 2:173–77.

74. José Manuel Pérez Prendes, "Las leyes de los adelantados mayores," *Hidalguía* 10 (1962): 365–84; Emilio Javier de Benito Fraile, "En torno a las leyes de los adelantados mayores," *CHD* 3 (1996): 287–314.

75. *Leyes nuevas dadas por el rey D. Alfonso el Sabio después del Fuero real*, in *Opúsculos legales*, 2:181–209; José López Ortiz, "La colección conocida con el título 'Leyes Nuevas' y atríbuida a Alfonso X el Sabio," *AHDE* 16 (1945): 5–70.

76. *Leyes del estilo et declaraciones sobre las Leyes del Fuero*, in *Opúsculos legales*, 2:235–352.

77. Pérez López, "Prólogos," 139–43.

78. Georg Gross, "Las Cortes de 1252: Ordenamiento otorgado al concejo de Burgos en las Cortes celebradas en Sevilla el 12 de octubre de 1252 (según el original)," *BRAH* 182 (1985): 95–114; Ismael García Ramila, "Ordenamientos de posturas y otros capítulos generales otorgados a la ciudad de Burgos por el rey Alfonso X," *Hispania: Revista española de historia* 5 (1945): 204–22; Antonio Ballesteros, "Las Cortes de 1252," *Anales de la Junta para Ampliación de Estudios e Investigaciones científicas* 3 (1911): 114–43; Carlos Sáez, *Los pergaminos del Archivo Municipal de Alcalá de Henares* (Alcalá de Henares: Universidad de Alcalá de Henares, 1990), 31–46, no. 1; Vicente

Argüello, "Memoria sobre el valor de las monedas de d. Alfonso el sabio," *Memorias de la Real Academia de la Historia* 8 (1852): 1–58.

79. López Ferreiro, *Fueros municipales,* 1:347–72; Procter, *Curia and Cortes,* 273–84, no 4; Alberto Martín Expósito and José María Monsalvo Antón, *Documentación medieval del Archivo municipal de Ledesma* (Salamanca: Universidad de Salamanca, 1986), 19–36; Matías Rodríguez Díez, *Historia de la ciudad de Astorga,* 2nd ed. (Astorga: Porfirio López, 1909), 697–713.

80. García Ramila, "Ordenamientos," 224–35; *CLC* 1:54–63; Emilio Sáez, *Colección diplomática de Sepúlveda* (Segovia: Diputación provincial de Segovia, 1956), 18–29, no. 8.

81. Manuel González Jiménez, "Cortes de Sevilla de 1261," *HID* 25 (1998): 295–312; Rodríguez Díez, *Historia de la ciudad de Astorga,* 715–20.

82. *CLC,* 1:64–85.

83. Joseph F. O'Callaghan, *The Cortes of Castile-León, 1188–1350* (Philadelphia: University of Pennsylvania Press, 1989), 56, 112–29; Carlos de Ayala Martínez and Francisco Javier Villalba Ruiz de Toledo, "Las Cortes bajo el reinado de Alfonso X," in *Las Cortes de Castilla y León, 1188–1988,* ed. Cortes de Castilla y León (Valladolid: Cortes de Castilla y León, 1990), 239–70.

84. Post, *Studies in Medieval Legal Thought,* 163–240; José Antonio Maravall, "La corriente democrática medieval en España y la fórmula *quod omnes tangit,*" in *Estudios de historia del pensamiento español. Edad media. Serie primera* (Madrid: Cultural Hispánica, 1967), 157–75.

85. *Inst.* 1, 1, 2; Joseph Canning, *A History of Medieval Political Thought, 300–1450* (London: Routledge, 1996), 119, 164–66.

86. Kenneth Pennington, *The Prince and the Law, 1200–1600: Sovereignty and Rights in the Western Legal Tradition* (Berkeley: University of California Press, 1993), 77–90; Canning, *History of Medieval Political Thought,* 8, 11, 118.

87. *Justinian's Institutes,* ed. Paul Krueger, trans. Peter Birks and Grant McLeod (Ithaca, NY: Cornell University Press, 1987), 1, 1, 2; Isidore of Seville, *Etymologiarum sive Originum Libri XX,* ed. W. M. Lindsay, 2 vols. (Oxford: Clarendon Press, 1911), bk. 5, chaps. 2–6; Pennington, *The Prince and the Law,* 119–64.

88. García Gallo, *Manual,* 1:155–71, esp. 155–56; José Sánchez-Arcilla Bernal, "La 'teoría de la ley' en la obra legislativa de Alfonso X el Sabio," *Alcanate* 6 (2008–9): 81–123; Panateri, *Discurso del rey,* 94–158.

89. Isidore, *Etymologiarum,* bk. 10, chap. 69; Pennington, *The Prince and the Law,* 123.

90. *PPBM* 1, 1, 7; *MHE,* 1:102–3, no. 47.

91. González, *Reinado y diplomas de Fernando III,* 3:387–89, no. 809.

92. For definitions, see *Espéculo,* ed. MacDonald, 339–434, appendix 1; María Nieves Sánchez González de Herrero, *Diccionario español de documentos alfonsíes* (Madrid: Arco Libros, 2000).

93. *MHE,* 1:333–35, no 148, and 2:29–31, no. 179.

94. *Fuero de Cuenca,* 861–62.

95. *MHE,* 1:175–80, 187–91, 211–12, 252–55, nos. 83, 86, 96, 115; Antonio Malalana Ureña, *Escalona Medieval (1083–1400)* (Escalona: Ayuntamiento de Escalona, n.d.), 34–36, 135–37.

96. *MHE,* 1:139–44, no. 65; López Ferreiro, *Fueros municipales,* 1:248–61.

97. Ballesteros, "Itinerario," 107:21–76, esp. 59, n. 1; Francisco Cantera Burgos, "Miranda en tiempos de Alfonso el Sabio," *Boletín de la Comisión provincial de Monumentos históricos y artísticos de Burgos* 17 (1938): 137–50, esp. 146–47.

98. Emiliano González Díez, *Colección diplomática del concejo de Burgos (884–1369)* (Burgos: Ayuntamiento de Burgos, 1984), 116–23, 163–64, 174, 204, nos. 36, 38, 80, 91, 117; Teófilo F. Ruiz, *Sociedad y poder real en Castilla (Burgos en la baja edad media)* (Barcelona: Ariel, 1981), 181.

99. César González Mínguez, "La concesión del Fuero real a Vitoria," *HID* 28 (2001): 217–29, esp. 227–29; Rafael Floranes, *Memorias y privilegios de la muy noble y muy ilustre ciudad de Vitoria* (Madrid: Vicente Rico, 1922), 182–88.

100. Palacio, Millares Carlo, and Varela Hervias, *Documentos del Archivo general de la villa de Madrid*, 1:113–17; *Privilegios reales y viejos documentos*, 17 vols. (Madrid: Joyas Bibliográficas, 1963–80), 10, no. 6; Ángel Barrios García and Alberto Martin Expósito, *Documentación medieval de los Archivos municipales de Béjar y Candelario* (Salamanca: Universidad de Salamanca), 218–31, no. 6; Emilio Sáez, Rafael Gibert, Manuel Alvar, and Atilano G. Ruiz-Zorrilla, *Los fueros de Sepúlveda* (Sepúlveda: Diputación Provincial de Segovia, 1953), 196–98, no. 13; Ballesteros y Beretta, *Alfonso X*, 581, 1102, no. 865; Procter, *Curia and Cortes*, 180, 191, 198.

101. *DAAX*, 426–27, no. 400.

102. *CAX(GJ)*, 76–123, 132–34, 153–57, 170–73, chaps. 23–42, 47, 53–54, 59; O'Callaghan, *Learned King*, 42–43, 222–23; González Jiménez, *Alfonso X*, 239–57; Julio Escalona, "Los nobles contra su rey: Argumentos y motivaciones de la insubordinación nobiliaria de 1272–1273," *CLCHM* 25 (2002): 131–62.

103. MacDonald, "Law and Politics," 180.

104. Américo Castro and Federico de Onís, *Fueros leoneses de Zamora, Salamanca, Ledesma y Alba de Tormes* (Madrid: Junta para Ampliación de Estudios e Investigaciones Científicas, 1916), 290.

3. Creating a Dynasty

1. O'Callaghan, *Alfonso X and the Cantigas*, 50–55.

2. Andrés Giménez Soler, *Don Juan Manuel: Biografía y estudio crítico* (Madrid: Real Academia Española, 1932), 221, no. 1; *PCG*, 2:773–74, chap. 1134; *Crónicas anónimas de Sahagún*, ed. Antonio Ubieto Arteta (Zaragoza: Anubar, 1987), 149, chap. 85; *CAX(GJ)*, 4, chap. 1; González Jiménez, *Alfonso X*, 44–46.

3. Ballesteros y Beretta, *Alfonso X*, 54–55; Peter Linehan, *History and the Historians of Medieval Spain* (Oxford: Clarendon Press, 1993), 426–30, 439–45.

4. Lucas of Túy, *Crónica de España*, ed. Julio Puyol (Madrid: Revista de Archivos, Bibliotecas y Museos, 1926), 449–50, chap. 103.

5. Gross, "Las Cortes de 1252"; Rodríguez Díez, *Historia de la ciudad de Astorga*, 698–713.

6. *DAAX*, 83, no. 80.

7. Ballesteros y Beretta, *Alfonso X*, 54–55.

8. Peter Linehan, "The Accession of Alfonso X (1252) and the Origins of the War of the Spanish Succession," in *God and Man in Medieval Spain: Essays in Honor of J. R. L. Highfield*, ed. Derek W. Lomax and David Mackenzie (Warminster: Aris and Phillips, 1989), 59–80.

9. *Crónica latina de los reyes de Castilla*, ed. Luis Charlo Brea (Cadiz: Universidad de Cádiz, 1984), 60; *The Latin Chronicle of the Kings of Castile*, trans. Joseph F. O'Callaghan (Tempe: Arizona Center for Medieval and Renaissance Studies, 2002), 85, chap. 40.

10. Teofilo F. Ruiz, "Une royauté sans sacre: La monarchie castillane du bas Moyen Âge," *Annales: Economies, Societés, Civilisations* 39 (1984): 429–53; Joseph F. O'Callaghan, "The *Cantigas de Santa Maria* as an Historical Source: Two Examples (nos. 321 and 386)," in *Studies on the Cantigas de Santa Maria: Art, Music and Poetry*, ed. Israel Katz and John E. Keller (Madison: Hispanic Seminary, 1987), 387–93; O'Callaghan, *Learned King*, 24–25; and O'Callaghan, *Alfonso X and the Cantigas*, 72–83.

11. Bernard F. Reilly, *The Kingdom of León-Castilla under King Alfonso VII, 1126–1157* (Philadelphia: University of Pennsylvania Press, 1998), 49; Julio González, *Regesta de Fernando II* (Madrid: Consejo Superior de Investigaciones Científicas, 1943), 21–22; González, *Alfonso IX*, 1:44–46; González, *El reino de Castilla en la época de Alfonso VIII*, 1:150, 180; and González, *Reinado y diplomas de Fernando III*, 1:232–39, 255–63.

12. Carlos Alvar, *Textos trovadorescos sobre España y Portugal* (Madrid: CUPSA, 1978), 259.

13. *Partida Segunda de Alfonso X el Sabio: Manuscrito 12794 de la B.N.*, ed. Aurora Juárez Blanquer and Antonio Rubio Flores (Granada: Impredisur, 1992).

14. José Manuel Nieto Soria, *Fundamentos ideológicos del poder real en Castilla (siglos XIII–XVI)* (Madrid: EUDEMA, 1988), 62–63, and Nieto Soria, "La coronación del rey: los símbolos y la naturaleza de su poder," in *Alfonso X y su época: el siglo del rey sabio*, ed. Miguel Rodríguez Llopis (Barcelona: Caroggio, 2001), 127–52; Panateri, *Discurso del rey*, 189–200.

15. Giraldus Cambrensis, *De principis instructione*, bk. 1, chap. 20, ed. George F. Warner, in *Giraldi Cambrensis Opera*, 8 vols. (London: Eyre & Spottiswood, 1891), 8:138; Jean Leclercq, *Jean de Paris et l'ecclésiologie du XIIIe siècle* (Paris: J. Vrin, 1942), 229; Peter Linehan, "The Politics of Piety: Aspects of the Castilian Monarchy from Alfonso X to Alfonso XI," *Revista canadiense de estudios hispánicos* 9 (1985): 386–404, and Linehan, "Pseudo-historia."

16. Pedro Fernández del Pulgar, *Historia secular y eclesiástica de la ciudad de Palencia*, 4 vols. (Madrid: F. Nieto, 1679–80), 2:344–45; Diego Catalán, *La Estoria de España de Alfonso X: Creación y Evolución* (Madrid: Universidad Autónoma de Madrid, 1992), 124–25; O'Callaghan, *Learned King*, 147–50; Ballesteros y Beretta, *Alfonso X*, 688–90; Linehan, *History*, 455–60.

17. Bernard F. Reilly, *The Kingdom of León-Castilla under King Alfonso VI, 1065–1109* (Princeton: Princeton University Press, 1988), 103–4.

18. Manuel Rodríguez Lapa, *Cantigas d'Escarnho e de Maldezir dos Cancioneiros medievais galego-portugueses* (Coimbra: Galaixa, 1970), 261, no. 167.

19. *Crónica del Rey don Sancho el Bravo*, in *BAE*, 66:69, chap. 1; Jofré de Loaysa, *Crónica*, 110, chap. 221.

20. *Crónica del Rey don Fernando Cuarto*, in *BAE*, 66:93, chap. 1; Linehan, *History*, 446–48.

21. Marc Bloch, *Les rois thaumaturges* (Paris: Armand Colin, 1961).

22. Álvaro Pelayo, *Speculum regum (Espelho dos Reis)*, ed. Miguel Pinto de Meneses (Lisbon: Universidade de Lisboa, 1955), 54; Procter, *Alfonso X of Castile*, 33–34; Nieto Soria, *Fundamentos ideológicos*, 68; Américo Castro, *La realidad histórica de España* (Mexico City: Porrua, 1962), 370–71.

23. Connie L. Scarborough, *A Holy Alliance: Alfonso X's Political Use of Marian Poetry* (Newark, DE: Juan de la Cuesta, 2009).

24. Walter Ullmann, *Principles of Government and Politics in the Middle Ages* (New York: Barnes and Noble, 1966), 117–20.

25. *PCG*, prologue, 1:4; *E* 1; *FR* 6; *SP* 3; *Setenario*, 1, 9; *CSM* 183.

26. *CAX(GJ)*, 12–14, chap. 4; González, *Repartimiento*, 1:85–91; O'Callaghan, *Learned King*, 156–62, 174–78; and O'Callaghan, *Alfonso X and the Cantigas*, 59–65.

27. Rafael Cómez Ramos, "El retrato de Alfonso X, el Sabio en la primera Cantiga de Santa María," in Katz and Keller, *Studies on the Cantigas de Santa Maria*, 35–52; Percy Ernst Schramm, *Las insignias de la realeza en la edad media española* (Madrid: Instituto de Estudios Políticos, 1960), 35–40.

28. *Inst.* 35; *PPBM*, laminas, fols. 1r, 1v, 79r, 80v, 86v, 89r.

29. *Castigos del rey don Sancho IV*, ed. Hugo Oscar Bizzarri (Frankfurt am Main: Vervuert, 2001), 142–45, 174, chaps. 11, 37; *Alfonso X: Toledo 1984* (Toledo: Ministerio de Cultura, 1984), 18, 135, fig. 59; Isidro G. Bango Torviso, "La llamada corona de Sancho IV y los emblemas de poder real," *Alcanate* 9 (2014–15): 261–83; Amparo García Cuadrado, *Las Cantigas: El Códice de Florencia* (Murcia: Universidad de Murcia, 1993), 80–81; Schramm, *Insignias*, 41–55; Linehan, *History*, 444–47.

30. García Cuadrado, *Cantigas*, 77–83; *Alfonso X: Toledo 1984*, 117, fig. 9; Gonzalo Menéndez Pidal, *La España del Siglo XIII leída en imagines* (Madrid: Real Academia de la Historia, 1986), 38–48.

31. O'Callaghan, *Alfonso X and the Cantigas*, 65–68; Ana Domínguez, "Retratos de Alfonso X en el Libro de los Juegos de Ajedrez, Dados y Tablas," *Alcanate* 7 (2010–11): 147–61; and Domínguez, "La miniatura del 'Scriptorium' Alfonsí," in *Estudios Alfonsíes: Lexicografía, lírica, estética y política de Alfonso el Sabio*, ed. José Mondéjar and Jesús Montoya (Granada: Universidad de Granada, 1985), 127–61.

32. Teofilo F. Ruiz, "Images of Power in the Seals of the Castilian Monarchy: 1135–1469," in *Estudios en Homenaje a Don Claudio Sánchez Albornoz*, 4:455–63, esp. 459–60; Menéndez Pidal, *España*, 154.

33. *CSM* 169, 292.58–59; García Cuadrado, *Cantigas*, 240–41.

34. Cómez Ramos, "Retrato," 37, 44–46, plates 2, 7, 8, 9, and Rafael Cómez Ramos, *Las empresas artísticas de Alfonso X el Sabio* (Seville: Diputación Provincial de Sevilla, 1979), 171, fig. 32; *CSM* 90; Menéndez Pidal, *España*, 39; *Castigos del rey don Sancho IV*, ed. Bizzarri, 104, chap. 17; Schramm, *Insignias*, 54–55; *Alfonso X: Toledo 1984*, 79–80.

35. Cómez Ramos, *Empresas*, 181–82, 185–86, and 73–85, figs. 34–35; María Elena Gómez Moreno, *La Catedral de León* (León: Everest, 1973), figs. 24–26.

36. Ibn Khaldūn, *Histoire des Berbères et des dynasties musulmanes de l'Afrique Septentrionale*, trans. Baron de Slane, 4 vols. (Paris: P. Geutner, 1852–56), 4:104–6.

37. *DAAX*, 559, no. 521.

38. Diego Ortiz de Zúñiga, *Anales eclesiásticos y seculares de la muy noble y muy leal ciudad de Sevilla, Metropoli de Andalucía*, ed. Antonio María Espinosa y Carzel, 2 vols. (Madrid: Imprenta real, 1795; repr., Seville: Guadalquivir, 1988), 1:306–7, 4:95, 5:321; Juan Delgado Roig, "Examen médico-legal de unos restos históricos: Los cadaveres de Alfonso X el Sabio y Doña Beatriz de Suabia," *Archivo Hispalense* 9 (1948): 135–53.

39. *MHE*, 1:1–2, nos. 1–2; Jofré de Loaysa, *Crónica*, 62, chap. 2; González, *Reinado y diplomas de Fernando III*, 1:102–4, 276–77; González Jiménez, *Alfonso X*, 36–39;

Francisco de Moxó y Montoliu, "El enlace de Alfonso de Castilla con Violante de Aragón: Marco político y precisiones cronológicas," *Hispania: Revista española de historia* 49 (1989): 69–110; Ferran Valls Taberner, "Relacions familiars i polítiques entre Jaume el Conqueridor i Alfons el Savi," *Bulletin Hispanique* 21 (1919): 9–42.

40. David Arbesú, "Alfonso X el Sabio, Beatriz de Portugal y el sepulcro de doña Mayor Guillén de Guzmán," *eHumanista* 24 (2013): 300–20.

41. Jaime Salazar y Acha, "Precisiones y nuevos datos sobre el entorno familiar de Alfonso X el Sabio, fundador de Ciudad Real," *Cuadernos de Estudios Manchegos* 20 (1990): 211–23; González Jiménez, *Alfonso X*, 368.

42. Richard Kinkade, "Violante of Aragon (1236?–1300?): An Historical Overview," *Exemplaria Hispanica* 2 (1992–93): 1–37; Melissa R. Katz, "The Final Testament of Violante of Aragón (ca. 1236–1300/01): Agency and (Dis)Empowerment of a Dowager Queen," in *Queenship in the Mediterranean: Negotiating the Role of the Queen in the Medieval and Early Modern Eras*, ed. Elena Woodacre (New York: Palgrave Macmillan, 2013), 51–71.

43. *Castigos del rey don Sancho IV*, ed. Bizzarri, 189–96, chap. 19.

44. Joseph F. O'Callaghan, "The Many Roles of the Medieval Queen: Some Examples from Castile," in *Queenship and Political Power in Medieval and Early Modern Spain*, ed. Theresa Earenfight (Burlington, VT: Ashgate, 2005), 21–32.

45. John Esten Keller and Annette Grant Cash, *Daily Life Depicted in the Cantigas de Santa Maria* (Lexington: University Press of Kentucky, 1998), plate 1; García Cuadrado, *Cantigas*, 152–62.

46. *PCG*, 2:772–73, chap. 1132.

47. *Espéculo*, ed. MacDonald, 347.

48. González Díez, *Colección diplomática del concejo de Burgos*, 196–97, no. 109; Ballesteros y Beretta, *Alfonso X*, 48.

49. *Espéculo*, ed. MacDonald, 394, 399.

50. Juan Manuel, *Tratado de las armas*, in *BAE*, 51:257–64, esp. 258, and Juan Manuel, *Libro de los castigos*, in *BAE*, 51:264–75, esp. 268, chap. 3.

51. Juan Gil de Zamora, *Liber de preconiis Hispaniae*, ed. Castro y Castro (Madrid: Universidad de Madrid, 1955); my references are to this edition. Juan Gil de Zamora, *Liber de preconiis Hispanie, o educación del príncipe*, ed. and trans. Jenaro Costas Rodríguez and José Luis Martín (Zamora: Ayuntamiento de Zamora, 1996); Georges Cirot, *De operibus historicis Iohannis Aegidii Zamorensis* (Bordeaux: Feret, 1913).

52. Keller and Cash, *Daily Life*, 25–26.

53. *Espéculo*, ed. MacDonald, 430.

54. *Espéculo*, ed. MacDonald, 374.

55. O'Callaghan, *Learned King*, 151–52.

56. Claudio Sánchez Albornoz, "Señoríos y ciudades: Dos diplomas para el estudio de sus recíprocas relaciones," *AHDE* 6 (1929): 454–61; Antonio López Ferreiro, *Historia de la santa a.m. iglesia de Santiago de Compostela*, 11 vols. (Santiago de Compostela: Imprenta del Seminario conciliar y central, 1898–1909), 5:91–92, no. 31; Georges Daumet, *Mémoire sur les relations de la France et de la Castille de 1255 à 1320* (Paris: Bibliothèque de l'École des Hautes Études, 1913), 1–9.

57. Gonzalo de la Hinojosa, *Crónica de España del Arzobispo Don Rodrigo Jiménez de Rada*, in *Colección de documentos inéditos para la historia de España*, ed. Martín Fernández de Navarrete et al., 112 vols. (Madrid: Cadera et al., 1841–95), 106:13.

58. Ballesteros y Beretta, *Alfonso X*, 130–31, 305–6, 543.

59. Manuel Espadas Burgos, ed., *VII centenario del Infante don Fernando de la Cerda: Jornadas de Estudio, Ciudad Real, Abril 1975* (Ciudad Real: Instituto de Estudios Manchegos, 1976); González Jiménez, *Alfonso X*, 215–24.

60. Nieto Soria, *Sancho IV*, 17–24; Ballesteros y Beretta, *Alfonso X*, 511, 520; Mercedes Gaibrois de Ballesteros, *María de Molina, tres veces reina* (Madrid: Espasa-Calpe, 1936); María Antonia Carmona Ruiz, *María de Molina* (Madrid: Plaza y Janés, 2005); Paulette L. Pepin, *María de Molina, Queen and Regent: Life and Rule in Castile-León* (Lanham MD: Lexington Books, 2016).

61. Ballesteros y Beretta, *Alfonso X*, 486, 804, 934.

62. González, *Reinado y diplomas de Fernando III*, 1:106–10; O'Callaghan, *Learned King*, 73–75; González Jiménez, *Alfonso X*, 58–60, and González Jiménez, "Alfonso X y sus hermanos (I)," *Boletín de la Real Academia Sevillana de Buenas Letras* 32 (2004): 203–14; Valeria Bertolucci Pizzorusso, "Don Enrique / Don Arrigo: un infante di Castiglia tra storia e Letteratura," *Alcanate* 4 (2004–5): 293–314.

63. Bruno Meyer, "El desarrollo de las relaciones políticas entre Castilla y el Imperio en tiempos de los Staufen," *ELEM* 21 (1998): 29–48; Máximo Diago Hernando, "La monarquía castellana y los Staufer: Contactos políticos y diplomáticos en los siglos XII y XIII," *ETF* 8 (1995): 51–84; Olga Pérez Monzón, "La imagen del poder y el poder de la imagen: Alfonso X de Castilla y el infante don Felipe," *Nuevo Mundo Mundos Nuevos*, 30 June 2009, http://nuevomundo.revues.org/56517.

64. *CAX(GJ)*, 98, chap. 29.

65. O'Callaghan, *History of Medieval Spain*, 134–36, 194–200, 235–36, 335, 340.

66. Bernard F. Reilly, *The Kingdom of León-Castilla under Queen Urraca, 1109–1126* (Princeton: Princeton University Press, 1982).

67. González, *Reinado y diplomas de Fernando III*, 1:81–85; Miriam Shadis, *Berenguela of Castile (1180–1246) and Political Women in the High Middle Ages* (New York: Palgrave Macmillan, 2010); Janna Bianchini, *The Queen's Hand: Power and Authority in the Reign of Berenguela of Castile* (Philadelphia: University of Pennsylvania Press, 2012).

68. Lucan, *The Civil War Books I–X (Pharsalia)*, trans. J. D. Duff (Cambridge, MA: Harvard University Press, 1962), 9, bk. 1, ll. 92–93.

69. Daumet, *Mémoire*, 1–9, 143–46, no, 1; Wladimir Piskorski, *Las Cortes de Castilla en el período de tránsito de la edad media a la moderna 1188–1520*, trans. Claudio Sánchez Albornoz (Barcelona 1930; repr., Barcelona: Ediciones El Albir, 1977), 196–97, no. 1.

70. Craddock, "Cronología," 367–71.

71. González, *El reino de Castilla en la época de Alfonso VIII*, 1:217–38; O'Callaghan, *History of Medieval Spain*, 235–36, 335–36, 401–4.

72. O'Callaghan, *Learned King*, 234–36; González Jiménez, *Alfonso X*, 295–303.

73. Robert A. MacDonald, "Alfonso the Learned and Succession: A Father's Dilemma," *Speculum* 40 (1965): 647–53, esp. 651; Jerry R. Craddock, "Dynasty in Dispute: Alfonso X of Castile and León in History and Legend," *Viator* 17 (1986): 197–219, and Craddock, "Cronología," 400–415.

74. González Jiménez, *Alfonso X*, 307–8.

75. *CAX(GJ)*, 170–72, chap. 59; Bernat Desclot, *Crònica*, ed. M. Coll i Alentorn, 5 vols. (Barcelona: Barcino, 1949–51), 3:10–13, chap. 66; Guillaume de Nangis, *Gesta Philippi tertii Francorum regum*, in *Recueil des Historiens des Gaules et de la France*, 24 vols.

(Paris: Victor Palmé, 1869–1904), 20:496–500; Gonzalo de la Hinojosa, *Crónica*, 106:6, chap. 238; Craddock, "Cronología," 401–3.

76. *CAX(GJ)*, 190–91, chap. 67; González Jiménez, *Alfonso X*, 310, 314–15; O'Callaghan, *Learned King*, 236–40.

77. Jofré de Loaysa, *Crónica*, 90–92, chap. 219.19–20; *CAX(GJ)*, 193–94, chap. 68.

78. *DAAX*, 549, no. 518.

79. Juan Gil de Zamora, *Liber de preconiis civitatis numantine*, ed. Fidel Fita, "Dos libros (inéditos) de Gil de Zamora," *BRAH* 5 (1884): 146; *DAAX*, 550, no. 518; O'Callaghan, *Learned King*, 246–47; González Jiménez, *Alfonso X*, 327–28.

80. *CAX(GJ)*, 216–30, chaps. 75–76; *DAAX*, 532–34, no. 503 bis.

81. *DAAX*, 557–64, no. 521; O'Callaghan, *Learned King*, 251–69; González Jiménez, *Alfonso X*, 342–69.

4. The King and His People

1. Gibert, *Historia*, 43; José Luis Bermejo Cabrera, "Notas sobre la Segunda Partida," in Espadas Burgos, *VII centenario*, 265–71; Procter, *Alfonso X of Castile*, 63.

2. Marta Haro Cortés, *La imagen del poder real a través de los compendios de castigos castellanos del siglo XIII* (London: Department of Hispanic Studies, Queen Mary and Westfield College, 1996); Hugo Oscar Bizzarri, "Las colecciones sapienciales castellanos en el proceso de reafirmación del poder monárquico (siglos XIII y XIV)," *CLHM* 20 (1995): 35–73; Hugo Oscar Bizzarri and Adeline Rucquoi, "Los espejos de principes en Castilla: Entre Oriente y Occidente," *CHE* 79 (2005): 7–30; David Nogales Rincón, "Los espejos de príncipes en Castilla (siglos XIII–XV): Un modelo literario de la realeza bajomedieval," *Medievalismo* 16 (2006): 9–39.

3. *Secreto de los secretos. Poridat de las poridades: Versiones castellanas del Pseudo-Aristóteles Secretum Secretorum*, ed. Hugo Oscar Bizzarri (Valencia: Universitat de València, 2011); Lloyd A. Kasten, *Seudo Aristóteles. Poridat de las poridades* (Madrid: S. Aguirre, 1957).

4. Mechthild Crombach, *Bocados de oro: Kritische Ausgabe des altspanischen Textes* (Bonn: Romanisches Seminar, 1971).

5. Thomas Aquinas, *On Kingship: To the King of Cyprus*, trans. Gerald B. Phelan, rev. I. T. Eschmann (Toronto: Pontifical Institute of Mediaeval Studies, 1949); Martin, "Alphonse X de Castille, Roi et Empereur," esp. 339–48.

6. José Luis Martín, Luis Miguel Villar García, Florencio Marcos Rodríguez, and Marciano Sánchez Rodriguez, *Documentos de los archivos catedralicios y diocesano de Salamanca (S. XII–XIII)* (Salamanca: Universidad de Salamanca, 1977), 352, no. 262; *MHE*, 1:70–72, no. 34.

7. Ullmann, *Principles*, 57–58; Nieto Soria, *Fundamentos ideológicos*, 127–34; Canning, *History of Medieval Political Thought*, 49–50, 99–100; Panateri, *Discurso del rey*, 170–74, 212–14.

8. Jaime Ferreiro Alemparte, "Recepción de las *Éticas* y de la *Política* de Aristóteles en las *Siete Partidas* del rey Sabio," *Glossae* 1 (1988): 97–133, esp. 102, 123. Martin, "Alphonse X de Castille, Roi et Empereur," 323–24.

9. José Iturmendi Morales, "En torno a la idea de imperio en Alfonso X el Sabio," *Revista de Estudios Políticos* 182 (1972): 83–157, esp. 147–55.

10. Adolf Berger, "Encyclopedic Dictionary of Roman Law," *Transactions of the American Philosophical Society*, n.s., 43 (1953): 437; Ernst Kantorowicz, *The King's Two Bodies: A Study in Medieval Political Theology* (Princeton: Princeton University Press, 1957), 383–450.

11. *Inst.*, 1, 1, 2; Canning, *History of Medieval Political Thought*, 8–9, 117–18.

12. Martin, "Alphonse X de Castille, Roi et Empereur," 325–31, 338–39.

13. Lucan, *Civil War*, 9, bk. 1, ll. 92–93.

14. *CAX(GJ)*, 3, pr.; Juan Manuel, *Libro del caballero et del escudero*, in *BAE*, 51:235, chap. 3; Kantorowicz, *King's Two Bodies*, 34–40; Panateri, *Discurso del rey*, 179–81.

15. Ullmann, *Principles*, 121–22; Nieto Soria, *Fundamentos ideológicos*, 55–58.

16. This citation raises the question: Did Alfonso X have a copy of the *Politics* in Greek or in translation? Ferreiro Alemparte, "Recepción," 121–23; Martin, "Alphonse X de Castille, Roi et Empereur," 345–48.

17. 1 Tm 6:15; Rv 17:14, 19:16.

18. José Antonio Maravall, "Del régimen feudal al régimen corporativo en el pensamiento de Alfonso X," *BRAH* 157 (1965): 213–68, esp. 223–25.

19. Ullmann, *Principles*, 205–6; Post, *Studies in Medieval Legal Thought*, 453–81; Maravall, "Del régimen," 220–22.

20. Canning, *History of Medieval Political Thought*, 125; Alejandro Torres Gutiérrez, "Orígenes canónico-medievales del concepto moderno de estado," in *Escritos en honor a Javier Hervada* (Pamplona: Universidad de Navarra, 1999), 987–98, esp. 990–92.

21. Post, *Studies in Medieval Legal Thought*, 481–93; Maravall, "Del régimen," 219–20.

22. Lucas of Túy, *Chronicon Mundi*, 9, *De excellentia Hispaniae*; Juan Gil de Zamora, *Liber de preconiis Hispanie*, 183, tract. 7, chap. 3.

23. Maravall, "Del régimen," 219; Iturmendi Morales, "En torno a la idea de imperio," 139–45; Panateri, *Discurso del rey*, 182–86.

24. Maravall, "Del régimen," 223–25; Nieto Soria, *Fundamentos ideológicos*, 112–16.

25. Ullmann, *Principles*, 135–37.

26. *E* 2, 1, 1; 2, 5, 1; *FR* 1, 2, 1; *PPBM* 1, 1, 1; *SP* 3, 28, 1; *PCG*, 2:494, chap. 813.

27. *PCG*, 2:653, chap. 973; *E* 5, 11, 33; *PPBM* pr.; *SP* 1, 1, 12; 2, 5, 5; Daniel Berjano, "Antigua carta de hermandad entre Plasencia y Talavera," *BRAH* 35 (1899): 317–18; Maravall, "Del régimen," 246.

28. *DAAX*, 548–54, 557–64, nos. 518, 521.

29. Lucan, *Civil War*, 9, bk. 1, ll. 92–93.

30. *FR* 2, 11, 5; *E* 5, 5, 14; *PPBM* 1, 6, 78; *FV* 1, 1, 1.

31. Berger, "Encyclopedic Dictionary," 437, 523, 607; Kantorowicz, *King's Two Bodies*, 384.

32. Vulgate, Prv 29:4: "rex iustus erigit terram vir avarus destruet eam."

33. *Secreto de los secretos*, ed. Bizzarri, 67, chap. 1, and *Poridat de las poridades*, ed. Bizzarri, 106 (unnumbered capítulo corresponding to tractado 1).

34. Juan Gil de Zamora, *Liber de preconiis Hispanie*, 25–41, tract. 3, chaps. 1–4.

35. Nilda Guglielmi, "La curia regia en León y Castilla," *CHE* 23–24 (1955): 116–267, and 28 (1958): 43–l01; Procter, *Curia and Cortes*, 1–93; Claudio Sánchez Albornoz, *La curia regia portuguesa: Siglos XII y XIII* (Madrid: Junta para ampliación de estudios e investigaciones científicas, 1920).

36. Manuel González Jiménez, "La corte de Alfonso X el Sabio," *Alcanate* 5 (2006–7): 13–30; Rogelio Pérez Bustamante, "Las reformas de la administración central en el reino de Castilla y León en la época de Alfonso X (1252–1284)," *RFDUC* 9 Extra (1985): 83–102; Jaime de Salazar y Acha, "La evolución de la Casa del Rey en el siglo XIII," in *Evolución y estructura de la Casa Real de Castilla*, ed. Andrés Gambra Gutiérrez and Félix Labrador Arroyo, 2 vols. (Madrid: Polifemo, 2010), 1:65–80, and Salazar y Acha, *La Casa del Rey de Castilla y León en la edad media* (Madrid: Centro de Estudios Políticos y Constitucionales, 2000).

37. O'Callaghan, *Learned King*, 37–48.

38. *Poridat de las poridades*, ed. Bizzarri, 122–33, tract. 4.

39. Seneca, *Epistulae morales*, ed. Richard Gummere, 3 vols. (Cambridge, MA: Harvard University Press, 1917–25), Epp. 4, 5, 20.

40. *CAX(GJ)*, 85, chap. 25; O'Callaghan, *Learned King*, 216–19; González Jiménez, *Alfonso X*, 249.

41. *MHE*, 1:122, no. 228.

42. Francisco Veas Arteseros and María del Carmen Veas Arteseros, "Alférez y mayordomo real en el siglo XIII," *MMM* 13 (1986): 29–48, and in *Alfonso X el Sabio: Vida, obra y época*, ed. Juan Carlos de Miguel Rodríguez, Ángela Múñoz Fernández, and Cristina Segura Graiño (Madrid: Sociedad Española de Estudios Medievales, 1989), 55–66.

43. *CAX(GJ)*, 240, chap. 77; Delgado Roig, "Examen médico-legal de unos restos históricos"; Juan Torres Fontes, "Un médico alfonsí: Maestre Nicolás," *Revista Murgetana* 6 (1954): 9–16.

44. Hilda Grassotti, "El repostero en León y Castilla (siglos XII–XIV)," *CHE* 69 (1987): 41–76.

45. Garcí Jufre, *copero mayor*, and Lope Alonso, *portero mayor en el reyno de Gallizia*, witnessed the royal will of 1283; *MHE*, 1:122, no. 228.

46. Nilda Guglielmi, "Posada y Yantar: Contribución al estudio del léxico de las instituciones medievales," *Hispania: Revista española de historia* 26 (1966): 5–29.

47. *Poridat de las poridades*, ed. Bizzarri, 134–35, chap. 5.

48. Reilly, *Kingdom of León-Castilla under King Alfonso VII*, 146–51.

49. Marina Kleine, *La Cancillería Real de Alfonso X: Actores y prácticas en la producción documental* (Seville: Universidad de Sevilla, 2015), and Kleine, "Los orígenes de la burocracia regia en Castilla: la especialización de los oficiales de Alfonso X y Sancho IV," *e-Spania*, 20 February 2015, https://journals.openedition.org/e-spania/; Evelyn Procter, "The Castilian Chancery during the Reign of Alfonso X, 1252–1284," in *Oxford Essays in Medieval History Presented to Herbert Edward Salter*, ed. F. M. Powicke (Oxford: Clarendon Press, 1934), 104–21; Jaime de Salazar y Acha, "La cancillería real en la Corona de Castilla," in *Monarquía, crónicas, archivos y cancillerías en los reinos hispano-cristianos*, ed. Esteban Sarasa (Zaragoza: Institución Fernando el Católico, 2014), 309–24.

50. Luis Rubio García, "Del latín al castellano en la cancillería de Alfonso X el Sabio," *Glossae* 5–6 (1993–94): 225–41.

51. Antonio J. López Gutiérrez, "Oficio y funciones de los escribanos en la cancillería de Alfonso X," *HID* 31 (2004): 353–67.

52. Antonio J. López Gutiérrez, "Registros y registradores en la Cancilleria de Alfonso X," *Estudis castellonenses* 6 (1994–1995): 709–20.

53. Rodríguez Llopis, *Alfonso X*, 39, 113, 195; *Alfonso X: Toledo 1984*, figs. 44, 162.

54. Matthew Paris, *Chronica Majora*, ed. H. R. Luard, 7 vols., Rolls Series (London: Longman, 1872–83), 5:397; Joseph O. Baylen, "John Maunsell and the Castilian Treaty of 1254: A Study of the Clerical Diplomat," *Traditio* 17 (1961): 482–91; Anthony Goodman, "Alfonso X and the English Crown," in Miguel Rodríguez, Múñoz Fernández, and Segura Graiño, *Alfonso X el Sabio*, 1:39–54.

55. Robert I. Burns, SJ, *Diplomatarium of the Crusader Kingdom of Valencia: The Registered Charters of Its Conqueror Jaume I, 1257–1276*, 4 vols. (Princeton: Princeton University Press, 1985–2007), 1:151–81.

56. Rodríguez Llopis, *Alfonso X*, 98, 101.

57. *Secreto de los secretos*, ed. Bizzarri, 122, tract. 3.

58. Maravall, "Del régimen," 223–25.

59. Berger, "Encyclopedic Dictionary," 418, 626.

60. Aquilino Iglesia Ferreirós, *Historia de la traición: La traición regia en León y Castilla* (Santiago de Compostela: Universidad de Compostela, 1971).

61. Jofré de Loaysa, *Crónica*, 96, chap. 191.23; *CAX(GJ)*, 194, chap. 68; *Anales Toledanos III*, in *ES*, 23:420; González Jiménez, *Alfonso X*, 316–22; Ballesteros y Beretta, *Alfonso X*, 819–27; Richard P. Kinkade, "Alfonso X, *Cantiga 235*, and the Events of 1269–1278," *Speculum* 67 (1992): 284–323, esp. 313–18; O'Callaghan, *Learned King*, 241–43; and O'Callaghan, *Alfonso X and the Cantigas*, 144–51.

62. Juan Gil de Zamora, *Liber de preconiis Hispanie*, 331, tract. 9, chap. 11, and *Liber de preconiis civitatis numantine*, 199, bk. 7 chap. 31.

63. Juan Gil de Zamora, *Liber de preconiis Hispanie*, 329–46, tract. 10, chaps. 1–3.

64. *CAX(GJ)*, 220–30, chap. 76; O'Callaghan, *Learned King*, 258–62; González Jiménez, *Alfonso X*, 342–49.

65. *DAAX*, 532–35, no. 503 bis. The quotations in this and the following two paragraphs are taken from the king's denunciation of Sancho.

66. *DAAX*, 532–35, no. 503 bis; Georges Martin, "Alphonse X maudit son fils," *Atalaya: Revue française d'études médiévales hispaniques romanes* 5 (1994): 153–78.

67. *DAAX*, 548–55, no. 518: *MHE*, 2:110–22, no. 228.

68. John of Salisbury, *Policraticus*, ed. and trans. Cary J. Nederman (New York: Cambridge University Press, 1990), 25, 206–8, bk. 3, chap. 15, bk. 8, chap. 20.

69. González, *Reinado y diplomas de Fernando III*, 3:287–89, no. 809; Seville 1252, art. 14; Valladolid 1258, arts. 28, 37; Seville 1261, art. 27; Jerez 1268, art. 41.

70. *MHE*, 2:67–70, nos. 202–3.

71. Juan Torres Fontes, *Documentos del siglo XIII* (Murcia: Academia Alfonso X el Sabio,1969), 70–71, no. 77.

72. Augusto Quintana Prieto, *Tumbo Viejo de San Pedro de Montes* (León: Centro de Estudios e Investigaciones "San Isidoro," 1971), 482–87, no. 375; Romualdo Escalona, *Historia del real monasterio de Sahagún* (Madrid, 1782; repr., León: Ediciones Leonesas, 1982), 618–22, no. 266; Antonio Álvarez de Morales, *Las hermandades expresión del movimiento comunitario en España* (Valladolid: Universidad de Valladolid, 1974), 207–8, no. 1.

73. Thomas Rymer, *Foedera, conventiones, litterae et cuiuscunque acta publica inter reges Angliae et alios quovis imperatores, reges, pontifices, principes*, 3rd ed., 10 vols. (The Hague: Joannes Neaulme, 1739–45), 1.2:230; *CAX(GJ)*, 240–42, chap. 77; O'Callaghan, *Learned King*, 267–69.

74. Juan Manuel, *Tratado de las armas*, in *BAE*, 51:257–64, esp. 263.

75. Ullmann, *Principles*, 232–36; Joseph R. Strayer, *On the Medieval Origins of the Modern State* (Princeton: Princeton University Press, 1970).

76. Maravall, "Del régimen," 250–51; Post, *Studies in Medieval Legal Thought*, 494–560; María Isabel Pérez de Tudela Velasco, "Ideario político y orden social en las Partidas de Alfonso X," *ELEM* 14 (1991): 183–200.

77. Ángel Ferrari, "La secularización de la teoría del estado en las Partidas," *AHDE* 11 (1934): 449–56.

78. *MHE*, 1:252–53, no. 115, and 2:131, no. 229; Juan Gil de Zamora, *Liber de preconiis civitatis numantine*, 197–99, bk. 7 chaps. 29, 31; *Castigos del rey don Sancho IV*, ed. Bizzarri, 100, chap. 5.

79. Juan Gil de Zamora, *Liber de preconiis Hispanie*, 30–32, 46, 71, tract. 2, chaps. 3–4; tract. 4, chaps. 2, 5.

80. María Dolores Guerrero Lafuente, *Historia de la ciudad de Benavente en la edad media* (Benavente: Lancia, 1983), 422, no. 3; Procter, *Curia and Cortes*, 284–86, no. 6; Rodríguez Díez, *Historia de la ciudad de Astorga*, 715; *MHE*, 2:29, no. 179.

81. *DAAX*, 534, no. 503 bis.

82. Agapito Rey, ed., *Libro de los cien capítulos* (Bloomington: Indiana University Press, 1960), 8, chap. 1.

83. Gaibrois, *Historia del reinado de Sancho IV*, 3:cdx, no. 596; *CAX(GJ)*, 57, chap. 19; Kantorowicz, *King's Two Bodies*, 336–82; Nieto Soria, *Fundamentos ideológicos*, 139–46.

84. Juan Gil de Zamora, *De preconiis Hispanie*, 253–54, 272, tract. 8, chaps. 10, 11.

85. John of Salisbury, *Policraticus*, 66–67, bk. 5, chap. 2; Kantorowicz, *King's Two Bodies*, 193–273.

86. Maravall, "Del régimen," 244.

87. Piskorski, *Cortes*, 196–97, no. 1; Lucan, *Civil War*, 9, bk. 1, ll. 92–93.

88. *PCG*, 2:494, chap. 813.

89. *Castigos del rey don Sancho IV*, ed. Bizzarri, 150, 165, chaps. 11.104, 15.16.

90. Juan Gil de Zamora, *Liber de preconiis Hispanie*, 31, tract. 3, chap. 3.

91. *DAAX*, 532, no. 503 bis.

92. *MHE*, 2:68–70, 94, nos. 203, 220; Post, *Studies in Medieval Legal Thought*, 247, 253; Ullmann, *Principles*, 67–68, 88, 133.

93. González, *Reinado y diplomas de Fernando III*, 3:387–89, no. 809.

94. Procter, *Curia and Cortes*, 284–86, no. 6; *MHE*, 1:252–53, no. 115.

95. J. M. Escudero de la Peña, "Súplica hecha a Papa Juan XXI para que absolviese al Rey de Castilla, D. Alfonso X, del juramento de no acuñar otra moneda que los dineros prietos," *RABM*, ser. 1, 2 (1872): 58–59; *MHE*, 2:78–80, no. 219.

96. *DAAX*, 533, no. 503 bis.

97. Seville 1252, pr.; Seville 1261, pr.; *MHE*, 1:71, 187–91, 252, nos. 34, 86, 115; Procter, *Curia and Cortes*, 284, no. 6.

98. *DAAX*, 553, no. 518; *CAX(GJ)*, 111–12, 144–51, chaps. 6, 52; Nieto Soria, *Fundamentos ideológicos*, 146–51.

99. *Leyes nuevas*, in *Opúsculos legales*, 2:181.

100. Escudero de la Peña, "Súplica," 59; Post, *Studies in Medieval Legal Thought*, 23, 319.

101. *DAAX*, 532–35, no. 503 bis.

102. Maravall, "Del régimen," 247–49.

5. Defender of the Faith

1. Joseph F. O'Callaghan, "Alfonso X and the Castilian Church," *Thought* 60 (1985): 417–29, and O'Callaghan, "The Ecclesiastical Estate in the Cortes of León-Castile, 1252–1350," *Catholic Historical Review* 67 (1981), 185–213; repr. in *Alfonso X, the Cortes and Government*, nos. VI, XII; José Manuel Nieto Soria, "Principios teóricos y evolución de la política eclesiástica de Alfonso X," *Mayorga* 22 (1989): 465–74.

2. Peter Linehan, *The Spanish Church and the Papacy in the Thirteenth Century* (Cambridge: Cambridge University Press, 1971); O'Callaghan, *Learned King*, 48–63.

3. Linda A. McMillin, "Alfonso el Sabio and the *Primera Partida*: A Thirteenth-Century Vision of the Church," *Comitatus* 17 (1986): 51–68.

4. José Giménez y Martínez de Carvajal, "El Decreto y las Decretales: Fuentes de la Primera Partida de Alfonso X el Sabio," *Anthologica Annua* 2 (1954): 239–48, and Giménez y Martínez de Carvajal, "San Raimundo de Peñafort y las Partidas de Alfonso X el Sabio," *Anthologica Annua* 3 (1955): 201–338.

5. *Setenario*, ed. Vanderford.

6. Rafael Lapesa, "Símbolos y palabras en el Setenario de Alfonso X," *Nueva Revista de Filología hispánica* 29 (1980): 247–61.

7. Margherita Morreale, "El canon de la misa en lengua vernácula y la Biblia romanceada del siglo XIII," *Hispania Sacra* 15 (1962): 203–19.

8. Norman Tanner, *Decrees of the Ecumenical Councils* (Washington, DC: Georgetown University Press, 1990), Constitution 1, Confession of Faith; Emilio Mitre Fernández, "Iglesia, salvación y teocracia romana en el Medievo (Un apunte en torno al axioma Extra Ecclesiam nulla salus)," *'Ilu: Revista de Ciencias de las Religiones* 18 (2013): 135–73.

9. *Catechism of the Catholic Church* (Vatican City: Libreria Editrice Vaticana, 1994), 846–51.

10. Sergi Grau Torras, *Cátaros e Inquisición en los reinos hispánicos (siglos XII–XIV)* (Madrid: Cátedra, 2012).

11. *De altera vita fideique controversiis adversus Albigensium errores*, ed. Juan de Mariana (Ingolstadt: Andreas Angermarius, 1612); Bonifacio Palacios Martín, "La circulación de los cátaros por el Camino de Santiago y sus implicaciones socioculturales: Una fuente para su conocimiento," *ELEM* 3 (1982): 219–30; Francisco Javier Fernández Conde, "Albigenses en León y Castilla a comienzos del siglo XIII," in *León medieval: doce estudios; Ponencias y comunicaciones presentadas al coloquio "El reino de León en la Edad Media"* (León: Colegio Universitario, 1978), 95–114, and Fernández Conde, "Un noyau actif d'Albigeois en León au commencement du XIIIᵉ siècle? Approche critique d'une œuvre de Luc de Tuy écrite entre 1230 et 1240," *Heresis* 17 (1991): 35–50.

12. Santiago Domínguez Sánchez, *Documentos de Gregorio IX (1227–1241) referentes a España* (León: Universidad de León, 2004), 441–42, 470, 621–22, nos. 539, 580, 79; González, *Reinado y diplomas de Fernando III*, 1:14–15.

13. Emilio Mitre Fernández, "Hérésie et culture dirigeante dans la Castille de la fin du XIIIᵉ siècle: le modèle d'Alphonse X," *Heresis* 9 (1987): 33–47.

14. *DAAX*, 548, 557–58, nos. 518, 521; *MHE*, 1:110–22, nos. 228–29; Georges Daumet, "Les testaments d'Alphonse X le Savant, roi de Castille," *Bibliothèque de l'Ecole des Chartes* 67 (1906): 73–87.

15. Argüello, "Memoria sobre," esp. 33.

16. E-mail communication of 7 October 2013.

17. O'Callaghan, *Cortes*, 21–22, and O'Callaghan, "Catálogo de los cuadernos de las Cortes de Castilla y León, 1252–1348," *AHDE* 62 (1992): 501–31; repr. in *Alfonso X, the Cortes and Government*, no. XIV.

18. Joseph F. O'Callaghan, "Una ley de las Cortes de Sevilla de 1252 incorporada en la Primera Partida del rey don Alfonso X, el Sabio," *AHDE* 84 (2014): 789–96.

19. James A. Brundage, *Medieval Canon Law and the Crusader* (Madison: University of Wisconsin Press, 1969), 11–18.

20. González, *Alfonso IX*, 2:739–41, nos. 666, 667; López Ferreiro, *Historia*, 5:43–45, no. 14.

21. *The Pilgrim's Guide to Santiago de Compostela*, trans. William Melczer (New York: Italica, 1993), 132; *LFC* 2, 20, 55, 56, 58, 59, 274.

22. González, *Alfonso IX*, 2:619–20, no. 519; López Ferreiro, *Historia*, 5:46–47, no. 15.

23. *The Pilgrim's Guide*, 92.

24. Luis Vázquez de Parga, José María Lacarra, and Juan Uria, *Las peregrinaciones a Santiago de Compostela*, 3 vols. (Madrid: Consejo Superior de Investigaciones Científicas, 1948–49), 3:111–12, no. 78.

25. Vázquez de Parga, Lacarra, and Uria, *Peregrinaciones*, 1:132–34; López Ferreiro, *Historia*, 5:95–96, 109, nos. 33, 39.

26. Ballesteros, "Itinerario," 107:22–23, n. 1.

27. *CAX(GJ)*, 90–92, chap. 26.

28. Ángel Barrios García, *Documentación medieval de la catedral de Ávila* (Salamanca: Universidad de Salamanca, 1981), 90–91, no. 101; Mateo Escagedo Salmón, *Colección diplomática: Privilegios, escrituras, y bulas en pergamino de la Insigne Real Iglesia Colegial de Santillana*, 2 vols. (Santoña: Dialco Mnemaen, 1927), 1:155–58; Ramón Menéndez Pidal, *Documentos lingüísticos de España: Reino de Castilla* (Madrid: Junta para Ampliación de Estudios e Investigaciones científicas, 1919), 300–302, no. 229; María Luisa Pardo Rodríguez, *La cancillería de Don Fernando de la Cerda, Infante de Castilla y León (1255–1275)* (León: Universidad de León, 2009), 175–83, nos. 34–36.

29. Santiago Domínguez Sánchez, *Documentos de Nicolás III (1277–1280) referentes a España* (León: Universidad de León, 1999), 334–40, nos. 114–17; Carlos de Ayala Martínez, "Las relaciones de Alfonso X con la santa sede durante el pontificado de Nicolás III (1277–10)," in Miguel Rodríguez, Múñoz Fernández, and Segura Graiño, *Alfonso X el Sabio*, 137–51.

30. Domínguez Sánchez, *Documentos de Nicolás III*, 340–45, no. 118; Linehan, *Spanish Church*, 209, 217–20.

31. Juan Torres Fontes, "La Orden de Santa María de España," *MMM* 3 (1977): 78–118.

32. Peter Linehan, "The Spanish Church Revisited: The Episcopal Gravamina of 1279," in *Authority and Power: Studies on Medieval Law and Government Presented to Walter Ullmann on his Seventieth Birthday*, ed. Brian Tierney and Peter Linehan (Cambridge: Cambridge University Press, 1980), 127–47, esp. 144–47. "Art. 5" refers to the *memoriale* and "E, G, H, I, K, M, N" refer to the text in Linehan's appendix.

33. Linehan, "Spanish Church Revisited," 133, n. 27.

34. González Díez, *Colección diplomática del concejo de Burgos*, 179–83, nos. 96, 98, 99.

35. Linehan, *Spanish Church*, 220–21.

36. José Manuel Nieto Soria, *Iglesia y poder real en Castilla: El episcopado, 1250–1350* (Madrid: Universidad Complutense, 1988), 197–204.

37. *PPBM* 1, 5, 18 mistakenly reads *amparador* as *emperador*.

38. Linehan, *Spanish Church*, 108, n. 2; José Manuel Nieto Soria, *Las relaciones monarquía-episcopado castellano como sistema de poder (1252–1312)*, 2 vols. (Madrid: Universidad Complutense de Madrid, 1983), 1:700, n. 13.

39. Demetrio Mansilla, *Iglesia castellano-leonesa y curia romana en los tiempos del rey san Fernando* (Madrid: Consejo Superior de Investigaciones Científicas, 1945), 311–12, no. 45; Ildefonso Rodríguez de Lama, *La documentación pontificia de Alejandro IV (1254–1261)* (Rome: Instituto Español de Historia Eclesiástica, 1976), 41–42, nos. 14–15; *Espéculo*, ed. MacDonald, 496, 500, nos. 180, 230.

40. Antonio Ballesteros, *Sevilla en el siglo XIII* (Madrid; Juan Pérez Torres, 1913), 89–100; *Espéculo*, ed. MacDonald, 483, no. 11.

41. Santiago Domínguez Sánchez, *Documentos de Clemente IV (1265–1268) referentes a España* (León: Universidad de León, 1996), 183–84, 188–200, nos. 76, 81–84, 87, 88; *Espéculo*, ed. MacDonald, 495, no. 176.

42. Domínguez Sánchez, *Documentos de Nicolás III*, 404–14, nos. 153–59; *Espéculo*, ed. MacDonald, 496–97, nos. 181, 193.

43. Domínguez Sánchez, *Documentos de Nicolás III*, 415–22, nos. 161–65.

44. Santiago Domínguez Sánchez, *Documentos de Gregorio X (1272–1276) referentes a España* (León: Universidad de León, 1997), 159–67, nos. 49–55; *Espéculo*, ed. MacDonald, 497–98, nos. 194–95.

45. François Olivier Martin, *Les registres de Martin IV (1281–1285)* (Paris: Bibliothèque des Écoles françaises d'Athènes et de Rome, 1901), 2–3, nos. 2–3; López Ferreiro, *Fueros municipales*, 304–5.

46. *Espéculo*, ed. MacDonald, 482–83, nos. 9, 12.

47. Linehan, "Spanish Church Revisited," 142–45, and Linehan, "La iglesia de León a mediados del siglo XIII," *León y su historia* 3 (1975): 13–76; José Manuel Nieto Soria, "Los obispos de la diócesis de León en sus relaciones con la monarquía, 1250–1350," *Archivos Leoneses* 74 (1983): 201–62.

48. *Espéculo*, ed. MacDonald, 482, 497, nos. 8, 194.

49. *DAAX*, 281–82, no. 254; *Espéculo*, ed. MacDonald, 500, nos. 7, 22.

50. Domínguez Sánchez, *Documentos de Nicolás III*, 288–93, nos. 82–86; Juan Torres Fontes, "El obispado de Cartagena en el siglo XIII," *Hispania: Revista española de historia* 13 (1953): 339–401, 515–80, esp. 515–18; *Espéculo*, ed. MacDonald, 495, 497, 499, nos. 174, 188, 218–19.

51. Manuel Nieto Cumplido, "La elección de obispos de Córdoba en la baja edad media," in Cristóbal Torres Delgado et al., *Andalucía medieval: Nuevos estudios* (Córdoba: Monte de Piedad y Caja de Ahorros de Córdoba, 1979), 75–103; *Espéculo*, ed. MacDonald, 496, 498, nos. 182, 204.

52. Diego de Colmenares, *Historia de la insigne ciudad de Segovia*, new ed., 3 vols. (Segovia: Academia de Historia y Arte de San Quirce, 1969–75), 1:407, 420; *Espéculo*, ed. MacDonald, 496, no. 186.

53. Toribio Minguella, *Historia de la diócesis de Sigüenza*, 3 vols. (Madrid: RABM, 1900–13), 1:214, 225–26; *Espéculo*, ed. MacDonald, 495, 499, nos. 165, 208.

54. Jean Guiraud, *Les registres d'Urbain IV (1261–1264)* (Paris: Albert Fontemoing, 1892–1958), 256, 302, 331, 333–35, 357, 388, 458, nos. 1080, 1915, 2061, 1076–77,

2080–82, 2093, 2100, 2346, 2728; Peter Linehan, "The *Gravamina* of the Castilian Church in 1262–3," *EHR* 85 (1970):730–54.

55. Linehan, "Spanish Church Revisited," 143.

56. Nieto Soria, *Iglesia*, 206–7.

57. López Ferreiro, *Fueros municipales*, 284–88.

58. Linehan, *Spanish Church*, 175–76.

59. González, *El reino de Castilla en la época de Alfonso VIII*, 2:582–84, no. 144; González, *Alfonso IX*, 2:127, 307, nos. 84, 221; and González, *Reinado y diplomas de Fernando III*, 2:428–29, no. 372.

60. F. Javier Pereda Llarena, *Documentación de la catedral de Burgos (1254–1293)* (Burgos: J. M. Garrido Garrido, 1984), 38–41, no. 25; *MHE*, 1:77–79, no. 37; Minguella, *Historia de la diócesis de Sigüenza*, 1:572–74, no.209; Martín et al., *Documentos de los archivos catedralicios y diocesano de Salamanca*, 350–52, no. 261; Fernández del Pulgar, *Historia secular y eclesiástica de la ciudad de Palencia*, 2: 336–8; Loperráez, *Descripción histórica del obispado de Osma*, 3:81–83, no. 58; Luis Miguel Villar Garcia, *Documentación medieval de la catedral de Segovia, 1115–1300* (Salamanca: Universidad de Salamanca, 1990), 268–71, no. 160; Francisco Santos Coco, "Documentos del Archivo-Catedral de Badajoz," *Revista de Estudios Extremeños* 1 (1927): 78–85, esp. 80–82; Ballesteros y Beretta, *Alfonso X*, 1071–72, nos. 256–57, 259–61, 263, 265, 270, 276, 278.

61. Pereda Llarena, *Documentación de la catedral de Burgos*, 168–70, 173–74, nos. 121–22, 125.

62. Linehan, "Spanish Church Revisited," 141–42.

63. González, *El reino de Castilla en la época de Alfonso VIII*, 1:357–61, and González, "Sobre la fecha de las Cortes de Nájera"; Bermejo Castro, "En torno a las Cortes de Nájera."

64. González, *Alfonso IX*, 2:23–26, esp. 26, no. 11; Joseph F. O'Callaghan, "Una nota sobre las llamadas Cortes de Benavente," *Archivos Leoneses* 73 (1983): 97–100; Rafael González Rodríguez, "Las cortes de Benavente de 1202 y 1228," in *El Reino de León en la época de las cortes de Benavente: Jornadas de Estudios Históricos, Benavente, 7, 8, 9, 10, 15, 16 y 17 de mayo de 2002* (Benavente: Institución Ledo del Pozo, 2002), 191–221.

65. *MHE*, 1:18, 21–22, nos. 9, 11; *DAAX*, 116, no. 117.

66. Ballesteros y Beretta, *Alfonso X*, 1078, no. 394.

67. Barrios Garcia, *Documentación medieval de la catedral de Ávila*, 90–91, no. 101; Escagedo Salmón, *Colección diplomática*, 1:155–58; Menéndez Pidal, *Documentos*, 300–302, no. 229.

68. Pereda Llarena, *Documentación de la catedral de Burgos*, 210–11, no. 148.

69. David Romano, *Judíos al servicio de Pedro el Grande de Aragón (1276–1285)* (Barcelona: Universidad de Barcelona, 1983), 209–10.

70. *Leyes nuevas*, in *Opúsculos legales*, 2:199.

71. Minguella, *Historia de la diócesis de Sigüenza*, 1:574–75, no. 210; *MHE*, 1:288–89, no. 129.

72. Pardo Rodríguez, *Cancillería*, 172–75, 183–85, nos. 31–32, 37.

73. Pardo Rodríguez, *Cancillería*, 185–86, 189–90, nos. 38, 40; Barrios García, *Documentación medieval de la catedral de Ávila*, 90–91, no. 101; Escagedo Salmón, *Colección diplomática*, 1:155–58; Menéndez Pidal, *Documentos*, 300–302, no. 229.

74. Pardo Rodríguez, *Cancillería*, 185–86, 189–90, nos. 38, 40; *LEst* 118.

75. González, *Reinado y diplomas de Fernando III*, 1:223–24, 3:374–76, 378–79, nos. 795, 798.

76. López Ferreiro, *Fueros municipales*, 235–44, 251–60, 262–77, 279–97; José Barreiro Somoza, *El señorío de la iglesia de Santiago de Compostela (siglos IX–XIII)* (La Coruña: Editorial Diputación Provincial, 1987), 415, 423.

77. Domínguez Sánchez, *Documentos de Nicolás III*, 183–84, no. 9; López Ferreiro, *Historia*, 5:242–43.

78. Linehan, "Spanish Church Revisited," 141–42; Domínguez Sánchez, *Documentos de Nicolás III*, 341, no. 118; Barreiro Somoza, *Señorío*, 452–56.

79. Linehan, "Spanish Church Revisited," 144, 146–47.

80. Pardo Rodríguez, *Cancillería*, 185–86, no. 38; Pareda Llarena, *Documentación de la catedral de Burgos*, 211–12, no. 149.

81. Linehan, "Spanish Church Revisited," 144; Domínguez Sánchez, *Documentos de Nicolás III*, 341–42, no. 118.

82. Martín et al., *Documentos de los archivos catedralicios y diocesano de Salamanca*, 352–54, no. 262; *MHE*, 1:70–75, no. 35; Pereda Llarena, *Documentación de la catedral de Burgos*, 35–38, no. 24; José Luis Martín, *Documentos zamoranos*, vol. 1, *Documentos del Archivo Catedralicio de Zamora, Primera Parte (1128–1261)* (Salamanca: Universidad de Salamanca, 1982), 126–28, no. 153; Antonio Ballesteros, *El Itinerario de Alfonso el Sabio* (Madrid: Tipografía de Archivos, 1935), 133–34, 139, 203, and Ballesteros y Beretta, *Alfonso X*, 1071–72, nos. 262, 264, 272; *DAAX*, 181–82, no. 164; Linehan, *Spanish Church*, 121–23.

83. *CLC*, 1:154–55; Rodríguez de Lama, *Documentación pontificia de Alejandro IV*, 364, no. 309.

84. *DAAX*, 447, 458, nos. 422, 435; Ballesteros, *Sevilla*, ccvii, ccxiii, nos. 195, 207.

85. Linehan, "Spanish Church Revisited," 146–47; Domínguez Sánchez, *Documentos de Nicolás III*, 341–42, no. 118.

86. Norah B. Ramos, "La iglesia a través de las cortes castellanas: Uso y abuso de la excomunión (Ss. XIII–XIV)," *CHE* 69 (1987): 97–107.

87. González, *Alfonso IX*, 2:236–37, no. 167; José Antonio García Luján, *Privilegios reales de la catedral de Toledo (1086–1462): Formación del patrimonio de la S.I.C.P. a través de las donaciones reales*, 2 vols. (Toledo: Imprenta Torres, 1982), 2:180–82, no. 74; *MHE*, 1:5–8, no. 4; Luis Sánchez Belda, *Documentos reales de la Edad media referentes a Galicia: Catálogo de los conservados en la Sección de Clero del Archivo Histórico Nacional* (Madrid: Dirección General de Museos y Bibliotecas, 1953), 309, no. 719; Nieto Soria, "Obispos," 251–53, nos. 1, 3; Pereda Llarena, *Documentación de la catedral de Burgos*, 10–12, no. 7; Mingüella, *Historia de la diócesis de Sigüenza*, 1:576–78, no. 211; Fernández del Pulgar, *Historia secular y eclesiástica de la ciudad de Palencia*, 2:336–38, and 3:27–28; Mateo Hernández Vegas, *Ciudad Rodrigo: La catedral y la ciudad*, 2 vols. (Salamanca: Imprenta Comercial Salmantina, 1935), 1:169; Colmenares, *Historia de la insigne ciudad de Segovia*, 2:214–15; Martín et al., *Documentos de los archivos catedralicios y diocesano de Salamanca*, 347–50, no. 260; Mateo Villar y Macías, *Historia de Salamanca*, 3 vols. (Salamanca: Librería Cervantes, 1887), 4:97–98; *DAAX*, 179–80, 230–31, nos. 163, 208; Martínez Marina, *Teoría*, 3:87–88, nos. 5–6; Ballesteros, *Itinerario*, 93, 132, and Ballesteros y Beretta, *Alfonso X*, 1087, no. 582; Marius Ferotin, *Histoire de l'Abbaye de Silos* (Paris: Ernest Leroux, 1897), 102, n. 3; Loperráez, *Descripción histórica del*

obispado de Osma, 3:79–81, no. 57; Antonio Benavides, *Memorias de D. Fernando IV de Castilla,* 2 vols. (Madrid: José Rodríguez, 1860), 2:332–33, no. 221; Ciriaco López de Silanes and Eliseo Sáinz Ripa, *Colección diplomática calceatense: Archivo Catedral (años 1125–1397)* (Logroño: Consejo Superior de Investigaciones Científicas, 1985), 66–68, no. 34; José Benavides Checa, *El Fuero de Plasencia* (Rome: Lobesi, 1896), 170; Villar Garcia, *Documentación medieval de la catedral de Segovia,* 265–66, no. 159; Menéndez Pidal, *Documentos,* 384–85, no. 284; Luciano Serrano, *Cartulario del Infantadgo de Covarrubias* (Madrid: Gregorio del Amo, 1907), 101–2, no. 58.

88. Nieto Soria, "Obispos," 253–54, no. 4; Sánchez Belda, *Documentos reales de la Edad media referentes a Galicia,* 327, no. 753; Pereda Llarena, *Documentación de la catedral de Burgos,* 41–42, no. 26; Fernández del Pulgar, *Historia secular y eclesiástica de la ciudad de Palencia,* 2:340–41; Villar Garcia, *Documentación medieval de la catedral de Segovia,* 265–68, no. 159.

89. Linehan, *Spanish Church,* 123.

90. Barrios García, *Documentación medieval de la catedral de Ávila,* 90–91, no. 101; Escagedo Salmón, *Colección diplomática,* 1:155–58; Menéndez Pidal, *Documentos,* 300–302, no, 229.

91. Domínguez Sánchez, *Documentos de Gregorio X,* 240–43, 341–42, nos. 110–11, 193.

92. Menéndez Pidal, *Documentos,* 257, no. 20; Villar Garcia, *Documentación medieval de la catedral de Salamanca,* 323, no, 98: Ubieto Arteta, *Colección diplomática de Cuéllar,* 78–79, no. 34.

93. Linehan, "Spanish Church Revisited," 143–44, 147; Domínguez Sánchez, *Documentos de Nicolás III,* 341, no. 118.

94. Manuel Segura Moreno, *Estudio del códice gótico (siglo XIII) de la catedral de Jaén* (Jaén: Instituto de Estudios Giennenses, 1976), 202–3, no. 16; Manuel Nieto Cumplido, *Orígenes del regionalismo andaluz (1235–1325)* (Córdoba: Monte de Piedad y Caja de Ahorros de Córdoba, 1979), 118–21, no. 3; *DAAX,* 262–64, no. 238.

95. Procter, *Curia and Cortes,* 286–87, no. 7.

96. Torres Fontes, "El obispado de Cartagena," 561–62, no. 7, and 549–50, 564, nos. 4, 11.

97. *MHE,* 1:109–10, 144–47, 160–63, nos. 50–52, 66, 76, 78; *DAAX,* 237–38, 246–47, nos. 213, 224.

98. Julio González, "La clerecía de Salamanca durante la edad media," *Hispania: Revista española de Historia* 3 (1943): 409–30.

99. Ballesteros, "Itinerario," 107:413; Pereda Llarena, *Documentación de la catedral de Burgos,* 114–15, no. 79; Barrios Garcia, *Documentación medieval de la catedral de Ávila,* 84–85, no. 93; Villar Garcia, *Documentación medieval de la catedral de Segovia,* 323–24, no 109; *DAAX,* 304–5, 330, 378–79, 385–86, nos. 278, 306, 350–51, 356.

100. Nieto Soria, *Iglesia,* 118–23.

101. Elie Berger, *Les Registres d'Innocent IV,* 4 vols. (Paris: Bibliothèque des Écoles françaises d'Athènes et de Rome, 1884–1921), 1:377, no. 2538; Linehan, *Spanish Church,* 111–12.

102. *MHE,* 1:308–23, esp. 319, no. 140.

103. *DAAX,* 126–28, no. 125; *MHE,* 1:33–36, 160–61, nos. 18, 76.

104. Martín et al., *Documentos de los archivos catedralicios y diocesano de Salamanca,* 341–42, 352–54, nos. 255, 262; *MHE,* 1:70–75, 108–10, nos. 34–35, 50–52; Marciano Sánchez Rodríguez, *Tumbo blanco de Zamora* (Salamanca: Varona, 1985), no. 20; María

Soledad Beltrán Suárez, "Privilegios de Alfonso X a la catedral de Oviedo," *Asturiensia medievalia* 5 (1986): 155–69, esp. 161; José Manuel Ruiz Asencio and José Antonio Martín Fuertes, *Colección documental del Archivo de La Catedral de León (1230–1269)* (León: Centro de Estudios e Investigación "San Isidoro," 1993), no. 2163; Pareda Llarena, *Documentación de la catedral de Burgos*, 35–38, no. 24; Martín, *Documentos zamoranos*, 1:126–28, no. 153; José Carlos de Lera Maillo, *Catálogo de documentos de la catedral de Zamora* (Zamora: Instituto de Estudios Zamoranos, 1999), no. 634 reg.; *DAAX*, nos. 164–65, 167; Antonio López Ferreiro, *Colección diplomática de Galicia Histórica* (Santiago de Compostela: Tipografía Galaica, 1901), 1:409–11; Ildefonso Rodríguez de Lama, *Colección diplomática medieval de la Rioja: Documentos siglo XIII* (Logroño: Instituto de Estudios Riojanos, 1989), no. 226; Santos Coco, "Documentos," 82–85, no. 2; Ballesteros, *Itinerario*, 123, n. 1, 133–34, 139, and Ballesteros y Beretta, *Alfonso X*, 1071–72, nos. 244, 262, 264, 269, 272; Menéndez Pidal, *Documentos*, 299–300, no. 228; Linehan, *Spanish Church*, 121–23.

105. Domínguez Sánchez, *Documentos de Clemente IV*, 140–44, nos. 32–33.

106. Clementino Sanz y Diaz, *Reseña cronológica de algunos documentos conservados en el Archivo de la Catedral de Cuenca* (Cuenca: Calasanz, 1965), 20, no. 135.

107. *MHE*, 1:313–14, no. 140.

108. Domínguez Sánchez, *Documentos de Gregorio X*, 368–89, no. 214, and Domínguez Sánchez, *Documentos de Nicolás III*, 334–45, nos. 114–18; Linehan, *Spanish Church*, 207–8.

109. Domínguez Sánchez, *Documentos de Nicolás III*, 341, no. 118; Linehan, "Spanish Church Revisited," 141.

110. *MHE*, 2:67–68, no. 202; Marius Ferotin, *Recueil des chartes de l'abbaye de Silos* (Paris: Imprimerie Nationale 1897), 272–73, no. 243; Escalona, *Historia del real monasterio de Sahagún*, 618–22, no. 266.

111. *MHE*, 2:59–63, no. 198; Linehan, *Spanish Church*, 220–21.

112. *DAAX*, 544–46, 555–57, nos. 515, 529. Linehan, *Spanish Church*, 137.

113. *MHE*, 2: 94–97, no. 220; Francisco José Díaz Marcilla, "Lealtades y deslealtades eclesiásticas durante la 'cuestión sucesoria' entre Alfonso X y Sancho IV (1282–1284)," *Edad Media* 18 (2017): 177–206.

6. The Defense of the Realm

1. Joseph F. O'Callaghan, "War (and Peace) in the Law Codes of Alfonso X," in *Crusaders, Condottieri, and Cannon: Medieval Warfare in Societies around the Mediterranean*, ed. Donald J. Kagay and L. J. Andrew Villalon (Leiden: Brill, 2003), 3–17.

2. Flavius Renatus Vegetius, *Epitoma rei militaris*, ed. Carl Lang (Leipzig: B. G. Teubner, 1885), and Vegetius, *Epitome of Military Science*, trans. N. P. Milner (Liverpool: Liverpool University Press, 1993); Juan Gil de Zamora, *Liber de preconiis Hispanie*, 347–76. bk. 11.

3. Julio Gerardo Martínez Martínez, *Acerca de la guerra y de la paz, los ejércitos, las estrategías y las armas según el Libro de las Siete Partidas* (Cáceres: Universidad de Extremadura, 1984).

4. Isidore of Seville, *Etymologiarum*, bk. 18, chaps. 2–4.

5. José María Gárate Córdoba, "El pensamiento militar en el Código de las Siete Partidas," *Revista de Historia Militar* 13 (1963): 7–60, esp. 19–21; Ana Belén

Sánchez Prieto, *Guerra y guerreros en España según las fuentes canónicas de la edad media* (Madrid: E.M.E., 1990).

6. *Crònica de Jaume I*, ed. J. M. Casacuberta and E. Bague, 9 vols. (Barcelona: Barcino, 1926–62), 7:42–44, chap. 382.

7. Eloy Benito Ruano, *Hermandades en Asturias durante la edad media* (Oviedo: La Cruz, 1972), 57–58, no. 1; Escudero de la Peña, "Súplica," 58–59.

8. Ariel Guiance, "Morir por la patria, por la fe: La ideología de la muerte en la *Historia de rebus Hispaniae*," *CHE* 73 (1991): 75–106, esp. 91–100; Gárate Córdoba, "Pensamiento," 12–13, 43.

9. *Poema de Fernán González*, ed. Alonso Zamora Vicente (Madrid: Espasa-Calpe, 1946), 161, vv. 549–62; *PCG*, 2:404–5, chap. 700.

10. Hilda Grassotti, "El deber y el derecho de hacer guerra y paz en León y Castilla," *CHE* 59–60 (1976): 221–96; repr. in her *Estudios medievales españolas* (Madrid: Fundación Universitaria Española, 1981), 43–132.

11. Gárate Córdoba, "Pensamiento," 31–32.

12. *Poema de Fernán González*, 18, 21, 131, vv. 66, 75, 444.

13. Rodríguez Lapa, *Cantigas d'Escarnho*, 2, 5–6, 11–2, 27–8, 37–9, 44–5, 49–50, nos. 2, 6, 9, 16, 21, 24, 26; Juan Paredes Núñez, *Alfonso X el Sabio: Cantigas profanes* (Granada: Universidad de Granada, 1988), 23, 25, 27, 30–31, 41–42, 48–49, 53, 55–56.

14. Francisco García Fitz, "La reconquista y formación de la España medieval (De mediados del siglo XI a mediados del siglo XIII)," in *Historia militar de España*, gen. ed. Hugo O'Donnell y Duque de Estrada, vol. 2, *Edad media*, ed. Miguel Ángel Ladero Quesada (Madrid: Laberinto, 2010), 142–216, and García Fitz, "La composición de los ejércitos medievales," in *La Guerra en la Edad media: XVII Semana de Estudios Medievales*, ed. José Ignacio de la Iglesia Duarte (Logroño: Instituto de Estudios Riojanos, 2007), 85–146.

15. González, *Repartimiento*, 2:234–35.

16. *CAX(GJ)*, 180–83, chap. 63; O'Callaghan, *Learned King*, 234–35; González Jiménez, *Alfonso X*, 300–303.

17. Carlos de Ayala Martínez, "La monarquía y las Ordenes militares durante el reinado de Alfonso X," *Hispania: Revista española de historia* 51 (1991): 409–65, and Ayala Martínez, *Las órdenes militares hispánicas en la Edad media (siglos XII–XV)* (Madrid: Marcial Pons, 2007), 405–610; Philippe Josserand, *Église et Pouvoir dans la Péninsule Ibérique: Les Ordres Militaires dans le Royaume de Castille (1252–1369)* (Madrid: Casa de Velázquez 2004), 233–99; Manuel González Jiménez, "Alfonso X y las órdenes militares: Historia de un desencuentro," *Alcanate* 2 (2000–2001): 209–21; Torres Fontes, "La Orden de Santa María de España" (1977); Enrique Rodríguez-Picavea, "The Armies of the Military Orders in Medieval Iberia," *Mediterranean Studies* 20 (2012): 28–58.

18. Salvador de Moxo, "De la nobleza vieja a la nobleza nueva: La transformación nobiliaria en la baja edad media," *Cuadernos de Historia* 3 (1969): 1–110, and Moxo, "La nobleza castellano-leonesa en la edad media: Problemática que suscita su estudio en el marco de la historia social," *Hispania: Revista española de historia* 30 (1970): 5–68; Isabel Beceiro Pita and Ricardo Córdoba de la Llave, *Parentesco, poder y mentalidad: La nobleza castellana, Siglos XII–XV* (Madrid: Consejo Superior de Investigaciones Científicas, 1990).

19. *CAX(GJ)*, 7, chap. 1; *MHE*, 1:209–10, no. 95.

20. John Esten Keller and Richard P. Kinkade, *Iconography in Medieval Spanish Literature* (Lexington: University Press of Kentucky, 1984), plate 15; Keller and Cash, *Daily Life*, 16–18, 52, plates 60, 68; García Cuadrado, *Cantigas*, 264–307.

21. Juan Manuel, *Libro del caballero et del escudero*, in *BAE*, 51:234–56; Noel Fallows, *The Chivalric Vision of Alfonso de Cartagena: Study and Edition of the Doctrinal de los caualleros* (Newark, DE: Juan de la Cuesta, 1995); Gárate Córdoba, "Pensamiento," 12–19.

22. Georges Martin, "Control regio de la violencia nobiliaria: La caballería según Alfonso X de Castilla (comentario al título XXI de la *Segunda Partida*)," *Annexes de CLCHM* 6 (2004): 219–34; Jesús D. Rodríguez Velasco, "De oficio a estado: La caballería entre el *Espéculo* y las *Siete Partidas*," *CLHM* 16 (1993–04): 49–77.

23. *Crónica latina*, 60; *The Latin Chronicle*, 85, chap. 40; Rodrigo Jiménez de Rada, *Historia de rebus Hispanie*, 291, bk. 8, chap. 10.

24. Giménez Soler, *Don Juan Manuel*, 221, no. 1; *DAAX*, 83, no. 80.

25. *CAX(GJ)*, 49–50, 55, chaps. 18, 19; *Chronicon de Cardeña*, in *ES*, 23:380.

26. Georges Martin, "Control regio de la violencia nobiliaria: La caballería según Alfonso X de Castilla (comentario al título XXI de la *Segunda Partida*." *Annexes des CLCHM* 6 (2004): 230–32.

27. Nelly Raquel Porro Girardi, *La investidura de armas en Castilla del Rey Sabio a los Católicos* (Valladolid: Junta de Castilla y León, 1998).

28. *CAX(GJ)*, 50, chap. 18; *Crònica de Jaume I*, 9:7–8, chaps. 495–96.

29. James F. Powers, *A Society Organized for War: The Iberian Municipal Militias in the Central Middle Ages, 1000–1284* (Berkeley: University of California Press, 1988), 112–35, and Powers, "Two Warrior Kings and Their Municipal Militias: The Townsman-Soldier in Law and Life," in Burns, *Worlds of Alfonso the Learned and James the Conqueror*, 95–117.

30. González Díez, *Colección diplomática del concejo de Burgos*, 93–96, 106–11, nos. 26, 32; *MHE*, 1:89–100, 187–91, 224–28, nos. 43–44, 86, 102; *Fuero de Cuenca*, 861–62; Benavides Checa, *El Fuero de Plasencia*, 170; Amando Represa Rodríguez, "Notas para el estudio de la ciudad de Segovia en los siglos XII–XIV," *Estudios Segovianos* 1 (1949): 273–319, esp. 290–94.

31. Carramolino, *Historia de Avila*, 2:491; Ubieto Arteta, *Colección diplomática de Cuéllar*, 60–66, no. 21; Palacio, Millares Carlo, and Varela Hervias, *Documentos del Archivo general de la villa de Madrid*, 1:96–102; *MHE*, 1:224–28, no.102; Juan Agapito y Revilla, *Los privilegios de Valladolid* (Valladolid: Sociedad Castellana de Escursiones, 1906), 54, 78.

32. *CAX(GJ)*, 26–28, chap. 9; *Crónica de la población de Ávila*, ed. Amparo Hernández Segura (Valencia: Anubar, 1966), 49.

33. Iglesia Ferreirós, "Privilegio general"; Ubieto Arteta, *Colección diplomática de Cuéllar*, 60–66, no. 21; Carramolino, *Historia de Ávila*, 2:492; Ballesteros, "Itinerario," 107:413; *Bullarium Ordinis Militiae de Alcántara* (Madrid: Antonio Marín, 1759), 107; Procter, *Curia and Cortes*, 211–12, 250–59, no. 7.

34. Ballesteros, "Itinerario," 109:416; Ángel Barrios Garcia, José María Monsalvo, and Gregorio del Ser Quijano, *Documentación medieval del Archivo municipal de Ciudad Rodrigo* (Salamanca: Diputación Provincial de Salamanca, 1988), 18–19, no. 5; *Fuero de Cuenca*, 867–68; Fernández del Pulgar, *Historia secular y eclesiástica de la ciudad de Palencia*, 3:330–32; Antonio Floriano, *Documentación histórica del Archivo municipal de*

Cáceres (1229–1471) (Cáceres: Diputación provincial, 1987), 21, no. 9.0; Juan Torres Fontes, *Documentos de Alfonso X el Sabio* (Murcia: Real Academia Alfonso el Sabio, 2008), 60, 81, nos. 50, 62.

35. *DAAX*, 369–70, 429–30, 497–98, nos. 342, 404, 471.

36. Ballesteros y Beretta, *Alfonso X*, 791–93.

37. José Antonio Martín Fuertes and César Álvarez Álvarez, *Archivo histórico municipal de León: Catálogo de los documentos* (León: Centro de Estudios e Investigación "San Isidoro," 1998), no. 17; Ángel Barrios García, Alberto Martin Expósito, and Gregorio del Ser Quijano, *Documentación medieval del Archivo municipal de Alba de Tormes* (Salamanca: Universidad de Salamanca, 1982), 51, no. 13.

38. Barrios Garciá, Monsalvo, and Ser Quijano, *Documentación medieval del Archivo municipal de Ciudad Rodrigo*, 18–19, no. 5; *Fuero de Cuenca*, 867–68; Fernández del Pulgar, *Historia secular y eclesiástica de la ciudad de Palencia*, 3:330–32; Floriano, *Documentación histórica del Archivo municipal de Cáceres*, 21, no. 9.0; *DAAX*, 369–70, 429–30, 497–98, nos. 342, 404, 471; Ballesteros y Beretta, *Alfonso X*, 791–93.

39. *MHE*, 1:314–16, no. 140.

40. Inés Carrasco, *Los cargos de la hueste real en tiempos de Alfonso X: Estudio onomasiológico* (Granada: Universidad de Granada, 1992), 59–70; Gárate Córdoba, "Pensamiento," 26–35.

41. Vegetius, *Epitoma*, 4–30, bk. 1.

42. *CSM* 277 and 374; O'Callaghan, *Alfonso X and the Cantigas*, 90–91, 132–33; Carrasco, *Cargos*, 79–83.

43. Carrasco, *Cargos*, 71–78, 85–88; González, *Repartimiento*, 2:249, 271, 274–79, 282–87.

44. *CSM* 63, 165A–B, 205.

45. González, *Reinado y diplomas de Fernando III*, 3:388, no. 809.

46. Powers, *Society Organized for War*, 188–206.

47. María Isabel Pérez de Tudela y Velasco, "Las construcciones militares y su función en la época de Alfonso X," *Castillos de España* 88 (1984): 37–42; Juan Muñoz Ruano, "El tratamiento de las fortalezas en las Cantigas de Santa Maria," *Castillos de España* 93 (1987): 15–34; Hilda Grassotti, "Sobre la retenencia de castillos en la Castilla medieval," in her *Estudios medievales españolas*, 261–81; Gonzala Plaza Serrano, "La tenencia de castillos y su entrega al señor en la II Partida de Alfonso X," in *Alarcos, 1195: Actas del Congreso Internacional Conmemorativo del VII Centenario de la Batalla de Alarcos*, ed. Ricardo Izquierdo Benito and Francisco Ruiz Gómez (Cuenca: Universidad de Castilla-LaMancha, 1996), 589–96.

48. María de la Concepción Castrillo Llamas, "Monarquía y nobleza en torno a la tenencia de fortalezas en Castilla durante los siglos XIII–XIV," *ELEM* 17 (1994): 95–112.

49. *CAX(GJ)*, 12–13, 31, 99–102, chaps. 4, 10, 30; O'Callaghan, *Alfonso X and the Cantigas*, 110–21.

50. Francisco García Fitz, *Castilla y León frente al Islam: Estrategias de expansión y tácticas militares (siglos XI–XIII)* (Seville: Universidad de Sevilla, 1998), 59–169.

51. *CAX(GJ)*, 149, chap. 52.

52. García Fitz, *Castilla*, 171–278.

53. Paul E. Chevedden, "The Hybrid Trebuchet: The Halfway Step to the Counterweight Trebuchet," in *On the Social Origins of Medieval Institutions: Essays in Honor*

of Joseph F. O'Callaghan, ed. Donald J. Kagay and Theresa Vann (Leiden: Brill, 1998), 179–222, and Paul E. Chevedden, Zvi Shiller, Samuel R. Gilbert, and Donald J. Kagay, "The Traction Trebuchet: A Triumph of Four Civilizations," *Viator* 31 (2000): 433–86.

54. O'Callaghan, *Learned King*, 174–78, 182–84, 187–88.

55. *CAX(GJ)*, 195–204, chaps. 69–72; Ibn Khaldūn, *Histoire des Berbères*, 4:101–2; O'Callaghan, *Learned King*, 247–49.

56. García Fitz, *Castilla*, 279–404.

57. *CAX(GJ)*, 175–87, chaps. 61–65; *Anales Toledanos III*, in *ES*, 23:420; Jofré de Loaysa, *Crónica*, 84–86, chap. 219.

58. *CAX(GJ)*, 207–9, chap. 74; *Anales Toledanos III*, in *ES*, 23:413–14; Ibn Khaldūn, *Histoire des Berbères*, 4:102–3.

59. *CAX(GJ)*, 212–20, chap. 75; *Anales Toledanos III*, in *ES*, 23:421; O'Callaghan, *Learned King*, 235–36, 249–50, 255.

60. *CSM* 28c–28d, 63, 86, 99, 165, 181, 187; O'Callaghan, *Alfonso X and the Cantigas*, plates 6, 7A–7B, 9, 11.

61. *PCG*, 2:748–50, 755–56, 760–61, 765–66, chaps. 1075, 1078–80, 1093–97, 1108–9, 1119–20. Florentino Pérez Embid, "La marina real castellana en el siglo XIII," *AEM* 6 (1969): 141–85, esp. 158–65, and Pérez Embid, *El almirantazgo de Castilla* (Seville: Universidad de Sevilla, 1944), 3–6.

62. Gonzalez, *Reinado y diplomas de Fernando III*, 3:408–12, no. 825.

63. Leopoldo Torres Balbás, "Atarazanas hispanomusulmanas," *Al-Andalus* 11 (1946): 179–205.

64. Ballesteros, *Sevilla*, lxxi–lxxii, no. 69; González, *Repartimiento*, 1:293–98; and González, "Origen de la marina real de Castilla," *RABM* 54 (1948): 229–53.

65. Paul Scheffer-Boichorst, "Kleinere Forschungen zur Geschichte Alfons X von Castilien," *Mitteilungen des Instituts für Österreichische Geschichtsforschung* 9 (1888): 226–48, esp. 241–46; Ballesteros y Beretta, *Alfonso X*, 155–56, 159–60, 169.

66. Ciriaco Miguel Vigil, *Colección histórico-diplomática del ayuntamiento de Oviedo* (Oviedo: Pardo Gusano, 1889), 46, no. 22.

67. *MHE*, 1:26–29, no. 15; Juan Torres Fontes, *Fueros y privilegios de Alfonso X el Sabio al Reino de Murcia* (Murcia: Academia Alfonso X el Sabio, 1973), 3:69–71, no. 52.

68. *DAAX*, 253–54, no. 231; *MHE*, 1:164–65, no. 79; Pérez Embid, *Almirantazgo*, 6–13, 86–89.

69. *CAX(GJ)*, 200–204, chap. 72; Pérez Embid, *Almirantazgo*, 13, 90–92.

70. Valdeavellano, *Curso*, 628.

71. Pérez Embid, *Almirantazgo*, 25–28.

72. *CSM* 5, 9, 33, 35, 36, 95, 193, 264, 328, 279; García Cuadrado, *Cantigas*, 339–50.

73. Ballesteros y Beretta, *Alfonso X*, 367; Pérez Embid, "La marina real," 175–77.

74. Hilda Grassotti, "Para la historia del botín y de las parias en Castilla y León," *CHE* 39–40 (1964): 43–132; repr. in her *Miscelánea de estudios sobre instituciones castellano-leonesas* (Bilbao: Nájera, 1978), 135–221; Gárate Córdoba, "Pensamiento," 39–41.

75. Powers, *Society Organized for War*, 162–87.

76. Ayala de Martínez, *Órdenes*, 604–12; Gárate Córdoba, "Pensamiento," 24–25, 41–42, 44–46; Powers, *Society Organized for War*, 136–61, 188–206.

77. *CSM* 95, 176, 192, 227, 325, 359.

78. Manuel González Jiménez, "Esclavos andaluces en el reino de Granada," in *Actas del III coloquio de historia medieval andaluza: La sociedad medieval andaluza; Grupos*

no privilegiados (Jaén: Diputación provincial, 1984), 327–38; Manuel González Jiménez and Ángel Luís Molina Molina, *Los Milagros Romanzados de Santo Domingo de Silos de Pero Marín* (Murcia: Real Academia Alfonso X El Sabio, 2008); María de los Llanos Martínez Carrillo, "Historicidad de los 'Miraculos Romançados' de Pedro Marín (1232–1293): El territorio y la esclavitud granadinos," *AEM* 21 (1991): 69–96.

79. Francisco García Fitz, "Captives in Mediaeval Spain: The Castilian-Leonese and Muslim Experience (XI–XIII Centuries," *E-Stratégica* 1 (2017): 205–21; José Manuel Calderón Ortega and Francisco Javier Díaz González, "El rescate de prisioneros y cautivos durante la edad media hispánica: Aproximación a su estudio," *HID* 38 (2011): 9–66, esp. 19–28; Francisco Javier Díaz González, "La normativa sobre los prisioneros y los cautivos en la España cristiana medieval," *REHJ* 32 (2010): 281–308, and Díaz González, "La base jurídica romana en la regulación del cautivo en las Partidas," *Revista General de Derecho Romano* 4 (2010): 1–27.

80. José Alemany, "Milicias cristianas al servicio de los sultanes musulmanes del Almagreb," in *Homenaje a D. Francisco de Codera en su jubilación del profesorado: Estudios de erudición oriental*, ed. Eduardo Saavedra (Zaragoza: Mariano Escar, 1904), 133–69.

81. James Brodman, "Military Redemptionism and the Castilian Reconquest, 1180–1250," *Military Affairs* 44 (1980): 24–27; Brodman, "Municipal Ransoming Law on the Medieval Spanish Frontier," *Speculum* 60 (1985): 318–30; Brodman, "Community, Identity and the Redemption of Captives: Comparative Perspectives Across the Mediterranean," *AEM* 36 (2006): 241–52; Brodman, "Captives or Prisoners: Society and Obligation in Medieval Iberia," *Anuario de Historia de la Iglesia* 20 (2011): 201–19; and Brodman, *Ransoming Captives in Crusader Spain: The Order of Merced on the Christian–Islamic Frontier* (Philadelphia: University of Pennsylvania Press, 1986).

7. Litigants, Judges, and Lawyers

1. Miguel Ángel Pérez de la Canal, "La justicia de la corte de Castilla durante los siglos XIII al XV," *HID* 2 (1975): 383–481; José Sánchez-Arcilla Bernal, "La administración de justicia en León y Castilla durante los siglos X al XIII," in *Jornadas sobre Documentación jurídico-administrativa, económico-financiera y judicial del reino castellano-leonés (Siglos X–XIII)* (Madrid: Universidad Complutense de Madrid, 2002), 1:13–49, and Sánchez-Arcilla Bernal, *La administración de justicia en León y Castilla durante la baja edad media (1252–1504)* (Madrid: Universidad Complutense de Madrid, 1980).

2. García Gallo, "El Libro de las leyes," 423–45, esp. 488–512; Burns, *Las Siete Partidas*, 3:ix–xxxiv.

3. González, *El reino de Castilla en la época de Alfonso VIII*, 2:628–31, no. 365, and González, *Alfonso IX*, 2:23–26, no. 11.

4. García Gallo, *Manual*, 1:149–54.

5. Quintana Prieto, *Tumbo Viejo de San Pedro de Montes*, 482–87, no. 375; O'Callaghan, *Learned King*, 241–43, 262–64; and O'Callaghan, *Alfonso X and the Cantigas*, 144–51.

6. *FJ* 2, 1, 10; 2, 2, 1–10.

7. Burns, "King Alfonso and the Wild West," 89.

8. González Jiménez, "La corte de Alfonso X el Sabio"; Julio Gerardo Martínez Martínez, "Tres ensayos sobre algunas cuestiones de historia del derecho español,"

Anuario de la Facultad el Derecho 22 (2004): 249–80, esp. 251–73, "El origen y evolución de los términos de la 'Corte' y de las 'Cortes' en el medioevo hispano."

9. *MHE*, 1:139–44, esp. 141.

10. Rafael Gibert, "La paz del camino en el derecho medieval español," *AHDE* 27–28 (1957–58): 831–52.

11. Iglesia Ferreirós, "Cortes de Zamora de 1274."

12. González Díez, *Colección diplomática del concejo de Burgos*, 173–74, no. 90.

13. Valladolid 1258, art. 9; Seville 1261, art. 17; OZ 1274, arts. 16–17.

14. *Leyes nuevas*, in *Opúsculos legales*, 2:199.

15. *C* 1, 49, 1, has forty days; *FJ* 2, 1, 11–32.

16. Juan Torres Fontes, "La Orden de Santa María de España," *AEM* 11 (1981): 794–821, and Torres Fontes, "La Orden de Santa María de España" (1977).

17. *Espéculo*, ed. MacDonald, 482–91, nos. 1–6, 29–93.

18. González, *Repartimiento*, 2:64, 176, 238, 263.

19. Antonio J. López Gutiérrez, "La tradición documental en la cancillería de Alfonso X," *HID* 19 (1992): 253–66, and López Gutiérrez, "Oficio y funciones de los escribanos."

20. W. W. Buckland, *A Textbook of Roman Law from Augustus to Justinian* (Cambridge: Cambridge University Press, 1921), 665; Berger, "Encyclopedic Dictionary," 364–65.

21. Ubieto Arteta, *Colección diplomática de Cuéllar*, 60–66, no. 21; OZ 1274, art. 27.

22. *LFC* 142, 150, 186, 203, 209, 241, 296; Rogelio Pérez Bustamante, *El gobierno y la administración territorial de Castilla (1230–1474)*, 2 vols. (Madrid: Universidad Autónoma, 1976).

23. González, *Alfonso IX*, 2:23–27, 125–29, nos. 11–12, 84–85.

24. José Sánchez-Arcilla Bernal, "Las reformas de Alfonso X en la organización territorial de la Corona de Castilla," *RFDUC* 9 Extra (1985): 115–27; Braulio Vázquez Campos, *Los adelantados mayores de la frontera o Andalucía (siglos XIII–XIV)* (Seville: Diputación provincial de Sevilla, 2006); Vázquez Campos, "Sobre los orígenes del Adelantamiento de Andalucía," *HID* 27 (2000): 333–73; Vázquez Campos, "El Adelantamiento Murciano en el contexto de las reformas alfonsinas, 1258–1283," *MMM* 27–28 (2003–4): 157–77, and 29–30 (2005–6):105–21; and Vázquez Campos, *Adelantados y lucha por el poder en el reino de Murcia* (Alcalá la Real: Editorial Zumaque, 2009), 23–34.

25. Pérez Bustamante, *Gobierno*, 1:235, 238, 289, 292, 342, 345, 389, 439.

26. José María Ortuño Sánchez-Pedreño, *El adelantado de la Corona de Castilla* (Murcia: Universidad de Murcia, 1997), and Ortuño Sánchez-Pedreño, "El adelantado en las Partidas," *MMM* 18 (1994): 161–74.

27. *CAX(GJ)*, 76–79, chap. 23.

28. Pérez Prendes, "Las leyes de los adelantados mayores"; Benito Fraile, "En torno a las leyes de los adelantados mayores."

29. Valdeavellano, *Curso*, 518–28.

30. Carlos de Ayala Martínez, ed., *Libro de privilegios de la Orden de San Juan de Jerusalén en Castilla y León (siglos XII–XV)* (Madrid: Editorial Complutense, 1995), 547–49, 562–63, nos. 334, 343.

31. Pardo Rodríguez, *Cancillería*, 146–47, 172–75, 183–86, 204–5, 209–10, 213–14, nos. 12, 31–32, 37–38, 48, 51, 54.

32. López Ferreiro, *Fueros municipales*, 235–90.

33. López Ferreiro, *Fueros municipales*, 365.

34. *CAX(GJ)*, 90–123, 132–34, 153–57, 170–73, chaps. 26–42, 47, 53–54, 59.

35. Múñoz y Romero, *Colección*.

36. *MHE*, 1:57–62, 68–70, nos. 27, 33.

37. González Díez, *Colección diplomática del concejo de Burgos*, 116–19, no. 36; Ruiz, *Sociedad*, 181.

38. *MHE*, 1:65, no. 30.

39. *MHE*, 1:211–12, no. 96.

40. González Díez, *Colección diplomática del concejo de Burgos*, 116–19, 119–23, 163–64, 174, 204, nos. 36, 38, 80, 91, 117; Ruiz, *Sociedad*, 181.

41. González Mínguez, "La concesión del Fuero real a Vitoria," 227–29; Floranes, *Memorias y privilegios*, 182–88.

42. González Díez, *Colección diplomática del concejo de Burgos*, 133–37, 164–65, 173–74, nos. 48–52, 81, 90.

43. *MHE*, 1:265–66, nos. 121–22.

44. Martín Fuertes and Álvarez Álvarez, *Archivo histórico municipal de León*, nos. 21–22.

45. *MHE*, 1:38, 124–25, nos. 20, 59, and 2:71–72, no 104.

46. López Ferreiro, *Fueros municipales*, 266–73.

47. Miguel Vigil, *Colección histórico-diplomática del ayuntamiento de Oviedo*, 50–51, no. 26.

48. Palacio, Millares Carlo, and Varela Hervias, *Documentos del Archivo general de la villa de Madrid*, 95–102, esp. 97–99.

49. Iglesia Ferreirós, "Labor legislativa," 328–30.

50. Antonio Merchán Álvarez, "La alcaldía de avenencia como forma de justicia municipal en el Derecho de León y Castilla," *ELEM* 6 (1985): 65–91.

51. James A. Brundage, *The Medieval Origins of the Legal Profession: Canonists, Civilians, and Courts* (Chicago: University of Chicago Press, 2008).

52. Kantorowicz, *King's Two Bodies*, 121–24, and Ernst Kantorowicz, "Kingship under the Impact of Scientific Jurisprudence," in *Twelfth-Century Europe and the Foundations of Modern Society*, ed. Marshall Clagett, Gaines Post, and Robert Reynolds (Madison: University of Wisconsin Press, 1966), 89–111, esp. 91–92, 106, n. 12.

53. *CLC*, 2:473, art. 3; Kantorowicz, "Kingship," 93, 108, n. 25.

54. *DO* pr.; Torres Fontes, *Documentos del Siglo XIII*, 52, no. 57.

55. *DO* 2, 1, 1–10; *FD* 2, 3.

56. Buckland, *Textbook of Roman Law*, 700–704; Berger, "Encyclopedic Dictionary," 653; Gaines Post, "Roman Law and Early Representation in Spain and Italy, 1150–1250," and "*Plena Potestas* and Consent in Medieval Assemblies," in his *Studies in Medieval Legal Thought*, 61–90, 91–160.

57. *FJ* 2, 3, 1–10.

58. González, *Reinado y diplomas de Fernando III*, 3:374–75, no. 795; López Ferreiro, *Fueros municipales*, 216–18, 220, 225–26, 231–34.

59. González, *Repartimiento*, 1:347, 2:65, 175, 239, 263, 325, 347, 356, 363; *DAAX*, 168–69, 207, 220–21, 435–36, 491–92, 522, nos. 155, 187, 200, 411, 463, 491.

60. López Ferreiro, *Historia*, 5:91–93, no. 31.

61. Sánchez Albornoz, "Señoríos y ciudades."

62. La Coruña: *Privilegios reales y viejos documentos*, 18, no. 4; Ubieto Arteta, *Colección diplomática de Cuéllar*, 66, no. 23; Tardajos: Pereda Llarena, *Documentación de la catedral de Burgos*, 185–87, no. 132; González Díez, *Colección diplomática del concejo de Burgos*, 152, no. 69; Frías and the abbey of Oña: Isabel Oceja Gonzalo, *Documentación del monasterio de San Salvador de Oña (1032–1284)* (Burgos: Ediciones J. M. Garrido Garrido, 1983), 235, no. 231; Order of the Hospital: Ayala Martínez, *Libro de privilegios de la Orden de San Juan de Jerusalén*, 572–74, no. 352.

63. *CAX(GJ)*, 216, chap. 75; González Díez, *Colección diplomática del concejo de Burgos*, 199–201, nos. 112–13.

64. Evelyn Procter, "The Towns of León and Castile as Suitors before the King's Court," *EHR* 74 (1959): 1–22.

65. Berger, "Encyclopedic Dictionary," 352.

66. González, *Regesta de Fernando II*, 334–35, no. 57; González, *El reino de Castilla en la época de Alfonso VIII*, 2:141 and 3:157, 506–7, 541–46, 611, nos. 83, 653, 858, 882, 922; and González, *Alfonso IX*, 2:692, no. 596; Alamo, *Colección diplomática de San Salvador de Oña*, 204, no. 409; *Fuero de Cuenca*, 855.

67. Castro and Onís, *Fueros leoneses*, 138, 160, 165, 181, 236, 313, 328; José Maldonado and Emilio Sáez, *El Fuero de Coria* (Madrid: Instituto de Estudios de Administración Local, 1949), 69, 76–77; Hayward Keniston, *Fuero de Guadalajara* (New York: Kraus Reprint, 1965), 3; Galo Sánchez, *El Fuero de Madrid* (Madrid: Ayuntamiento de Madrid, 1963), 51, 56.

68. Seville 1253, art. 60; Valladolid 1258, art. 40; Seville 1261, art. 30; OZ 1274, arts. 1–16.

69. José María Ortuño Sánchez-Pedreño, "El oficio de abogado en las Partidas de Alfonso X el Sabio," *Revista jurídica de la Región de Murcia* 21 (1996): 29–46.

70. *MHE*, 1:39–43, no. 21.

71. López Ferreiro, *Fueros municipales*, 252, 256, 274.

72. Burns, "King Alfonso and the Wild West," 89.

73. *MHE*, 1:39–43, no. 21.

74. González Díez, *Colección diplomática del concejo de Burgos*, 102–3, no. 102; *LEst* 18, 20.

8. The Judicial Process

1. Raúl Orellana Calderón, "La Tercera Partida de Alfonso X el Sabio: Estudio y edición crítica de los Títulos XVIII al XX" (PhD thesis, Universidad de Madrid, 2006). See his "La 'Tercera Partida' de Alfonso X el Sabio: Estudio y edición crítica de los títulos XVIII al XX. Contextos en torno a la edición de la 'Tercera Partida' de Alfonso X el Sabio," *Revista jurídica del notariado* 64 (2007): 183–278; 65 (2008): 159–274; 66 (2008): 191–328; 67 (2008): 297–494; 68 (2008): 45–226.

2. Buckland, *Textbook of Roman Law*, 599–740; José Maldonado y Fernández del Torco, "Líneas de influencia canónica en la historia del proceso español," *AHDE* 23 (1953): 467–93.

3. Antonio Pérez Martín, *El derecho procesal del "ius commune" en España* (Murcia: Universidad de Murcia, 1999); Martínez Marina, *Ensayo*, 244–52.

4. López Ferreiro, *Fueros municipales*, 292–96; María Teresa González Balasch, *Tumbo B de La Catedral de Santiago* (Santiago de Compostela: Edicios de Castro, 2004), nos. 25, 103.

5. *LEst* 21–39; *SNTP*, 1; *FD* 1, 4–10.

6. Seville 1252, arts. 34–36; Seville 1253, arts. 6, 18, 21, 58, 60.

7. *MHE*, 1:39–43, no. 21; *FD* 1, 12, 1–6.

8. Isabel Ramos Vázquez, "El proceso en rebeldía en el derecho castellano," *AHDE* 75 (2005): 721–54, esp. 728–37.

9. Jesús Vallejo, "La regulación del proceso en el Fuero Real: Desarrollo, precedentes y problemas," *AHDE* 55 (1985): 495–704.

10. *MHE*, 1:40, no. 21; *FD* 2, 1–2; *SNTP* 2.

11. *DO* 3, 2, 1; *FD* 1, 15, 1–5; *SNTP* 3; *LEst* 235–36; Buckland, *Textbook of Roman Law*, 648–58; Berger, "Encyclopedic Dictionary," 459.

12. *FD* 2, 1–2; *SNTP* 4.

13. *DO* 3, 3, 1; *FD* 2, 3, 1–2; *SNTP* 5; *LEst* 136; Juan García González, "El juramento de manquadra," *AHDE* 25 (1955): 211–55.

14. Berger, "Encyclopedic Dictionary," 534.

15. Manuel Muro García, "En el Archivo municipal de Úbeda: Un precedente de 'Las Partidas.' Como debían jurar los cristianos, judíos y moros," *BRAH* 91 (1927): 376–84; *DAAX*, 247–49, no. 225; Jerez 1268, arts. 45–47; *Libro de las Tahurerías*, ed. MacDonald, leyes 41–43; and *Leyes nuevas*, in *Opúsculos legales*, 28–29.

16. María Josefa Sanz Fuentes, "Repartimiento de Écija," *HID* 3 (1976): 535–51, esp. 543.

17. *FD* 2, 5–7; *SNTP* 6; Marta Madero, "Causa, creencia y testimonios: La prueba judicial en Castilla durante el siglo XIII," *Bulletin du Centre d'Études médiévales d'Auxerre*, Hors-série 2 (2008), http://journals.openedition.org/cem/9672; Sebastián Martín-Retortillo y Baquer, "Notas para un estudio de la prueba en la Tercera Partida," *Argensola: Revista de Ciencias sociales del Instituto de Estudios altoaragoneses* 22 (1955): 101–22.

18. *DO* 3, 3, 4–7; *FD* 2, 3, 2; 2, 4, 1–2; Rafael Pérez Molina, "La prueba de confesión en la legislación castellano" (PhD thesis, Universidad de Córdoba, 2012), 17–125.

19. Marta Madero, "El juez y los testigos," in her *Las verdades de los hechos: Proceso, juez y testimonios en la Castilla del siglo XIII* (Salamanca: Universidad de Salamanca, 2004), 47–75; Berger, "Encyclopedic Dictionary," 735.

20. *DO* 4, 2, 1–18; *FD* 2, 8, 1–3.

21. Evelyn Procter, *The Judicial Use of Pesquisa (Inquisition) in León and Castille, 1157–1369*, *English Historical Review*, Supplement 2 (London: Longmans, 1966); Joaquín Cerdá Ruiz-Funes, "En torno a la pesquisa y procedimiento inquisitivo en el derecho castellano-leonés de la edad media," *AHDE* 32 (1962): 483–518.

22. *LFC* 32, 42, 61, 73, 117, 146, 218, 227, 229, 232; *FV* 2, 4, 1–6; Jerry R. Craddock, "La pesquisa en Castilla y Aragón: Un caso curioso del *Libre des feyts* de Jaume I," *AEM* 27 (1997): 369–79.

23. *MHE*, 1:22, no. 12.

24. *MHE*, 1:44–51, no. 23.

25. Miguel Vigil, *Colección histórico-diplomática del ayuntamiento de Oviedo*, 52, 62, nos. 27, 35.

26. Pereda Llarena, *Documentación de la catedral de Burgos*, 211–12, no. 149.

27. López Ferreiro, *Fueros municipales*, 264–77, esp. 268–71; Bermejo Cabrero, "En torno a la aplicación de las Partidas."

28. Oceja Gonzalo, *Documentación del monasterio de San Salvador de Oña (1032–1284)*, 291–336, no. 231; Isabel Alfonso Antón and Cristina Jular Pérez-Alfaro, "Oña contra Frías o el pleito de los cien testigos: una pesquisa en la Castilla del siglo XIII," *Edad Media* 3 (2000): 61–88.

29. *CSM*, 2:331–33, no. 386; O'Callaghan, *Learned King*, 258.

30. Torres Fontes, *Documentos de Alfonso X*, 337–38, no. 303.

31. *CLC*, 1:96–97.

32. *DO* 4, 2, 1–6; *FD* 2, 9, 2.

33. *OZ* 1274, art. 40; García Gallo, "El Libro de las leyes," 436–43; Procter, *Alfonso X of Castile*, 63.

34. López Ferreiro, *Fueros municipales*, 251–60.

35. Pereda Llarena, *Documentación de la catedral de Burgos*, 208–10, 219–21, nos. 147, 156–57.

36. Oceja Gonzalo, *Documentación del monasterio de San Salvador de Oña (1032–1284)*, 243–46, no. 231.

37. *MHE*, 1:39–43, no. 21; *SNTP* 7.

38. Buckland, *Textbook of Roman Law*, 631–64.

39. *DO* 5, 1, 1–19; *FD* 2, 9, 1–2; 3, 1, 1–9; *SNTP* 8–9.

40. López Ferreiro, *Fueros municipales*, 264–77; González Balasch, *Tumbo B*, no. 28.

41. *MHE*, 1:22, no. 2.

42. *FD* 3, 3, 1–3; 3, 4, 1–2.

43. López Ferreiro, *Fueros municipales*, 364.

44. *MHE*, 1:39–43, no. 21.

45. Buckland, *Textbook of Roman Law*, 665–67.

46. *DO* 6, 1, 1–27; *FD* 3, 2, 1–8.

47. *Espéculo*, ed. MacDonald, 485.

48. Oceja Gonzalo, *Documentación del monasterio de San Salvador de Oña (1032–1284)*, 189–92, 219–20, 231–36, nos. 195, 219, 231; González Díez, *Colección diplomática del concejo de Burgos*, 112, 126, 189, nos. 34, 41, 104.

49. Vicente Vignau, *Cartulario del monasterio de Eslonza* (Madrid: Viuda de Hernando, 1885), 40–42, no. 21; Pardo Rodríguez, *Cancillería*, 152–56, nos. 16–17; also see 141–42, no. 7.

50. Bonifacio Palacios Martín, *Colección diplomática de la Orden de Alcántara (1157?–1494): De los orígenes a 1454* (Madrid: Editorial Complutense, 2000), 128–30, 189–90, nos. 239, 300.

51. *Bullarium Ordinis Militiae de Alcántara*, 105–109, nos. 33, 35.

52. *DAAX*, 169–71, 210–11, nos. 157, 189.

53. *MHE*, 1:195–200, no. 89.

54. Ubieto Arteta, *Colección diplomática de Cuéllar*, 49–50, 74, nos. 18, 31.

55. *DAAX*, 208–9, 281–82, 284, nos. 188, 253, 256, 260–61, 287–92.

56. *MHE*, 1:131–32, no. 61.

57. Loperráez, *Descripción histórica del obispado de Osma*, 3:84–86, no. 59.

58. *DAAX*, 347–48, no. 319.

59. Miguel Vigil, *Colección histórico-diplomática del ayuntamiento de Oviedo*, 60, no. 33.

60. Ayala Martínez, *Libro de privilegios de la Orden de San Juan de Jerusalén*, 534–36, 539–40, 542–44, nos. 323, 327, 329, 330.

61. *MHE*, 1:200–201, no. 90.

62. Pardo Rodríguez, *Cancillería*, 143–44, 203–4, 207–8, nos. 9, 47, 50.

63. Palacios Martín, *Colección diplomática de la Orden de Alcántara*, 133–36, nos. 245, 249; Alonso Torres y Tapia, *Crónica de la Orden de Alcántara*, 2 vols. (Madrid: Gabriel Ramírez, 1773), 1:347–48, 353.

64. Palacios Martín, *Colección diplomática de la Orden de Alcántara*, 174–76, no. 285.

65. Merchán Álvarez, "La alcaldía de avenencia."

66. Pereda Llarena, *Documentación de la catedral de Burgos*, 31–33, 46–47, 79–81, 86–89, nos. 21, 31, 59, 62, 63; Floriano, *Documentación histórica del Archivo municipal de Cáceres*, 12–13, no. 3; Oceja Gonzalo, *Documentación del monasterio de San Salvador de Oña (1032–1284)*, 147–48, 185–87, 342–45, nos. 170, 235; Palacios Martín, *Colección diplomática de la Orden de Alcántara*, 177–78, 192, 206–8, 216–18, nos. 287, 326, 339; *DAAX*, 310–11, 333–34, nos. 283, 311; Miguel Vigil, *Colección histórico-diplomática del ayuntamiento de Oviedo*, 74, 77, nos. 40, 43; Ubieto Arteta, *Colección diplomática de Cuéllar*, 77–78, no. 33.

67. Oceja Gonzalo, *Documentación del monasterio de San Salvalor de Oña (1032–1284)*, 189–92, 219–20, 291, nos. 195, 219, 231.

68. Oceja Gonzalo, *Documentación del monasterio de San Salvador de Oña (1032–1284)*, 231–34, no. 229; Alfonso Antón and Jular Pérez-Alfaro, "Oña contra Frias o el pleito de los cien testigos."

69. Oceja Gonzalo, *Documentación del monasterio de San Salvador de Oña (1032–1284)*, 235–36, 284–85.

70. Alamo, *Colección diplomática de San Salvador de Oña*, 2:830–31, no. 699; Oceja Gonzalo, *Documentación del monasterio de San Salvador de Oña (1285–1310)*, 6–7, no. 269.

71. Oceja Gonzalo, *Documentación del monasterio de San Salvador de Oña (1032–1284)*, 337–41, no. 233.

72. Oceja Gonzalo, *Documentación del monasterio de San Salvador de Oña (1032–1284)*, 337–41, no. 233.

73. *MHE*, 1:39–43, no 21.

9. Marriage, Family, and Inheritance

1. Heath Dillard, *Daughters of the Reconquest: Women in Castilian Town Society, 1100–1300* (Cambridge: Cambridge University Press, 1984); Cristina Segura Graíño, "Historia de las mujeres en la Edad Media," *Medievalismo* 18 (2008): 249–72.

2. Esteban Martínez Marcos, *Las causas matrimoniales en las Partidas de Alfonso el Sabio* (Salamanca: Consejo Superior de Investigaciones Científicas, 1966), and Martínez Marcos, "Fuentes de la doctrina canónica de la IV Partida del código del rey Alfonso el Sabio," *Revista Española de Derecho Canónico* 18 (1963): 897–926; José Maldonado y Fernández del Torco, "Sobre la relación entre el derecho de las Decretales y el de las Partidas en materia matrimonial," *AHDE* 15 (1944): 589–643; Eduardo Fernández Regatillo, "El derecho matrimonial en las Partidas y en las Decretales," in *Acta Congressus Iuridici Internationalis VII saeculo a Decretalibus Gregorii IX et XIV a Codice Iustiniano promulgatis* (Rome: Pontificum Institutum Utriusque Iuris, 1936): 3:315–84; *Las Siete Partidas, Título II, "De los casamientos" de Alfonso X, el Sabio: Edición crítica y exposición analítica*, ed. Patricia T. Ramos Anderson (New York: Edwin Mellen Press, 2009).

3. James A. Brundage, *Law, Sex, and Christian Society in Medieval Europe* (Chicago: University of Chicago Press, 1987), esp. chaps. 6–8; Berman, *Law and Revolution*, 226–30.

4. María del Carmen Carlé, "Apuntes sobre el matrimonio en la edad media española," *CHE* 63–64 (1980): 115–77; Yves-René Fonquerne and Alfonso Esteban, eds., *La Condición de la mujer en la Edad media: Actas del coloquio celebrado en la Casa de Velázquez, del 5 al 7 de noviembre de 1984* (Madrid: Casa de Velázquez, 1986); Marilyn Stone, *Marriage and Friendship in Medieval Spain: Social Relations according to the Fourth Partida of Alfonso X* (New York: Peter Lang, 1990), 33–114.

5. Beceiro Pita and Córdoba de la Llave, *Parentesco, poder y mentalidad*, 125–70; Burns, *Las Siete Partidas*, 4:xix.

6. Buckland, *Textbook of Roman Law*, 114; Dillard, *Daughters of the Reconquest*, 36–67.

7. Pardo Rodríguez, *Cancillería*, 133–36, nos. 1–2bis.

8. Keller and Kinkade, *Iconography*, plate 2.

9. Buckland, *Textbook of Roman Law*, 113–14; Rafael Gibert, "El consentimiento familiar en el matrimonio según el Derecho medieval español," *AHDE* 18 (1947): 706–61.

10. González, *Reinado y diplomas de Fernando III*, 2:268–69, no. 224; González Díez, *Colección diplomática del concejo de Burgos*, 83–84, no. 21; *LFC* 1.

11. Keller and Cash, *Daily Life*, 34–37, plates 35–36; Connie L. Scarborough, *Women in Thirteenth-Century Spain as Portrayed in Alfonso X's Cantigas de Santa Maria* (Lewiston, NY: Edwin Mellen Press, 1993), 92–97.

12. O'Callaghan, *Learned King*, 92–93.

13. Dillard, *Daughters of the Reconquest*, 96–126; Marjorie Ratcliffe, "'Así donde no hay varón, todo bien fallece': La viuda en la legislación medieval española," in *Actas del X Congreso de la Asociación Internacional de Hispanistas, Barcelona 21–26 de agosto de 1989*, 4 vols. (Barcelona: Promociones y Publicaciones Universitarias, 1992), 1:311–18.

14. Torres Fontes, *Documentos del Siglo XIII*, 35, 46–48, nos. 38, 52, and Torres Fontes, *Documentos de Alfonso X*, 262–63, no. 225.

15. Dillard, *Daughters of the Reconquest*, 60–67.

16. González, *Reinado y diplomas de Fernando III*, 3:387–89, 398–400, nos. 809, 819; González Jiménez, *Fernando III el Santo*, 257–59; Procter, *Curia and Cortes*, 216–17.

17. Sánchez, *Fuero de Madrid*, 72, no. 115.

18. González Díez, *Colección diplomática del concejo de Burgos*, 155–56, nos. 73–74.

19. José Antonio López Nevot, *La aportación marital en la historia del derecho castellano* (Almería: Universidad de Almería, 1998), esp. 65–73.

20. Beceiro Pita and Córdoba de la Llave, *Parentesco, poder y mentalidad*, 181–96.

21. Pardo Rodríguez, *Cancillería*, 137, 165, nos. 3, 25.

22. Pereda Llarena, *Documentación de la catedral de Burgos*, 243, no. 176; Ruiz, *Sociedad*, 59, 61, 132.

23. Berger, "Encyclopedic Dictionary," 444; Buckland, *Textbook of Roman Law*, 107–11.

24. *Inst.* 1, 10, 12; 2, 7, 3; 2, 20, 15; 3, 19, 4; 3, 24, 3; 4, 6, 39; Berger, "Encyclopedic Dictionary," 443; Buckland, *Textbook of Roman Law*, 111; Alfonso Otero Varela, "Las arras en el Derecho español medieval," *AHDE* 25 (1955): 189–210; María Luz Alonso, "La dote en los documentos toledanos de los siglos XII–XV," *AHDE* 48 (1978): 379–456; Beceiro Pita and Córdoba de la Llave, *Parentesco, poder y mentalidad*, 173–80.

25. González, *Reinado y diplomas de Fernando III*, 1:114–16; González Jiménez, *Alfonso X*, 414; Alfonso Sánchez de Mora, "Doña Juana de Ponthieu, reina de Castilla y señora de Marchena," in *La mujer en la Historia de Marchena*, ed. Juan Luis Carriazo Rubio and Ramón Ramos Alfonso (Marchena: Cajasol, 2007), 11–24.

26. Pereda Llarena, *Documentación de la catedral de Burgos*, 179, no. 127; Ruiz, *Sociedad*, 35–36.

27. Maximiliano Soler, "Derecho, narración y racionalidad jurídica: El caso de la fazaña bajomedieval," *Cuadernos Electrónicos de Filosofía y Derecho* 22 (2011):162–89, esp. 173.

28. *MHE*, 1:132–34, no. 62.

29. Berger, "Encyclopedic Dictionary," 617.

30. Buckland, *Textbook of Roman Law*, 106.

31. Torres Fontes, *Documentos de Alfonso X*, 261–62, no. 224.

32. Burns, "King Alfonso and the Wild West," 90–91, 94–95.

33. Buckland, *Textbook of Roman Law*, 128–30; María Teresa Arias Bautista, *Barraganas y concubinas en la España medieval* (Seville: ArCiBel, 2010).

34. González Jiménez, *Alfonso X*, 28–29, 156–57.

35. Ana Arranz Guzmán, "Celibato eclesiástico, barraganas y contestación social en la Castilla bajomedieval," *ETF* 21 (2008): 13–39.

36. *ES*, 36:216–30, esp. 218–19; Linehan, *Spanish Church*, 28–31, 186; Ángel Luis Molina Molina, "Aspectos de la vida cotidiana en Las Partidas," *Glossae* 5–6 (1993–94): 171–85, esp. 174–77.

37. *MHE*, 1:193–95, no. 88.

38. Loperráez, *Descripción histórica del obispado de Osma*, 3:204–5, no. 71.

39. Juan Ruiz, *Libro de Buen Amor*, ed. María Brey Mariño (Madrid: Castalia, 2012), vv. 1690–1712.

40. González, *Repartimiento*, 2:339.

41. Buckland, *Textbook of Roman Law*, 129–31.

42. Iain M. Lonie, *The Hippocratic Treatises, "On Generation," "On the Nature of the Child," "Diseases IV"* (Berlin: Walter de Gruyter, 1981), 19.

43. Jacqueline Leclercq-Marx, "Los monstruos antropomorfos de origen antiguo en la Edad media: Persistencias, mutaciones y recreaciones," *Anales de Historia del Arte*, 2010 extra, *II Jornadas complutenses de Arte Medieval*, 259–74.

44. *Inst.* 1, 11, 1–12; Alfonso Otero Varela, "La adopción en la historia del derecho español," in his *Estudios histórico-jurídicos*, 2 vols. (Madrid: Colegio de Registradores de la Propiedad y Mercantiles de España, 2005), 2:9–92. Salvador Ruiz Pino, "Régimen jurídico de la adopción en derecho romano y su recepción en el derecho español" (PhD thesis, Universidad de Córdoba, 2010), 312–44.

45. Berger, "Encyclopedic Dictionary," 350–51; Buckland, *Textbook of Roman Law*, 122–28.

46. Walenka Arévalo Caballero, "*Adoptio a muliere facta* en derecho romano y en la tradición jurídica española," *Revista Internacional de Derecho Romano* 7 (2011): 156–98.

47. Burns, "King Alfonso and the Wild West," 90–91.

48. *Espéculo*, ed. MacDonald, 490, no. 103.

49. *CAX(GJ)*, 61, 96–98, chaps. 20, 29; González Jiménez, *Alfonso X*, 250; Mercedes Gaibrois de Ballesteros, "La reina doña Mencía," *Revista da Universidade de Coimbra* 11 (1933): 501–39.

50. *Inst.* 1, 13–26; Buckland, *Textbook of Roman Law*, 143–74; Antonio Merchán Álvarez, *La tutela de los menores en Castilla hasta fines del siglo XV* (Seville: Universidad de Sevilla, 1976).

51. Berger, "Encyclopedic Dictionary," 420–21, 747–49.

52. González, *Repartimiento*,1:83, 250, 278, 347; 2:54, 175, 239, 263, 325, 356, 363.

53. *Inst.* 1, 9, 1–3; 1, 12, 1–10; Alfonso Otero Varela, "La patria potestad en el derecho histórico español," *AHDE* 26 (1956): 209–41; Berger, "Encyclopedic Dictionary," 621.

54. Berger, "Encyclopedic Dictionary," 624; Buckland, *Textbook of Roman Law*, 279–80.

55. Buckland, *Textbook of Roman Law*, 71.

56. Buckland, *Textbook of Roman Law*, 133–35.

57. *Inst.* 2, 10–12; Berger, "Encyclopedic Dictionary," 732–33; Buckland, *Textbook of Roman Law*, 281–402.

58. Berman, *Law and Revolution*, 230–37; María Angustias Martos Calabrús, *Aproximación histórica a las solemnidades del testamento Público* (Almería: Universidad de Almería, 1998).

59. Burns, *Las Siete Partidas*, 5:xvi; *Inst.* 2, 9, 10–25. Carmen Pujal Rodríguez, "La recepción el derecho romano testamentario en las Partidas," *Anales de la Universidad de Alicante. Facultad de Derecho 5* (1990): 175–207.

60. González, *Alfonso IX*, 2:619–20, no. 519.

61. Vázquez de Parga, Lacarra, and Uria, *Peregrinaciones*, 3:111–12, no. 78.

62. Teofilo Ruiz, "The Business of Salvation: Castilian Wills in the Late Middle Ages, 1200–1400," in Kagay and Vann, *On the Social Origins of Medieval Institutions*, 63–92.

63. *Inst.* 2, 13, 1–12. Buckland, *Textbook of Roman Law*, 324–30; Tomás Montagut Estragués, "El testamento inoficioso en las Partidas y sus fuentes," *AHDE* 62 (1992): 239–326.

64. DAAX, 548–54, 567–74, nos. 518, 521.

65. Berman, *Law and Revolution*, 233–34.

66. James Brodman, "The *Siete Partidas* and the Law of Charity in Thirteenth-Century Castile," in *The Emergence of León-Castile, c. 1065–1500: Essays Presented to J. F. O'Callaghan*, ed. James Todesca (Burlington, VT: Ashgate, 2015), 81–92, and Brodman, "What Is a Soul Worth? Pro anima Bequests in the Municipal Legislation of Reconquest Spain," *Medievalia et Humanistica*, n.s., 20 (1993): 15–23.

67. *Inst.* 2, 22; *D* 35, 2; *C* 6, 50; Berger, "Encyclopedic Dictionary," 552; Buckland, *Textbook of Roman Law*, 338.

68. *Inst.* 2, 25, 1–3; *D* 29, 7; *C* 6, 36; Berger, "Encyclopedic Dictionary," 392; Buckland, *Textbook of Roman Law*, 356–57.

69. *Inst.* 3, 1–7; Buckland, *Textbook of Roman Law*, 361–63; Francisco Tomás y Valiente, "La sucesión de que muere sin parientes y sin disponer de sus bienes," *AHDE* 36 (1966): 189–254, esp. 224–27.

70. DAAX, 548–54, 567–74, nos. 518, 521.

71. Ballesteros, *Sevilla*, lxvi–vii, lxxii–iii, clviii–ix, nos. 65, 70, 152.

72. Barrios García, *Documentación medieval de la catedral de Ávila*, 75–77, no. 87. Also Pereda Llarena, *Documentación de la catedral de Burgos*, 182–84, 198–99, nos. 130, 240; López de Silanes and Sainz Ripa, *Colección diplomática Calceatense*, 58–60.

73. Pereda Llarena, *Documentación de la catedral de Burgos*, 148–50, no. 104.

74. Pereda Llarena, *Documentación de la catedral de Burgos*, 174–79, 200–207, 216–18, nos. 126, 142–43, 154; Beltrán de Heredia, *Cartulario*, 619–20, no. 39; *MHE*, 1:277–78, no. 127; Linehan, *Spanish Church*, 320.

75. Juan Torres Fontes, "El testamento del Infante don Manuel," *MMM* 7 (1981): 10–21.

76. *MHE*, 1:264–66, nos. 121–22.

77. Isabel Beceiro Pita, "Parentesco y consolidación de la aristocracia en los inicios de la Corona de Castilla (Siglos XI–XIII)," *Meridies* 2 (1995): 49–71.

10. The Law of Persons

1. Barry Nicholas, *An Introduction to Roman Law* (Oxford: Oxford University Press, 1962), 60–97; Buckland, *Textbook of Roman Law*, 56–181.

2. *Inst.* 3, 13; Berger, "Encyclopedic Dictionary," 603–4; Buckland, *Textbook of Roman Law*, 403–6.

3. Alfonso García Gallo, *Curso de Historia del derecho español*, 7th ed., 2 vols. (Madrid: A.G.E.S.A, 1958), 1:478–572; Manuel Salvat Monguillot, "Factores que determinan la capacidad civil en el derecho castellano leonés alto medieval," *Revista Chilena de Historia del Derecho* 2 (1961): 22–35.

4. Berger, "Encyclopedic Dictionary," 620–21, 628; Buckland, *Textbook of Roman Law*, 174–81.

5. Canning, *History of Medieval Political Thought*, 172–73.

6. José Maldonado y Fernández del Torco, *La condición jurídica del "Nasciturus" en el derecho Español* (Madrid: Instituto Nacional de Estudios Jurídicos, 1946).

7. Berger, "Encyclopedic Dictionary," 500, 573; Nicholas, *Introduction to Roman Law*, 91, 93.

8. Berger, "Encyclopedic Dictionary," 469.

9. Almudena Bermejo Díaz, "La mujer en la edad media: Su condición jurídica en las Partidas" (Trabajo fin de grado, Universidad de la Rioja, 2014); María Teresa Bouzada Gil, "El privilegio de las viudas en el derecho castellano," *CHD* 4 (1997): 203–42.

10. Valdeavellano, *Curso*, 317–26; Ignacio Álvarez Borge, "La nobleza castellana en la edad media: Patrimonio, familia, y poder," in *La familia en la edad media: XI Semana de Estudios Medievales, Nájera, del 31 de julio al 4 de agosto de 2000*, ed. José Ignacio de la Iglesia Duarte (Nájera: Instituto de Estudios Riojanos, 2001), 221–52.

11. Valdeavellano, *Curso*, 326–28, 330–38.

12. Nicholas, *Introduction to Roman Law*, 95–97.

13. Berger, "Encyclopedic Dictionary," 491.

14. Valdeavellano, *Curso*, 308–12.

15. Rafael Gibert y Sánchez de la Vega, "La condición de los extranjeros en el antiguo derecho español," *Recueils de la Société Jean Bodin* 9 (1958): 150–99; Moisés García Rives, "Condición jurídica de los extranjeros en Castilla y León desde el Fuero de León (1020) al Código de las Partidas," *Revista de Ciencias Jurídicas y Sociales* 3 (1920): 245–83, 320–55; Manuel Álvarez-Valdés y Valdés, *La extranjería en la historia del derecho español* (Oviedo: Universidad de Oviedo, 1992).

16. Torres Fontes, *Documentos de Alfonso X*, 59, 79, nos. 42, 59.

17. Jesús Vallejo, "Vida castellana de la muerte civil: En torno a la ley cuarta de Toro," *HID* 31 (2004): 671–85, esp. 674–80; Berger, "Encyclopedic Dictionary," 588.

18. Joaquín Cerdá Ruiz-Funes, "Consideraciones sobre el hombre y sus derechos en las Partidas de Alfonso el Sabio," *Anales de la Universidad de Murcia. Derecho* 22 (1964): 9–55; Juan Beneyto, "Los derechos fundamentales en la España medieval," *Revista de Estudios Políticos*, n.s., 26 (1982): 99–117.

19. González, *Alfonso IX*, 2:22–26, esp. 23. no. 11.

20. Georges Martin, "Le concept de 'naturalité' (*naturaleza*) dans les *Sept parties* d'Alphonse X le Sage," *e-Spania*, 5 June 2008, https://journals.openedition.org/e-spania/, and Martin, "De lexicología jurídica alfonsí: naturaleza," *Alcanate* 6 (2008–9), 125–38.

21. Berger, "Encyclopedic Dictionary," 592–93.

22. Berger, "Encyclopedic Dictionary," 499, 613.

23. Procter, *Curia and Cortes*, 286, no. 7.

24. *DAAX*, 557–64, esp. 562, no. 521.

25. Valdeavellano, *Curso*, 383–84, 390–91, 413.

26. *El Fuero viejo de Castilla*, ed. Barrios García, Ser Quijano, and González Alonso; Jordán de Asso y del Río and Manuel y Rodríguez, *El Fuero Viejo de Castilla*.

27. Román Riaza, "Las Partidas y los '*Libri feudorum*,'" *AHDE* 10 (1933): 5–18.

28. Claudio Sánchez Albornoz, "El 'juicio del Libro' en León durante el siglo X y un feudo castellano del XIII," *AHDE* 1 (1924): 382–90: Ramón Paz, "Un nuevo feudo castellano," *AHDE* 5 (1928): 445–48; Valdeavellano, *Curso*, 370–77; Julio Valdeón, *El feudalismo* (Madrid: Alba, 1992); Ignacio Álvarez Borge, "Señorío y feudalismo en Castilla: Una revisión de la historiografía entre los años 1989–2004," in *Estudios sobre señorío y feudalismo: Homenaje a Julio Valdeón*, ed. Esteban Sarasa Sánchez and Eliseo Serrano Martín (Zaragoza: Institución Fernando el Católico, 2010), 107–96.

29. Berger, "Encyclopedic Dictionary," 494.

30. García Gallo, "Textos," 317–32; Claudio Sánchez Albornoz, "Diviseros y propietarios: un documento castellano que los equipara," *CHE* 5 (1946): 170–72.

31. *FV* 1, 8, 1–21; 1, 9, 1–6; Valdeavellano, *Curso*, 245–56, 330–46, 518–28; Carlos Estepa Díez, *Las behetrías castellanas*, 2 vols. (Valladolid: Junta de Castilla y León, 2003); Cristina Jular Pérez-Alfaro and Carlos Estepa Díez, eds., *Land, Power, and Society in Medieval Castile: A Study of Behetría Lordship* (Turnhout: Brepols, 2009).

32. Rodrigo Jiménez de Rada, *Historia de rebus Hispanie*, 246, bk. 7, chap. 24; *Crónica latina*, 12; *The Latin Chronicle*, 22, chap. 11.

33. Reilly, *Kingdom of León-Castilla under King Alfonso VI*, 129–30; Richard Fletcher, *The Quest for El Cid* (New York: Alfred A. Knopf), 125–33.

34. *CAX(GJ)*, 92–111, chaps. 27–36; O'Callaghan, *Alfonso X and the Cantigas*, 218–25; González Jiménez, *Alfonso X*, 239–72.

35. Carlos Heusch, "Les fondements juridiques de l'amitié à travers les *Partidas* d'Alphonse X et la droit médiéval," *CLHM* 18–19 (1993–94): 5–48; Antonella Liuzzo Scorpo, *Friendship in Medieval Iberia: Historical, Legal and Literary Perspectives* (Farnham: Ashgate, 2014); Stone, *Marriage and Friendship*, 115–30.

36. Aristotle, *Nicomachaean Ethics*, bk. 8, in *The Complete Works of Aristotle: The Revised Oxford Translation*, ed. Jonathan Barnes, 2 vols. (Princeton: Princeton University Press, 1984), 2:1729–1867, esp. 1825C–29.

37. Cicero, *Laelius de amicitia*, ed. C. F. W. Müller (Leipzig: Teubner, 1884), bks. 25–26, chaps. 89–99.

38. Cicero, *Laelius*, bk. 28, chap. 65.

39. Aristotle, *Nicomachaean Ethics*, 1828.

40. Sirach 6:1–17 (formerly Ecclesiasticus) speaks of friendship, but the phrase cited does not appear there. Compare Proverbs 11:9 and 11:13.

41. Cicero, *Laelius*, bks. 19–20, chaps. 70–71.

42. Cicero, *Laelius*, bks. 12–13, chaps. 40–44; bk. 7, chap. 24.

43. Berger, "Encyclopedic Dictionary," 563.

44. Olivia Remie Constable, *Trade and Traders in Muslim Spain: The Commercial Realignment of the Iberian Peninsula, 900–1500* (Cambridge: Cambridge University Press, 1994), 203–8, 234–35.

45. María del Carmen Carlé, "La servidumbre en las Partidas," *CHE* 12 (1949): 105–20; William D. Phillips, *Slavery in Medieval and Early Modern Iberia* (Philadelphia: University of Pennsylvania Press, 2014), and Phillips, *Slavery from Roman Times to the Early Transatlantic Trade* (Minneapolis: University of Minnesota Press, 1985).

46. *Inst.* 1, 2, 2; 1, 3; Nicholas, *Introduction to Roman Law*, 69–76; Buckland, *Textbook of Roman Law*, 63–73; Berger, "Encyclopedic Dictionary," 704–6.

47. Francisco Pons Boigues, *Apuntes sobre las escrituras mozárabes toledanas que se conservan en el Archivo Histórico Nacional* (Madrid: Tello, 1897), 258–61.

48. *Inst.* 1, 5; *C* 1, 13, 2; *FJ* 5, 7, 1–2.

49. Berger, "Encyclopedic Dictionary," 574–76; Buckland, *Textbook of Roman Law*, 73–87.

50. Berger, "Encyclopedic Dictionary," 564; Buckland, *Textbook of Roman Law*, 89–91.

11. The Law of Property

1. Berger, "Encyclopedic Dictionary," 441–42.

2. Buckland, *Textbook of Roman Law*, 182–92; Nicholas, *Introduction to Roman Law*, 98–116.

3. Nicholas, *Introduction to Roman Law*, 130–31; Buckland, *Textbook of Roman Law*, 184–88.

4. Torres Fontes, *Documentos del Siglo XIII*, 23, 37, nos. 36, 41.

5. Burns, "King Alfonso and the Wild West."

6. Livy, *The History of Rome, Books 1–5*, trans. Valerie M. Warrior (Indianapolis: Hackett Publishing, 2006), 12–13, bk.1, chaps. 6–7.

7. Buckland, *Textbook of Roman Law*, 206–32; Nicholas, *Introduction to Roman Law*, 130–33.

8. Buckland, *Textbook of Roman Law*, 213–21; Nicholas, *Introduction to Roman Law*, 133–40.

9. Buckland, *Textbook of Roman Law*, 249–51; Nicholas, *Introduction to Roman Law*, 120–22; Berger, "Encyclopedic Dictionary," 645; *FJ* 10, 2, 6–7.

10. Buckland, *Textbook of Roman Law*, 198–205; Nicholas, *Introduction to Roman Law*, 107–15; Berger, "Encyclopedic Dictionary," 636–38.

11. Buckland, *Textbook of Roman Law*, 258–68; Nicholas, *Introduction to Roman Law*, 140–48; Berger, "Encyclopedic Dictionary," 702–704; Margarita Serna Vallejo,

"Servidumbres prediales y limitaciones de dominio: Entre la diferenciación y la confusión," in *Historia de la propiedad: Servidumbres y limitaciones de dominio*, ed. Salustiano de Dios, Javier Infante, Ricardo Robledo, Eugenia Torijano (Madrid: Fundación Registral, 2009), 852–83, esp. 859–66.

12. Buckland, *Textbook of Roman Law*, 268–74; Berger, "Encyclopedic Dictionary," 755.

13. Buckland, *Textbook of Roman Law*, 213–15.

14. Buckland, *Textbook of Roman Law*, 403–598; Nicholas, *Introduction to Roman Law*, 158–207; Berger, "Encyclopedic Dictionary," 413–15, 603–4.

15. *Justinian's Institutes*, ed. Krueger, trans. Birks and McLeod, 13–15; Berger, "Encyclopedic Dictionary," 399, 591.

16. *FJ* 5, 5, 1–10; *FV* 3, 4, 1–19; Buckland, *Textbook of Roman Law*, 459–62.

17. Beltrán de Heredia, *Cartulario*, 2:68, no. 37; *MHE*, 1:267–68, no. 123; Linehan, *Spanish Church*, 128–41.

18. González, *Reinado y diplomas de Fernando III*, 3:336, no. 765; Hilda Grassotti, "Un empréstito para la conquista de Sevilla," *CHE* 45–46 (1967): 191–247, and Grassotti, "Alfonso IX y el origen de los empréstitos," *CHE* 69 (1987): 217–24; Joseph F. O'Callaghan, "La financiación de la conquista de Sevilla," in *Sevilla 1248: Congreso Internacional Conmemorativo del 750 Aniversario de la Conquista de la Ciudad de Sevilla por Fernando III, Rey de Castlla y León*, ed. Manuel González Jiménez (Madrid: Fundación Ramón Areces, 2001), 191–206, esp. 203–5.

19. *MHE*, 1:68–70, no. 33; Martín Expósito and Monsalvo Antón, *Documentación medieval del Archivo municipal de Ledesma*, 36–40, no. 3; Agapito y Revilla, *Los privilegios de Valladolid*, 48–49, no. 29-XI.

20. Miguel Vigil, *Colección histórico-diplomática del ayuntamiento de Oviedo*, 46, no. 22.

21. *FJ* 5, 5, 1–7; Buckland, *Textbook of Roman Law*, 467–70.

22. *MHE*, 1:56–57, no. 26; *DAAX*, 455–56, no. 432.

23. John T. Noonan, *The Scholastic Analysis of Usury* (Cambridge, MA: Harvard University Press 1957).

24. Pereda Llarena, *Documentación de la catedral de Burgos*, 144–47, 180, nos. 101–2, 128.

25. *Inst.* 3, 14, 3; 4, 6, 17, 23, 30; Buckland, *Textbook of Roman Law*, 464–67; Berger, "Encyclopedic Dictionary," 432; Juan Antonio Arias Bonet, "El depósito en las Partidas," *AHDE* 32 (1962): 543–66.

26. Torres Fontes, *Documentos del Siglo XIII*, 14–15, no. 16.

27. *DAAX*, 14, no. 15; O'Callaghan, *Learned King*, 73–75; González Jiménez, *Alfonso X*, 58–60.

28. *Inst.* 2, 7; Buckland, *Textbook of Roman Law*, 253–58; Berger, "Encyclopedic Dictionary" 442–43; José María Ortuño Sánchez-Pedreño, "Las fuentes del régimen de la donación en las Partidas," *REHJ* 23 (2001): 369–90.

29. Berger, "Encyclopedic Dictionary," 624.

30. *Inst.* 2, 7, 2.

31. González, *Repartimiento*, 1:257–301, 2:13–178; *MHE*, 1:9–17, 26–29, nos. 6–8, 15.

32. González Díez, *Colección diplomática del concejo de Burgos*, 100–105, no. 30; *MHE*, 1:68–70, no. 33.

33. *DAAX*, 255–57, no. 233; *MHE*, 1:166–69, no. 81.

34. *MHE*, 1:107–8, no. 49.

35. *Inst.* 3, 13; Buckland, *Textbook of Roman Law*, 478–95; Nicholas, *Introduction to Roman Law*, 171–82; Berger, "Encyclopedic Dictionary," 452–53; Ramón Fernández Espinar, "La compraventa en el Derecho medieval español," *AHDE* 25 (1955): 293–528.

36. *FJ* 5, 4, 1–23; *FV* 4, 1, 1–12; 4, 2, 1–4.

37. *MHE*, 1:32–33, 81, 151–52, nos. 17, 39, 70.

38. Ballesteros, *Sevilla*, xlii–iv, no. 39. Also see nos. 45, 47, 48, 49, 51, 53, 64, 66, 69, 82, 83, 89, 100, 103, 105, 106, 124, 125, 128, 129, 130, 131, 135, 138, 142, 146, 147, 159, 162, 163, 170, 171.

39. Torres Fontes, *Documentos del Siglo XIII*, 52–53, no. 57.

40. Teofilo F. Ruiz, *Crisis and Continuity: Land and Town in Late Medieval Castile* (Philadelphia: University of Pennsylvania Press, 1994), 140–74.

41. Oceja Gonzalo, *Documentación del monasterio de San Salvador de Oña (1032–1284)*, 135, 144–46, 175–76, 179–80, 188–89, 193–94, 198–99, 201–5, 207–9, 225–26, 345–46, nos. 158, 166, 168, 183, 186, 194, 198, 202, 204–5, 209, 224, 236.

42. *Inst.* 3, 23, 2; Buckland, *Textbook of Roman Law*, 520–21; Berger, "Encyclopedic Dictionary," 628; *FJ* 5, 4, 1.

43. Buckland, *Textbook of Roman Law*, 518–20; Berger, "Encyclopedic Dictionary," 414; Nicholas, *Introduction to Roman Law*, 189–91.

44. *MHE*, 1:117–20, 127–30, nos. 66, 69; *DAAX*, 221–23, no. 202.

45. Oceja Gonzalo, *Documentación del monasterio de San Salvador de Oña (1032–1284)*, 137–38, 175–76, 223–25, 227–28, 348–49, nos. 160, 183, 223, 225, 238.

46. *Inst.* 3, 24; Buckland, *Textbook of Roman Law*, 494–503; Nicholas, *Introduction to Roman Law*, 182–85; Berger, "Encyclopedic Dictionary," 567; José Antonio Martínez Vela, "El contrato de 'Locatio Conductio': Notas sobre su recepción en el derecho castellano medieval, con especial referencia al código de 'Las Partidas,'" *Revista de Derecho UNED* 11 (2012): 601–34; Rafael Gibert, "El contrato de servicios en el derecho medieval español," *Revista de Política Social* 101 (1974): 5–134.

47. *Inst.* 3, 24, 3; Buckland, *Textbook of Roman Law*, 275; Nicholas, *Introduction to Roman Law*, 148–49; Berger, "Encyclopedic Dictionary," 452; José María Ortuño Sánchez-Pedreño, "Origen romano de la enfiteusis en las Partidas," *Anales de la Universidad de Alicante. Facultad de Derecho* 8 (1993): 63–74.

48. *Fulan* (ar. *fulān*) was used to refer to someone whose name was unknown.

49. Oceja Gonzalo, *Documentación del monasterio de San Salvador de Oña (1032–1284)*, 130–31, 135–36, 176–78, 183–84, 216–17, 346–47, 350, nos. 154, 159, 184, 190, 217, 237, 239; Pereda Llarena, *Documentación de la catedral de Burgos*, 34–35, 158–59, nos. 23, 111.

50. *Inst.* 3, 15; 3, 17–19; Buckland, *Textbook of Roman Law*, 431–540; Berger, "Encyclopedic Dictionary," 657, 716–18; Rafael Núñez Lagos, *La estipulación en las Partidas y el Ordenamiento de Alcalá* (Madrid: Real Academia de Jurisprudencia y Legislación, 1950); Juan Antonio Arias Bonet, "Recepción de las formas estipulatorias en la baja edad media: Un estudio sobre las 'promisiones' de las Siete Partidas," *Boletim da Faculdade de Direito de Coimbra* 42 (1966): 285–334; Alejandro Guzmán Brito, "La promesa obligacional en las 'Partidas' como sede de la doctrina general de las obligaciones," *Revista Chilena de Derecho* 34 (2007): 395–404.

51. Berger, "Encyclopedic Dictionary," 624.

52. *Inst.* 3, 20; Buckland, *Textbook of Roman Law*, 441–58; Nicholas, *Introduction to Roman Law*, 204–5; Berger, "Encyclopedic Dictionary," 471; *FJ* 5, 4, 2; José María

Ortuño Sánchez-Pedreño, "Origen romano de la fianza en las Partidas," *Ius fugit: Revista interdisciplinar de Estudios histórico-jurídicos* 7 (1998): 89–122.

53. Berger, "Encyclopedic Dictionary," 604.

54. I want to thank Jerry Craddock for his kind assistance with the meaning of these words.

55. Oceja Gonzalo, *Documentación del monasterio de San Salvador de Oña (1032–1284)*, 135, 144–46, 175–76, 179–80, 188–89, 193–94, 198–99, 201–9, 225–26, 345–46, nos. 158, 166, 168, 183, 186, 194, 198, 202, 204–6, 209, 224, 236; Pereda Llarena, *Documentación de la catedral de Burgos*, 34–35, 180, nos. 23, 128.

56. Buckland, *Textbook of Roman Law*, 470–77; Berger, "Encyclopedic Dictionary," 630–31.

57. González Díez, *Colección diplomática del concejo de Burgos*, 105–6, no. 31.

58. *MHE*, 1:68–70, no. 33; Torres Fontes, *Documentos de Alfonso X*, 317, no. 283.

59. Buckland, *Textbook of Roman Law*, 560–62; Berger, "Encyclopedic Dictionary," 710.

60. *Inst.* 4, 6, 30, 39; Buckland, *Textbook of Roman Law*, 558–59; Berger, "Encyclopedic Dictionary," 401.

12. Trade and Commerce

1. Joseph F. O'Callaghan, "Paths to Ruin: The Economic and Financial Policies of Alfonso the Learned," in Burns, *Worlds of Alfonso the Learned and James the Conqueror*, 41–67, repr. in *Alfonso X, the Cortes, and Government*, no. V; Miguel Ángel Ladero Quesada, "Aspectos de la política económica de Alfonso X," *RFDUC* 9 (1985): 69–82; José Luis Martín, "Economía y sociedad de la época Alfonsina," *Revista de Occidente* 43 (1984): 29–41; Teofilo F. Ruiz, "Expansion et changement: La conquête de Castille et la société castillane (1248–1350)," *Annales: Economies, Sociétés, Civilisations* 35 (1979): 548–65.

2. Claudio Sánchez Albornoz, *España, un enigma histórico*, 2 vols. (Buenos Aires: Sudamericana, 1962), 2:123–24.

3. Ana Arranz Guzmán, "Alfonso X y la conservación de la naturaleza," in Miguel Rodríguez, Múñoz Fernández, and Segura Graiño, *Alfonso X el Sabio*, 1:127–36; Vázquez de Parga, Lacarra, and Uria, *Peregrinaciones*, 3:111–14, nos. 78–79.

4. Seville 1252, arts. 21–22, 29–30, 33, 39; Valladolid 1258, arts. 34–35, 41–43; Seville 1261, arts. 22–25, Jerez 1268, arts. 16–17, 20–39; *FR* 4, 5, 11; Miguel Ángel Ladero Quesada, "La caza en la legislación municipal castellana: Siglos XIII a XVIII," *ELEM* 1 (1980): 193–222, esp. 208–9, 211.

5. Jesús García Díaz, "El fenómeno del mercado en la obra legislativa de Alfonso X el Sabio." *HID* 38 (2011): 111–40.

6. González, *Reinado y diplomas de Fernando III*, 3:380, 387–90, nos. 800, 809.

7. Valladolid 1258, arts. 36–37; Seville 1261, arts. 27–28; Jerez 1268, arts. 27, 41.

8. Escalona, *Historia del real monasterio de Sahagún*, 603; *Fuero de Cuenca*, 861–62; Represa Rodríguez, "Notas para el estudio de la ciudad de Segovia," 290–94.

9. María del Carmen Carlé, "Mercaderes en Castilla (1252–1512)," *CHE* 21–22 (1954): 146–328.

10. López Ferreiro, *Fueros municipales*, 237, ley 4.

11. González Díez, *Colección diplomática del concejo de Burgos*, 184–85, no. 101.

12. Layna Serrano, *Historia de la villa de Atienza*, 502–503; Antonio Collantes de Terán, "La formación de los gremios sevillanos: A propósito de unos documentos sobre los tejedores," *ELEM* 1 (1980): 89–104, esp.101–2, nos. 1–2; Loperráez, *Descripción histórica del obispado de Osma*, 3:217–21, no. 81; González Díez, *Colección diplomática del concejo de Burgos*, 197–98, no. 110.

13. *MHE*, 2:18–19, no. 170.

14. *CAX(GJ)*, 7, chap. 1; María del Carmen Carlé, "El precio de la vida en Castilla del rey sabio al emplazado," *CHE* 15 (1951): 132–56, esp. 136–37, 143–44; Reyna Pastor, "Ganadería y precios: Consideraciones sobre la economía de León y Castilla (siglos XI–XIII)," *CHE* 35–36 (1962): 37–55.

15. Sáez et al., *Los fueros de Sepúlveda*, 193–94, no. 12.

16. González Jiménez, "Cortes de Sevilla de 1261," 307–8, no. 20; Andrés Marcos Burriel, *Informe de la imperial ciudad de Toledo al Real y Supremo Consejo de Castilla sobre igualación de pesos y medidas en todos los Reynos y Señorios de su Majestad según las leyes* (Toledo: Joachin Ibarra, 1758), 391–92; Ramón Álvarez de Brana, "La igualación de pesos y medidas por don Alfonso el Sabio," *BRAH* 38 (1901): 134–44; José Antonio Martín Fuertes, María del Carmen Rodríguez López, and María Jesús Pradal Garcia, *Colección documental del Archivo Municipal de León, 1219–1400* (León: Centro de Estudios e Investigación "San Isidoro," 1998), 11; Martín Fuertes and Álvarez Álvarez, *Archivo histórico municipal de León*, 29, no. 6.

17. *Fuero de Cuenca*, 867–68.

18. González Díez, *Colección diplomática del concejo de Burgos*, 165, no. 82; *MHE*, 2:26–27, no. 176.

19. Luis G. de Valdeavellano, "El mercado: Apuntes para su estudio en León y Castilla durante la Edad Media," *AHDE* 8 (1931): 201–405; repr. at Seville: Universidad de Sevilla, 1975; González Díez, *Colección diplomática del concejo de Burgos*, 84–85, no. 22; Torres Fontes, *Documentos de Alfonso X*, 141, no. 113.

20. Escalona, *Historia del real monasterio de Sahagún*, 603.

21. Pereda Llarena, *Documentación de la catedral de Burgos*, 67–68, no. 47; González Díez, *Colección diplomática del concejo de Burgos*, 113–16, no. 35.

22. *MHE*, 2:46–48, no. 189.

23. Loperráez, *Descripción histórica del obispado de Osma*, 3:187–88, no. 64; Ballesteros y Beretta, *Alfonso X*, 1090, 1006, nos. 624, 955.

24. Barrios García, Expósito, and Ser Quijano, *Documentación medieval del Archivo municipal de Alba de Tormes*, 48–51, nos. 10–12; González Díez, *Colección diplomática del concejo de Burgos*, 198–99, no. 11.

25. José Miguel Gual López, "La política ferial alfonsí y el ordenamiento general de ferias castellanas en su época," in Miguel Rodríguez, Múñoz Fernández, and Segura Graiño, *Alfonso X el Sabio*, 1:94–114; Miguel Ángel Ladero Quesada, "Las ferias de Castilla: Siglos XII a XV," *CHE* 67–68 (1982): 269–347 (repr. at Madrid: Comité español de Ciencias Históricas, 1994).

26. José Miguel Gual López, "Bases para el estudio de las ferias murcianas en la edad media," *MMM* 9 (1982): 9–55, esp. 29–34, nos. 1, 5, 8; Torres Fontes, *Documentos de Alfonso X*, 29–31, 77, 141–43, 259–61, nos. 25, 77, 114, 223; Torres Fontes, *Fueros y privilegios*, 105–6, 141, nos. 95, 134; Tomás González, *Colección de cédulas, cartas patentes, provisiones, reales ordenes y documentos concernientes las provincias vascongadas*, 6 vols. (Madrid: Imprenta real, 1829–33), 6:112, 124, 404, nos. 258,

261, 316; *DAAX*, 116–18, 169, nos. 118, 156; Floriano, *Documentación histórica del Archivo municipal de Cáceres*, 19–20, no. 7; Guerrero Lafuente, *Historia de la ciudad de Benavente*, 422, no. 3; Villar y Macías, *Historia de Salamanca*, 1:256; Barrios García, Expósito, and Ser Quijano, *Documentación medieval del Archivo municipal de Alba de Tormes*, 37–41, 45–46, 49–51, nos. 4, 7, 11–12; Cantera Burgos, "Miranda"; Agapito y Revilla, *Los privilegios de Valladolid*, 51–52, no. 31-xii; Ángel Casimiro de Govantes, *Diccionario geográfico-histórico de España* (Madrid: Jordán 1846), 309–10; *MHE*, 1:37, no. 19; Francisco Layna Serrano, *Historia de Guadalajara y sus Mendozas en los s. XV y XVI*, 4 vols. (Madrid: Instituto Jerónimo Zurita, 1942), 1:30, 262; Juan Ignacio Ruíz de la Peña, "Poblamientos y cartas pueblas de Alfonso X y Sancho IV en Galicia," in *Homenaje a José María Lacarra*, 3 vols. (Zaragoza: Anubar, 1978), 3:27–51, esp. 36–37.

27. *DAAX*, 116–18, no. 118; Guerrero Lafuente, *Historia de la ciudad de Benavente*, 422, no. 3; Barrios García, Expósito, and Ser Quijano, *Documentación medieval del Archivo municipal de Alba de Tormes*, 37–38, 45–46, nos. 4, 7; Torres Fontes, *Documentos de Alfonso X*, 152, 242, nos. 121, 213.

28. Valladolid 1258, art. 33; Seville 1261, art. 34; César González Mínguez, *El portazgo en la edad media: Aproximación a su estudio en la Corona de Castilla* (Bilbao: Universidad del País Vasco, 1989); Pedro A. Porras Arboledas, "Los portazgos en León y Castilla durante la Edad Media: Política real y circuitos comerciales," *ELEM* 15 (1992): 161–21, esp. 171–73.

29. *DAAX*, 169, no. 156; Alamo, *Colección diplomática de San Salvador de Oña*, 2:681, 700–701, 781–82, 789, 791, nos. 565, 587, 659, 665, 667; Sánchez Belda, *Documentos reales de la Edad media referentes a Galicia*, 338, no. 779; González, *Colección*, 5:190–91, no. 60; Pereda Llarena, *Documentación de la catedral de Burgos*, 154–55, 159–68, nos. 107, 112–20; Escagedo Salmón, *Colección diplomática*, 1:147–48; Ferotin, *Recueil*, 143, no. 216: Pardo Rodríguez, *Cancillería*, 138–39, no. 4; Julio González, "Aranceles del portazgo de Sahagún en el siglo XIII," *AHDE* 14 (1943): 573–78.

30. González, *Colección*, 5:170–71, no. 51; Juan Ignacio Fernández Marco, *La muy noble y muy leal villa de Briones: estudio biográfico* (Logroño: Instituto de Estudios Riojanos, 1976), 341–44, no. 1; González Mínguez, *Portazgo*, 219–20, nos. 3–5; Miguel Vigil, *Colección histórico-diplomática del ayuntamiento de Oviedo*, 53, 58, nos. 28, 31; José Damián González Arce, "La evolución del almojarifazgo de Córdoba entre los siglos XIII y XV," *ELEM* 37 (2014): 165–204.

31. *DAAX*, 171–72, 191–92, nos. 171, 173; Torres Fontes, *Documentos de Alfonso X*, 134, 152–57, 156–57, 338, nos. 107, 122–23, 127, 304; Isabel Pérez Valera, *Indice de los documentos del Archivo municipal de Ciudad Real, 1255–1899* (Ciudad Real: Instituto de Estudios Manchegos, 1962), 9, 11, nos. 2, 8.

32. Miguel Pino Abad, "La saca de cosas vedadas en el derecho territorial castellano," *AHDE* 70 (2000): 195–241; Asunción López Dapena, "Exportación castellana del mineral de hierro en el siglo XIII," *CEM* 12–13 (1984): 119–254; Yves Renouard, "Un sujet de recherches: l'exportation de chevaux de la péninsule ibérique en France et en Angleterre au moyen âge," in *Homenaje a Jaime Vicens Vives*, ed. Juan Maluquer de Motes, 2 vols. (Barcelona: Universidad de Barcelona, 1965–67), 1:571–77; Teofilo Ruiz. "Castilian Merchants in England, 1248–1350," in *Order and Innovation in the Middle Ages: Essays in Honor of Joseph R. Strayer* (Princeton: Princeton University Press, 1976), 173–85, esp. 181–82.

33. Wendy R. Childs, *Anglo-Castilian Trade in the Later Middle Ages* (Manchester: Manchester University Press, 1978), 11–15, 72, 77–78.

34. Américo Castro, "Unos aranceles de aduanas del siglo XIII," *RFE* 8 (1921): 1–29; Enrique de Vedia y Goossens, *Historia y descripción de la ciudad de La Coruña* (La Coruña: Domingo Puga, 1845), 148–50, no. 7; Torres Fontes, *Documentos de Alfonso X*, 257–58, no. 221.

35. *CAX(GJ)*, 87, 115, 132–34, chaps. 25, 40, 47; *CLC*, 1:85–86; *MHE*, 1:321, no. 140; Sánchez Belda, *Documentos reales de la Edad media referentes a Galicia*, 350, no. 808.

36. Torres Fontes, *Fueros y privilegios*, 152–53, no. 141, and Torres Fontes, *Documentos de Alfonso X*, 307–309, nos. 269–70; *MHE*, 2:7–8, no. 163.

37. González Díez, *Colección diplomática del concejo de Burgos*, 191–96, nos. 106–8; *MHE*, 2:29–31, no. 179; *LEst* 204.

38. Juan Antonio Arias Bonet, "Derecho marítimo en las Partidas," *Revista de Derecho mercantil* 41 (1966): 91–108; José Martínez Gijón, "La jurisdicción maritima en Castilla durante la baja edad media," *Historia* 8 (1969): 309–22; Pedro Andrés Porras Arboledas, "El derecho marítimo en el Cantábrico durante la baja edad media: *Partidas y Rôles d'Oléron*," in *Ciudades y villas portuarias del Atlántico en la Edad media: Nájera. Encuentros Internacionales del Medievo, Nájera, 27–30 de julio de 2004*, ed. Beatriz Arizaga Bolumburu and Jesús Ángel Solórzano Telechea (Nájera: Instituto de Estudios Riojanos, 2005), 231–55; esp. 234–37; Jennifer L. Green, "The Development of Maritime Law in Medieval Spain: The Case of Castile and the *Siete Partidas*," *The Historian* 58 (1996): 575–87.

39. Manuel González Jiménez, "Genoveses en Sevilla (siglos XIII–XV)," in *Presencia italiana en Andalucía: siglos XIV–XVII. Actas del I Coloquio Hispano-Italiano*, ed. Bibiano Torres Ramírez and José J. Hernández Palomo (Madrid: Consejo Superior de Investigaciones Científicas, 1989), 115–30.

40. *CSM*, 15, 33, 36, 72; Keller and Cash, *Daily Life*, plate 63 (*CSM* 36); García Cuadrado, *Cantigas*, 339–50.

41. *DAAX*, 518, no. 487, arts. 12–13; O'Callaghan, *Alfonso X and the Cantigas*, 172–91, esp. 177–80.

42. Buckland, *Textbook of Roman Law*, 504–12; Berger, "Encyclopedic Dictionary," 708–9.

43. *D* 17, 2, 29, 2. In Aesop's *Fables* a lion refused to share prey with other animals.

44. *CAX(GJ)*, 5–7, chap. 1; Jean Gautier-Dalché, "La politique monétaire d'Alphonse X," *CHE* 69 (1987): 77–95, and Gautier-Dalché, "Remarques sur les premières mutations monétaires d'Alphonse X de Castille," in his *Économie et société dans les pays de la Couronne de Castille* (London: Variorum, 1982), 147–56; James Todesca, "The Monetary History of Castile-León (ca. 1100–1300) in Light of the Bourgey Hoard," *American Numismatic Society Museum Notes* 33 (1988): 129–203, and Todesca, "The Crown Renewed: The Administration of Coinage in León-Castile, c. 1065–1200," in Todesca, *Emergence of León-Castile*, 9–32.

45. Joseph F. O'Callaghan, "The Cortes and Royal Taxation during the Reign of Alfonso X of Castile," *Traditio* 27 (1971): 379–98, esp. 382–83; Todesca, "Monetary History," 160–62.

46. Todesca, "Monetary History," 168–70.

47. Gautier-Dalché, "Politique monétaire," 85–88; Todesca, "Monetary History," 162–66.

48. Todesca, "Monetary History," 167–73; Escudero de la Peña, "Súplica," 58–59; Gautier-Dalché, "Politique monétaire," 89–92.

49. Torres Fontes, *Documentos de Alfonso X*, 266–67, no. 227; *CAX(GJ)*, 73, chap. 22; Gautier-Dalché, "Politique monétaire," 90–91.

50. *CAX(GJ)*, 136, chap. 48.

51. Escudero de la Peña, "Súplica," 58–59.

52. Todesca, "Monetary History," 174–75.

53. *CAX(GJ)*, 216, chap. 75.

54. González Díez, *Colección diplomática del concejo de Burgos*, 205–8, nos. 118, 120; *MHE*, 2:78–80, no. 209.

55. Miguel Ángel Ladero Quesada, "Crédito y comercio de dinero en la Castilla medieval," *Acta historica et archaeologica mediaevalia* 11–12 (1991): 145–59.

56. Macarena Crespo Álvarez, "Judíos, préstamos y usuras en la Castilla medieval: De Alfonso X a Enrique III," *Edad Media* 5 (2002): 179–215, esp. 189–93.

57. Valladolid 1258, arts. 29–30; Seville 1261, art. 20; Jerez 1268, art. 44; *Leyes Nuevas*, 1; José "Amador de los Ríos, *Historia social, política y religiosa de los judíos de España*, 2 vols. (Madrid: T. Fontanet, 1875–76), 1:587–88, no. 12; Villar Garcia, *Documentación medieval de la catedral de Segovia*, 250–51, no. 151; González Jiménez, "Cortes de Sevilla de 1261," 309–10, no. 3.

58. González Jiménez, "Cortes de Sevilla de 1261," 305–6, no. 1; Justiniano Rodríguez Fernández, "Juderías de León," *Archivos Leoneses* 2 (1947): 33–72, esp. 49–50, and Rodríguez Fernández, *Las Juderías de la provincia de León* (León: Consejo Superior de Investigaciones Científicas, 1976), 197–99; Barrios García and Expósito, *Documentación medieval de los Archivos municipales de Béjar*, 20–22, no. 4, and Barrios García, Expósito, and Ser Quijano, *Documentación medieval del Archivo municipal de Alba de Tormes*, 41–44, no. 6; Procter, *Curia and Cortes*, 284–86, no. 6; Juan Manuel del Estal, *Documentos inéditos de Alfonso X el sabio y el Infante su hijo don Sancho* (Alicante: Juan Manuel del Estal, 1984), 106–10, no. 4.

59. González Díez, *Colección diplomática del concejo de Burgos*, 141–49, 151–55, 157, 161–62, nos. 57, 59–62, 64–66, 68, 70–72, 75, 79; Barrios García, Expósito, and Ser Quijano, *Documentación medieval del Archivo municipal de Alba de Tormes*, 52–53, no. 14; Torres Fontes, *Documentos de Alfonso X*, 285–86, no. 245.

60. Francisco Layna Serrano, *Historia de la villa de Cifuentes* (Guadalajara: Institución Provincial de Cultura "Marqués de Santillana," 1979), 267–68, no. 2, and Layna Serrano, *Historia de la villa de Atienza*, 502–3; Mingüella, *Historia de la diócesis de Sigüenza*, 1:593–95, no. 221; Palacio, Millares Carlo, and Varela Hervias, *Documentos del Archivo general de la villa de Madrid*, 1:111–13; Barrios García and Expósito, *Documentación medieval de los Archivos municipales de Béjar*, 19–20, no. 3; *DAAX*, 388–89, no. 362; Nieto Cumplido, *Orígenes*, 126–30, nos. 6–8.

61. Julius Klein, *The Mesta: A Study in Spanish Economic History, 1273–1836* (Cambridge, MA: Harvard University Press, 1920).

62. Valladolid 1258, arts. 31–32, 40, 66, 68; *MHE*, 1:62–63, no. 28.

63. Represa Rodríguez, "Notas para el estudio de la ciudad de Segovia," 304.

64. *DAAX*, 262–64, 405–6, 487, nos. 238, 444, 460; Torres Fontes, *Fueros y privilegios*, 76, no. 57.

65. *DAAX*, 420–24, no. 398; Carmen Argente del Castillo Ocaña, "Precedentes de la organización del concejo de la Mesta," in Miguel Rodríguez, Múñoz Fernández, and Segura Graiño, *Alfonso X el Sabio*, 1:115–25.

66. *DAAX*, 420–24, no. 398.

67. *MHE*, 1:314, no. 140; González, *Colección*, 6:117–18, no. 258; Klein, *Mesta*, 256–57; Miguel Ángel Ladero Quesada, "Las transformaciones de la fiscalidad regia castellano-leonesa en la segunda mitad del siglo XIII (1252–1312), " in *Historia de la hacienda española: Homenaje al Profesor García de Valdeavellano* (Madrid: Instituto de Estudios Fiscales, 1982), 356–58.

68. *DAAX*, 420–24, no. 398.

69. *CAX(GJ)*, 121, chap. 41; *DAAX*, 428, no. 403.

70. Klein, *Mesta*, 12–13; Charles J. Bishko, "The Castilian as Plainsman: The Medieval Ranching Frontier in La Mancha and Extremadura," in *The New World Looks at Its History*, ed. Archibald R. Lewis and Thomas F. McGann (Austin: University of Texas Press, 1963), 47–69, esp. 61.

71. Barrios García and Expósito, *Documentación medieval de los Archivos municipales de Béjar*, 34–39, nos. 8–11; *LEst* 137; Julius Klein, "Los privilegios de la Mesta de 1273 y 1276," *BRAH* 64 (1914): 202–18.

72. Barrios García and Expósito, *Documentación medieval de los Archivos municipales de Béjar*, 39–41, nos. 12–13; *MHE*, 1:333–35, no. 148; J. Rodríguez Molina, "La mesta de Jaén y sus conflictos con los agricultores," *CEM* 1 (1973): 77–79; Floriano, *Documentación histórica del Archivo municipal de Cáceres*, 21–22, nos. 9–10.

73. Luciano Serrano, *Cartulario de San Pedro de Arlanza* (Madrid: Junta para Ampliación de Estudios e Investigaciones Científicas, 1925), 274–75, no. 155; Ballesteros, "Itinerario," 107:406–8, n. 2; Alamo, *Colección diplomática de San Salvador de Oña*, 2:719–20, no. 604; Amancio Rodríguez López, *El real monasterio de Las Huelgas de Burgos y el Hospital del Rey*, 2 vols. (Burgos: Centro Católico, 1907), 1:478, 482–83, nos. 97, 101; Ferotin, *Recueul*, 252–53, no. 222; Pereda Llarena, *Documentación de la catedral de Burgos*, 194–95, 231, nos. 137, 169.

13. Crime and Punishment

1. Román Riaza Martínez Osorio, "El derecho penal en las Partidas," in *Trabajos del Seminario del derecho penal: curso 1916–17*, ed. Luis Jiménez de Asúa (Madrid: Reus, 1922), 19–65; María Paz Alonso, *El proceso penal en Castilla (siglos XIII–XVIII)* (Salamanca: Universidad de Salamanca, 1982), 3–63; Enrique Álvarez Cora, "El derecho penal de Alfonso X," *Initium: Revista catalana d'Historia del Dret* 16 (2011): 223–96; Ángel López Amo Marín, "El derecho penal español de la baja edad media," *AHDE* 26 (1956): 337–67.

2. Berger, "Encyclopedic Dictionary," 340.

3. González Díez, *Colección diplomática del concejo de Burgos*, 178, 189–90, nos. 95, 104; Ruiz, *Sociedad*, 183, n. 77.

4. *Espéculo*, ed. MacDonald, 345.

5. Irene Zadorenko, "El procedimiento judicial de riepto entre nobles y la fecha de composición de la *Historia Roderici* y el *Poema de Mio Cid*," *RFE* 78 (1998): 183–94; Alfonso Otero Varela, "El riepto en el derecho castellano-leonés," in his *Estudios histórico-jurídicos*, 1:173–260, and Otero Varela, "El riepto en los fueros municipales," *AHDE* 29 (1959):153–73, and in his *Estudios histórico-jurídicos*, 1:273–98; Manuel Torres Aguilar, "Naturaleza jurídico-penal y procesal del desafio y riepto en León y Castilla en la edad media," *AHDE* 10 (1933): 161–74.

6. Marta Madero, "El *duellum* entre la honra y la prueba según las *Siete Partidas* de Alfonso X y el comentario de Gregorio López," *CLCHM* 24 (2001): 343–52.

7. *Poem of the Cid (El poema del mio Cid),* trans. William S. Merwin (New York: New American Library, 1962), 268–99, cantos 139–51.

8. Juan Antonio Alejandre García, "Estudio histórico del delito de falsedad documental," *AHDE* 42 (1972): 117–87, esp. 161–62; Pilar Ostos Salcedo and María Luisa Pardo Rodríguez, "La teoría de la falsedad documental en la Corona de Castilla," in Comision Internacional de Diplomatica, *Falsos y falsificaciones de documentos diplomáticos en la Edad Media* (Zaragoza: Real Sociedad Económica Aragonesa de Amigos del País, 1991), 161–76.

9. Ernst Jaffe and Heinrich Finke, "La dispensa de matrimonio falsificada para el rey Sancho IV y María de Molina," *AHDE* 4 (1927): 298–318; Alejandro Marcos Pous, "Los dos matrimonios de Sancho IV de Castilla," *Cuadernos de Trabajos de la Escuela Española de Historia y Arqueología en Roma* 8 (1956): 1–108; Santiago Domínguez Sánchez, "Falsificaciones medievales: Una 'Bula' de Nicolás IV falsificada por el rey Sancho IV de Castilla," *Estudios humanísticos. Historia* 2 (2003): 13–26; Nieto Soria, *Sancho IV*, 21–24, 47–49; César González Mínguez, *Fernando IV de Castilla (1295–1312): La guerra civil y el predominio de la nobleza* (Valladolid: Universidad de Valladolid, 1976), 117–19.

10. Jaime Lluis y Navas, "Los principios sobre la falsificación de moneda en el código de las Partidas," *Numisma* 4 (1954): 87–95, and Lluis y Navas, "El sistema de penas sobre falsificación de moneda en el código de las Partidas," *Numisma* 4 (1954): 109–23.

11. González, *Reinado y diplomas de Fernando III*, 2:282–83, 425–27, nos. 242, 370.

12. Berger, "Encyclopedic Dictionary," 487–88; José Sánchez-Arcilla Bernal, "Notas para el estudio del homicidio en el derecho histórico español," *RFDUC* 72 (1986–87): 513–74.

13. González Díez, *Colección diplomática del concejo de Burgos*, 138–39, no. 54.

14. Berger, "Encyclopedic Dictionary," 382.

15. Victoria Rodríguez Ortíz, *El aborto hasta fines de la Edad Media castellana: Su consideración social y jurídica* (Madrid: Aranzadi, 2014); José Sánchez-Arcilla Bernal, "Notas para el estudio del aborto en el Derecho histórico español," *Icade: Revista de las Facultades de Derecho y Ciencias Económicas y Empresariales* 8 (1986): 13–40.

16. Berger, "Encyclopedic Dictionary," 419, 618; Manuel Torres Aguilar, *El parricidio: del pasado al presente de un delito* (Madrid: Editorial de Derecho Reunidas SA, 1991).

17. Berger, "Encyclopedic Dictionary," 382.

18. Marta Madero, *Manos violentas, palabras vedadas: La injuria en Castilla y León, siglos XIII–XV* (Madrid: Taurus Humanidades, 1992); Rafael Serra Ruiz, "Honor, honra e injuria en el Derecho medieval español," *Anales de la Universidad de Murcia. Derecho* 23 (1965): 55–155; Antonio Pérez Martín, "La protección del honor y de la fama en el derecho hstórico español," *AD* 11 (1991): 117–56, esp. 127–31; Berger, "Encyclopedic Dictionary," 502.

19. Professor Raymond S. Willis, on the request of Teofilo F. Ruiz, explained the meaning of *fide fududincul* as *fi* (son) *de* (of) *foder* (to fornicate) *in* (in) *cul* (anus). See Teofilo F. Ruiz, "The Transformation of the Castilian Municipalities: The Case of Burgos, 1248–1350," *Past and Present: A Journal of Historical Studies* 77 (1977): 3–32, esp. 23, n. 73; repr. in his *The City and the Realm: Burgos and Castile, 1080–1492* (Brookfield, VT: Ashgate, 1992), no. VII.

20. González Díez, *Colección diplomática del concejo de Burgos*, 119–23, 166, nos. 38, 83; *Leyes Nuevas*, 11.

21. Juan Paredes Núñez, *Alfonso X el Sabio: Cantigas profanas* (Granada: Universidad de Granada, 1988).

22. Berger, "Encyclopedic Dictionary," 767.

23. González, *Alfonso IX*, 2:23–26, no. 11.

24. Ajo G. y Saínz de Zúñiga, *Historia*, 1:438, nos. 7–8.

25. Pardo Rodríguez, *Cancillería*, 149–50, no. 14.

26. Berger, "Encyclopedic Dictionary," 480–81, 667; Nicholas, *Introduction to Roman Law*, 211, 215.

27. González Díez, *Colección diplomática del concejo de Burgos*, 180–81, no. 97; Ruiz, *Sociedad*, 133.

28. González, *Alfonso IX*, 2:26–27, no. 12.

29. Berger, "Encyclopedic Dictionary," 424; Nicholas, *Introduction to Roman Law*, 218–20.

30. Berger, "Encyclopedic Dictionary," 440; Nicholas, *Introduction to Roman Law*, 223.

31. *Poem of the Cid*, 42–52, 144, cantos 5–11, 83; Nicasio Salvador Miguel, "Reflexiones sobre el episodio de Rachel y Vidas en el Cantar de mio Cid," *RFE* 59 (1977): 183–224.

32. Brundage, *Law, Sex, and Christian Society*.

33. Berger, "Encyclopedic Dictionary," 352; María José Collantes de Terán, "El delito de adulterio en el derecho general de Castilla," *AHDE* 66 (1996): 201–28.

34. *LEst* 62, 93; Alejandro Morín, "Matar a la adúltera: el homicidio legítimo en la legislación castellana medieval," *CLHM* 24 (2001): 353–77.

35. Marjorie Ratcliffe, "Adulteresses, Mistresses, and Prostitutes: Extramarital Relationships in Medieval Castile," *Hispania* 67 (1984): 346–50.

36. Molina Molina, "Aspectos," esp. 180–82: Dillard, *Daughters of the Reconquest*, 196–201; Eukene Lacarra Lanz, "Legal and Clandestine Prostitution in Medieval Spain," *Bulletin of Hispanic Studies* 79 (2002): 265–85.

37. Molina Molina, "Aspectos," 181–82; Iñaki Bazán, "La construcción del discurso homofóbico en la Europa cristiana medieval," *ELEM* 30 (2007): 433–54, esp. 436–37.

38. *CAX(GJ)*, 194, chap. 68; Jofré de Loaysa, *Crónica*, 96, chap. 219.23; Kinkade, "Alfonso X, *Cantiga* 235," 313–18; O'Callaghan, *Learned King*, 241–43; and O'Callaghan, *Alfonso X and the Cantigas*, 144–51.

39. Molina Molina, "Aspectos," 182–85; Dillard, *Daughters of the Reconquest*, 201–2; Francisco Corti, "Cantiga 125: La nigromancia y las relaciones entre imágenes y textos," *Alcanate* 5 (2006–7): 293–305.

40. *Crónica geral de 1344*, ed. L. F. Lindley Cintra, 6 vols. (Lisbon: Academia Portuguesa da História, 1952–83), 6:382–83, chap. 791.

41. Manuel González Jiménez, "Unos Anales del Reinado de Alfonso X," *BRAH* 192 (1995): 461–92, esp. 482–86, chaps. 18–19, and 486–91; Derek W. Lomax, "Una crónica inédita de Silos," in *Homenaje a Fray Justo Pérez de Urbel*, 2 vols. (Silos: Abadía de Silos, 1976), 1:323–37, esp. 328; Craddock, "Dynasty in Dispute," 204–9, 214–19; Ballesteros y Beretta, *Alfonso X*, 209–11.

42. Isabel de Barros Días, "La blasfemia del rey sabio: Vicisitudes de una leyenda (Nuevas hipótesis respecto a la datación y la posición relativa del texto portugués)," *AEM* 45 (2015): 733–52, and Barros Días, "A blasfémia do Rei Sábio: os antecedentes

da lenda," in *Estudios de Literatura Medieval: 25 años de la AHLM*, ed. Antonia Martinez Perez and Ana Luisa Baquero Escudero (Murcia: Universidad de Murcia, 2012), 189–96; Leonardo Funes, "La blasfemia del rey sabio: Itinerario narrativo de una leyenda," *Incipit* 13 (1993): 51–70, and 14 (1994): 69–101; Maarten Franssen, "Did King Alfonso of Castile Really Want to Advise God against the Ptolemaic System," *Studies in History and Philosophy of Science* 24 (1993): 313–25.

43. Miguel Pino Abad, "Los andadores de concejo en los fueros municipales castellano-leoneses," *CHD* 6 (1999): 273–300.

44. José María Ortuño Sánchez-Pedreño, "El derecho de asilo en iglesias y sus cementerios en la legislación de Partidas," *Glossae* 5–6 (1993–94): 187–93.

45. *DAAX*, 359–61, 530–31, nos. 330 (21 July 1267), 502 (21 July 1282). Ballesteros, "Itinerario," 107:388, has Saturday, 21 July 1263, the only date that corresponds to the royal itinerary.

46. Torres Fontes, *Fueros y privilegios*, 81, no. 63; *LEst* 97.

47. Isabel Ramos Vázquez, *Arrestos, cárceles y prisiones en los derechos históricos españoles* (Madrid: Ministerio de Interior, 2008), and Ramos Vázquez, "Cárceles públicas y privadas en el derecho medieval y castellano: El delito de cárceles particulares," *REHJ* 28 (2006): 338–86.

48. Berger, "Encyclopedic Dictionary," 738.

49. Gonzalo Martínez Díez, "La tortura judicial en la legislación histórica," *AHDE* 32 (1962): 223–300; Daniel Panateri, "La tortura en las Siete Partidas: la pena, la prueba y la majestad. Un análisis sobre la reinstauración del tormento en la legislación castellana del siglo XIII," *Estudios de Historia de España* 14 (2012): 83–108, and Panateri, "La tortura judicial en las *Siete Partidas* de Alfonso X, el Sabio (un análisis sobre el prólogo al trigésimo título de la *Partida VII*)," in *Palimpsestos: Escrituras y reescrituras de las culturas antigua y medieval*, ed. Gisela Coronado-Schwindt, Viviana Gastaldi, Gabriela Marrón, and Gerardo Rodríguez (Bahía Blanca: EdiUNS, 2013), 267–76.

50. Rafael Serra Ruiz, "Finalidad de la pena en la legislación de las Partidas," *Anales de la Universidad de Murcia. Derecho* 21 (1963): 199–257; Patricia Zambrana Moral, "Rasgos generales de la evolución histórica de la tipología de las penas corporales," *REHJ* 27 (2005): 197–229.

51. Manuel Torres Aguilar, "La pena de exilio: Sus orígenes en el derecho romano," *AHDE* 63–64 (1993–94): 701–86; Augusto Prego de Lis, "La pena de exilio en la legislación Hispanogoda," *Espacio y tiempo en la Percepción de la Antigüedad Tardía* 23 (2006): 515–29.

52. Berger, "Encyclopedic Dictionary," 418–19, 633–34.

53. Keller and Cash, *Daily Life*, plate 67; Sagrario Medrano del Pozo, "'Marisaltos,' la judía segoviana protagonista de la Cantiga CVII de Alfonso X el Sabio," *Iacobus: Revista de Estudios Jacobeos y Medievales* 33–34 (2015): 95–128.

54. Berger, "Encyclopedic Dictionary, 300; Aniceto Masferrer Domingo, *La pena de infamia en el derecho histórico español: Contribución al estudio de la tradición penal europea en el marco del ius commune* (Madrid: Dykinson, 2001); Jeffrey A. Bowman, "Infamy and Proof in Medieval Spain," in *Fama: The Politics of Talk and Reputation in Medieval Europe*, ed. Thelma S. Fenster and Daniel Lord Smail (Ithaca: Cornell University Press, 2005), 95–117; Edward Peters, "Wounded Names: The Medieval Doctrine of Infamy," in *Law in Mediaeval Life and Thought*, ed. Edward B. King and Susan J. Ridyard (Sewanee, TN: Press of the University of the South, 1990), 43–89.

55. *DAAX*, 532–35, no. 503 bis.

56. Emilio de la Cruz Aguilar, "Los juglares en las Partidas," *RFDUC* 9 (1985): 25–33.

57. María Inmaculada Rodríguez Flores, *El perdón real en Castilla (siglos XIII–XVIII)* (Salamanca: Universidad de Salamanca, 1971).

58. *E* 4, 12, 19 in the Martínez Díez edition. *LEst* 38.

59. *CAX(GJ)*, 12–13, 31, 100, chaps. 4, 10, 30; *CSM* 345; O'Callaghan, *Alfonso X and the Cantigas*, 114–20.

60. *CAX(GJ)*, 60–170, chaps. 20–58; O'Callaghan, *Learned King*, 214–33; González Jiménez, *Alfonso X*, 239–72.

14. The Law of the Non-Christian Peoples

1. Manuel González Jiménez, "Alfonso X y las minorías confesionales de mudéjares y judíos," in Rodríguez Llopis, *Alfonso X*, 71–90.

2. Raimundus de Pennaforte, *Summa de poenitentia*, 1,4, in *Summa de iure canonico*, ed. Xavier Ochoa and Aloisio Díez, 2 vols. in 1 (Rome: Universalis Bibliotheca Iuris, 1975), 1:308–17.

3. Dwayne E. Carpenter, *Alfonso X and the Jews: An Edition of and Commentary on "Siete Partidas" 7.24 "De los judíos"* (Berkeley: University of California Press, 1986), 57–61.

4. *CSM* 22.17–18; *CSM* 133.5–8; *CSM* 149.43–46; Elvira Fidalgo Francisco, "Consideración social de los judíos a través de las *Cantigas de Santa Maria*," *Revista de Literatura Medieval* 8 (1996): 91–103, esp. 98–100.

5. L. P. Harvey, *Islamic Spain, 1250 to 1500* (Chicago: University of Chicago Press, 1990), 59–67.

6. Kenneth B. Wolf, "The Earliest Christian Views of Islam," *Church History* 55 (1986): 281–93, and Wolf, "Christian Views of Islam in Early Medieval Spain," in *Medieval Christian Perceptions of Islam*, ed. John V. Tolan (New York: Garland, 1995); Ron Barkai, *Cristianos y musulmanes en la España medieval (El enemigo en el espejo)* (Madrid: Rialp, 1984), 19–53.

7. Norman Daniel, *Islam and the West: The Making of an Image* (Edinburgh: Edinburgh University Press 1960); John Victor Tolan, *Saracens: Islam in the Medieval European Imagination* (New York: Columbia University Press, 2002), 14–93.

8. *Libro de Alexandre*, in *Poetas castellanos anteriores al siglo XV*, ed. Tomás Antonio Sánchez, Pedro José Pidal, and Francisco Janer (Madrid: M. Rivadeneyra, 1864), 219, v. 2346.

9. Rodrigo Jiménez de Rada, *Historia Arabum*, in *Opera* (Valencia: Anubar, 1968), 242–48, chaps. 1–6; Katarzyna Krystyna Starczewska, *El retrato de Mahoma en la Historia Arabum de Jiménez de Rada y en el Prologus Alcorani de Marcos de Toledo: Ejemplos de literatura y confrontación islamo-cristiana* (Barcelona: Universitat Autònoma de Barcelona, 2009); Lucy K. Pick, *Conflict and Coexistence: Archbishop Rodrigo and the Muslims and Jews of Medieval Spain* (Ann Arbor: University of Michigan Press, 2004).

10. Marie Thérèse D'Alverny, "Deux traductions latines du Coran au Moyen Âge," *Archives d'Histoire Doctrinale et Littéraire du Moyen Âge* 16 (1947): 69–131.

11. Lucas of Túy, *Chronicon Mundi*, 166–69, bk. 3, chaps. 5–6.

12. *PCG*, 1:254, 261–65, 267–74, chaps. 451, 466–67, 469, 471–72, 475, 478, 483, 486–89, 493–94.

13. Juan Manuel, *Libro de la caza*, 1, prologue; José Múñoz Sendino, *La escala de Mahoma* (Madrid: Ministerio de Asuntos Exteriores, 1949).

14. Yitzhak Baer, *A History of the Jews in Christian Spain*, 2 vols. (Philadelphia: Jewish Publication Society, 1966), 1:111–85, esp. 115–18; David Romano, "Los judíos y Alfonso X," *Revista de Occidente* 43 (1984): 203–17, and Romano, *De historia judía hispánica* (Barcelona: Universitat de Barcelona, 1991), 162–78; Ezequiel Borgognoni, "Los judíos en la legislación castellana medieval: Notas para su estudio (siglos X–XIII)," *Estudios de Historia de España* 14 (2012): 53–68.

15. *Leyes nuevas*, in *Opúsculos legales*, 2:201–2; Pilar León Tello, *Los judíos de Toledo*, 2 vols. (Madrid: Consejo Superior de Investigaciones Científicas, 1980), 2:378, 382, nos. 9, 13.

16. Amador de los Ríos, *Historia social, política y religiosa*, 2:553–54, no. 3.

17. Demetrio Mansilla, *La documentación pontificia hasta Inocencio III (965–1216)* (Rome: Instituto Español de Estudios eclesiásticos, 1955), 38, no. 22; Álvaro Pelayo, *Speculum regum*, 120, 128.

18. Torres Fontes, *Fueros y privilegios*, 124, no. 114.

19. Torres Fontes, *Documentos del Siglo XIII*, 49–52, 54–56, nos. 55–56, 59.

20. *DAAX*, 128–29, no. 126; Torres Fontes, *Fueros y privilegios*, 57, 74–75, nos. 39, 55; *CSM*, no. 358.

21. Joseph F. O'Callaghan, "The Mudéjars of Castile and Portugal in the Twelfth and Thirteenth Centuries," in *Muslims under Latin Rule, 1100–1300*, ed. James M. Powell (Princeton: Princeton University Press, 1990), 11–56; Manuel González Jiménez and Isabel Montes Romero-Camacho, "Los mudéjares andaluces (siglos XIII–XV): Aproximación al estado de la cuestión y propuesta de un modelo teórico," *Revista d'Historia Medieval* 12 (2001–2): 47–78; Ana Echevarría, "La 'mayoría' mudéjar en León y Castilla: legislación real y distribución de la población (siglos XI–XIII)," *ELEM* 29 (2006): 7–30; Francisco Fernández y González, *Estado social y politico de los mudéjares de Castilla* (Madrid: J. Muñoz, 1866).

22. *MHE*, 1:43, no. 22; Torres Fontes, *Documentos del Siglo XIII*, 76, no. 84; Estal, *Documentos*, 181, no. 5.

23. Torres Fontes, *Fueros y privilegios*, 74–75, no. 55.

24. *DAAX*, 158–60, no.147, and 151, 298–99, nos. 139, 270.

25. Manuel González Jiménez, *En torno a los orígenes de Andalucía*, 2nd ed. (Seville: Universidad de Sevilla, 1988), 69–72, 187–90.

26. Torres Fontes, *Documentos del Siglo XIII*, 78–79, nos. 87–88, and Torres Fontes, *Fueros y privilegios*, 77, 156, nos. 39, 146; Gaibrois de Ballesteros, *Historia del reinado de Sancho IV*, 1:153–54, 179–80.

27. Torres Fontes, *Documentos del Siglo XIII*, 64–65, 108–9, nos. 69, 110.

28. IV Lateran Council 1215, canon 68; Carpenter, *Alfonso X and the Jews*, 91–93.

29. Seville 1252 (art. 41); Valladolid 1258 (art. 38); Seville 1261 (art. 25); Jerez 1268 (art. 30).

30. Dillard, *Daughters of the Reconquest*, 188–90, 206.

31. Carpenter, *Alfonso X and the Jews*, 85–89; James F. Powers, "Frontier Municipal Baths and Social Interaction in Thirteenth-Century Spain," *American Historical Review* 84 (1979): 649–67.

32. Javier Gorosterratzu, *Don Rodrigo Jiménez de Rada, Gran estadista, escritor y prelado* (Pamplona: Bescansa, 1925), 429, 433, 436, nos. 51, 69–70, 77; Mansilla, *Iglesia*, 141–43; Baer, *History*, 1:116–17.

33. Linehan, *Spanish Church*, 4, 6, 11.

34. Valladolid 1258 (art. 26); Seville 1261 (art. 29); Jerez 1268 (arts. 7–8).

35. Albert Bagby, "The Jew in the *Cantigas* of Alfonso X el Sabio," *Speculum* 46 (1971): 670–88; Vikki Hatton and Angus MacKay, "Anti-Semitism in the *Cantigas de Santa María*," *Bulletin of Hispanic Studies* 60 (1983): 189–99, esp. 194.

36. *CLC*, 1:227, 231.

37. González Díez, *Colección diplomática del concejo de Burgos*, 116–18, no. 36, dated incorrectly in 1269 in *Leyes nuevas* in *Opúsculos legales*, 2:203; Norman Roth, "Dar una voz a los judíos: Representación en la España medieval," *AHDE* 56 (1986): 943–52.

38. *Leyes nuevas*, in *Opúsculos legales*, 2:185, 198, 201–2.

39. González Díez, *Colección diplomática del concejo de Burgos*, 150–51, no, 67; Ruiz, *Sociedad*, 181–82.

40. *CLC*, 1:99.

41. Torres Fontes, *Fueros y privilegios*, 17, 57–58, 126, nos. 13, 40, 114, and Torres Fontes, *Documentos del Siglo XIII*, 69–70, no. 85; Estal, *Documentos*, 170, no 2.4; González Díez, *Colección diplomática del concejo de Burgos*, 245–48, 280–81, nos. 153–54, 168.

42. Torres Fontes, *Fueros y privilegios*, 57–58, no. 40.

43. *Leyes Nuevas*, in *Opúsculos legales*, 2:194–96, leyes 27–29; Jerez 1268, arts. 45–47.

44. *LFC* 107; Cortes of Valladolid 1322, art. 60, in *CLC*, 1:344.

45. *MHE*, 1:4–5, 33–36, 263–65, nos. 3, 18, 120; González Díez, *Colección diplomática del concejo de Burgos*, 167, 186–88, nos. 84, 103.

46. León Tello, *Judíos*, 2:382–83, no. 13; Amador de los Ríos, *Historia social, política y religiosa*, 2:531–52.

47. Torres Fontes, *Fueros y privilegios*, 74–75, no. 55.

48. *DAAX*, 114, 126–27, nos. 115, 125; *MHE*, 1:33–36, no. 18.

49. *MHE*, 1:4–5, no. 3; González Díez, *Colección diplomática del concejo de Burgos*, 167, 186–88, nos. 84, 103.

50. *DAAX*, 118, no. 119; Torres Fontes, *Fueros y privilegios*, 35, 57, 74–78, 148, nos. 23, 39, 55, 59–60, 135.

51. *DAAX*, 126–27, 171–73, 246–47, nos. 125, 158, 224; Torres Fontes, *Fueros y privilegios*, 35, 113, nos. 23, 103.

52. *CAX(GJ)*, 210, chap. 74; Baer, *History*, 1:104.

53. Cortes of Palencia 1313 (arts. 32–33); Valladolid 1322 (art. 60), in *CLC*, 1:220, 230, 356–57.

54. Fritz Baer, *Die Juden im christlichen Spanien*, 2 vols. (Berlin: Schocken, 1936), 1:81–87, no. 96; León Tello, *Judíos*, 2:382–84, no. 13; Amador de los Ríos, *Historia social, política y religiosa*, 2:531–52, no. 2.

55. Asunción López Dapena, *Cuentas y Gastos (1292–1294) del Rey D. Sancho IV el Bravo (1284–1295)* (Córdoba: Monte de Piedad y Caja de Ahorros, 1984), 197–99, 635–36; Gaibrois de Ballesteros, *Historia del reinado de Sancho IV*, 3:cccxcvi, no. 583; Ladero Quesada, "Las transformaciones de la fiscalidad," esp. 335.

56. Amador de los Ríos, *Historia social, política y religiosa*, 2:553–54, no. 3 (1289).

57. Gorosterratzu, *Don Rodrigo*, 460, no. 151; Mansilla, *Iglesia*, 146.

58. Dwayne E. Carpenter, "Tolerance and Intolerance: Alfonso X's Attitude towards the Synagogue as Reflected in the *Siete Partidas*," *Kentucky Romance Quarterly* 31 (1984): 31–39.

59. Carpenter, *Alfonso X and the Jews*, 71–74; Fidel Fita, "La sínagoga de Córdoba," *BRAH* 5 (1884) 361–99; Mansilla, *Iglesia*, 145.

60. Dwayne E. Carpenter, "Alfonso el Sabio y los moros: Algunas precisiones legales, históricas y textuales con respecto a Siete Partidas 7.25," *Al-Qantara: Revista de estudios árabes* 7 (1986): 229–52.

61. *Crónica latina*, 100; *The Latin Chronicle*, 141, chap. 73.

62. Manuel González Jiménez, Mercedes Borrero Fernández, and Isabel Montes Romero-Camacho, *Sevilla en tiempos de Alfonso X el Sabio* (Seville: Ayuntamiento de Sevilla, 1987), 84; *Crònica de Jaume I*, 8:34, chap. 441; Gaibrois de Ballesteros, *Historia del reinado de Sancho IV*, 3:lxv, no. 100.

63. Torres Fontes, *Documentos del Siglo XIII*, 19–20, 29–32, 37, nos. 21, 32, 34, 40.

64. Raimundus de Pennaforte, *Summa de poenitentia*, 1, 4, 6–7.

65. *Libro de las Tahurerías*, ed. MacDonald, 1.

66. *Anales Toledanos I*, in *ES*, 23:387, reported an incident of this sort in 1108.

67. Bagby, "The Jew in the *Cantigas*," 675–76; Hatton and MacKay, "Anti-Semitism," 191.

68. Carpenter, *Alfonso X and the Jews*, 79–81.

69. Juan Manuel, *Libro de los estados*, ed. R. B. Tate and I. R. Macpherson (Oxford: Clarendon Press, 1974), 45, bk. 1, chap. 30.

70. Echevarría, "La 'mayoría' mudéjar en León y Castilla," 26.

71. José Sánchez Herrero, *Concilios provinciales y sínodos toledanos de los siglos XIV y XV* (Seville: Consejo Superior de Investigaciones Científicas, 1976), const. 10.

72. *DAAX*, 52–54, no. 142.

73. *Castigos del rey don Sancho IV*, ed. Bizzarri, 205, chap. 21.

74. Estal, *Documentos*, 104, no. 2; Juan Torres Fontes, "El Estatuto concejil murciano en la época de Alfonso X," in *Documentos del Siglo XIII*, xxxi–lxxvi.

75. O'Callaghan, *Learned King*, 181–96, and O'Callaghan, "Mudejars," 21–25; González Jiménez, *Alfonso X*, 163–90; Miguel Ángel Ladero Quesada, "Los mudéjares de Castilla en la baja edad media," *HID* 5 (1978): 257–304.

76. Norman Roth, "Two Jewish Courtiers of Alfonso X called Zag (Isaac)," *Sefarad* 43 (1983):75–85, and Roth, "Jewish Collaborators in Alfonso's Scientific Work," in Burns, *Emperor of Culture*, 59–71.

77. *MHE*, 1:308–21, no. 140; Baer, *History*, 1:124–28.

78. González Díez, *Colección diplomática del concejo de Burgos*, 158–60, no. 77.

79. *CAX(GJ)*, 209–10, chap. 74; Baer, *History*, 1:129–30; González Jiménez, *Alfonso X*, 338.

80. David Goldstein, *The Jewish Poets of Spain* (Baltimore: Penguin Books, 1965), 177.

81. *FJ* 12, 2, 3–18; 12, 3, 1–28; III Toledo (589), canon 14; IV Toledo (633) canons 63–66; VI Toledo (636) canon 3; VIII Toledo (653), canon 12; X Toledo (656) canon 7; *Concilios visigóticos e hispano-romanos*, ed. José Vives, Tomás Marín, Gonzalo Martínez (Barcelona-Madrid: Consejo Superior de Investigaciones Científicas, 1963), 129, 213–14, 236–37, 285, 313–14.

15. The Juridical Achievement of Alfonso X

1. Burns, *Las Siete Partidas*, 1:xix.
2. *CLC*, 4:194–219.
3. *Recopilación de Leyes destos reynos* (Alcalá de Henares: Juan Iñiguez Lequerica, 1598).
4. *Los Códigos españoles*, vols. 7–12.
5. E. N. Van Kleffens, *Hispanic Law until the End of the Middle Ages with a Note on the Continued Validity after the Fifteenth Century of Medieval Hispanic Legislation in Spain, the Americas, Asia and Africa* (Edinburgh: Edinburgh University Press, 1968), 255–85.
6. Burns, *Las Siete Partidas*, 1:xii–xiii.
7. *Alphonse X, Primeyra Partida: Edition et Étude*, ed. José de Azevedo Ferreira (Braga: Instituto Nacional de Investigação Científica, 1980).
8. José Domingues, "A tradição medieval das Sete Partidas em Portugal," *7 Partidas Digital: Edición crítica de las Siete Partidas*, 1 June 2017, https://7partidas.hypotheses. org/; Domingues, "As Partidas de Afonso X e a natureza jurídico-política do estado portugués," in *Natura e natureza no tempo de Afonso X o Sabio*, ed. José Carlos Ribeiro Miranda and Maria Rosário Ferreira (Porto: Humus, 2015), 31–49; and Domingues, "O elemento castelhano-leonês na formação do Direito Medieval portugués," *CHD* 21 (2014): 213–27, esp. 218–22; Clara Araujo Barros, *Versões portuguesas da legislação de Afonso X: Estudo linguístico-Discursivo* (Porto: Universidade do Porto, 2010).
9. Ramon Llull, *The Book of the Order of Chivalry / Llibre de l'Ordre de Cavalleria, / Libro de la Orden de Caballería*, ed. and trans. by Antonio Cortijo Ocaña (Amsterdam: John Benjamins, 2015).
10. Ramon d'Abadal, *Las Partidas a Catalunya durant l'edat mitja* (Barcelona: Masso, Casas, 1914), 11.
11. Gemma Avenoza, "Las Partidas en catalán," *7 Partidas Digital: Edición crítica de las Siete Partidas*, 21 December 2017, https://7partidas.hypotheses.org/; David A. Cohen, "Secular Pragmatism and Thinking about War in Some Court Writings of Pere III el Cerimoniós," in Kagay and Villalon, *Crusaders, Condottieri, and Cannon*, 21–53, esp. 35–53.
12. John T. Vance, "The Old Spanish Code of 'Las Siete Partidas' in Mexico," *American Bar Association Journal* 14 (1928): 219–24; Helen L. Glagett and David M. Valderrama, *A Revised Guide to the Law and Legal Literature of Mexico* (Washington, DC: Library of Congress, 1973), 62–388.
13. Bernardino Bravo Lira, "Vigencia de las Partidas en Chile," *REHJ* 10 (1985): 43; *Leyes del Ecuador, de procedimiento civil* (Quito: F. Bermeo, 1855), 1, chap. 1; José Francisco Gálvez, "Aproximación al estudio de la pervivencia de las Partidas en el derecho Peruano," in *XIII Congreso del Instituto Internacional de Historia del Derecho Indiano: Actas y estudios*, 2 vols. (San Juan: Asamblea Legislativa de Puerto Rico, 2003), 2:707–28.
14. Timothy G. Kearley, "The Enigma of Samuel Parsons Scott," *Roman Legal Tradition* 10 (2014): 1–37.
15. Louis Moreau-Lislet and Henry Carleton, *The Laws of the Siete Partidas which are still in Force in the State of Louisiana*, 2 vols. (New Orleans: James McKarraher, 1820).
16. Agustín Parise, "Translators' Preface to the Laws of Las Siete Partidas which are Still in Force in the State of Louisiana," *Journal of Civil Law Studies* 7 (2014): 311–53.

17. Burns, "King Alfonso and the Wild West"; and Burns, *Las Siete Partidas*, 1:xix–xxix; Marilyn Stone, "Desde las Siete Partidas a los códigos civiles norteamericanos," *Actas del Congreso de la Asociación internacional de Hispanistas* 11 (1992): 25–33.

18. Joseph W. McKnight, "The Spanish Watercourses of Texas," in *Essays in Legal History in Honor of Felix Frankfurter* (New York: Bobbs-Merrill, 1966), 373–86.

19. Peter Reich, "Western Courts and the Privatization of Hispanic Mineral Rights since 1850: An Alchemy of Title," *Columbia Journal of Environmental Law* 23 (1998): 57–87, and Reich, "Siete Partidas in My Saddlebags: The Transmission of Hispanic Law from Antebellum Louisiana to Texas and California," *Tulane European And Civil Law Forum* 22 (2007): 79–88.

20. Joseph W. McKnight, "Protection of the Family Home from Creditors: The Sources and Evolution of a Legal Principle," *Southwestern Historical Quarterly* 86 (1982): 370–99, and McKnight, "Spanish Law for the Protection of Surviving Spouses in North America," *AHDE* 57 (1987): 365–406.

21. Márquez Villanueva, *El concepto cultural alfonsí*, 19–27.

22. "Pence Praises Arpaio in Arizona," http://www.youtube.com.

23. *MHE*, 2:7–8, no. 163.

24. Pedro López de Ayala, *Crónica del Rey don Juan, primero de Castilla é de Leon*, Año 7, chap. 5, in *BAE* 68:95.

✒ Bibliography

Narrative Sources

Anales Toledanos III. In *ES*, 23:411–24.

Biblioteca de Autores Españoles desde la formación del lenguaje hasta nuestros días. 302 vols. to date. Madrid: Imprenta de los Sucesores de Hernando et al., 1846–1993.

Chronicle of Alfonso X. Trans. Shelby Thacker and José Escobar. Lexington: University Press of Kentucky, 2002.

Chronicon de Cardeña. In *ES*, 23:370–80.

Crónica de Alfonso X según el Ms. II/2777 de la Biblioteca del Palacio Real (Madrid). Ed. Manuel González Jiménez. Murcia: Real Academia Alfonso X el Sabio, 1998.

Crònica de Jaume I. Ed. J. M. Casacuberta and E. Bague. 9 vols. Barcelona: Barcino, 1926–62.

Crónica de la población de Ávila. Ed. Amparo Hernández Segura. Valencia: Anubar, 1966.

Crónica del Rey don Alfonso Décimo. In *BAE*, 66:3–66.

Crónica del Rey don Fernando Cuarto. In *BAE*, 66:91–170.

Crónica del Rey don Sancho el Bravo. In *BAE*, 66:69–90.

Crónica geral de 1344. Ed. L. F. Lindley Cintra. 6 vols. Lisbon: Academia Portuguesa da História, 1952–83.

Crónica latina de los reyes de Castilla. Ed. Luis Charlo Brea. Cádiz: Universidad de Cádiz, 1984.

Crónicas anónimas de Sahagún. Ed. Antonio Ubieto Arteta. Zaragoza: Anubar, 1987.

Desclot, Bernat. *Crònica*. Ed. M. Coll i Alentorn. 5 vols. Barcelona: Barcino, 1949–51.

Estoria de España. See *Primera Crónica General*.

Fita, Fidel. "Biografías de San Fernando y de Alfonso el Sabio por Juan Gil de Zamora." *BRAH* 5 (1884): 308–28.

General Estoria: Primera Parte. Ed. Antonio García Solalinde. Madrid: Centro de Estudios Históricos, 1930.

González Jiménez, Manuel. "Unos Anales del Reinado de Alfonso X." *BRAH* 192 (1995): 461–92.

González Jiménez, Manuel, and Ángel Luís Molina Molina. *Los Milagros Romanzados de Santo Domingo de Silos de Pero Marín*. Murcia: Real Academia Alfonso X El Sabio, 2008.

Gonzalo de la Hinojosa. *Crónica de España del Arzobispo Don Rodrigo Jiménez de Rada*. In *Colección de documentos inéditos para la historia de España*, ed. Martín Fernández de Navarrete et al., vols. 105–6. Madrid: José Perales y Martínez, 1893.

Guillaume de Nangis. *Gesta Philippi tertii Francorum regum*. In *Recueil des Historiens des Gaules et de la France*, 20:466–539. Paris: Victor Palmé, 1894.

Ibn Khaldūn. *Histoire des Berbères et des dynasties musulmanes de l'Afrique Septentrionale.* Trans. Baron de Slane. 4 vols. Paris: P. Guethner, 1852–56.

Jofré de Loaysa. *Crónica de los reyes de Castilla, Fernando III, Alfonso X, Sancho IV y Fernando IV, 1248–1305.* Ed. Antonio García Martínez. Murcia: Academia Alfonso X el Sabio, 1982.

The Latin Chronicle of the Kings of Castile. Trans. Joseph F. O'Callaghan. Tempe: Arizona Center for Medieval and Renaissance Studies, 2002.

Livy. *The History of Rome, Books 1–5.* Trans. Valerie M. Warrior. Indianapolis: Hackett Publishing, 2006.

Lomax, Derek W. "Una crónica inédita de Silos." In *Homenaje a Fray Justo Pérez de Urbel,* 1:323–37. Silos: Abadía de Silos, 1976.

López de Ayala, Pedro. *Crónica del Rey don Juan, primero de Castilla é de Leon.* In *BAE,* 68:65–159.

Lucan. *The Civil War Books I–X (Pharsalia).* Trans. J. D. Duff. Cambridge, MA: Harvard University Press, 1962.

Lucas of Túy. *Chronicon Mundi.* Ed. Emma Falque. Corpus Christianorum, Continuatio Medievalis 74. Turnhout: Brepols, 2003.

——. *Crónica de España.* Ed. Julio Puyol. Madrid: Revista de Archivos, Bibliotecas y Museos, 1926.

Matthew Paris. *Chronica Majora.* Ed. H. R. Luard. 7 vols. Rolls Series. London: Longman, 1872–83.

Pedro Marín. "Miraculos romanzados." In Sebastián Vergara, *Vida e milagros de Santo Domingo de Silos,* 128–229. Madrid: Francisco del Hierro, 1736.

Primera Crónica General. Ed. Ramón Menéndez Pidal. 2 vols. Madrid: Editorial Gredos, 1955.

Rodrigo Jiménez de Rada. *Historia Arabum.* In *Opera.* Valencia: Anubar, 1968.

——. *Historia de rebus Hispanie sive Historia Gothica.* Ed. Juan Fernández Valverde. Corpus Christianorum, Continuatio Mediaevalis 72. Turnhout: Brepols, 1987.

Documentary Sources

Agapito y Revilla, Juan. *Los privilegios de Valladolid.* Valladolid: Sociedad Castellana de Escursiones, 1906.

Alamo, Juan del. *Colección diplomática de San Salvador de Oña (822–1284).* 2 vols. Madrid: Consejo Superior de Investigaciones Científicas, 1950.

Ayala Martínez, Carlos de. *Libro de privilegios de la Orden de San Juan de Jerusalén en Castilla y León (siglos XII–XV).* Madrid: Editorial Complutense, 1995.

Baer, Fritz. *Die Juden im christlichen Spanien.* 2 vols. Berlin: Schocken, 1936.

Ballesteros, Antonio. "El Fuero de Atienza." *BRAH* 68 (1916): 264–70.

——. *El Itinerario de Alfonso el Sabio.* Madrid: Tipografía de Archivos, 1935.

——. "El itinerario de Alfonso X, rey de Castilla." *BRAH* 104 (1934): 49–88, 455–516; 105 (1934): 123–80; 106 (1935): 83–150; 107 (1935): 21–76, 381–418; 108 (1936): 15–42; 109 (1936): 377–460.

Barrios García, Ángel. *Documentación medieval de la catedral de Ávila.* Salamanca: Universidad de Salamanca, 1981.

Barrios García, Ángel, and Alberto Martin Expósito. *Documentación medieval de los Archivos municipales de Béjar y Candelario.* Salamanca: Universidad de Salamanca, 1986.

Barrios García, Ángel, Alberto Martin Expósito, and Gregorio del Ser Quijano. *Documentación medieval del Archivo municipal de Alba de Tormes*. Salamanca: Universidad de Salamanca, 1982.

Barrios García, Ángel, José María Monsalvo, and Gregorio del Ser Quijano. *Documentación medieval del Archivo municipal de Ciudad Rodrigo*. Salamanca: Diputación Provincial de Salamanca, 1988.

Beltrán de Heredia, Vicente. *Cartulario de la Universidad de Salamanca (1218–1600)*. 6 vols. Salamanca: Ediciones Universidad, 1970–73.

Beltrán Suárez, María Soledad. "Privilegios de Alfonso X a la catedral de Oviedo." *Asturiensia medievalia* 5 (1986): 155–69.

Benavides, Antonio. *Memorias de D. Fernando IV de Castilla*. 2 vols. Madrid: José Rodríguez, 1860.

Berger, Elie. *Les Registres d'Innocent IV*. 4 vols. Paris: Bibliothèque des Écoles françaises d'Athènes et de Rome, 1884–1921.

Berjano, Daniel. "Antigua carta de hermandad entre Plasencia y Talavera." *BRAH 35* (1899): 317–18.

Bourel de la Roncière, Charles. *Les registres d'Alexandre IV (1254–1261)*. Paris: Bibliothèque des Écoles françaises d'Athènes et de Rome, 1902–59.

Bullarium Ordinis Militiae de Alcántara. Madrid: Antonio Marín, 1759.

Burns, Robert I., SJ. *Diplomatarium of the Crusader Kingdom of Valencia: The Registered Charters of Its Conqueror Jaume I, 1257–1276*. 4 vols. Princeton, NJ: Princeton University Press, 1985–2007.

Daumet, Georges. "Les testaments d'Alphonse X le Savant, roi de Castille." *Bibliothèque de l'Ecole des Chartes* 67 (1906): 75–99.

Domínguez Sánchez, Santiago. *Documentos de Clemente IV (1265–1268) referentes a España*. León: Universidad de León, 1996.

——. *Documentos de Gregorio IX (1227–1241) referentes a España*. León: Universidad de León, 2004.

——. *Documentos de Gregorio X (1272–1276) referentes a España*. León: Universidad de León, 1997.

——. *Documentos de Nicolás III (1277–1280) referentes a España*. León: Universidad de León, 1999.

Escagedo Salmón, Mateo. *Colección diplomática: Privilegios, escrituras, y bulas en pergamino de la Insigne Real Iglesia Colegial de Santillana*. 2 vols. Santoña: Dialco Mnemaen, 1927.

Escudero de la Peña, J. M. "Súplica hecha al Papa Juan XXI para que absolviese al Rey de Castilla, D. Alfonso X, del juramento de no acuñar otra moneda que los dineros prietos." *RABM* ser. 1, 2 (1872): 58–60.

España Sagrada: Teatro geográfico-histórico de la Iglesia de España. 51 vols. Madrid: A. Marin, 1754–1879.

Estal, Juan Manuel del. *Documentos inéditos de Alfonso X el sabio y el Infante su hijo don Sancho*. Alicante: Juan Manuel del Estal, 1984.

Ferotin, Marius. *Recueil des chartes de l'abbaye de Silos*. Paris: Imprimerie Nationale 1897.

Floriano, Antonio. *Documentación histórica del Archivo municipal de Cáceres (1229–1471)*. Cáceres: Diputación provincial, 1987.

García Luján, José Antonio. *Privilegios reales de la catedral de Toledo (1086–1462): Formación del patrimonio de la S.I.C.P. a través de las donaciones reales*. 2 vols. Toledo: Imprenta Torres, 1982.

González, Julio. *Repartimiento de Sevilla*. 2 vols. Madrid: Consejo Superior de Investigaciones Científicas, 1951. Reprint, Seville: Ayuntamiento de Sevilla 1998.

González, Tomás. *Colección de cédulas, cartas patentes, provisiones, reales ordenes y documentos concernientes las provincias vascongadas*. 6 vols. Madrid: Imprenta real, 1829–33.

González Balasch, María Teresa. *Tumbo B de La Catedral de Santiago*. Santiago de Compostela: Edicios de Castro, 2004.

González Díez, Emiliano. *Colección diplomática del concejo de Burgos (884–1369)*. Burgos: Ayuntamiento de Burgos, 1984.

González Jiménez, Manuel. *Diplomatario Andaluz de Alfonso X*. Seville: El Monte. Caja de Huelva y Sevilla, 1991.

González Jiménez, Manuel, and María Antonia Carmona Ruiz. *Documentación e itinerario de Alfonso X el Sabio*. Seville: Universidad de Sevilla, 2012.

Guiraud, Jean. *Les registres d'Urbain IV (1261–1264)*. Paris: Albert Fontemoing, 1892–1958.

Lera Maillo, José Carlos de. *Catálogo de documentos de la catedral de Zamora*. Zamora: Instituto de Estudios Zamoranos, 1999.

López Dapena, Asunción. *Cuentas y Gastos (1292–1294) del Rey D. Sancho IV el Bravo (1284–1295)*. Córdoba: Monte de Piedad y Caja de Ahorros, 1984.

López de Silanes, Ciriaco, and Eliseo Sainz Ripa. *Colección diplomática Calceatense: Archivo Catedral (años 1125–1397)*. Logroño: Consejo Superior de Investigaciones Científicas, 1985.

López Ferreiro, Antonio. *Colección diplomática de Galicia Histórica*. Santiago de Compostela: Tipografía Galaica, 1901.

Mansilla, Demetrio. *La documentación pontificia hasta Inocencio III (965–1216)*. Rome: Instituto Español de Estudios eclesiásticos, 1955.

Martin, François Olivier. *Les registres de Martin IV (1281–1285)*. Paris: Bibliothèque des Écoles françaises d'Athènes et de Rome, 1901.

Martín, José Luis. *Documentos zamoranos*. Vol. 1, *Documentos del Archivo Catedralicio de Zamora, Primera Parte (1128–1261)*. Salamanca: Universidad de Salamanca, 1982.

Martín, José Luis, Luis Miguel Villar García, Florencio Marcos Rodríguez, and Marciano Sánchez Rodriguez. *Documentos de los archivos catedralicios y diocesano de Salamanca (S. XII–XIII)*. Salamanca: Universidad de Salamanca, 1977.

Martín Expósito, Alberto, and José María Monsalvo Antón. *Documentación medieval del Archivo municipal de Ledesma*. Salamanca: Universidad de Salamanca, 1986.

Martín Fuertes, José Antonio, and César Álvarez Álvarez. *Archivo histórico municipal de León: Catálogo de los documentos*. León: Centro de Estudios e Investigación "San Isidoro," 1998.

Martín Fuertes, José Antonio, María del Carmen Rodríguez López, and María Jesús Pradal Garcia. *Colección documental del Archivo Municipal de León, 1219–1400*. León: Centro de Estudios e Investigación "San Isidoro." 1998.

Memorial Histórico Español: Colección de documentos, opúsculos y antigüedades. 49 vols. Madrid: Real Academia de la Historia, 1851–1948.

Menéndez Pidal, Ramón. *Documentos lingüísticos de España: Reino de Castilla*. Madrid: Junta para Ampliación de Estudios e Investigaciones científicas, 1919.

Miguel Vigil, Ciriaco. *Colección histórico-diplomática del ayuntamiento de Oviedo.* Oviedo: Pardo Gusano, 1889.

Muñoz y Romero, Tomás. *Colección de fueros municipales y cartas pueblas de los reinos de Castilla, León, Corona de Aragón y Navarra.* Madrid: José María Alonso, 1847.

Oceja Gonzalo, Isabel. *Documentación del monasterio de San Salvador de Oña (1032–1284).* Burgos: J. M. Garrido Garrido, 1983.

——. *Documentación del monasterio de San Salvador de Oña (1285–1310).* Burgos: J. M. Garrido Garrido, 1986.

Palacio, Timoteo Domingo, Agustin Millares Carlo, and Eulogio Varela Hervias. *Documentos del Archivo general de la villa de Madrid.* 6 vols. Madrid: Imprenta Municipal, 1888–1943.

Palacios Martín, Bonifacio. *Colección diplomática de la Orden de Alcántara (1157?–1494): De los orígenes a 1454.* Madrid: Editorial Complutense, 2000.

Pereda Llarena, F. Javier. *Documentación de la catedral de Burgos (1254–1293).* Burgos: J. M. Garrido Garrido, 1984.

Pérez Valera, Isabel. *Indice de los documentos del Archivo municipal de Ciudad Real, 1255–1899.* Ciudad Real: Instituto de Estudios Manchegos, 1962.

Pons Boigues, Francisco. *Apuntes sobre las escrituras mozárabes toledanas que se conservan en el Archivo Histórico Nacional.* Madrid: Tello, 1897.

Privilegios reales y viejos documentos. 17 vols. Madrid: Joyas Bibliográficas, 1963–80.

Quintana Prieto, Augusto. *Tumbo Viejo de San Pedro de Montes.* León: Centro de Estudios e Investigaciones "San Isidoro," 1971.

Represa Rodríguez, Amando. "Notas para el estudio de la ciudad de Segovia en los siglos XII–XIV." *Estudios Segovianos* 1 (1949): 273–319.

Rodríguez de Lama, Ildefonso. *Colección diplomática medieval de la Rioja: Documentos siglo XIII.* Logroño: Instituto de Estudios Riojanos, 1989.

——. *La documentación pontificia de Alejandro IV (1254–1261).* Rome: Instituto Español de Historia Eclesiástica, 1976.

Ruiz Asencio, José Manuel, and José Antonio Martín Fuertes. *Colección documental del Archivo de La Catedral de León (1230–1269).* León: Centro de Estudios e Investigación "San Isidoro," 1993.

Sáez, Carlos. *Los pergaminos del Archivo Municipal de Alcalá de Henares.* Alcalá de Henares: Universidad de Alcalá de Henares, 1990.

Sáez, Emilio. *Colección diplomática de Sepúlveda.* Segovia: Diputación provincial de Segovia, 1956.

Sáez, Emilio, Rafael Gibert, Manuel Alvar, and Atilano G. Ruiz-Zorrilla. *Los fueros de Sepúlveda.* Sepúlveda: Diputación Provincial de Segovia, 1953.

Sánchez Albornoz, Claudio. "Diviseros y proprietarios: un documento castellano que los equipara." *CHE* 5 (1946): 170–72.

Sánchez Belda, Luis. *Documentos reales de la Edad media referentes a Galicia: Catálogo de los conservados en la Sección de Clero del Archivo Histórico Nacional.* Madrid: Dirección general de Museos y Bibliotecas, 1953.

Sánchez Rodríguez, Marciano. *Tumbo blanco de Zamora.* Salamanca: Varona, 1985.

Santos Coco, Francisco. "Documentos del Archivo-Catedral de Badajoz." *Revista de Estudios Extremeños* 1 (1927): 78–85.

Sanz Fuentes, María Josefa. "Repartimiento de Écija." *HID* 3 (1976): 535–51.

Sanz y Diaz, Clementino. *Reseña cronológica de algunos documentos conservados en el Archivo de la Catedral de Cuenca*. Cuenca: Calasanz, 1965.

Scheffer-Boichorst, Paul. "Kleinere Forschungen zur Geschichte Alfons X von Castilien." *Mitteilungen des Instituts für Osterreichische Geschichtsforschung 9* (1888): 226–48.

Segura Moreno, Manuel. *Estudio del códice gótico (siglo XIII) de la catedral de Jaén*. Jaén: Instituto de Estudios Giennenses, 1976.

Serrano, Luciano. *Cartulario del Infantadgo de Covarrubias*. Madrid: Gregorio del Amo, 1907.

——. *Cartulario de San Pedro de Arlanza*. Madrid: Junta para Ampliación de Estudios e Investigaciones Científicas, 1925.

Tanner, Norman. *Decrees of the Ecumenical Councils*. Washington, DC: Georgetown University Press, 1990.

Torres Fontes, Juan. *Documentos de Alfonso X el Sabio*. Murcia: Real Academia Alfonso el Sabio, 2008.

——. *Documentos del Siglo XIII*. Murcia: Academia Alfonso X el Sabio, 1969.

——. *Fueros y privilegios de Alfonso X el Sabio al Reino de Murcia*. Murcia: Academia Alfonso X el Sabio, 1973.

Ubieto Arteta, Antonio. *Colección diplomática de Cuéllar*. Segovia: Diputación provincial de Segovia, 1961.

Vignau, Vicente. *Cartulario del monasterio de Eslonza*. Madrid: Viuda de Hernando, 1885.

Villar Garcia, Luis Miguel. *Documentación medieval de la catedral de Segovia (1115–1300)*. Salamanca: Universidad de Salamanca, 1990.

Legal Sources

Afonso X: Foro real. Ed. José de Azevedo Ferreira. 2 vols. Lisboa: Instituto Nacional de Investigação Científica, 1987.

Alphonse X, Primeyra Partida: Edition et Étude. Ed. José de Azevedo Ferreira. Braga: Instituto Nacional de Investigação Cientifica, 1980.

Argüello, Vicente. "Memoria sobre el valor de las monedas de d. Alfonso el sabio." *Memorias de la Real Academia de la Historia* 8 (1852): 1–58.

Ballesteros, Antonio. "Las Cortes de 1252." *Anales de la Junta para Ampliación de Estudios e Investigaciones cientificas* 3 (1911): 114–43.

Beaumanoir, Philippe de. *Coutumes de Beauvaisis*. Ed. A. Salmon. 2 vols. Paris: Picard, 1899–1900.

——. *The Coutumes de Beauvaisis of Philippe de Beaumanoir*. Trans. F. R. P. Akehurst. Philadelphia: University of Pennsylvania Press, 1992.

Benavides Checa, José. *El Fuero de Plasencia*. Rome: Lobesi, 1896.

Bermejo Cabrero, José Luis. "Un nuevo texto afin al Fuero Viejo de Castilla: 'El Fuero de los fijosdalgos y las Fazañas del Fuero de Castilla.'" *AHDE 69* (1999): 240–74.

Bracton, Henry de. *De legibus et consuetudinibus regni Angliae*. Ed. Samuel Thorne. 4 vols. Cambridge, MA: Harvard University Press, 1968–77.

Burns, Robert I., ed. *Las Siete Partidas*. Trans. Samuel Parsons Scott. 5 vols. Philadelphia: University of Pennsylvania Press, 2001.

Castro, Américo, and Federico de Onís. *Fueros leoneses de Zamora, Salamanca, Ledesma y Alba de Tormes*. Madrid: Junta para Ampliación de Estudios e Investigaciones Científicas, 1916.

Cerdá Ruiz-Funes, Joaquín. "La Margarita de los pleitos de Fernando Martínez de Zamora." *AHDE* 20 (1950): 634–738.

The Code of Cuenca: Municipal Law on the Twelfth-Century Castilian Frontier. Trans. James F. Powers. Philadelphia: University of Pennsylvania Press, 2000.

Los Códigos españoles concordados y anotados. 2nd ed. 12 vols. Madrid: Antonio de San Martín, 1873–74.

Concilios visigóticos e hispano-romanos. Ed. José Vives, Tomás Marín, and Gonzalo Martínez. Barcelona-Madrid: Consejo Superior de Investigaciones Científicas, 1963.

Corpus iuris canonici. Ed. E. A. Friedberg. 2 vols. Leipzig: Bernhard Tauchnitz, 1879–81.

Corpus Iuris Civilis. Ed. Paul Kreuger, Theodor Mommsen, Rudolf Schoell, and Wilhelm Kroll. 3 vols. Berlin: Weidmann, 1877–88.

The Digest of Justinian. Trans. Alan Watson. 2 vols. Philadelphia: University of Pennsylvania Press, 1985.

Espéculo. Ed. Gonzalo Martínez Díez and José Manuel Ruiz Asencio. Ávila: Fundación Sánchez Albornoz, 1985.

Espéculo: Texto jurídico atribuído al rey de Castilla don Alfonso el Sabio. Ed. Robert A. MacDonald. Madison: Hispanic Seminary of Medieval Studies, 1990.

Floranes, Rafael. "Flores de las Leyes: Suma legal del Maestre Jacobo Ruiz, llamado de las Leyes." In *MHE*, 2:138–248.

Fuero de Cuenca: Formas primitiva y sistemáticas. Texto latín, texto castellano y adaptación del Fuero de Iznatoraf. Ed. Rafael Ureña y Smenjaud. Madrid: Tipografía de Archivos, 1935.

Fuero Juzgo en latín y castellano. Ed. Real Academia Española. Madrid: Ibarra, 1815.

Fuero real. Ed. Gonzalo Martínez Díez, José Manuel Ruiz Asencio, and C. Hernández Alonso. Ávila: Fundación Claudio Sánchez Albornoz, 1988.

Fuero real del rey d. Alonso el Sabio. In *Opúsculos legales,* 2:1–169.

Fuero real del Rey Don Alonso el Sabio, copiado del Códice del Escorial señalado ij.z.8. Ed. Real Academia de la Historia. Madrid: Imprenta Real, 1836.

El Fuero viejo de Castilla. Ed. Ángel Barrios García, Gregorio del Ser Quijano, and Benjamín González Alonso. Salamanca: Junta de Castilla y León-Europa, 1996.

García Gallo, Alfonso. "Aportación al estudio de los Fueros." *AHDE* 26 (1956): 387–446.

——. "El Concilio de Coyanza: Contribución al estudio del Derecho canónico español en la alta edad media." *AHDE* 20 (1950): 275–633.

——. "Textos de derecho territorial castellano." *AHDE* 13 (1936–41): 308–96.

——. "Una colección de fazañas castellanas del siglo XII." *AHDE* 11 (1934): 522–31.

García Ramila, Ismael. "Ordenamientos de posturas y otros capítulos generales otorgados a la ciudad de Burgos por el rey Alfonso X." *Hispania: Revista española de historia* 5 (1945): 179–235.

González Jiménez, Manuel. "Cortes de Sevilla de 1261." *HID* 25 (1998): 295–312.

Gross, Georg. "Las Cortes de 1252: Ordenamiento otorgado al concejo de Burgos en las Cortes celebradas en Sevilla el 12 de octubre de 1252 (según el original)." *BRAH* 182 (1985): 95–114.

Hernández Sánchez, Francisco Javier. "Las Cortes de Toledo de 1207." In *Las Cortes de Castilla y León en la Edad media,* ed. Julio Valdeón, 1: 221–63. Valladolid: Cortes de Castilla y León 1988.

——. "Las posturas publicadas por las Cortes de Toledo de 1207 (Nueva edición)." *HID* 38 (2011): 253–66.

Iglesia Ferreirós, Antonio. "El Privilegio general concedido a las Extremaduras en 1264 por Alfonso X: Edición del ejemplar enviado a Peñafiel en 15 de abril de 1264." *AHDE* 53 (1983): 456–521.

Jacobo de las leyes. *Dotrinal de los pleitos.* In Ureña y Smenjaud and Bonilla San Martín, *Obras del Maestre Jacobo de las leyes,* 185–376.

——. *Flores de derecho.* In Ureña y Smenjaud and Bonilla San Martín, *Obras del Maestre Jacobo de las leyes,* 1–184.

——. *Summa de los nueve tiempos de los pleitos.* Ed. Jean Roudil. Paris: Klincksieck, 1986.

Jordán de Asso y del Río, Ignacio, and Miguel de Manuel y Rodríguez. *El Fuero Viejo de Castilla.* Madrid: Joachín Ibarra, 1771.

——. *El Ordenamiento de leyes que d. Alfonso XI hizo en las Cortes de Alcalá de Henares el año de mil trescientos y cuarenta y ocho.* Madrid: Antonio Calleja, 1847.

Justinian's Institutes. Ed. Paul Krueger. Trans. Peter Birks and Grant McLeod. Ithaca: Cornell University Press, 1987.

Keniston, Hayward. *Fuero de Guadalajara.* New York: Kraus Reprint, 1965.

Leyes del Ecuador, de procedimiento civil. Quito: F. Bermeo, 1855.

Leyes del estilo et declaraciones sobre las Leyes del Fuero. In *Opúsculos legales,* 2:235–352.

Leyes nuevas dadas por el rey D. Alfonso el Sabio después del Fuero real. In *Opúsculos legales,* 2:181–209.

Leyes para los Adelantados mayores dadas por el rey d. Alonso el Sabio. In *Opúsculos legales,* 2:173–77.

Liber Augustalis. In Jean L. A. Huillard-Breholles, *Historia Diplomatica Friderici II,* 4.1:1–178. Paris: H. Plon, 1854.

Liber Augustalis or Constitutions of Melfi Promulgated by the Emperor Frederick II for the Kingdom of Sicily in 1231. Trans. James M. Powell. Syracuse: Syracuse University Press, 1971.

Liber Iudiciorum. In *Leges Visigothorum,* ed. Karl Zeumer, Monumenta Germaniae Historica. Leges 1, 33–456. Hannover: Hahn, 1902.

Libro de las Tahurerías: A Special Code of Law, Concerning Gambling, Drawn Up by Maestro Roldán at the Command of Alfonso X of Castile. Ed. Robert A. MacDonald. Madison: Hispanic Seminary, 1995.

Libro de los Adelantados Mayores: Regulations Attributed to Alfonso X of Castile, Concerning the King's Vicar in the Judiciary and in Territorial Administration. Ed. Robert A. MacDonald. New York: Hispanic Seminary, 2000.

Libro de los fueros de Castiella. Ed. Galo Sánchez. Barcelona, 1924. Reprint, Barcelona: El Albir, 1981.

López Ferreiro, Antonio. *Fueros municipales de Santiago y de su tierra.* Santiago de Compostela: Seminario Central, 1895. Reprint, Madrid: Ediciones Castilla, 1975.

López Ortiz, José. "La colección conocida con el título 'Leyes Nuevas' y atríbuída a Alfonso X el Sabio." *AHDE* 16 (1945): 5–70.

Majada Neila, Jesús. *Fuero de Zamora.* Salamanca: Librería Cervantes, 1983.

Maldonado, José, and and Emilio Sáez. *El Fuero de Coria.* Madrid: Instituto de Estudios de Administración Local, 1949.

Millares Carlo, Agustín, and Agustín Gómez Iglesias. *El Fuero de Madrid.* Madrid: Raycar, 1963.

Moreau-Lislet, Louis, and Henry Carleton. *The Laws of the Siete Partidas which are still in Force in the State of Louisiana.* 2 vols. New Orleans: James McKarraher, 1820.

Múñoz y Romero, Tomás. *Colección de fueros municipales y cartas públicas.* Madrid: J. M. Alonso, 1847.

O'Callaghan, Joseph F. "Una ley de las Cortes de Sevilla de 1252 incorporada en la Primera Partida del rey don Alfonso X, el Sabio." *AHDE* 84 (2014): 789–96.

Opúsculos legales del Rey Don Alfonso el Sabio. Ed. Real Academia de la Historia. 2 vols. Madrid: Imprenta Real, 1836.

Ordenamiento de Alcalá. In *CLC,* 1:492–593.

Ordenamiento de las leyes que D. Alfonso XI hizo en las Cortes de Alcalá el año de mil trescientos y cuarenta y ocho. Ed. Ignacio Jordán de Asso y del Río and Miguel de Manuel y Rodríguez. Madrid: Calleja, 1847.

Ordenamiento de las Tafurerías que fue fecho en la era de mil e trescientos e quatorse años por el rey don Alfonso X. In *Opúsculos legales,* 2:213–31.

Orellana Calderón, Raúl. "La Tercera Partida de Alfonso X el Sabio: Estudio y edición crítica de los Títulos XVIII al XX." PhD thesis, Universidad de Madrid, 2006.

——. "La 'Tercera Partida' de Alfonso X el Sabio: Estudio y edición crítica de los títulos XVIII al XX. Contextos en torno a la edición de la 'Tercera Partida' de Alfonso X el Sabio." *Revista jurídica del notariado* 64 (2007): 183–278; 65 (2008): 159–274; 66 (2008): 191–328; 67 (2008): 297–494; 68 (2008): 45–226.

Pardo Rodríguez, María Luisa. *La cancillería de Don Fernando de la Cerda, Infante de Castilla y León (1255–1275).* León: Universidad de León, 2009.

Partida Segunda de Alfonso X el Sabio: Manuscrito 12794 de la B.N. Ed. Aurora Juárez Blanquer, and Antonio Rubio Flores. Granada: Impredisur, 1992.

Primera Partida (MS HC 397/573) Hispanic Society of America. Ed. Francisco Ramos Bossini. Granada: Universidad de Granada, 1984.

Primera Partida según el Manuscrito Add. 20787 del British Museum. Ed. Juan Antonio Arias Bonet. Valladolid: Universidad de Valladolid, 1975.

Raimundus de Pennaforte. *Summa de poenitentia.* Vol. 1 of *Summa de iure canonico,* ed. Xavier Ochoa and Aloisio Díez, 2 vols. in 1. Rome: Universalis Bibliotheca Iuris, 1975.

Recopilación de Leyes destos reynos. Alcalá de Henares: Juan Iñiguez Lequerica, 1598.

Rymer, Thomas. *Foedera, conventiones, litterae et cuiuscunque acta publica inter reges Angliae et alios quovis imperatores, reges, pontífices, principes.* 3rd ed. 10 vols. The Hague: Joannes Neaulme, 1739–45.

Sáez, Emilio, Rafael Gibert, Manuel Alvar, and Atilano G. Ruiz-Zorrilla. *Los Fueros de Sepúlveda.* Segovia: Diputación provincial de Segovia, 1953.

Sánchez, Galo. "Colección de fórmulas jurídicas castellanas de la edad media." *AHDE* 3 (1926): 476–502.

——. *El Fuero de Madrid.* Madrid: Ayuntamiento de Madrid, 1963.

Sánchez-Arcilla Bernal, José. *Las Siete Partidas.* Madrid: Reus, 2003.

Sánchez Herrero, José. *Concilios provinciales y sínodos toledanos de los siglos XIV y XV.* Seville: Consejo Superior de Investigaciones Científicas, 1976.

Sanz García, Juan. *El Fuero de Verviesca y el Fuero real.* Burgos: Imprenta el Castellano, 1927.

Scott, Samuel Parsons, trans. *Las Siete Partidas.* Chicago: Commerce Clearing House, 1931.

Setenario. Ed. Kenneth Vanderford. Buenos Aires, 1945. Reprint, Barcelona: Crítica, 1984.

Las Siete Partidas de Alfonso X el Sabio. Ed. Alfonso Díaz de Montalvo. 2 vols. Sevilla: Ungut and Polono, 1491.

Las Siete Partidas del Rey Don Alfonso el Sabio. Ed. Real Academia de la Historia. 3 vols. Madrid: Imprenta Real, 1807. Reprint, Madrid: Atlas, 1972.

Las Siete Partidas del Sabio rey Don Alonso el nono, nuevamente glosadas por el Licenciado Gregorio López. 4 vols. Salamanca: Andrea de Portonaris, 1555; facsimile, Madrid: Boletín Oficial del Estado, 1974.

Las Siete Partidas, Título II, "De los casamientos" de Alfonso X, el Sabio: Edición crítica y exposición analítica. Ed. Patricia T. Ramos Anderson. Lewiston, NY: Edwin Mellen Press, 2009.

The Statutes of the Realm. 12 vols. London: Public Record Office, 1810–28.

Ureña y Smenjaud, Rafael, and Adolfo Bonilla San Martín. *Obras del Maestre Jacobo de las leyes, jurisconsulto del siglo XIII*. Madrid: Reus, 1924.

The Visigothic Code (Forum Iudicum). Trans. Samuel Parsons Scott. Boston: Boston Book Company, 1910.

Literary and Scientific Sources

Alvar, Carlos. *Textos trovadorescos sobre España y Portugal*. Madrid: CUPSA, 1978.

Álvaro Pelayo. *Speculum regum (Espelho dos Reis)*. Ed. Miguel Pinto de Meneses. Lisbon: Universidade de Lisboa, 1955.

Aly Aben Ragel. *El Libro conplido en los iudizios de las Estrellas: Traducción hecha en la corte de Alfonso el Sabio*. Ed. Gerold Hilty. Madrid: Real Academia Española, 1954.

Aristotle. *Nicomachaean Ethics*. In *The Complete Works of Aristotle: The Revised Oxford Translation*, ed. Jonathan Barnes, 2:1729–1867. Princeton: Princeton University Press, 1984.

Cantigas de Santa Maria. Ed. Walter Mettmann. 4 vols. Coimbra: Universidade de Coimbra, 1959–74. Reprint, 2 vols., Vigo: Edicions Xerais de Galicia, 1981.

Castigos del rey don Sancho IV. Ed. Hugo Oscar Bizzarri. Frankfurt am Main: Vervuert, 2001.

Chabas, José, and Bernard R. Goldstein. *The Alfonsine Tables of Toledo*. Dordrecht: Kluwer, 2003.

Cicero. *Laelius de amicitia*. Ed. C. F. W. Müller. Leipzig: Teubner, 1884.

Cirot, Georges. *De operibus historicis Iohannis Aegidii Zamorensis*. Bordeaux: Feret, 1913.

Crombach, Mechthild. *Bocados de oro: Kritische Ausgabe des altspanischen Textes*. Bonn: Romanisches Seminar, 1971.

Fallows, Noel. *The Chivalric Vision of Alfonso de Cartagena: Study and Edition of the Doctrinal de los caualleros*. Newark, DE: Juan de la Cuesta, 1995.

García Cuadrado, Amparo. *Las Cantigas: El Códice de Florencia*. Murcia: Universidad de Murcia, 1993.

García Morencos, Pilar. *Libro de ajedrez, dados y tablas de Alfonso X el Sabio: Estudio*. Madrid: Patrimonio Nacional, 1977.

Giraldus Cambrensis. *De principis instructione*. Ed. George F. Warner. Vol. 8 of *Giraldi Cambrensis Opera*. London: Eyre & Spottiswood, 1891.

Goldstein, David. *The Jewish Poets of Spain*. Baltimore: Penguin Books, 1965.

Isidore of Seville. *Etymologiarum sive Originum Libri XX*. Ed. W. M. Lindsay. 2 vols. Oxford: Clarendon Press, 1911.

John of Salisbury. *Policraticus*. Ed. and trans. Cary J. Nederman. New York: Cambridge University Press, 1990.

Juan Gil de Zamora. *Liber de preconiis civitatis numantine*. Ed. Fidel Fita. "Dos libros (inéditos) de Gil de Zamora." *BRAH* 5 (1884): 131–200.

———. *Liber de preconiis Hispaniae*. Ed. Manuel de Castro y Castro. Madrid: Universidad de Madrid, 1955.

———. *Liber de preconiis Hispanie, o educación del príncipe*. Ed. and trans. Jenaro Costas Rodríguez and José Luis Martín. Zamora: Ayuntamiento de Zamora, 1996.

Juan Manuel. *El Libro de la caza*. Ed. G. Baist. Halle: Max Niemeyer, 1880.

———. *Libro de los castigos*. In *BAE*, 51:264–75.

———. *Libro de los estados*. Ed. José María Castro Calvo. Barcelona: Consejo Superior de Investigaciones Científicas, 1968.

———. *Libro de los estados*. Ed. R. B. Tate and I. R. Macpherson. Oxford: Clarendon Press, 1974.

———. *Libro del caballero et del escudero*. In *BAE*, 51:234–57.

———. *Tratado de las armas*. In *BAE*, 51:257–64.

Juan Ruiz. *Libro de Buen Amor*. Ed. María Brey Mariño. Madrid: Castalia, 2012.

Kasten, Lloyd A. *Seudo Aristóteles. Poridat de las poridades*. Madrid: S. Aguirre, 1957.

Leclercq, Jean. *Jean de Paris et l'ecclésiologie du XIIIe siècle*. Paris: J. Vrin, 1942.

Libro de Alexandre. In *Poetas castellanos anteriores al siglo XV*, ed. Tomás Antonio Sánchez, Pedro José Pidal, and Francisco Janer, 147–224. Madrid: M. Rivadeneyra, 1864.

Llull, Ramon. *The Book of the Order of Chivalry / Llibre de l'Ordre de Cavalleria / Libro de la Orden de Caballería*. Ed. and trans. by Antonio Cortijo Ocaña. Amsterdam: John Benjamins, 2015.

Lonie, Iain M. *The Hippocratic Treatises, "On Generation," "On the Nature of the Child," "Diseases IV."* Berlin: Walter de Gruyter, 1981.

Lucas of Tuy. *De altera vita fideique controversiis adversus Albigensium errores*. Ed. Juan de Mariana. Ingolstadt: Andreas Angermarius, 1612.

Múñoz Sendino, José. *La escala de Mahoma*. Madrid: Ministerio de Asuntos Exteriores, 1949.

Paredes Núñez, Juan. *Alfonso X el Sabio: Cantigas profanas*. Granada: Universidad de Granada, 1988.

The Pilgrim's Guide to Santiago de Compostela. Trans. William Melczer. New York: Italica, 1993.

Poem of the Cid (El poema del mio Cid). Trans. William S. Merwin. New York: New American Library, 1962.

Poema de Fernán González. Ed. Alonso Zamora Vicente. Madrid: Espasa-Calpe, 1946.

Rey, Agapito. *Libro de los cien capítulos*. Bloomington: Indiana University Press, 1960.

Rodríguez Lapa, Manuel. *Cantigas d'Escarnho e de Maldezir dos Cancioneiros medievais galego-portugueses*. Coimbra: Galaixa, 1970.

Secreto de los secretos. Poridat de las poridades: Versiones castellanas del Pseudo-Aristóteles Secretum Secretorum. Ed. Hugo Oscar Bizzarri. Valencia: Universitat de València, 2011.

Seneca. *Epistulae morales*. Ed. Richard Gummere. 3 vols. Cambridge, MA: Harvard University Press, 1917–25.

Thomas Aquinas. *On Kingship: To the King of Cyprus*. Trans. Gerald B. Phelan. Revised by I. T. Eschmann. Toronto: Pontifical Institute of Mediaeval Studies, 1949.

Vegetius, Flavius Renatus. *Epitoma rei militaris*. Ed. Carl Lang. Leipzig: B. G. Teubner, 1885.

———. *Epitome of Military Science*. Trans. N. P. Milner. Liverpool: Liverpool University Press, 1993.

Modern Works

Abadal, Ramon d'. *Las Partidas a Catalunya durant l'edat mitja*. Barcelona: Masso, Casas, 1914.

Ajo G. y Saínz de Zúñiga, C. M. *Historia de las universidades hispánicas*. 11 vols. Madrid: Centro de Estudios e Investigaciones "Alonso de Madrigal," 1957–79.

Alejandre García, Juan Antonio. "Estudio histórico del delito de falsedad documental." *AHDE* 42 (1972): 117–87.

Alemany, José. "Milicias cristianas al servicio de los sultanes musulmanes del Almagreb." In *Homenaje a D. Francisco de Codera en su jubilación del profesorado: Estudios de erudición oriental*, ed. Eduardo Saavedra, 133–69. Zaragoza: Mariano Escar, 1904.

Alfonso X: Toledo 1984. Toledo: Ministerio de Cultura, 1984.

Alfonso Antón, Isabel, and Cristina Jular Pérez-Alfaro. "Oña contra Frías o el pleito de los cien testigos: una pesquisa en la Castilla del siglo XIII." *Edad Media* 3 (2000):61–88.

Alonso, María Luz. "La dote en los documentos toledanos de los siglos XII–XV." *AHDE* 48 (1978): 379–456.

———. "La perduración del Fuero Juzgo y el derecho de los castellanos de Toledo." *AHDE* 48 (1978): 335–77.

Altisent, Agustín. "Otra referencia a las Cortes de Nájera." *AEM* 5 (1968): 473–78.

Alvarado Planas, Javier. "A modo de conclusiones: el Liber Iudiciorum y la aplicación del Derecho en los siglos VI a XI." *Mélanges de la Casa de Velázquez* 41, no. 2 (2011): 109–27.

Álvarez Borge, Ignacio. "La nobleza castellana en la edad media: Patrimonio, familia, y poder." In *La familia en la edad media: XI Semana de Estudios Medievales, Nájera, del 31 de julio al 4 de agosto de 2000*, ed. José Ignacio de la Iglesia Duarte, 221–52. Nájera: Instituto de Estudios Riojanos, 2001.

———. "Señorío y feudalismo en Castilla: Una revisión de la historiografía entre los años 1989–2004." In *Estudios sobre señorío y feudalismo: Homenaje a Julio Valdeón*, ed. Esteban Sarasa Sánchez and Eliseo Serrano Martín, 107–96. Zaragoza: Institución "Fernando el Católico," 2010.

Álvarez Cora, Enrique. "El derecho penal de Alfonso X." *Initium: Revista catalana d'Historia del Dret* 16 (2011): 223–96.

Álvarez de Brana, Ramón. "La igualación de pesos y medidas por don Alfonso el Sabio." *BRAH* 38 (1901): 134–44.

Álvarez de Morales, Antonio. *Las hermandades expresión del movimiento comunitario en España*. Valladolid: Universidad de Valladolid, 1974.

Álvarez-Valdés y Valdés, Manuel. *La extranjería en la historia del derecho español*. Oviedo: Universidad de Oviedo, 1992.

Amador de los Ríos, José. *Historia crítica de la literatura española*. 7 vols. Madrid: Impr. de J. Rodriguez, 1861–65.

——. *Historia social, política y religiosa de los judíos de España.* 2 vols. Madrid: T. Fontanet, 1875–76.

Araujo Barros, Clara. *Versões portuguesas da legislação de Afonso X: Estudo linguístico-Discursivo.* Porto: Universidade do Porto, 2010.

Arbesú, David. "Alfonso X el Sabio, Beatriz de Portugal y el sepulcro de doña Mayor Guillén de Guzmán." *eHumanista* 24 (2013): 300–20.

Arévalo Caballero, Walenka. "*Adoptio a muliere facta* en derecho romano y en la tradición jurídica española." *Revista Internacional de Derecho Romano* 7 (2011): 156–98.

Argente del Castillo Ocaña, Carmen. "Precedentes de la organización del concejo de la Mesta." In Miguel Rodríguez, Múñoz Fernández, and Segura Graiño, *Alfonso X el Sabio*, 1:115–25.

Arias Bautista, María Teresa. *Barraganas y concubinas en la España medieval.* Seville: ArCiBel, 2010.

Arias Bonet, Juan Antonio. "El depósito en las Partidas." *AHDE* 32 (1962): 543–66.

——. "Derecho marítimo en las Partidas." *Revista de Derecho mercantil* 41 (1966): 91–108.

——. "Recepción de las formas estipulatorias en la baja edad media: Un estudio sobre las 'promisiones' de las Siete Partidas." *Boletim da Faculdade de Direito de Coimbra* 42 (1966): 285–334.

Arranz Guzmán, Ana. "Alfonso X y la conservación de la naturaleza." In Miguel Rodríguez, Múñoz Fernández, and Segura Graiño, *Alfonso X el Sabio*, 1:127–36.

——. "Celibato eclesiástico, barraganas y contestación social en la Castilla bajomedieval." *ETF* 21 (2008): 13–39.

Avenoza, Gemma. "Las Partidas en catalán." *7 Partidas Digital: Edición crítica de las Siete Partidas*, 21 December 2017. https://7partidas.hypotheses.org/.

Ayala Martínez, Carlos de. *Directrices fundamentales de la política peninsular de Alfonso X (Relaciones castellano-aragonesas de 1252 a 1263).* Madrid: Universidad Autónoma de Madrid, 1986.

——. "La monarquía y las Ordenes militares durante el reinado de Alfonso X." *Hispania: Revista española de historia* 51 (1991): 409–65.

——. *Las órdenes militares hispánicas en la Edad media (siglos XII–XV).* Madrid: Marcial Pons, 2007.

——. "Las relaciones de Alfonso X con la santa sede durante el pontificado de Nicolás III (1277–10)." In Miguel Rodríguez, Múñoz Fernández, and Segura Graiño, *Alfonso X el Sabio*, 1:137–51.

Ayala Martínez, Carlos de, and Francisco Javier Villalba Ruiz de Toledo. "Las Cortes bajo el reinado de Alfonso X." In *Las Cortes de Castilla y León 1188–1988*, ed. Cortes de Castilla y León, 239–70. Valladolid: Cortes de Castilla y León, 1990.

Baer, Yitzhak. *A History of the Jews in Christian Spain.* 2 vols. Philadelphia: Jewish Publication Society, 1966.

Bagby, Albert. "The Jew in the *Cantigas* of Alfonso X el Sabio." *Speculum* 46 (1971): 670–88.

Ballesteros, Antonio. *Sevilla en el siglo XIII.* Madrid; Juan Pérez Torres, 1913.

Ballesteros y Beretta, Antonio. *Alfonso X, el Sabio.* Barcelona: Espasa-Calpe, 1963. Reprint, Barcelona: El Albir, 1984.

Bango Torviso, Isidro G. "La llamada corona de Sancho IV y los emblemas de poder real." *Alcanate* 9 (2014–15): 261–83.

Barkai, Ron. *Cristianos y musulmanes en la España medieval (El enemigo en el espejo).* Madrid: Rialp, 1984.

Barreiro Somoza, José. *El señorío de la iglesia de Santiago de Compostela (siglos IX–XIII).* La Coruña: Editorial Diputación Provincial, 1987.

Barros Días, Isabel de. "La blasfemia del rey sabio: Vicisitudes de una leyenda (Nuevas hipótesis respecto a la datación y la posición relativa del texto portugués)." *AEM* 45 (2015): 733–52.

——. "A blasfémia do Rei Sábio: os antecedentes da lenda." In *Estudios de Literatura Medieval: 25 años de la AHLM,* ed. Antonia Martínez Pérez and Ana Luisa Baquero Escudero, 189–96. Murcia: Universidad de Murcia, 2012.

Baylen, Joseph O. "John Maunsell and the Castilian Treaty of 1254: A Study of the Clerical Diplomat." *Traditio* 17 (1961): 482–91.

Bazán, Iñaki. "La construcción del discurso homofóbico en la Europa cristiana medieval." *ELEM* 30 (2007): 433–54.

Beceiro Pita, Isabel. "Parentesco y consolidación de la aristocracia en los inicios de la Corona de Castilla (Siglos XI–XIII)." *Meridies* 2 (1995): 49–71.

Beceiro Pita, Isabel, and Ricardo Córdoba de la Llave. *Parentesco, poder y mentalidad: La nobleza castellana, Siglos XII–XV.* Madrid: Consejo Superior de Investigaciones Científicas, 1990.

Bellomo, Manlio. *The Common Legal Past of Europe, 1000–1800.* Trans. Lydia G. Cochrane. Washington, DC: Catholic University of America Press, 1995.

Beneyto, Juan. "Los derechos fundamentales en la España medieval." *Revista de Estudios Políticos,* n.s., 26 (1982): 99–117.

Benito Fraile, Emilio Javier de. "En torno a las leyes de los adelantados mayores." *CHD* 3 (1996): 287–314.

Benito Ruano, Eloy. *Hermandades en Asturias durante la edad media.* Oviedo: La Cruz, 1972.

Berger, Adolf. "Encyclopedic Dictionary of Roman Law." *Transactions of the American Philosophical Society,* n.s., 43 (1953): 333–809.

Berman, Harold J. *Law and Revolution: The Formation of the Western Legal Tradition.* Cambridge, MA: Harvard University Press, 1983.

Bermejo Cabrero, José Luis. "En torno a la aplicación de las Partidas: Fragmentos del 'Espéculo' en una sentencia real de 1261." *Hispania: Revista española de historia* 30 (1970): 169–80.

——. "En torno a las Cortes de Nájera." *AHDE* 70 (2000): 245–50.

——. "Notas sobre la Segunda Partida." In Espadas Burgos, *VII centenario,* 265–71.

Bermejo Díaz, Almudena. "La mujer en la edad media: Su condición jurídica en las Partidas." Trabajo Fin de Grado. Universidad de la Rioja, 2014.

Bertolucci Pizzorusso, Valeria. "Don Enrique / Don Arrigo: un infante di Castiglia tra storia e Letteratura." *Alcanate* 4 (2004–5): 293–314.

Bianchini, Janna. *The Queen's Hand: Power and Authority in the Reign of Berenguela of Castile.* Philadelphia: University of Pennsylvania Press, 2012.

Bidagor, Ramón. "El derecho de las Decretales y las Partidas de Alfonso X el Sabio de España." In *Acta Congressus Iuridici Internationalis VII saeculo a Decretalibus Gregorii IX et XIV a Codice Iustiniano promulgatis,* 3:297–313. Rome: Pontificum Institutum Utriusque Iuris, 1936.

Bishko, Charles J. "The Castilian as Plainsman: The Medieval Ranching Frontier in La Mancha and Extremadura." In *The New World Looks at Its History*, ed. Archibald R. Lewis and Thomas F. McGann, 47–69. Austin: University of Texas Press, 1963.

——. "The Peninsular Background of Latin American Cattle Ranching." In his *Studies in Medieval Spanish Frontier History*, no. VI. London: Variorum Reprints, 1980.

Bizzarri, Hugo Oscar. "Las colecciones sapienciales castellanos en el proceso de reafirmación del poder monárquico (siglos XIII y XIV)." *CLHM* 20 (1995): 35–73.

Bizzarri, Hugo Oscar, and Adeline Rucquoi. "Los espejos de principes en Castilla: Entre Oriente y Occidente." *CHE* 79 (2005): 7–30.

Bloch, Marc. *Les rois thaumaturges*. Paris: Armand Colin, 1961.

Bono y Huerta, José. "La legislación notarial de Alfonso X el Sabio: Sus características." *Anales de la Academia Matritense del Notariado* 27 (1987): 27–44.

Borgognoni, Ezequiel. "Los judíos en la legislación castellana medieval: Notas para su estudio (siglos X–XIII)." *Estudios de Historia de España* 14 (2012): 53–68.

Bouzada Gil, María Teresa. "El privilegio de las viudas en el derecho castellano." *CHD* 4 (1997): 203–42.

Bowman, Jeffrey A. "Infamy and Proof in Medieval Spain." In *Fama: The Politics of Talk and Reputation in Medieval Europe*, ed. Thelma S. Fenster and Daniel Lord Smail, 95–117. Ithaca: Cornell University Press, 2005.

Bravo Lira, Bernardino. "Vigencia de las Partidas en Chile." *REHJ* 10 (1985): 43–105.

Brodman, James. "Captives or Prisoners: Society and Obligation in Medieval Iberia." *Anuario de Historia de la Iglesia* 20 (2011): 201–19.

——. "Community, Identity and the Redemption of Captives: Comparative Perspectives Across the Mediterranean." *AEM* 36 (2006): 241–52.

——. "Military Redemptionism and the Castilian Reconquest, 1180–1250." *Military Affairs* 44 (1980): 24–27.

——. "Municipal Ransoming Law on the Medieval Spanish Frontier." *Speculum* 60 (1985): 318–30.

——. *Ransoming Captives in Crusader Spain: The Order of Merced on the Christian–Islamic Frontier*. Philadelphia: University of Pennsylvania Press, 1986.

——. "The *Siete Partidas* and the Law of Charity in Thirteenth-Century Castile." In *The Emergence of León-Castile, c. 1065–1500: Essays Presented to J. F. O'Callaghan*, ed. James Todesca, 81–92. Burlington, VT: Ashgate, 2015.

——. "What Is a Soul Worth? Pro anima Bequests in the Municipal Legislation of Reconquest Spain." *Medievalia et Humanistica*, n.s., 20 (1993): 15–23.

Brundage, James A. *Law, Sex, and Christian Society in Medieval Europe*. Chicago: University of Chicago Press, 1987.

——. *Medieval Canon Law*. London: Longman, 1995.

——. *Medieval Canon Law and the Crusader*. Madison: University of Wisconsin Press, 1969.

——. *The Medieval Origins of the Legal Profession: Canonists, Civilians, and Courts*. Chicago: University of Chicago Press, 2008.

Buckland, W. W. *A Textbook of Roman Law from Augustus to Justinian*. Cambridge: Cambridge University Press, 1921.

Burns, Robert I., SJ, ed. *Emperor of Culture: Alfonso X the Learned of Castile and His Thirteenth-Century Renaissance*. Philadelphia: University of Pennsylvania Press, 1990.

——. "King Alfonso and the Wild West: Medieval Hispanic Law on the U.S. Frontier." *Medieval Encounters* 6 (2000): 80–100.

——. "*Stupor Mundi*: Alfonso X of Castile, the Learned." In Burns, *Emperor of Culture*, 1–13.

——, ed. *The Worlds of Alfonso the Learned and James the Conqueror: Intellect and Force in the Middle Ages*. Princeton: Princeton University Press, 1985.

Burriel, Andrés Marcos. *Informe de la imperial ciudad de Toledo al Real y Supremo Consejo de Castilla sobre igualación de pesos y medidas en todos los Reynos y Señorios de su Majestad según las leyes*. Toledo: Joachin Ibarra, 1758.

Calderón Ortega, José Manuel, and Francisco Javier Díaz González. "El rescate de prisioneros y cautivos durante la edad media hispánica: Aproximación a su estudio." *HID* 38 (2011): 9–66.

Canning, Joseph. *A History of Medieval Political Thought, 300–1450*. London: Routledge, 1996.

Cantera Burgos, Francisco. "Miranda en tiempos de Alfonso el Sabio." *Boletín de la Comisión provincial de Monumentos históricos y artísticos de Burgos* 17 (1938): 137–50.

Carlé, María del Carmen. "Apuntes sobre el matrimonio en la edad media española." *CHE* 63–64 (1980): 115–77.

——. "El bosque en la edad media (Asturias-León-Castilla)." *CHE* 59–60 (1976): 297–374.

——. "Mercaderes en Castilla (1252–1512)." *CHE* 21–22 (1954): 146–328.

——. "El precio de la vida en Castilla del rey sabio al emplazado." *CHE* 15 (1951): 132–56.

——. "La servidumbre en las Partidas." *CHE* 12 (1949): 105–20.

Carmona Ruiz, María Antonia. *María de Molina*. Madrid: Plaza y Janés, 2005.

Carpenter, Dwayne E. "Alfonso el Sabio y los moros: Algunas precisiones legales, históricas y textuales con respecto a Siete Partidas 7.25." *Al-Qantara: Revista de estudios árabes* 7 (1986): 229–52.

——. *Alfonso X and the Jews: An Edition of and Commentary on "Siete Partidas" 7.24 "De los judíos."* Berkeley: University of California Press, 1986.

——. "Tolerance and Intolerance: Alfonso X's Attitude towards the Synagogue as Reflected in the *Siete Partidas*." *Kentucky Romance Quarterly* 31 (1984): 31–39.

Carramolino, Juan Martín. *Historia de Ávila, su provincia y obispado*. 3 vols. Madrid: Librería Española, 1872.

Carrasco, Inés. *Los cargos de la hueste real en tiempos de Alfonso X: Estudio onomasiológico*. Granada: Universidad de Granada, 1992.

Castrillo Llamas, María de la Concepción. "Francisco Martínez Marina: El hombre y su obra." *Medievalismo* 2 (1992): 219–25.

——. "Monarquía y nobleza en torno a la tenencia de fortalezas en Castilla durante los siglos XIII–XIV." *ELEM* 17 (1994): 95–112.

Castro, Américo. *La realidad historica de España*. Mexico City: Porrua, 1962.

——. "Unos aranceles de aduanas del siglo XIII." *RFE* 8 (1921): 1–29.

Catalán, Diego. *La Estoria de España de Alfonso X: Creación y Evolución*. Madrid: Universidad Autónoma de Madrid, 1992.

Catechism of the Catholic Church. Vatican City: Libreria Editrice Vaticana, 1994.

Cerdá Ruiz-Funes, Joaquín. "Consideraciones sobre el hombre y sus derechos en las Partidas de Alfonso el Sabio." *Anales de la Universidad de Murcia. Derecho* 22 (1964): 9–55.

——. "En torno a la pesquisa y procedimiento inquisitivo en el derecho castellano-leonés de la edad media." *AHDE* 32 (1962): 483–518.

Chevedden, Paul E. "The Hybrid Trebuchet: The Halfway Step to the Counterweight Trebuchet." In *On the Social Origins of Medieval Institutions: Essays in Honor of Joseph F. O'Callaghan*, ed. Donald J. Kagay and Theresa Vann, 179–222. Leiden: Brill, 1998.

Chevedden, Paul E., Zvi Shiller, Samuel R. Gilbert, and Donald J. Kagay. "The Traction Trebuchet: A Triumph of Four Civilizations." *Viator* 31 (2000): 433–86.

Childs, Wendy R. *Anglo-Castilian Trade in the Later Middle Ages*. Manchester: Manchester University Press, 1978.

Clavero, Bartolomé. *Mayorazgo: Propiedad feudal en Castilla 1369–1836*. Madrid: Siglo XXI de España, 1974.

Cohen, David A. "Secular Pragmatism and Thinking about War in Some Court Writings of Pere III el Cerimoniós." In *Crusaders, Condottieri, and Cannon: Medieval Warfare in Societies around the Mediterranean*, ed. Donald J. Kagay and L. J. Andrew Villalon, 21–53. Leiden: Brill, 2003.

Collantes de Terán, Antonio. "La formación de los gremios sevillanos: A propósito de unos documentos sobre los tejedores." *ELEM* 1 (1980): 89–104.

Collantes de Terán, María José. "El delito de adulterio en el derecho general de Castilla." *AHDE* 66 (1996): 201–28.

Collins, Roger. *Visigothic Spain, 409–711*. Malden, MA: Blackwell, 2004.

Colmeiro, Manuel. *Cortes de los antiguos reinos de Castilla y León: Introducción*. 2 vols. Madrid: Rivadeneyra, 1883–84.

Colmenares, Diego de. *Historia de la insigne ciudad de Segovia*. New ed. 3 vols. Segovia: Academia de Historia y Arte de San Quirce, 1969–75.

Cómez Ramos, Rafael. *Las empresas artísticas de Alfonso X el Sabio*. Seville: Diputación Provincial de Sevilla, 1979.

——. "El retrato de Alfonso X, el Sabio en la primera Cantiga de Santa María." In *Studies on the Cantigas de Santa Maria: Art, Music and Poetry*, ed. Israel Katz and John E. Keller, 35–52. Madison: Hispanic Seminary, 1987.

Constable, Olivia Remie. *Trade and Traders in Muslim Spain: The Commercial Realignment of the Iberian Peninsula, 900–1500*. Cambridge: Cambridge University Press, 1994.

Corti, Francisco. "Cantiga 125: La nigromancia y las relaciones entre imágenes y textos." *Alcanate* 5 (2006–7): 293–305.

Craddock, Jerry R. "La cronología de las obras legislativas de Alfonso X el Sabio." *AHDE* 51 (1981): 365–418.

——. "Dynasty in Dispute: Alfonso X of Castile and León in History and Legend." *Viator* 17 (1986): 197–219.

——. "How Many *Partidas* in the *Siete Partidas*?" In *Hispanic Studies in Honor of Alan D. Deyermond: A North American Tribute*, ed. John S. Miletich, 83–92. Madison: Hispanic Seminary of Medieval Studies, 1986.

——. "The Legislative Works of Alfonso el Sabio." In Burns, *Emperor of Culture*, 182–97.

——. *The Legislative Works of Alfonso X, el Sabio: A Critical Bibliography*. London: Grant & Cutler, 1986.

——. "Must the King Obey His Laws?" In *Florilegium Hispanicum: Medieval and Golden Age Studies Presented to Dorothy Clotelle Clarke*, 71–79. Madison: Hispanic Seminary of Medieval Studies, 1983.

——. "La nota cronológica inserta en el prólogo de las *Siete Partidas*: edición crítica y comentario." *Al-Andalus* 39 (1974): 363–90.

——. "The *Partidas*: Bibliographical Notes." In Burns, *Las Siete Partidas*, xli–xlviii.

——. "Los pecados veniales en las Partidas y en el Setenario: dos versiones de Graciano, Decretum D.25 c.3." *Glossae* 3 (1992):103–16.

——. "La pesquisa en Castilla y Aragón: Un caso curioso del *Libre des feyts* de Jaume I." *AEM* 27 (1997): 369–79.

——. "Setenario: última e inconclusa refundición alfonsina de la primera Partida." *AHDE* 56 (1986): 441–66.

——. "El Texto del *Espéculo* de Alfonso X el Sabio." *Initium: Revista catalana d'Historia del Dret* 3 (1998): 221–74.

Crespo Álvarez, Macarena. "Judíos, préstamos y usuras en la Castilla medieval: De Alfonso X a Enrique III." *Edad Media* 5 (2002): 179–215.

Cruz Aguilar, Emilio de la. "Los juglares en las Partidas." *RFDUC* 9 Extra (1985): 25–33.

D'Alverny, Marie Thérèse. "Deux traductions latines du Coran au Moyen Âge." *Archives d'Histoire Doctrinale et Litteraire du Moyen Âge* 16 (1947): 69–131.

Daniel, Norman. *Islam and the West: The Making of an Image.* Edinburgh: Edinburgh University Press 1960.

Daumet, Georges. *Mémoire sur les relations de la France et de la Castille de 1255 à 1320.* Paris: Bibliothèque de l'École des Hautes Études, 1913.

Delgado Roig, Juan. "Examen médico-legal de unos restos históricos: Los cadaveres de Alfonso X el Sabio y Doña Beatriz de Suabia." *Archivo Hispalense* 9 (1948): 135–53.

Diago Hernando, Máximo. "La monarquía castellana y los Staufer: Contactos políticos y diplomáticos en los siglos XII y XIII." *ETF* 8 (1995): 51–84.

Díaz González, Francisco Javier. "La base jurídica romana en la regulación del cautivo en las Partidas." *Revista General de Derecho Romano* 4 (2010): 1–27.

——. "La normativa sobre los prisioneros y los cautivos en la España cristiana medieval." *REHJ* 32 (2010): 281–308.

Díaz Marcilla, Francisco José. "Lealtades y deslealtades eclesiásticas durante la 'cuestión sucesoria' entre Alfonso X y Sancho IV (1282–1284)." *Edad Media* 18 (2017): 177–206.

Dillard, Heath. *Daughters of the Reconquest: Women in Castilian Town Society, 1100–1300.* Cambridge: Cambridge University Press, 1984.

Domingues, José. "A tradição medieval das Sete Partidas em Portugal." *7 Partidas Digital: Edición crítica de las Siete Partidas*, 1 June 2017. https://7partidas. hypotheses.org/.

——. "As Partidas de Afonso X e a natureza jurídico-política do estado português." In *Natura e natureza no tempo de Afonso X o Sabio*, ed. José Carlos Ribeiro Miranda and Maria Rosário Ferreira, 31–49. Porto: Humus, 2015.

——. "O elemento castelhano-leonês na formação do Direito Medieval português." *CHD* 21 (2014): 213–27.

Domínguez, Ana. "La miniatura del 'Scriptorium' Alfonsí." In *Estudios Alfonsíes: Lexicografía, lírica, estética y política de Alfonso el Sabio*, ed. José Mondéjar and Jesús Montoya, 127–61. Granada: Universidad de Granada, 1985.

——. "Retratos de Alfonso X el Sabio en la Primera Partida (British Library, Add. Ms. 20.787)." *Alcanate* 6 (2008–9): 239–51.

Domínguez Sánchez, Santiago. "Falsificaciones medievales: Una 'Bula' de Nicolás IV falsificada por el rey Sancho IV de Castilla," *Estudios humanísticos. Historia* 2 (2003): 13–26.

Dufourcq, Charles Emmanuel, and Jean Gautier-Dalché. *Histoire économique et sociale de l'Espagne chrétienne au moyen âge.* Paris: Armand Colin, 1976.

———. *Historia económica y social de la España cristiana en la edad media.* Barcelona: El Albir, 1983.

Echevarría, Ana. "La 'mayoría' mudéjar en León y Castilla: legislación real y distribución de la población (siglos XI–XIII)." *ELEM* 29 (2006): 7–30.

Escalona, Julio. "Los nobles contra su rey: Argumentos y motivaciones de la insubordinación nobiliaria de 1272–1273." *CLCHM* 25 (2002): 131–62.

Escalona, Romualdo. *Historia del real monasterio de Sahugún.* Madrid, 1782; repr. León: Ediciones Leonesas, 1982.

Espadas Burgos, Manuel, ed. *VII centenario del Infante don Fernando de la Cerda: Jornadas de Estudio, Ciudad Real, Abril 1975.* Ciudad Real: Instituto de Estudios Manchegos, 1976.

Estepa Díez, Carlos. *Las behetrías castellanas.* 2 vols. Valladolid: Junta de Castilla y León, 2003.

Estudios en homenaje a Don Claudio Sánchez Albornoz en sus 90 años. 4 vols. Buenos Aires: Instituto de Historia de España, 1983–86.

Fernández Conde, Francisco Javier. "Albigenses en León y Castilla a comienzos del siglo XIII." In *León medieval: doce estudios; Ponencias y comunicaciones presentadas al coloquio "El reino de León en la Edad Media,"* 95–114. León: Colegio Universitario, 1978.

———. "Un noyau actif d'Albigeois en León au commencement du XIIIᵉ siècle? Approche critique d'une œuvre de Luc de Tuy écrite entre 1230 et 1240." *Heresis* 17 (1991): 35–50.

Fernández del Pulgar, Pedro. *Historia secular y eclesiástica de la ciudad de Palencia.* 4 vols. Madrid: F. Nieto, 1679–80.

Fernández Duro, Cesáreo. *Memorias históricas de la ciudad de Zamora.* 4 vols. Madrid: Sucesores de Rivadeneyra, 1882–83.

Fernández Espinar, Ramón. "La compraventa en el Derecho medieval español." *AHDE* 25 (1955): 293–528.

Fernández Fernández, Laura. *Arte y ciencia en el scriptorium de Alfonso X el Sabio.* Seville: Universidad de Sevilla, 2013.

Fernández Marco, Juan Ignacio. *La muy noble y muy leal villa de Briones: estudio biográfico.* Logroño:Instituto de Estudios Riojanos, 1976.

Fernández Regatillo, Eduardo. "El derecho matrimonial en las Partidas y en las Decretales." In *Acta Congressus Iuridici Internationalis VII saeculo a Decretalibus Gregorii IX et XIV a Codice Iustiniano promulgatis,* 3:315–84. Rome: Pontificum Institutum Utriusque Iuris, 1936.

Fernández y González, Francisco. *Estado social y politico de los mudéjares de Castilla.* Madrid: J. Muñoz, 1866.

Ferotin, Marius. *Histoire de l'Abbaye de Silos.* Paris: Ernest Leroux, 1897.

Ferrari, Ángel. "La secularización de la teoría del estado en las Partidas." *AHDE* 11 (1934): 449–56.

Ferreiro Alemparte, Jaime. "Recepción de las *Éticas* y de la *Política* de Aristóteles en las *Siete Partidas* del rey Sabio." *Glossae* 1 (1988): 97–133.

Fidalgo Francisco, Elvira. "Consideración social de los judíos a través de las *Cantigas de Santa Maria*." *Revista de Literatura Medieval* 8 (1996): 91–103.

Fita, Fidel. "Madrid desde el año 1235 hasta el de 1275." *BRAH* 9 (1886): 11–157.

——. "La sínagoga de Córdoba." *BRAH* 5 (1884) 361–99.

Fletcher, Richard. *The Quest for El Cid*. New York: Alfred A. Knopf, 1990.

Floranes, Rafael. *Memorias y privilegios de la muy noble y muy ilustre ciudad de Vitoria*. Madrid: Vicente Rico, 1922.

Fonquerne, Yves-René, and Alfonso Esteban, eds. *La Condición de la mujer en la Edad media: Actas del coloquio celebrado en la Casa de Velázquez, del 5 al 7 de noviembre de 1984*. Madrid: Casa de Velázquez, 1986.

Franssen, Maarten. "Did King Alfonso of Castile Really Want to Advise God against the Ptolemaic System?" *Studies in History and Philosophy of Science* 24 (1993): 313–25.

Funes, Leonardo. "La blasfemia del rey sabio: Itinerario narrativo de una leyenda." *Incipit* 13 (1993): 51–70; 14 (1994): 69–101.

Gaibrois de Ballesteros, Mercedes. *Historia del reinado de Sancho IV*. 3 vols. Madrid: Revista de Archivos, Bibliotecas y Museos, 1922–28.

——. *María de Molina, tres veces reina*. Madrid: Espasa-Calpe, 1936.

——. "La reina doña Mencía." *Revista da Universidade de Coimbra* 11 (1933): 501–39.

Gálvez, José Francisco. "Aproximación al estudio de la pervivencia de las Partidas en el derecho Peruano." In *XIII Congreso del Instituto Internacional de Historia del Derecho Indiano: Actas y estudios*, 2:707–28. San Juan: Asamblea Legislativa de Puerto Rico, 2003.

Gárate Córdoba, José María. "El pensamiento militar en el Código de las Siete Partidas." *Revista de Historia Militar* 13 (1963): 7–60.

García Cuadrado, Amparo. *Las Cantigas: El códice de Florencia*. Murcia: Universidad de Murcia, 1993.

García Díaz, Jesús. "El fenómeno del mercado en la obra legislativa de Alfonso X el Sabio." *HID* 38 (2011): 111–40.

García Fitz, Francisco. "Captives in Mediaeval Spain: The Castilian-Leonese and Muslim Experience (XI–XIII Centuries." *E-Stratégica* 1 (2017): 205–21.

——. *Castilla y León frente al Islam: Estrategias de expansión y tácticas militares (siglos XI–XIII)*. Seville: Universidad de Sevilla, 1998.

——. "La composición de los ejércitos medievales." In *La Guerra en la Edad media: XVII Semana de Estudios Medievales*, ed. José Ignacio de la Iglesia Duarte, 85–146. Logroño: Instituto de Estudios Riojanos, 2007.

——. "La reconquista y formación de la España medieval (De mediados del siglo XI a mediados del siglo XIII)." In *Historia militar de España*, gen. ed. Hugo O'Donnell y Duque de Estrada, vol. 2, *Edad media*, ed. Miguel Ángel Ladero Quesada, 142–216. Madrid: Laberinto, 2010.

García Gallo, Alfonso. *Curso de Historia del derecho español*. 7th ed. 2 vols. Madrid: A.G.E.S.A, 1958.

——. "El Libro de las leyes de Alfonso el Sabio: Del Espéculo a las Partidas." *AHDE* 21–22 (1951–52): 345–528.

——. *Manual de Historia del Derecho Español*. 3rd ed. 2 vols. Madrid: Artes Gráficas y Ediciones, 1967.

——. "Nacionalidad y territorialidad del derecho en la época visigoda." *AHDE* 13 (1936–41): 168–264.

——. "Nuevas observaciones sobre la obra legislativa de Alfonso X." *AHDE* 46 (1976): 609–70.

——. "La obra legislativa de Alfonso X: Hechos y hipótesis." *AHDE* 54 (1984): 97–161.

García González, Juan. "El Fuero Viejo asistemático." *AHDE* 41 (1971): 767–86.

——. "El juramento de manquadra." *AHDE* 25 (1955): 211–55.

García Rives, Moisés. "Condición jurídica de los extranjeros en Castilla y León desde el Fuero de León (1020) al Código de las Partidas." *Revista de Ciencias Jurídicas y Sociales* 3 (1920): 245–83, 320–55.

García y García, Antonio. *Derecho común en España: los juristas y sus obras.* Murcia: Universidad de Murcia, 1991.

——. "En torno al derecho romano en la España medieval." In *Estudios en homenaje a Don Claudio Sánchez Albornoz,* 3:59–72.

——. "Fuentes canónicas de las Partidas." *Glossae* 3 (1992): 93–101.

——. *Laurentius Hispanus: Datos biográficos y estudio crítico de sus obras.* Rome: Consejo Superior de Investigaciones Científicas, 1956.

——. "Tradición manuscrita de las Siete Partidas." In *Iglesia, Sociedad y Derecho,* 249–83. Salamanca: Universidad Pontificia de Salamanca, 1985.

Gautier-Dalché, Jean. "La politique monétaire d'Alphonse X." *CHE* 69 (1987): 77–95.

——. "Remarques sur les premières mutations monétaires d'Alphonse X de Castille." In his *Économie et société dans les pays de la Couronne de Castille,* 147–56. London: Variorum, 1982.

Gibert, Rafael. "El contrato de servicios en el derecho medieval español." *Revista de Política Social* 101 (1974): 5–134.

——. *Historia general del derecho español.* Granada: F. Román, 1968.

——. "La paz del camino en el derecho medieval español." *AHDE* 27–28 (1957–58): 831–52.

Gibert y Sánchez de la Vega, Rafael. "La condición de los extranjeros en el antiguo derecho español." *Recueils de la Société Jean Bodin* 9 (1958): 150–99.

——. "El consentimiento familiar en el matrimonio según el Derecho medieval español." *AHDE* 18 (1947): 706–61.

——. "Jacobo el de las Leyes en el estudio jurídico hispánico." *Glossae* 5–6 (1993–94): 255–77.

Giménez Soler, Andrés. *Don Juan Manuel: Biografía y estudio crítico.* Madrid: Real Academia Española, 1932.

Giménez y Martínez de Carvajal, José. "El Decreto y las Decretales. Fuentes de la Primera Partida de Alfonso X el Sabio." *Anthologica Annua* 2 (1954): 239–48.

——. "San Raimundo de Peñafort y las Partidas de Alfonso X el Sabio." *Anthologica Annua* 3 (1955): 201–338.

Glagett, Helen L., and David M. Valderrama. *A Revised Guide to the Law and Legal Literature of Mexico.* Washington, DC: Library of Congress, 1973.

Gómez Moreno, María Elena. *La Catedral de León.* León: Everest, 1973.

González, Julio. *Alfonso IX.* 2 vols. Madrid: Consejo Superior de Investigaciones Científicas, 1945.

——. "Aranceles del portazgo de Sahagún en el siglo XIII." *AHDE* 14 (1943): 573–78.

——. "La clerecía de Salamanca durante la edad media." *Hispania: Revista española de historia* 3 (1943): 409–30.

——. "Origen de la marina real de Castilla." *RABM* 54 (1948): 229–53.

——. *Regesta de Fernando II*. Madrid: Consejo Superior de Investigaciones Científicas, 1943.

——. *Reinado y diplomas de Fernando III*. 3 vols. Córdoba: Monte de Piedad y Caja de Ahorros, 1980–86.

——. *El reino de Castilla en la época de Alfonso VIII*. 3 vols. Madrid: Consejo Superior de Investigaciones Científicas, 1960.

——. "Sobre la fecha de las Cortes de Nájera." *CHE* 61–62 (1977): 357–61.

González Arce, José Damián. "El consulado genovés de Sevilla (siglos XIII–XV): Aspectos jurisdiccionales, comerciales y fiscales." *Studia Historica: Historia Medieval* 28 (2010): 179–206.

——. "La evolución del almojarifazgo de Córdoba entre los siglos XIII y XV." *ELEM* 37 (2014): 165–204.

González Jiménez, Manuel. *Alfonso X, el Sabio*. Barcelona: Ariel, 2004.

——. "Alfonso X y las minorías confesionales de mudéjares y judíos." In Rodríguez Llopis, *Alfonso X*, 71–90.

——. "Alfonso X y las órdenes militares: Historia de un desencuentro." *Alcanate* 2 (2000–2001): 209–21.

——. "Alfonso X y sus hermanos (I)." *Boletín de la Real Academia Sevillana de Buenas Letras* 32 (2004): 203–14.

——. "La corte de Alfonso X el Sabio." *Alcanate* 5 (2006–7): 13–30.

——. *En torno a los orígenes de Andalucía*. 2nd ed. Seville: Universidad de Sevilla, 1988.

——. "Esclavos andaluces en el reino de Granada." In *Actas del III coloquio de historia medieval andaluza: La sociedad medieval andaluza; Grupos no privilegiados*, 327–38. Jaén: Diputación provincial, 1984.

——. *Fernando III el Santo: El Rey que marcó el destino de España*. Seville: Fundación José Manuel Lara, 2006.

——. "Genoveses en Sevilla (siglos XIII–XV)." In *Presencia italiana en Andalucía: siglos XIV–XVII. Actas del I Coloquio Hispano-Italiano*, ed. Bibiano Torres Ramírez and José J. Hernández Palomo, 115–30. Madrid: Consejo Superior de Investigaciones Científicas, 1989.

González Jiménez, Manuel, and Isabel Montes Romero-Camacho. "Los mudéjares andaluces (siglos XIII–XV): Aproximación al estado de la cuestión y propuesta de un modelo teórico." *Revista d'Historia Medieval* 12 (2001–2): 47–78.

González Jiménez, Manuel, Mercedes Borrero Fernández, and Isabel Montes Romero-Camacho. *Sevilla en tiempos de Alfonso X el Sabio*. Seville: Ayuntamiento de Sevilla, 1987.

González Mínguez, César. "La concesión del Fuero real a Vitoria." *HID* 28 (2001): 217–29.

——. *Fernando IV de Castilla (1295–1312): La guerra civil y el predominio de la nobleza*. Valladolid: Universidad de Valladolid, 1976.

——. *El portazgo en la edad media: Aproximación a su estudio en la Corona de Castilla*. Bilbao: Universidad del País Vasco, 1989.

González Rodríguez, Rafael. "Las cortes de Benavente de 1202 y 1228." In *El Reino de León en la época de las cortes de Benavente: Jornadas de Estudios Históricos, Benavente, 7, 8, 9, 10, 15, 16 y 17 de mayo de 2002*, 191–221. Benavente: Institución Ledo del Pozo, 2002.

Goodman, Anthony. "Alfonso X and the English Crown." In Miguel Rodríguez, Múñoz Fernández, and Segura Graiño, *Alfonso X el Sabio*, 1:39–54.

Gorosterratzu, Javier. *Don Rodrigo Jiménez de Rada, Gran estadista, escritor y prelado.* Pamplona: Bescansa, 1925.

Govantes, Ángel Casimiro de. *Diccionario geográfico-histórico de España.* Madrid: Jordán 1846.

Grassotti, Hilda. "Alfonso IX y el origen de los empréstitos." *CHE* 69 (1987): 217–24.

——. "El deber y el derecho de hacer guerra y paz en León y Castilla." *CHE* 59–60 (1976): 221–96. Reprinted in her *Estudios medievales españolas* (Madrid: Fundación Universitaria Española, 1981), 43–132.

——. *Miscelánea de estudios sobre instituciones castellano-leonesas.* Bilbao: Nájera, 1978.

——. "Para la historia del botín y de las parias en Castilla y León." *CHE* 39–40 (1964): 43–132. Reprinted in *Miscelánea*, 135–221.

——. "El recuerdo de las Cortes de Nájera." *CHE* 70 (1988): 255–72.

——. "El repostero en León y Castilla (siglos XII–XIV)." *CHE* 69 (1987): 41–76.

——. "Sobre la retenencia de castillos en la Castilla medieval." In her *Estudios medievales españolas*, 261–81. Madrid: Fundación Universitaria Española, 1981.

——. "Un empréstito para la conquista de Sevilla." *CHE* 45–46 (1967): 191–247. Reprinted in *Miscelánea*, 225–73.

Grau Torras, Sergi. *Cátaros e Inquisición en los reinos hispánicos (siglos XII–XIV).* Madrid: Cátedra, 2012.

Green, Jennifer L. "The Development of Maritime Law in Medieval Spain: The Case of Castile and the *Siete Partidas.*" *The Historian* 58 (1996): 575–87.

Gual Camarena, Miguel. "Para un mapa de la sal hispana en la edad media." In *Homenaje a Jaime Vicens Vives*, ed. Juan Maluquer de Motes, 1:483–97. Barcelona: Universidad de Barcelona, 1965.

Gual López, José Miguel. "Bases para el estudio de las ferias murcianas en la edad media." *MMM* 9 (1982): 9–55.

——. "La política ferial alfonsí y el ordenamiento general de ferias castellanas en su época." In Miguel Rodríguez, Múñoz Fernández, and Segura Graiño, *Alfonso X el Sabio*, 1:94–114.

Guerrero Lafuente, María Dolores. *Historia de la ciudad de Benavente en la edad media.* Benavente: Lancia, 1983.

Guglielmi, Nilda. "La curia regia en León y Castilla." *CHE* 23–24 (1955): 116–267; 28 (1958): 43–101.

——. "Posada y Yantar: Contribución al estudio del léxico de las instituciones medievales." *Hispania: Revista española de historia* 26 (1966): 5–29.

Guiance, Ariel. "Morir por la patria, por la fe: La ideología de la muerte en la *Historia de rebus Hispaniae.*" *CHE* 73 (1991): 75–106.

Guzmán Brito, Alejandro. "La promesa obligacional en las 'Partidas' como sede de la doctrina general de las obligaciones." *Revista Chilena de Derecho* 34 (2007): 395–404.

Haro Cortés, Marta. *La imagen del poder real a través de los compendios de castigos castellanos del siglo XIII.* London: Department of Hispanic Studies, Queen Mary and Westfield College, 1996.

Hartmann, Wilfried, and Kenneth Pennington, eds. *The History of Medieval Canon Law in the Classical Period, 1140–1234: From Gratian to the Decretals of Pope Gregory IX.* Washington, DC: Catholic University of America Press, 2008.

Harvey, L. P. *Islamic Spain, 1250 to 1500*. Chicago: University of Chicago Press, 1990.

Hatton, Vikki, and Angus MacKay. "Anti-Semitism in the *Cantigas de Santa María*." *Bulletin of Hispanic Studies* 60 (1983): 189–99.

Hernández Vegas, Mateo. *Ciudad Rodrigo: La catedral y la ciudad*. 2 vols. Salamanca: Imprenta Comercial Salmantina, 1935.

Heusch, Carlos. "Les fondements juridiques de l'amitié à travers les *Partidas* d'Alphonse X et la droit medieval." *CLHM* 18–19 (1993–94): 5–48.

Hinojosa, Eduardo de. *El elemento germánico en el derecho español*. Madrid: Imprenta Clásica Española, 1915.

Ibáñez de Segovia, Gaspar, Marqués de Mondéjar. *Memorias históricas del Rey D. Alonso el Sabio i observaciones a su chrónica*. Madrid: Joaquin Ibarra, 1777.

Iglesia Ferreirós, Aquilino. "Alfonso X, su labor legislativa y los historiadores." *HID* 9 (1982): 9–113.

——. "Alfonso X el Sabio y su obra legislativa: Algunas reflexiones." *AHDE* 50 (1980): 531–61.

——. "Las Cortes de Zamora de 1274 y los casos de corte." *AHDE* 41 (1971): 945–71.

——. "Cuestiones Alfonsinas." *AHDE* 55 (1985): 95–149.

——. "Derecho municipal, derecho señorial, derecho regio." *HID* 4 (1977): 115–98.

——. "Fuero real y Espéculo." *AHDE* 52 (1982): 111–91.

——. "¿Hay juristas en el Medioevo Peninsular?" *Initium: Revista catalana d'Historia del Dret* 16 (2011): 3–25.

——. *Historia de la traición: La traición regia en León y Castilla*. Santiago de Compostela: Universidad de Compostela, 1971.

——. "La labor legislativa de Alfonso X el Sabio." In Pérez Martín, *España y Europa*, 275–599.

Iradiel Murugarren, Paulino. *Evolución de la industria textil castellana en los siglos XIII–XVI*. Salamanca: Universidad de Salamanca, 1974.

Iturmendi Morales, José. "En torno a la idea de imperio en Alfonso X el Sabio." *Revista de Estudios Políticos* 182 (1972): 83–157.

Jaffe, Ernst, and Heinrich Finke. "La dispensa de matrimonio falsificada para el rey Sancho IV y María de Molina." *AHDE* 4 (1927): 298–318.

Jenks, Edward. *Edward Plantagenet (Edward I), the English Justinian: or, The Making of the Common Law*. New York: G. P. Putnam's Sons, 1902.

Josserand, Philippe. *Église et Pouvoir dans la Péninsule Ibérique: Les Ordres Militaires dans le Royaume de Castille (1252–1369)*. Madrid: Casa de Velázquez, 2004.

Jular Pérez-Alfaro, Cristina, and Carlos Estepa Díez, eds. *Land, Power, and Society in Medieval Castile: A Study of Behetría Lordship*. Turnhout: Brepols, 2009.

Kantorowicz, Ernst. *The King's Two Bodies: A Study in Medieval Political Theology*. Princeton: Princeton University Press, 1957.

——. "Kingship under the Impact of Scientific Jurisprudence." In *Twelfth-Century Europe and the Foundations of Modern Society*, ed. Marshall Clagett, Gaines Post, and Robert Reynolds, 89–111. Madison: University of Wisconsin Press, 1966.

Katz, Melissa R. "The Final Testament of Violante of Aragón (ca. 1236–1300/01): Agency and (Dis)Empowerment of a Dowager Queen." In *Queenship in the Mediterranean: Negotiating the Role of the Queen in the Medieval and Early Modern Eras*, ed. Elena Woodacre, 51–71. New York: Palgrave Macmillan, 2013.

Kearley, Timothy G. "The Enigma of Samuel Parsons Scott." *Roman Legal Tradition* 10 (2014): 1–37.

Keller, John Esten, and Annette Grant Cash. *Daily Life Depicted in the Cantigas de Santa Maria*. Lexington: University Press of Kentucky, 1998.

Keller, John Esten, and Richard P. Kinkade. *Iconography in Medieval Spanish Literature*. Lexington: University Press of Kentucky, 1984.

Kibre, Pearl. "Scholarly Privileges: Their Roman Origins and Medieval Expression." *American Historical Review* 59 (1954): 543–67.

King, P. D. *Law and Society in the Visigothic Kingdom*. Cambridge: Cambridge University Press, 1972.

Kinkade, Richard. "Alfonso X, *Cantiga* 235, and the Events of 1269–1278." *Speculum* 67 (1992): 284–323.

——. "Violante of Aragon (1236?–1300?): An Historical Overview." *Exemplaria Hispanica* 2 (1992–93): 1–37.

Klein, Julius. *The Mesta: A Study in Spanish Economic History, 1273–1836*. Cambridge, MA: Harvard University Press, 1920.

——. "Los privilegios de la Mesta de 1273 y 1276." *BRAH* 64 (1914): 202–18.

Kleine, Marina. *La Cancillería Real de Alfonso X: Actores y prácticas en la producción documental*. Seville: Universidad de Sevilla, 2015.

——. "Los orígenes de la burocracia regia en Castilla: la especialización de los oficiales de Alfonso X y Sancho IV." *e-Spania*, 20 February 2015, https://journals.openedition.org/e-spania/.

Lacarra Lanz, Eukene. "Legal and Clandestine Prostitution in Medieval Spain." *Bulletin of Hispanic Studies* 79 (2002): 265–85.

Ladero Quesada, Miguel Ángel. "Aspectos de la política económica de Alfonso X." *RFDUC* 9 Extra (1985): 69–82.

——. "La Casa real en la baja edad media." *HID* 25 (1998): 327–50.

——. "La caza en la legislación municipal castellana: Siglos XIII a XVIII." *ELEM* 1 (1980): 193–222.

——. "Crédito y comercio de dinero en la Castilla medieval." *Acta historica et archaeologica mediaevalia* 11–12 (1991): 145–59.

——. "Las ferias de Castilla: Siglos XII a XV." *CHE* 67–68 (1982): 269–347. Reprinted at Madrid: Comité español de Ciencias Históricas, 1994.

——. "Los mudéjares de Castilla en la baja edad media." *HID* 5 (1978): 257–304.

——. "Las transformaciones de la fiscalidad regia castellano-leonesa en la segunda mitad del siglo XIII (1252–1312)." In *Historia de la hacienda española: Homenaje al Profesor García de Valdeavellano*, 319–406. Madrid: Instituto de Estudios Fiscales, 1982.

Lapesa, Rafael. "Símbolos y palabras en el Setenario de Alfonso X." *Nueva Revista de Filología hispánica* 29 (1980): 247–61.

Layna Serrano, Francisco. *Historia de Guadalajara y sus Mendozas en los s. XV y XVI*. 4 vols. Madrid: Instituto Jerónimo Zurita, 1942.

——. *Historia de la villa de Atienza*. Madrid: Consejo Superior de Investigaciones Científicas, 1945.

——. *Historia de la villa de Cifuentes*. Guadalajara: Institución Provincial de Cultura "Marqués de Santillana." 1979.

Leclercq-Marx, Jacqueline. "Los monstruos antropomorfos de origen antiguo en la Edad media: Persistencias, mutaciones y recreaciones." *Anales de Historia del Arte*, 2010 extra, *II Jornadas complutenses de Arte Medieval*, 259–74.

León Tello, Pilar. *Los judíos de Toledo*. 2 vols. Madrid: Consejo Superior de Investigaciones Científicas, 1980.

Lewis, Archibald R., and Timothy J. Runyan. *European Naval and Maritime History,* *300–1500.* Bloomington: Indiana University Press, 1990.

Linehan, Peter. "The Accession of Alfonso X (1252) and the Origins of the War of the Spanish Succession." In *God and Man in Medieval Spain: Essays in Honor of J. R. L. Highfield,* ed. Derek W. Lomax and David Mackenzie, 59–80. Warminster: Aris and Phillips, 1989.

——. "The *Gravamina* of the Castilian Church in 1262–3." *EHR* 85 (1970): 730–54.

——. *History and the Historians of Medieval Spain.* Oxford: Clarendon Press, 1993.

——. "La iglesia de León a mediados del siglo XIII." *León y su historia* 3 (1975): 13–76.

——. "The Politics of Piety: Aspects of the Castilian Monarchy from Alfonso X to Alfonso XI." *Revista canadiense de estudios hispánicos* 9 (1985): 386–404.

——. "Pseudo-historia y pseudo-liturgia en la obra Alfonsina." In Pérez Martín, *España y Europa,* 259–74.

——. *The Spanish Church and the Papacy in the Thirteenth Century.* Cambridge: Cambridge University Press, 1971.

——. "The Spanish Church Revisited: The Episcopal Gravamina of 1279." In *Authority and Power: Studies on Medieval Law and Government Presented to Walter Ullmann on his Seventieth Birthday,* ed. Brian Tierney and Peter Linehan, 127–47. Cambridge: Cambridge University Press, 1980.

Liuzzo Scorpo, Antonella. *Friendship in Medieval Iberia: Historical, Legal and Literary Perspectives.* Farnham: Ashgate, 2014.

Llanos Martínez Carrillo, María de los. "Historicidad de los 'Miraculos Romançados' de Pedro Marín (1232–1293): El territorio y la esclavitud granadinos." *AEM* 21 (1991): 69–96.

Lluis y Navas, Jaime. "Los principios sobre la falsificación de moneda en el código de las Partidas." *Numisma* 4 (1954): 87–95.

——. "El sistema de penas sobre falsificación de moneda en el código de las Partidas." *Numisma* 4 (1954): 109–23.

Loperráez, Juan. *Descripción histórica del obispado de Osma.* 3 vols. Madrid: Imprenta real, 1788.

López Amo Marín, Ángel. "El derecho penal español de la baja edad media." *AHDE* 26 (1956): 337–67.

López Dapena, Asunción. "Éxportación castellana del mineral de hierro en el siglo XIII." *CEM* 12–13 (1984): 119–254.

López Ferreiro, Antonio. *Historia de la santa a.m. iglesia de Santiago de Compostela.* 11 vols. Santiago de Compostela: Imprenta del Seminario conciliar y central, 1898–1909.

López Gutiérrez, Antonio J. "Oficio y funciones de los escribanos en la cancillería de Alfonso X." *HID* 31 (2004): 353–67.

——. "Registros y registradores en la Cancilleria de Alfonso X." *Estudis castellonenses* 6 (1994–95): 709–20.

——. "La tradición documental en la cancillería de Alfonso X." *HID* 19 (1992): 253–66.

López Nevot, José Antonio. *La aportación marital en la historia del derecho castellano.* Almería: Universidad de Almería, 1998.

López Pérez, José Luis. "Las Siete Partidas según el códice de los Reyes Católicos de la Biblioteca Nacional de Madrid." *Dicenda: Cuadernos de FilologíaHispánica* 14 (1996): 235–58.

Luchía, Corina. "Reflexiones metodológicas sobre la propiedad privilegiada en la baja edad media: el mayorazgo castellano." *ETF* 27 (2014): 305–26.

MacDonald, Robert A. "Alfonso the Learned and Succession: A Father's Dilemma." *Speculum* 40 (1965): 647–53.

——. "The Editing of Alfonsine Juridical Texts: An Addendum." *La Corónica* 7 (1979): 119–20.

——. "El Espéculo atribuído a Alfonso X, su edición y problemas que plantea." In Pérez Martín, *España y Europa*, 636–44.

——. "Law and Politics: Alfonso's Program of Political Reform." In Burns, *Worlds of Alfonso the Learned and James the Conqueror*, 150–209.

——. "Progress and Problems in Editing Alfonsine Juridical Texts." *La Corónica* 6 (1978): 74–81.

Madero, Marta. "Causa, creencia y testimonios: La prueba judicial en Castilla durante el siglo XIII." *Bulletin du Centre d'Études médiévales d'Auxerre*, Hors-série 2 (2008), http://journals.openedition.org/cem/9672.

——. "El *duellum* entre la honra y la prueba según las *Siete Partidas* de Alfonso X y el comentario de Gregorio López." *CLCHM* 24 (2001): 343–52.

——. "Formas de justicia en la obra juridical de Alfonso X el Sabio." *Hispania: Revista española de historia* 56 (1996): 447–66.

——. "El juez y los testigos." In her *Las verdades de los hechos: Proceso, juez y testimonios en la Castilla del siglo XIII*, 47–75. Salamanca: Universidad de Salamanca, 2004.

——. *Manos violentas, palabras vedadas: La injuria en Castilla y León, siglos XIII–XV*. Madrid: Taurus Humanidades, 1992.

Malalana Ureña, Antonio. *Escalona Medieval (1083–1400)*. Escalona: Ayuntamiento de Escalona, n.d.

Maldonado y Fernández del Torco, José. *La condición jurídica del "Nasciturus" en el derecho Español*. Madrid: Instituto Nacional de Estudios Jurídicos, 1946.

——. "Líneas de influencia canónica en la historia del proceso español." *AHDE* 23 (1953): 467–93.

——. "Sobre la relación entre el derecho de las Decretales y el de las Partidas en materia matrimonial." *AHDE* 15 (1944): 589–643.

Mansilla, Demetrio. *Iglesia castellano-leonesa y curia romana en los tiempos del rey san Fernando*. Madrid: Consejo Superior de Investigaciones Científicas, 1945.

Maravall, José Antonio. "La corriente democrática medieval en España y la fórmula quod omnes tangit." In *Estudios de historia del pensamiento español. Edad media. Serie primera*, 157–75. Madrid: Cultural Hispánica, 1967.

——. "Del régimen feudal al régimen corporativo en el pensamiento de Alfonso X." *BRAH* 157 (1965): 213–68.

Marcos Pous, Alejandro. "Los dos matrimonios de Sancho IV de Castilla." *Cuadernos de Trabajos de la Escuela Española de Historia y Arqueología en Roma* 8 (1956): 1–108.

Marichalar, Amalio, and Cayetano Manrique. *Historia de la legislación y recitaciones del derecho civil de España*. 9 vols. Madrid: Imprenta Nacional, 1861–72.

Márquez Villanueva, Francisco. *El concepto cultural alfonsí*. Madrid: Mapfre, 1995.

Martin, Georges. "Alphonse X de Castille, Roi et Empereur: Commentaire du premier titre de la Deuxième Partie." *CLHM* 23 (2000): 323–48.

——. "Alphonse X maudit son fils." *Atalaya: Revue française d'études médiévales hispaniques romanes* 5 (1994): 153–78.

——. "Alphonse X ou la science politique (*Septénaire*, 1–11)." *CLHM* 18–19 (1993–94): 79–100; 20 (1995): 7–33.

——. "Le concept de 'naturalité' (*naturaleza*) dans les *Sept parties* d'Alphonse X le Sage." *e-Spania*, 5 June 2008, https://journals.openedition.org/e-spania/.

——. "Control regio de la violencia nobiliaria: La caballería según Alfonso X de Castilla (comentario al título XXI de la *Segunda Partida*)." *Annexes des CLCHM* 6 (2004): 219–34.

——. "De lexicología jurídica alfonsí: naturaleza." *Alcanate* 6 (2008–9): 125–38.

——. "De nuevo sobre la fecha del Setenario," *e-Spania*, 2 December 2006, https://journals.openedition.org/e-spania/.

Martín, José Luis. "Economía y sociedad de la época Alfonsina." *Revista de Occidente* 43 (1984): 29–41.

Martín-Retortillo y Baquer, Sebastián. "Notas para un estudio de la prueba en la Tercera Partida." *Argensola: Revista de Ciencias sociales del Instituto de Estudios altoaragoneses* 22 (1955): 101–22.

Martínez Díez, Gonzalo. "Cortes y ordenamientos de Alfonso X el Sabio (1252–1284)." In *Annals of the Archive of Ferran Valls i Taberner's Library: Studies in the History of Political Thought, Political & Moral Philosophy, Business & Medical Ethics, Public Health and Juridical Literature*, ed. Manuel J. Peláez, nos. 11–12, 123–68. Málaga: Universidad de Málaga, 1991.

——. "La tortura judicial en la legislación histórica." *AHDE* 32 (1962): 223–300.

Martínez Gijón, José. "La jurisdiccíon marítima en Castilla durante la baja edad media." *Historia* 8 (1969): 309–22.

Martínez Marcos, Esteban. *Las causas matrimoniales en las Partidas de Alfonso el Sabio.* Salamanca: Consejo Superior de Investigaciones Científicas, 1966.

——. "Fuentes de la doctrina canónica de la IV Partida del código del rey Alfonso el Sabio." *Revista Española de Derecho Canónico* 18 (1963): 897–926.

Martínez Marina, Francisco. *Ensayo histórico-crítico sobre la antigua legislación y principales cuerpos legales de los Reynos de León y Castilla, especialmente sobre el Código de las Siete Partidas de Don Alfonso el Sabio.* 2 vols. Madrid: Hijos de don Joaquín Ibarra, 1808; 2nd ed., Madrid: D. E. Aguado, 1834; 3rd ed., Madrid: Sociedad Literaria y Tipográfica, 1845.

——. *Obras escogidas de don Francisco Martínez Marina.* Ed. José Martínez Cardós. 3 vols. Madrid: Atlas, 1966–69.

——. *Teoría de las Cortes o Grandes Juntas Nacionales.* Madrid: Fermín Villalpando, 1813. Reprinted in *Obras escogidas*, vols. 2–3.

Martínez Martínez, Julio Gerardo. *Acerca de la guerra y de la paz, los ejércitos, las estrategías y las armas según el Libro de las Siete Partidas.* Cáceres: Universidad de Extremadura, 1984.

——. "Tres ensayos sobre algunas cuestiones de historia del derecho español." *Anuario de la Facultad del Derecho* 22 (2004): 249–80.

Martínez Vela, José Antonio. "El contrato de 'Locatio Conductio': Notas sobre su recepción en el derecho castellano medieval, con especial referencia al código de 'Las Partidas.'" *Revista de Derecho UNED* 11 (2012): 601–34.

Martos Calabrús, María Angustias. *Aproximación histórica a las solemnidades del testamento Público*. Almería: Universidad de Almería, 1998.

Masferrer Domingo, Aniceto. *La pena de infamia en el derecho histórico español: Contribución al estudio de la tradición penal europea en el marco del ius commune*. Madrid: Dykinson, 2001.

McKnight, Joseph W. "Protection of the Family Home from Creditors: The Sources and Evolution of a Legal Principle." *Southwestern Historical Quarterly* 86 (1982): 370–99.

———. "Spanish Law for the Protection of Surviving Spouses in North America." *AHDE* 57 (1987): 365–406.

———. "The Spanish Watercourses of Texas." In *Essays in Legal History in Honor of Felix Frankfurter*, ed. Morris D. Forkosch, 373–86. New York: Bobbs-Merrill, 1966.

McMillin, Linda A. "Alfonso el Sabio and the *Primera Partida*: A Thirteenth-Century Vision of the Church." *Comitatus* 17 (1986): 51–68.

Medrano del Pozo, Sagrario. "'Marisaltos,' la judía segoviana protagonista de la Cantiga CVII de Alfonso X el Sabio." *Iacobus: Revista de Estudios Jacobeos y Medievales* 33–34 (2015): 95–128.

Menéndez Pidal, Gonzalo. *La España del Siglo XIII leída en imágenes*. Madrid: Real Academia de la Historia, 1986.

Menjot, Denis. *Murcie castillane: une ville au temps de la frontière (1243-milieu du XVe s.)*. 2 vols. Madrid: Casa de Velázquez, 2002.

Merchán Álvarez, Antonio. "La alcaldía de avenencia coma forma de justicia municipal en el Derecho de León y Castilla." *ELEM* 6 (1985): 65–91.

———. *La tutela de los menores en Castilla hasta fines del siglo XV*. Seville: Universidad de Sevilla, 1976.

Meyer, Bruno. "El desarrollo de las relaciones políticas entre Castilla y el Imperio en tiempos de los Staufen." *ELEM* 21 (1998): 29–48.

Miguel Rodríguez, Juan Carlos de, Ángela Múñoz Fernández, and Cristina Segura Graiño, eds. *Alfonso X el Sabio: Vida, obra y época*. Madrid: Sociedad Española de Estudios Medievales, 1989.

Minguella, Toribio. *Historia de la diócesis de Sigüenza*. 3 vols. Madrid: RABM, 1900–13.

Mitre Fernández, Emilio. "Hérésie et culture dirigeante dans la Castille de la fin du XIIIᵉ siècle: le modèle d'Alphonse X." *Heresis* 9 (1987): 33–47.

———. "Iglesia, salvación y teocracia romana en el Medievo (Un apunte en torno al axioma Extra Ecclesiam nulla salus)." *'Ilu: Revista de Ciencias de las Religiones* 18 (2013): 135–73.

Molina Molina, Ángel Luis. "Aspectos de la vida cotidiana en Las Partidas." *Glossae* 5–6 (1993–94): 171–85.

Montagut Estragués, Tomás. "El testamento inoficioso en las Partidas y sus fuentes." *AHDE* 62 (1992): 239–326.

Montoya, María Isabel. "La caza en el medievo peninsular." *Revista electrónica de Estudios Filológicos* 6 (2003), http://www.um.es/tonosdigital/znum6/index.htm.

Morín, Alejandro. "Matar a la adúltera: el homicidio legítimo en la legislación castellana medieval." *CLHM* 24 (2001): 353–77.

Morreale, Margherita. "El canon de la misa en lengua vernácula y la Biblia romanceada del siglo XIII." *Hispania Sacra* 15 (1962): 203–19.

Moxo, Salvador de. "De la nobleza vieja a la nobleza nueva: La transformación nobiliaria en la baja edad media." *Cuadernos de Historia* 3 (1969): 1–110.

———. "La nobleza castellano-leonesa en la edad media: Problemática que suscita su estudio en el marco de la historia social." *Hispania: Revista española de historia* 30 (1970): 5–68.

Moxó y Montoliu, Francisco de. "El enlace de Alfonso de Castilla con Violante de Aragón: Marco político y precisiones cronológicas." *Hispania: Revista española de historia* 49 (1989): 69–110.

Muñoz Ruano, Juan. "El tratamiento de las fortalezas en las Cantigas de Santa Maria." *Castillos de España* 93 (1987): 15–34.

Muro García, Manuel. "En el Archivo municipal de Úbeda: Un precedente de 'Las Partidas.' Como debían jurar los cristianos, judíos y moros." *BRAH* 91 (1927): 376–84.

Nelson, Benjamin N. *The Idea of Usury, from Tribal Brotherhood to Universal Otherhood.* Princeton: Princeton University Press, 1950.

Nicholas, Barry. *An Introduction to Roman Law.* Oxford: Oxford University Press, 1962.

Nieto Cumplido, Manuel. "La elección de obispos de Córdoba en la baja edad media." In Cristóbal Torres Delgado et al., *Andalucía medieval: Nuevos estudios*, 75–103. Córdoba: Monte de Piedad y Caja de Ahorros de Córdoba, 1979.

———. *Orígenes del regionalismo andaluz (1235–1325).* Córdoba: Monte de Piedad y Caja de Ahorros de Córdoba, 1979.

Nieto Soria, José Manuel. "La coronación del rey: los símbolos y la naturaleza de su poder." In *Alfonso X y su época: el siglo del rey sabio*, ed. Miguel Rodríguez Llopis, 127–52. Barcelona: Caroggio, 2001.

———. *Fundamentos ideológicos del poder real en Castilla (siglos XIII–XVI).* Madrid: EUDEMA, 1988.

———. Iglesia y poder real en Castilla: El episcopado, 1250–1350. Madrid: Universidad Complutense, 1988.

———. "Los obispos de la diócesis de León en sus relaciones con la monarquía, 1250–1350." *Archivos Leoneses* 74 (1983): 201–62.

———. "Principios teóricos y evolución de la política eclesiástica de Alfonso X." *Mayorga* 22 (1989): 465–74.

———. *Las relaciones monarquía-episcopado castellano como sistema de poder (1252–1312).* 2 vols. Madrid: Universidad Complutense de Madrid, 1983.

———. *Sancho IV, 1284–1295.* Palencia: Diputación Provincial de Palencia, 1994.

Nogales Rincón, David. "Los espejos de príncipes en Castilla (siglos XIII–XV): Un modelo literario de la realeza bajomedieval." *Medievalismo* 16 (2006): 9–39.

Noonan, John T. *The Scholastic Analysis of Usury.* Cambridge, MA: Harvard University Press 1957.

Núñez Lagos, Rafael. *La estipulación en las Partidas y el Ordenamiento de Alcalá.* Madrid: Real Academia de Jurisprudencia y Legislación, 1950.

O'Callaghan, Joseph F. "Alfonso X." In *Great Christian Jurists in Spanish History*, ed. Rafael Domingo and Javier Martínez-Torrón, 69–83. New York: Cambridge University Press, 2018.

———. *Alfonso X and the Cantigas de Santa Maria: A Poetic Biography.* Leiden: Brill, 1998.

———. "Alfonso X and the Castilian Church." *Thought* 60 (1985): 417–29; repr. in *Alfonso X, the Cortes and Government,* no. VI.

——. *Alfonso X, the Cortes and Government in Medieval Spain.* Brookfield, VT: Ashgate, 1998.

——. "The Beginnings of the Cortes of León-Castile." *American Historical Review* 74 (1969): 1503–37.

——. "The *Cantigas de Santa Maria* as an Historical Source: Two Examples (nos. 321 and 386)." In *Studies on the Cantigas de Santa Maria: Art, Music and Poetry*, ed. Israel Katz and John E. Keller, 387–93. Madison: Hispanic Seminary, 1987.

——. "Catálogo de los cuadernos de las Cortes de Castilla y León, 1252–1348." In *Alfonso X, the Cortes and Government*, no. XIV.

——. "The Cortes and Royal Taxation during the Reign of Alfonso X of Castile." *Traditio* 27 (1971): 379–98. Reprinted in *Alfonso X, the Cortes and Government*, no. IV.

——. *The Cortes of Castile-León, 1188–1350.* Philadelphia: University of Pennsylvania Press, 1989.

——. "The Ecclesiastical Estate in the Cortes of León-Castile, 1252–1350." *Catholic Historical Review* 67 (1981), 185–213; repr. in *Alfonso X, the Cortes and Government*, no. XII.

——. "La financiación de la conquista de Sevilla." In *Sevilla 1248: Congreso Internacional Conmemorativo del 750 Aniversario de la Conquista de la Ciudad de Sevilla por Fernando III, Rey de Castlla y León*, ed. Manuel González Jiménez, 191–206. Madrid: Fundación Ramón Areces, 2001.

——. *The Gibraltar Crusade: Castile and the Battle for the Strait.* Philadelphia: University of Pennsylvania Press, 2011.

——. *A History of Medieval Spain.* Ithaca: Cornell University Press, 1975.

——. "Image and Reality: The King Creates his Kingdom." In Burns, *Emperor of Culture*, 14–32.

——. *The Learned King: Alfonso X of Castile.* Philadelphia: University of Pennsylvania Press, 1993.

——. "The Many Roles of the Medieval Queen: Some Examples from Castile." In *Queenship and Political Power in Medieval and Early Modern Spain*, ed. Theresa Earenfight, 21–32. Burlington, VT: Ashgate, 2005.

——. "The Mudéjars of Castile and Portugal in the Twelfth and Thirteenth Centuries." In *Muslims under Latin Rule, 1100–1300*, ed. James M. Powell, 11–56. Princeton: Princeton University Press, 1990.

——. "On the *Ordenamiento de Zamora*, 1274," *HID* 44 (2017): 297–312.

——. "On the Promulgation of the *Espéculo* and the *Fuero Real*." In *Alfonso X, the Cortes and Government*, no. III:1–12.

——. "Paths to Ruin: The Economic and Financial Policies of Alfonso the Learned." In Burns, *Worlds of Alfonso the Learned and James the Conqueror*, 41–67.

——. *Reconquest and Crusade in Medieval Spain.* Philadelphia: University of Pennsylvania Press, 2003.

——. "Sobre la promulgación del Espéculo y del Fuero real." In *Estudios en homenaje a Don Claudio Sánchez Albornoz*, 3:167–79.

——. "Una nota sobre las llamadas Cortes de Benavente." *Archivos Leoneses* 73 (1983): 97–100.

——. "War (and Peace) in the Law Codes of Alfonso X." In *Crusaders, Condottieri, and Cannon: Medieval Warfare in Societies around the Mediterranean*, ed. Donald J. Kagay and L. J. Andrew Villalon, 3–17. Leiden: Brill, 2003.

Ochoa Sanz, Javier. *Vincentius Hispanus: Canonista boloñes del siglo XIII.* Rome: Cuadernos del Instituto Jurídico Español, 1960.

Ors, Álvaro d'. "La territorialidad del derecho de los visigodos." *Estudios Visigóticos* 1 (1956): 91–124.

Ortiz de Zúñiga, Diego. *Anales eclesiásticos y seculares de la muy noble y muy leal ciudad de Sevilla, Metropoli de Andalucía.* Ed. Antonio María Espinosa y Carzel. 5 vols. Madrid: Imprenta real, 1795. Reprint, Seville: Guadalquivir, 1988.

Ortuño Sánchez-Pedreño, José María. *El adelantado de la Corona de Castilla.* Murcia: Universidad de Murcia, 1997.

——. "El adelantado en las Partidas." *MMM* 18 (1994): 161–74.

——. "El derecho de asilo en iglesias y sus cementerios en la legislación de Partidas." *Glossae* 5–6 (1993–94): 187–93.

——. "Las fuentes del régimen de la donación en las Partidas." *REHJ* 23 (2001): 369–90.

——. "El oficio de abogado en las Partidas de Alfonso X el Sabio." *Revista jurídica de la Región de Murcia* 21 (1996): 29–46.

——. "Origen romano de la enfiteusis en las Partidas." *Anales de la Universidad de Alicante. Facultad de Derecho* 8 (1993): 63–74.

——. "Origen romano de la fianza en las Partidas." *Ius fugit: Revista interdisciplinar de Estudios histórico-jurídicos* 7 (1998): 89–122.

Ostos Salcedo, Pilar, and María Luisa Pardo Rodríguez. "La teoría de la falsedad documental en la Corona de Castilla." In Comision Internacional de Diplomatica, *Falsos y falsificaciones de documentos diplomáticos en la Edad media,* 161–76. Zaragoza: Real Sociedad Económica Aragonesa de Amigos del País, 1991.

Otero Varela, Alfonso. "La adopción en la historia del derecho español." In his *Estudios histórico-jurídicos,* 2:9–92.

——. "Las arras en el Derecho español medieval." *AHDE* 25 (1955): 189–210.

——. *Estudios histórico-jurídicos.* 2 vols. Madrid: Colegio de Registradores de la Propiedad y Mercantiles de España, 2005.

——. "Las Partidas y el Ordenamiento de Alcalá en el cambio del ordenamiento medieval." *AHDE* 63–64 (1993–94): 451–548.

——. "La patria potestad en el derecho histórico español." *AHDE* 26 (1956): 209–41.

——. "El riepto en el derecho castellano-leonés." In his *Estudios histórico-jurídicos,* 1:173–260.

——. "El riepto en los fueros municipales." *AHDE* 29 (1959):153–73; also in his *Estudios histórico-jurídicos,* 1:273–98.

Palacios Martín, Bonifacio. "La circulación de los cátaros por el Camino de Santiago y sus implicaciones socioculturales: Una fuente para su conocimiento." *ELEM* 3 (1982): 219–30.

Panateri, Daniel. *El discurso del rey: El discurso jurídico alfonsí y sus implicancias políticas.* Madrid: Universidad Carlos III de Madrid, 2017.

——. "El Prólogo de *Siete Partidas*: Entropía, edición y uso político." *Medievalia* 47 (2015): 54–81.

——. "La tortura en las Siete Partidas: la pena, la prueba y la majestad. Un análisis sobre la reinstauración del tormento en la legislación castellana del siglo XIII." *Estudios de Historia de España* 14 (2012): 83–108.

——. "La tortura judicial en las *Siete Partidas* de Alfonso X, el Sabio (un análisis sobre el prólogo al trigésimo título de la *Partida* VII)." In *Palimpsestos: Escrituras y reescrituras de las cultura antigua y medieval*, ed. Gisela Coronado-Schwindt, Viviana Gastaldi, Gabriela Marrón, and Gerardo Rodríguez, 267–76. Bahía Blanca: EdiUNS, 2013.

Parise, Agustín. "Translators' Preface to the Laws of Las Siete Partidas which are Still in Force in the State of Louisiana." *Journal of Civil Law Studies* 7 (2014): 311–53.

Pastor, Reyna. "Ganadería y precios: Consideraciones sobre la economía de León y Castilla (siglos XI–XIII)." *CHE* 35–36 (1962): 37–55.

——. "La sal en Castilla y León: Un problema de la alimentación y del trabajo y una política fiscal (siglos X–XIII)." *CHE* 37–38 (1963): 42–87.

Paz, Ramón. "Un nuevo feudo castellano." *AHDE* 5 (1928): 445–48.

Paz Alonso, María. *El proceso penal en Castilla (siglos XIII–XVIII)*. Salamanca: Universidad de Salamanca, 1982.

Paz Alonso Romero, María. *El régimen de la abogacía en Castilla (Siglos XIII–XVII)*. Madrid: Dykinson, 2013.

Pennington, Kenneth. "Laurentius Hispanus." In *Dictionary of the Middle Ages*, ed. Joseph R. Strayer, 7:385–86. New York: Scribner's, 1986.

——. *The Prince and the Law, 1200–1600: Sovereignty and Rights in the Western Legal Tradition*. Berkeley: University of California Press, 1993.

Pepin, Paulette L. *María de Molina, Queen and Regent: Life and Rule in Castile-León*. Lanham MD: Lexington Books, 2016.

Pérez Bustamante, Rogelio. *El gobierno y la administración territorial de Castilla (1230–1474)*. 2 vols. Madrid: Universidad Autónoma, 1976.

——. "Las reformas de la administración central en el reino de Castilla y León en la época de Alfonso X (1252–1284)." *RFDUC* 9 Extra (1985): 83–102.

Pérez de la Canal, Miguel Ángel. "La justicia de la corte de Castilla durante los siglos XIII al XV." *HID* 2 (1975): 383–481.

Pérez de Tudela y Velasco, María Isabel. "Las construcciones militares y su función en la época de Alfonso X." *Castillos de España* 88 (1984): 37–42.

——. "Ideario político y orden social en las Partidas de Alfonso X." *ELEM* 14 (1991): 183–200.

Pérez Embid, Florentino. *El almirantazgo de Castilla*. Seville: Universidad de Sevilla, 1944.

——. "La marina real castellana en el siglo XIII." *AEM* 6 (1969): 141–85.

Pérez Gil, Julio. *La acusación popular*. Granada: Comares, 1998.

Pérez López, José Luis. "Los prólogos del *Libro de las Leyes* y el fragmento llamado *Setenario* en la obra jurídica alfonsí." *Revista de Literatura Medieval* 14 (2002): 109–43.

Pérez Martín, Antonio. "Los colegios de doctores de Bolonia y su relación con España." *AHDE* 48 (1978): 5–90.

——. *El derecho procesal del "ius commune" en España*. Murcia: Universidad de Murcia, 1999.

——, ed. *España y Europa: Un pasado jurídico común; Actos del I simpósio internacional del Instituto de Derecho común*. Murcia: Instituto de Derecho Común, 1986.

——. "El estudio de la recepción del derecho común en España." In *I Seminario de historia del derecho y derecho privado: Nuevas técnicas de investigación*, ed. Pablo Salvador Coderch and Joaquín Cerdá Ruiz-Funes, 241–325. Barcelona: Universitat Autònoma de Barcelona, 1982.

——. "Fuentes romanas en las Partidas." *Glossae* 4 (1992): 215–46.

——. "El Fuero Real y Murcia." *AHDE* 54 (1984): 55–96.

——. "Hacia un Derecho Común Europeo: La obra jurídica de Alfonso X." In Rodrí- guez Llopis, *Alfonso X*, 109–35.

——. "Importancia de las universidades en la recepción del derecho romano en la Península ibérica." *Studi Sassaresi* 8 (1980–81): 255–332.

——. "La institución real en el 'ius commune' y en las Partidas." *CLHM* 23 (2000): 305–21.

——. "El ius commune: artificio de juristas." In *Història del pensament jurídic: Curs 1996–1997 dedicat a la memoria del professor Francisco Tomás y Valiente*, ed. Tomàs de Montagut, 69–93. Barcelona: Universitat Pompeu Fabra, 1999.

——. "Jacobo de las leyes: datos biográficos." *Glossae* 5–6 (1993–94): 279–331.

——. "Jacobo de las leyes: Ureña tenía razón." *AD* 26 (2008): 251–73.

——. "Murcia y la obra legislativa alfonsina: pasado y presente." *AD* 8 (1985): 93–128.

——. "La obra jurídica de Jacobo de las Leyes: las Flores de Derecho." *CLHM* 22 (1998–99): 247–70.

——. "La obra legislativa alfonsina y puesto que en ella ocupan las Siete Partidas. *Glossae* 3 (1992): 9–63.

——. "El *Ordo iudiciarius 'ad summarium notitiam'* y sus derivados: Contribución a la historia de la literatura procesal castellana." *HID* 8 (1981): 195–266; 9 (1982): 327–423.

——. "La protección del honor y de la fama en el derecho histórico español." *AD* 11 (1991): 117–56.

——. "Las redacciones de la primera Partida de Alfonso X el Sabio." *Revista española de Derecho Canónico* 71 (2014): 21–37.

——. "La republica christiana medieval: Pontificado, Imperio y Reinos." In Jesús Lalinde Abadía et al., *El estado español en su dimensión histórica*, 61–128. Barce- lona: Promociones y Publicaciones Universitarias, 1984.

Pérez Molina, Rafael. "La prueba de confesión en la legislación castellano." PhD thesis, Universidad de Córdoba, 2012.

Pérez Monzón, Olga. "La imagen del poder y el poder de la imagen: Alfonso X de Castilla y el infante don Felipe." *Nuevo Mundo Mundos Nuevos*, 30 June 2009, http://nuevomundo.revues.org/56517.

Pérez Prendes, José Manuel. "La frialdad del texto: Comentario al prólogo del *Fuero viejo de Castilla*," *CLHM* 22 (1998–99): 297–322.

——. "Las leyes de los adelantados mayores." *Hidalguía* 10 (1962): 365–84.

Peters, Edward. "Wounded Names: The Medieval Doctrine of Infamy." In *Law in Mediaeval Life and Thought*, ed. Edward B. King and Susan J. Ridyard, 43–89. Sewanee, TN: Press of the University of the South, 1990.

Phillips, William D. *Slavery from Roman Times to the Early Transatlantic Trade*. Minne- apolis: University of Minnesota Press, 1985.

——. *Slavery in Medieval and Early Modern Iberia*. Philadelphia: University of Pennsyl- vania Press, 2014.

Pick, Lucy K. *Conflict and Coexistence: Archbishop Rodrigo and the Muslims and Jews of Medieval Spain*. Ann Arbor: University of Michigan Press, 2004.

Pino Abad, Miguel. "Los andadores de concejo en los fueros municipales castellano- leoneses." *CHD* 6 (1999): 273–300.

——. *La pena de confiscación de bienes en el derecho histórico español*. Madrid: Dykinson, 2014.

———. "La saca de cosas vedadas en el derecho territorial castellano." *AHDE* 70 (2000): 195–241.

Piskorski, Wladimir. *Las Cortes de Castilla en el período de tránsito de la edad media a la moderna 1188–1520.* Trans. Claudio Sánchez Albornoz. Barcelona, 1930. Reprint, Barcelona: Ediciones El Albir, 1977.

Plaza Serrano, Gonzala. "La tenencia de castillos y su entrega al señor en la II Partida de Alfonso X." In *Alarcos, 1195: Actas del Congreso Internacional Conmemorativo del VII Centenario de la Batalla de Alarcos,* ed. Ricardo Izquierdo Benito and Francisco Ruiz Gómez, 589–96. Cuenca: Universidad de Castilla-LaMancha, 1996.

Porras Arboledas, Pedro Andrés. "El derecho marítimo en el Cantábrico durante la baja edad media: *Partidas* y *Rôles d'Oléron.*" In *Ciudades y villas portuarias del Atlántico en la Edad media: Nájera. Encuentros Internacionales del Medievo, Nájera, 27–30 de julio de 2004,* ed. Beatriz Arizaga Bolumburu and Jesús Ángel Solórzano Telechea, 231–55. Nájera: Instituto de Estudios Riojanos, 2005.

———. "Los portazgos en León y Castilla durante la Edad Media. Política real y circuitos comerciales." *ELEM* 15 (1992): 161–212.

Porro Girardi, Nelly Raquel. *La investidura de armas en Castilla del Rey Sabio a los Católicos.* Valladolid: Junta de Castilla y León, 1998.

Post, Gaines. "*Plena Potestas* and Consent in Medieval Assemblies." In his *Studies in Medieval Legal Thought,* 61–90.

———. "Roman Law and Early Representation in Spain and Italy, 1150–1250." In his *Studies in Medieval Legal Thought,* 91–161.

———. *Studies in Medieval Legal Thought: Public Law and the State, 1100–1322.* Princeton: Princeton University Press, 1964.

Powers, James F. "Frontier Municipal Baths and Social Interaction in Thirteenth-Century Spain." *American Historical Review* 84 (1979): 649–67.

———. *A Society Organized for War: The Iberian Municipal Militias in the Central Middle Ages, 1000–1284.* Berkeley: University of California Press, 1988.

———. "Two Warrior Kings and Their Municipal Militias: The Townsman-Soldier in Law and Life." In Burns, *Worlds of Alfonso the Learned and James the Conqueror,* 95–117.

Prego de Lis, Augusto. "La pena de exilio en la legislación Hispanogoda." *Espacio y tiempo en la Percepción de la Antigüedad Tardía* 23 (2006): 515–29.

Procter, Evelyn. *Alfonso X of Castile: Patron of Literature and Learning.* Oxford: Clarendon Press, 1951.

———. "The Castilian Chancery during the Reign of Alfonso X, 1252–1284." In *Oxford Essays in Medieval History Presented to Herbert Edward Salter,* ed. F. M. Powicke, 104–21. Oxford: Clarendon Press, 1934.

———. *Curia and Cortes in León and Castille, 1072–1295.* Cambridge: Cambridge University Press, 1980.

———. *The Judicial Use of Pesquisa (Inquisition) in Léon and Castille, 1157–1369. English Historical Review.* Supplement 2. London: Longmans, 1966.

———. "The Towns of León and Castile as Suitors before the King's Court." *EHR* 74 (1959): 1–22.

Pujal Rodríguez, Carmen. "La recepción el derecho romano testamentario en las Partidas." *Anales de la Universidad de Alicante. Facultad de Derecho* 5 (1990): 175–207.

Ramos, Norah B. "La iglesia a través de las cortes castellanas: Uso y abuso de la excomunión (Ss. XIII–XIV)." *CHE* 69 (1987): 97–107.

Ramos Vázquez, Isabel. *Arrestos, cárceles y prisiones en los derechos históricos españoles.* Madrid: Ministerio de Interior, 2008.

——. "Cárceles públicas y privadas en el derecho medieval y castellano: El delito de cárceles particulares." *REHJ* 28 (2006): 338–86.

——. "El proceso en rebeldía en el derecho castellano." *AHDE* 75 (2005): 721–54.

Ratcliffe, Marjorie. "Adulteresses, Mistresses, and Prostitutes: Extramarital Relationships in Medieval Castile." *Hispania* 67 (1984): 346–50.

——. "'Así donde no hay varón, todo bien fallece': La viuda en la legislación medieval española." In *Actas del X Congreso de la Asociación Internacional de Hispanistas: Barcelona 21–26 de agosto de 1989*, 1:311–18. Barcelona: Promociones y Publicaciones Universitarias, 1992.

Reich, Peter. "Siete Partidas in My Saddlebags: The Transmission of Hispanic Law from Antebellum Louisiana to Texas and California." *Tulane European and Civil Law Forum* 22 (2007): 79–88.

——. "Western Courts and the Privatization of Hispanic Mineral Rights since 1850: An Alchemy of Title." *Columbia Journal of Environmental Law* 23 (1998): 57–87.

Reilly, Bernard F. *The Kingdom of León-Castilla under King Alfonso VI, 1065–1109.* Princeton: Princeton University Press, 1988.

——. *The Kingdom of León-Castilla under King Alfonso VII, 1126–1157.* Philadelphia: University of Pennsylvania Press, 1998.

——. *The Kingdom of León-Castilla under Queen Urraca, 1109–1126.* Princeton: Princeton University Press, 1982.

Renouard, Yves. "Un sujet de recherches: l'exportation de chevaux de la péninsule ibérique en France et en Angleterre au moyen âge." In *Homenaje a Jaime Vicens Vives*, Juan Maluquer de Motes, 1:571–77. Barcelona: Universidad de Barcelona, 1965.

Riaza, Román. "Las Partidas y los *Libri feudorum*." *AHDE* 10 (1933): 5–18.

Riaza Martínez Osorio, Román. "El derecho penal en las Partidas." In *Trabajos del Seminario del derecho penal: curso 1916–17*, ed. Luis Jiménez de Asúa, 19–65. Madrid: Reus, 1922.

Rico, Francisco. *Alfonso X y la General Estoria: Tres Lecciones.* Barcelona: Ariel, 1972.

Rodríguez Díez, Matías. *Historia de la ciudad de Astorga.* 2nd ed. Astorga: Porfirio López, 1909.

Rodríguez Fernández, Justiniano. "Juderías de León." *Archivos Leoneses* 2 (1947): 33–72.

——. *Las Juderías de la provincia de León.* León: Consejo Superior de Investigaciones Científicas, 1976.

Rodríguez Flores, María Inmaculada. *El perdón real en Castilla (siglos XIII–XVIII).* Salamanca: Universidad de Salamanca, 1971.

Rodríguez Llopis, Miguel, ed. *Alfonso X: Aportaciones de un rey castellano a la construcción de Europa.* Murcia: Editora Regional de Murcia, 1997.

Rodríguez López, Amancio. *El real monasterio de Las Huelgas de Burgos y el Hospital del Rey.* 2 vols. Burgos: Centro Católico, 1907.

Rodríguez Molina, José. "La mesta de Jaén y sus conflictos con los agricultores." *CEM* 1 (1973): 67–82.

Rodríguez Ortíz, Victoria. *El aborto hasta fines de la Edad media castellana: Su consideración social y jurídica.* Madrid: Aranzadi, 2014.

Rodríguez-Picavea, Enrique. "The Armies of the Military Orders in Medieval Iberia." *Mediterranean Studies* 20 (2012): 28–58.

Rodríguez Velasco, Jesús D. "De oficio a estado: La caballería entre el *Espéculo* y las *Siete Partidas.*" *CLHM* 18–19 (1993–94): 49–77.

Romano, David. *De historia judía hispánica.* Barcelona: Universitat de Barcelona, 1991.

——. *Judíos al servicio de Pedro el Grande de Aragón (1276–1285).* Barcelona: Universidad de Barcelona, 1983.

——. "Los judíos y Alfonso X." *Revista de Occidente* 43 (1984): 203–17.

Rosa Pereira, Isaías da. "Livros de direito na Idade Média." *Lusitania Sacra* 7 (1964–66): 7–60.

Roth, Norman. "Dar una voz a los judíos: Representación en la España medieval." *AHDE* 56 (1986): 943–52.

——. "Jewish Collaborators in Alfonso's Scientific Work." In Burns, *Emperor of Culture,* 59–71.

——. "Two Jewish Courtiers of Alfonso X called Zag (Isaac)." *Sefarad* 43 (1983):75–85.

Rubio García, Luis. "Del latín al castellano en la cancillería de Alfonso X el Sabio." *Glossae* 5–6 (1993–94): 225–41.

Rüfner, Thomas. "The Roman Concept of Ownership and the Medieval Doctrine of *Dominium Utile.*" In *The Creation of the Ius Commune: From Casus to Regula,* ed. John W. Cairns and Paul J. du Plessis, 127–42. Edinburgh: University of Edinburgh Press, 2010.

Ruiz, Teofilo F. "The Business of Salvation: Castilian Wills in the Late Middle Ages, 1200–1400." In *On the Social Origins of Medieval Institutions: Essays in Honor of Joseph F. O'Callaghan,* ed. Donald J. Kagay and Theresa Vann, 63–92. Leiden: Brill, 1998.

——. "Castilian Merchants in England, 1248–1350." In *Order and Innovation in the Middle Ages: Essays in Honor of Joseph R. Strayer,* 173–85. Princeton: Princeton University Press, 1976.

——. *The City and the Realm: Burgos and Castile, 1080–1492.* Brookfield, VT: Ashgate, 1992.

——. *Crisis and Continuity: Land and Town in Late Medieval Castile.* Philadelphia: University of Pennsylvania Press, 1994.

——. "Expansion et changement: La conquête de Castille et la société castillane (1248–1350)." *Annales: Economies, Sociétés, Civilisations* 35 (1979): 548–65.

——. "Images of Power in the Seals of the Castilian Monarchy: 1135–1469." In *Estudios en homenaje a Don Claudio Sánchez Albornoz,* 4:455–63.

——. *Sociedad y poder real en Castilla (Burgos en la baja edad media).* Barcelona: Ariel, 1981.

——. "The Transformation of the Castilian Municipalities: The Case of Burgos, 1248–1350." *Past and Present: A Journal of Historical Studies* 77 (1977): 3–32. Reprinted in *The City and the Realm,* no. VII.

——. "Une royauté sans sacre: La monarchie castillane du bas Moyen Âge." *Annales: Economies, Sociétés, Civilisations* 39 (1984): 429–53.

Ruíz de la Peña, Juan Ignacio. "Poblamientos y cartas pueblas de Alfonso X y Sancho IV en Galicia." In *Homenaje a José María Lacarra,* 3:26–60. Zaragoza: Anubar, 1978.

Ruiz Pino, Salvador. "Régimen jurídico de la adopción en derecho romano y su recepción en el derecho español." PhD thesis, Universidad de Córdoba, 2010.

Salazar y Acha, Jaime. "La cancillería real en la Corona de Castilla." In *Monarquía, crónicas, archivos y cancillerías en los reinos hispano-cristianos*, ed. Esteban Sarasa, 309–24. Zaragoza: Institución Fernando el Católico, 2014.

——. *La Casa del Rey en Castilla y León en la edad media*. Madrid: Centro de Estudios Políticos y Constitucionales, 2002.

——. "La evolución de la Casa del Rey en el siglo XIII." In *Evolución y estructura de la Casa Real de Castilla*, ed. Andrés Gambra Gutiérrez and Félix Labrador Arroyo, 1:65–80. Madrid: Polifemo, 2010.

——. "Precisiones y nuevos datos sobre el entorno familiar de Alfonso X el Sabio, fundador de Ciudad Real." *Cuadernos de Estudios Manchegos* 20 (1990): 211–31.

Salvador Miguel, Nicasio. "Reflexiones sobre el episodio de Rachel y Vidas en el Cantar de mio Cid." *RFE* 59 (1977): 183–224.

Salvat Monguillot, Manuel. "Factores que determinan la capacidad civil en el derecho castellano leonés alto medieval." *Revista Chilena de Historia del Derecho* 2 (1961): 22–35.

Sánchez, Galo. *Curso de historia del derecho: Introducción y fuentes*. 9th ed. Madrid: Reus 1960.

——. "Para la historia de la redacción del antiguo derecho territorial castellano." *AHDE* 6 (1929): 260–328.

——. "Sobre el Ordenamiento de Alcalá (1348) y sus fuentes." *Revista de Derecho Privado* 9 (1922): 351–68.

Sánchez Albornoz, Claudio. *La curia regia portuguesa: Siglos XII y XIII*. Madrid: Junta para ampliación de estudios e investigaciones científicas, 1920.

——."Dudas sobre el ordenamiento de Nájera." *CHE* 35–36 (1962): 315–34.

——. *España, un enigma histórico*. 2 vols. Buenos Aires: Sudamericana, 1962.

——. "El 'juicio del Libro' en León durante el siglo X y un feudo castellano del XIII." *AHDE* 1 (1924): 382–90.

——. "Menos dudas sobre el ordenamiento de Nájera." *AEM* 3 (1966): 465–68.

——. "Señoríos y ciudades: Dos diplomas para el estudio de sus recíprocas relaciones," *AHDE* 6 (1929): 454–61.

Sánchez-Arcilla Bernal, José. *La administración de justicia en León y Castilla durante la baja edad media (1252–1504)*. Madrid: Universidad Complutense de Madrid, 1980.

——. "La administración de justicia en León y Castilla durante los siglos X al XIII." In *Jornadas sobre Documentación jurídico-administrativa, económico-financiera y judicial del reino castellano-leonés (Siglos X–XIII)*, 1:13–49. Madrid: Universidad Complutense de Madrid, 2002.

——. "Notas para el estudio del aborto en el Derecho histórico español." *Icade: Revista de las Facultades de Derecho y Ciencias Económicas y Empresariales* 8 (1986): 13–40.

——. "Notas para el estudio del homicidio en el Derecho histórico español." *RFDUC* 72 (1986–87): 513–74.

——. "Las reformas de Alfonso X en la organización territorial de la Corona de Castilla." *RFDUC* 9 Extra (1985): 115–27.

——. "La 'teoría de la ley' en la obra legislativa de Alfonso X el Sabio." *Alcanate* 6 (2008–9): 81–123.

Sánchez de Mora, Alfonso. "Doña Juana de Ponthieu, reina de Castilla y señora de Marchena." In *La mujer en la Historia de Marchena*, ed. Juan Luis Carriazo Rubio and Ramón Ramos Alfonso, 11–24. Marchena: Cajasol, 2007.

Sánchez González de Herrero, María Nieves. *Diccionario español de documentos alfonsíes*. Madrid: Arco Libros, 2000.

Sánchez Prieto, Ana Belén. *Guerra y guerreros en España según las fuentes canónicas de la edad media*. Madrid: E.M.E., 1990.

Scarborough, Connie L. *A Holy Alliance: Alfonso X's Political Use of Marian Poetry*. Newark, DE: Juan de la Cuesta, 2009.

——. *Women in Thirteenth-Century Spain as Portrayed in Alfonso X's Cantigas de Santa Maria*. Lewiston, NY: Edwin Mellen Press, 1993.

Schramm, Percy Ernst. *Las insignias de la realeza en la edad media española*. Madrid: Instituto de Estudios Políticos, 1960.

Segura Graiño, Cristina. "Historia de las mujeres en la Edad media." *Medievalismo* 18 (2008): 249–72.

——. "Las mujeres en el medioveo hispano." *Cuadernos de Investigación Medieval* 1 (1984): 7–56.

Serna Vallejo, Margarita. "Servidumbres prediales y limitaciones de dominio: Entre la diferenciación y la confusión." In *Historia de la propiedad: Servidumbres y limitaciones de dominio*, ed. Salustiano de Dios, Javier Infante, Ricardo Robledo, and Eugenia Torijano, 852–83. Madrid: Fundación Registral, 2009.

Serra Ruiz, Rafael. "Finalidad de la pena en la legislación de las Partidas." *Anales de la Universidad de Murcia. Derecho* 21 (1963): 199–257.

——. "Honor, honra e injuria en el Derecho medieval español." *Anales de la Universidad de Murcia. Derecho* 23 (1965): 55–155.

Shadis, Miriam. *Berenguela of Castile (1180–1246) and Political Women in the High Middle Ages*. New York: Palgrave Macmillan, 2010.

Socarras, Cayetano J. *Alfonso X of Castile: A Study on Imperialistic Frustration*. Barcelona: Hispam, 1976.

Soler, Maximiliano. "Derecho, narración y racionalidad jurídica: El caso de la fazaña bajomedieval." *Cuadernos Electrónicos de Filosofía y Derecho* 22 (2011):162–89.

Solórzano Telechea, Jesús Ángel. "Justicia y ejercicio del poder: La infamia y los 'delitos de lujuria' en la cultura legal de la Castilla medieval." *CHD* 12 (2005): 313–53.

Starczewska, Katarzyna Krystyna. *El retrato de Mahoma en la Historia Arabum de Jiménez de Rada y en el Prologus Alcorani de Marcos de Toledo: Ejemplos de literatura y confrontación islamo-cristiana*. Barcelona: Universitat Autònoma de Barcelona, 2009.

Stickler, Alfons Maria. "Il Decretista Laurentius Hispanus." *Studia Gratiana* 9 (1966): 461–549.

Stone, Marilyn. "Desde las Siete Partidas a los códigos civiles norteamericanos." *Actas del Congreso de la Asociación internacional de Hispanistas* 11 (1992): 25–33.

——. *Marriage and Friendship in Medieval Spain: Social Relations according to the Fourth Partida of Alfonso X*. New York: Peter Lang, 1990.

Strayer, Joseph R. *On the Medieval Origins of the Modern State*. Princeton: Princeton University Press, 1970.

Todesca, James. "The Crown Renewed: The Administration of Coinage in León-Castile, c. 1065–1200." In *The Emergence of León-Castile, c. 1065–1500: Essays Presented to J. F. O'Callaghan*, ed. James Todesca, 9–32. Burlington, VT: Ashgate, 2015.

——. "The Monetary History of Castile-León (ca. 1100–1300) in Light of the Bourgey Hoard." *American Numismatic Society Museum Notes* 33 (1988): 129–203.

Tolan, John Victor. *Saracens: Islam in the Medieval European Imagination.* New York: Columbia University Press, 2002.

Tomás y Valiente, Francisco. *Manual de historia del derecho español.* 4th ed. Madrid: Tecnos, 1983.

——. *Martínez Marina, Historiador del derecho.* Madrid: Real Academia de la Historia, 1991.

——. "La sucesión de que muere sin parientes y sin disponer de sus bienes." *AHDE* 36 (1966): 189–254.

Torres Aguilar, Manuel. "Naturaleza jurídico-penal y procesal del desafío y riepto en León y Castilla en la edad media." *AHDE* 10 (1933): 161–74.

——. *El parricidio: del pasado al presente de un delito.* Madrid: Editorial de Derecho Reunidas SA, 1991.

——. "La pena de exilio: Sus orígenes en el derecho romano." *AHDE* 63–64 (1993–94): 701–86.

Torres Balbás, Leopoldo. "Atarazanas hispanomusulmanas." *Al-Andalus* 11 (1946): 179–205.

Torres Fontes, Juan. "La familia de Maestre Jacobo de las Leyes." *Glossae* 5–6 (1993–94): 333–49.

——. "El obispado de Cartagena en el siglo XIII." *Hispania: Revista española de historia* 13 (1953): 339–401, 515–80.

——. "La Orden de Santa María de España." *AEM* 11 (1981): 794–821.

——. "La Orden de Santa María de España." *MMM* 3 (1977): 75–118.

——. "Un médico alfonsí: Maestre Nicolás." *Revista Murgetana* 6 (1954): 9–16.

——. "El testamento del Infante don Manuel." *MMM* 7 (1981): 10–21.

Torres Gutiérrez, Alejandro. "Orígenes canónico-medievales del concepto moderno de estado." In *Escritos en honor a Javier Hervada,* 987–98. Pamplona: Universidad de Navarra, 1999.

Torres y Tapia, Alonso. *Crónica de la Orden de Alcántara.* 2 vols. Madrid: Gabriel Ramírez, 1773.

Ullmann, Walter. *Principles of Government and Politics in the Middle Ages.* New York: Barnes and Noble, 1966.

Valdeavellano, Luis García de. *Curso de historia de las instituciones españolas de los orígines al final de la edad media.* Madrid: Revista de Occidente, 1968.

——. "El desarrollo del derecho en la península ibérica hasta alrededor del año 1300." *Cahiers d'Histoire Mondiale* 3 (1957): 833–53.

——. *Historia de España: De los orígenes a la baja edad media.* 2 vols. 2nd ed. Madrid: Revista de Occidente, 1955.

——. "Martínez Marina y las 'Partidas' de Alfonso el Sabio." *BRAH* 181 (1984): 371–85.

——. *El mercado: Apuntes para su estudio en León y Castilla durante la Edad media.* Seville: Universidad de Sevilla, 1975.

Valdeón, Julio. *El feudalismo.* Madrid: Alba, 1992.

Vallejo, Jesús. "Fuero Real 1, 7,4: Pleitos de justicia." *HID* 11 (1984): 343–74.

——. "La regulación del proceso en el Fuero Real: Desarrollo, precedentes y problemas." *AHDE* 55 (1985): 495–794.

——. "Vida castellana de la muerte civil: En torno a la ley cuarta de Toro." *HID* 31 (2004): 671–85.

Valls Taberner, Ferran. "Le juriste catalan Pierre de Cardona." In *Mélanges Paul Fournier*, 743–46. Paris: Recueil Sirey, 1929.

——. "Relacions familiars i polítiques entre Jaume el Conqueridor i Alfons el Savi." *Bulletin Hispanique* 21 (1919): 9–42.

Van Kleffens, E. N. *Hispanic Law until the End of the Middle Ages with a Note on the Continued Validity after the Fifteenth Century of Medieval Hispanic Legislation in Spain, the Americas, Asia and Africa*. Edinburgh: Edinburgh University Press, 1968.

Vance, John T. "The Old Spanish Code of 'Las Siete Partidas' in Mexico." American Bar Association Journal 14 (1928): 219–24.

Vanderford, Kenneth. "El 'Setenario' y su relación con las 'Siete Partidas'" *Revista de Filología hispánica* 3 (1941): 233–62.

Vázquez Campos, Braulio. *Los adelantados mayores de la frontera o Andalucía (siglos XIII–XIV)*. Seville: Diputación provincial de Sevilla, 2006.

——. *Adelantados y lucha por el poder en el reino de Murcia*. Alcalá la Real: Editorial Zumaque, 2009.

——. "El Adelantamiento Murciano en el contexto de las reformas alfonsinas, 1258–1283." *MMM* 27–28 (2003–4): 157–77, and 29–30 (2005–6):105–21.

——. "Sobre los orígenes del Adelantamiento de Andalucía." *HID* 27 (2000): 333–73.

Vázquez de Parga, Luis, José Maria Lacarra, and Juan Uria. *Las peregrinaciones a Santiago de Compostela*. 3 vols. Madrid: Consejo Superior de Investigaciones Científicas, 1948–49.

Veas Arteseros, Francisco, and María del Carmen Veas Arteseros. "Alférez y Mayordomo real en el siglo XIII." In Miguel Rodríguez, Múñoz Fernández, and Segura Graiño, *Alfonso X el Sabio*, 55–66.

Vedia y Goossens, Enrique de. *Historia y descripción de la ciudad de La Coruña*. La Coruña: Domingo Puga, 1845.

Villar y Macías, Mateo. *Historia de Salamanca*. 3 vols. Salamanca: Librería Cervantes, 1887.

Wolf, Kenneth B. "Christian Views of Islam in Early Medieval Spain." In *Medieval Christian Perceptions of Islam*, ed. John V. Tolan, 85–108. New York: Garland, 1995.

——. "The Earliest Christian Views of Islam." *Church History* 55 (1986): 281–93.

Zadorenko, Irene. "El procedimiento judicial de riepto entre nobles y la fecha de composición de la *Historia Roderici* y el *Poema de Mio Cid*." *RFE* 78 (1998):183–94.

Zambrana Moral, Patricia. "Rasgos generales de la evolución histórica de la tipología de las penas corporales." *REHJ* 27 (2005): 197–229.

INDEX

CPSIA information can be obtained
at www.ICGtesting.com
Printed in the USA
BVHW032137290319
544133BV00005B/26/P

9 781501 735899